THOUSAND OAKS LIBRARY

THOUSAND OAKS LIBRARY

3 2052 00003 1739

FEB - - 1999

W9-AUE-073

DISCARD

Collection Development Information

6/00	2	4/00
7/00	2	4/00
1-07	10-1	10-05
4/09	11-1	1/08
12/2011	13-1	6/2011

THOUSAND OAKS LIBRARY
1401 E. JANSS ROAD
THOUSAND OAKS, CA 91362

Manhood in America

A CULTURAL HISTORY

by MICHAEL KIMMEL

THE FREE PRESS

New York   London   Toronto   Sydney   Singapore

The Free Press
A Division of Simon & Schuster Inc.
1230 Avenue of the Americas
New York, N.Y. 10020

Copyright © 1996 by Michael Kimmel
All rights reserved,
including the right of reproduction
in whole or in part in any form.

First Paperback Edition 1997

THE FREE PRESS and colophon are trademarks
of Simon & Schuster Inc.

Designed by Carla Bolte

Manufactured in the United States of America

The Library of Congress has catalogued the Free Press hardcover edition as follows:

Kimmel, Michael S.
    Manhood in America: a cultural history / Michael Kimmel.
        p.   cm.
    Includes bibliographical references and index.
    1. Men—United States—Psychology.   2. Masculinity (Psychology—
United States.   I. Title.
HQ1090.3.K553   1996
305.31—dc20   95–32619
                                                                              CIP

ISBN 0–02–874067–X
0–684–83712–9 (Pbk)

305.31

FOR MY PARENTS,
WITH GRATITUDE AND LOVE

An American will build a house in which to pass his old age and sell it before the roof is on; he will plant a garden and rent it just as the trees are coming into bearing; he will clear a field and leave others to reap the harvest; he will take up a profession and leave it, settle in one place and soon go off elsewhere with his changing desires....At first sight there is something astonishing in this spectacle of so many lucky men restless in the midst of abundance. But it is a spectacle as old as the world; all that is new is to see a whole people performing in it.

—Alexis de Tocqueville
Democracy in America (1835)

Contents

Preface   vii

Acknowledgments   xi

Introduction: Toward a History of Manhood in America   1

PART ONE
THE MAKING OF THE SELF-MADE MAN IN AMERICA, 1776–1865

1. The Birth of the Self-Made Man   13

2. Born to Run: Self-Control and Fantasies of Escape   43

PART TWO
THE UNMAKING OF THE SELF-MADE MAN AT THE TURN OF THE
CENTURY

3. Men at Work: Captains of Industry, White Collars,
   and the Faceless Crowd   81

4. Playing for Keeps: Masculinity as Recreation
   and the Re-creation of Masculinity   117

5. A Room of His Own: Socializing the New Man   157

PART THREE
THE NEW MAN IN A NEW CENTURY, 1920–1950

6. Muscles, Money, and the M-F Test:
Measuring Masculinity Between the Wars   191

7. "Temporary About Myself": White-Collar Conformists
and Suburban Playboys, 1945–1960   223

PART FOUR
THE CONTEMPORARY "CRISIS" OF MASCULINITY

8. The Masculine Mystique   261

9. Wimps, Whiners, and Weekend Warriors:
The Contemporary Crisis of Masculinity and Beyond   291

Epilogue: Toward Democratic Manhood   329

Appendix: Attitude-Interest Analysis Test   337
Notes   363
Bibliography   483
Index   533

Preface

Clarence Thomas. William Kennedy Smith. Senator Bob Packwood. The names fairly leap off the front pages of recent newspapers. Mike Tyson. Woody Allen. O.J. Simpson. Michael Jackson. Overnight, heroes become villains, accused of rape, murder, sexual abuse. Tailhook. Spur Posse. The Citadel. Male bonding run amok.

These names and so many others have become part of our collective vocabulary in recent years. Barely a month goes by without a new set of allegations about some prominent man, or a new scandal that erupts in some all-male organization.

What all these names share, of course, is masculinity. Suddenly, it seems, masculinity is a problem, an issue. "Years ago," humorist Garrison Keilor writes in his recent book, The Book of Guys, "manhood was an opportunity for achievement, and now it is a problem to be overcome."

And the headlines echo this problem: "Manhood on Trial." "Masculinity Under Siege."

How have men responded to this siege, this trial? Only Hollywood could give us Michael Douglas's character D-Fens in the film Falling Down, conducting his own little one-man riot in Los Angeles, confronting representatives of all the awful forces arrayed against modern American manhood: Chicano gangs, effete rich snobs, nonnative speaking Asian immigrant store owners, and an indifferent bureaucracy.

A lot of men have dealt with this new "crisis" of masculinity by getting tougher, pumping up like Schwarzenegger wanna-bes—impenetrable, impervious to external threat. Leaner and meaner. Harder. Stronger. And if the body would not cooperate, yuppies donned power ties for their power lunches, as if that inner sense of self-possession could be achieved by accessorizing.

Some men feel so besieged that they declare themselves to be the new victims of reverse sexism. It's men, they say, who are the victims of discrimination—in divorce courts, custody hearings, and the military. It's men who lose their jobs to women and minorities. And it's men who are portrayed as ignorant louts, drunken oafs, or violent dangerous rapists. It's time, the cadres of "angry white males" tell us, for men's rights, for men's liberation even, for men to stand up to those "feminazis" and welfare queens. Forget about Thoreau's observation about how men lead lives of "quiet desperation." Men's rightists shout (and whine) as noisily as they can. These guys are mad as hell and they're not going to take it anymore! It's time for men to stand up for themselves!

Other men aren't so sure about who's to blame, but they are sure that they are unsure. And so off they go into the woods, like Thoreau did over a century ago, there to retrieve that deep essence of manhood that they seem to have lost along the path growing up. The American media had a pleasant collective chuckle at the sight of all these middle-class, middle-age white guys trooping off like so many lost lemmings after the sage elder poet Robert Bly and other New Age gurus, drumming and chanting and whooping up a "mythopoetic" masculine storm.

Most observers have dismissed such efforts as the vain preoccupations of the already privileged, or they've heard an anguished cry of pain and despair from the collective mouths of American manhood. But few have observed that these three responses—efforts at self-control, reactive exclusion, and escape—have been the dominant themes of American manhood for the last two centuries.

That observation is the starting point for this book: that the current malaise among men has a long history, and that the way men are responding these days bears a startling resemblance to men's responses over the course of American history. Only by examining this

crisis of masculinity through this historical perspective can we illuminate its deep, underlying structure.

This book began as such an inquiry. I sought to chart the history
of a gender—that is, to write a cultural history of the changing ideals
of manhood in America. As the research for the book developed,
however, I realized that these patterns of response to real or perceived
threats to manhood had been startlingly consistent throughout American history, that men today were doing similar things and for similar
reasons that they had done for a very long time.

This work in cultural interpretation of the changing definition of
American manhood thus kept bumping up against a larger set of
questions about the gendered nature of much of American history.
Though Manhood in America cannot hope to revise the entirety of
that history, nor reduce its complexity to a single overarching factor, I
do believe that a comprehensive historical account of the American
experience can no longer ignore the importance of masculinity—and
especially of men's efforts to prove their manhood—in the making of
America.

This theme—proving manhood, manhood as a relentless test—
has been and continues to be a dominant one in American life. The
drive to "prove" it and the heroic and not-so-heroic efforts we have
made to do so are the subjects of this book. As a historical sociologist, I set out by asking if we were, as Henry Clay called us, "a nation
of self-made men," then how did one make one's self? How did one
prove it? What were the visible outward signs of having successfully
achieved manhood? Over our two centuries of history, American
manhood became less and less about an inner sense of self, and more
and more about a possession that needed to be acquired.

In this book, I've sought to locate the sources of the current male
malaise in the historical record of men's efforts to prove their manhood. A psychologist might pose these questions differently, but our
analyses are easily compatible. Freud argued that gender identity for
men is a perilous accomplishment, achieved only after a traumatic
separation from mother and identification with father, who was perceived as a distant, often frightening figure. Of course, once the
young boy links his sense of masculinity to being separate from
mother, can he ever get far enough away? How much distance from

the feminine is enough? Psychologically, his sense of masculinity becomes a constant test to demonstrate the fact of that separation. But how does he prove it? And to whom?

Such psychological theories of child development often assumed an ahistorically transcendent family constellation of homebound mother, distant working father, and children, as if the nuclear family of the late nineteenth century was eternal. But why was the father absent? When did he leave? Didn't he have to prove his manhood also?

A more historically informed analysis of these processes suggests that Freud's brilliant dissection of fin-de-siècle middle-class gendered neuroses may have mistaken consequence for cause. The family form that produced such young men struggling to prove their manhood was, itself, the product of earlier efforts to prove manhood, efforts that transformed family life and personal identity in the first half of the nineteenth century. Already by the 1830s, as Tocqueville reminds us, American men were busy building, planting, and clearing but still somehow "restless in the midst of abundance."

This book begins at the beginning of our nation's history in an effort to tell the story of American men's efforts to prove themselves. It is a story of a chronically anxious, temperamentally restless manhood—a manhood that carries with it the constant burdens of proof.

Acknowledgments

Completing this project leaves me humbled. I am happy to acknowledge the work of so many other scholars whose careful research has provided the foundation for my work. For most, I hope the notes and references serve as sufficient acknowledgment. But I must record a special debt to the work of George Chauncey, Nancy Cott, Joe Dubbert, Martin Duberman, Peter Filene, Robert Griswold, David Leverenz, Joseph Pleck, Michael Rogin, and E. Anthony Rotundo.

This work stands on the foundation laid by these and other scholars; its girders and beams are the support of friends, colleagues, and institutions. Much of the research and writing was accomplished while I was a Visiting Scholar at the Institute for the Study of Social Change and a Visiting Professor of Political Economy of Industrial Societies and of Sociology at the University of California at Berkeley. I am grateful to Troy Duster, director of ISSC, for providing me with such a congenial base of operations, and to Albert Fishlow, director of the PEIS teaching program, Neil Fligstein, chairman of the Sociology department, and to their staffs, especially Vida Prater, Barbara Peavey, and Janice Tanigawa for making my stay such a pleasure. I am also grateful to Hagit Elul and Claudia Teran for research assistance.

Back at SUNY at Stony Brook, my colleagues have been invariably supportive and, well, collegial. My departmental chair, Andrea Tyree, has tried to loosen what support she could from an ever-shrinking pie. I also thank John Gagnon, Ian Roxborough, and Bob Zussman. My assistant Pat Carson helped in so many ways; valuable last-minute help was provided by Kevin Maillard. The National Science Foundation's small grant program through the American Sociological Association provided some needed support.

My editor at The Free Press, Bruce Nichols, has been a pleasure to work with, believing in the project from the beginning, and reading the manuscript with such care and dedication. I am amazed at his ability to keep one eye on the big picture and the other on the smallest detail. My literary agents, Frances Goldin and Sydelle Kramer, have advocated for this project for a very long time and have been among its strongest supporters, caring critics, and persistent promoters.

My friends have constantly buttressed my work, creatively and caringly blurring the distinctions between colleagueship and friendship. I am grateful to Mitch Allen and Vida Prater, Amy Aronson, Bob and Joanne Brannon, Judith Brisman, Shelby Chodos, Sandra Laub and Emma Laub-Chodos, Martin Duberman and Eli Zal, Andreas Gailus, John Gagnon and Cathy Greenblat, Michael Kaufman, David, Deborah and Drew Levin, Mike Messner, Mary Morris, Katie Morris and Larry O'Connor, Tim Nonn, George Robinson and Margo Fox, Lillian and Hank Rubin, Mitchell Tunick, Pam Hatchfield, and H. Perry Tunick-Hatchfield. For much of the time I worked on this book, Iona Mara-Drita shared my life. I am grateful for the love and support she offered. I am saddened that Martin Levine, who was such a loving friend and ally, did not live to see its publication. I will always miss him.

Special thanks to those friends—Amy Aronson, Tim Beneke, Harry Brod, Martin Duberman, Joy Johanassen, Michael Kaufman, Paul Kivel, Iona Mara-Drita, Mike Messner, Joe Pleck, Michael Rogin, Lillian Rubin—who read the entire manuscript and provided such helpful feedback and supportive criticism. I probably should have followed their sage advice more often.

I usually find acknowledgments fascinating. I read them at least as carefully as the work itself, trying to locate the author, to fashion together that web of institutional and interpersonal networks that compose a writer's life. But I also find them incomplete; authors cheerfully thank foundations for institutional support and libraries for research assistance, relatives and friends for moral support and guidance and love—as I have just done.

So now that I've discharged these obligations, however pleasurably, shouldn't I also mention that during the writing of this book I was sustained by the soulful stirrings of Sam Cooke, inspired by the passionate longings of Bruce Springsteen, or soothed by the sweetness of Brahms's string quartets? Shouldn't I also mention how I was electrified by John Starks's three-pointers, or by Jason Kidd's passes? Shouldn't I also mention how often I returned to the visionary didacticism of films by Bernardo Bertolucci or Oliver Stone? I suppose so. Without them, how much less would have been the life I've lived while working on this book. And in these days of political assault on our cultural institutions, it seems even more pressing to thank them publicly.

Finally, my family, in all its recombinant forms, has always been very supportive of me. This book is for my parents, who early on taught me the principles of a democratic manhood, a vision based more on the values one embodies than on the external markers of one's relentless efforts to prove it.

INTRODUCTION

TOWARD A HISTORY OF MANHOOD IN AMERICA

> And what is our Ideal Man? On what grand and luminous mythological figure does contemporary humanity attempt to model itself? The question is embarrassing. Nobody knows.
> —Aldous Huxley *Texts and Pretexts*

> A man would never get the notion of writing a book on the peculiar situation of the human male.
> —Simone de Beauvoir *The Second Sex* (1953)

American men have no history. Sure, we have libraries filled with the words of men about the works of men—stacks of biographies of the heroic and famous, and historical accounts of events in which men took part, like wars, strikes, or political campaigns. We have portraits of athletes, scientists, and soldiers, histories of unions and political parties. And there are probably thousands of histories of institutions that were organized, staffed, and run entirely by men.

So how can I claim that men have no history? Isn't virtually every history book a history of men? After all, as we have learned from feminist scholars, it's been *women* who have had, until recently, no history. In fact, if the book doesn't have the word *women* in the title, it's

1

a good bet that the book is largely about men. Yet such works do not explore how the experience of being a man, of *manhood*, structured the lives of the men who are their subjects, the organizations and institutions they created and staffed, the events in which they participated. American men have no history of themselves *as men*.[1]

What does it mean, then, to write of men *as men*? It requires two things: first, to chart how the definition of masculinity has changed over time; second, to explore how the experience of manhood has shaped the activities of American men. When we do that, we find some startling news—that the sources of the current confusion, defensiveness, and malaise among American men lie deep in our nation's past. Beginning in the early part of the nineteenth century, the idea of testing and proving one's manhood became one of the defining experiences in American men's lives. The long-term causes of the idea of proving one's manhood were structural—change in the work world, the political arena, and the family. The consequences of those changes, however, have been both social and psychological, carried out both in the relationships between different groups throughout our history as well as in men's sense of themselves as men. And the idea of proving one's manhood continues to reverberate to the present day.

That's not to say that charting the history of manhood will become a catchall cornucopia, that by injecting gender into the standard historical narrative, we will suddenly, magically, illuminate the entire American historical pageant. We cannot understand manhood without understanding American history. But I believe we also cannot fully understand American history without understanding masculinity. How has American history been shaped by the efforts to test and prove manhood—the wars we Americans have waged, the frontier we have tamed, the work we have done, the leaders we admire? Why do so many contemporary American men feel that they have to "prove it" all the time? These are big questions, and in this book I hope only to suggest some of the larger patterns that such a detailed historical inquiry into the meaning of manhood might observe.

American men still have no history in part, I believe, because we haven't known what questions to ask. In the past twenty-five years the pioneering work of feminist scholars, both in traditional disciplines and in women's studies, has made us increasingly aware of the centrality of gender in shaping social life. By gender I mean the sets of cultural meanings and prescriptions that each culture attaches to one's biological sex. And these meanings become one of the poles around which our experiences revolve.[2]

The women's movement made gender visible—at least to women. Courses on gender in the universities are populated largely by women, as if the term only applied to them. "Woman alone seems to have 'gender' since the category itself is defined as that aspect of social relations based on difference between the sexes in which the standard has always been man," writes the historian Thomas Lacquer.[3] Consider the evolution of Women's Studies, which originally focused on what Catharine Stimpson, one of the field's founders, called the "omissions, distortions, and trivializations" of women's experiences.[4] Women's Studies rescued from obscurity the lives of notable women who had been ignored or whose work had been minimized by traditional scholarship and also examined the everyday lives of women in the past—the efforts, for example, of laundresses, factory workers, pioneer homesteaders, or housewives to carve out lives of meaning and dignity in a world controlled by men. Only gradually have scholars seen the patterns among these female subjects and realized the different meanings that being a woman has taken throughout our history.

Eventually it will be time to go further, to explore the history of both women and men. "We should not be working on the subjected sex any more than a historian of class can focus exclusively on peasants," writes the historian Natalie Zemon Davis. "Our goal is to understand the significance of the *sexes*, of gender groups in the historical past."[5] Such a perspective understands the relations among men or among women, or the relationships between women and men as gendered relationships, not simply relationships in which men and/or women happen to be participating.

But first we must make gender visible to men. We continue to treat our male military, political, scientific, or literary figures as if their gender, their masculinity, had nothing to do with their military exploits, policy decisions, scientific experiments, or writing styles and subjects. As the Chinese proverb has it, the fish are the last to discover the ocean.

This problem was made clear to me in a seminar on Feminist Theory I attended several years ago. There, in a discussion between two women, I first confronted the invisibility of gender to men. During one meeting, a white woman and a black woman were discussing whether all women were, by definition, "sisters" because they all had essentially the same experiences and because all women faced a common oppression by men. The white woman asserted that the fact that they were both women bonded them, in spite of racial differences. The black woman disagreed.

"When you wake up in the morning and look in the mirror, what do you see?" she asked.

"I see a woman," replied the white woman.

"That's precisely the problem," responded the black woman. "I see a *black* woman. To me, race is visible every day, because race is how I am *not* privileged in our culture. Race is invisible to you, because it's how you are privileged. It's a luxury, a privilege, not to see race all the time. It's why there will always be differences in our experience."

As I witnessed this exchange, I was startled, and groaned—more audibly, perhaps, than I had intended. Someone asked what my response meant.

"Well," I said, "when I look in the mirror, I see a human being." I'm universally generalizable. As a middle-class white man, I have no class, no race, no gender. I'm the generic person!

Sometimes I like to think it was on that day that I *became* a middle-class white man. Sure, I had been a member of all those groups before, but they had not meant much to me. That was, itself, a form of privilege. Since then, I've begun to understand that race, class, and gender do not refer only to the marginalized "others"; they also describe me.

Writing a history of men in America, I have placed gender in the center of my historical analysis. I argue that the quest for manhood—the effort to achieve, to demonstrate, to prove our masculinity—has been one of the formative and persistent experiences in men's lives. That we remain unaware of the centrality of gender in our lives only helps to perpetuate gender inequality.

Even when we do acknowledge gender, we often endow manhood with a transcendental, almost mythic set of properties that still keep it invisible. We think of manhood as eternal, a timeless essence that resides deep in the heart of every man. Either we think of manhood as innate, residing in the particular anatomical organization of the human male, or we think of manhood as a transcendent tangible property that each man manifests in the world, the reward presented with great ceremony to a young novice by his elders for having successfully completed an arduous initiation ritual. In the words of Robert Bly, "the structure at the bottom of the male psyche is still as firm as it was twenty thousand years ago."[6]

Putting manhood in historical context presents it differently, as a constantly changing collection of meanings that we construct through our relationships with ourselves, with each other, and with our world. Manhood is neither static nor timeless. Manhood is not the manifestation of an inner essence; it's socially constructed. Manhood does not bubble up to consciousness from our biological constitution; it is created in our culture. In fact, the search for a transcendent, timeless definition of manhood is itself a sociological phenomenon—we tend to search for the timeless and eternal during moments of crisis, those points of transition when the old definitions no longer work and the new definitions are yet to be firmly established.

Manhood means different things at different times to different people. Some cultures encourage a manly stoicism we might find familiar. Many men in many cultures seem preoccupied with demonstrating sexual prowess. But some cultures prescribe a more relaxed definition of masculinity, a more emotional and familial man. Nor are all American men alike. What it means to be a man in America depends heavily on one's class, race, ethnicity, age, sexuality, region of the country. To acknowledge these differences among men, we must speak of *masculinities*. At the same time, though, all American men must also contend with a singular vision of masculinity, a particular definition that is held up as the model against which we all measure ourselves. As the sociologist Erving Goffman once wrote:

In an important sense there is only one complete unblushing male in America: a young, married, white, urban, northern, heterosexual, Protestant, father, of college education, fully employed, of good complexion, weight, and height, and a recent record in sports. . . . Any male who fails to qualify in any one of these ways is likely to view himself—during moments at least—as unworthy, incomplete, and inferior.[7]

A history of manhood must, therefore, recount two histories: the history of the changing "ideal" version of masculinity and the parallel and competing versions that coexist with it.[8]

It is this tension between the multiplicity of masculinities that collectively define American men's actual experiences and this singular "hegemonic" masculinity that is prescribed as the norm that forms one of the organizing dynamics of this book. In a sense, this is a history of that "complete" male that Goffman describes—straight, white, middle class, native-born—the story of his great accomplishments and his nagging anxieties. Yet in another sense, it is at least indirectly the story of the marginalized "others"—working class men, gay men, men of color, immigrant men—how these different groups of men and, of course, women were used as a screen against which those "complete" men projected their fears and, in the process, constructed this prevailing definition of manhood. I do not tell the story of these "others" from their point of view nor in their own voices; rather, I trace the ways that they were set up as everything that "straight white men" were not, so as to provide public testimony and private reassurance that those "complete" men were secure in their gender identity. Thus, this book describes only one version of "Manhood in America"—albeit the dominant version.

There have been some attempts to tell the story of American manhood—by women. But many feminist analyses failed to resonate with men's own experiences. Not a surprise, since women theorized about masculinity from *their* point of view, from the way women experienced masculinity. And women theorized that men's relationships with women were the pivotal relationship in the lives of both women and men. Masculinity, we were told, was defined by the drive for power, for domination, for control.[9]

I began the historical research for this book guided by that feminist perspective. But the historical record has revealed a somewhat different picture. Manhood is less about the drive for domination and more about the fear of others dominating us, having power or control over us. Throughout American history American men have been afraid that others will see us as less than manly, as weak, timid, frightened. And men have been afraid of not measuring up to some vaguely defined notions of what it means to be a man, afraid of failure. Here's how novelist John Steinbeck put it in *Of Mice and Men* (1937):

> "Funny thing," [Curley's wife] said. "If I catch any one man, and he's alone, I get along fine with him. But just let two of the guys get together an' you won't talk. Jus' nothin' but mad." She dropped her fingers and put her hands on her hips. "You're all scared of each other, that's what. Ever'one of you's scared the rest is goin' to get something on you."[10]

Curley's wife sees clearly what we've often missed: In large part, it's other men who are important to American men; American men define their masculinity, not as much in relation to women, but in relation to each other. Masculinity is largely a homosocial enactment. "Women have, in men's minds, such a low place on the social ladder of this country that it's useless to define yourself in terms of a woman," noted playwright David Mamet. "What men need is men's approval."[11]

Such a bold claim does not mean that women are incidental to men's efforts to prove their manhood. Far from it. As I will show in the pages that follow, men often go to elaborate lengths and take extraordinary risks to prove their manhood in the eyes of women. Women are not incidental to masculinity, but they are not always its central feature, either. At times, it is not women as corporeal beings but the "idea" of women, or femininity—and most especially a perception of effeminacy by other men—that animates men's actions. Femininity, separate from actual women, can become a negative pole against which men define themselves. Women themselves often serve as a kind of currency that men use to improve their ranking with other men.[12]

The historical record underscores this homosociality. From the early nineteenth century until the present day, much of men's relentless effort to prove their manhood contains this core element of homosociality. From fathers and boyhood friends to teachers, coworkers, and bosses, the evaluative eyes of other men are always upon us, watching, judging. As one Army general put it, every soldier fears "losing the one thing he is likely to value more highly than life—his reputation as *a man among other men*."[13] Our real fear, writes the literary critic David

Leverenz, "is not fear of women but of being ashamed or humiliated in front of other men, or being dominated by stronger men."[14]

Masculinity defined through homosocial interaction contains many parts, including the camaraderie, fellowship, and intimacy often celebrated in male culture. It also includes homophobia. Homophobia is more than the irrational fear of homosexuals, more than the fear that we might (mistakenly) be perceived as gay. It is these, of course, but it is also something deeper. Homophobia is the fear of other men—that other men will unmask us, emasculate us, reveal to us and the world that we do not measure up, are not real men, that we are, like the young man in a poem by Yeats, "one that ruffles in a manly pose for all his timid heart." "The word 'faggot' has nothing to do with homosexual experience or even with fears of homosexuals," writes David Leverenz. "It comes out of the depths of manhood: a label of ultimate contempt for anyone who seems sissy, untough, uncool."[15]

My task in this book is to set these constant efforts to prove manhood, the burdens of proof, within the context of American history and to do so by holding American history up to the prism of gender. Like all prisms, this works in two ways. First, I take the disparate strands of economic, political, social, cultural, and literary events, focus them into one beam, and shed the brightest light possible on one aspect of American society—men. But the prism will also refract that light to fragment what seems to be a unitary vision of masculinity in a rainbow of different colors, shades, and hues.

The history of American manhood is many histories at once. It is the story of spectacular technological and military triumphs and of the sobering dullness of everyday life. It is the inspiring story of heroic efforts to overcome adversity through feats of dazzling brilliance, astonishing physical strength, or remarkable courage and the story of ordinary men in ordinary circumstances shouldering the responsibilities of quotidian routine, seeking moments of comfort and solace in the face of their personal daily grind. It is a history of energy and excitement, of sadness and silences.

And always also a history of fears, frustration, and failure. At the grandest social level and the most intimate realms of personal life, for individuals and institutions, American men have been haunted by fears that they are not powerful, strong, rich, or successful enough.

And many of our actions, on both the public and private stages, have been efforts to ward off these demons, to silence these fears. I argue that there have been certain patterns to these actions: American men try to *control themselves*; they project their fears onto *others*; and when feeling too pressured, they attempt an *escape*. These three themes recur frequently in the following pages, as men return to self-control, exclusion, and escape in their efforts to ground a secure sense of themselves as men.

In rough outline my argument will look something like this: At the turn of the nineteenth century, American manhood was rooted in landownership (the Genteel Patriarch) or in the self-possession of the independent artisan, shopkeeper, or farmer (the Heroic Artisan).[16] In the first few decades of the nineteenth century, though, the Industrial Revolution had a critical effect on those earlier definitions. American men began to link their sense of themselves as men to their position in the volatile marketplace, to their economic success—a far less stable yet far more exciting and potentially rewarding peg upon which to hang one's identity. The Self-Made Man of American mythology was born anxious and insecure, uncoupled from the more stable anchors of landownership or workplace autonomy. Now manhood had to be proved. This "*self-maker*, self-improving, is always a construction in progress," writes cultural historian Garry Wills. "He must ever be tinkering, improving, adjusting; starting over, fearful his product will get out of date, or rot in the storehouse."[17] This book is a history of the Self-Made Man—ambitious and anxious, creatively resourceful and chronically restive, the builder of culture and among the casualties of his own handiwork, a man who is, as the great French thinker Alexis de Tocqueville wrote in 1832, "restless in the midst of abundance."

In the first part of this book (chapters 1 and 2), I describe this fitful birth of the Self-Made Man and observe how he sought to secure his sense of himself in the years before the Civil War. In part 2 (chapters 3, 4, and 5) I trace his experiences from the end of the Civil War to the first decades of the twentieth century as he confronted new challenges in an increasingly industrialized, urban, and crowded society. His working life became too precarious to provide a firm footing, so the Self-Made Man turned to leisure activities, like sports, to give his man-

hood the boost he needed and strove to develop some all-male preserves where he could both be alone with other men and teach his
sons to become Self-Made Men themselves. Part 3 (chapters 6 and 7)
traces his efforts during the first half of this century, following him
through two world wars, one Depression, and adding the new media
of film and television, while part 4 (chapters 8 and 9) follows his
move to postwar suburbia and brings his saga up to the present day.

To map the meanings of manhood over the past two centuries, I've
relied upon an eclectic reading of a variety of sources—advice books
for young parents, and for anxious young men about to go off and
seek their fortunes; records of public displays of manly prowess and
recollections of private moments in masculine preserves; novels and
popular fiction in magazines and comic books, film and television;
political pamphlets engaged with questions raised by the women's
movement, as well as from electoral campaigns and union struggles;
and finally, more conventional political and economic history. I'm interested especially in moments of crisis when masculinity was seen as
threatened and people worked hard to try and salvage, revitalize, and
resurrect it. These crisis points in the meaning of manhood were also
crisis points in economic, political, and social life—moments when
men's relationships to their work, to their country, to their families,
to their visions, were transformed.

The advice of experts, the claims of politicians, and the flights of
literary or cinematic fantasy—these are the materials from which I
construct a history of the changing ideals of American manhood.
This book is less about what boys and men actually *did* than about
what they were told that they were *supposed* to do, feel, and think
and what happened in response to those prescriptions. America and
American masculinity evolved together, each in relation to the other,
a dynamic that has made of this country the wealthiest and most
powerful that the world has ever known and laid the possibilities for
unlimited personal success, strength, power, and achievement on the
shoulders of every Self-Made Man. Such possibilities have been both
our freedom and our imprisonment, propelling us forward toward
new horizons, and keeping us racing on treadmills, unable to stop.

Part One

THE MAKING OF THE SELF-MADE MAN, 1776–1865

CHAPTER 1

The Birth of the Self-Made Man

Nothing conceivable is so petty, so insipid, so crowded with
paltry interests—in one word, so anti-poetic—as the life of a
man in the United States.
—Alexis de Tocqueville *Democracy in America* (1832)

On April 16, 1787, a few weeks before the opening of the Constitutional Convention, the first professionally produced play in American history opened in New York. *The Contrast*, a five-act comedy by Royall Tyler, centered around two men—one, a disingenuous womanizing fop, and the other, a courageous American army officer—and the woman for whose affections they competed.[1] Tyler parodied the dandy's pretensions at the same time that he disdained the superficial vanities of women, contrasting both with an ideal of chaste and noble love. A patriotic play, *The Contrast* offered a kind of Declaration of Independence of Manners and Morals a decade after the original Declaration had spelled out political and economic rights and responsibilities.

The Contrast posed the most challenging question before the newly independent nation: What kind of nation were we going to be?

13

The sharply drawn differences between the two leading male characters, Billy Dimple and Colonel Manly, allowed the playwright to set (in names worthy of Dickens) the Old World against the New. Dimple was a feminized fop, an Anglophilic, mannered rogue who traveled to England and returned a dandy. "The ruddy youth, who washed his face at the cistern every morning, and swore . . . eternal love and constancy, was now metamorphosed into a flippant, pallid, polite beau, who devotes the morning to his toilet, reads a few pages of Chesterfield's letters [on the art of seduction], and then minces out to put the infamous principles in practice on every woman he meets."[2] His rival, the virtuous Colonel Manly, is a former military officer, modeled after George Washington, fresh from the victory over the British—a man loyal to his troops and to honor and duty. Dimple and Manly compete for the hand of Maria, daughter of Mr. Van Rough, a successful urban businessman who is looking to solidify his newly prosperous economic position with a marriage to the well-positioned Dimple. Van Rough's motto is "Money makes the mare go; keep your eye upon the main chance."[3]

While audiences were quick to see the political choices before them—pitting ill-gained wealth and dubious morality against hard work and civic virtue—Tyler was also presenting another contrast, the answer to a different set of questions: What kind of men would populate this new nation? What vision of manhood would be promoted? What would it mean to be a man in the newly independent United States? Dimple, Manly, and Van Rough offered the audience a contrast among three types of men, three versions of manhood; each embodied different relationships to his work, to his family, to his nation. The signal work in the history of American theater is also one of the earliest meditations on American manhood.

When we first meet Maria Van Rough in the play's opening scene, she is disconsolate, extolling the manly virtues that her fiancé, Dimple, lacks:

The manly virtue of courage, that fortitude which steels the heart against the keenest misfortunes, which interweaves the laurel of glory amidst the instruments of torture and death, displays something so noble, so exalted, that in despite of the prejudices of education I cannot but admire it, even in a savage.

Maria sees Dimple as "a depraved wretch, whose only virtue is a polished exterior; who is actuated by the unmanly ambition of conquering the defenseless; whose heart, insensible to the emotions of patriotism, dilates at the plaudits of every unthinking girl; whose laurels are the sighs and tears of the miserable victims of his specious behavior."[4]

Enter Colonel Manly. When he and Maria meet by accident in the second act, they are smitten, but Manly's virtue precludes any action on his part.[5] As the play builds to the inevitable confrontation between Dimple and Manly, Tyler provides brief exchanges between the two men (and their manservants) to maintain the audience's interest. In one exchange they parry over the question of whether aristocratic wealth saps virility. Manly warns that no one "shall convince me that a nation, to become great, must first become dissipated. Luxury is surely the bane of a nation: Luxury! which enervates both soul and body, . . . which renders a people weak at home and accessible to bribery, corruption and force from abroad."

Dimple responds by describing the pleasures of seduction. "There is not much pleasure when a man of the world and a finished coquette meet, who perfectly know each other; but how delicious it is to excite the emotions of joy, hope, expectation, and delight in the bosom of a lovely girl who believes every tittle of what you say to be serious!" (We learn later that Dimple's disquisition was more than theoretical, as he has seduced all three of the play's leading women.) Manly's retort is angry and virtuous. "The man who, under pretensions of marriage, can plant thorns in the bosom of an innocent, unsuspecting girl is more detestable than a common robber, in the same proportion as private violence is more despicable than open force."[6]

Finally, Dimple is exposed as a phony and denounced by all. Even in defeat, though, he asks that those assembled consider "the contrast between a gentleman who has read Chesterfield and received the polish of Europe and an unpolished, untravelled American." Manly gets Maria's hand and also has the last word, closing the play with what he has learned, that "probity, virtue, honour, though they should not have received the polish of Europe, will secure to an honest American the good graces of his fair countrywomen."[7]

Maria's father, Mr. Van Rough, presents still another masculine archetype; indeed, each of the three—Dimple, Manly, and Van Rough—embodies one of the three dominant ideals of American manhood available at the turn of the nineteenth century.[8] Despite the play's focus on the other two, it is Van Rough who would come to dominate the new country in a new century. Dimple represents what I will call the Genteel Patriarch. Though Tyler's critical characterization sets Dimple out as a flamboyant fop, the Genteel Patriarch was a powerful ideal through the early part of the nineteenth century. It was, of course, an ideal inherited from Europe. At his best, the Genteel Patriarch represents a dignified aristocratic manhood, committed to the British upper-class code of honor and to well-rounded character, with exquisite tastes and manners and refined sensibilities. To the Genteel Patriarch, manhood meant property ownership and a benevolent patriarchal authority at home, including the moral instruction of his sons. A Christian gentleman, the Genteel Patriarch embodied love, kindness, duty, and compassion, exhibited through philanthropic work, church activities, and deep involvement with his family. For an illustration of the Genteel Patriarch, think of Thomas Jefferson at Monticello, George Washington, John Adams, or James Madison.

Colonel Manly embodies a second type of manhood—the Heroic Artisan.[9] This archetype was also inherited from Europe, despite Royall Tyler's attempt to Americanize him. Independent, virtuous, and honest, the Heroic Artisan is stiffly formal in his manners with women, stalwart and loyal to his male comrades. On the family farm or in his urban crafts shop, he was an honest toiler, unafraid of hard work, proud of his craftsmanship and self-reliance. With a leather apron covering his open shirt and his sleeves rolled up, Boston silversmith Paul Revere, standing proudly at his forge, well illustrates this type.

The newcomer to this scene is Mr. Van Rough, the wealthy entrepreneur, whose newly acquired financial fortune leads to his social aspirations of marrying his daughter to the well-placed aristocratic Dimple. Van Rough represents the Self-Made Man, a model of man-

hood that derives identity entirely from a man's activities in the public sphere, measured by accumulated wealth and status, by geographic and social mobility. At the time, this economic fortune would
have to be translated into permanent social standing—Van Rough
must try to become Mr. Smooth. Since a man's fortune is as easily
unmade as it is made, the Self-Made Man is uncomfortably linked to
the volatile marketplace, and he depends upon continued mobility.
Of course, Self-Made Men were not unique to America; as the natural
outcome of capitalist economic life, they were known as *nouveaux
riches* in revolutionary France (and also known as *noblesse de robe*, as
well as other, less pleasant, terms, in the preceding century), and
they had their counterparts in every European country. But in America, the land of immigrants and democratic ideals, the land without
hereditary titles, they were present from the start, and they came to
dominate much sooner than in Europe.

In the growing commercial and, soon, industrial society of the
newly independent America, the Self-Made Man seemed to be born
at the same time as his country. A man on the go, he was, as one
lawyer put it in 1838, "made for action, and the bustling scenes of
moving life, and not the poetry or romance of existence."[10] Mobile,
competitive, aggressive in business, the Self-Made Man was also temperamentally restless, chronically insecure, and desperate to achieve
a solid grounding for a masculine identity.

Royall Tyler hoped that the republican virtue of the Heroic Artisan
would triumph over the foppish Genteel Patriarch, just as democratic
America defeated the aristocratic British. But it was not to be: It was
the relatively minor character, Van Rough, who would emerge triumphant in the nineteenth century, and the mobility and insecurity
of the Self-Made Man came to dominate the American definition of
manhood.

This book is the story of American manhood—how it has changed
over time and yet how certain principles have remained the same. I
believe some of its most important characteristics owe their existence
to the timing of the Revolution—the emergence of the Self-Made
Men at that time and their great success in the new American democracy have a lot to do with what it is that defines a "real" man even
today.

Let's look at the Self-Made Man's first appearance on the historical stage, which will help us limn the shifts in the definitions of manhood in the first half of the nineteenth century. An old standard rooted in the life of the community and the qualities of a man's character gave way to a new standard based on individual achievement, a shift in emphasis "from service to community and cultivation of the spirit to improvement of the individual and concern with his body."[11] From a doctrine of "usefulness" and "service" to the preoccupation with the "self," American manhood got off to a somewhat disturbing start.

Part of this start, the American Revolution, brought a revolt of the sons against the father—in this case, the Sons of Liberty against Father England.[12] And this introduced a new source of tension in the act of resolving an old one. The relatively casual coexistence of the Genteel Patriarch and the Heroic Artisan had been made possible by the colonies' relationship with England. Many Genteel Patriarchs looked to England not just for political and economic props but also for cultural prescriptions for behavior. Patriarchs had the right to lead their country by virtue of their title. The American colonies had few noblemen, like Sir William Randolph, but they had plenty of substitutes, from upper-class political elites to Dutch landed gentry in New York and the large plantation owners in Virginia and around Chesapeake Bay. There was little tension between them and the laborers who worked for or near them. The real problem was that as long as the colonies remained in British hands, it seemed to all that manly autonomy and self-control were impossible. Being a man meant being in charge of one's own life, liberty, and property.

Being a man meant also not being a boy. A man was independent, self-controlled, responsible; a boy was dependent, irresponsible, and lacked control. And language reflected these ideas. The term *manhood* was synonymous with "adulthood." Just as black slaves were "boys," the white colonists felt enslaved by the English father, infantilized, and thus emasculated.

The American Revolution resolved this tension because, in the terms of the reigning metaphor of the day, it freed the sons from the tyranny of a despotic father. The Declaration of Independence was a declaration of manly adulthood, a manhood that was counterposed to the British version against which American men were revolting. Jefferson and his coauthors accused the king of dissolving their representative assemblies because they had opposed "with manly firmness, his invasions on the rights of the people." (Of course, the rebellion of the sons did not eliminate the need for patriarchal authority. George Washington was immediately hailed as the Father of our Country, and many wished he would become king.)

By contrast, British manhood and, by extension, aristocratic conceptions of manhood (which would soon come to include the Genteel Patriarch) were denounced as feminized, lacking manly resolve and virtue, and therefore, ruling arbitrarily. Critiques of monarchy and aristocracy were tainted with a critique of aristocratic luxury as effeminate. John Adams posed the question about how to prevent the creation of a new aristocracy in a letter to Thomas Jefferson in December 1819. "Will you tell me how to prevent riches becoming the effects of temperance and industry? Will you tell me how to prevent riches from producing luxury? Will you tell me how to prevent luxury from producing effeminacy, intoxication, extravagance, vice and folly?"[13]

Works of fiction and essays exploited the Lockean theme of America as the state of nature in which individual morality could emerge, a contrast between virtue born of nature and vice born of luxury and refinement. In the preface to *Edgar Huntley*, the first work of fiction written by an American specifically about the American experience, novelist Charles Brockden Brown claimed that he had replaced the "puerile superstitions and exploded manner, Gothic castles and chimeras" of the European novel with "the incidents of Indian hostility and the perils of the Western wilderness." And Washington Irving echoed these themes a few decades later, writing that "[w]e send our youth abroad to grow luxurious and effeminate in Europe; it appears to me, that a previous tour on the Prairies would be more likely to produce that manliness, simplicity and self-dependence, most in unison with our political institutions." In politics and in culture, in both fiction and fact, American men faced a choice between effeminacy and manliness, between aristocracy and republicanism.[14]

To retrieve their manhood from its British guardians, the Sons of Liberty carried out a symbolic patricide. "Having left the British parent as a child, America miraculously becomes capable of its own nurturing; independence transforms the son into his own parent, a child into an adult."[15] The American man was now free to invent himself. The birth of the nation was also the birth of a New Man, who, as Hector St. John de Crèvecoeur put it in his marvelous *Letters from an American Farmer* (1782), "leaving behind him all his ancient prejudices and manners, receives new ones from the new mode of life he has embraced, the new government he obeys, and the new rank he holds. The American is a new man who acts upon new principles. . . . Here individuals of all nations are melted into a new race of men."[16]

At first, the American new man at the turn of the nineteenth century cautiously tried to fit in, either as a Genteel Patriarch, Heroic Artisan, or even Van Roughian Self-Made Man. In the early American magazines, for example, heroism was defined by a man's usefulness and service, his recognition of responsibilities. Between 1810 and 1820, the term *breadwinner* was coined to denote this responsible family man. The breadwinner ideal would remain one of the central characteristics of American manhood until the present day. At its moment of origin, it meant that a man's "great aim" was "to fill his station with dignity, and to be useful to his fellow beings"; in another magazine, a man's death was lamentable because of "his desire of usefulness—his wish to be one of those by whom society is enlightened and made better."[17]

This is well illustrated in *The Farmer's Friend*, an advice book written by the Reverend Enos Hitchcock in 1793. In recounting the story of the well-named Charles Worthy, Hitchcock describes the Heroic Artisan as young farmer and recounts his gradual rise as he diligently pursues his calling. Worthy, Hitchcock writes, "never felt so happy as when conscious of industriously following his occupation. . . . In order to merit the esteem of others, we must become acquainted with the duties of our particular professions, occupations, or stations in life, and discharge the duties of them in the most useful and agreeable manner." Virtue inheres in the work virtuously performed, the calling followed, not in the financial rewards that accrue to the virtuous worker. Benjamin Franklin, perhaps the first American prototype of the Self-Made Man, underscored this theme. "In order to secure my credit and character as a tradesman," he wrote in his *Autobiogra-phy*, first published in 1791, "I took care not only to be in *reality* in-dustrious and frugal, but to avoid all appearances to the contrary." To Franklin, as to many other early Self Made Men, image may not have been everything, but it was of importance.[18]

But patricide has significant costs, including the loneliness of the fatherless son and the burden of adult responsibilities placed upon his shoulders.[19] American men's chief fear at the time was that the overthrown effeminate aristocracy would return to haunt them. Samuel Adams articulated this fear in an article in the *Massachusetts Sentinel* in January 1785. "Did we consult the history of Athens and Rome, we should find that so long as they continued their frugality and simplicity of manners, they shone with superlative glory; but no sooner were effeminate refinements introduced amongst them, than they visibly fell from whatever was elevated and magnanimous, and became feeble and timid, dependent, slavish and false." In other words, aristocratic luxury and effeminacy threatened the Revolution's moral edge. The post-Revolutionary American man had to be con-stantly vigilant against such temptation, eternally distancing himself from feminized indulgence.[20]

A few years later, Benjamin Rush saw the threat to the newly emerging republican manhood as coming from both sides—from ef-feminate aristocrats as well as from lazy laborers. In his "Address to the Ministers of the Gospel of Every Denomination in the United States upon Subjects Interesting to Morals" (1788), Rush advocated that American men turn themselves into "republican machines." He called for the elimination of fairs, racehorses, cockfighting, and clubs of all kinds, argued that all forms of play be banned on Sundays, and that all intoxicating spirits, including liquor and wine, the "parents of idleness and extravagance," be prohibited.

But Adams and Rush, like Royall Tyler, were wrong. Neither effemi-nate aristocrats nor lazy laborers were the real threats. Billy Dimple's time was slowly passing, and Colonel Manly could never be as domi-nant as Cincinnatus. Instead, the economic boom of the new coun-try's first decades produced the triumph of the Self-Made Men, the Van Roughs, men who were neither aristocratic fops nor virtuous drones—far from it. These Self-Made Men built America.

Between 1800 and 1840 the United States experienced a market revolution. Freed from colonial dependence, mercantile capitalism remade the nation. America undertook the construction of a national transportation system and developed extensive overseas and domestic commerce. Between 1793 and 1807 American exports tripled, while between 1800 and 1840 the total amount of free labor outside the farm sector rose from 17 to 37 percent.[21] The fiscal and banking system expanded rapidly; from eighty-nine banks in 1811 to 246 five years later and 788 by 1837. The economic boom meant westward expansion as well as dramatic urban growth.

Such dramatic economic changes were accompanied by political, social, and ideological shifts. Historian Nancy Cott notes that the period 1780–1830 witnessed a demographic transition to modern patterns of childbirth and childcare, development of uniform legal codes and procedures, expansion of primary education, the beginning of the democratization of the political process, and the "invention of a new language of political and social thought." Democracy was expanding, and with it, by the end of the first half of the century, America was "converted to acquisitiveness," a conversion that would have dramatic consequences for the meanings of manhood in industrializing America. In the third decade of the century, between 1825 and 1835, a bourgeoisie worthy of the name came into being in the Northeast, a self-consciously self-made middle class.[22]

The emerging capitalist market in the early nineteenth century both freed individual men and destabilized them. No longer were men bound to the land, to their estates, to Mother England, or to the tyrannical father, King George. No longer did their manhood rest on their craft traditions, guild memberships, or participation in the virtuous republic of the New England small town. America was entering a new age, and men were free to create their own destinies, to find their own ways, to rise as high as they could, to write their own biographies. God had made man a "moral free agent," according to revivalist minister Charles Finney in a celebrated sermon in 1830. The American Adam could fashion himself in his own image. This new individual freedom was as socially and psychologically unsettling as it was exciting and promising. To derive one's identity, and especially one's identity as a man, from marketplace successes was a risky proposition.

Yet that is precisely what defined the Self-Made Man: success in the market, individual achievement, mobility, wealth. America expressed political autonomy; the Self-Made Man embodied economic autonomy. This was the manhood of the rising middle class. The flip side of this economic autonomy is anxiety, restlessness, loneliness. Manhood is no longer fixed in land or small-scale property ownership or dutiful service. Success must be earned, manhood must be proved—and proved constantly.

Contemporary observers of early nineteenth century American life noticed the shift immediately. One of the most popular tracts of the 1830s was Thomas Hunt's *The Book of Wealth* (1836), which went through several printings while proving to its readers that the Bible mandates that men strive for wealth. "No man can be obedient to God's will as revealed in the Bible without, as the general result, becoming wealthy," Hunt wrote. The drive for wealth penetrated everything. "Nearly all Americans trade and speculate," observed Thomas Nichols in 1837. "They are ready to swap horses, swap watches, swap farms; and to buy and sell anything. . . . Money is the habitual measure of all things." One English traveler in 1844 remarked that Americans used the phrase "I calculate" as a synonym for "I believe" or "I think." "Things are in the saddle, and ride mankind," quipped Ralph Waldo Emerson in an 1847 ode, which commented on the reversal of priorities encouraged by the emerging capitalist market.[23]

In the early republic, as today, equal opportunity meant equal opportunity to either succeed or to fail. "True republicanism requires that every man shall have an equal chance—that every man shall be free to become as unequal as he can," was the way one advice manual, *How to Behave*, expressed it. "Some are sinking, others rising, others balancing, some gradually ascending toward the top, others flamingly leading down," wrote a young Daniel Webster. In his 1837 book *The Americans*, Francis Grund commented on the "endless striving," the "great scramble in which all are troubled and none are satisfied." "A man, in America, is not despised for being poor in the outset . . . but every year which passes, without adding to his prosperity, is a reproach to his understanding of industry" and, he might have added, a stain on his sense of manliness.[24]

The contrast with European manhood was a constant theme, and one that European observers noted with special relish. The Frenchman Michel Chevalier wrote, after a visit to Jacksonian America, of its "universal instability." "Here is all circulation, motion, and boiling agitation. . . . Men change their houses, their climate, their trade, their laws, their officers, their constitutions."[25] Even after ten years as a resident of Boston, the Viennese immigrant Francis Grund still couldn't figure it out:

> There is probably no people on earth with whom business constitutes pleasure, and industry amusement, in an equal degree with the inhabitants of the United States of America. Active participation is not only the principal source of their happiness, and the foundation of their national greatness, but they are absolutely wretched without it. . . . Business is the very soul of an American: he pursues it, not as a means of procuring for himself and his family the necessary comforts of life, but as the fountain of all human felicity.[26]

The acclaimed British novelist Charles Dickens expected to be delighted when he visited the United States in 1842 but found himself increasingly disappointed with the American people both for their self-congratulatory myopia and defensiveness and for their energy and restlessness. As he chronicled in his rambling work *American Notes for General Circulation* (1842), Dickens was awestruck in this "great emporium of commerce" as much by the "national love of trade" as by the "universal distrust" that accompanied it, which Americans "carry into every transaction of public life." Dickens told the American people,

> It has rendered you so fickle, and so given to change, that your inconstancy has passed into a proverb; for you no sooner set up an ideal firmly, than you are sure to pull it down and dash it into fragments: and this, because directly you reward a benefactor, or a public servant, you distrust him, merely because he *is* rewarded; and immediately apply yourselves to find out, either that you have been too bountiful in your acknowledgements, or he remiss in his deserts.[27]

Dickens found Americans "dull and gloomy," without either joy or humor, and found himself "oppressed by the prevailing seriousness and melancholy air of business" among these strange people, "restless and locomotive, with an irresistible desire for change."[28]

The era's most perceptive visitor—perhaps the most observant visitor in our history—was a young French nobleman, Alexis de Tocqueville. When Tocqueville arrived in America in 1830, he was instantly struck by the dramatically different temperament of the American, a difference he attributed to the difference between aristocracies and democracies. Unlike his European counterpart, Tocqueville observed, the American man was a radical democrat— equal and alone, masterless and separate, autonomous and defenseless against the tyranny of the majority. Each citizen was equal, and "equally impotent, poor and isolated." In Europe caste distinctions between nobles and commoners froze social positions but also connected them; "aristocracy links everybody, from peasant to king, in one long chain." Democracy meant freedom but disconnection; it "breaks the chain and frees every link." American democracy also meant a great sliding towards the center; all Americans tended to "contract the ways of thinking of the manufacturing and trading classes."[29]

Tocqueville's dissection of the double-edged quality of the democratic personality remains as incisive today as it was in the early nineteenth century. The middle-class man was an anxious achiever, constantly striving, casting his eyes nervously about as he tried, as Mr. Van Rough put it in The Contrast, to "mind the main chance." The American man was "restless in the midst of abundance." In a passage that eloquently defines this restlessness of the Self-Made Man, Tocqueville writes:

> An American will build a house in which to pass his old age and sell it before the roof is on; he will plant a garden and rent it just as the trees are coming into bearing; he will clear a field and leave others to reap the harvest; he will take up a profession and leave it, settle in one place and soon go off elsewhere with his changing desires. . . . [H]e will travel five hundred miles in a few days as a distraction from his happiness.[30]

Like Dickens, Tocqueville also found the American marked by a "strange melancholy"; every American "is eaten up with a longing to rise, but hardly any of them seem to entertain very great hopes or to aim very high." The American man was a man in a hurry but with not very far to go.[31]

Even the term *self-made man* was an American neologism, first coined by Henry Clay in a speech in the U.S. Senate in 1832. Defending a protective tariff that he believed would widen opportunities for humble men to rise in business, he declared that in Kentucky "almost every manufactory known to me is in the hands of enterprising, self-made men, who have whatever wealth they possess by patient and diligent labor."[32]

The term immediately caught on. Rev. Calvin Colton noted in 1844 that America "is a country where men start from a humble origin, and from small beginnings gradually rise in the world, as the reward of merit and industry. . . . One has as good a chance as another, according to his talents, prudence, and personal exertions. . . . [T]his is a country of *self-made men* [in which] work is held in the highest respect [while] the idle, lazy, poor man gets little pity in his poverty."[33] By the 1840s and 1850s a veritable cult of the Self-Made Man had appeared, as young men devoured popular biographies and inspirational homilies to help future self-made men create themselves. John Frost's *Self Made Men in America* (1848), Charles Seymore's *Self-Made Men* (1858) and Freeman Hunt's *Worth and Wealth* (1856) and *Lives of American Merchants* (1858) provided self-making homilies, packaged between brief biographies of poor boys who had made it rich.

The central characteristic of being self-made was that the proving ground was the public sphere, specifically the workplace. And the workplace was a man's world (and a native-born white man's world at that). If manhood could be proved, it had to be proved in the eyes of other men. From the early nineteenth century until the present day, most of men's relentless efforts to prove their manhood contain this core element of homosociality. From fathers and boyhood friends to our teachers, coworkers, and bosses, it is the evaluative eyes of other men that are always upon us, watching, judging. It was in this regime of scrutiny that such men were tested. "Every man you meet has a rating or an estimate of himself which he never loses or forgets," wrote Kenneth Wayne in his popular turn-of-the-century advice book, *Building the Young Man* (1912). "A man has his own rating, and instantly he lays it alongside of the other man." Almost a century later, another man remarked to psychologist Sam Osherson that "[b]y the time you're an adult, it's easy to think you're always in competition with men, for the attention of women, in sports, at work."[34]

In the early decades of the nineteenth century, the Self-Made Man competed with the two other archetypes from Tyler's play. The Genteel Patriarch had to be displaced, and the Heroic Artisan had to be uprooted and brought into the new industrial marketplace. In the rush of the new century, Self-Made Men did indeed triumph, but neither the patriarch nor the laborer disappeared overnight.

First, the Genteel Patriarch. While the richest tenth of all Americans held slightly less (49.6%) than half the wealth in 1774, they held 73 percent in 1860, and the richest 1 percent more than doubled their share of the wealth, from 12.6 to 29 percent, and then to about 50 percent by mid-century. The period 1820–1860 was "probably the most unequal period in American history."[35] But these new wealthy were no longer the landed aristocracy but the new merchants and industrialists.[36] Economically, Van Rough simply blew away Billy Dimple.

American culture followed suit. Gone were the powder, wigs, and richly ornamented and colorfully patterned clothing that had marked the old gentry; the new man of commerce wore plain and simple clothing "to impart trust and confidence in business affairs."[37] Countless pundits recast the Genteel Patriarch as a foppish dandy as they railed against Europe, against traditional feudal society, against historical obligation.[38] Even older, venerated Genteel Patriarchs were not immune to the feminization of the landed gentry. Jefferson himself was castigated as dandified, the product of aristocratic and chivalric Virginia, "America's Athens." He was accused of "timidity, whimsicalness," "a wavering of disposition" and a weakness for flattery, a man who "took counsel in his feelings and imagination," and the Jeffersonians were condemned for their "womanish resentment" against England and their "womanish attachment to France."[39]

Leading the charge against the Genteel Patriarch was Ralph Waldo Emerson, who signaled the shifting taste in his seminal essay "The American Scholar" (1837). Emerson "enshrined psychic self-sovereignty as the essential manly virtue," according to literary critic T. Walter Herbert, and the theme of his essays "of self-reliant struggle from humble origins to high position became the ruling narrative of manly worth, supplanting that of the well-born lad demonstrating his superior breeding in the exercise of responsibilities that were his birthright."[40] Nathaniel Hawthorne even suggested that a young man could be crippled by inheriting "a great fortune." Here was a "race of non-producers," warned S. C. Allen in 1830, a "new sort of aristocracy, of a more uncompromising character than the feudal, or any landed aristocracy can ever be."[41]

Such efforts were not altogether successful, but certainly indicated a trend. Even in the mid-nineteenth century cultural observers venerated a "romantic consumptiveness" as the preferred male body type—composed of a thin physique, pale complexion and languid air. (Muscular bodies were snubbed as artisanal, a sign of a laborer.) "An American exquisite must not measure more than 24 inches round the chest; his face must be pale, thin and long; and he must be spindle-shanked," wrote the venerable observer Francis Grund in 1839. "There is nothing our women dislike so much as corpulency; weak and refined are synonymous." (Even then there was a difference between a manhood constructed for women's approval and the masculinity of a man's man.) It was in the Old South where the Genteel Patriarch made his last stand, at least until the Civil War. While Southern manhood was increasingly caricatured as effeminate and dandified in the Northern press, even in the South the old cavalier's time was passing.

Meanwhile, the Heroic Artisan was losing his independence, which he so dearly prized. He "looks the whole world in the face / For he owes not any man," as Henry Wadsworth Longfellow put it in "The Village Blacksmith" (1844).[42] Disciplined and responsible, the Heroic Artisan believed that "independent men of relatively small means were both entitled to full citizenship and best equipped to exercise it." A firm believer in self-government, the Heroic Artisan was the embodiment of Jeffersonian liberty; the virtuous "yeoman of the city," as he had called them. Before the Civil War nine of every ten American men owned their own farm, shop, or small crafts workshop. About half of all workmen were employed in shops of ten or fewer; four-fifths worked in shops of no more than twenty. His body was his own, his labor a form of property.[43]

The independence of the Heroic Artisan did not mean that he was isolated, reclusive, nor on the other hand, overly competitive; both in his daily interactions in the workplace and as he strolled through the city or town, the Heroic Artisan saw himself as deeply embedded within a community of equals, a "shirtless democracy," in the words of Mike Walsh. On the occasion of the dedication of the Apprentice's Library in 1820, Thomas Mercein said that "[e]very man looks with independent equality in the face of his neighbor; those are exalted whose superior virtues entitle them to confidence; they are revered as legislators, obeyed as magistrates, but still considered as equals." One bit of verse used equality before God as another foundation for political equality:

> Of rich and poor the difference what?—
> In working or in working not
> Why then on Sunday we're as great
> As those who own some vast estate.

Sure, the Heroic Artisan wanted to get ahead in the market, and he was not immune to its rewards or temptations. Even Tocqueville remarked that the craftsman's goal was not "to manufacture as well as possible" but to "produce with great rapidity many imperfect commodities." But he was just as determined to retain his independence and protect the independence of the community of equals in the republic of virtue.[44]

The cement of this republican virtue was the coupling of economic autonomy to political community and workplace solidarity. This combination is the essence of *producerism*, an ideology that claimed that virtue came from the hard work of those who produce the world's wealth. Producerism held that there was a deep-rooted conflict in society between the producing and the nonproducing classes and that work was a source of moral instruction, economic success, and political virtue. "We ask that every man become an independent proprietor, possessing enough of the goods of this world, to be able by his own moderate industry to provide for the wants of his body," wrote Orestes Brownson in his tract "The Laboring Classes" (1840). The doctrines of producerism resurface constantly through the century as rural and urban workingmen, from the Populists to the Knights of Labor and early union organizers, cast their resistance to proletarianization in terms of preservation of economic autonomy and political community.[45]

The British historian E. P. Thompson's explorations of the emergence of the British working class revealed an easy flow between the workplace and leisure in the British villages of the pre-Industrial Revolution, even in the actual length and organization of the working day.[46] In their workshops, apprentices, journeymen, and master craftsmen integrated work and leisure. Customers would appear, contract for specific tasks, and socialize and wait while it was being done; when no customers appeared, masters and journeymen would continue to train young apprentices while jugs of hard cider were constantly passed around. At leisure the Heroic Artisan was communitarian, participating regularly in "evenings of drink, merriment, and ceremony that were part of longstanding premodern traditions" and that provided ample opportunities for artisans to meet in a mood of "mutual self-esteem and exaltation."[47]

Workplace solidarity and ease of movement between work and leisure also spilled over into the organization of the trades. Many trades resembled fraternal orders in which artisans developed modest welfare systems for their sick and needy brethren or for the families of deceased brethren. Each volunteer fire department, for example, was its own fraternal society with its own insignias, mottoes, "freshly minted traditions," "fiercely masculine rituals," and sacred emblems like the fire hose, company crest, and fire chief's trumpet.[48]

These independent artisans, craftsmen, and small shopkeepers were on the defensive throughout the first half of the century. Each of the periodic economic crises had struck these artisans especially hard. Older skills became obsolete and factory employment grew— from an average of eight women and men to anywhere between fifty and five hundred men.[49] Masters increased the scale, pace, and routine of production, hiring young strangers, with whom they shared only contractual relations, rather than the sons of their neighbors.[50] Real wages of skilled workers declined, and workplace autonomy seemed to be disappearing everywhere. New forms of labor control, including the putting-out system, sweated labor, and wages, all eroded the virtuous republic.

In Philadelphia in 1819, three of four workers were idle, and nearly two thousand were jailed for unpaid debts. By 1836 ten major strikes hit the skilled trades, and convulsive strikes took place on the waterfront and the building sites. In June of that year, thirty thousand men showed up for a demonstration in New York, the single largest protest gathering in American history to that point. Also in New York six thousand masons and carpenters were discharged in April 1837 alone.[51]

The sons of the Sons of Liberty were fast becoming, as they put it in a letter of protest to President John Tyler, "mere machines of labor." Ironically, the same experiences that cemented their solidarity and underscored their autonomy now left them isolated and defensive. While, politically, democracy had "hastened the destruction of onerous forms of personal subordination to masters, landlords, and creditors that American working people had historically faced," writes the labor historian David Montgomery, it also left them unprotected from unscrupulous masters and conniving employers and disconnected from others who shared a similar fate.[52]

Many workingmen tried to combat this trend by organizing the nation's first workingmen's political parties, there to redress their economic and political grievances in parties like the Mechanics Union of Trade Associations (1827), the Workingmen's Party (1828), and the Equal Rights Party (1833). These organizations' rhetoric was saturated with equations of autonomy and manhood. Loss of autonomy was equated with emasculation; economic dependence on wages paid by an employer was equivalent to social and sexual dependency. The factory system was "subversive of liberty," according to one worker in the fledgling National Trades Union in 1834, "calculated to change the character of a people from bold and free to enervated, dependent and slavish." Under such circumstances, held an editorialist in the union newspaper *The Man*, it would have been "unmanly" and undignified, "an abdication of their responsibilities as citizens" if they did *not* organize.[53]

Newspapers like *The Man* inveighed regularly against three groups: women, immigrants, and black slaves. Women had earlier been excluded (of course) from craft guilds and apprenticeships, but the emerging working class supported women's complete exclusion from the public sphere, even though only around 2 percent of all females over the age of ten worked in any type of industry. These formerly independent small shopkeepers and craftsmen opposed women's rights to education, property ownership, and suffrage.[54] It was as if workplace manhood could only be retained if the workplace had only men in it.

And only native-born men at that. Immigration had increased rapidly through the first half of the century, from 140,439 in the 1820s to 599,125 in the 1830s. During the 1840s immigration more than tripled to 1,713,251, and 2,598,214 more immigrants arrived during the 1850s. Anti-immigrant demonstrations and riots followed as the native-born artisans felt increasingly threatened by these lessskilled workers, who were willing to work longer hours for lower wages.[55] In antebellum America Irish immigrants were especially stamped with a problematic masculinity. Imagined as rough and primitive, uncivilized and uncivilizable, the Irish were ridiculed as a subhuman species, born to inferiority and incapable of being true American men.[56]

Of course, not all native-born men were real men. In an arresting book the historian David Roediger argues that, from the moment of its origins, the white working class used black slaves as the economic and moral "other," whose economic dependency indicated emasculation and moral degeneracy. Whiteness, Roediger argues, served as a secondary "wage" for white workers who were resisting the view of wage labor as a form of wage slavery. By asserting their whiteness, workers could compensate for their loss of autonomy; the "status and privileges conferred by race could be used to make up for alienating and exploitative class relationships."[57]

What Roediger describes economically, social historian Eric Lott discusses symbolically in his analysis of blackface minstrel shows in antebellum America. Minstrel shows performed a double mimesis;

the minstrel show was, Lott argues, both love and theft. The projection of white men's fears onto black men was simultaneously for "whites insecure about their whiteness" and for men insecure about their manhood. "Mediating white men's relations with other white men, minstrel acts certainly made currency out of the black man himself," he writes. The "pale gaze" of the white audience faced with a caricatured black identity paralleled the "male gaze" of this now conscious audience of men reasserting their manhood through the symbolic appropriation of the black man's sexual potency.[58]

In these literal and symbolic ways the American working class that emerged in the decades before the Civil War was self-consciously white, native-born, and male, rooted as much in racism, sexism, and xenophobia as in craft pride and workplace autonomy—a combination that has haunted its efforts to retrieve its lost dignity and organize successfully against industrial capitalists throughout American history. The rage of the dying class of Heroic Artisans took many forms.

In the 1830s, however, something remarkable happened. The working class saw its salvation in the presidential campaign of one of its own. Andrew Jackson was both the last gasp of Jeffersonian republican virtue and the first expression of the politics of class-based resentment.

Andrew Jackson was not the first American leader to combine virulent hypermasculinity with vengeful, punitive political maneuvers nor, certainly, was he (nor will he be) the last. But he was one of the most colorful and charismatic of such, and he embodied the hopes and fears of many men. The emotions that seem to have animated Jacksonian America were fear and rage. When Jackson first arrived in the Senate, he was unable to speak because of "the rashness of his feelings," then–Vice President Thomas Jefferson recalled. "I have seen him attempt it repeatedly and as often choke with rage." A "choleric, impetuous" man, according to turn-of-the-century historian Frederick Jackson Turner, Jackson was a "tall, lank, uncouth-looking personage, with long locks of hair hanging over his face and a cue [ponytail] down his back tied in an eel skin; his dress singular, his manners those of a rough backwoodsman."[59]

It is difficult not to see Jackson and the men he stood for in starkly Freudian terms. Here was the fatherless son, struggling without guidance to separate from the mother and, again, for adult mastery over his environment. Terrified of infantilization, of infantile dependency, his rage propelled the furious effort to prove his manhood against those who threatened it, notably women and infantilized "others." It was as if America found an adolescent leader to preside over its own adolescence as a nation. Here was "the nursling of the wilds," a "pupil of the wilderness," according to George Bancroft; a man, as Tocqueville put it, "of violent character and middling capacities." Andrew Jackson was the consummate schoolyard bully.[60]

The hero of the War of 1812 and the Creek War of 1813/14, Jackson saw his military exploits as an effort to overcome his own "indolence" and achieve republican purification through violence. He came to power as the champion of the Heroic Artisan, whether rural yeoman farmer or urban artisan, against the effete aristocracy of the Eastern urban entrepreneur and the decadent Europeanized landed gentry. One laudatory biography of Jackson from 1820 began with alarm over the "voluptuousness and effeminacy" that was attendant upon the sudden rise of new wealth in America, characteristics that were "rapidly diminishing that exalted sense of national glory."[61]

The Heroic Artisans embraced Jackson. He campaigned in 1828, in the words of a campaign song, as one "who can fight" against John Quincy Adams, "who can write," pitting "the plowman" against "the professor."[62] As president his hostility towards paper currency, his opposition to corporate charters, his deep suspicion of public enterprise and public debt—all elements of American producerism—appealed to small planters, farmers, mechanics, and laborers, the "bone and sinew of the country." His administration was saturated with the rhetoric of the violent, short-tempered, impulsively democratic artisanate, especially in his struggle against the savage nature of primitive manhood (Indians) and the effete, decadent institutions that signaled Europeanized overcivilization (the Bank).

In his brilliant, psychoanalytically informed biography and cultural history of Jackson and his historical era, Michael Rogin focuses on these twin peaks of the Jacksonian landscape. Jackson projected his own and the nation's fears of dependency onto the Indians, who were cast as the passive, helpless children that the Heroic Artisan was attempting to avoid becoming. A simple pattern emerged: Appropriate their land and abridge their freedom because you see them as passive and helpless. This makes them passive and helpless, which then allows you to justify the whole thing by referring to the passivity and helplessness you have just caused.

It was as if, by making these independent Indian tribes dependent upon the benevolent paternalism of a centralizing state, white artisans and farmers could avoid becoming dependent. "Like a kind father," James Gadsden said to the Seminoles in Florida, "the President says to you, there are lands enough for both his white and his red children. His white are strong, and might exterminate his red, but he will not permit them. He will preserve his red children." And Jackson told three chiefs that the bad counsel they had heeded "compelled your Father the President to send his white children to chastise and subdue you, and thereby give peace to his children both red and white." Now, Jackson continued, it was necessary for the Indians to come under the President's care, where "your Father the President may be enabled to extend to you his fatherly care and assistance." No sooner had the sons of liberty thrown off their own tyrannical monarchical father than they set themselves up as the benevolent fathers they had never had and, tragically, were utterly unable to become.[63]

If the Indian symbolized the savage brute transformed into a helpless dependent child, the Bank symbolized the devouring mother from whose grasp the adolescent nation was trying to escape. The "Mother Bank," was a "monster Hydra," a "hydra of corruption," as Jackson himself put it, and it became a symbol of corporate power— paper money, monopoly privilege, complex credit—that turned men from "the sober pursuits of honest industry." The Bank represented centralized economic and political power, which threatened to overwhelm the virtue of the republic. If the Bank was able to consolidate credit, control a single paper currency, and control all business transactions, the independence of the Heroic Artisan would be compromised, and he would be returned to helpless childhood dependency. As Vice President Martin Van Buren warned, the Bank would "produce throughout society a chain of dependence . . . in preference to the manly virtues that give dignity to human nature, a craving desire for luxurious enjoyment and sudden wealth [and] substitute for republican simplicity and economical habits a sickly appetite for effeminate indulgence." The freeborn sons of liberty would be turned into the dependent daughters of the Mother Bank.[64]

Jackson's flight from feminizing influences illustrates a psychodynamic element in the historical construction of American manhood. Having killed the tyrannical father, American men feared being swallowed whole by an infantilizing and insatiable mother—voluptuous, voracious, and terrifyingly alluring. Jackson projected those emotions onto "others" so that by annihilating or controlling them, his own temptations to suckle helplessly at the breast of indolence and luxury could be purged. Jackson's gendered rage at weakness, feminizing luxury, and sensuous pleasure resonated for a generation of symbolically fatherless sons, the first generation of American men born after the Revolution.

Historically, such flight from feminization produced its opposite as the Heroic Artisan became wedded to exclusionary policies that left him increasingly defenseless against unscrupulous capitalist entrepreneurs, just as Jackson's effort to reconcile simple yeoman values with the free pursuit of economic interest ultimately cleared the path for the expansion of laissez-faire capitalist development. The heroic resistance of the artisan against the feminizing Bank was ironically the mechanism by which he was eventually pushed aside and transformed into a proletarian.

That process was begun in the 1830s but by no means quickly completed. In the presidential campaign of 1836, Jackson had picked his vice president, Martin Van Buren, as his successor to continue the struggle against the forces of feminization and proletarianization. The son of an innkeeper, Van Buren was praised by Jackson as "frank, open, candid, and manly . . . *able and prudent*." But after one term in office, Van Buren was outmasculinized in the campaign of 1840 by his Whig opposition as they seized upon the very sentiments that Jackson and Van Buren had aroused. The rhetoric of that campaign, which pitted William Henry Harrison, the hero of Tippecanoe, against Van Buren, was a political masterpiece of gendered speech. Harrison's manly virtues and log cabin birth were contrasted with Van Buren's ruffled shirts and his cabinet composed of "eastern officeholder pimps." In a sense, the presidential campaign of 1840 was the first—but certainly not the last—national presidential campaign characterized by dirty tricks, race-baiting, and the promotion of form over substance, and it continued the great American tradition of using manhood as political currency.[65]

Rather than articulate Harrison's position on specific issues, the Whigs chose to denigrate his opponent and promote their man by attaching to him two symbols of the Heroic Artisan: the log cabin, symbolizing the humble birth of a self-made man of the people—Harrison was labeled the Cincinnatus of the West—and the hard cider jug, symbolizing his alliance with the traditional artisanal work world and his opposition to the new discipline of the market. Images of log cabins were everywhere—"hung on watches, earrings, in parlor pictures and shop windows, mounted on wheels, decorated with coonskins, and hauled in magnificent parades."[66]

The chief task for the Whigs was to dissociate Van Buren from his predecessor. Congressman Charles Ogle's speech, "The Regal Splendor of the Presidential Palace," delivered in April 1840, signaled the beginning of perhaps the most gendered rhetorical barrage in the history of American politics. Ogle freely mixed gender and class in his effort to discredit Van Buren. In vain imitation of European aristocratic tastes, Ogle observed, the president's table was not "provided with those old and unfashionable dishes *hog and hominy, fried meat and gravy, schnitz, kneop and sourcrout* with a mug of *hard cider*." Instead, Van Buren's "French cooks" furnished the president's table in "massive gold plate and French sterling silver services." Van Buren was, moreover, the first president who insisted upon "the pleasures of the warm or tepid bath." Perhaps most shocking was Ogle's contention that a recent appropriation of $3,665 for alterations and repairs to the President's home "may be expended in the erection of a *throne* within the 'Blue Elliptical Saloon' [the Oval Office] and for the purchase of a *crown, diadem, sceptre* and *royal jewels*" so that this president, "although deprived of the *title* of royalty, will be invested, not only with its *prerogatives* but with its *trappings* also."[67]

The tone for the campaign was set, and pundits quickly fell into step. The *Louisville Journal* reported that when Van Buren read this outrageous attack, "he actually *burst his corset*." Davy Crockett penned an incendiary faux biography of Van Buren, damning the President as traveling in "an English coach" with liveried "English servants." "He is laced up in corsets, such as women in town wear, and, if possible, tighter than the best of them," wrote Crockett, so that "[i]t would be difficult to say from his personal appearance, whether he was man or woman, but for his large *red* and *gray* whiskers."[68]

As the log cabin dwellers and drinkers of hard cider campaigned against "Vanocracy," they sang newly penned campaign songs. (This campaign marked the political songbook's first appearance.) Like the journalists, songwriters went after his physical appearance and his manner and style, chastising "little Van" as a "used up man," a man "who wore corsets, put cologne on his whiskers, slept on French beds, rode in a British coach, and ate from golden spoons from silver plates when he sat down to dine in the White House." According to the song lyrics, Van Buren "had no taste for fighting" but adored "scheming" and "intrigue."[69] Of Harrison, by contrast, they sang:

> No ruffled shirt, no silken hose
> No airs does TIP display
> But like the "pith of worth" he goes
> In homespun "hoddin-grey."

> Upon his board there ne'er appeared
> The costly "sparkling wine"
> But plain "hard cider" such as sheered
> In days of old lang syne.

The strategy paid off handsomely, sending an incumbent to defeat for only the third time in American history. Over 80 percent of the eligible white male voters turned out for the election—a turnout rarely, if ever, equaled before or since. And it set a dubious precedent: Since 1840 the president's manhood has always been a question, his manly resolve, firmness, courage, and power equated with the capacity for violence, military virtues, and a plain-living style that avoided cultivated refinement and civility.

The campaign of 1840 had a sad, if well-known, coda. Harrison apparently believed his own hype. Taking the oath of office on one of the most bitterly cold days on record in Washington, Harrison refused to wear a topcoat lest he appear weak and unmanly. He caught pneumonia as a result, was immediately bedridden, and died one month later—the shortest term in office of any president in our history.

But gender had become political currency, and subsequent campaigns continued to trade in manly rhetoric. Of Zachary Taylor, Old Rough and Ready, for example, it was said that his education on the frontier had developed his manly character, while Taylor's supporters castigated his opponent, Lewis Cass, for his service as Jackson's ambassador to France. Cass was a "common man" if ever there was one—the son of a New Hampshire blacksmith who had fought in the Revolution, he rose to fame as a soldier and frontiersman, fought the British at Detroit, and made peace with the Indians.[70] Yet even he could be smeared by the association with France. In the following election, General Winfield Scott attempted to "clothe military aristocracy in frontier buckskin."[71] By 1860 one newspaper chastised James Buchanan for his "shrill, almost female voice, and wholly beardless cheeks," while the bearded and deep voiced Abraham Lincoln parlayed his plain-spoken humble origins into a national myth of probity, economy, and virtue that come from a log cabin president.[72] Our president could never be some Europeanized dandy who dreamed of aristocracy or monarchy; he would, for many years, claim the mantle of the artisanate, a descendent of the agrarian yeoman farmer.

In the last decade before the outbreak of Civil War, it was still unclear which model of manhood would emerge as triumphant. Already the Heroic Artisans were in retreat though they still exerted significant influence in local urban politics. And though Genteel Patriarchs had been discredited politically, at least as a political symbol, they still controlled a significant proportion of the nation's property. Their decline and the Self-Made Man's ascendancy were still in question, as was made abundantly clear in a shocking series of events that took place in May 1849. As with Royall Tyler's *The Contrast*, the stage was set, literally, in the New York City theater. Or rather in the Opera House at Astor Place and the surrounding square and city streets.

In May the celebrated British actor William Macready was preparing to perform *Macbeth* at the tony Astor Place Opera House. At the same time, Edwin Forrest, perhaps the most acclaimed American actor of his era, was taking up theatrical residence at the Broadway Theater for a run of his own. What might have begun as a personal squabble between the two premier actors of their respective countries turned into a clash between the patriotic, xenophobic nationalism of the New York working classes and the contemptuous elitism of the powerful. To the emerging urban elite, the working classes were nothing but gutter rabble, "sanguinary ruffians," filthy and uncouth; those same workingmen branded the bankers and merchants as "the dandies of Uppertendom."[73]

The actors themselves had squared off before. Macready was pompous, elegant, and extraordinarily gifted; an "actor autocrat," according to one critic. Forrest was a man of the people, "born in humble life," who "worked his way up from poverty and obscurity." In short, the man hailed as "the American Tragedian" was a self-made man; and as the *Boston Mail* put it in 1848:

> he is justly entitled to that honor—he has acquired it by his own labors; from a poor boy in a circus he has arisen to be a man of fame and wealth, all of which he has lastingly gained by enterprise and talent, and secured both by economy and temperance.[74]

Stylistically and sartorially, the two men were as different as a leather-aproned artisan and a liveried aristocrat. When Macready played Hamlet, one critic observed, he "wore a dress, the waist of which nearly reached his arms; a hat with a sable plume big enough to cover a hearse; a pair of black silk gloves, much too large for him; a ballet shirt of straw coloured satin," which, combined with his angular facial features, made him appear "positively hideous." Forrest's rugged appearance and muscular acting style stood in sharp contrast; Forrest had, in the words of one London reviewer, "shot up like the wild mountain pine and prairie sycamore, amid the free life and spontaneous growths of the west, not rolled in the garden-bed of cities to a dead level, nor clipped of all proportion by too careful husbandry." The two actors captured the contrast of national cultures and of versions of manhood, pitting, as one critic put it, "the unsophisticated energy of the daring child of nature" against the "more glossy polish of the artificial European civilian."[75]

The two played their parts superbly. Neither especially liked the other, either as an actor or as a man. Macready was struck by the "vehemence and rude force" of Forrest's performances, which favorable critics attributed to Forrest's manly vigor and oracular power. Macready was criticized as a "high-hatted" player, "craven-hearted, egotistical, cold, selfish, inflated," and obsessed with his "aristocratic importance."[76] Forrest had earlier hissed at Macready's performance of *Hamlet* ostensibly because the Englishman, castigated as a "super-annuated driveller," had tinkered with the play somewhat, introducing into one scene a "fancy dance" that was excoriated by Forrest as a "pas de mouchoir—dancing and throwing up his handkerchief across the stage."

When Macready and Forrest were each booked to perform in New York in May 1849, both stages were set for an explosive confrontation. The opening night performance of Macready's *Macbeth* was punctuated by noisy demonstrations and efforts by the rowdy throngs in the balconies to disrupt the performance. Tossing rotten eggs, "pennies, and other missiles" and eventually throwing a few chairs, they succeeded in driving Macready from the stage of that "aristocratic, kid-glove Opera House."[77] Disgusted, the stalwart English actor determined to cancel his performances and sail the next night for England. The plebeian crowds were jubilant in their assumed victory. The next day, though, Macready changed his mind after being entreated by several New York notables, including bankers, merchants, and writers like Washington Irving and Herman Melville.

The next night, May 10, thousands of workingmen and young working-class teenagers, known colloquially as B'hoys and renowned for their "virtuous contempt" for all things aristocratic, gathered in front of the Opera House.[78] Ned Buntline, the organizer of the infamous nativist organizations the United Sons of America and the Patriotic Order of Sons of America, whipped the "mobbish nativism" of the crowds to a fever pitch; the group now intended to prevent the performance or at least to disrupt its conclusion. Meanwhile the New York City police, joined by the local battalions of the state militia, were determined to keep the enormous crowd in check. By the end of the performance, as the crowds were whisked away via side exits, tempers were flaring. There was the expected shouting back and forth and even a few projectiles launched in the direction of the police and soldiers. Suddenly and unexpectedly the soldiers opened fire on the crowd. Twenty-two were killed, thirty more wounded, and over sixty more arrested.[79]

The Astor Place riot marked the first time in American history that American troops had ever opened fire on American citizens. To some it signaled the beginning of the great class struggle. A year after Marx and Engels had published *The Communist Manifesto* in Germany, one eyewitness saw the Astor Place riots in these terms:

> [I]t was the rich against the poor—the aristocracy against the people; and this hatred of wealth and privilege is increasing all over the world, and ready to burst out whenever there is the slightest occasion. The rich and well bred are too apt to despise the poor and ignorant; and they must not think it strange if they are hated in return.[80]

Those killed and arrested were all local artisans or small shopkeepers, including printers, clerks, grocers, ship joiners, butchers, plumbers, sailmakers, carpenters, and gunsmiths.[81] And their opponents were the newly moneyed urban entrepreneurs, flexing their political muscles, able to harness military and police power for their side and able to fend off efforts to taint them as aristocratic dandies.

It had taken scarcely twenty years for the Self-Made Man to establish a foothold in the consciousness of American men and to stake a claim for dominance in American politics and culture. He had gone from being the new kid on the block to owning the street. Avoiding the taint of aristocracy and subduing the working classes, the Self-Made Man was now, at mid-century, the dominant American conception of manhood. And in the decades following the Civil War, he would transform the nation.

CHAPTER 2

Born to Run

SELF-CONTROL AND FANTASIES OF ESCAPE

> The mass of men lead lives of quiet desperation. What is
> called resignation is confirmed desperation. From the
> desperate city you go to the desperate country. . . . A
> stereotyped but unconscious despair is concealed even under
> what are called the games and amusements of mankind.
> There is no play in them, for this comes after work. But it is a
> characteristic of wisdom not to do desperate things.
> —Henry David Thoreau *Walden* (1854)

> Where lies the final harbor, whence we unmoor no more?
> —Herman Melville *Moby Dick* (1851)

In the middle of the nineteenth century, the Self-Made Man began
to remake America in his own image—restless, insecure, striving,
competitive, and extraordinarily prosperous. Thrown into the anarchy of the marketplace, a place Thoreau had described as a "site of
humiliation," American men's economic, political, and social identity
was no longer fixed. If social order, permanence, could no longer be
taken for granted and a man could rise as high as he aspired, then his
sense of himself as a man was in constant need of demonstration.

Everything became a test—his relationships to work, to women, to nature, and to other men.

No wonder Thoreau penned his now-famous line that the "mass of men lead lives of quiet desperation" when he took off for Walden Pond.[1] As such a relentless test, civilization can be unbearable. One must be completely self-controlled, since in the new democracy there was no one else to look to for such control. Society was chock full of equals—which is another way of saying it was full of *competitors*. Two choices seemed possible: Stay and compete, or try to escape.

American men chose both. They struggled to build themselves into powerful, impervious machines, capable of victory in any competition. And they ran away to the frontier, to the West, to start over, to make their fortunes and thus to remake themselves, to escape the civilizing constraints of domestic life represented by the Victorian woman.

More than these, though, American men also tried to stack the decks in their favor. Although America has been from its birth a multicultural society, American manhood has often been built on the exclusion of others from equal opportunity to work, to go to school, to vote—to do any of the things that allow people to compete equally. It seemed as though men believed that by keeping the public worlds of work, education, or politics as the homosocial preserves of native-born white men, they could more reliably prove their manhood. Exclusion also allowed men a kind of domestic version of escape; everytime they went off to work, they ran away from women to prove themselves with other men. These solutions—self-control, exclusion, and escape—have been the dominant themes in the history of American masculinity until the present day.

THE DOCTRINE OF SELF-CONTROL

The drive for control, for order, stems from experiencing the world as *dis*ordered, as out of control. And to middle-class American men the mid-nineteenth century world often felt like it was spinning out of control, rushing headlong towards an industrial future. For a young man seeking his fortune in such a free and mobile society, identity was no longer fixed, and there was no firm patriarchal lineage to ground a secure sense of himself as a man. For the first time in American history, young men experienced "identity crises." "Sons had to compete for elusive manhood in the market rather than grow into secure manhood by replicating fathers. Where many could never attain the self-made manhood of success, middle class masculinity pushed egotism to extremes of aggression, calculation, self-control and unremitting effort."[2] The Self-Made Man was a control freak.

First he had to gain control over himself. In the 1830s and 1840s a spate of advice manuals counseled young men on how to do just that. This mania for self-control focused, perhaps not surprisingly, on sexual appetites and how to avoid the temptation of masturbation.[3] Concerns about "self-abuse" were not new—as early as 1724, an anonymous work was published in Boston entitled *Onania*; it carried a self-explanatory subtitle, "The Heinous Sin of Self-Pollution, and all its Frightful Consequences, in both Sexes, Considered. With Spiritual and Physical Advice to Those who have already injur'd themselves by this Abominable Practice." But in the mid-nineteenth century, the scope and scale of these works was unprecedented, as was the basis for their advice. Earlier, writers had stressed the immoral causes of sinful sexual behaviors; now they were more concerned with the secular effects of those behaviors, the debility, enervation, and sapping of vigor. When an English translation of S. A. Tissot's classic French work, *A Treatise on the Diseases Produced by Onanism*, appeared in 1832, it was an instant hit.[4]

To the medical experts of the time, the willful sexual control of a body was the ultimate test of mind over matter. Conservation of sperm was the single best way to conserve energy for other, more productive uses. It was believed that a body's total energy was finite, and the world of work demanded a full measure of it.[5] The link between economic and sexual behavior was so explicit, in fact, that a recent writer coined the phrase "spermatic economy" to describe the fusion of sexual and marketplace activities. "Sturdy manhood," one mid-century writer claimed, "loses its energy and bends under too frequent expenditure of this important secretion."[6]

The body was a well of carnal desires and diffuse energies. Advice-manual writers sought to control these desires and harness the energy toward productive activity. If some of their prescriptions sound silly to modern ears, they nonetheless sprang from an admirable impulse. The new, self-made man in the newly formed democracy was embarking on an experiment in social anarchy. With no birthrights, no one "knew his place." In such a self-made world, control must come from *somewhere*, and it could only come from within.

By the 1850s several advice books—among them William Alcott's *The Young Man's Guide* (1846), George Burnap's *Lectures to Young Men* (1848), George Peck's *The Formation of a Manly Character* (1853), and Timothy Arthur's *Advice to Young Men* (1855)—addressed men's need for self-control over passion, temptation, and masturbation, which would sap their vital energies and leave "effeminated" men's bodies, as Sophia Hawthorne worried, and thus render them unfit for the tasks ahead.[7]

Among the most successful of these advice books were Sylvester Graham's *A Lecture to Young Men* (1834), his later *Lectures on Science and Human Life* (1839), and John Todd's *The Student's Manual* (1835). Todd, a New England minister who became one of the nation's foremost campaigners against women's rights, and Graham, a health reformer and the inventor of the cracker that bears his name, were the preeminent experts who addressed themselves to the problems of becoming and remaining a successful man in the mid-nineteenth century. In his autobiographical work, *John Todd, The Story of His Life, Told Mainly by Himself* (1876), Todd claimed to have been "an orphan, shelterless, penniless" as a boy; he was, therefore, a prime example of the Self-Made Man. (Except that it was not entirely true. Todd had been raised by his mother and two aunts after his father had died.) *The Student's Manual* struck a nerve among American youth; by 1854 it had gone through twenty-four editions. Todd claimed that masturbation enfeebled the mind, debased and polluted the heart and feelings; the so-called "solitary vice" was, as he saw it, "almost inseparable from the habit of revery"—the province of the idle. As far as he could see, masturbation had claimed more healthy lives than war.[8]

Graham laid out an elaborate plan for dietary and behavioral reforms that would allow men to live secure, upright, productive and healthy lives. Desire, he believed, "disturbs and disorders all the functions of the system," so Graham offered a set of bodily dos and

don'ts, a prescription of dietary and sexual temperance. He advocated a diet of farinaceous foods, properly prepared, like "good
bread, made of coarsely ground, unbolted wheat, or rye-meal, and
hominy, made of cracked wheat, or rye, or Indian corn." Young men
should avoid full and large suppers and should eat no animal meat
whatever, since he was convinced that one is more susceptible to sins
of the flesh if one eats another's flesh. (For this, Graham was twice
attacked by a mob of Boston butchers, who claimed that he was ruin-
ing their business.)

Graham advocated strenuous exercise, the avoidance of "every
kind of stimulating and heating substances" and sleeping on a hard
wood bed, since feather beds would wrap the sleeper in indolent luxury and thereby enervate him. Graham warned that socializing boys
to bad habits of "luxury, indolence, voluptuousness and sensuality"
would lead them to surrender their "nobleness, dignity, honor, and
manhood" and reenact the fall from grace into a debased near dev-
ilry, becoming:

> the wretched transgressor [who] sinks into a miserable fatuity, and fi-
> nally becomes a confirmed and degraded idiot, whose deeply sunken
> and vacant, glossy eye, and livid shrivelled countenance, and ulcerous,
> toothless gums, and fetid breath, and feeble, broken voice, and emaci-
> ated and dwarfish and crooked body, and almost hairless head—cov-
> ered perhaps with suppurating blisters and running sores—denote a
> premature old age! a blighted body—and a ruined soul![9]

Sexual relations between husbands and wives also needed to be
regulated and their frequency curtailed—Graham suggested no more
than once a month—lest a variety of illnesses befall the husband.[10]
Even sexual fantasies—"those lascivious day-dreams and amorous
reveries"—must be suppressed.[11]

There were many other members of this antebellum vice squad.
Dr. Augustus Kingsley Gardner advised parents that even if their children attempt to hide their practice of the solitary vice, sooner or later,
"hysterias, epilepsies, spinal irritations, and a train of symptoms"
would give them away. Another writer counseled parents to employ
several innovative treatments for sexual intemperance and especially
masturbation to help boys keep their hands to themselves. These in-

cluded using a straitjacket and tying the feet such that the thighs would remain apart. If these methods didn't work, he contrived "cork cushions," which could be placed inside the thighs to pry them apart, and a "genital cage," a metal truss of silver or tin in which the boy's penis and scrotum were placed and held by springs. R. J. Culverwell invented a chair that served as a kind of bidet for the sexually tempted. An armchair was fitted with an open seat, beneath which a pan of cold water, or "medicated refrigerant fluid," would be placed. By means of a pump, a young man could direct this cold water to his genitals, thus "cooling" his sexual urges and making himself more capable of self-control.[12]

Some advice manuals took up some of Graham's nonsexual counsel and dietary regimens.[13] Even Charles Dickens suggested a few healthful reforms Americans might adopt, including greater personal cleanliness and exercise, as well as changing "the custom of hastily swallowing large quantities of animal food, three times a day, and rushing back to sedentary pursuits after each meal."[14] G. W. Docine's *Manners Maketh Man* (1852) and Eliza W. R. Farrar's *The Young Man's Own Book* (1832) advised men to avoid "anything which brings weariness and exhaustion, and fatigue," including dancing, theatrical performances, gambling, and alcohol.[15]

Alcohol was perhaps the second greatest challenge for the new ethic of self-control since, by today's standards, American men of the early national period were hopeless sots. Men would routinely wash down meals with hard cider (or peach brandy in the South), and frequent drams in the shop or in the field fortified young men for bursts of heavy labor in the cold or in the heat. In the South men took a break from work in midmorning for what they called "eleveners," the antebellum version of the coffee break, during which they drank a mixture of whiskey and berry flavorings. Workingmen, historians Paul Johnson and Sean Wilentz write, "liked to drink, at all times of the day, in stupefying quantities." Traditionally, the successful drank wine, while the unambitious or unsuccessful drank cider or, later, beer. One itinerant minister, James Finley, wrote in his *Autobiography* in 1854 that "a house could not be raised, a field of wheat cut down, nor could there be a log rolling, a husking, a quilting, a wedding, or a funeral without the aid of alcohol." Alcohol was a way of life; even

the Founding Fathers drank heavily. "Neighborhood sociability centered on taverns," writes historian Charles Sellers, "and strong waters
cheered funerals, ministerial ordinations, militia musters, elections,
corn huskings, and houseraisings." Drink "made them men," they
thought, and "gave them strength."[16]

In the first decades of the nineteenth century, though, American
men went on a national bender, especially imbibing hard liquor. Historian William Rorabaugh surveys the scene in this way:

> A western husbandman tarried at the tavern until drunk; an eastern
> harvest laborer received daily a half pint or pint of rum; a southern
> planter was considered temperate enough to belong to the Methodist
> Church if he restricted his daily intake of alcohol to a quart of peach
> brandy. A city mechanic went directly from work to the public house
> where he stayed late and spent his day's wages. Alcohol was such an
> accepted part of American life that in 1829 the secretary of war esti-
> mated that three-quarters of the nation's laborers drank daily at least 4
> ounces of distilled spirits.[17]

All that drinking signaled more than workplace conviviality and
smalltown democracy. Americans drank more—far more—hard alcoholic beverages between 1790 and 1830 than at any other time in
our history before or since. (See figures 2-1 and 2-2, p. 51.) This was
"the great American whiskey binge." By 1830 hard liquor consumption had climbed to 9.5 gallons a year for every American over fourteen, and over 5 gallons per capita overall, plus 30.3 gallons of hard
cider and other intoxicants. Rorabaugh speculates that the reason
for such constant intoxication was that Americans' economic aspirations were so high that they were constantly warding off feelings of
failure. The volatility of the marketplace, the fortunes to be won and
lost, and the general economic uncertainty of the early Industrial
Revolution left this generation of working Americans fretting constantly over their plight. As Edward Bourne noted at mid-century,
American men's drinking habits "grew out of the anxiety of their
condition."[18]

Advice manuals bravely promoted temperance in the face of this
tradition. Following the founding of the American Society for the Promotion of Temperance in 1826, begun largely by clergymen opposed

to Andrew Jackson, writers like Henry Ward Beecher and health reformers like Graham railed against the dangers of drink and frequently peppered their tales of woe by contrasting two friends who embark on the path of life together. When one succumbs to drink and the other doesn't, their lives diverge, but not before the drunkard steals from or otherwise harms the temperate young man. In the end the drunkard is either lying dissolute by the side of the road or is dead of his own cause, while the pure young man continues on, his fortune assured.

Other social reformers promoted temperance as part of larger reforms. Abolitionists William Lloyd Garrison and Theodore Weld, for example, linked intemperance and slavery; each, they argued, was economically wasteful as well as immoral. Fueled by ministerial leaders and followers of the Second Great Awakening, temperance advocates sought to stem the tide. They had their work cut out for them, especially since so many of the reformers were women; drinking became an expression of masculine protest against feminization at the same time as it was an artisanal protest against proletarianization.[19]

The urge for self-control and the need for social control were easily fused in the new republic—and with serious social consequences. Beyond sexual and alcoholic temperance there was also the possibility that those "repressed middle-class sexual energies were channeled into a xenophobic hostility toward the immigrant and the black, then projected into fantasies incorporating the enviable and fully expressed sexuality of these alien groups" and projected onto women, who were cast as seductive temptresses, brimming with carnal desires they were unable to control, and at the same time, as pious, asexual angels who, at the merest mention of the body and its desires, would faint straight away.[20] These projections led to what was perhaps the most significant development in the relations between the sexes prior to the birth of feminism.

THE SEPARATION OF SPHERES

When Tocqueville came to the United States in the early 1830s, he was amazed by the way this new democratic society had affected relations within the family. In particular, he noticed startling differ-

Figure 1. Annual Consumption of Distilled Spirits (i.e., rum, whiskey, gin, brandy) per Capita, in U.S. Gallons

Figure 2. Annual Consumption of Alcohol Contained in All Alcoholic Beverages per Capita, in U.S. Gallons

SOURCE: William Rorabaugh, *The Alcoholic Republic* (New York: Oxford University Press, 1979), pp. 28, 29.

ences between Europe and America in the treatment of women and the relationship between fathers and sons. He observed that what begins as greater freedom and intimacy in the New World actually soon changes into its opposite. In Europe women were far more dependent before marriage, unable to move about freely beyond the boundaries of the home, whereas in America unmarried women were relatively independent as girls. Marriage changed all that—"the independence of woman is irrecoverably lost in the bonds of matrimony: if an unmarried woman is less constrained [in America] than elsewhere, a wife is subjected to stricter obligations." She "never leaves her domestic sphere, and is in some respects very dependent within it."[21]

A similar paradox could be seen in the relationship between fathers and sons. American democracy dramatically reduced the distance between them, relaxing filial bonds of obedience, as "relations between father and sons become more intimate and gentle; there is less of rule and authority, often more of confidence and affection." Sons addressed their fathers "with a tang of freedom, familiarity and tenderness all at once." And yet these tender and intimate relations ended quickly as the sons grew up. Preparation for manhood required that the son become independent quickly, "master of his thoughts" and soon "master of his conduct." He was raised to shed his familial dependence like a snake sheds its old skin.[22]

Tocqueville was thus among the first of many commentators to confront the American separation of spheres. "In America, more than anywhere else in the world," he wrote, "care has been taken to constantly trace clearly the distinct spheres of action of the two sexes and both are required to keep in step, but along paths that are never the same."[23] It is significant that the doctrine of separate spheres was "a male creation," first promoted by male writers of advice books and said to "serve men's needs."[24] Only later was it picked up, embraced, and elaborated by women writers celebrating domesticity. Separate spheres allowed insecure middle-class men to feel like men, both in the homosocial workplace and when they returned to their homes.

There had always been, of course, a division of labor between the sexes, from hunting and gathering to agricultural to these early industrial societies, on both sides of the Atlantic. What was new—and distinctly American—were the strictness and the degree to which women and men were now seen as having a separate sphere. The home became entirely the domain of wives; husbands were even less involved than before. Men ceded both responsibility and authority over household management. In the early part of the century, men performed some work around the home—gathering fuel, leather work, grain processing—that could not be done elsewhere. "Virtually all the stereotypically male household occupations were eliminated by technological and economic innovations," writes historian Ruth Schwartz Cowan. This was not so for women, who saw their work "either untouched or augmented." Advice manuals once written primarily to fathers were now geared exclusively to mothers.[25]

And some services and functions that husbands and wives had performed together could now be delegated elsewhere. Middle-class children had once been educated at home but now increasingly went to school, and to a lesser degree the new asylums served a caretaking function that had earlier fallen on the family.[26] To modern eyes, of course, the family still had lots to do: early childhood socialization and the shaping of emotion and morality, acting like a "shrine for upholding and exemplifying all the softer virtues—love, generosity, tenderness, altruism, harmony, repose."[27] But at the time, this represented a significant retrenchment.

Thus the separation of spheres: The workplace became harder, the home softer. The casual conviviality of the workplace was fast disappearing in the new world of the factory system and mass production. Time and work discipline increasingly ruled. Outside the home was the "turmoil and bustle of an active, selfish world," explained Thomas Drew, where a man has to "encounter innumerable difficulties, hardships and labors."[28] The home would be a balm to soothe men from the roughness of the working day. The workplace was masculinized, the home feminized.

Whenever men have felt threatened by social change, some of them have resorted to arguments based on the natural distinctions between women and men as the justification for the newly endangered status quo. In the early nineteenth century men resorted to religious doctrine and scientific and medical evidence that "proved" that women were neither theologically nor biologically capable of moving into the public sphere. Religious fanatics, such as the Prophet Matthias, who drew zealous followers during the Second Great Awakening, preached the imminent restoration of a kind of "divine patriarchy" which utterly excluded women as God's plan. Other, more mainstream, ministers agreed that women were ordained by God and their bodies to remain at home.[29]

Women got the message. "If you are thinking of entering the matrimonial state," wrote Rebeccah Root Buell to her friend Weltha Brown in 1822, "you had better come [visit] while you can, as there is no certainty attending [marriage] but confinement."[30] Advice manuals for these newly domesticated women flooded the market in Jacksonian America; historian Nancy Cott lists dozens of these books published in New England between 1830 and 1840 alone, by both male and female authors, including *The Mother at Home, The Mother's Book, The Young Mother, Domestic Education, Familiar Letters on Subjects Interesting to the Minds and Hearts of Females*, and *Letters to Young Ladies*.[31] "Because women remain out of the world, men can safely enter into it," writes one historian, while another observes that "by making the women and children of the society the guardians of virtue, the male was released to act amorally in the world outside the home." The separation of spheres thus bolstered men's identities on both the home front and in the workplace.[32]

To justify this spatial and emotional segregation, writers of advice manuals invented the Cult of True Womanhood.[33] Women were not to be excluded from participation in the public sphere as much as exempted from participation in such a competitive and ugly world. Delicate and fragile, women were not subservient but "chosen vessels" requiring protection from the world, said Henry Harrington in *Ladies Companion* in 1838. Woman was a "moral, a sexual, a germiferous, gestative, and parturient creature" whose head is "almost too small for intellect but just big enough for love," declared Philadelphia gynecologist Dr. Charles Meigs. And Dr. William Acton's *Functions and Disorders of the Reproductive System* taught that "love of home, children and domestic duties are the only passions [women] feel."[34]

It was a woman's job to act as moral restraint, since men, alone, were not capable of restraining their baser emotions, their violence, their aggressive, competitive, acquisitive edge. "There is but little of the genuine emotion in our [sex]," observed Sylvester Judd in 1839.

"The habits of men are too commercial and restrained, too bustling and noisy, too ambitious and repellent." The world outside the home was "a vast wilderness" fueled by the "rage of competitive battle," wrote one minister in 1827. Home, then, became the place where man "seeks a refuge from the vexation and embarrassments of business."[35] If men were going to be able to exercise any self-control and yet take necessary risks in the work world, then women were going to have to help. Women were the "moralizers," who would elicit moral behavior from men. "The purity of women is the everlasting barrier against which the tides of man's sensual nature surge," was how Eliza Farnham put it in 1864.[36]

The strictures of Self-Made Manhood filtered down to younger and younger men, making their boyhoods appear increasingly to be little manhoods. No wonder Tocqueville lamented how quickly and sadly Americans are forced to renounce their boyhoods. What historian E. Anthony Rotundo calls "boy culture" came increasingly to imitate adult male culture as young boys were taught the "aggressive, self-reliant qualities needed for men's work" so that each one could "assert himself and stand emotionally alone while away from his family." Such prescriptions transformed the carefree tenderness of male friendships in the nineteenth century as the carefree play of youth was renounced for more instrumental relationships. The transition to manhood, then, was a sustained loss as the "crude aggressions and the raw boisterousness of boyhood" were transformed into the "refined self-assertion and purposeful self-discipline of manhood."[37]

This loss continued through the American man's adult life. Although industrialization pushed more and more men together in the workplace, it also increased the distance they each felt from one another. Gone were the casual intimacies of boyhood. Gone too was a view that other men—coworkers and friends—could act as moral constraints on excessive behavior. Instead, other men were potential economic rivals. "Between man and man," wrote Nathaniel Hawthorne in *The Marble Faun*, "there is always an insuperable gulf. They can never quite grasp each other's hands; and therefore man never derives any intimate help, any heart sustenance, from his brother man, but from woman—his mother, his sister, or his wife."[38] Men's reliance on women to meet all their emotional needs is a sad product of the separation of spheres.

The widening chasm between men produced a deep yearning for the intimacies that had earlier marked men's lives. "As networks of mutual trust and support among males gave way to individualist self-reliance, a prohibition was placed on physical intimacies between men that had earlier been accepted without qualm," writes literary critic T. Walter Herbert in a perceptive aside to his revealing portrait of Nathaniel and Sophia Hawthorne.[39] Such tenderness and intimacy were now tainted by fears of dependency; by the end of the century, those fears would be more fully sexualized into a fear of homosexuality.

The separation of spheres also affected the laboring classes, although these groups stressed female virtue less and male authority more than the middle class. "In their labor organizations they spoke in behalf of a rejuvenated patriarchal family, with men in the workplace and women in their rightful and natural place—the home."[40] The National Trade Union elaborated an artisanal version of separate spheres when it took up the question of female labor in the mid-1830s. Women, they argued, were incapable of pressing the demands of unionized labor. "The natural weakness of the sex—their modesty and bashfulness—their ignorance of the forms and conduct of public meetings and of the measures necessary to enable them to resist the oppression under which they labor—will ever prevent them from obtaining any melioration or improvement of their condition," observed one report in July 1835. The next year the report of the Committee on Female Labor noted how women's "hysterical organization, the natural responsibilities and the moral sensibility . . . prove conclusively that her labors should be only of a domestic nature."[41]

What these male workers also realized was that women workers would suppress wages and make it harder for men to find jobs. "When the females are found capable of performing duties generally performed by the men, as a natural consequence, from the cheapness of their habits and dependent situation, they acquire complete control of that particular branch of labor." Ironically, the National Trade

Union advocated equal wages for women, in part so that men's wages would remain high. Equal wages were "the only means of curtailing or arresting the evil" of female labor in the first place—curious and circuitous logic to reach a position of support for women's rights.[42]

Most men followed less circuitous logic to arrive at more antifeminist conclusions. Women's brains, they argued, were neither large nor strong enough to handle the enormity of the intellectual challenge of the collegiate curriculum. Education "would only confuse these feebleminded creatures, bring them into contact with polluting ideas whose misunderstood complexity would contaminate the virginal purity of their minds, and hence interfere with their role as soul-keepers." According to the Reverend John Todd, a Calvinist minister who became one of the best-selling advice-book authors of mid-century, "the great danger of our day is forcing the intellect of woman beyond what her physical organization will possibly bear."[43]

Efforts by women to educate themselves met with no better reception. When Emma Willard opened her seminary, one man remarked that "[t]hey'll be educating the cows next." E. A. Andrews attacked the founding of Mount Holyoke in 1837, warning of gender inversion: "[I]n place of all which is most attractive in female manners, we see characters expressly formed for acting a *manly* part upon the theater of life. Under such influences, the female character is fast becoming masculine." In 1854 a young James Garfield, then an Ohio schoolteacher, listened to a speech by Antoinette Brown, who had been ordained into the ministry a year earlier. Garfield wrote that "there is something about a woman speaking in public that unsexes her in my mind, and how much soever I might admire the talent, yet I could never think of the female speaker as the gentle sister, the tender wife, or the loving mother."[44]

Reverend John Todd also used gender inversion as a theme in the fight against woman suffrage, especially after the First Woman's Rights Convention was held in Seneca Falls, New York, in 1848. Suffrage is a civil right, which cannot contravene women's natural right "to be exempted from certain things which men must endure." Thus, he argued, woman suffrage is a "rebellion against God's law of the sexes, against marriage . . . and against the family organization, the holiest thing that is left from Eden." James Long went further, to naturalize the continuing power of white men: "How did woman first become subject to man as she now is all over the world? By her nature, her sex, just as the negro is and always will be, to the end of time, inferior to the white race, and therefore, doomed to subjection; but happier than she would be in any other condition, just because it is the law of her nature."[45]

Finally, the separation of spheres between women and men had enormous consequences for the relations between men and their families. If, as contemporary feminist writers would have it, women had become prisoners in the home, then men were increasingly exiled from the home, unable to return without fear of feminization. And so American fathers were increasingly estranged from the lives of their children, just as the workplace demanded an increasing amount of time and energy.[46] "Most men are so entirely engrossed by business as to have but little opportunity of fully understanding the characters of their children," complained Sarah Pierce in 1818. Just as motherhood was advancing, "fatherhood was in retreat." The term *father* no longer had unequivocally positive connotations. Charles Francis Adams yearned to "know" his father but never did and confessed that he "suffered from it all through life." Theodore Dwight's *The Father's Book* (1834) tried to persuade fathers to resume their responsibilities in the home. "Paternal neglect at the present time is one of the most abundant sources of domestic sorrow," wrote the Reverend John S. C. Abbott in an article in *Parents Magazine* in 1842. The father, "eager in the pursuit of business, toils early and late, and finds no time to fulfill . . . duties to his children."[47] If a man's home was his castle, by the mid-1800s he was becoming an absentee landlord.

American manhood had been born as the Sons of Liberty threw off the yoke of a tyrannical father. In but one generation the sons had grown to manhood and had turned themselves into fathers without sons:

> In terms of male-male interaction, the old unity was shattered. Sons found themselves within a world neither they nor their fathers understood. The young man stood alone. The men of Jacksonian America

experienced themselves both as sons loosed from the fathers' ways, and as fathers increasingly troubled as to how to provide for, control, or even to understand the experiences of their sons.[48]

The Self-Made Man's constant drive for self-control helped to create what we think of as the modern nuclear family: the Breadwinner Father and Homemaker Mother and children who remained under their mother's immediate charge. If life in the public sphere left him battered and bruised and his efforts to assert his manly will over both his body and his fortune left him exhausted, these domestic arrangements could provide a needed balm, a haven in a heartless world. "It is at home where man . . . seeks a refuge from the vexation and embarrassments of business," claimed New Hampshire minister Charles Burroughs in a sermon in 1827.[49]

Many men chafed at what they felt was a loss—of freedom, of casual homosocial intimacies, of authority. These Self-Made Men longed to make themselves all over again; they yearned for a place where they could reestablish their manhood and replace market competition with male camaraderie. In both fiction and fact, they ran away.

ON THE ROAD

In the last lines of the novel that bears his name, Huckleberry Finn anxiously plans an escape. "I reckon I got to light out for the territory ahead of the rest, because Aunt Sally she's going to adopt me and sivilize me, and I can't stand it. I been there before." Huck eloquently expresses the sentiments of many young American men. Women constrained manhood—through temperance, Christian piety, sober responsibility, sexual fidelity. Women set the tone of those institutions that restrained masculine excess—schoolroom, parlor, church. "Woman" meant mother, the one responsible for curtailing boyish rambunctiousness; later, "woman" meant wife, the wellspring of emotional and moral strength. If men wanted relief from the demands for self-control, they had to "light out for the territory."

Part of the struggle was simply to get out of the middle-class house, now a virtual feminine theme park, where well-mannered and well-dressed children played quietly in heavily draped and carpeted parlors and adults chatted amiably over tea served from porcelain services. This contrast with the frantic and aggressive business world made men feel uneasy in their own homes. A man's house "is a prison, in which he finds himself oppressed and confined, not sheltered and protected," wrote Thoreau. "His muscles are never relaxed. It is rare that he overcomes the house, and learns to sit at home in it."[50]

Women were not only domestic, they were domesticators, expected to turn their sons into virtuous Christian gentlemen—dutiful, well-mannered, and feminized. Orestes Brownson growled about "female religion" as well as male ministers who were the domesticated pets of widows and spinsters, "fit only to balance teacups and mouth platitudes." It fell increasingly to women to teach their sons how to be men.[51]

Thus did a portion of the definition of American manhood become the repudiation of the feminine, a resistance to mothers' and wives' efforts to civilize men.[52] Part of the struggle was one of appearance. Beards and moustaches proliferated in the 1840s and 1850s, while critics lampooned feminized styles among urban men.[53] Preachers during the Second Great Awakening excluded "men who wear spectacles" from their lists of Americans scheduled to enter the Kingdom of Heaven (as well as those merchants who hire women to work). Walt Whitman chastised the painted urban male who "looks like a doll," and a writer in Harper's Monthly described the human "poodles" who paraded in the cities with their "velvet tunics" and "long glossy locks." And Oliver Wendell Holmes foresaw the end of our race in 1858, convinced that a "set of black-coated, stiff-jointed, soft-muscled, paste-complexioned youth as we can boast from our Atlantic cities never before sprang from loins of Anglo-Saxon lineage."[54]

The ultimate relief was simply to get out of town. When Horace Greeley gave his famous advice in 1837—the full text of which was "Go West, young man, and grow up with the country"—men perked up their ears and followed in droves.[55] The West was a safety valve, siphoning off excess population, providing an outlet for both the ambitious and the unsuccessful. "All the past we leave behind," Walt Whitman wrote in "Pioneers! O Pioneers!" in 1865. As Frederick Jackson Turner put it:

To the peasant and artisan of the Old World, bound by the chains of social class, as old as custom and as inevitable as fate, the West offered an
exit into a free life and greater well-being among the bounties of nature,
into the midst of resources that demanded manly exertion and that
gave in return the chance for indefinite ascent in the scale of social advance.[56]

Timothy Flint suggested, in 1831, that these "shrinking and effeminate spirits, the men of soft hands and fashionable life" ought to follow the pioneers, for "there is a kind of moral sublimity in the
contemplation of the adventures and daring of such men" with their
"manly hardihood." This was a far cry from Yale president Timothy
Dwight's four-volume *Travels in New England and New York* (1821/2),
in which the author regretted that as the pioneer pushed further and
further into the wilderness, he became "less and less a civilized
man," or J. Hector St. John Crèvecoeur's lament that on the frontier,
men "degenerated altogether into the hunting state" and became, ultimately, "no better than carnivorous animals of a superior rank."[57]

Reports from the field of this westward rush all celebrated the return to manly virtues. Francis Parkman's *The Oregon Trail: Sketches of
Prairie and Rocky Mountain Life* (1849) was an immediate best-seller,
as was his later *Discovery of the Great West* (1869). A scrawny, feeble-
bodied rich boy, Parkman saw his masculine salvation in the repudiation of all things civilized. Rejecting his own class as a bunch of "soft
hearted philanthropists," Parkman sought out Indians and frontiersmen as manly examples to hold up to effete Bostonians. The "vigorous life of the nation springs from the deep soil at the bottom of
society," he wrote from the trail.[58] And Parkman wasn't alone in repudiating the educated elite and idealizing the rough-hewn working
classes in their ability to confront life's "incessant battle." Ruling-class
weakling Richard Henry Dana penned a masculinist escape memoir,
Two Years Before the Mast in 1840. Charles Webber's *Old Hicks, the
Guide; or, Adventures in the Comanche Country in Search of a Gold Mine*
(1848) also celebrated the "philosophy of the savage life."[59]

The rush westward reached its apotheosis with the California Gold
Rush of 1849. Never before or since have men created such a homosocial preserve on such a scale. Nearly 200,000 men came to California

in 1849 and 1850 alone, composing 93 percent of the state's population, 71 percent of whom were younger men, aged twenty to forty.[60] Though they had been lured by the exciting possibilities of sudden and exorbitant wealth, money alone did not keep them there. It was the homosocial life, a world of "rude freedom" outside the conventional boundaries of civilization and away from wives. "There was no female society," wrote Reverend John Todd, "no homes to soften and restrain." "The condition of the mining population, especially their carelessness in regard to appearances, mode of life, and habits in general," observed C. W. Haskins, "showed conclusively that man, when alone, and deprived of that influence which the presence of woman only can produce, would in a short time degenerate into a savage and barbarous state." With women scarcer than gold, one doctor explained that in California, "all the *restrictive influence* of fair women is lost, and the ungoverned tempers of men run wild."[61]

And they looked and acted the part. Forty-niners cast off the cultural baggage they brought from the East. They took new names, manly and rough, like Texas Jack, Whiskey Tom, French Flat Pete, Buckeye, and Sawbones (a doctor); they neither bathed nor changed their clothes, but they gambled, drank incessantly, swore, and attended bare-knuckle prizefights more often than they attended church services. A deck of cards was called the "California prayer book." Three years after leaving home, one prospector informed his family that he was now a "bull necked, horny handed, whiskered backwoodsman" unable to function "under the eye and hand of a boss." The forty-niners may have found what they were really looking for in those gold mines: they discovered a "pure" manhood—even if they didn't find any gold.[62]

Of course, one needn't go to all the trouble of traveling across the country to confront nature. One could find it in one's own backyard, the way Henry David Thoreau did. Thoreau, too, rejected a definition of masculinity that pushed men into "such desperate haste to succeed and in such desperate enterprises" that their lives are "frittered away by detail." The fear of failure suffocated urban businessmen and left workingmen with neither time nor inclination to develop their manly integrity. Men, Thoreau believed, needed liberation.[63] "We should come home from far, from adventures, and perils, and discoveries every day, with new experience and character." In short, we need the "tonic of the wilderness," as an antidote to the lockstep inanity of civilization.[64]

So Thoreau set out to live at Walden Pond in 1845, shunning the company of women in order to create himself, to become a Self-Made Man in the wilderness. In a sense, Thoreau conducted his own initiation into this new version of manhood. First, he rejected as a model the old aristocratic father, England. "I look on England today as an old gentleman who is travelling with a great deal of baggage, trumpery which has accumulated from long housekeeping, which he has not the courage to burn." Then he baptized himself. "I got up early and bathed in the pond; that was a religious exercise, and one of the best things which I did." And finally, he took communion, in a rather brutal fashion. "I caught a glimpse of a woodchuck stealing across my path, and felt a strange thrill of savage delight, and was strongly tempted to seize and devour him raw; not that I was hungry then, except for that wildness which he represented." Ingesting the wildness, Thoreau suggests, allows middle-class men to free themselves.[65]

If middle-class men were unable to venture to the West, or even to the local pond, the tonic virtues of the wilderness could be brought to their homes; they could escape through fantasy. In the first half of the century, two forms of fantasy were available—popular biographies of pioneers and backwoodsmen, elevated to the level of national myths, and general fiction, both of which allowed men to escape through fantasies of identification. For example, although Kit Carson and Daniel Boone were each active in the first two decades of the century and Davy Crockett active in the 1830s, all became mythic heroes in the 1840s and especially in the 1850s, when their biographies were rewritten as primitivist narratives of innate, instinctual manhood. All three were in constant retreat from advancing civilization.

Boone was the "natural man," uninterested in accumulation of wealth, always on the move, never weighted down. "Boone used to say to me," declared one backwoodsman, who claimed to be Boone's hunting buddy, "that when he could not fell the top of a tree near enough to his door for firewood, it was time to move to a new place."

Another legend held that when Boone heard that someone was clearing a farm twelve miles west of him, he declared the area "too thickly settled" and prepared his next move. Lionizing such misanthropic grumpiness seems to be a peculiarly American trait.[66]

Equally distinctive was the creation of the American myth of mobility and especially the link between geographic mobility, social mobility, and self-re-creation as men. The Heroic Artisan here returns in the guise of the pioneer, the masculine primitive, but he is still humble and beholden to his origins. As Richard Slotkin, who has traced what he calls the "frontier fable" as a dominant theme in American culture, writes:

> The protagonist is usually represented as having marginal connections to the Metropolis and its culture. He is a poor and uneducated borderer or an orphan lacking the parental tie to anchor him to the Metropolis and is generally disinclined to learn from book culture when the book of nature is free to read before him. His going to the wilderness breaks or attenuates the Metropolitan tie, but it gives him access to something far more important than anything the Metropolis contains—the wisdom, morality, power, and freedom of Nature in its pure wild form.[67]

This myth contains an obvious irony—the very activity in moving west to escape civilization transforms the protagonists into culture's advance guard as they tame the West for future settlement.[68] Yet even today, with little admission of irony, it remains a most potent myth. When one historian dared, in 1989, to debunk aspects of the myth about how and when Crockett died at the Alamo, he was berated by irate writers as a "wimp," fit for nothing better than the lowly profession of college teaching. In the 1992 Presidential campaign Republican challenger Pat Buchanan donned a coonskin cap as he campaigned in Crockett's native Tennessee.[69]

These real-life historical figures were transformed into mythic heroes within a decade or two of their deaths; early nineteenth-century American novelists made them up as they went along. Heroic men, to be sure, populated their pages, but antebellum fiction by men is also marked by the startling absence of sexuality, of marriage, of families—the virtual absence of women entirely.[70] American novels were

about "adventure and isolation plus an escape at one point or another, or a flight from society to an island, a woods, the underworld,
a mountain fastness—some place, at least, where mothers do not
come."[71]

Take Washington Irving's famous story "Rip Van Winkle" (1820).
What appears to be a surface treatment of progress—Van Winkle
sleeps for twenty years and comes back to find everything changed—
is also the story of poor Rip's escape from his shrewish wife. "Morning, noon, and night her tongue was incessantly going, and
everything he did or said was sure to produce a torrent of household
eloquence." Usually, Rip simply "shrugged his shoulders, shook his
head, and cast up his eyes" in response. But finally he had to get
away. "Poor Rip was at last reduced almost to despair; and his only
alternative, to escape from the labor of the farm and clamor of his
wife, was to take gun in hand and stroll away into the woods." Rip's
musket-laden stroll culminates in a twenty-year alcoholic reverie and
confrontation with the homosocial world of the mountain trolls.
Upon his return Rip is most struck by the changes in the gender
order that his absence—and his wife's death—has elicited:

> Rip, in fact, was no politician; the changes of states and empires made
> but little impression on him; but there was one species of despotism
> under which he had long groaned, and that was—petticoat govern-
> ment. Happily that was at an end; he had got his neck out of the yoke
> of matrimony, and could in and out whenever he pleased, without
> dreading the tyranny of Dame Van Winkle. Whenever her name was
> mentioned, however, he shook his head, shrugged his shoulders, and
> cast up his eyes; which might pass either for an expression of resigna-
> tion to his fate, or joy at his deliverance.

The story's last line extends Irving's fable to the "common wish of all
hen-pecked husbands in the neighborhood, when life hangs heavy
on their hands, that they might have a quieting draught of Rip Van
Winkle's flagon." Rip is the first of this fictional American archetype
of the man in flight—he is the fugitive, born to run.[72]

By the mid-nineteenth century this new American male hero
began to encounter another man, usually a man of color, as a sort of
spirit guide to this world without women. From Natty Bumppo and

Chingachgook, Huck and Jim, Ishmael and Queequeg, Billy Budd and Claggart, all the way to the Lone Ranger and Tonto, Captain Kirk and Mr. Spock, Lt. John Dunbar and Kicking Bird in *Dances with Wolves*, and Murtaugh and Riggs in the *Lethal Weapon* series, American fiction has celebrated male bonding, "a love between males, more enduring and purer than any heterosexual passion," which culminates in an asexual countermarriage "in which the white refugee from society and the dark skinned primitive are joined till death do them part."[73]

Literary critic Leslie Fiedler attributes this tradition of cross-race male bonding to a search for redemption for white guilt, but I believe it is also a way to present screens against which white manhood is projected, played out, and defined.[74] The nonwhite male stands in for women—as dependent child (Jim), male mother (Chingachgook, Tonto), spiritual guide and moral instructor (Queequeg, Chingachgook)—sometimes all at once. Their homoerotic passion is never the passion of equals; the nonwhite is either the guide and exemplar or the Rousseauian "noble savage" who, in his childlike innocence, is more susceptible to the wiles of civilization.[75] Murtaugh and Riggs are the only ones who seem to play against type, as Danny Glover plays a stable sober policeman, a mature and responsible black family man, in contrast to Mel Gibson's Riggs, who plays the masculine primitive in whiteface. This is not as inverted, however, as it might at first appear. Chingachgook, Tonto, Jim, Queequeg—all of them are closer to both nature and nurture. They are male mothers, nurturing their younger, wilder white charges into the deeply spiritual world of the primitive. One must be sane, sober, and soulful to remain so close to nature; one must be tame to be primitive and wild to be so tame.[76]

Sexuality—succumbing to the lustful temptations of the body—would ruin everything. Transforming homoerotic bonding into homosexual union would destroy the charged but chaste basis for the bond.[77] Nowhere is this more clear than in the five-novel saga of the *Leatherstocking Tales* by James Fenimore Cooper, certainly among the most popular male novelists of antebellum America.[78] In Natty Bumppo—the hero of *The Pioneers* (1823), *The Last of the Mohicans*

(1826), *The Prairie* (1827), *The Pathfinder* (1840), and *The Deerslayer* (1841)—Cooper created the prototype of masculinist flight and "showed how the solitary hunter, unencumbered by social responsibilities, utterly self-sufficient, uncultivated but endowed with a spontaneous appreciation of natural beauty, could become the central figure in the great American romance of the West."[79] "And Natty, what sort of man is he?" asked D. H. Lawrence. "Why, he is a man with a gun. He is a killer, a slayer. Patient and gentle, as he is, he is a slayer. Self-effacing . . . still he is a killer." Natty Bumppo is the first "last real man in America," created, ironically, by an author who was a leading Manhattan socialite.[80]

When we first meet Natty, he and his Indian companion Chingachgook are engaged in a debate about whether whites have any rights to take the Indians' land. At first, Natty says that whites are only doing to the Indians what the Indians used to do to each other, although he acknowledges that it does seem a bit unfair to be using bullets. But then Natty launches into a critique of feminization that seems to come out of nowhere. Modern white men no longer publicly shame the "cowardly" and applaud bravery; nowadays they "write in books" instead of telling their deeds in the villages, "where the lie can be given to the face of a cowardly boaster, and the brave soldier can call on his comrades to witness for the truth of his words." As a result, "a man who is too conscientious to misspend his days among the women, in learning the names of black marks [reading], may never hear of the deeds of his fathers, nor feel a pride in striving to outdo them."[81]

Women are but helpless and frail creatures in this telling. Throughout the novel, men spend a lot of time in the forests, risking all manner of danger, to rescue women who they believe cannot survive without male protection. Enemies are also feminized: "The Delawares are women!" exclaims Hawkeye (Natty). "The Yengeese, my foolish countrymen, have told them to take up the tomahawk, and strike their fathers in the Canada, and they have forgotten their sex. Does my brother wish to hear Le Cerf Agile ask for his petticoats, and see him weep before the Hurons, at the stake?"[82] Though Hawkeye delivers the masculinist attacks on effeminate mama's boys and disdains women, it falls to Chingachgook, the Indian, to deliver the most stinging critique of Self-Made Manhood in the guise of a critique of the white man:

> Some [The Great Spirit] made with faces paler than the ermine of the forests: and these he ordered to be traders; dogs to their women and wolves to their slaves. He gave this people the nature of the pigeon; wings that never tire: young, more plentiful than the leaves on the trees, and appetites to devour the earth. He gave them tongues like the false call of the wildcat; hearts like rabbits; the cunning of the hog . . . and arms to fight his battles; his cunning tells him how to get together the goods of the earth; and his arms inclose the land from the shore of the salt water to the islands of the great lake. His gluttony makes him sick. God gave him enough, and yet he wants all. Such are the pale-faces.[83]

Such was the masculinity expressed by the urban entrepreneur, against which Cooper was rebelling; he celebrated, in his sentimental style, the return of the virtuous hunter, the Heroic Artisan in the wilderness. Cooper's strength lies in his ability to combine an elegy for the fast-receding state of nature (and its native inhabitants) with the tragic irony of the white men, whose very idealizing of the natives was part of the process of their disappearance.[84]

Other antebellum writers were similarly more ambivalent about the triumph of the Self-Made Man. Walt Whitman celebrated the Heroic Artisan's vibrant sensuality and the nation's "athletic Democracy" as a counterpoint to the stoic self-control of the Self-Made Man, as in his homoerotic adulation of artisanal comradeship—both physical and spiritual:

> I will plant companionship thick as trees along the rivers of America,
>   and along the shores of the Great Lakes, and all over the prairies.
> I will make inseparable cities with their arms about each other's necks,
> By the love of comrades
> By the manly love of comrades.[85]

Some observers were suspicious of masculine escape. Charles Russell Lowell questioned the celebration of the West, writing in 1858 that "the West may make a man strong, massy, rock-like—never large

and generous and manly."[86] Nathaniel Hawthorne was especially critical of the Self-Made Man's drive to dominate. His novels, especially
Blithedale Romance (1852), equate competitive manhood with de-
monic possession (as did Sylvester Graham earlier) but make it clear
that neither the yeoman ideal nor Genteel Patriarch offered much alternative.[87]

More perhaps than any other single work, Herman Melville's *Moby
Dick* reveals men's uncomfortable ambivalence about the possibilities
of escape, while providing a compelling analysis of the mid-century
crisis of masculinity. Captain Ahab's "desperate narcissistic rage" and
"mesmerizing coerciveness" are the marks of "a man obsessed with
avenging his shattered manhood."[88] In Ahab, Melville provides a portrait of gendered madness, a blind rage fueled by sexualized obsession, the self-destruction of the Self-Made Man. Here is a man driven
to dominate, compulsively competitive, obsessively insecure—in
short, the archetypal capitalist man, a nineteenth-century type A
power broker. His monomania, that obsession with domination that
is the disease of the driven, is the nineteenth-century male version of
hysteria.[89]

The great whale is both the more powerful man against which
masculinity is measured and, simultaneously, the archetypal
woman—carnal, sexually insatiable, other.[90] What are we to make,
after all, of the fact that Ahab, who had lost his "leg" trying to plunge
his "six inch blade" into the whale, is now engaged in a "crazed flight
to prove his manhood"? *Moby Dick* is "the most extravagant projection of male penis envy" in American literature.[91] Ahab's inevitable
failure is both economic and sexual; the Self-Made Man is no match
for the forces of nature, and so the relations are inverted, revealing
the terror of being dominated that lies beneath the drive to dominate.
Ahab is the male Dora, seducing and seduced, rapist and raped, willing to partake of the savage butchery of his entire crew to avoid humiliation at the hands of his rival. Like Andrew Jackson, the fictional
Ahab is finally hysterically mute, incapable of speech. He dies stran-
gled in the harpoon's ropes, choking—voiceless and terrified.

These violent passions offer a startling contrast to the tender artisanal homoeroticism between the narrator, Ishmael, and the harpoon-
ist, Queequeg, who discover, as they lie asleep in bed, wrapped in

each other's arms, that chaste, yet eroticized, homosocial fraternalism that characterizes the purified male bond. To Melville those bonds were impossible if one adopted the competitive drive of the marketplace. When Ishmael, alone, survives, he has become, as the book's final words tell us, "another orphan." But buoyed by Queequeg's coffin and eventually saved by the "feminized" sailing ship, the *Rachel*, this orphan finally understands the seductive fatal trappings of the Self-Made Man and knows how to remake himself. He sails for home.

WAS THERE AN ALTERNATIVE?

American men were uncertain which model of masculinity would emerge triumphant in the second half of the century. As America drifted slowly toward Civil War and the contrasts between North and South sharpened, the national debates about slavery and woman suffrage also allowed a small group of men to articulate an alternative to the strategies that had been the stock responses to the antebellum masculine identity crisis. Instead of self-control, exclusion, and escape, these men proposed a broadly democratic vision, a manhood based on inclusion and self-expression. Such men were to be found among the abolitionists, especially those who also advocated women's rights. By advocating abolition and suffrage, several of these men also advanced an alternative vision of American manhood.[92]

Some of them challenged the separation of spheres and supported women's entry into the public sphere.[93] Others championed women's sexual autonomy and men's responsibility. Several founders of spiritual communes in the 1830s and 1840s, for example, included women as spiritual or even sexual equals. John Humphrey Noyes, founder of the Oneida commune, promoted sexual equality between women and men and male continence as a form of birth control.[94] Robert Dale Owen's *Moral Physiology* (1831) and Thomas Gove Nichols's *Esoteric Anthropology* (1853) provided counterweights to the many advice manuals that supported the separation of spheres and sexual self-control.[95]

Still others supported male bonding and homosocial intimacies but eschewed the fantasies of escape from women. Though Walt

Whitman sang of the "muscular urge" of manly comradeship and friendship as a counter to "limber tongued lawyers, very fluent but empty, feeble old men, professional politicians, dandies, dyspeptics, and so forth," he also insisted that women were "not one jot less" than he was.[96]

The debates over the abolition of slavery offer a fascinating window into the antebellum debate about masculinity. Abolitionists— like Wendell Phillips, William Lloyd Garrison, Thomas Wentworth Higginson, Martin Delany, Theodore Tilton, Parker Pillsbury—extended their antislavery vision to women's position and thus entered a debate about manhood as well. For Garrison, founder of the New England Anti-Slavery Society in 1831 and the American Anti-Slavery Society in 1833 and publisher of the *Liberator*, an imperious definition of manhood was indissolubly linked to women's subordination. In his speech to the Fourth Woman's Rights Convention in Cleveland in 1853, Garrison railed against sexist injustice. "I believe that man has done this through calculation, accentuated by a spirit of spite, *a desire for domination which has made him degrade woman* in her own eyes, and thereby tend to make her a mere vassal."[97]

Frederick Douglass linked his struggle to claim his manhood as a free black man to the struggles of women for full equality.[98] To be a man meant autonomy and meant denying full autonomy to no one. His critics, however, believed that support of women's rights indicated a failure of manhood. The Syracuse papers called Douglass an "Aunt Nancy Man" in an editorial the week after his speech at the Seneca Falls Convention, and other supporters were vilified as "man-milliners" and "Miss-Nancys." The next year the *Syracuse Daily Star* opined in an editorial:

> The poor creatures who take part in the silly rant of "brawling women" and Aunt Nancy men, are most of the "ismizers" of the rankest stamp, Abolitionists of the most frantic and contemptible kind, and Christian sympathizers with such heretics as Wm. Lloyd Garrison, Parker Pillsbury, C. C. Burleigh, and S. S. Foster. These men are all Woman's Righters, and preachers of such damnable doctrines and accursed heresies, as would make demons of the pit shudder to hear.[99]

Support for women's rights and opposition to slavery had brought their manhood into question. For example, a defense of slavery by James Gordon Bennett, editor of the *New York Herald*, was saturated with gendered language. Bennett feared that middle-class pieties would feminize the nation. "They would snatch the convivial tankard from the honest toiler, close down the dance halls and theaters, shut up the Post Offices and railroad depots on Sundays, encourage blacks to seek white mates, and bring on a return to the theocratic tyrannies of puritan New England." The *New York Daily World* lampooned male supporters as "crack-brained, rheumatic, dyspeptic, henpecked men, vainly striving to achieve the liberty to open their heads in the presence of their wives." And the *Baltimore Patriot* declared that abolitionist lecturers had to be escorted to their lecterns by "a life guard of elderly ladies, and protected by a rampart of whale bones and cotton padding," i.e. a hoop skirt.[100]

For their part, abolitionists defended their manhood against such slanders; slavery's supporters were "cringing wretches," according to Wendell Phillips, while Garrison promoted a virile Christian manliness against slavery. "Men of natural softness and timidity, of a sincere and effeminate virtue, will be apt to look on these bolder, hardier spirits" of the antislavery crusade as "violent, perturbed, and uncharitable."[101] John Brown's raid on Harpers Ferry was experienced by many abolitionists as redemptive of their manhood.

Such a debate illustrates a theme we encounter again and again throughout American history. Support for feminism or civil rights has been seen as an indication that a man is less than manly—as if support for inequality somehow made one *more* of a man.

The Civil War propelled that debate into the nation's consciousness. To be sure, the Civil War centered around the morality of slavery, political questions of states' rights, economic struggles between industrial capitalism and agrarian slave-based economies, and the rending of American families in fratricidal struggle.[102] But the Civil War was also a gendered war in which the meanings of manhood were bitterly contested.

All wars, of course, are meditations on masculinity. And the Civil War was no different. Take, for example, the metaphors we use to describe it. The American Revolution was a rebellion of the Sons of Liberty against the tyrannical Father; in the Civil War brother fought against brother in "the house divided." Those fatherless sons had grown out of their Jacksonian adolescence and now faced each other to determine which vision of manhood would dominate for the rest of the century.

Four different groups of men pressed their case, each plagued by different questions about their manhood. For the northern upper classes the war provided an opportunity to reclaim a manhood that had been dismissed as enervated and effete. Some even prescribed war as an antidote for the overcivilized indolent luxury of the eastern educated elite. Emerson snarled at his age "of fops and toys / Wanting Wisdom, void of right" as he began his poem "Voluntaries"; he believed that the war would "restore intellectual and moral power to these languid and dissipated populations." The editor of *Harper's Monthly* promised in 1861 that the "discipline of the camp is a wonderful check upon effeminacy and self-indulgence." A Philadelphia minister claimed:

> this war promises to arrest in a measure the extravagance and parade, the epicurianism and effeminacy into which we are fast running. It puts our young men upon a training which will nourish their manly virtues. It inculcates, as no moralist could, lessons of economy, of moderation, of patience, of self-control.

And one editor heralded the substitution of a purer manhood for the "commercial estimate of virtue now existing," while another chided upper-class Bostonians who lived "in safe and cowardly ease."[103]

The Civil War also represented a claim for manhood on the part of black men. Many abolitionists, both white and black, saw the struggle against slavery, as the governor of Wisconsin put it in 1859, "a question of manhood, not of color."[104] "The negro is a man, and has all the elements of manhood, like other men," claimed H. Ford Douglass. What's more, he added, "he has the *highest* elements of manhood."[105] Frederick Douglass (no relation) explicitly linked his critique of manhood to his experience as a black man. The turning point in Douglass's powerful autobiography comes when he finds himself a free man, "my own master," capable of self-respect earned through freedom and hard work. "Personal independence is the soul out of which comes the sturdiest manhood," he wrote.[106] Independence from slavery provided the material foundation, but it was violent physical confrontation that added the mortar to that foundation. After he beats a slavebreaker named Covey, Douglass claims that he "was a changed being." He had been "*nothing* before; I was A MAN NOW," he writes in *My Bondage and My Freedom*. Later, in his *Narrative of the Life . . .*, he looks back at the fight almost nostalgically, recognizing that it "revived within me a sense of my own manhood." Douglass reveled in his discovery. In a speech entitled "Self-Made Men," he placed himself in a long line of men who

> owe little or nothing to birth, relationship, friendly surroundings; to wealth inherited or to early approved means of education; who are what they are, without the aid of any of the favoring conditions by which other men usually rise in the world and achieve great results.[107]

For both black men and the northern upper classes, the deployment of the 54th Massachusetts regiment, the famed all-black Union army regiment under the command of Boston Brahmin Robert Gould Shaw, was heroically redemptive. Shaw represented the innate heroism of the aristocratic *noblesse oblige*, which assuaged a "deep seated anxiety among the members of the cultivated classes about their own ability . . . to meet some undefined challenge," according to the historian George Frederickson.[108] And free black men also sensed this reclamation of manhood. "This was the biggest thing that ever happened in my life," said one former slave. "I feel like a man with a uniform on and a gun in my hand."[109]

At the war's end black manhood had been formally established via emancipation, though asserting their manhood would continue to be a central struggle for black American men throughout American history. Black poet Albery A. Whitman celebrated that moment in his epic poem *Not a Man, and Yet a Man* (1877):

> This was the day when Southern chivalry
> Beheld black manhood clothed in liberty,
> Step from the shadow of his centuries
> Of bondage, shake dejection from his eyes,

And to the awful verge of valor rise.
The day that heard the negro, scarred and maimed,
Of sovereign battle's lips a man proclaimed.

"When God made me I wasn't much," said a former slave."But I's a man now."[110]

In addition, northern and southern men questioned each other's manhood, both on the battlefield and in rhetorical skirmishes. The Civil War pitted Confederate chivalry against Self-Made Yankees and signaled the triumph of the urban industrial entrepreneur over the genteel southern patrician. Contemporaries saw northerners and southerners as distinctly different species, different expressions of manhood. Georgian William Lowndes Yancey explained in 1855 that

> The Creator has beautified the face of this Union with sectional features. Absorbing all minor subdivisions, He has made the North and the South; the one the region of frost, ribbed with ice and granite; the other baring its generous bosom to the sun and ever smiling under its influence. The climate, soil, and productions of these two grand divisions of the land, have made the character of their inhabitants. Those who occupy the one are cool, calculating, enterprising, selfish and grasping; the inhabitants of the other are ardent, brave, and magnanimous, more disposed to give than to accumulate, to enjoy ease rather than to labor.[111]

Southern planters represented a "doomed aristocrat," free of any taint of "new wealth or old European corruption." "Each planter is in fact a Patriarch—his position compels him to be a ruler in his household," noted G. Memminger in a lecture in Georgia in 1852. As Daniel Huntley, a southerner with extensive experience in the North put it in 1860, some northerners believed

> that the citizens of our Southern States are so many Chevalier Bayards, *sans peur et sans reproche*; living upon their broad estates in all baronial splendor and hospitality, but, being nevertheless—like the slave-holding Catos and Brutuses of republican Rome, and the equally slave-holding Solons and Leonidases of democratic Greece—still true to the Constitution, the Commonwealth, and the Laws.

As southerners saw it, the legend of the Old South was a world where:

> gesturing gentlemen moved soft-spokenly against a background of rose gardens and dueling grounds, through always gallant deeds, and lovely ladies, in farthingales, never for a moment lost that exquisite remoteness which has been the dream of all men and the possession of none. Its social pattern was manorial, its civilization that of the Cavalier, its ruling class an aristocracy coextensive with the planter group.[112]

Southern conservative men offered a profound challenge to Self-Made Manhood, perhaps, as the historian Eugene Genovese wrote, "the only politically powerful challenge to liberal capitalism to emanate from within the United States." Only men like John C. Calhoun and the lawyer and journalist George Fitzhugh "questioned the assumptions of liberal society, denounced the hypocrisy and barbarism of the marketplace, and advanced a vision of an organic society and a collective community."[113] Southerners saw northerners as crassly commercial, avaricious, unscrupulous, aggressive, and mercenary; "Yankee" was a decidedly negative term, denoting unethical business practices and concern only for the bottom line.[114] Northern men had abandoned honor for money, morality for mobility, community values for self-improvement. Southerners saw themselves as a doomed aristocracy, falling in the wake of the triumph of the Self-Made Man, who, it turns out, was a northerner. Sarah Hale wrote:

> It is not the love of pleasure, the taste for amusements, that constitute the love of the world. It is the love of money, the craving desire to accumulate property, the entire devotion of the heart and soul, mind, might, and strength, to the one object of increasing or preserving an estate, that bows down to lofty intellect of men, and makes their sordid souls as grovelling as the appetites of the brutes that perish. This inordinate thirst for riches is the besetting sin of Americans' situation, institutions, education, all combine to foster it.[115]

For southerners the Civil War represented the last stand of the Genteel Patriarch, now a Confederate cavalier.

The war's denouement offers a particularly interesting example of this vilification of southern manhood as feminized. At the end of the war, it was believed that Jefferson Davis, president of the Confederacy, sought to escape from his capital in Richmond disguised in a woman's clothing. Northern cartoonists and popular songwriters immediately set to work, producing dozens of illustrations and lampoons of Davis. One popular song, "Jeff in Petticoats," recounted the story like this:

> Jeff Davis was a warrior bold,
> And vowed the Yanks should fall;
> He jumped into his pantaloons
> And swore he'd rule them all.
> But when he saw the Yankees come
> To hang him if they could
> He jumped into a petticoat
> And started for the wood.

By lampooning "Jeffie" Davis, the "Belle of Richmond," as one cartoon had it, the victorious northerners could ridicule southern manhood, its feminized Genteel Patriarchal pretense, and the "Petticoat Confederacy" at the same time.[116]

The Union triumph ensured that American men would ground their identities in the shifting sands of the marketplace. It was a Pyrrhic victory. This intrafamilial squabble between brothers led to an unprecedented mobilization of resources and manpower, and left the nation drenched in the blood of those brothers—over 600,000 of them, with over $15 billion gone up in smoke.

What did it mean for American manhood? Instead of resolving the antebellum anxieties of American men, the Civil War only seemed to keep them momentarily at bay. "Instead of purging the nation once and for all of self-seeking materialism and corruption, the war opened the floodgates for the greatest tide of personal and political selfishness the nation had ever seen," writes the historian George Frederickson.[117] More than ever, self-making men would find the going tough; they still had something to prove.

For southern men, defeat meant a kind of gendered humiliation—the southern gentleman was discredited as a "real man." Southern soldiers returned to a barren and broken land of untilled farms, broken machinery, gutted and burned buildings, and a valueless currency. Schools, banks, and businesses were closed, unemployment was high, and inflation crippling. For the rest of the century and well into the twentieth century, southern manhood would continually attempt to assert itself against debilitating conditions, northern invaders (from carpetbaggers to civil rights workers), and newly freed blacks. The southern rebel, waving the Confederate flag at collegiate football games, is perhaps his most recent incarnation.

The forces transforming the meanings of manhood lay beyond class and region. The last decades of the century witnessed the unleashing of forces that had taken shape in the Civil War years, now given free reign to flourish. Three coincident processes shifted the terrain upon which manhood had been traditionally grounded—an unprecedented level of industrialization; the entry into the public sphere of large numbers of women, newly freed blacks, and immigrants; and the closing of the frontier—and the meanings of manhood were once again uncertain. The combined impact of these processes led many men to feel frightened, cut loose from the traditional moorings of their identities, adrift in some anomic sea. By the last decades of the century, manhood was widely perceived to be in crisis.

This fin de siècle crisis of masculinity was a popular theme for critics and experts.[118] All agreed that it was increasingly difficult to be a real man. Who was a man? What did manhood mean? How could one tell that he was a real man? As experts debated, American men still struggled to carve out a world in which they could successfully experience their manhood. Such a large-scale loss of control as a civil war, the new political and social claims of women and freed blacks, and failed attempts at escape all signaled the inadequacy of the various strategies American men had developed upon which to ground a secure sense of themselves as men. Something had forever changed. Mark Twain captured this in his eloquent eulogy for lost manhood as Tom Sawyer and his band of young men searched for their lost boyhoods. "The boys dressed themselves, hid their accoutrements, and went off grieving that there were no outlaws anymore, and wondering what modern civilization could claim to have done to compensate them for their loss."[119]

Part Two

THE UNMAKING OF THE SELF-MADE MAN AT THE TURN OF THE CENTURY

CHAPTER 3

Men at Work

CAPTAINS OF INDUSTRY, WHITE COLLARS, AND THE FACELESS CROWD

> A man's business makes him,—it hardens his muscle . . .
> wakes up his inventive genius, puts his wits to work, arouses
> ambition, makes him feel that he is a man, and must show
> himself a man by taking a man's part in life.
> —Madison Peters *The Strenuous Career* (1908)

> In this fiercely competitive age, when the law of the survival
> of the fittest acts with seemingly merciless rigor, no one
> can afford to be indifferent to the smallest detail of dress,
> or manner, or appearance, that will add to his chance
> of success.
> —Orison Swett Marden *Power of Personality* (1899)[1]

The end of the Civil War ushered in an era of unprecedented economic transformation. Between 1870 and 1900 industrial output in the United States increased by 500 percent. The demands of war had been "technology forcing"; the growth of the steel industry, the laying of a railroad and transportation infrastructure, and the substitution of petroleum for whale oil were spurred by the war and in turn fueled this enormous growth.

Both agriculture and industry were jolted by what the historian Alan Trachtenberg calls "the incorporation of America." In 1800 over 80 percent of American men had been farmers; by 1880 only one-half the nation's labor force was in agriculture. Although four of every five American men were self-employed in the first decades of the century, by 1870 only one-third were self-employed.[2] Large factories, not small shops, now dominated the industrial landscape. On the eve of the Civil War, the McCormick factory employed three hundred to four hundred workers and was the largest factory of its kind in the world. In 1870 Best and Company (which eventually became the Pabst Brewing Company) was the nation's second largest brewery and employed no more than a hundred workers. Even in the early 1880s only the railroads and the New England textile mills employed more than a thousand workers. But within the decade all this had changed markedly. By 1884 Best Brewery had fourteen hundred workers, and by 1899 more than four thousand. Carnegie Steel employed more than four thousand at its Homestead works alone. Edison Electric, precursor to General Electric, employed one thousand workers in the early 1880s, two thousand four hundred by 1890, and over ten thousand by 1892.[3]

Most importantly, perhaps, America was increasingly an urban society. In 1830 about one American in fifteen lived in a city of over eight thousand. Between 1860 and 1890 the proportion of Americans living in municipalities with more than two thousand five hundred doubled to about 30 percent; by 1900 one-third of Americans lived in cities of at least eight thousand people; and by 1910 one-half lived there.[4] In short, the great new fact in American life was the crowd. And crowds created a new problem for self-made, self-controlled men.

For one thing, changes in scale, location, and level of technology transformed men's working lives. Workers increasingly seemed to lose control of their labor and the production process, which was transferred upwards to a new class of managers and supervisors. New technological advances sped up production but invaded men's sphere of control. "Machinery has advanced, apprenticeship has declined," lamented a carpentry union official in 1886.[5] The application of military discipline to production, epitomized by Frederick Winslow Taylor's "scientific management" based on the "soldiering" of workers, led to standardization of tools and jobs, increased use of semiskilled and unskilled workers, and fragmentation of jobs into minute and discrete tasks. Taylor's famous time-and-motion studies, using time clocks, reduced jobs into their principal components to determine the minimum amount of time for each task. Workers were becoming human machines. The new managers were elated since these shifts, as two observers gloated in their report to the Ford Motor Company in 1915, tended to

> make the workmen absolutely docile. New regulations, important or trivial, are made almost daily; workmen are studied individually and changed from place to place with no cause assigned, as the bosses see fit, and not one word of protest is ever spoken, because every man knows the door to the street stands open for any man who objects in any way, shape, or manner to instant and unquestioning obedience to any directions whatsoever.

Workers, of course, were far less sanguine. "There are men standing over you all the time, and of course you are almost drove to it. You have got to keep pegging at it and working," commented one worker at the Watertown strike in 1911. Such conditions, he observed, were "getting down to slavery."[6]

Rapid industrialization, technological transformation, capital concentration, urbanization, and immigration—all of these created a new sense of an oppressively crowded, depersonalized, and often emasculated life. Manhood had meant autonomy and self-control, but now fewer and fewer American men owned their own shops, controlled their own labor, owned their own farms. More and more men were economically dependent, subject to the regime of the time clock. By the turn of the century, less-skilled workers began to outnumber the highly skilled and more self-ruling members of the labor force. In these impersonal factories former apprentices and journeymen were placed alongside semiskilled workers, and by the end of the century, no one spoke of mechanics, artisans, journeymen, or master craftsmen anymore. Family farmers were, of course, far from extinct, but their decline was dramatic.

These changes had gender consequences. Samuel Eliot, writing in the *Journal of Social Science* in 1871, observed that to "put a man upon wages is to put him in the position of a dependent" and that the longer he holds that position, the more his capacities atrophy and "the less of a man . . . he becomes." Horace Greeley claimed that the separation of wage work from management reversed traditional craftsman-apprentice relations, further humiliating adult men. "I dislike to see men in advanced years working for salaries in places where perhaps they are ordered about by boys." And Anthony Ludovici observed the "steady degeneration of men" brought on by the "spectacle of men working at tasks which every woman knows she could easily undertake." "It was different then," one wage worker looked back nostalgically while testifying before a U.S. Senate panel on the relations between labor and capital in 1885. "A mechanic was considered somebody and he felt he was somebody." The era of the Heroic Artisan was over.[7]

The world of the merchant would likewise never be the same. "The one-man ownership stage of capitalism" was disappearing, noted a professor at the newly founded (1908) Harvard Business School. What was needed now was training in administrative organization, investment banking, large sales organization—thus the need for the nation's first business school.[8] The postbellum world, Henry Adams argued, was a crowded "banker's world," and one's place in it was both less valuable and more competitive than before. A man in this world knew what that meant:

> He was for sale, in the open market. So were many of his friends. All the world knew it, and knew too that they were cheap; to be bought at the price of a mechanic. . . . The young man was required to impose himself, by the usual business methods, as a necessity on his elders, in order to compel them to buy him as an investment.[9]

And just as he himself became a marketable commodity, the pressure to make good increased markedly. "Life is a sharp conflict of man with man, a remorseless struggle for existence . . . in which the men of greatest skill and perseverance still defeat their fellows," wrote James Platt in 1889, in the seventy-fifth edition of his book *Business*. It is "your duty to get rich," Rev. Russell Conwell admonished his listeners. His best-seller *Acres of Diamonds* was drafted as a sermon in 1870 and delivered over six thousand times, reaching an audience of millions. He preached that every man's worth was entirely up to him. "There is not a poor person in the United States who was not made so by his own shortcomings."[10]

The possibilities for self-making were also complicated by dramatic social changes. As new groups entered the public arena, the competitive field became increasingly crowded. In the last decades of the century, unprecedented numbers of immigrants and recently freed blacks poured into northern industrializing cities, demanding recognition and rights, challenging native-born white men for dominance on what had been their turf. The war's end catapulted the country into the position of world economic power, full of economic opportunity and a beacon of hope for the "huddled masses, yearning to breathe free," as Emma Lazarus's poem, inscribed on the Statue of Liberty, put it in 1886. This resulted in the most massive immigration of Europeans in U.S. history. In 1870, of the nearly one million people living in New York City, almost half were foreign-born (mostly Irish and German). More than a half-million immigrants came to New York City alone in 1902. In the 1870s 115,000 Chinese arrived on the West Coast, joined by another fifty thousand in 1881 and 1882, until Congress passed the Chinese Exclusion Act. Over 130,000 Japanese arrived in the United States between 1891 and 1907. A total of nine million immigrants came to the United States between 1880 and 1900, and fourteen million more arrived by 1914.[11]

Postbellum black migration also swelled northern and eastern cities and changed the complexion of America's urban population. Between 1870 and 1890, 156,000 came north, and another 185,000 came north in the 1890s. The Great Migration was to come later, after 1914, when the combination of wartime industrial opportunity in the North and Midwest and a devastating boll weevil attack on southern cotton in 1914 pressed many to seek their fortunes elsewhere. Between 1910 and 1920 the black population of the North increased from 850,000 to 1.4 million; it reached 2.3 million by

1930. In the first few decades of the twentieth century, the black population of Chicago and New York grew at approximately five times the rate of the white population: from 43,103 to 109,458 in Chicago and from 91,709 to 152,467 in New York City, a 66 percent increase between 1910 and 1920. In the next decade the black population grew another 115 percent to 327,706, while the white population grew 20 percent.[12]

Black men saw their new lives in terms of economic opportunity and survival, and also in gender terms, as they escaped the emasculation of Jim Crow laws, first enacted in the 1880s.[13] And they escaped the literal emasculation of despicably gendered torture, in which many victims of lynching were first castrated. Between 1900 and 1917 more than eleven hundred black men were lynched in the South. Escape from such conditions meant the opportunity to be a real man as well as a free man. One man commented that he left because he wanted to "go anywhere you want to go . . . [and you] don't have to look up to the white man, get off the street for him, and go to the buzzard roost at shows." Another told a journalist, "I want to be a free man, come when I please, and nobody say nothing to me, nor order me around." And still another put it most simply and eloquently; in the North, he said, "a man could feel more like a man."[14]

It was hard enough that America was more urban, more heavily populated, more diverse, and more bureaucratized at work. The additional postbellum surge of women into the public arena was almost too much to bear. The first wave of the women's movement really picked up momentum after the Civil War, with concurrent campaigns for entry into the workplace, university, and voting booth. The opening of several women's colleges, notably Vassar (1865), Wellesley (1872), Bryn Mawr (1885), Smith (1875), and Mount Holyoke (1837), provided new opportunities for women's education.[15] In 1870 21 percent of all enrolled college students were women. By 1890 36 percent were women; by 1920 the number was over 47 percent, and women received one-third of all graduate degrees.[16] The passage of the Morrill Act in 1862 established many public universities as coeducational institutions, prompting new political and ideological struggles about the virtues and vices of coeducation.

Women were also entering the workforce. Between 1870 and 1900 the female percentage of the workforce edged up from 16 percent to 20 percent (1.8 million women in 1870, 5.3 million in 1900). Ten years later one-fourth of all workers were women; by 1920 the percentage was closer to 40 percent, and by 1930, nearly 50 percent of the workforce. The number of married white women in the labor force rose from about 4 percent in 1900 to about 10 percent by the end of the 1920s.[17] In the expanding world of white-collar offices, this increase was startling and rapid. In 1870 women made up 2.5 percent of the clerical labor force and 5 percent of all stenographers and typists. By 1930 women accounted for 52.5 percent of the total clerical workforce and 96 percent of all stenographers and typists. Other working women campaigned for entry into the growing labor unions and proved dedicated and fierce unionists, leading the famous strikes in Paterson and Lawrence; one Philadelphia newspaper warned that the "governor may have to call out the militia to prevent a gynecocracy."[18]

Men no longer worried only about controlling their own passions; now they were fretting that the new crowds surrounding them would put them in a straitjacket. And sadly, at least to many of them, escape was increasingly difficult. For two centuries the ever-receding frontier had been a place where men could achieve their manhood or re-prove it after failure. The frontier had offered "perennial rebirth" to both men and nation, according to Frederick Jackson Turner. In this midwestern-educated Harvard professor the frontier found its historian and its most enthusiastic booster. Turner "discovered" the frontier's significance in American history at the moment of its disappearance, the turn of the century.[19]

Turner's original thesis was actually quite progressive, articulated as a corrective to his mentor Herbert Baxter Adams's "germ theory," which explained American culture by reference to its Germanic and Anglo-Saxon antecedents, or "germs." According to Turner, too much attention had been paid to European antecedents, and too little to the distinctive shaping influence of the American continent itself. Echoing Ralph Waldo Emerson's arguments in Nature (1836), Turner claimed that it was the frontier that had provided American democracy's literal grounding, liberating men from European influence, and imbued a "forest philosophy" that was anti-intellectual, anticonsumerist, and anti–European refinement.[20]

The late nineteenth century was full of commentary on how the frontier made men. If the workplace could not inspire the "manly independence" of the earlier Heroic Artisan, escape to the primitive conditions of existence on the frontier might do the trick. In a magazine essay, General Horace Porter invited his audience to compare two men:

> Let one remain in a quiet city, playing the milksop . . . leading to an unambitious namby-pamby life, . . . while the other goes out on the frontier, runs his chance in encounters with wild animals, finds that to make his way he must take his life in his hands, and assert his rights, if necessary with deadly weapons. . . .

Porter's conclusion was unavoidable. He "will become the superior of the lad who has remained at home." "The wilderness will take hold of you," added George Evans. "It will give you good red blood; it will turn you from a weakling into a man."[21]

Commentators also recognized that the frontier provided a cultural safety valve, siphoning off potentially rebellious young men whose economic futures were clouded or stymied. Geographic mobility might compensate for failed social mobility—if one couldn't rise in the economic system, one could at least head west. "For more than a half century, the outlet toward the free lands of the West has been the escape valve of social discontent in the great cities of America," wrote Hamlin Garland, in 1892. "Whenever the conditions of his native place pressed too hard on him, the artisan or the farmer has turned his face toward the prairies and forests of the West."[22]

The same commentators who were championing the virtues of the frontier were also lamenting its passing. Francis Parkman, who had earlier celebrated frontier manhood, now wrote mournfully:

> The buffalo is gone, and of all his millions nothing is left but bones. Tame cattle and fences of barbed wire have supplanted his vast herds and boundless grazing grounds. The wild Indian is turned into an ugly caricature of his conqueror; and that which made him romantic, terri-

ble, and hateful is in large measure scourged out of him. The slow cavalcade of horsemen armed to the teeth have disappeared before parlor cars and the effeminate comforts of modern travel.[23]

An article in the *North American Review* in 1906 noted that

the old cabins and dugouts are replaced by modern dwellings. The great ranges are fast passing into orderly farms, where cultivated crops take the place of wild grasses. Steadily is man's rational selection directing the selection of nature. Even the cowboy, the essential creation of Western conditions, is rapidly passing away. Like the buffalo, he has had his place in the drama of civilization. The Indian of the plain must yield to civilization or pass away. Custer, Cody, Bridger, and Carson did their work and passed on. Pioneers of the old school are giving place to a young and vigorous group of men of intellect, will and ceaseless activity, who are turning the light of scientific discovery on plain and mountain.[24]

The Self-Made Man had tamed the wilderness, and so it could no longer be relied upon to make him wild.[25]

EXCLUSION AS MASCULINE RETREAT

In the rush of the new at the turn of the century, the old way of life was passing quickly from view—and with it the possibilities to test and prove manhood in the time-honored ways that American men had historically used. But that didn't stop them from trying. The turn of the century city was overcrowded and bustling, and men were overwhelmed by the changes. After all, aristocratic honor was unreachable, and moral self-control didn't help explain a gilded age in which some men's success was so visibly the result of other skills, like self-promotion, avarice, or outright theft. And yet sheer economic worth neither seemed very scientific nor very fair—most Americans ranked well below the captains of industry.

For many men, resistance meant retreat to a bygone era. To some, the restorative tonic would be found in a return to earlier historical notions of masculine virtue. To others, that era could only be restored by stemming what one writer called "the rising tide of color."

To that writer, it meant both the masses of immigrants flooding America's cities and the streams of blacks migrating north at the same time. But to many men, that tide that threatened to wash over American manhood and dash their hopes for self-making included other groups as well, among them women and homosexuals.

Racism, antifeminism, and nativism fed off these fears, as though by excluding the "others," gender identity could be preserved.[26] American manhood had earlier been grounded upon the exclusion of blacks and women, the non-native-born (immigrants) and the genuinely native-born (Indians), each on the premise that they weren't "real" Americans and couldn't, by definition, be real men. The ideas of Social Darwinism provided the perfect ideological justification for such exclusion. No sooner had Darwin's *Origin of the Species* been published in 1859 than social thinkers on both sides of the Atlantic attempted to apply his theories of natural selection and the survival of the fittest to human societies—something Darwin himself had been hesitant to do. Herbert Spencer in England and Yale's William Graham Sumner in the United States developed Social Darwinism as a doctrine that explained social inequality as evidence of natural superiority. "Let it be understood that we cannot go out of this alternative," wrote Sumner, "liberty, inequality, survival of the fittest; non-liberty, equality, survival of the unfittest. The former carries society forward and favors all its best members; the latter carries society downwards and favors all its worst members."[27]

It has often been noted that such principles were applied to the racial and ethnic diversity of the crowded nation. What has been ignored is how they were also linked to gender, to the greater or lesser degrees of manhood among different peoples. For example, opposing the Emancipation Proclamation in 1862, Ohio Congressman Samuel Sullivan Cox argued:

> Our statistician boasts that Ohio has men of greater height . . . than England, Belgium or Scotland, and in breadth of chest nearly equal to that of Scotland, and above all others. I do not offer myself as a specimen [laughter]. But how long before the manly, warlike people of Ohio of fair hair and blue eyes, in a large preponderance, would become, in

spite of Bibles and morals, degenerate under the wholesale emancipation and immigration [of black slaves]?

Francis Parkman believed that white Anglo-Saxons were "peculiarly
masculine," while in *Democracy and the Overman* (1910) Charles Zueblin fused Social Darwinism and a bastardized Nietzschean evocation
of the Overman when he argued that the survival of the fittest resulted in the "raw, sturdy Saxon of primitive England." The danger
would be to dilute it by diffusion to those below.[28]

Survival of the most manly was also used against blacks. Georges
Clemenceau, the future French prime minister, commented on a visit
to the United States in 1869 that blacks "must gird up their loins and
struggle for their existence, in Darwin's phrase, for their physical as
well as their moral existence. In a word, they must become men."[29]
But Social Darwinian hierarchies implied that some groups were
more manly than others. Self-Made Men were supposed to be "frugal
and productive"; it was argued that black men represented "laziness
and license."[30]

Intermarriage was particularly terrifying because it would dilute
the purity of the race and, hence, pure manhood. Lathrop Stoddard's
Rising Tide of Color (1920), Homer Lea's *The Day of the Saxon* (1912),
and Madison Grant's *The Passing of the Great Race* (1916) bordered
on hysteria. "The whole white race is exposed . . . to the possibility of
social sterilization and final replacement or absorption by the teem-
ing colored races," which would be an "unspeakable catastrophe,"
wrote Stoddard. "The white man is being rapidly bred out by negroes," Grant echoed, resulting in an "ever thinning veneer of white
culture." Racial mixing leads to "disintegration and dissolution,"
wrote Lea, which will result in an "apocalypse of the white man's ignorance." Grant's terrors were grounded in racialist ideas that "the
cross between a white man and a Negro is a Negro" and between a
"European and a Jew is a Jew."[31] Here, too, groupthink was a form of
gender-think.

Grant's anti-Semitism added a new group to the ranks of the less
manly. The Jew was effeminate, bookish, and conniving; he got his
way insidiously, by passing himself off as a real man, and thereby

sabotaging the purity of the race. And what was this pure race? The men "of the old stock" comprised a "race of soldiers, sailors, adventurers and explorers, but above all, of rulers, organizers, and aristocrats." Perhaps, if Grant had been less focused on genetics, he would not have feared that urbane, bookish Jews could have any impact on those men of action. But the new Darwinian world was one of racial bloodlines, not behavior.

There were two ways in which the new pseudoscientific doctrines of racial superiority were cloaked as comparative levels of masculinity. Many believed that men were at a higher stage of Darwinian evolution than women. Thus, one common strategy was to link the men of other races to women and children, to make them Darwinian throwbacks, lower down the evolutionary ladder from white Anglo-Saxon or Teutonic men. The Negro was "next below man in the zoological scale," noted one St. Louis physician in 1882. One anatomist argued that the adult Negro men are intellectually the equals of "the child, the female and the senile white."[32] One method to demonstrate innate intelligence was the weighing of brains, which became a booming business during the 1880s and 1890s. One anatomist "proved" conclusively that black men "have a brain scarcely heavier than that of white women"; while other scientists compared men's and women's brains to demonstrate that in men's heavier brain weight lay the justification for exclusion of women from education and voting.[33]

The perceived—or, just as frequently, projected—effeminacy of nonwhite men was a standard racialist theme. Ignatius Donnelly railed, in his novel *Caesar's Column* (1890), against those "wretched yellow under-fed coolies, with women's garments over their effeminate limbs, [who] will not have the courage or the desire or the capacity to make soldiers and defend their oppressors." Samuel Gompers had contempt for the Chinese because they would "allow themselves to be barbarously tyrannized over in their own country," without the gumption to fight back. Harvard zoologist Louis Agassiz was alarmed at the possibility that "the manly populations" descended from Nordic stock would be replaced by the "effeminate progeny of mixed races, half Indian, half Negro, sprinkled with white blood." Mexican acquiescence to U.S. domination was attributed to

Mexicans' lack of "all the manlier virtues," which made them "perfectly accustomed to being conquered," wrote an editor of the *New York Sun*.[34]

Yet there was a noteworthy confusion in this group assignment of virtue, a confusion that has remained to this day. Black men and immigrants were seen simultaneously as less manly than native-born whites and as *more* manly, especially as more sexually voracious and potent. Some Social Darwinists who claimed that blacks and immigrants were lower on the evolutionary scale placed them alongside primitive beasts rather than women and children. And these beasts sounded a lot like the hypermasculine men of the old frontier. The Chinese were depicted as "invariably degenerate," a "savage, vicious, idol-worshiping and barbarous race" against which "every man in America should be at work." Dr. William English noted that blacks' instinctual composition was toward "bestiality and gratification" and the "innate tendency to sex appetite."[35] Immigration, one advice book warned, "tends to lower the standards of morality," because

> year after year Europe pours into the United States multitudes of degenerate human beings [including Italians, Germans, Huns, Poles, Frenchmen, and Austrians] who, incited by the freedom of American institutions, and without the deterrent fear of summary punishment, immediately give free reign to their atavistic imaginations, and whenever they think that the favorable moment has arrived, plunge into anarchy and lawlessness.[36]

One critic wanted it both ways, drawing on images of both hypermasculinity and effeminacy when he labeled the Chinese "a barbarous race, devoid of energy."[37]

Two groups of men were singled out as especially threatening. "Indians," of course, had to be continually pushed aside in the headlong scramble toward the receding frontier. In the last decades of the century, Native-American life was completely and finally transformed. The Homestead Act (1862) brought large numbers of settlers to claim free land, while the completion of the railroads and the annihilation of the great buffalo herds obliterated the traditional Native-American economy. Through the 1870s tribes were forcibly consolidated, removed, and destroyed, acts justified because they were no longer fierce men, men whose virility could rival that of the settlers, but were now, in the words of one editorialist in the *New York Daily Graphic*, "a degraded relic of a decayed race." It was unclear, the writer continued,

> whether he is worth civilizing, even if he is capable of civilization. . . .
> Were the money and effort wasted in trying to civilize the Indians
> wisely expended in reclaiming and educating the savages in our cities
> the world would be vastly better off in the end. The globe is none too
> large for the civilized races to occupy, and all others are doomed by a
> law that is irrevocable and that it is folly to resist.

Now that the "Indian" had been stripped of his dignity and manhood, he was on his own.[38]

For themselves, Native-Americans developed new, symbolic ways to ease the pain of emasculation at the hand of the white man. Increasing alcoholism and the growth of the peyote cult provided a kind of temporary anesthesia for these men, and the Ghost Dance and Sun Dance religions allowed hope and enthusiasm, especially the possibility of spiritual transcendence of depraved temporal life. One ritual in the Sun Dance religion (popularized in the 1970s movie *A Man Called Horse*) is particularly striking in its efforts to retrieve a sense of power and virility. Sun Dance festivals consisted of days of fasting and dancing after which rituals of self-mutilation by the men would begin. Warriors would slice open the skin on their chests, pass rawhide skewers through these cuts, and then tie the rawhide to poles. At a signal, they would step back forcefully from the poles until the skewers ripped through their skin. These rituals of individual heroism—the ability to withstand self-initiated torture in the hope of experiencing some form of transcendence—were all that was left for these men who had been stripped of the traditional expressions of their manhood by white society.

Such rituals seemed to confirm the Darwinists' notions that non-white men were primitive beasts. Black men, too, were a screen against which white men projected their own fears of emasculation. In the South, recall, military defeat was experienced as the emasculation of Southern manhood, the chivalrous and gallant Southern cavalier, although those ideals of honor continued to dominate. The organization of the Ku Klux Klan and other fraternal orders, the founding of and expansion of military schools designed to produce "officers and gentlemen," and a revival of dueling to preserve personal honor all temporarily gave southern white men a respite from this perceived assault on their manhood.

The Klan's goal was the reclamation of southern manhood, whose principles included "all that is chivalric in conduct, noble in sentiment, generous in manhood, and patriotic in purpose" and whose purpose, according to the *Prescript of the Order of the Ku Klux Klan* (1868), was

> to protect the weak, the innocent, and the defenseless, from the indignities, wrongs and outrages of the lawless, the violent and the brutal; to relieve the injured and oppressed; to succor the suffering and unfortunate, and especially the widows and orphans of Confederate soldiers.[39]

Klan rhetoric was saturated with images of heroic and chivalrous Southern manhood. Members were required to demonstrate "manly" character and courage, and initiation rituals were punctuated by prayers that "God, give us Men!"[40] Playing on traditional images of the emasculated southern gentleman and his fears of rapacious blacks and conniving northern reformers, the Klan mobilized southern white men into its "invisible empire" for many decades. At its peak, in 1926, the Klan numbered over five million members, and with other groups, like the American Protective Association and the American Super-Race Foundation, it was memorialized in, among others, Thomas Dixon's novel *The Clansman* (1905) and the film based on it, D. W. Griffiths's *Birth of a Nation* (1915).[41]

The new and powerful fear of the black rapist revealed more about southern white men's fears of lost manhood than about any propensity on the part of black men. George Lydston's 1904 study of vice and crime attributed the frequency of rape in the South to the "primitive impulses of the black race," for which he proposed what was conceived of as a "progressive" solution: castration—"the total ablation of the sexual organs." The criminal would be "incapacitated," prevented from repeating the crime or perpetuating his kind, as well as becoming a walking deterrent to other would-be rapists. Others' solutions were more conventional, simply advocating lynching and murder.[42]

Social Darwinists also lent new force to biological arguments about the differences between women and men. They had plenty of opportunities to make their case in reaction to the first wave of feminism, from Seneca Falls in 1848 to the ratification of woman suffrage in 1920. In 1880 one speaker claimed:

> I am opposed to woman's sufferage [sic] on account of the burden it will place on her. Her delicate nature has already enough to drag it down. Her slender frame, naturally weakened by the constant strain attendant upon her nature is too often racked by the diseases that are caused by a too severe tax upon her mind. The presence of passion, love, ambition is all too potent for her enfeebled constitution and wrecked health and early death are all too common.[43]

Here was a heightened reliance on biological difference, complete with disease and fears of extinction. Women should not be deprived of the vote, opponents argued, as much as exempted from it. Antisuffrage organizations abounded, such as the national Man Suffrage Association and state-level associations.[44]

Antifeminists argued that college-educated women had already lost their delicate feminine virtue. The publication of Edward Clarke's *Sex in Education* in 1873 galvanized the opposition to higher education for women. Clarke rehearsed biological arguments in the guise of protecting women from the injurious effects of education beyond their biological capacities. The result of college education, Clarke argued, was that women were losing their ability to breed, developing "monstrous brains and puny bodies" with "flowing brains and constipated bowels." Wombs and brains seemed in direct competition; as women's brains grew heavier and larger due to education, their wombs would atrophy and they would cease to reproduce.[45]

All participation in the public sphere would harm women by "masculinizing" them so that women would "feebly imitate" men in their social clubs, on the streets, in the schoolrooms, and in the workplace. "The number of women in business who lose their gentleness and womanliness is far greater than those who retain what, after all, are woman's best and chief qualities," warned Edward Bok, editor of the *Ladies' Home Journal* in 1893.[46] Another writer claimed that women's independence would make men lose interest in them. "A state of independence always begets more or less of jealous rivalry and hostility. A man loves his children because they are weak, helpless, and dependent. He loves his wife for similar reasons. When his children grow up and assert their independence, he is apt to transfer his affection to his grand-children. He ceases to love his wife when she becomes masculine or rebellious."[47]

What men seemed to fear at least as much was that "the newly civilized worker had lost his manhood in the gendered office." And many men believed that they could retrieve it only by pushing women back out of the labor force, that "the sense of subordination and vulnerability endemic to corporate work could only be overcome by reasserting their position relative to women—by attempting to reinforce a traditional gender hierarchy by separating themselves from women and behaviors ascribed to women."[48] Thus, it appears that other sentiments motivated such apparent concern for women's protection. For one thing, manhood was seen as noble sacrifice. Work is unpleasant, painful, difficult, and cruel—a dirty job that someone has to do. Women should be placed on a pedestal glorifying feminine delicacy, for which men must sacrifice themselves. This was a new twist on the definition of manhood: It was no picnic of power and privilege; it was dirty and demanding, and men went through it because they loved their wives and children.

However defensive such arguments were, it was through them that masculinity became an "issue." Men wanted to be taken into consideration *as men*. "We hear so much about the rights of women, that just for the sake of variety it ought not to be displeasing to hear a little something about the rights of men," suggested Harry Thurston Peck in 1899. And the editor of *Harper's* magazine added that, given all the women's magazines "devoted to the aspirations and the wants of women alone," it was time to consider a Men's Journal, "which should try to keep his head above water in the struggle for social supremacy."[49]

That struggle was increasingly difficult as so many newcomers demanded recognition. As Sojourner Truth had earlier demanded inclusion into the women's struggle with the ringing cry of "Ain't I a Woman," a growing chorus of black and immigrant men asked angrily if they, too, weren't men. One of the more revealing moments of this struggle came in 1893 at Chicago's Columbian Exposition. The organizers of the exposition planned a glorious White City to celebrate the progress of civilization and promoted a "vision of Strong Manhood and Perfection of Society." Outside the White City, down the midway, exposition organizers placed exhibits of other cultures with "authentic" reproductions of Egyptian, Dahoman, and Turkish villages—ostensibly to demonstrate how far modern white American civilization had come. These other races were uncivilized and "unmanly" compared with the White City, and the layout allowed visitors, as the *Chicago Tribune* enthused, to trace "humanity in its highest phases down almost to its animalistic origins." Black reformers Ida Wells and Frederick Douglass demanded that black Americans be included in the White City, instead of on the midway. "We are men and our aim is perfect manhood, to be men among men," wrote Douglass in a flyer handed to exposition attendees. The organizers refused, and black men thus remained excluded from full manhood, both in reality and in the nation's representation of itself to itself.[50]

The emergence of another group of men—homosexuals—onto the public stage at the turn of the century further fueled men's anxieties. A visible gay subculture had already emerged in the nation's cities as early as the 1850s; by the end of the century, gay men had "resorts in every large city," places "where the 'queens' hung out." George Beard had noted "great numbers" of gay men in New York City in 1884; by 1911 the Chicago Vice Commission observed "whole colonies" of them.[51] In his impressive study of "Gay New York," historian George Chauncey described "an organized, multilayered, and self-conscious gay subculture, with its own meeting places, language, folklore and moral codes." At the turn of the century, he writes:

> an extensive gay world took shape in the streets, cafeterias, saloons, and apartments of New York, and gay men played an integral role in the social life of certain neighborhoods. Fairies drank with sailors and other workingmen at waterfront dives and entertained them at Bowery

resorts; "noted faggots" mixed with other patrons at Harlem's rent parties and basement cabarets; and lesbians ran speakeasies where Greenwich Village Bohemians—straight and queer alike—gathered to read
their verse.[32]

Gay men were defined almost entirely in terms of their masculinity, or rather, in terms of its absence. Homosexuality involved a "comprehensive gender role inversion (or reversal)," writes Chauncey.
These men—called "fairies" or "queers" at that time—"act effemi-
nately; most of them are painted and powdered . . . [and] ape the female character," noted one police investigator in 1899. Psychiatrists
routinely diagnosed men as homosexual if they exhibited traits that
were seen as less than manly—an "abnormal dread of dust and dirt,"
for example, or a finicky attention to clothing and personal appearance. On the streets, too, gay men's "irrepressible desire to act the
part of the opposite sex" resulted in "effeminacy of voice, dress, and
manner"; they could thus be easily spotted by their imitation of
women. "He acted sort of peculiar, walking around with his hands on
his hips," noted one sailor at a criminal trial. "His manner was not
masculine." One fairy confessed that he had "never been one who
felt like taking a man's place among men."[53]

Chauncey argues that such flagrant flouting of traditional masculinity came less from some internal drive to express innate effeminacy; gay effeminacy was more a behavioral strategy to signal other
homosexual men. "Effeminacy was one of the few sure means they
had to identify themselves to others," he writes. Thus, it may have
been that a man "chose to be effeminate precisely because he wanted
to identify himself to other men."[54] Ironically, such overt repudiation
of traditional masculine behaviors permitted a more casual relationship between many heterosexual and homosexual men at the turn of
the century. Gay male effeminacy simultaneously exaggerated the differences between themselves and "normals" and between women
and men and thus "served to confirm rather than threaten the masculinity of other men."[55] For many straight men, then, homosexuality
did not threaten their masculinity but reinforced it.

Such casual coexistence was relatively short lived. As the nature of
work changed and as women, immigrants, and black men "invaded"

men's spheres, masculinity was experienced as increasingly difficult to prove. Sexuality emerged as a central element of American manhood. "Middle class men increasingly conceived of their sexuality— their heterosexuality, or exclusive desire for women—as one of the hallmarks of a real man," writes Chauncey. "It was as if they had decided that no matter how much their gender comportment might be challenged as unmanly, they were normal men because they were heterosexual." Homosexuality and effeminacy were thus added to the repertoire of men's anxieties. Terms like "pussyfoot" and "sissy" became increasingly prominent, and negative. "Sissy," for example, had originally been coined in the 1840s as an affectionate term for "sister." By the 1880s the term had become a derisive description for spineless boys and men and by 1900 had become clearly associated with effeminacy, cowardice, and lack of aggression. Heterosexual men had begun to define themselves in opposition to all that was soft and womanlike.[56]

With such definitions came campaigns of exclusion, concerted attacks on homosexuals for gender deviance. Health reformer Bernarr Macfadden, for example, praised men who practiced turn of the century gay-bashing; in 1904 he denounced "the shoals of painted, perfumed, Kohl-eyed, lisping, mincing youths that at night swarm on Broadway in the Tenderloin section, or haunt the parks and 5th Avenue, ogling every man that passes and—it is pleasant to relate—occasionally getting a sound thrashing or an emphatic kicking."[57] Even though the larger social debates about homosexuality were still some decades away, the association between masculinity and heterosexuality was now firmly embedded in public perception. "If a man was walking around and did not act real masculine, I would think he was a cocksucker," observed a sailor who was testifying in a criminal trial. Such an observation illustrates my central themes about American manhood at the turn of the century: that masculinity was increasingly an act, a form of public display; that men felt themselves on display at virtually all times; and that the intensity of the need for such display was increasing. To be considered a real man, one had better make sure to always be walking around and acting "real masculine."

THE PROBLEM OF BUSINESS CIVILIZATION

The reassertion of this version of masculinity, whether through Social Darwinism or some other ideology, was a conservative reaction against real and perceived threats to increasingly anxious Self-Made Men, as if pushing others out could reassure those who were left that they were, in fact, real men. There were other responses as well. Former Heroic Artisans asserted manly pride in workmanship as they united to fight against becoming faceless workers. And they were backed by liberal theorists who celebrated both the virility and the dignity of craftsmanship. Others sought to accommodate anxious men to the crowd, and thereby both soothe their insecurities and redefine manhood away from marketplace success.

Of course, some men didn't buy the idea of Self-Made Masculinity at all and simply dropped out of the struggle, resigned to workplace failure. For example, new social problems emerged in decaying urban neighborhoods—problems such as chronic alcoholism among the "bums" who lived on Seattle's Skid Row or New York's Bowery. Here were men who had given up in their work or family lives, who were now creating a community of failed men. Itinerant hobos who rode the rails and lived by the sides of the tracks were not only escaping economic dislocation but running away from Self-Made Manhood, away from the settled responsibility of a boring, unpleasant job that such a gender ideal seemed to require. There was also a peculiar solace among them, a collective nursing of wounds, as if having been declared failures as men had suddenly freed these men from having to maintain the social and physical distance and the emotional neutrality that masculinity required. On the margins, on the skids, men held one another, wept openly, and shared their momentary pleasures and their constant despair. Out of the rat race, they had no one to turn to but themselves.[58]

Other men were ambivalent about the entire project of being Self-Made Men. Why should manhood require having power over other men and over women? And if so many men were casualties of these relentless efforts to prove their manhood in the marketplace, then perhaps something was wrong with American culture itself. Throughout the nineteenth century there were men who were less sanguine about the virilizing effects of the market and urged a redefinition of success so that it would be possible for ordinary men to grasp.[59] Henry Ward Beecher's popular *Twelve Lectures to Young Men* (1888) argued that industry, not wealth, was the real the key to manhood, that one should strive for "the applause of conscience, the self-respect of pride, the consciousness of independence, the manly joy of usefulness, the consent of every faculty of the mind to one's occupation"—these were the emotions which should animate men. The blind pursuit of money was a blind alley. Another advice book counseled that "money getting under competitive conditions is by no means the indispensable motive power that impels men to their best activity," while another observed that "no matter how much a man has, when he comes to a point where he stops getting richer, he is scared."[60]

In place of the scramble for wealth, men were advised to return to more stately and Protestant virtues, such as industry, usefulness, and thrift; to substitute virtues of personality for success; and do a good job. "Manhood is greater than wealth, grander than fame," wrote Orison Swett Marden. His *Pushing to the Front* (1894) was a collection of homey platitudes, designed to help men who feel like failures feel like successes by returning to the antebellum value of character. (It went through twelve editions in its first year of publication alone.) His other books—including *Success* (1897), *The Secrets of Achievement* (1898), *Character, the Greatest Thing in the World* (1899), *The Power of Personality* (1899), *The Young Man Entering Business* (1903), *He Who Can Thinks He Can* (1908), and *How to Get What You Want* (1917)—made Marden perhaps the era's most successful self-help writer.[61]

Marden himself was a self-made success story. He was originally invited to Harvard to establish a dining service on campus and later admitted to the college. After the enormous success of *Pushing to the Front*, he founded a magazine, *Success*, in which he preached a gospel of hard work, dedication, and relentless sublimation. Men, he argued in *The Optimistic Life* (1907), had to be healthy and strong and develop "manly qualities" like vigor, energy, and enthusiasm. But ultimately, Marden preached a gospel of individual achievement through acceptance of limited possibilities. It was far better to know one's place, he counseled, to be the "Napoleon of bootblacks, the Alexander the Great of chimney sweeps," and do a great job there. "It matters not whether the boy is born in a log cabin or in a mansion; if he is dominated by resolute purpose and upholds himself, neither men nor demons can keep him down." Every business opportunity, win or lose, was an opportunity "to be polite . . . to be manly . . . to be honest . . . to make friends."[62] Standing out was a matter of fitting in.

Middle-class men found the going tough; managers and white-collar salaried employees were particularly hard hit by these newly gendered anxieties. For them the question was how to participate in the business world, find their rung upon the ladder, and still maintain a sense of their manhood. One writer defined a government clerk in 1873 as someone who "has no independence while in office, no manhood . . . he must openly avow his implicit faith in all his superiors, on pain of dismissal, and must cringe and fawn upon them." By 1910 about 20 percent of the adult male population was working in such white-collar jobs in large companies, banks, and retail firms. But they remained dependent upon the corporation as paternal authority, and just as much in need of manly validation.[63]

With office work increasingly feminized, aspiring white-collar men were counseled to enter the newly expanding field of sales. Salesmen were heralded as the self-made men of the new century. Sales reinforced "independence and individuality," wrote one salesman. Life insurance was described as a "manly calling." The Equitable Company recruited would-be salesmen to a world in which their possibilities for success were "almost limitless," in which an ambitious young man could "reach the top if he have but the requisite ability and energy." America became "a nation of salesmen," and what those salesmen sold was themselves, their winning personalities, their smiles and shoeshines.[64]

Two of the more prescient observers of these changes in American business life were the stolid German economist and sociologist Max Weber and Thorstein Veblen, an irascible economist from the midwestern American heartland. Weber's observations on American society at the turn of the century offer a chilling portrait of men's psyches. In *The Protestant Ethic and the Spirit of Capitalism*, written in 1902 after a visit to the United States, Weber looked deeply into the heart of modern society and into the anxious soul of modern American manhood. Like Tocqueville seventy years earlier, Weber saw the Americans' frantic scramble for wealth as a kind of proof of salvation, an insatiable quest that both animated American life and left individual Americans feeling bewildered and trapped. One would have thought that the material wealth produced by advanced capitalist economic organization would have brought great happiness. But the most successful, he observed, "were characterized by the exact opposite of the joy of living." Borrowing heavily from Benjamin Franklin's epigrams, Weber decried the perversion of the Protestant work ethic into "the earning of more and more money, combined with the strict avoidance of all spontaneous enjoyment of life," so that a man would be "dominated by the making of money, by acquisition as the ultimate purpose of his life."[65]

This corruption of the work ethic traps us in an "iron cage." Devoid of meaning, bereft of hope, we scurry about in "economic compulsion," unable to make sense of the world. We become, Weber argues, "specialists without spirit, sensualists without heart"—a condemnation of characterological emptiness that rings as true today as at the beginning of the century. Thus, "the pursuit of wealth, stripped of its religious and ethical meaning, tends to become associated with purely mundane passions, which often actually give it the character of sport." Or, in the words of a bumper sticker from the Reagan era: He who has the most toys when he dies, wins.[66]

The grandsons of those antebellum Self-Made Men now found themselves trapped in that iron cage. The very strategies they had used to resolve the earlier identity crisis now led them to scramble relentlessly to grasp that elusive ideal. To Veblen this signaled an endless cycle of "conspicuous consumption"—the frenzied and competitive consumption of expensive items that demonstrate high status. His controversial book *The Theory of the Leisure Class* (1899) revealed the shift—from the realm of production to the realm of consumption—of the arena in which men proved their worth. Men consume conspicuously to demonstrate "that the wearer can afford to consume freely and uneconomically," that money is no object. Beneath his satiric view of consumerist culture lay a bitter antipathy to parasitic upper-class men. Veblen claimed that traditional ideals of producerism, ideals of thrift and hard work and dedication that had earlier animated the Heroic Artisan, were now in too short supply. American manhood required a return to artisanal values of republican virtue, simplicity, and hard work.[67]

For others, though, it was the achievement of wealth and success by American men that was proving to be their undoing, producing the very effeminacy that was eroding manhood. "No nation becomes rich and prosperous without becoming also luxurious and debilitated," noted Edward Hitchcock, a professor at Amherst College. In *Democratic Vistas* (1876) Walt Whitman warned against "extreme business energy" leading to an "almost maniacal appetite for wealth." Luxury and wealth "produces national effeminacy and effeteness," warned Homer Lea, which produces "whole tribes of theorists, feminists," and other examples of "opulent decadence."[68] In an astonishing inversion of his own position, Andrew Carnegie joined the chorus of those who warned that wealth leads to feminization; in a 1902 article in *Success* magazine, he scorned the genteel aristocrat as an object of pity:

> The youth who is reared in a luxurious home, who, from the moment of his birth is waited on by an army of servants, pampered and indulged by overfond parents, and deprived of every incentive . . . is more to be pitied than the poorest, most humbly born boy or girl in the land. Unless he is gifted with an unusual mind, he is in danger of becoming a degenerate, a parasite, a creature who lives on the labor of others, whose powers ultimately atrophy from disuse.[69]

And Dr. James Weir warned that such luxury leaves the door open for the less highly evolved working class. "The rich become effeminate, weak and immoral," Weir wrote, "and the lower classes, taking advantage of this moral lassitude, and led on by their savage inclinations, undertake strikes, mobs, boycotts, and riots."[70] All the more reason to slam that door shut again.

Workingmen, for their part, used manhood to turn upper-class ideals on their heads. Frank James, the celebrated outlaw, put it like this:

If there is ever another war in this country, which may happen, it will be between capital and labor, I mean between greed and manhood, and I'm as ready to march now in defense of American manhood as I was when a boy in defense of the south.[71]

Workers must "stand erect in the full majesty of our manhood" observed the writer of a letter to *Miner's Magazine* in 1904, and against the "effeminate monopolistic system" and "effete methods of tyranny," as another correspondent had written in 1887.[72]

Some workers' organizations considered the plight of the wage laborer to be analogous to that of a feudal serf. "We claim, that although the masses have advanced towards independence, they will never be completely free from vassalage until they have thrown off the system of working for hire," observed the Knights of St. Crispin, a shoemakers' union, in 1870. Other workers used prostitution as a metaphor for wage labor, as men were forced to sell their bodies to the capitalist in the same way that a prostitute sells her body to her well-heeled customer. Unemployment emasculated men who could not support their families. "I have no more desire to be idle," commented one iron puddler, "than I do to wear women's clothes." Thus, women (as prostitutes), blacks (as slaves), and European peasants (as indentured serfs) served as the screens against which late nineteenth-century "artisans" sought to reconfigure their claims to independent manhood.[73]

The development of the labor movement in the United States was built on such contrapuntal images of masculinity. Within the ranks of organized labor, the Heroic Artisan returned as a vision of resistance to the workers' degradation into a proletariat, a form of symbolic resistance to their emasculation as independent, self-made men. The artisanal community of the Jeffersonian yeoman's republic resurfaced as the basis for the American working-class movement. The appeal of socialism, observed one worker in 1899, was that it promised to instill a sympathetic solidarity in the face of that "wasteful war of competition between man and his brother in the wilderness of anarchical production in which people blindly wander."[74]

Of course, organizing these fiercely independent men proved difficult, since groups each held onto their craft or skill as the mark of autonomy and were often indifferent to the claims of other groups in perilously similar positions. (This prevented the much-sought-after worker-farmer alliance in the last decades of the century.) Exclusion remained a potent organizing principle in many developing unions. Blacks were a "scab race," and were therefore not to be admitted. At a meeting of the Bricklayers National Union in 1871, for example, a heated argument developed about the incorporation of black workers. "I wouldn't let a nigger into our union, and if he came in I would go out," one delegate remarked. "We will not recognize a nigger bricklayer in Baltimore," he roared, to great approval of the assembled. The making of the American working class was the making of a distinctly white, male, and native-born class.[75]

A surprising exception to grounding working-class masculinity on racist, sexist, and nativist foundations was also one of the most successful organizations of the era. In the 1870s and 1880s the Knights of Labor took up where earlier, smaller unions left off. Organized in 1869 as a secret society by Philadelphia garment workers, the Noble and Holy Order of the Knights of Labor grew to become America's first mass-membership labor organization, counting between two and three million members over its twenty-year life and numbering over 750,000 at its peak in 1886. The Knights harkened back to an era in which labor was dignified, chivalric, and even heroic. Their language was the language of the Jeffersonian yeoman transplanted into the industrial sphere. Wage earners were "producers," and factory owners were "accumulators" or "monopolists." Their goal was to uphold "the dignity of labor"—the abolition of "wage slavery," not the overthrow of capitalism. In short, the Knights sought to return America to the virtuous republic of producerism, a true "workingman's democracy" of the "noblest and bravest of our race."[76]

Apparently, these "noblest and bravest" knew neither race, skill, nor gender; all workers could take pride in honest and useful work. Free blacks were welcome, as were women. "The rights of the sexes are co-equal, their privileges should be the same, and I can see no reason why women should not be entitled to giving to the world its products as well as men," commented Knights' president Terrence

Powderly.[77] Unfortunately, the Knights were not so inclusionary for nonnative workers, as they encouraged and participated in anti-Chinese riots and supported the Chinese Exclusion Act in 1882.

Among rural yeomen, those independent small family farmers, the consolidation of American capitalism and industrial development was no less serious a threat. As the railroads created a national market, these small farmers were increasingly squeezed between falling farm prices and rising costs of transportation and machinery, and many were transformed into tenants and hired laborers. "Once the domain of yeomen freeholders," the Georgia upcountry was fast becoming a "territory of the dispossessed."[78]

The Populist movement—a broad-based agrarian resistance to rural proletarianization—organized these rural discontents into local producer cooperatives to set transport and grain prices. Populism's backbone was "the yeomanry of the country," as the *People's Party Paper* put it in 1892—"the small landed proprietors, the working farmers, the intelligent artisans, the wage workers, men who own homes and want a stable government." And these independent farmers expressed the Jeffersonian republicanism of small-scale producers seeking the restoration of the cooperative commonwealth with its noble vision of manhood. At their mass meetings and rallies, wagon trains and encampments, Populists expressed their belief that the farmer wasn't a peasant but rather a "peer of the realm," "as much of a business man as his employer," as William Jennings Bryan put it—and that his contribution was fundamental to society. In the presidential campaign of 1896, the Populists, as the People's Party, mounted "the largest and most threatening third party movement" since the Civil War for candidate Bryan. His thundering orations chastising aggressive, rapacious finance capitalists—the "idle holders of idle capital"—and his pleas in defense of rural innocence "against the encroachments of organized wealth," revealed a vision of the rural Heroic Artisan, the independent farmer as autonomous worker and family man, virtuous and virile.[79]

This vision of republican, artisanal manhood was also expressed in fiction, particularly in one of America's best-loved children's stories.[80] Although L. Frank Baum's *The Wizard of Oz* (1900) has long been understood as a Populist parable as well as a beloved children's tale, this distinctly American story can also be read as a parable on the meanings of manhood at the turn of the century. Each of the men in the story undertakes a quest to reclaim his manhood.

When we first meet them, Dorothy's relatives are as cold and gray as the dreary Kansas landscape where they still try to eke out a living as independent farmers before a cyclone literally dispossesses them of their house.[81] Dorothy's companions on her odyssey are initially losers, too—particularly losers as men. The Scarecrow (farmer) is incapable of doing his job, scaring away the crows, and is down on himself because he has no brains. The Tin Woodsman (the industrial worker) is the literal embodiment of alienated labor. Under the spell of the Wicked Witch of the East (manufacturers and bankers), he has been hacking himself to bits, cutting off each of his limbs, and replacing them with tin. His labor is literally alienated. A formerly independent craftsman, he now has no control over his work, which is turned against him in graphic self-mutilation. He has been transformed into a machine that needs a heart, without which he will not have the compassion to make common cause with the farmer. And the Cowardly Lion (the well-known symbol of Bryan's presidential campaign) lacks only the courage to be powerful.

Off they go down the Yellow Brick Road (the gold standard) to Oz (abbreviation for "ounce") to seek redemption from the Wizard of Oz, a carnival confidence man, a humbug who stands in for all the U.S. presidents since the Civil War. "I think you are a very bad man," says Dorothy to the wizard as he is unmasked as a fraud. "Oh no, my dear; I'm really a very good man; but I'm a very bad wizard, I must admit."

Through the course of the story, each of these symbolic representations proves himself as a real man. The Tin Woodsman kills a swarm of bees and a pack of wolves sent by the Wicked Witch of the West to kill the stalwart troop and later chops off the branches of trees that grab those who seek to enter the forest. The Scarecrow finally scares off some crows, and the Lion decapitates a gigantic spider which had terrified the entire forest. And so each of them receives the validation of his virility that he seeks from the Wizard, who gives them, as Baum puts it, "exactly what they thought they wanted."[82] In the end, they each return to the scenes of their respective triumphs to become the ruler over the local residents. As political allegory, Baum's *The Wizard of Oz* represents hope that Bryan's Populist campaign would restore the manhood of these symbolic characters; as a meditation on gender, it is a tale of that masculine revival, set in motion by a protofeminist heroine.[83]

One last effort to retrieve a form of manhood for the heroic toiler came from the Arts and Crafts Movement.[84] Originally a British movement following art critic John Ruskin and, later, William Morris, the Arts and Crafts Movement in the United States also damned industrialization for eliminating the hearty fellowship and craft pride among working men. Factory production had "reduced the workman to such a skinny and pitiful existence that he scarcely knows how to frame a desire for any life much better than that which he now endures," wrote Morris. He argued that work should be "pleasurable as well as useful" with the product a "joy to the maker and the owner."[85] In the arts and crafts workshop independent craftsmen would enjoy both the process and the product of their labor; work would be a "calling" whose outcome would be, as Horace Traubel put it in 1906, "manhood."[86] For some leading figures of the movement, such as C. R. Ashbee, the workshop was also an eroticized homosocial Eden where vigorous young men worked, played, and lived together. Influenced by Edward Carpenter and Walt Whitman, Ashbee fused a critique of modernity's enervating effects on manhood with an exploration of homosexuality. Ashbee promised to keep "the sacred lamp of the New Socialism always before me . . . making the bulwarks of real human love so strong in the hearts of our men and boys that no castrated affection shall dare face it."[87]

While the British wing of the movement was sympathetic to women's dissatisfaction with their role in society (arts and crafts workshops became staging grounds for British feminism), the American wing launched a critique of "the feminization of American culture."[88] Syracuse-based Gustav Stickley, guild organizer, furniture maker, and editor of the *Craftsman* (begun in 1901), saw his mission as providing the homes for men who embraced Theodore Roosevelt's "strenuous life." Stickley despised the typical American home—"built to meet the needs of women, whose tendency is still to emphasize emotion—to minimize reason"—and his designs, with their disciplined geometry, generous proportions, and sturdiness offered men the possibility of return to their castles. "It is the place to which a man comes home when his day's work is done and where he expects to find himself comfortable and at ease in surroundings that are in harmony with his daily life, thought and pursuits." The message to women was equally clear: "Place Craftsman furniture in your parlor or sitting room and men will remain at home instead of leaving for the club or the saloon."[89]

Turn-of-the-century designers carved out a distinctly male space in the home as an antidote to feminized Victorian parlors—the den, "the man's special room." By 1905 Montgomery Ward offered a Morris chair for "manly comfort," and others suggested furniture and paneling of solid oak—"a robust, manly sort of wood," wrote Stickley. Brown leather seat covers, smoking paraphernalia on the well-wrought tables, and perhaps a few hunting trophies on the walls—all made it clear that man was not in the least feminized by returning to his lair, his den, after hunting in the corporate jungle all day.[90]

Finally, other men sought to revive manhood in the real jungle. If the frontier was closed, some reasoned, why not extend its boundaries beyond the borders of the continental United States and create new frontiers where men could test and prove their manhood? No sooner was there no frontier left on the continent than Alfred Thayer Mahan argued that America should develop overseas colonies to serve as coaling stations for the Navy and to increase the nation's commerce. In *The Influence of Sea Power upon History* (1890), Mahan's idea of "race patriotism" linked a desire for frontier manhood to racial terrors of the Asian countries whose conquest he was urging.[91]

Imperialist expansion could create the new frontier. The annexation of Hawaii, the Philippine Islands, Puerto Rico, and Guam (all in 1898), the division of the Samoan Islands with the Germans, (1899), and the suppression of the Boxer Rebellion (1900) all signaled a new imperial strategy. Others believed that decades of peace had made American men effeminate and effete; only by being constantly at war could frontier masculinity be retrieved. General Homer Lea—short, physically deformed, and nearly blind—was one of the most virulent warmongers; his books *The Valor of Ignorance* (1909) and *The Day of the Saxon* (1912) made the analogy between man and nation explicit. "As manhood marks the height of physical vigor among mankind, so the militant successes of a nation mark the zenith of its physical greatness," he wrote.[92] After the sinking of the *Maine*, one journalist wrote that "a nation needs a war from time to time to prevent it from becoming effeminate, to shake it up from demoralizing materialism, and to elevate the popular heart by awakening heroic emotions and the spirit of patriotic self-sacrifice."[93]

For William James militarism was "the greatest preserver of our ideals of hardihood, and human life with no use for hardihood would be contemptible"; his search was, therefore, for the "moral equivalent" of war—"something heroic that will speak to men as universally as war does." In his landmark book *The Varieties of Religious Experience* (1902), James argued that the martial virtues "must be the enduring cement; intrepidity, contempt for softness, surrender of private interest, obedience to command, must still remain the rock upon which states are built." He found such a moral equivalent in the person of the ascetic monk, whose voluntary poverty was an example of the "strenuous life."[94]

The celebration of the military spirit was more than an attempt to redraw the boundaries of the frontier—it was an attempt to re-create the experience of the frontier, a virulent reaction against the perceived feminization of American manhood by the deadening routine of office work or the loss of autonomy and other craft values among the growing proletariat.[95] But the costs were great. When Joyce Kilmer, the poet best known for "Trees," was killed in battle in the First World War, a eulogy in a magazine indicated how he had redeemed his manhood. "Kilmer was young, only 32, and the scholarly type of man," it read. "One did not think of him as a warrior. And yet from the time he entered the war, he could think of but one thing—that he must, with his own hands, strike a blow at the Hun. He was a man."[96]

A PROFEMINIST ALTERNATIVE

Several of these liberal efforts to challenge the rise of both the corporation and the crowd ended up unintentionally reinforcing them—in part because their proponents linked their challenge to restoring masculinity by exclusion, or by retrieving outmoded definitions. One liberal thinker at the turn of the century daringly tried to use conservative Darwinian arguments in the service of a redefinition of masculinity. Using evolutionism, anthropology, and sociology, Lester Ward expounded a theory he called "gynecocracy," claiming that the female sex was both the primary and the original sex in evolutionary development. The origins of human life were matriarchal and matrilineal; woman "is the unchanging trunk of the great genealogic tree." The origins of male domination lay in women's selection of larger and stronger men for mates, who had then usurped political and social power by virtue of their strength, thus ushering in an era defined by patriarchy and monogamous sexual relations. Male domination and monogamy were not some divinely sanctioned moral law, Ward reasoned, but simply a temporary stage of evolution—a stage out of which we were, fortunately, beginning to pass.[97]

Ward also argued that the state should regulate family and marriage to ensure equality between women and men and that sexual relationships should be free of all political, social, or moral encumbrances. Women's position was both morally insupportable and unnatural. "Throughout all human history," he wrote in *Pure Sociology* (1903), "woman has been powerfully discriminated against and held down by custom, law, literature and public opinion." Sexism—not biology, not evolutionary inferiority—held women back. "The universal prevalence of the androcentric world view acts as a wet blanket on all the genial fire of the female sex," he argued in *Applied Sociology* (1906). "Let this be at once removed and woman's true relation to society will be generally perceived, and all this will be changed."[98]

Ward would have few takers, even in our own times, although a recent popularity of feminist anthropologists in search of prehistoric matriarchies, not to mention feminists who attack the gender biases of sciences generally, suggests that Ward's model of redefinition is still very much with us.

At the time, though, Ward's reliance on evolutionary biology was an oddity among the liberal wing of respondents to the crisis of masculinity. Most of his fellow travelers were decidedly unscientific, and some were eager to try to practice what they preached. The Greenwich Village radicals of the turn of the century developed a new vision of masculinity that in many ways set the stage for the new century; what's more, they tried to implement their ideas in the lives they were living. Unlike earlier male supporters of feminism, the Greenwich Village radicals drew less on abstract conceptions of justice or on women's putative monopoly on morality as the basis for their support of feminism.[99] Both feminist and socialist, this group embraced feminist ideas as much for self-interest as anything else; they saw their potential to liberate men as their importance to the liberation of women.

The Bohemian radicals who clustered around Greenwich Village attempted to create new relationships while they promoted and supported feminist causes. In this "moral health resort," as Floyd Dell called it, they confronted issues of monogamy and sexual fidelity, women's sexual autonomy, and women's rights to birth control and abortion while they supported women's entry into the economic sphere, increased educational opportunities, and of course, suffrage. Feminism wasn't a threat; it was an exciting challenge. The New Woman of the century was about to meet the New Man—a man who could thrill to woman's sexual autonomy, who was outraged at economic and political discrimination, and who worked in both public and private spheres to bring about a system of sexual equality and gender justice.

Men like the young Max Eastman, Floyd Dell, Hutchins Hapgood, William Sanger, and Randolph Bourne. Eastman, the editor of *Masses* and secretary and organizer of the Men's League for Woman Suffrage, was (in his early years) an exemplary figure, organizing other men around feminist issues and struggling toward equality in his personal life. Eastman and his wife, Ida Rauh, caused a scandal when, on their return from a trip to Europe in the fall of 1911, they began a Village custom by posting Rauh's full name on their mailbox. Eastman linked his support for feminism with his understanding of masculinity. "There was nothing harder for a man with my mamma's-boy complex to do than stand up and be counted as a 'male suffragette'," he wrote in *Enjoyment of Living*. "It meant not only that I had asserted my manhood, but that I had passed beyond the need of asserting it."[100]

In the political sphere the Greenwich Village radicals were very visible in their campaigns for women's equality. Officers of the Men's League for Woman Suffrage (founded by Eastman in 1910) included Oswald Garrison Villard, publisher of the *New York Evening Post*, Columbia professor John Dewey, and Rabbi Stephen Wise. The Men's League was the first organized profeminist men's organization in the United States; its purpose was to organize men's contingents in suffrage marches and parades and to visibly support, as men, woman suffrage. An editorial in *La Follette's* in May 1911 praised the eighty-five "courageous and convinced men" who had marched in a recent demonstration; one marcher counted being "booed and hissed down the Avenue a very thrilling experience" and indicated his determination that "if I can help to that end, there shall be a thousand men in line next year." He wasn't very far off. An editorial in the *New York Times* one year later predicted that eight hundred men would march the next day in a suffrage demonstration.

Many of these men saw the social revolution offered by feminist demands for personal autonomy as the personal complement to the socialist revolution. And such personal autonomy required sexual freedom; Greenwich Village radicals linked socialist economic critiques of American capitalism with a feminist critique of sexual repression. Thus, Floyd Dell argued in "Feminism for Men" (1914), an article in *The Masses*, that capitalism is opposed to feminism because "it wants men with wives and children who are dependent on them for support." But feminism will allow men to rediscover women as equals, which means to discover women all over again; the home, he argues is "a little dull":

> When you have got a woman in a box, and you pay rent on the box, her relationship to you insensibly changes character. It loses the fine excitement of democracy. It ceases to be companionship, for companionship is only possible in a democracy. It is no longer a sharing of life together—it is a breaking of life apart. Half a life—cooking, clothes, and children; half a life—business, politics, and baseball. . . . It is in the great world that a man finds his sweetheart, and in that narrow little box outside of the world that he loses her. When she has left that box and gone back into the great world, a citizen and a worker, then with surprise and delight he will discover her again, and never let her go.[101]

Eastman claimed a similar motive for supporting feminism and was equally certain that feminism held an important message for men. In one short item in *The Masses*, Eastman recounted a brief (and possibly apocryphal) exchange with a new stenographer:

"Are you a feminist?" we asked the stenographer.
She said she was.
"What do you mean by Feminism?"
"Being like men," she answered.
"Now you are joking!"
"No, I'm not. I mean real independence. And emotional independence too—living in relation to the universe rather than in relation to some other person."
"All men are not like that," we said sadly.
"Then they should join the Feminist movement!"[102]

For all their contradictory arguments and eventual abandonment of the feminist cause, Dell, Eastman, and other Greenwich Village radicals had discovered the fusion of the personal and the political. And what's more, some men had come to see that the success of feminism contained within it both a critique of traditional masculinity and the seeds of male liberation. Men had come to understand that feminism, as Dell wrote, "is going to make it possible for the first time for men to be free."[103]

Possible, perhaps, but not likely—at least for another century. Not even the Greenwich Village bohemians could fully implement their vision of feminism and socialism as building blocks of a new masculinity.[104] In the meantime, conservatives would continue to use race, sex, and place of birth as criteria for exclusion from the masculine testing ground and extol the virtues of the Heroic Artisan even as he receded into historical memory. And new strategies would develop in the new century—strategies that relied on the growing culture of consumption to enable American men to re-create their masculinity at their leisure.

CHAPTER 4

Playing for Keeps

MASCULINITY AS RECREATION AND THE RE-CREATION OF MASCULINITY

The curse of our age is its femininity, its lack, not of barbarism, but of virility.
—Orestes Brownson (1884)

In his popular novel *The Bostonians* (1885), Henry James captured the anger and resentment many men had come to feel at the turn of the century. After pursuing the young feminist visionary Verena Tarrant for what seems like an eternity, Basil Ransome explodes in a rhetorical torrent:

> The whole generation is womanized; the masculine tone is passing out of the world; it's a feminine, nervous, hysterical, chattering, canting age, an age of hollow phrases and false delicacy and exaggerated solicitudes and coddled sensibilities, which, if we don't soon look out, will usher in the reign of mediocrity, of the feeblest and flattest and most pretentious that has ever been. The masculine character, the ability to dare and endure, to know and yet not fear reality, to look the world in the face and take it for what it is . . . that is what I want to preserve, or

117

rather . . . recover; and I must tell you that I don't in the least care what becomes of you ladies while I make the attempt![1]

Through Ransome, James here expresses a powerful current of malaise and resentment felt by turn-of-the-century American men, railing against what they perceived as the feminization of American culture.[2] Something had happened to American society that had led to a loss of cultural vitality, of national virility. That spirit had to be retrieved and revived for a new century.

But not in the workplace, now a site of uneasiness. What had formerly been the central arena in which self-making men had made themselves had now become unreliable, tenuous. Changes in the nature of work itself and changes in the composition of the workforce combined to make these self-making men uncertain of their futures. As historian Elliot Gorn recently asked:

> Where would a sense of maleness come from for the worker who sat at a desk all day? How could one be manly without independence? Where was virility to be found in increasingly faceless bureaucracies? How might clerks or salesmen feel masculine doing 'women's work'? What became of rugged individualism inside intensively rationalized corporations? How could a man be a patriarch when his job kept him away from home for most of his waking hours?[3]

With so many breadwinners faced with becoming breadlosers, what was a man to do?

One answer, as we've seen, was to try and clear away those newcomers to the workplace and to thus reestablish marketplace success as still possible. Another answer was to pretend. "As men felt their real sense of masculinity eroding, they turned to fantasies that embodied heroic physical action, reading novels of the Wild West and cheering the exploits of baseball and football players."[4] If manhood could no longer be directly experienced, then perhaps it could be vicariously enjoyed by appropriating the symbols and props that signified earlier forms of power and excitement.

Such attempts played out the well-worn psychological axiom that what we lose in reality we re-create in fantasy. In our psychological development, the theory goes, those relationships and experiences that give life meaning, that make us feel full, satisfied, secure, are snatched from us, leaving us insecure, frightened, and desperate. Part of the normal, garden-variety neurosis that is the human condition is the creation of a stockpile of symbols that remind us of those lost objects, a secret symbolic treasure chest we can occasionally raid to re-create those earlier moments of fulfillment. As individuals struggling to find meaning in the world, we create those symbols to help us return to those earlier experiences so that we can again feel secure and without anxiety.

The analogy between individual development and cultural development holds—and at no time more clearly than the turn of the century. Just as the realm of production had been so transformed that men could no longer anchor their identity in their position in the market, we created new symbols, the consumption of which "reminded" men of that secure past, evoking an age before identity crises, before crises of masculinity—a past when everyone knew what it meant to be a man and achieving one's manhood was a given. In the culture of consumption, identity was based less on what one did and who one was and more upon how one appeared and lived. In his classic study *The Lonely Crowd*, sociologist David Riesman discerned the shift in identities and ethics from the "inner directed" nineteenth-century man—a man of strong character animated by an inner sense of morality, fixed principles by which he grounded his identity—to the twentieth-century "other directed" man—a sensitive personality, animated by a need to fit in, to be liked. Inner-directed men went their own way, could stand alone, tuned to the hum of an internal gyroscope; other-directed men scanned a mental radar screen for fluctuations in public opinion. For the other-directed man, having a good personality was the way to win friends and influence people.[5]

Such a shift was reflected in the terms men used to describe themselves. *Manhood* had been understood to define an inner quality, the capacity for autonomy and responsibility, and had historically been seen as the opposite of *childhood*. Becoming a man was not taken for granted; at some point the grown-up boy would demonstrate that he had become a man and had put away childish things. At the turn of the century, *manhood* was replaced gradually by the term *masculinity*, which referred to a set of behavioral traits and attitudes that were contrasted now with a new opposite, *femininity*. Masculinity was something that had to be constantly demonstrated, the attainment of which was forever in question—lest the man be undone by a perception of being too feminine.

Masculinity required proof, and proof required serious effort, whether at the baseball park, the gymnasium, or sitting down to read *Tarzan* or a good western novel. Suddenly, books about the urban "jungle" or "wilderness" appeared, which allowed men to experience manly risk and excitement without ever leaving the city—books like Upton Sinclair's classic muckraking exposé of the Chicago meatpacking industry, *The Jungle* (1906), or Robert Wood's work on settlement houses, *The City Wilderness* (1898). Or they could flip through *National Geographic* (1888 on) to encounter the primitive "other."

One could replace the inner experience of manhood—a sense of manly confidence radiating outward from the virtuous self into a sturdy and muscular frame that had taken shape from years of hard physical labor—and transform it into a set of physical characteristics obtainable by persistent effort in the gymnasium. The ideal of the Self-Made Man gradually assumed increasingly physical connotations so that by the 1870s the idea of "inner strength" was replaced by a doctrine of physicality and the body. By the turn of the century, a massive, nationwide health and athletics craze was in full swing as men compulsively attempted to develop manly physiques as a way of demonstrating that they possessed the interior virtues of manhood. The self-made man of the 1840s "shaped himself by acting upon the material world and [testing] himself in the crucible of competition"; by century's end he was making over his physique to *appear* powerful physically, perhaps to replace the lost real power he imagined that he—or at least his father or grandfather—once felt. If the body revealed the virtues of the man, then working on the body could demonstrate the appearance of the possession of the very virtues that one was no longer certain one possessed.[6]

What had caused such anxiety and insecurity among American men? Why were they so afraid of being feminized? And what could they do to combat such physical, psychological, and spiritual erosion? Some writers believed that cultural feminization was the natural consequence of the invasion of cultural outsiders, the "others," whose manhood was suspect to begin with. Fears of cultural degeneration were fueled by the entry of supposedly weaker and less virile races and ethnicities into the growing northern industrial city. To some commentators it was the city itself that bred feminization, with its conformist masses scurrying to work in large bureaucratic offices, which sapped innate masculine vitality and harnessed it to the service of the corporation. The great architect Frank Lloyd Wright had excoriated the urban world as an "enormity *devouring manhood.*" "Our cities are populated by weaklings," complained health reformer Bernarr Macfadden in a letter to President Theodore Roosevelt a few years later.[7]

Many men believed that cultural feminization was the direct result of the feminization of American boyhood, the predominance of women in the lives of young boys—mothers left alone at home with their young sons and teachers in both elementary and Sunday schools. In 1910 four of every five elementary-school teachers were women, up from three-fourths in 1900 and two-thirds in 1870.[8] The "preponderance of women's influence in our public schools," warned Rabbi Solomon Schindler in 1892, is feminizing our boys; a "vast horde of female teachers" were teaching boys how to become men, added psychologist J. McKeen Cattell. A 1904 report of a British group that was sent to the United States to observe American education and head off a similar problem in Britain concluded that the preponderance of women teachers meant that "the boy in America is not being brought up to punch another boy's head; or to stand having his own punched in an healthy and proper manner."[9]

Observers were alarmed about the effect of so many women teaching young boys. One writer posed two unpleasant outcomes, the "effeminate babyish boy" and "the bad boy," and suggested that masculine influence "is necessary for the proper development" of young boys. Another writer in the *Educational Review* in 1914 complained that women teachers had created "a feminized manhood, emotional, illogical, non-combative against public evils." This psychic threat to "masculine nature," he argued, was beginning to "warp the psyches of our boys and young men into femininity."[10]

To others the problem wasn't women but the demands of the culture itself that made men "weak, effeminate, decaying and almost ready to expire from sheer exhaustion and decrepitude," as an 1867 editorial in the *North Carolina Presbyterian* had earlier put it. Overcivilization had made men "over-sophisticated and effete"; their energies had been spent, not saved, their manhood dissipated. Suddenly, new words, such as "pussyfoot" and "stuffed shirt," entered into common parlance. Women "pity weakly men," O. S. Fowler warned, but they love and admire those "who are red faced, not white livered; right hearty feeders, not dainty; sprightly, not tottering; more muscular than exquisite, and powerful than effeminate, in mind and body."[11]

Most terrifying to men was the specter of the sissy. As we have seen, by the last decade of the century the term had come to mean weakness, dependency, and helplessness—all the qualities that men were not. The sissy was outwardly feminine in demeanor, comportment, and affect. If manhood is defined by courage, generosity, modesty, dignity, wrote Rafford Pyke in his 1902 diatribe against sissies in *Cosmopolitan* magazine, then the sissy was "flabby, feeble, mawkish . . . chicken-hearted, cold and fearful." He was "a slender youthful figure, smooth faced, a little vacuous in the expression of the countenance, with light hair and rather pale eyes a little wide apart; a voice not necessarily weak, but lacking timbre, resonance, carrying power." Real men, Pyke argued, "laugh at him," while women rightfully shun him, as he causes a general "moral nausea" among observers, "a vague yet insurmountable feeling of malaise." Dr. Alfred Stillé, president of the American Medical Association, weighed in with a claim that "a man with feminine traits of character, or with the frame and carriage of a female, is despised by both the sex he ostensibly belongs to, and that of which he is at once a caricature and a libel."[12]

The emergence of a visible gay male subculture in many large American cities at the turn of the century gave an even greater moral urgency to men's flight from being perceived a sissy. Here were real-live gender inverts, men acting like women, and therefore any manner of behavior or action that was reminiscent of these inverts might be a man's undoing. The increased fears of feminization eroded the casual coexistence between homosexual and heterosexual men that had characterized urban life in the 1870s and 1880s.[13]

By 1900 men would do whatever they could to appear manly. And, it appears, whatever they were told, no matter how contradictory. Take facial hair, for example. On the one hand, beards and moustaches experienced a cultural revival, as they had in the 1840s, as one of the easiest ways to sharpen the distinctions between the sexes. "There is nothing that so adds to native manliness as the full beard if carefully and neatly kept," counseled one advice book, *Decorum* in 1877. "The person who invented razors libeled nature."

At the same time, ads for shaving paraphernalia linked shaving to hard work and success. One Gillette advertisement proclaimed its product was

> typical of the American spirit. It is used by capitalists, professional men, business men—by men of action all over this country—three million of them.
>
> Its use starts habits of energy—of initiative. And men who *do* for themselves are men who *think* for themselves. Be master of your own time. Buy a Gillette and use it.

Perhaps more important than the rhetoric, the ad depicted five All-Star baseball players (who were "clean of action and clean of face").[14]

Yet the very act of purchasing these toiletries created some uneasiness. Had not consumption been branded as feminine, the new urban department store a female world of abundance and delight? Several of the newly established department stores developed separate entrances, separate elevators, and separate departments for male and female shoppers, partly to ease the psychological threat to men entering such spheres there to engage in such feminizing activities as shopping.[15]

This at the same time as men became increasingly concerned about the economic and social impact of manly appearance. Talent and motivation may have become unreliable predictors of success, but one could still make sure to look the part, to act as if one were already successful, to, as we might say today, "dress for success." As Kenneth Wayne advised his young male readers in 1912:

> A young man may have tons of virtue, talent, and ability, but he cannot get people to look for these things through a soiled, shabby dress, where there is no necessity for it to commend it. An indifferently

groomed young man is at a disadvantage among a group of well-groomed young men applicants for a position.

Appearances also mattered in one's work. "Do work as if you meant it," Wayne advised. "There is no substitute for enthusiasm." The inclusion of the words "as if" speaks volumes about men's lives at the turn of the century. Work could no longer be relied upon to express one's autonomy and success. But one had still to act as if it did![16]

Although fears of feminization were largely a preoccupation of middle-class men, the problem could also be acute among the working class. These men also had to prove that they were "men among men." The constancy of these efforts, the frequency with which they reassured themselves of their "regular guy" status, indicates a preoccupation with the obverse—"that men were in danger of being called something else: unmanly, a mollycoddle, a sissy, even a pansy. Whereas manhood could be achieved, it could also be lost; it was not simply a quality that resulted naturally and inevitably from one's sex."[17] Traditionally working-class institutions, like the billiard hall, the saloon, or the street corner, occupied an increasingly important place in working-class men's lives.

Take drinking, long a well-integrated part of such lives. In 1894 New York City had one saloon for every 200 residents, while the working-class districts averaged one saloon for every 129 residents. Chicago and Baltimore had similar figures: one saloon for every 212 in Chicago and one for every 229 in Baltimore, while their working-class neighborhoods offered one for every 127 and every 105 residents, respectively. Drinking together cemented manly solidarity, even as the traditional artisanal conviviality was superseded in impersonal factories. But more than that, drinking asserted "a glorious manhood unfettered by the nagging demands of women who would, had they their way, ensconce men at home, squander their wages, forbid them to drink—in short emasculate them." Drinking was a form of masculine resistance to feminization.[18]

This was as true in the rural South as it was in northern cities. In a revealing portrait of postbellum southern manhood, the historian Ted Ownby describes how drinking, brawling, hunting, swearing, and even a revival of dueling witnessed increased popularity as a tonic to restore lost manhood and provide manly solace and "respite from the constraints of female-centered evangelical life." The saloon, the street, the cockfighting and dogfighting rings were arenas of distinctly male vice, enjoyed lustily by men seeking to escape from the sweet virtue of the southern Christian home. It was the wife's Christian duty to convert and subdue these Rhett Butler wanna-bes, transforming them into dutiful Ashley Wilkeses. And it was men's duty to resist, lest Christian piety turn them into wimps.[19]

This world was attacked by the temperance movement, the Social Purity Movement, and other movements to clean up urban social problems; they all expressed a middle-class disdain for such working-class masculine sociability. "The Southern male who had once raised his hell, laughing at churchgoers while perhaps fearing occasionally for the state of his soul, now faced laws prohibiting much of his pursuit of pleasure." Campaigns against animal fighting and hunting further restrained a certain variety of masculine exuberance and problematized its homosocial bonding. Some reformers argued that these arenas expressed a psychologically unhealthy need for relations with other men. Perhaps homosociality was a breeding ground for homosexuality. Among the middle classes, of course, it was also feared that too *little* contact with other men and too much contact with women contributed to middle-class men's effeminacy and homosexuality.

Thus did psychologists and other reformers link the campaigns against vice, whether gaming, alcohol, or billiards, to sexual deviance. "The pool room diverts man power," wrote one representative of the Georgia Anti-Poolroom League. It encouraged moral and physical laxity—"idleness . . . dissipation . . . intoxicants . . . profanity . . . lascivious stories . . . [and] the love of chance"—particularly among young men. One psychological study of saloons frowned on any emotional expression of friendship between men as "abnormal" and likely due to the alcohol, since "to a healthy-minded man any kind of tender contact with other men is repugnant."[20] One psychologist suggested uneasily that alcohol also lowered men's guard around other men; that "when drinking, men fall on each other's necks and kiss one another; they feel that they are united by peculiarly intimate ties and this moves them to tears and intimate modes of address." And a psychoanalyst made the link between alcohol and homosexuality inescapable:

> Of recent years, there have been incidents which have led to a great deal of talk about "abnormal friendships between men." The expressions of feeling which in these cases were branded as morbid or immoral may be observed, by anyone who has eyes to see, wherever men are drinking heavily; and every drinking bout is tinged with homosexuality. The homosexual component-instincts, which education has taught us to repress and sublimate, reappear in no veiled form under the influence of alcohol.[21]

Fearing such a taint, many men—working- and middle-class, heterosexual or occasionally even homosexual—developed various strategies to insure that others would continue to see them as manly. For example, one young Italian man remarked that he was always sexually active with men where he would "act as a woman," but he tried to protect his reputation by developing a conventionally masculine style in other arenas. He did not carry himself as a "fairy" and sought to establish his masculinity with other young men at a neighborhood gym by deliberately "talk[ing] about women." This participation in the "collective sexualization and objectification of women" was one of the "rituals by which he established himself as a man," writes historian George Chauncey.[22]

This young man points us to a new masculine hangout, a new institution where men could pump up those listless, lethargic, feminized bodies—the gym. At the turn of the century, thousands of American men trooped off to gyms and athletic fields as part of a national health craze, there to acquire manly physiques, shore up flagging energy, and develop masculine hardiness as ways of countering the perceived feminization of culture. The health craze was vital to the perpetuation of a virile nation; unlike the street corner or the pub, it was as morally purifying as it was physically imposing. As one contemporary observer claimed:

> Gymnasiums, athletic clubs, outdoor sports, and methods of exercise and other artificial means of contributing to and continuing the physical vigor and virility of the race take the place of the hard physical labor

of the earlier periods, or the love of luxury and ease, when physical development is no longer a necessity, overcomes the promptings of intelligence and experience, and the moral illness of the civilization has begun its work of devastation and destruction.[23]

Or as G. Stanley Hall put it, "you can't have a firm will without firm muscles."[24] This preoccupation with physicality meant that men's bodies carried a different sort of weight than earlier. The body did not *contain* the man, expressing the man within; now, that body *was* the man.

Turn-of-the-century men flocked to healers who prescribed tonics and elixirs guaranteed to put hair on their chests and pep in their step. Men like Russell Trall, founder of the New York Hydropathic and Physiological School, who proclaimed the virtues of hydropathy—the famed "water cure," which involved steam-induced sweats or plunges in ice water. Or Robert Edis, who saw impurities hiding everywhere in the feminized household and railed against wallpaper, draperies, carpets and Europeanized furniture. Or Horace Fletcher, whose proposal that we masticate each bit of food one thousand times before swallowing was proclaimed as a way to recover health and challenge the "gobble, gulp, and go" table manners of the day. Or Bernarr Macfadden, the celebrated founder of Physical Culture, who promoted a new muscular manhood to be built from purified blood, deep breathing exercises, vigorous workouts with barbells, and large doses of his breakfast cereal, Strengthro. (Macfadden was also the proud inventor of a "peniscope," a cylindrical glass tube with a rubber hose at one end attached to a vacuum pump, designed to enlarge the male organ.)

And they consumed vast quantities of these manly concoctions. Like Sylvester Graham's crackers earlier in the century or C. W. Post's new Grape Nuts (1901), which was promoted as brain food for the burgeoning white-collar class because "brain workers must have different food than day laborers." Or J. H. Kellogg's rolled flakes of whole corn, which were but a part of his total health regimen. According to its promoters, such brain food also produced financial brawn. "What a man eats when he's twenty-five is more than likely to influence what he earns when he's fifty," noted one Post cereal advertisement. "If you hope for success, eat for success!" proclaimed another. An ad for Kellogg's All Bran warned about the other side, suggesting what might happen to those who failed to heed its advice. Underneath a pallid, drained man in a business suit was this caption:

> Lost . . . another big order . . . the fourth defeat of that day. All because he didn't have the energy to fight when his prospect said "No." Something had blunted his senses and stolen his strength. . . . That something was constipation, the world's most universal disease.[25]

And there was more. In 1900 one firm published a list of sixty-three imported and forty-two domestic bottled waters for sale, complete with the geographic source of each water and a brief note alerting potential purchasers to their specific medicinal properties and restorative powers. American men bought enormous numbers of advice manuals and guidebooks, such as William Haikie's *How to Get Strong and How to Stay So* (1879) and Macfadden's *The Virile Powers of Superb Manhood* (1900), both of which were best-sellers.[26]

As they had earlier in the century, many health reformers strove to control male sexuality, especially the body's fluids, as a way to gain control of the forces that were sapping men's energies. Self-making required self-control, and self-control required emotional control. So, for example, emotional outbursts of passion or jealousy, which had been associated with manhood in the eighteenth century, were now associated with lack of manhood; it was women, not men, who were now said to feel these emotions most acutely. Real men held their emotions in check, the better to channel them into workplace competition. A recurring economic metaphor marks many postbellum advice books as men were encouraged to "save," "conserve," and "invest" their seed, the fruits of their productive bodies, and to avoid unnecessary "expenditure" or profligate "waste." Masturbation would send a young man on an inevitable downward economic and social spiral. In his advice book, *The Crime of Silence* (1915), Orison Swett Marden told of a professor who was dragged slowly and inexorably down by self-abuse until at last he had no opinion on any topic whatever and ended up cleaning toilets in a large hotel. "The failure army is full of emasculated beings," he cautioned.[27]

Some books were concerned with preventing masturbation because of its association with enfeeblement and, hence, feminization. Joseph Conwell observed that muscles of masturbators become "flabby and weak" and the "enervated nervous system" loses its full virility. O. S. Fowler warned that masturbation "unsexes" the man, robbing boys of "future manliness" and leaving them "tame, discouraged, subdued, ungallant" drones. The quick discharge of semen leaves "its products extra nervous, yet minus the snap, vim, power, and condensed vigor they would otherwise have had." And Bernarr Macfadden observed that masturbation had "caused incomparably more sexual dilapidation, paralysis, and disease, as well as demoralization, than all the other sexual depravities combined," leaving men "maimed mentally, morally, and physically for life."[28]

Crusaders against masturbation were divided about the effects of the solitary vice. To some it resulted in the immediate onset of sexual depravity—consorting with prostitutes, unbridled lusts that the young man could no longer contain, and ultimately, insanity and early death. Masturbation was a crime that "blanches the cheek, that shakes the nervous system into ruin, that clouds the intellect, that breaks down the integrity of the will, that launches emasculated ruin into asylums of hopeless insanity, collapsing in premature death," wrote G. Douglas in the *Official Report of the Twelfth International Christian Endeavor Convention* in 1900. To others masturbation would so drain its practitioner that he would have no ardor left over for sexual activity. Winfield Hall's advice book, *From Youth to Manhood*, published by the YMCA in 1900, claimed that since masturbation is unnatural, it is "more depleting than is normal sexual intercourse." Thus, as if in compensation, nature would exact its revenge, "removing, step by step, his manhood."[29]

Specific physical and dietary regimens flourished to combat the scourge. Corn Flakes, for example, were designed by J. H. Kellogg as a massive anaphrodisiac to temper and eventually reduce sexual ardor in American men. Kellogg was perhaps the most successful and excessive of these health reformers. Like Sylvester Graham, Kellogg wrote books, like *Man the Masterpiece* (1886) and *Plain Facts for Young and Old* (1888), that were best sellers of popular self-improvement via self-restraint, providing a guide for young men and their parents about clean living.

Kellogg was fanatical in his pursuit of masculine purity. His general health regime included:

1. Kneading and pounding on the abdomen each day to promote evacuation before sleep and thus avoiding "irritating" congestions.
2. Drinking hot water, six to eight glasses a day (same end in view).
3. Urinating several times each night (same end in view).
4. Avoiding alcohol, tobacco, and tea because they stimulated lecherous thoughts.
5. Taking cold enemas and hot sitz baths each day.
6. Wearing a wet girdle to bed each night.[30]

But Kellogg's chief concern was masturbation. In *Plain Facts for Old and Young*, he provided anxious parents with a frighteningly systematic list of thirty-nine signs of masturbation, including physical and behavioral changes.[31] Such a list could provoke anxiety in virtually all parents. What could they do about this plague? In a chapter called "Treatment for Self-Abuse and Its Effects," Kellogg listed a set of chilling home remedies. In addition to bandaging the genitals, covering the organs with cages, and tying the hands, Kellogg also recommended circumcision "without administering an anaesthetic, as the brief pain attending the operation will have a salutary effect upon the mind, especially if it be connected with the idea of punishment." Older boys may be forced to have silver sutures placed over the foreskin to prevent erection. "The prepuce, or foreskin, is drawn forward over the glans, and the needle to which the wire is attached is passed through from one side to the other. After drawing the wire through, the ends are twisted together, and cut off close. It is now impossible for an erection to occur, and the slight irritation thus produced acts as a most powerful means of overcoming the disposition to resort to the practice."[32] (Although the extent to which Kellogg's sadistic suggestions were followed by terrified parents is impossible to know, one can only cringe at the possibility that *any* of them did.)

Nor was Kellogg alone. Other reformers suggested bloodletting or applying leeches or heated pneumatic cups to the genitals to draw out "congestion" which led to arousal. One writer advised punching a hole through the foreskin and inserting a metal ring, while another suggested cutting the foreskin apart with a jagged-edge scissors. Red iron, tartar emetic ointment, and Spanish fly-blister could all be applied to make the genitals painful to the touch. "It is better . . . to endure any physical discomfort than to sacrifice one's chastity," wrote Henry Guernsey, M.D., in his *Plain Talks on Avoided Subjects* in 1882.[33]

By the middle of the second decade of the twentieth century, much of this explicitly sexual panic began to subside, in part because of the popularization of Freud's ideas. Freud was a fierce opponent of sexual puritanism and the ideology of the spermatic economy. To Freud the sexual instinct was just that, an instinct, inherited and normal. In "Sexual Morality and Modern Nervousness" (1908), Freud argued that the notion of physical depletion had it backward—it was continence or abstinence, not expenditure of semen, that was injurious to men. The only harm from masturbation was the guilt that traditionally attended it. "Masturbation as a rule does not much harm beyond that which we believe it to be wrong," was how one physician put it—as close as one can come to an iatrogenic, or even more accurately, a cultural etiology of disease as has ever been advanced.

Yet no sooner was the fear of depletion through masturbation ushered out as a problem for men than problems with male sexuality found another new, or rather, a very old, cause. Dr. William Robinson's *Sexual Impotence* (1912) was an enormously popular treatment of male sexual problems, going through thirteen editions. Robinson argued that "older doctors" had exaggerated the ills associated with masturbation; it certainly was *not* the cause of impotence. In fact, men were not to be blamed for impotence; women were, since it was women's lack of responsiveness to male sexual ardor which exacerbated and sometimes even caused impotence. The problem was, as he coined the term, "frigidity" in women, which "will not call out his virility." Once again, male sexuality was women's problem.[34]

The popularization of Freudian psychoanalytic theory echoed many earlier fears of masculine humiliation and also gave us some new ones. After all, the centerpiece of Freud's theory is that the rational, autonomous ego is the architect of the personality, which it creates by "appropriating" parts of the individual's instinctual drives and directing them to more socially appropriate outlets. To make the ego independent of the id, the master of its own fate, was a lifelong project, the triumph of mind and will over body and society. For the little boy it entailed the separation from mother, identification with father, and the subsequent assumption of the ability to stand alone. Failure to separate from mother led, Freud believed, to sexual "inversion" (homosexuality), while failure to develop independently from father led to a neurotic need for the authority of groups or organizations, such as the army or the church. The goal of psychoanalysis was to strengthen the ego, make it independent of those forces that threatened to overwhelm it. Just at the moment that autonomy and independence were disappearing in men's experience in the corporation, along came a theory that proclaimed the autonomous ego as the mark of maturity. If work prevented our self-making, psychology could facilitate it.

This created a new set of anxieties, especially because it linked the origins of homosexuality to the individual boy's experiences within his family. In brief, Freud argued that failure to break with his mother and identify with his father left the boy psychologically identified with mother (feminine gender identity) and therefore predisposed to feel like women; that is, he could only be completed sexually by the presence of a father figure—a strong powerful man. By linking gender behavior to sexual orientation and locating both within the family, Freudian theory sent many anxious parents scurrying to advice columns and child-rearing manuals to make sure that they wouldn't raise their children to grow up to be homosexual. This was even more pressing than, and more pressured by, the perceived feminization of the culture—as if American culture was conspiring to turn its men into a bunch of effeminate wimps barely a generation after the Civil War.[35]

As the century progressed, psychiatrists and psychologists were blaming modern society for many of men's psychological problems.[36] Some reformers suggested that it was the pace of society that caused such problems—the rush of the modern, the clanking barrage of stimuli, the productive frenzy. Men simply wore themselves out mentally as well as physically. Dr. Edward Jarvis, speaking before the American Institutions for the Insane in 1851, pointed his finger at mobility and industrialization:

> No son is necessarily confined to the work . . . of his father . . . all fields are open . . . all are invited to join the strife. . . . They are strug-

gling . . . at that which they cannot reach . . . their mental powers are strained to their utmost tension. . . . Their minds stagger . . . they are perplexed with the variety of insurmountable obstacles; and they are exhausted with the ineffectual labor.

And Dr. Peter Bryce, head of the Alabama Insane Hospital, observed in 1872 that mental illness was most common among men "at the most active time of life," ages thirty-five to forty. "Habitual intemperance, sexual excesses, overstrain in business, in fact, all those habits which tend to keep up too rapid cerebral action, are supposed to induce this form of disease. It is especially a disease of *fast life*, and fast business in large cities." Philip Hamerton's popular book *The Intellectual Life* (1873) laid the blame at the doorstep of the workplace and university when he wrote that "the excessive exercise of the mental powers are injurious to bodily health."[37]

Mental illness was gendered illness. In some cases the same symptoms would be diagnosed differently; in other cases the same diagnosis would result in different cures. Take, for example, the question of hysteria. Freud had treated female hysterics as women who were afraid to be fully women, who shrank into somatic illness when confronted with the constraints of femininity. Hysteria was the result of sexual wishes or desires that the women could not confront or accept. For men the new somatic illness of shell shock was defined as a similar inability to meet the demands of one's gender. During World War I a large number of men froze, could not return fire, or experienced psychic breaks with reality. For some, shell shock included "great weariness and profuse weeping, even in otherwise strong men." According to a 1916 article in the *Lancet*, a British medical journal, 40 percent of all British casualties in the war were attributable to shell shock. Another two hundred thousand on each side of the war deserted. S. Weir Mitchell explored dozens of cases of unexplained male paralysis, which he discussed in *Gunshot Wounds and Other Injuries of Nerves*.[38]

Most psychiatric treatments for shell shock involved treating the disease as the result of insufficient manliness. T. J. Calhoun, assistant surgeon with the Army of the Potomac, argued that if the soldier could not be "laughed out of it by his comrades" or by "appeals to his manhood," then a good dose of battle was the best "curative." Literary critic Elaine Showalter argues that both hysteria and shell shock were double edged—failures to conform to gender demands that were so obvious and palpable that they also became expressions of resistance to traditional gender norms:

> If the essence of manliness was not to complain, then shell shock was the body language of the masculine complaint, a disguised male protest not only against the war but against the concept of "manliness" itself. [It was] a protest against the politicians, generals, and psychiatrists. The heightened code of masculinity that dominated in wartime was intolerable to surprisingly large numbers of men.[39]

Just as contemporary critics understood hysteria to be a form of resistance to excessive standards of femininity, so too was shell shock a form of resistance to militarized manhood.

No one understood the psychological and somatic effects of modern civilization better than George Beard and Dr. S. Weir Mitchell. Beard's *American Nervousness* (1881) and *Sexual Neurasthenia* (1884; revised 1902) introduced a new psychological malady into American life: neurasthenia, or as it quickly became known in the popular press, "brain sprain." Neurasthenia, Beard claimed, was the result of "overcivilization"—changes such as steam power, the periodical press, the telegraph, and the sciences had so speeded up the pace of social life that people simply couldn't keep up despite their tireless efforts. The outcome was a host of symptoms, including insomnia, dyspepsia, hysteria, hypochondria, asthma, headache, skin rashes, hay fever, baldness, inebriety, hot flashes, cold flashes, nervous exhaustion, and brain collapse. "Modern nervousness is the cry of the system struggling with its environment."[40]

Beard argued that youthful masturbation and sexual excess contributed to neurasthenia and that, in this sense, "men could be considered responsible for their own insanity." To cure spermatorrhea, the collapse of male sexual vitality due to neurasthenic energy depletion, Beard prescribed cold baths, outdoor exercise, wearing a urethral ring, sleeping on a hair mattress with little covering of the genitals, and avoiding all erotic novels or dalliances with women of compromised virtue. Brain workers were to avoid intimate dinners, spiced foods, oysters, and alcohol.[41]

Never before had a cultural diagnosis resulted in a more gendered prescription and cure. Neurasthenia tended to invert gendered health, masculinizing women and feminizing men. So neurasthenic women were thus to be confined to their beds, idle and unstimulated, there to retrieve femininity. For example, Charlotte Perkins Gilman was diagnosed as neurasthenic in 1885, when she was 25, by Dr. Mitchell. "Live as domestic a life as possible," he counseled. "Have your child with you all the time. Lie down an hour after each meal. Have but two hours intellectual life a day. And never touch a pen, brush, or pencil as long as you live." Gilman was obedient; she "went home, followed those directions rigidly for months, and came perilously close to losing my mind," she wrote in her diary. (Her short story "The Yellow Wallpaper" [1892] offers a chilling description of her experience and what might have happened had she not had the strength to get out of bed.)

Men, by contrast, were pushed out to western dude ranches to take in the masculinizing freshness of the out of doors. Men, after all, had to rediscover masculinity. Riding the range, breathing the fresh country air, and exerting the body and resting the mind were curative for men, and in the last two decades of the century, large numbers of weak and puny eastern city men—like Theodore Roosevelt, Owen Wister, Frederic Remington, and Thomas Eakins—all came west to find a cure for their insufficient manhood. That each returned a dedicated convert, trumpeting the curative value of the strenuous life, is part of the story of how America was won over to the West.[42]

The rugged outdoors was consistently trumpeted as restorative of the flagging manhood of modern civilized men. The pages of the diaries of teenagers, college students, and young male clerks were filled with an endless list of their outdoor activities—from boxing to hiking, from ice skating to football and baseball. One physician proposed that a certain cure for hay fever was a "season of farm work," not because contact with the allergen would cure the malady, but because outdoor work would cure virtually anything. "Get your children into the country," one real estate advertisement for Wilmington,

Delaware, urged potential buyers in 1905. "The cities murder children. The hot pavements, the dust, the noise, are fatal in many cases and harmful always. The history of successful men is nearly always the history of country boys." Naturalist John Muir added that thousands of "tired, nerve-shaken, over-civilized people are beginning to find out that going to the mountains is going home; that wilderness is a necessity." And George Evans advised that "[w]henever the light of civilization falls upon you with a blighting power, and work and pleasure become stale and flat, go to the wilderness. The wilderness with take hold on you. It will give you good red blood; it will turn you from a weakling into a man."[43]

In short, the turn of the century reinvented the frontier as simply the outdoors. Yet for many wilderness explorers or visitors to newly minted dude ranches—which were often nothing more than failed cattle ranches reopened as consumer health spas—the West had been transformed into a gigantic theme park, safely unthreatening, whose natural beauty was protected as in an art museum. The three men who so graphically memorialized the premodern West, who transformed nature into culture—novelist Owen Wister, painter Frederic Remington, and naturalist President Theodore Roosevelt— were all effete eastern intellectuals who spent time on these civilized western ranches and rediscovered their manhood.

Across the nation, hunting also experienced a renaissance at the turn of the century. Modern methods of slaughtering beef made the hunt no longer a material necessity for survival. It returned as recreation and proving ground. Theodore Roosevelt organized the Boone and Crockett Club to encourage big-game hunting. "Hunting big game in the wilderness," he and cofounder George Bird Grinnell wrote in 1893, "is a sport for a vigorous and masterful people." William Kent, a California congressman concerned about the degeneration of the race since the disappearance of the caveman, rejoiced in the savagery of the hunt. After a kill, Hunt declared, "you are a barbarian, and you're glad of it. It's good to be a barbarian . . . and you know that if you are a barbarian, you are at any rate a man."[44] Some commentators didn't care how the meat was obtained as long as it was consumed. Many health reformers, including Graham, had shunned meat eating, believing it to excite the system and stimulate animal passions. But others proclaimed meat eating as a potent answer to feminized manhood; some claimed that a diet devoid of red meat would prevent the building of full manly power. George Beard described his encounter with a vegetarian in gendered terms; the hiker's "pale and feminine features, tinged with an unnatural flush" repelled Beard. Following a popular medical belief, Woods Hutchinson claimed that one needs blood to make blood, muscle to make muscle, and that the way to health was through consumption of large quantities of barely cooked beef. Hutchinson taunted vegetarians for being repelled by "Meat! R-r-red meat, dr-r-ripping with b-l-lood, r-r-reeking of the shambles." Eating red meat, men were literally consuming manhood.[45]

Perhaps the most important vehicle to re-create manhood was sports. In the late nineteenth century America went "sports crazy" as the nation witnessed a bicycle craze, a dramatic increase in tennis playing, golfing, weightlifting, and boxing, new excitement over football and racing, keen interest in basketball, and the spectacular rise of baseball.[46] Sports were heralded as character building; health reformers promised athletic activity would make young men healthier and instill moral virtues. In short, sports made boys into men.[47] Sports were necessary, according to D. A. Sargent, to "counteract the enervating tendency of the times and to improve the health, strength, and vigor of our youth" since they provided the best kind of "general exercise for the body, and develop courage, manliness, and self-control." Sports aided youth in "the struggle for manliness," wrote G. Walter Fiske in *Boy Life and Self-Government*. If masculinity required proof, one English newspaper championed athletics for substituting the "feats of man for the 'freak of the fop,' hardiness for effeminacy, and dexterity for luxurious indolence."[48]

Sports were celebrated for instilling moral as well as physical virtue. Sports developed "courage, steadiness of nerve . . . resourcefulness, self-knowledge, self-reliance . . . the ability to work with others . . . [and] readiness to subordinate selfish impulses, personal desires, and individual credit to a common end," claimed Frances Walker, president of M.I.T., in an address to the Phi Beta Kappa at Harvard in 1893. The *Wesleyan University Bulletin* observed in 1895 that the end of the century "is an era of rampant athleticism. But these contests play their part in making sturdy citizens, and training men in the invaluable qualities of loyalty, self-sacrifice, obedience, and temperance." Sports could rescue American boys from the "haunts of dissipation" that seduced them in the cities—the taverns, gambling parlors, and brothels, according to the *Brooklyn Eagle*. Youth needs recreation, the *New York Herald* claimed, and "if they can't get it healthily and morally, they will seek it unhealthily and immorally at night, in drink saloons or at the gambling tables, and from these dissipations to those of a lower depth, the gradation is easy."[49]

Sports were also a way to resolve some class and racial tensions, offset others, and siphon off working-class or black discontent into other arenas. The playground movement put working-class children under the adult supervision of middle-class reformers to better control their behavior and socialization. "The free lands were used up. The cow country rose and fell. The safety valve was screwed down. But the explosion did not come," noted Frederic Paxson in 1917. How come? he wondered. "Because the safety valve of sport was designed, built and applied."[50]

It was through sports, not work, that self-making men could make themselves, at least physically, and demonstrate that "man was no longer fated to keep the body he was born with." Take Eugen Sandow, the German-born bodybuilder who gained an enormous following in the United States. "I know very well that I am not a perfect man as my manager frequently has for the purposes of advertising said, but I also know that by the application of certain broad principles I have acquired almost perfect control over myself."[51]

So off America went to the sporting green. The first tennis court was built in Boston in 1876, the first basketball court in 1891. The American Bowling Congress was founded in 1895, and the Amateur Athletic Union in 1890. "This vaunted age needs a saving touch of honest, old fashioned barbarism, so that when we come to die, we shall die leaving men behind us, and not a race of eminently respectable female saints," is what one boxing fan wrote in 1888.

Boxing was especially popular at the turn of the century. As were other sports, boxing was defended as a counter to the "mere womanishness" of modern, overcivilized society. But boxing was more than mere manhood; it heralded the triumphant return of the Heroic Artisan as mythic hero. No sooner had he virtually disappeared into enormous, impersonal factories than he staged his triumphant return in the boxing ring. If the workaday world undermined working-class manhood—requiring obedience to rules and docility towards managers—then boxing celebrated his traditional virtues: toughness, prowess, ferocity. If men could not make things with the skill of their hands, they could at least destroy things, or others, with them.[52]

In his fascinating study of bare-knuckle prizefighting in America, *The Manly Art*, the historian Elliot Gorn describes the way that working-class bachelor subcultures in the late nineteenth-century city resurrected the language of skilled artisans in their descriptions of boxing matches. Just as industrialization had destroyed traditional skills and crushed artisanal autonomy, boxing revived it in a frenzied fantasy of violence. Boxing was a "profession," and boxers were "trained" in various "schools" of fighting. Newspapers reported that the combatants "went to work" or one "made good work" of his opponent. Admirers spoke of the way that particular fighters "plied their trades" or understood the "arts and mysteries" of the pugilistic métier. Words like "art," "science," and "craft" were tossed about as often as in universities. Boxers controlled their own labor like individual proprietors. Here was a "manly art," an act of violence which required craftsmanlike skill and deftness.[53]

No one symbolized this cult of "elemental virility" better than John L. Sullivan, perhaps the "greatest American hero of the late nineteenth century." With his manly swagger and well-waxed moustache, this Irish fighter recalled a lost era of artisanal heroism and symbolized "the growing desire to smash through the fluff of bourgeois gentility and the tangle of corporate ensnarements to the throbbing heart of life." And at the other end of the spectrum, no one could better symbolize the demise of artisanal manhood than Jack Johnson, the first black heavyweight boxing champion. Flamboyant and powerful, Johnson was the black specter that had haunted white workingmen since antebellum days—the fear that unskilled free blacks would triumph over skilled white workers in the workplace, the bedroom, and now, in the sporting world.[54]

Baseball, too, would have its darker moments, at least rhetorically, with the infamous Chicago Black Sox scandal, which rocked the sporting world in 1919 at the close of the era. But before that, base-ball offered a rich palette of manly athletic expression for all of its players and fans. Theodore Roosevelt included baseball in his list of "the true sports for a manly race."[55] Just as horse racing had resulted in better horse breeding, Edward Marshall claimed in 1910, so base-ball "resulted in improvement in man breeding." "No boy can grow to a perfectly normal manhood today without the benefits of at least a small amount of baseball experience and practice," wrote William McKeever in his popular advice manual, *Training the Boy* (1913). Per-haps novelist Zane Grey said it best. "All boys love baseball," he wrote. "If they don't they're not real boys."[56]

Baseball replaced the desiccating immorality of a dissolute life, providing a "remedy for the many evils resulting from the immoral associations boys and young men of our cities are apt to become con-nected with" and therefore deserving "the endorsement of every cler-gyman in the country." Baseball was good for men's bodies and souls, imperative for the health and moral fiber of the body social. From pulpits and advice manuals the virtues of baseball were sounded.[57]

Those virtues stressed, on the surface, autonomy and aggressive in-dependence—but the game also required obedience, self-sacrifice, dis-cipline, and hierarchy. Baseball's version of masculinity thus cut with a contradictory edge: If the masculinity expressed on the baseball field was exuberant, fiercely competitive, and wildly aggressive, it was so only in a controlled and orderly arena, closely supervised by powerful adults. Psychologically, baseball would always be a boy's game.[58]

Like boxing, baseball recalled a bygone era of independent farmers and small shopkeepers. The first baseball parks were just that—parks or fields or grounds, all terms that referred to their bucolic rural ori-gins (like Philadelphia's Shibe Park [1909], Chicago's Comiskey Park [1910] and Wrigley Field [1914], Boston's Fenway Park [1912], Pitts-burgh's Forbes Field [1909], and New York's Polo Grounds [1911]; only Detroit's Tiger Stadium, built in 1912, broke this pattern until Yankee Stadium was built for the 1922 season). Here the pain and alienation of urban industrial work life was soothed, and the routine dull grayness of the urban landscape was broken up by these mani-cured patches of green.[59]

Baseball was fantasy; it was diversion, a safety valve, allowing the release of potential aggression in a healthy, socially acceptable way.[60] In 1912 President William Howard Taft proclaimed himself a baseball fan, especially because it had salubrious moral effects on young people:

> Baseball takes people into the open air—it draws out millions of factory hands, of tradesmen and interior laborers of all kinds, who spend their afternoons whenever possible in a healthful, genuinely inspiring contest in the warm sunshine and fresh air, when many other sports, and in fact all natural tendencies conspire to keep them indoors engaged in various kinds of unwholesome and unhealthful pastimes.[61]

By the end of the second decade of the century, some of this innocence was lost as baseball became mired in several of those "unwholesome and unhealthful pastimes," especially drinking, gambling, and sexual promiscuity. With the 1919 World Series scandal, involving the infamous Chicago "Black Sox," commercialism had "come to dominate the sporting quality of sports"; heroes were venal, and the pristine pastoral was exposed as corrupt, part of the emergent corporate order and not the alternative to it that people had imagined.[62] But by then it was too late: Baseball had facilitated a casual accommodation to the new industrial economic order. The geographic frontier was replaced by the outfield fence, workplace autonomy by watching a solitary pitcher and batter square off against one another.

USEFUL FICTIONS

Men could also retrieve the heroic masculine virtues without ever leaving their living rooms or, at least, their dens. The frontier might be too elusive, the world of sports too corrupt, but literature could help promote savagery in even the most timid man's breast. Boys' literature found avid young male readers. Popular biographies of self-made successes were enormously popular. Some celebrated the self-made power and wealth of the robber barons; others were more interested in the manly virtues of the robber barons' nemesis, the outlaw. Jesse James, for example, developed armed robbery into a craftsman's skill. "Highway robbery as a fine art has been cultivated only in a way that has tended to bring it into disrespect," observed a writer in the *Republic* in 1874, until the James gang "burst upon us, and revealed a new field of worthy labor."[63] The mythic figure of George Armstrong Custer was also seen as "the incarnation of the heroic, virile, self-restrained and tough minded American." Dashing, debonair, and dutiful, Custer was also ruthless and monomaniacal in his pursuit of his manhood through the conquest of Indians. His carefully constructed persona was part flamboyant aristocrat, part cold sober professional, and part wild savage hunter.[64]

Tall tales and legends also reveal these masculine themes. Casey Jones (1900), John Henry (ca. 1873), and Paul Bunyan (collected 1912–1914) were mythic representations of the heroic triumphs in the same arenas and against the same forces that had defeated the older Heroic Artisan in reality. Jones's track skills are necessary to keep the Illinois Central trains running; John Henry outperforms a steam drill in a masterpiece of suicidal craftsmanship, dying "with the hammer in his hand"; and the giant logger Paul Bunyan outcuts the most technically developed chainsaws with his mighty ax. They were "heroes of an industrial world" projected back to the moment of the artisan's demise.[65]

In boys' fiction heroes like Frank Merriwell embodied the strenuous ideal found in sports, excelling at every sport, always winning the big game for Yale when the chips were down—he could even throw a curve ball that curved twice!—without any compromise of his manly and moral virtues. Like Gilbert Patten (who wrote the Merriwell stories under the name Burt Standish), Horatio Alger offered his young readers fictional accounts of upward mobility gained through hard work, dedication, and a small dose of "luck and pluck." Alger's stories illustrate a distinctly American take on the making of the self-made man. Unlike nineteenth-century European novels, which often spend a good deal of time locating the young protagonist in a social landscape, these American novels begin with a dislocated individual, off to seek his fortune away from home. Horatio Alger's heroes are almost always orphans or at least living with and supporting their mothers.[66] Henry Fleming (*The Red Badge of Courage*) and a host of soldier heroes are at the battlefield, aboard ship, or running away.

And even after his transformation into a civilized man, Tarzan still is fatherless. "My mother was an Ape, and of course she couldn't tell me much about it. I never knew who my father was" is the last line of the novel. (Playwright Peter Schaffer noted also that "all cowboys are orphans.")

American novels often include a search for father—for legitimacy, perhaps, but also for the warmth and tenderness that readers felt lacking since their real fathers were preoccupied with their careers. This is particularly evident in Alger's stories. Richard Hunter, the hero of Alger's first book, *Ragged Dick* (1868), is an orphan whose honesty, hard work, and virtue earn him the respect of older men, who actually become his benefactors when Hunter rescues them from swindlers or their daughters from distress. What happy consolation to young male readers that in the world of work they may experience the love and largesse of the fathers whose absence they so painfully feel at home. These works obviously struck a nerve; Alger wrote at least 103 short novels, and their popularity made him perhaps history's most widely read novelist.[67]

Many of Alger's stories—such as *Risen from the Ranks, Strive and Succeed, Forging Ahead, Struggling Upward*, and *Slow and Sure*—describe the gradual ascent to respectability possible for the hardworking and dedicated young boy; others, like *Snares of New York*, document the "ominous geography" of the "urban juvenile underworld," warning young men of the "tricks, traps and pitfalls of city life" as the subtitle to another novel put it.[68] Alger constantly used descriptions of other young boys as the foils against which the hero undertakes his quest, his struggle "upward from a boyhood of privation and self-denial into a youth and manhood of prosperity and honor."[69] There's the lesser hero, a slightly younger and less vigorous boy who becomes our hero's apprentice; the snob, the son of a gentleman, who is "lazy, ignorant, arrogant, and unwilling to work because he considers it beneath his station" and who is both overtly contemptuous and secretly envious of the hero's success; and the poor boy, who lacks the intelligence or ability of the hero and is often susceptible to the corruption of his environment.[70]

Some writers posed masculinist strategies for coming of age as men, offering vicarious accounts of young men being tested and proving themselves. Stephen Crane's *The Red Badge of Courage* (1895) is perhaps the most famous of these.[71] When Henry Fleming first sees the enemy, he is "not a man, but a member" of the army because he "felt the subtle battle-brotherhood more potent even than the cause for which they were fighting." His experience is less about virtue than about the fear of shame, humiliation, and disgrace. His initiation involves the substitution of one form of fear—the fear of social humiliation in front of other men—for an earlier, childlike fear, the fear of death. Fleming tries to "measure himself by his comrades" and falls short. Following his shameful inability to prove his manhood in battle, he was "amid wounds," feeling that his shame "could be viewed." He "wished that he, too, had a wound." But eventually, he rediscovers what contemporary masculinists might call his "inner warrior," and his shame and humiliation lead him to fight like a "barbarian, a beast," a "pagan who defends his religion," so that, ultimately, he was a "hero" like other "proved men." As we leave Henry Fleming we see him now in the possession of

> a quiet manhood, nonassertive, but a sturdy and strong blood. He knew that he would no more quail before his guides wherever they should point. He had been to touch the great death, and found that, after all, it was but the great death. He was a man.[72]

Being seen as a man was important for adult men, too. And turn-of-the-century fiction offered a wide variety of masculine themes. Literary critics like W. Churchill Williams and Bliss Carman had fumed against "emasculated" literature; American writers "have become so over-nice in our feelings, so restrained and formal, so bound by habit and use in our devotion to the effeminate realists, that one side of our nature was starved. We must have a revolt at any cost."[73]

Frank Norris was among the chief rebels. He believed in a new masculinist fiction with less attention to style and more to action and adventure. "Who cares for fine style! Tell your yarn and let your style go to the devil. We don't want literature, we want life," Norris bellowed. The impulse for manly fiction must come "far from the studios of the aesthetes, the velvet jackets and the uncut hair, far from the sexless creatures who cultivate their little art of writing as the fancier cultivates his orchids" and lead one into "a world of Working

Two Archetypes of Masculinity at the Beginning of the Nineteenth Century: The Genteel Patriarch. Although George Washington was frequently depicted as a virtuous man of the people, the Father of the Country was also its *pater familias,* and represented the gentility of the landed gentry. (*The Washington Family* [1798] by Edward Savage; courtesy of General Research Division, The New York Public Library, Astor, Lenox and Tilden Foundations)

The Heroic Artisan is the mythical ideal of the honest hardworking man whose virtue stems from his commitment to industry. This myth has lasted many decades, only recently fading. (Illustration by Thomas Nast, published March 26, 1882; courtesy of The University of Chicago Press)

The Self-Made Man Appears on the Historical Stage: Although Thomas Cole intended his *Daniel Boone at his Cabin on the Great Osage Lake* (1826) to celebrate transcendental virtues, he also reveals the loneliness of the Self-Made Man's constant quest. (Courtesy of Mead Art Museum, Amherst College)

The Myth and the Reality of the Self-Made Man in Politics: "General Harrison, the true Friend of the People"—a Whig Party campaign poster from the Presidential campaign of 1840 portrays William Henry Harrison in front of his log cabin. (Lithograph from Dorothy Goebel, *William Henry Harrison*, Indianapolis, 1926; reproduced in Carl Fish, *The Rise of the Common Man* [New York: Macmillan, 1927])

The Reality: William Henry Harrison's estate at North Bend, Ohio. (From an engraving in *The Ladies' Repository* I, 193 [July 1841]; reproduced in Carl Fish, *The Rise of the Common Man* [New York: Macmillan, 1927])

Manly Nurture and Effeminacy at the End of the Civil War: After his assassination, Abraham Lincoln is received in the heavenly arms of George Washington, while Jefferson Davis tries to escape Union capture by dressing as a woman. *Top: Lincoln and Washington Apotheosis* (1865). *Bottom:* "Jefferson Davis as an Unprotected Female!" (*Harper's Weekly,* 27 May 1865). (Courtesy of General Research Division, The New York Public Library, Astor, Lenox and Tilden Foundations)

THE CLERK

A COUNTER-PART

Negative Images of Turn-of-the-Century Masculinity: At the turn of the century, Americans were presented with several negative images of manhood, from the dissolute and disheveled egghead intellectual and the brutish pinhead of this cartoon, to the effeminate clerk in a dry goods store who fixes his hair while his customers go unattended. *Right:* "A Counter-Part" (post-card, published ca. 1910, from the personal collection of Jonathan Ned Katz; reprinted by permission). *Bottom:* "Education: Is There No MIddle Course?" (Illustration by Thomas Nast, *Harper's Weekly*, 30 November 1879; courtesy of General Research Division, The New York Public Library, Astor, Lenox and Tilden Foundations)

Manly Nurture and Homosocial Solace in Fraternal Orders: Middle-class men found both hearty camaraderie and masculinist protest against feminization in turn-of-the-century fraternal orders. By 1897, one in five American men had joined. With rituals heavily laden with religious symbolism and myth, fraternalists were devoted to a form of manly nurture. Lodges were the only place where men would wear aprons or dresses. *Left:* Daguerreotype of early fraternalists, 1850. *Bottom:* Rocky Hill Lodge Knights of Pythias Degree Team, Portland, Maine, early twentieth century. (Both courtesy of Scottish Rite Masonic Museum of Our National Heritage [80.45 and 84.6]; photographs by John Miller)

Muscular Christianity Remasculinizes Jesus: Railing against cultural feminization, Muscular Christians recast Jesus as a hypermasculine savior, "no lick spittle proposition," but the "greatest scrapper who ever lived," according to evangelist preacher Billy Sunday. Others retrieved the image of the Heroic Artisan to transform Jesus into a working class socialist hero. *Top:* Billy Sunday preaches at a meeting for men in Atlanta, Georgia, 1917. (Courtesy of The Archives of the Billy Graham Center, Wheaton, Illinois). *Right:* "The Carpenter of Nazareth was 'a workman that needeth not to be ashamed.'" (Frontispiece illustration from *The Call of the Carpenter* by Bouck White [1913]; illustration by Balfour Ker)

Remaking Masculinity Through Western Fantasies: No sooner was the frontier "closed" in reality than it was reopened through fantasies of manly confrontation with the wild and untamed. Theodore Roosevelt recast himself from an asthmatic weakling into a more heroic mold in the Dakotas, while Ernest Thompson Seton invoked Native American rituals in the founding of the Boy Scouts of America in 1910. Each of these photographs was posed in a photographer's studio. For over a century, American boys have heartily embraced the myth. *Top:* Theodore Roosevelt as frontiersman. (Courtesy of Theodore Roosevelt Birthplace National Monument). *Right:* Ernest Thompson Seton in Indian costume, 1917. (Courtesy Julia M. Seton Trust and Ernst Thompson Seton Institute)

No writer was more convinced of the regenerative masculinizing capacities of western adventure than Owen Wister. Son of a wealthy Philadelphia merchant, Wister studied acting at Harvard before heading west. His 1902 novel, *The Virginian,* celebrated the cowboy and heralded the literary form of the Western. *Left:* Owen Wister in costume for a play at Harvard, 1880. *Bottom:* Wister at Yellowstone Park, 1887. (Both photographs courtesy of American Heritage Center, University of Wyoming)

Men, crude of speech, swift of action, strong of passion, straight to the heart of a new life, on the borders of a new time, and there only will you learn to know the stuff of which must come the American fiction of the future."[74]

In several of his novels, among them *Moran, Blix, A Man's Woman, Vandover and the Brute*, and *McTeague*, Norris fused two themes—the descent into animality and the civilizing influences of women—and claimed that manhood rests between both poles. In *McTeague*, perhaps his most famous work, Norris explores the seamy side of Self-Made Manhood and reveals the terrible consequences of greed on family and home life as well as in the society at large. McTeague is a modestly successful dentist, who is, as Norris describes him, a massive, powerful man, "immensely strong, stupid, docile, and obedient." His mantra is "you can't make small of me." McTeague is possessed by undercurrents of deep, dark, brooding animal brutality, which he struggles against but is unable to contain in the face of greed. Greed makes virtually everyone in McTeague's world psychotic—from Zerkow the pawnbroker, who listens to Maria the maid's incessant chattering about fantasy gold-plated china, to Trina, his wife, who wins $5,000 in the lottery and becomes a cruel miser, salting away whatever pennies she can rather than use them to help herself and her husband. McTeague is double-edged tragedy: His own tragic flaw—his animality that he cannot completely contain— becomes enmeshed with the tragic flaw of social life at the turn of the century, an unbridled greed which destroys all human relationships and ultimately claims his life.[75]

In *Vandover and the Brute* (written in 1896, published posthumously in 1914), Norris explored this split personality between the civilized man and his primal, deep manhood in a style reminiscent of Robert Louis Stevenson's *Dr. Jekyll and Mr. Hyde*. First "there was himself, the real Vandover of every day, the same familiar Vandover that looked back at him from his mirror." But then there was also "the wolf, the beast, whatever the creature that lived in his flesh, and that struggled within him now, striving to gain ascendancy, to absorb the real Vandover into his own hideous identity."[76]

In *A Man's Woman* (1900) Norris explored this split in two figures, counterposing Ward Bennett, a brutish Arctic explorer, to Lloyd

Searight, a strong-willed nurse with a masculine name, whose creed was "to *do* things." Bennett possesses a coarse but elemental masculinity. "The world wants men," he exclaims, "great, strong, harsh, brutish men—men with purposes who let nothing, nothing, nothing, stand in their way." Through the course of the novel, Lloyd discovers that it is the natural role of women to submit to men, while Ward learns that masculinity can consist of more than animal brutality.[77]

William Dean Howells agreed with Norris about cultural feminization, arguing that Americans had become a "weak and sniveling race," but he explored the cultural clash between the rising middle class and the traditional aristocracy in terms that found him labeled an "effeminate realist" himself. In his ironically titled *The Rise of Silas Lapham* (1885), the clash between these two classes, represented by two families, the Laphams and the Coreys, is also a clash between two forms of manhood, those of the genteel Bromfield Corey and the uncouth, brashly arrogant Lapham, whose demise is all the more pitiful because the Coreys have become effete and unable to help him when he falls. Silas Lapham is one of the first completely Self-Made Men in American literature, and his story is really about his unmaking—the fall of the Self-Made Man is, in the end, far more significant than his rise.[78]

The most famous novelist of the day, Henry James, was also pessimistic about the possibilities of revitalizing American manhood from the inherited models of manhood. Sentimental, prosaic, and favoring "genderless minds usually devoid of desire," as one critic put it, James's male characters seemed to embody everything that real men were not. For example, the floridly named Hyacinth Robinson in *The Princess Casamassima* is "small," with a "narrow chest," "delicate" hands, a "childishly slight" frame, and a "pale complexion." But even James also delivered a tirade against feminization through Basil Ransome in *The Bostonians* and then fled to a vision of natural aristocracy (although he remained contemptuous of aristocrats).[79] Norris descended to naive innocence and animal brutality, but could not offer it as hope in a world corrupted by greed. And Howells implied that both models of successful manhood—nouveaux riches businessmen and aristocrats of inherited wealth—were impotent for the twentieth century.

Other cultural media echoed the preoccupations of masculinist fiction. For example, painters such as Frederic Remington, Thomas Hart Benton, Thomas Eakins, and Ashcan School members like George Bellows, Robert Henri, and John Sloan challenged European painterly conventions of beauty with their stark evocations of the brutal reality of urban life, as in Bellows's painting of boxing matches or Remington's romanticized visions of western Indian slaughter and cowboy life. Whether painting the hurly-burly of the city streets or the rugged coast of Maine, Bellows's energetic style and rough-hewn subject matter brought appreciation from male viewers who felt excluded by dandified aesthetes. And Eakins finessed a homoerotic adoration of the male body into muscular shoulders and straining backs of scullers along the Schuylkill River, the studied determination of baseball players (*Baseball Players Practicing* [1875]), or the youthful sinewy male bonding (*The Swimming Hole* [1883–1885]). His paintings, one reviewer noted in 1875, were full of "pure natural force and virility."[80]

In music Charles Ives rejected what he heard as the "sweet" or "feminine" music of the impressionists—"easy music for the sissies, for the lilypad ears." Instead, Ives derived a masculine musical idiom, incorporating the manly dissonance of strong sounds and a virile patriotism. At the end of one composition he wrote, "To strengthen and give more muscle to the ear, brain, heart, limbs and FEAT! Atta boy!" Elsewhere he provides occasional marginal notation to "keep up the fight!" or "don't quit because the ladybirds don't like it."[81] And pioneer architect Louis Sullivan was also dissatisfied with the baroque forms of the late Victorian building and sought to create a distinctly masculine type of building, the skyscraper. A man who moved in an entirely homosocial world, Sullivan sought to recapture manly power in corporeal form. He claimed that he learned from Michelangelo "the power and possibility of being male, of being super male." Upon observing a warehouse of the Marshall Field Company, Sullivan wrote, "Here is a man for you to look at. A man that walks on two legs instead of four, has active muscles . . . lives and breathes . . . in a world of barren pettiness, a male," while at another retail store for the same company, he praised the building as a "virile force," a building with "red blood, a real man, a manly man . . . an entire male."

Sullivan's skyscrapers were symbolic attempts to create a real man, and his disciple Frank Lloyd Wright brought the ideal of space as masculine into the vernacular design of his prairie houses, challenging the home as a feminine preserve.[82]

But nowhere could American men find a better exemplar of rugged outdoor masculinity than out west with the cowboy, that noble denizen of the untamed frontier. The cowboy occupies an important place in American cultural history: He is America's contribution to the world's stock of mythic heroes. But the cowboy was not always a hero. In the 1860s and 1870s the cowboy was called a "herder," and he appeared in public prints and writing as a rough, uncouth, shaggy, and dirty man, whose behavior was violent, barbarous, and rowdy. He was the brutal outlaw, not the good guy. Writing in 1875, Laura Winthrop Johnson saw no glamour in these "rough men with shaggy hair and wild staring eyes, in butternut trousers stuffed into great rough boots." But around 1882 a cowboy named Buck Taylor at the First Wild West Show captured the attention of a writer, Prentiss Ingraham. The Wild West Show was a re-creation of the West in the form of a traveling circus. Organized by Buffalo Bill Cody, the show depicted the conquest and taming of the Wild West. When Ingraham wrote a fictional biography of Taylor in 1887, later expanded into a series of dime novels, the new cowboy was invented.[83]

By 1887 the great cattle drives that were his home had ended, and the "big die-up" of the winter of 1886–1887 had bankrupted many cattle outfits and so altered ranch life that the cowboy was "less a knight errant and more a hired man on horseback." In fiction the cowboy was all guts and glory. The cowboy thus emerged in literature at the exact moment of his disappearance as an independent craftsman and his transformation into a wage worker in a new industry of cattle ranching.[84]

The end of the century also witnessed the creation of the rodeo, a "celebration of the unique and daring sports indulged in and enjoyed by all the virile characters of the western frontier," as a promotional handbill for Cheyenne's Frontier Days put it. The first rodeo was held in 1883 in Pecos, Texas; five years later, folks in Prescott, Arizona, paid admission to see cowboys strut their cowpunching stuff in arenas. By the 1890s rodeos had defined formats and rules that governed the major competitions—steer wrestling, bareback riding, and bronco busting. Cheyenne's Frontier Days were inaugurated in 1897 as a self-conscious "annual resurrection of the west as it was, for the edification of the west as it is." One magazine writer explained the significance of Frontier Days in 1909:

> Civilization is pushing everything before it: thriving cities and well kept farms are taking the place of the cattle upon a thousand hills. But the pioneer still clings with a pathetic tenacity to the old customs . . . a pathetic but vigorous desire . . . to prove that strong arms and courageous hearts still existed on the range.[85]

Organizers had no doubts that it was rugged western manliness that was also being resurrected. Individual acts were extolled for their "peril to life and limb"; commentators were awed by the "sheer nerve" of the bareback rider, and one waxed poetic about broncos—"murderers that plunge with homicidal fury beneath the cinches of leather of a bucking saddle." For the participants the rodeo gave the "feeling of being part of the frontier that still lives in the professional rodeo arena. A cowboy on a bronco symbolizes the rugged individuality of the Western man and beast." For the spectators the rodeo was a "true taste of the wild and woolly."[86] The rodeo pen preserved the frontier as gladiatorial arena and its competitors as participants in a blood sport.

As a mythic creation the cowboy was fierce and brave, willing to venture into unknown territory, a "negligent, irrepressible wilderness," and tame it for women, children, and emasculated civilized men. As soon as the environment has been subdued, he must move on, unconstrained by the demands of civilized life, unhampered by clinging women and whining children and uncaring bosses and managers.[87] His is a freedom which cannot be "bounded by the fences of a too weak and timid conventionalism," as Harold Wright put it in his western novel *When a Man's a Man* (1916).[88] He is a man of impeccable ethics, whose faith in natural law and natural right is eclipsed only by the astonishing fury with which he demands rigid adherence to them. He is a man of action—"grim [and] lean, . . . of few topics, and not many words concerning these." He moves in a world of men, in which daring, bravery, and skill are his constant companions. He lives by physical strength and rational calculation; his compassion is social and generalized, but he forms no lasting emotional bonds with any single person. He lives alone, a "hermited horseman" out on the range, settling the West.[89]

But, of course, he doesn't really exist, except in the pages of the western, the literary genre heralded by the publication of Owen Wister's novel *The Virginian* in 1902.[90] Wister is not only the creator of the genre but one of its biggest boosters and celebrators. Born into an aristocratic Philadelphia family, Wister's first love was music, and he went to Harvard to study composition. When it became clear that he would never become a truly great composer, his father insisted that he return home to a position at Boston's largest brokerage house. Within a few months Wister had a nervous breakdown and developed Bell's palsy (a paralysis of the face). He consulted S. Weir Mitchell, who diagnosed Wister's problem as neurasthenia and prescribed a trip to a Wyoming dude ranch for a cure. At the ranch Wister slept outdoors in a tent, bathed in an icy creek each morning, spent hours in the saddle, hunted, fished, worked in the roundup, and helped to brand calves, castrate bulls, and deliver foals. "I am beginning to be able to feel I'm something of an animal and not a stinking brain alone," he wrote from the ranch in 1885. In three weeks Wister believed himself to be completely cured.[91]

And completely converted to western life, which he was now devoted to celebrating. The western was his creation, a vehicle for "an upper class composer–short-story-writer with doubts about his independence to claim a robust masculinity," according to literary critic Jane Tompkins.[92] As a genre the western represented the apotheosis of masculinist fantasy, a revolt not against women but against feminization. The vast prairie is the domain of male liberation from workplace humiliation, cultural feminization, and domestic emasculation. The saloon replaces the church, the campfire replaces the Victorian parlor, the range replaces the factory floor. The western is a purified, pristine male domain.[93]

What are the traits of such a mythic figure as a cowboy? Of course, he is manly.[94] He is a natural aristocrat—a "natural nobleman, formed not by civilization and its institutions but the spontaneous influence of the land working on an innate goodness." Like Natty Bumppo or Davy Crockett before him, the Virginian, as the narrator first meets him, is a "handsome, ungrammatical son of the soil"; "here in flesh and blood was a truth which I had long believed in words, but never met before. The creature we call a *gentleman* lies deep in the hearts of thousands that are born without a chance to master the outward graces of the type."[95] Having served his apprenticeship, he is now a master of his craft of riding, roping, and killing. His values are the old artisanal virtues: "self-discipline, unswerving purpose; the exercise of knowledge, skill, ingenuity, and excellent judgement; and a capacity to continue in the face of total exhaustion and overwhelming odds." He is free in a free country, embodying republican virtue and autonomy.[96]

And he is white. To Wister the West was "manly, egalitarian, self-reliant, and Aryan." A 1902 review of *The Virginian* in the *World's Work* saw this deeper theme in the western at the moment of its origins:

> To catch the deeper meaning of our life, one's path must be toward that Western verge of the continent where all white men are American born, because there only are the culture and conservatism of the East, the chivalrism and the fire-eating spirit of the South, and the broad, unhampered gambler's view of life native to raw Western soil, all transmuted into a democracy of no distinctions.[97]

Frederic Remington echoed such sentiments. He was, like Wister, an elite easterner whose first trip west was designed to cure neurasthenia. He rejected effete conceptions of beauty, of the "cards and custards" of the eastern establishment, and he hated Europe with its "collars, cuffs and foreign languages."[98] And like Wister, Remington's masculinist revival was an all-white affair. He loathed immigrants: "Jews, Injuns, Chinamen, Italians, Huns—the rubbish of the earth I hate," he wrote. "I've got some Winchesters and when the massacring begins, I can get my share of 'em, and what's more, I will." And he detested blacks; writing to Wister, he commented on the tragedy of the Civil War, when "so many Americans [had] to be killed to free a lot of damn niggers who are better off under the yoke. There is something fateful in our destiny that way." He closed his letter with some relief that in the Spanish-American war, at least, "we will kill a few Spaniards instead of Anglo-Saxons," a change that "will be proper and nice."[99]

The cowboy hero of the western novel was an anachronism, obsolete at the moment of his creation. Wister knew full well that this new genre was in fantasy mode, as he wrote in an editorial preface to *The Virginian*:

> What has become of the horseman, the cow-puncher, the last romantic figure upon our soil? For he was romantic. Whatever he did, he did with his might. The bread that he earned was earned hard, the wages that he squandered were squandered hard. . . . Well, he will be among us always, invisible, waiting his chance to live and play as he would like. His wild kind has been among us always, since the beginning, a young man with his temptations, a hero without wings.

To Remington the cowboy was the last cavalier; his illustrations for Wister's essay, "Evolution of the Cowpuncher" (1895), portrayed the cowboy as "the noble descendent of chivalric knights and crusaders." It was an image that resonated for generations of American men. *The Virginian* went through fourteen editions and sold over three hundred thousand copies between its initial publication in 1902 and 1904. Just as he had disappeared in real life, the cowboy had arrived in myth.[100]

No western writer of the era managed to cover all these themes as powerfully as Wister, but several writers plied a similar trade with powerful and popular results. For Jack London or Edgar Rice Burroughs the frontier could simply be transported elsewhere—for example, the African jungle or the Alaskan Klondike. Here men might reunite with their Darwinian ancestors and retrieve their pure masculinity by shedding all the trappings of modernity. Wrenched from effete, civilized life or born into the life of the primitive, Buck and Tarzan, two of the most popular male characters in American fiction, hear the call of their primitive instincts and return to become wolves and apes.

When we first meet Buck, in London's *Call of the Wild* (1903), he is a relatively tame house pet in California, dognapped by an impoverished gardener and sold to a Klondike expedition. There, in the wild, he learns quickly the "law of club and fang" and becomes the strongest and most successful and ferocious sled dog. He has a multitude of adventures, including a deep love for the man who saves him from a savage beating and then treats him kindly—a deep, manly love, not the love of a tame animal. But even that love could not "civilize" the "strain of the primitive":

> Deep in the forest a call was sounding, and as often as he heard this call, mysteriously thrilling and luring, he felt compelled to turn his back upon the fire and the beaten earth around it, and to plunge into the forest.[101]

To which he eventually succumbs, in a masterful regression that is at once evolutionary and developmental.[102] London revels in Buck's muscular power and brute ferocity and provides a potent antidote to overcivilization. Here's London at his most eloquent:

> There is an ecstasy that marks the summit of life, and beyond which life cannot rise. And such is the paradox of living, this ecstasy comes when one is most alive, and it comes as a complete forgetfulness of living, comes to the artist, caught up and out of himself in a sheet of flame; it comes to the soldier, war-mad on a stricken field and refusing quarter; and it came to Buck, leading the pack, sounding the old wolf-cry, straining after the food that was alive and that fled swiftly before him through the moonlight. He was sounding the deeps of his nature, and of the parts of his nature that were deeper than he, going back into the womb of Time. He was mastered by the sheer surging of life, the tidal wave of being, the perfect joy of each separate muscle, joint, and sinew and that it was everything that was not death, that it was aglow and rampant, expressing itself in movement, flying exultantly under the stars and over the face of dead matter that did not move.[103]

Another of London's novels, *The Sea Wolf* (1904), applied similar themes to the interaction among men. Humphrey Van Weyden, the effeminate, overcivilized narrator, receives his own initiation aboard the ship of the aptly-named Wolf Larsen, a working-class brute who possesses "a strength savage, ferocious, alive in itself, the essence of life . . . the potency of motion."[104] The narrator rejects his mentor's animal brutality as a way to shed his older, sissified identity and finally achieves a sense of himself as a man.[105]

This contrast of civilization and animality is the bedrock of Burroughs's *Tarzan of the Apes* (1912) and the subsequent series of books that saw Tarzan have every manly adventure known to Burroughs, including returning to the Old West and rocketing off to outer space. Tarzan is the personification, Burroughs writes, "of the primitive man, the hunter, the warrior," the Rousseauian innocent, the "naked savage" who is also, it turns out, a blue-blooded English nobleman. In his dramatic (and steamy) encounters with Jane, we fully understand the power of the primitive.[106] Tarzan embodies the "avenging hero, half animal and half human, fusing beast and patrician, [who] descend[s] into an evil underclass to save a helpless bourgeois civilization." Tarzan "has a man's figure and a man's brain, but he was an ape by training and environment." At the climax of this Darwinian nightmare, in which descending the evolutionary ladder is the only mechanism to retrieve manhood, Tarzan tells Jane that he has "come across the ages out of the dim and distant past from the lair of the primeval man to claim you—for your sake I have become a civilized man—for your sake I have crossed oceans and continents—for your sake I will be whatever you will me to be." Tarzan's triumph is that he will be civilized by a woman.[107]

This kind of civilization seemed perfectly reasonable to Burroughs and, in a sense, expressed the American ambivalence with the nobility. Genteel Patriarchs had been largely discredited as masculine role models, precisely because they were *already* tame. But what of Tarzan's aristocratic birth, the natural aristocracy of the cowboy avenger, or the primitive nobility of the reborn animal in Buck? The American middle-class man's fascination with natural aristocracy, a nobility of bearing, temperament, and demeanor that such a freeborn aristocrat possesses prior to his contact with the civilized world—this was a nobility worth retrieving. At times it appeared that any trait that was natural was virtuous, any trait gained through civilization was unmanly.

London and Burroughs transported the western to other, more exotic locales, but they did not transform it. The western remains the core cultural contribution of masculinist escapism, a vein mined no better than by Zane Grey. Like Wister, Remington, and other purveyors of the western motif, Grey came from a wealthy Philadelphia family but abandoned his career as a dentist to write westerns. In his first and most famous work, *Riders of the Purple Sage* (1912), the hero, Bern Venters, represents the nineteenth-century men who "have been enfeebled by the doctrines of a feminized Christianity," embodied by Jane Witherspoon, who has symbolically emasculated him in the opening pages by taking away his guns. Through his transformation "American men are taking their manhood back from the Christian women who have been holding it in thrall." "Harness the cave man— yes!" wrote Grey in 1924, "but do not kill him. Something of the wild and primitive should remain instinctive in the human race."[108]

Fantasies of western adventure, testing and proving manhood on the battlefield; the reclamation of the workplace for heroic artisans and the critiques of marketplace manhood and aristocratic snobbery; celebrating the manly in literature, music, and art and even going native in a Darwinian devolution to pure animality—these were the dominant themes of masculinist literature at the turn of the century. Like bodybuilding, becoming a sports or fitness fanatic, or perfecting the body as a way of perfecting the self, these were vigorous, desperate efforts to provide for men the possibility of imagining their manhood in its traditional settings, consuming their manhood in idealized versions of those settings—even as the real men who were its consumers had to find new ways to adjust to the changing circumstances that transformed their lives.

CHAPTER 5

A Room of His Own

SOCIALIZING THE NEW MAN

Manliness can only be taught by men, and not by those who
are half men, half old women.
—R. S. S. Baden-Powell (founder of the Boy Scouts)

The purpose of our institutions is to manufacture manhood.
—Sen. Albert J. Beveridge *The Young Man and the World* (1905)

By the beginning of the twentieth century, testing manhood had become increasingly difficult. The public arena was crowded and competitive, and heading west to start over was more the stuff of fiction than possibility. What was worse, many believed, a new generation of young boys was being raised entirely by women, who would turn America's future men into whiny little mama's boys. Men sought to rescue their sons from the feminizing clutches of mothers and teachers and create new ways to "manufacture manhood."

Their efforts were also somewhat self-serving. The separation of spheres, it has been argued, had left women domestic prisoners, locked into the home by an ideology of feminine domesticity and Christian piety and virtue. By the end of the century, I've suggested, men began to experience the separate spheres as painful to them as well. Men were excluded from domestic life, unable to experience the love, nurture, and repose that the home supposedly represented. How could a man return to the home without feeling like a wimp?

One solution, as we've seen, was to colonize the home, to find a small corner that could be unmistakably "his," like the den or the study in the nineteenth century or the basement, the workshop, the garage, or even the backyard barbecue pit today. But fears of feminization gave a new urgency to men's desires. Women were entirely in charge of socialization of young boys. The three principal institutions that dominate early childhood socialization—family, religion, and education—were completely staffed and run by women. Many men felt that they needed to wrest control over socialization and get more actively involved themselves. To that end men decided to inculcate manhood into the next generation and create some parallel institutions for themselves as well.

But first, American men needed to come home. Earlier in the century reformers had promoted the separation of spheres, in part to maintain the public arena as a masculine testing ground. This had been so successful that by century's end the family looked very different from its early nineteenth-century antecedent. Now husbands and wives spent their days in separate worlds—he, away all day at work, at increasing distances from home, and she, at home all day, looking after the house and children. Both arenas were increasingly industrialized and mechanized—his, by the assembly line, mass production, and growth of white-collar clerical positions, and hers, by innovations in household technology that made the home look like a little factory. Fathers' roles diminished in proportion to the distance and time they spent at work away from the home.[1] An increasing number of industrial products and services designed for the home turned the housewife into a "household engineer," as domestic reformer Christine Frederick termed her in her treatise *Household Engineering* (1910).[2]

At the moment of perhaps their greatest separation, husbands and wives were told they should establish what critics called companionate marriage. Husband and wife should be more devoted, more emotionally *connected*, than before. On the one hand, it meant fewer children—from nearly five children per wife (4.94) between 1800 and 1849 to less than three (2.77) between 1870 and 1900 and less than two (1.92) by 1915. The percentage of women who had only one child jumped from 4 percent in 1800–1849 to 8.1 percent by 1870–1900 and to 20 percent by 1915. On the other hand, it meant increasing sexual activity. Ironically, however, it also meant an increasing number of divorces, foreshadowing the second wave of feminism and companionate marriage in the 1970s and 1980s. Husbands and wives were more likely to part if the companionship faltered. In 1916 one in four marriages ended in divorce in San Francisco; in Los Angeles it was one in five and in Chicago one in seven. Psychologist John B. Watson predicted that "in fifty years there will be no such thing as marriage."[3]

Along with companionate marriage came a fatherhood movement. "It is far more needful for children that a father should attend to the formation of their character and habits, and end in developing their social, intellectual and moral nature, than it is that he should earn money to furnish them with handsome clothes and a variety of tempting food," wrote Catharine Beecher and her sister Harriet Beecher Stowe in *The American Woman's Home* (1869). "The home is man's affair as much as woman's," wrote Martha and Robert Brueres in 1912. "When God made homemakers, male and female created He them!" "The responsibility of the home is not [the wife's] alone, but equally the husband's," announced the editor of *American Homes and Gardens* in 1905. "There is no reason at all why men should not sweep and dust, make beds, clean windows, fix the fire, clean the grate, arrange the furniture and cook."[4]

Some men, it seems, heeded the advice. A large number of men participated in childbirth, often at the request of their wives, and despite much counsel against it.[5] In a new ideology of "masculine domesticity," men found

a model of behavior in which fathers would agree to take on increased responsibility for some of the day-to-day tasks of bringing up children and spending their time away from work in playing with their sons and daughters, teaching them, taking them on trips. A domestic man would also make his wife, rather than his male cronies, his regular companion on evenings out. And while he might not dust the mantel or make the bed except in special circumstances, he would take a significantly greater interest in the details of running the household and caring for the children that [sic] his father was expected to do.[6]

Even at home, however, men were still men. They focused on their wives, but they felt on surer ground with their sons. Domesticity "was incorporated in to the concept of manliness, as men became convinced that in order to have their sons grow up to be 'manly,' they should involve themselves more substantially in their children's upbringing." These men were perhaps not the sensitive "new men" feminist women keep hoping for; their domestic participation was an "alternative to feminism, a way to deflect and even sabotage women's advances."[7] For young boys, though, the effort ushered in a period of dramatic transformation.

Boys' and girls' spheres of play were, for the first time, completely separated. Fathers sought father-son togetherness and feared a young boy's identification with his mother and sissification by playing with his sisters. Part of the change was in the ways baby boys and girls were dressed. Prior to the 1880s little boys and little girls were dressed identically. Both wore what looked like white christening gowns during infancy and short, loose-fitting dresses in early childhood—that is, boys and girls looked like little girls. But that changed in the late 1880s as parents dressed their toddlers in gender-appropriate clothing, and knickerbockers and trousers made their first appearance for little boys.

In the first decades of the twentieth century, clothing became color coded. The only problem was choosing the right color scheme. A 1918 editorial entitled "Pink or Blue?" in the magazine *The Infants' Department* explained:

> there has been a great diversity of opinion on the subject, but the generally accepted rule is pink for the boy and blue for the girl. The reason is that pink being a more decided and stronger color is more suitable for the boy; while blue, which is more delicate and dainty, is prettier for the girl.

It is unclear exactly why these colors were subsequently reversed. At the time, boys wore pink or red because they were manly colors indicating strength and determination, and girls wore light blue, an airier color, like the sky, because girls were so flighty. Parents debated the question in the letters column of the Sears, Roebuck catalog and eventually flipped over to the present color arrangement. But as late as 1939 the debate continued, as "What Color for Your Baby?," an article in *Parents Magazine*, suggested that "red symbolizes zeal and courage, while blue is symbolic of faith and constancy."[8]

By the first decades of the new century, boys and girls were not only wearing different clothes but playing with different toys. Toys were increasingly marketed as appropriate only for boys or for girls.[9] One writer advised parents about boys' fighting:

> There are times when every boy must defend his own rights if he is not to become a coward, and lose the road to independence and true manhood. . . . The strong-willed boy needs no inspiration to combat, but often a good deal of guidance and restraint. If he fights more than, let us say, a half-dozen times a week,—except of course, during his first week at a new school—he is probably over-quarrelsome and needs to curb. The sensitive, retiring boy, on the other hand, needs encouragement to stand his ground and fight.[10]

So boys were to average a fight a day—except during the first week at a new school, during which, presumably, they would have to fight more often than that! By contrast, a boy with no interest in fighting was unnatural, a "nonentity," argued G. Stanley Hall in his celebrated work *Adolescence* (1904). It was "better even an occasional nose dented by a fist . . . than stagnation, general cynicism and censoriousness, bodily and psychic cowardice."[11]

For boys growing older, advice books returned to the same advice as that given earlier in the century, counseling parents to maintain the separation of spheres for boys and girls. Boys were to avoid dancing, sleeping on featherbeds, warm rooms, and reading books—these last because they were "artificial," providing only "second hand information" compared with "completely natural experience," the real instructor of manhood. "The tendency of novel reading is most pernicious," Mrs. S. B. Dana had written. "It enervates the mental powers, and unfits them for close study and serious contemplation. It promotes sickly sensibility, and renders its votaries unfit for the pursuits of real life"—just as it had done in the early nineteenth century.[12]

SCHOOLING FOR MANHOOD

There were two worries for men with young sons in school. As discussed in the previous chapter, teaching was dominated by women. The era also witnessed new pseudoscientific theories claiming to demonstrate that women and men were essentially different species and that the education of the two together would destroy both manhood and womanhood. Opponents believed that "constant intimacy between maturing boys and girls fosters an undesirable precocity and introduces unnecessarily perplexing problems." Namely, one presumes, sex.[13]

Most opponents believed that attending school together would harm girls "by assimilating them to boys' ways and work, robbing them of their sense of feminine character," and make boys "effeminate and unfit for the serious business of life in a man's world," as G. Stanley Hall put it. Hall's massive, two-volume, fourteen-hundred-page treatise *Adolescence* (1904) made him the instant expert on the topic and provided an important justification for opposing coeducation.[14] Hall based his arguments on the theory of recapitulation, a still-popular view that the lifelong development of each individual recapitulates the entire history of the species as a whole. Each child passed through all the evolutionary stages of human history, from savagery to civilization, through the course of development. "Ontogeny recapitulates phylogeny" is the theory's epigrammatic formulation. In this model, adolescence was pivotal, the moment of transition from the barbarian state of childhood to the civilized stage of mature adulthood. But according to Hall, women and men represented different stages of this evolutionary development. Women were evolutionarily older, more primitive, and conservative, while men were more modern, adaptive, and variable. In a sense, women were perpetual adolescents, representing "childhood and youth in the full meridian of its glory in all her dimensions and nature."[15]

Boys and girls thus had different educational needs and experiences though most schools forced them to be similar. The effect was disastrous: Boys protected their sexuality by channeling it into schoolwork, while girls destroyed their sexuality by sublimation. Studying too hard robbed them of their maternal capacities. Contemporary education had it entirely backward. Rather than being separated, young boys were being forced to absorb girl culture and young girls were being forced to absorb boy culture, processes that would "virify women and feminize men." Actually, Hall believed the consequences had been more severe for boys because they were forced to "sink to a standard purposely set low for girls." Children's literature was "flabby, nerveless, inactive" or "light and chatty" with "too many illustrations" or "goody Sunday school books"—exactly what young boys did not need. "All that rot they teach to children about the little raindrop fairies with their buckets washing down the window panes must go," he said in a speech to Chicago teachers in 1899. "We need less sentimentality and more spanking." Hall's mission was the restructuring of education to make "man more manly and woman more womanly."[16]

Adolescent boys should be recognized as being in a "hoodlum stage" of development, "young barbarians" to be relinquished by mother into the care of the father. "Never has the American boy been quite so wild as now, and never in the world have so many young cubs been so half-orphaned and left to female guidance in school, home, and church." Boys needed different forms of understanding and different forms of punishment—flogging was a good idea for boys, "coddling" for girls. Adolescent male rebellion is necessary and vital, the "natural revolution of the young male just beginning to sense his virility against the prim pedagogue propriety of petticoat control to which he has been too much committed," Hall wrote, with a flair for alliteration.[17] In college, Hall advised, boys should endure fraternity hazing and practical joking as ways of asserting manly independence. "The practical joke is war, cruelty, torture reduced to the level and intensity of play," he wrote. "A good course of rough and roistering treatment" by one's peers has made "many a callow youth" develop a more "flexible" nature and prevented "inspissation of the soul."

Others observers took up the celebration of male adolescent marauding. J. Adams Puffer's The Boy and His Gang (1912), written under Hall's guidance, suggested that gang membership was healthy for young boys, "the result of a group of instincts inherited from a distant past," a "natural and a necessary stage in normal development." When some critics urged restraints on rowdy forms of male bonding, like gangs and fraternity hazing, Senator Albert Beveridge retorted that we "cannot change our sex, or the nature and habits of it. A young man is like a male animal after all, and those who object to his rioting like a young bull are in a perpetual quarrel with Nature."[18]

Hall went further than most educators in his evocation of contra-Darwinian "devolution." If children represented the earlier stages of social development, then it was the innate primitive savagery of young boys that could point the way to the resolution of the crisis of masculinity—we should learn to be more like boys and less like over-civilized men. Perhaps the savage child could be father to the man and reinstill manly behavior. Toward that end, Hall became increasingly enamored of boxing and violence in general, claiming that men enjoy "a quite unparalleled tingling of fibre and a peculiar mental inebriation" from violence.[19]

The coeducation debate was hotly argued in the 1890s and 1900s.[20] Some antifeminists had earlier argued that women's admission to formerly men's colleges would unsex women. As one Wesleyan College student put it as that college began a short-lived experiment with coeducation:

And thus she makes a farce of this fair life
By stepping out of Nature's goodly plan
Into the dusty tumult and the strife
Absurdly trying to become a man.[21]

New arguments stressed the effects on the college and upon men— that, for example, educating women and men together would weaken the curriculum with subjects better omitted or by slowing down the pace to allow women to keep up. Or that coeducation would distract men from the discipline of their studies or that contact between the sexes would "dilute" the mysteries of heterosexual attraction and thus promote homosexuality among men. Or that the entry of women would sap the virility of the male students and thus the ranking of the school would fall. "Where coeducation exists, there is invariably a noticeable weakness in the calibre of the large majority of men attending such institutions and a corresponding loss of rank of such institutions among the colleges in the country," observed the editor of Wesleyan University's college newspaper, the *Argus*, in 1898. Still others were concerned that if men's institutions were to admit women, men would no longer want to come. "The average young man will not go to a coeducational institution if other things are anywhere near equal. . . . He is not comfortable with the women in the classroom," warned F. W. Hamilton, president of Tufts College, in 1907.[22]

It was also feared that alumni would stop giving funds. The *Hartford Courant* quoted a "prominent athlete" on the consequences. "Only last year," he said, "we lost a star pitcher for the baseball team, and this year four crack-a-jack football men, three of whom eventually entered Princeton, owing to their feeling on the matter of coeducation." Here's one Wesleyan graduate's fantasy, as he wrote it to the administration in 1890:

> Banish football! . . . Banish baseball! I expect you fellows, excuse me, you girls, will soon be sending little pink envelopes to the alumni soliciting subscriptions to the Wesleyan Croquet Club, Wesleyan Sewing Circles, and similar organizations. Say, girls, please take my name off the list, won't you?

The pink slips never came. Rather than risk it, Wesleyan's trustees abandoned their flirtation with coeducation (begun in 1872) in 1912.[23]

Other colleges and universities were similarly ambivalent, although some went through these wrenching debates earlier than others. Women had first entered the University of Wisconsin in 1863 but had been abruptly banned in 1867, when the university formed a female college, and then readmitted to segregated classes in 1873. When the University of Chicago opened in 1892, two-fifths of its entering class was women. By 1900 the enrollment of women was greater than that of men, and women earned more than half the Phi Beta Kappa awards, prompting fears that Chicago would soon turn into a women's college. In 1902, over the objections of women students and faculty, President William Harper instituted "segregation" to, as he put it, "solve the problem of effeminization," separating women into a separate junior college, separate sections of upper division courses, and separate chapels and laboratories.[24] Harvard president Charles Eliot believed that "girls and boys are better taught separately than together, especially after the age of puberty."[25] And Columbia's trustees thwarted President Barnard's plans to admit women to Columbia in 1882; they founded the college that bears his name seven years later. At the University of California, the student newspaper, the *Daily Californian*, which was edited by the fraternities, argued that since the "minds of men and women are radically different," they should be taught separately. And the yearbook, *The Blue and Gold*, added that "familiarity breeds contempt. The intimate associations which go with co-education prohibit forming the idealism about feminine charms which makes them charming." Therefore, "coeducation might destroy the dissimilarity between the sexes."[26]

Hall's theories informed several generations of educators, psychologists, and parents, and his legacy is still with us in recurring ideas of separation of the sexes. In 1899 Theodore Roosevelt was effusive in his praise of Hall's ideas:

> I must write to thank you for your sound common sense, decency, and manliness in what you advocate for the education of children. Oversentimentality, over-softness, in fact washiness and mushiness are the great dangers of this age and of this people. Unless we keep the barbarian virtue, gaining the civilized ones will be of little avail. I am particularly glad that you emphasize the probable selfishness of a milksop. . . . I feel we cannot too strongly insist upon the need for the rough, manly virtues. A nation that cannot fight is not worth its salt, no matter how cultivated and refined it may be. . . . It is just so with a boy.[27]

Others were not so sanguine about Hall or his opposition to coeducation. M. Carey Thomas, president of Bryn Mawr, for example, claimed she had "never chanced again upon a book that seemed to me so to degrade me in my womanhood as . . . President Stanley Hall's *Adolescence*." John Dewey, the noted philosopher and educator, argued that coeducation was beneficial to both girls and boys. "Boys learn gentleness, unselfishness, courtesy; their natural vigor finds helpful channels of expression instead of wasting itself in law-

less boisterousness." Girls, on the other hand, become less manipulative; they "acquire greater self-reliance and a desire to win approval
by deserving it instead of by 'working' others. Their narrowness of
judgment, depending on the enforced narrowness of outlook, is overcome; their ultra-feminine weaknesses are toned up." He found the
argument that women teachers feminize boys to be "nonsense," "utterly absurd."[28]

Other advocates of collegiate coeducation, like John Van Vleck and
William North Rice at Wesleyan, James Fairchild at Oberlin, Robert
Maynard Hutchins at Chicago, and Andrew D. White at Cornell, confronted Hall's and others' fears of emasculation. If men were uneasy
about educational equality or opposed to women's education, Dewey
had a simple response. "The kind of man that will be kept from the
University simply because he will have to associate upon equal terms
with his equals is not the kind the University wants or needs."[29]

PLAY

The possibilities of feminization lurked also outside the classroom. In
1886 a striking change swept through the Young Men's Christian Association, one that illustrates these fears. Founded in Boston in 1851,
the YMCA had originally been a sedentary place that spurned the
gymnasium and sporting field. In its early decades that attitude mod-
ified only slightly. After the first gym was built in the New York City
branch, for example, the organization began to promote "Athletic
Sundays," during which boys would gather for morning Bible study
and afternoon lectures by famous sports figures like Amos Alonzo
Stagg, the legendary Yale football coach, or members of the Princeton
football team, or Billy Sunday, the fleet right fielder of the Pittsburgh
baseball club. But when Luther Gulick took over the directorship of
the organization, the promotion of physical culture suddenly became
a major part of the YMCA program. Gulick wanted to create a "manly
boy," a potent combination of physical hardiness with Christian
morality and duty. "Activities calling for cooperation and self-sacrifice
form the natural basis upon which a life of service can be built," he
wrote. "This life for others is far more probable, natural and tangible,
when it comes as the natural unfolding or development of that in-

stinct which has its first great impulse of growth in the games of adolescence."[30]

The turn of the century also witnessed the birth of a handful of
"boys' lib" organizations. The Boys Brigades, the Boone and Crockett
Club, Knights of King Arthur, and the Men of Tomorrow all foreshad-
owed that major American institution of boyhood, the Boy Scouts of
America. The Boone and Crockett Club was founded originally in
1888 for adult men, to "promote manly sport with the rifle" and "to
promote travel and exploration in wild and unknown or partially
known lands." Membership in the club required shooting "at least
one adult male . . . of each of three of the various species of American
large game," including bears, cougars, buffalo, mountain sheep, elk,
or moose. Theodore Roosevelt soon transformed it into a training
club for boys.[31]

The Knights of King Arthur and the Men of Tomorrow were both
founded by Rev. William Forbush, author of *The Boy Problem* (1901)
and promoter of the single-sex summer camp for boys—"a place
where the boy will develop those savage virtues which are the admiration of boyhood." The Men of Tomorrow promoted a general fellowship of men who worked with boys to study boys and their needs,
and it provided a clearinghouse for information on adolescent male
development. The Knights, also for boys alone, was an order of
Christian knighthood designed to "bring back to the world, and especially to its youth, the spirit of chivalry, courtesy, deference to
womanhood, recognition of noblesse oblige, and Christian daring."
Modeled after collegiate Greek-letter fraternities, the Knights reveled
in "ritual, mystery, and parade" in an effort to bring fraternalism to
high-school and non-college-bound boys.[32]

By far the most important organization developed to rescue boys
from their mothers and reunite them with a virile ideal was the Boy
Scouts. Originally founded in England by Lord Baden-Powell, the
Scout vision stressed a kind of obedient and patriotic masculinism,
seeking to create strong men who were also reliable workers. "God
made men to be men," he wrote. "We badly need some training for
our lads if we are to keep up manliness in our race instead of lapsing
into a nation of soft, sloppy, cigarette suckers."[33] In the United
States, scouting achieved its greatest success—over sixty-six million

members since its founding in 1910 by Ernest Thompson Seton.[34] The Boy Scouts of America (BSA) yoked the development of manhood to a nostalgic re-creation of the frontier, partly through an evocation of Indian legend and lore and partly through the celebration of the white man's conquest.[35] The Scouts were thus "laying the foundation for a self-disciplined and virile generation worthy to follow the trail of the backwoodsman," wrote Frederick Jackson Turner in 1918. "It is an inspiring prophecy of the revival of the old pioneer conception of the obligations and opportunities of neighborliness." As Daniel Beard put it in the Boy Scout manual, *Scouting* (1914):

> Wilderness is gone, the Buckskin man is gone, the painted Indian has hit the trail over the Great Divide, the hardships and privations of pioneer life which did so much to develop sterling manhood are now but a legend in history, and we must depend upon the Boy Scout Movement to produce the MEN of the future.

This was well beyond Seton's intentions. In his mind the frontiersmen were "almost without exception, treacherous, murderous, worthless, without the shadow of a claim on our respect but this: at best, a measure of dull brute grit." Seton celebrated the other "real man" of the West, the noble savage, the Indian. From its origins the BSA minted several "traditional" Indian rituals. Headdress feathers became merit badges, symbolizing exemplary activity; Indian names or animal totems became symbolic representations of the troop.[36]

Seton's antimilitarism and his devotion to Native-American symbols and rituals combined with personal awkwardness, eventually clashed with other scouting leaders, who embraced both the idealized frontiersman and Baden-Powell's efforts to turn the Boy Scouts into a patriotic youth brigade. Beard claimed that Seton's love of the Indian was unpatriotic, and most other Scout leaders agreed. One critic told Seton that there were simply "too many Americans who think of Indians as dirty and loafing degenerates or as savages" for them to remain symbols of manly heroism to young boys. By 1915 Seton was forced to resign.[37]

What the Boy Scouts did take from Seton, however, was his critique of urban industrial society. "Not one boy in a thousand is born bad," he wrote. Boys have their badness thrust upon them. They are made bad by evil surroundings during the formative periods between school and manhood—evil surroundings that included "money grubbing machine politics, degrading sports, cigarettes, false ideals, moral laxity and lessening Church power—in a word 'City rot.'"[38] The urban, civilized life was unmanly: "I do not know that I ever met a boy that would not rather be John L. Sullivan than Darwin or Tolstoi," he wrote in *Boy Scouts of America: A Handbook of Woodcraft, Scouting, and Life-Craft* (1910), the first Boy Scout handbook and manual. The natural, gender-based division of labor had been compromised; in a chapter of his memoirs, "Primitive Home Life," he wrote:

> the home life of those frontier days was nearly ideal; and so sanely adjusted that it may have valuable lessons for those who are wrestling with modern problems of living. . . . Those who cooked and sewed did so in an atmosphere of fun and frolic. The men no more thought of serving food than the women did of cutting the firewood. When a woman was seen chopping or carrying in firewood it was understood to mean that she had failed as a man-charmer. When a man was seen washing the dishes it was understood . . . that he had absolutely surrendered, and become the service thrall of some female enchanter.

Modern society had instead given us the sissy—"more effeminate than his sister, and his flabby muscles are less flabby than his character."[39]

Seton loved play, but the city promoted indolence. A chief culprit, he believed, was spectator sports, which sapped virility; "spectatoritis," he wrote, was turning "robust, manly, self-reliant boyhood into a lot of flat chested cigarette smokers with shaky nerves and doubtful vitality." Like school and church, spectator sports created a "society for sitting still."[40] The Scouts were thus a kind of "boys' liberation movement" to free young men from mothers, teachers, and the more generally enervating experiences of the soft city life.[41]

For the college man collegiate fraternities promoted male bonding through rough play and Christian service. Although fraternities had existed at elite universities since the turn of the nineteenth century, they received their greatest push at large midwestern campuses in its last decades. In part this growth was an effort to retain a homosocial

white world in a rapidly diversifying collegiate environment, shield-
ing "traditional" students from women, blacks, and non-Protestants
(especially Jews) who now sought admission. Land-grant institutions, universities like Michigan, Wisconsin, and Illinois, were required to admit all state residents—and thus were ripe for
fraternities. Harvard's Hasty Pudding Club, founded in 1795 as a literary society, was transformed into a social club in 1875 in order to
keep out the newcomers. "The great glory of the American college
fraternity is that throughout a chaotic era of educational experimen-
tation, and throughout its own groping for its proper place and function, it has remained the one last stronghold where youth did for
itself and by itself" was the way fraternity historian and booster Francis Shepardson put it.[42] By the end of the century, fraternities had become an important part of collegiate life, with over 140,000 members
by 1898.[43]

MEN'S RITES

But what would become of these boys when they grew up to be men,
away from their college fraternity, their Scout troop, the other
Knights? What would become of the men trapped in cities and towns
across the country, locked into work lives and lifestyles that left them
sedentary, soft, without vigor? G. Stanley Hall might have suggested
that adult men were supposed to be more civilized, but few wanted
to lose the hardy camaraderie, the rough-edged naturalism, the tried
and tested brotherhood of their youth. Today, they might sign up for
a "Wildman" weekend retreat. At the turn of the century, they developed a variety of organizations that together provided a kind of masculinist alternative to the female-controlled home and church, places
where men could experience the succor of domestic life and Christian fellowship and still feel like men.

For one thing, American men joined fraternal organizations. The
turn of the century was "the Golden Age of Fraternity," according to
W. S. Harwood in 1897. By his count, over three hundred different
fraternal orders boasted a total membership of 5.5 million American
men out of a total adult male population of about nineteen million.
This included 810,000 Odd Fellows, 750,000 Freemasons, 475,000

Knights of Pythias, 165,000 Red Men, as well as members of the dozens of smaller orders that gathered weekly at the more than 70,000 fraternal lodges nationwide.[44] At a time of economic stagnation and thwarted economic mobility, fraternal orders provided a symbolic arena in which men were moving up the ladder. At virtually every meeting someone was being initiated into the next, highest, level of the order. (If they couldn't make it in the economic sphere, here, in the comfort of the lodge, American men experienced the mobility the nation had promised but had not delivered.) But more than that, fraternal orders allowed men to reinvent themselves as men, to experience the pleasures and comforts of each other's company and of cultural and domestic life without feeling feminized. The lodge was alternately the artisanal guild, the church, or the home—or all three simultaneously.

Most fraternal orders provided an innocuous brew of bogus medieval mysticism, symbolic frontier naturalism, and ritualistic birth and rebirth, providing middle-class men with the fellowship, friendship, and solace that they no doubt otherwise missed. Work in the Gilded Age, before Progressive social reforms, demanded cutthroat competition and aggression, while the family home made men feel enervated and feminized in the wife's domain, and the combination left them lonely for each other's company. Fraternal orders filled that gap, re-creating the artisanal brotherhood, the masculine parish, and the patriarchal family that had virtually disappeared from men's lives. But mostly they provided male friendship. As one member of the Knights of Pythias put it in a speech in Fall River, Massachusetts, in 1885:

> A man may be in a crowd and have no society. He stands within himself alone. He feels tremendously this loneliness, and is impelled to make friends, even if it be among the worst of mankind. Here appears one of the reasons why so many of our sons and daughters are rushed to their ruin on entering our large towns and cities . . . lack of socialness and the rarity of neighborhood society . . . is very marked in our large cities and towns. It is a growing evil of our times. . . .
>
> The world at large, cold in self-aggrandizement, eager in pursuit of wealth, careless of the comforts or even the lives of others, feels, per-

haps, no sympathy with our symbolic rites and ceremonies; laughs to scorn our friendship. . . . The wealth and pleasure of the outside world are but tinsel when compared with the pure gold of brotherly love.[45]

Some fraternal organizations that catered especially to working-class men provided death and sickness benefits and paid funeral costs in this era before life insurance, thus reinventing the craft guild's economic as well as social ties. If the ideals of craft brotherhood "could no longer be realized at work, they could instead be transferred to a purely social setting, the fraternal order."[46]

Fraternal orders attempted to create a domestic sanctuary outside the home—a place where men might experience fellowship and intimacy without the feminizing influence of women. The fraternal order was the motherless, wifeless, womanless family, the band of brothers. The lodge was also the unfeminized church, devoid of clucking mother hens and effete ministers. Victorian men felt deprived of a "religious experience with which they could identify" and a "family environment in which they could freely express nurturing and paternal emotions," writes the historian Mark Carnes. Fraternal orders filled both needs. They offered a "theology" that contrasted sharply with the milquetoast moralism of feminized Protestant doctrine and a "mass secret society" where men could express "feminine" emotions like compassion, nurturance, and charity.[47]

Male bonding promoted "the innate principles of man's nature," wrote a Reverend Mr. Beharrell about the Order of Odd Fellows. Here was a vehicle for men to reclaim emotion without feeling feminized in the process. Men needed "banding together to stimulate their better affections," noted Reverend A. B. Grosh of the Odd Fellows in 1871. But one could only experience these emotions in the company of other men; the man who was emotional with women was despised as effeminate. Men could publicly shun feminization and privately act like women.[48]

The centerpiece of fraternalism was the initiation ritual.[49] Nearly all initiation rituals were modeled on baptism, the symbolic death of the old profane (workaday) man and his symbolic rebirth into the community of believers. The initiate is not yet a man as he undertakes an arduous journey to prove his worthiness and "grow up" into a new family of brethren and patriarchs. Such ceremony rested on secrecy and inversion and the appropriation of symbols of those very groups against whom fraternal members were framing their identities. Thus did middle-class, white-collar men proclaim their artisanal brotherhood (Modern Woodmen, Mechanics of the World), complete with symbols of the Heroic Artisan, like hammers and compasses. And thus did white men call themselves Red Men, imitating warrior initiations of the very tribes their fathers had "pacified." And thus did men don aprons and dresses to symbolically give birth to other men.[50]

Across the Atlantic, Sigmund Freud was theorizing that women grow up envying men. In the lodges, however, men seemed to be the envious ones. They "played Indian," they pretended to be artisans, and they pretended to be women. But they refused to let women join, and they certainly acted manly at home—a place from which they could now, with justification, remain distant. The real purpose of fraternal orders, wrote suffragist Matilda Joslyn Gage, was "to set one sex against another."[51]

Some of them, unfortunately, also set one race against another. Several fraternal orders, such as the Order of United American Mechanics, the Red Men, Modern Woodmen, the Loyal Order of the Moose, and the Patriotic Order of the Sons of America, admitted only whites by charter. (The OUAM also had a paramilitary arm, the Loyal Legion, which marched in parades and was used as a racist and nativist goon squad.) In the first two decades of the century, a resurgent Ku Klux Klan deliberately linked fraternal brotherhood to a violent vision of American manhood dedicated to expunging "aliens" and destroying "commodity madness" as well as excessive taxation, religious infidelity, and political corruption. Klan rhetoric was soaked with masculine imagery.[52]

In addition to fraternal orders, there was at this time an explosion of men's organizations and clubs. Some like the Elks (1868), Eagles (1898), and the Sons of the American Revolution (1889), were middle-class service organizations that doubled as homosocial retreats for white, native-born men. These groups' "backslapping camaraderie helped meliorate the personal and community disturbances associated with modernization" and "countered the impersonality associated with an increasingly bureaucratic society."[53]

Others were exclusively patrician enclaves, like Boston's Somerset Club, New York's Knickerbocker Club, Philadelphia's Rittenhouse Club, San Francisco's Bohemian Club, and the Union Club in both Boston and New York. These clubs were conceived of as islands of "homogeneity in an ever-diversifying urban ocean," places where, according to one genteel member, a gentleman found "his peculiar asylum from the pandemonium of commerce and the bumptiousness of democracy." And they were alternative families, where each member could "seek the comforts of a home," according to one magazine article in 1876.[54] Some held weekend retreats, where the men could escape urban riffraff and experience the tonic freshness of the outdoors and the good fellowship of their upper-class comrades at the same time.[55]

Despite its continued popularity among some American men today, fraternalism had lost much of its luster by 1925. Membership declined precipitously, and many organizations folded. It wasn't that young men born after 1900 were any less "afflicted with the fathers' and grandfathers' gender anxieties"; those anxieties were as palpable as ever. But the institutional solutions that men used to ground their manhood and to dispel those gender anxieties moved from separate clubs outside the world of work to the corporation itself and to male bonding within the work world as well as in the world of leisure— from spectator sports to the local golf course.[56] By the 1950s Ralph Cramden and Ed Norton's weekly sojourns to the Loyal Order of the Raccoons had become a joke, a couple of pathetic men searching for something they could never find—that homosocial Eden away from their wives that would revirilize them to take command in the very homes that were supposed to have been their castles.

THE MANLY CHURCH

Just as men sought to re-enter their homes and to create islands of manly nurture outside the home, they also moved to reclaim religion and create an alternative institution for manly religious expression and the socialization of their sons. Religion had been women's domain, and the sentimental piety and obsessive moralism were experienced by men as a brake on manly exuberance and a constraining critique of marketplace competition. A typical Protestant minister catered to an increasingly female clientele; he "moved in a world of women," writes cultural historian Ann Douglas. And as religion became more feminized, men's attendance at church dropped precipitously. As early as 1832 Frances Trollope had commented that she'd never seen a country "where religion had so strong a hold upon the women or a slighter hold upon the men" than the United States, and Joel Hawes claimed that "the sword of the spirit" is "muffled up and decked out with flowers and ribbons." No one listened to ministers any longer "except women and superstitious men," as one critic put it. "Religion in the old virile sense has disappeared," lamented Henry James, Sr., at mid-century, "and been replaced by a feeble Unitarian sentimentality."[57]

Feminized religion was graphically illustrated by late nineteenth-century Protestant iconography. Jesus was commonly depicted as a thin, reedy man with long, bony fingers and a lean face with soft, doelike eyes and a beatific countenance—a man who could advise his congregations to love their enemies or turn the other cheek, while gazing dreamily heavenward. Ministers emulated this pacific angel; one was favorably described by contemporaries as having an "almost feminine sensibility," an expression as "bland and gentle as a woman's," with "a most amiable spirit, with much of the ethereal in his countenance," while another had "poetry in his countenance and manners as well as in his mind and heart."[58] Was this a model for turn-of-the-century manhood? One Methodist minister described a man's transformation upon accepting Jesus into his life:

> It is wonderful to see a great burly man, mostly animal, who has lived under the dominion of his lower nature and given rein to his natural tendencies, when he is born of God and begins to grow in an upward and better direction. His affections begin to lap over his passion. . . . The strong man becomes patient as a lamb, gentle as the mother, artless as the little child.

No wonder men had developed their clubs and fraternal orders as alternative religious institutions and used the saloon or the Grange Hall as their secular temples. "Have we a Religion for Men?" asked Howard Alan Bridgeman in 1890.[59]

Enter Muscular Christianity—a religious movement designed "to bring manliness in its various manifestations to church and to keep it awake when it got there." In its first incarnation Muscular Christianity was imported from England through the novels of Charles Kingsley and Thomas Hughes, which fused a hardy physical manliness with ideals of Christian service.[60] Thomas Wentworth Higginson picked up the call in a series of articles in the *Atlantic Monthly* from 1858 to 1861. "The professional or business man, what muscles has he at all?" Higginson inquired in "Saints and Their Bodies" (1858), an essay that promoted athleticism as a way to build manly and moral character. Higginson warned Protestants that Roman Catholics were far more hardy and had greater stamina and admonished parents who said of their "pallid, puny, sedentary, lifeless, joyless, little offspring, 'He is born for a minister,'" while the "ruddy, the brave and the strong are as promptly consigned to a secular career!"[61]

The goal of the Muscular Christians was to revirilize the image of Jesus and thus remasculinize the Church. Jesus was "no dough-faced, lick-spittle proposition," proclaimed evangelist Billy Sunday, but "the greatest scrapper who ever lived." Look to Jesus, counseled Luther Gulick of the YMCA, for an example of "magnificent manliness." Books such as *The Harvest Within* (1909), *Building the Young Man* (1912), *The Call of the Carpenter* (1913), *The Manhood of the Master* (1913), *The Manliness of Christ* (1900), *The Manly Christ* (1904), and *The Masculine Power of Christ* (1912) portrayed Jesus as a brawny carpenter, whose manly resolve challenged the idolaters, kicked the money changers out of the temple, and confronted the most powerful imperium ever assembled. This was no "Prince of peace at any price."[62]

One common strategy was to recast Jesus as the first Heroic Artisan, a "working man," whose "bench work gave him experimental knowledge of life" where he "toiled but never whimpered."[63] Pictures and drawings of Jesus at his carpenter's bench, with sleeves rolled up, leather apron around his torso, and his strong set eyes gazing heavenward, fused the sacred and the muscular. Bouck White's *The Call of the Carpenter* (1913) went further, retelling Jesus's story as a socialist allegory. According to White, Rome was "a world wide confederation of aristocracies for the perpetuation of human servitude," composed of effeminate parasites.[64] Jesus was the working-class hero, "a skilled artisan," a "master of his craft . . . who took pride in his work." Roman oppression made it impossible for him to earn his living by the sweat of his brow, and so he became a "working class agitator," whose mission it was to "awaken the proletariat."[65]

Jesus was not, however, simply some testosterone-juiced, muscle-bound lout. "The Carpenter did not make his impress upon history through any advantages of physique, but through a master intellect, coupled with a master heart and will." And those who followed him were not passive little sheep. They burned Rome, didn't they? So today, White claims, as civilization is "threatened with the sleeping sickness," the working class, led by a masculine Jesus, will be the nation's savior. "Stiffened by manly fibre, refusing doles of charity, the working class shall be the saviors of a civilization threatened with dry rot."[66]

This revirilized Jesus was remarkably adaptable to other political agendas. Some Muscular Christians sounded a more militaristic tone, recasting Jesus as a kind of religious Rambo, always ready to fight. The Ku Klux Klan signed on to its own version of Muscular Christianity, invoking the manly Christ, who was "a robust, toil-marked young man" who "purged the temple with a whip," according to Hiram Wesley Evans, a Georgia Imperial Wizard. The Church of Christ in America would be tempered by "the red blooded and virile" into a "thing of rugged steel . . . forged in the terrific stress . . . of wresting a continent from savages and from the wilderness."[67] Others retained the emphasis on Christian service and social reform but towards decidedly different purposes, including ministering to the poor and to unemployed black men.[68]

In the Muscular Christian iconography, Jesus had dark hair, calloused hands, and a well-developed physique. Gone was the sad, sweet man with flowing robes and pacific gaze. And gone was the image of the religious life as sedentary and feminizing. Muscular Christians looked for the "exacting masculine pages of their Bible," the study of which was "worthy of the best time and mightiest effort of the manliest man," writes the historian Gail Bederman. Bible study "produces a virility, a ruggedness of character, an altruistic spirit, a hopeful temper, a power of patience and endurance, a fearlessness, a stability of manhood that nothing else gives," gushed Rev. Luther Peacock in 1915. Sunday schools must offer a "ruddy religious reality" to students. Prayer was "a manly duty"; faith was "mountain moving, galvanic," according to Rev. Billy Sunday.[69]

Sunday was the most famous of all Muscular Christian—that former professional baseball player who became America's foremost itinerant evangelical preacher. The fleet, former right fielder for the Chicago and, later, Pittsburgh baseball teams left his lucrative athletic career for the ministry not because baseball was immoral but because it was amoral—because "morality was not an essential to success; one may be a consummate rogue and a first class ball player," as he explained in 1893. Triumphing over childhood physical frailty—he was sickly and scarcely able to walk as a child and had to be carried around on a specially made pillow—Sunday transformed himself into a strong, sinewy physical specimen whose boundless energy was injected into his rousing tent sermons. Sunday "brought bleacher-crazy, frenzied aggression to religion"; one journalist effusively described a Billy Sunday sermon thus:

> He stands up like a man in the pulpit and out of it. He speaks like a man. He works like a man. . . . He is manly with God and with everyone who comes to hear him. No matter how much you disagree with him, he treats you after a manly fashion. He is not an imitation, but a manly man giving all a square deal.[70]

Sunday's mission was the complete transformation of feminized religion, to "strike the death blow at the idea that being a Christian takes a man out of the busy whirl of the world's life and activity and makes him a spineless effeminate proposition," he claimed. A Christian cannot be "some sort of dishrag proposition, a wishy-washy, sissified sort of galoot, that lets everybody make a doormat out of him. Let me tell you, the manliest man is the man who will acknowledge Jesus Christ." Sunday offered his followers a "hard muscled, pick-axed religion, a religion from the gut, tough and resilient," not some "dainty, sissified, lily-livered piety."[71]

Sunday took on the church establishment in colorful rhetoric, from biblical scholars (those "anemic rank skeptics" who would "dissolve the atoning blood of Jesus into mist and vapor") to their cronies, intellectuals ("fudge-eating mollycoddles" who would rather eat "fried oysters and tea" than red meat). Protestant ministers had become "pretentious, pliable mental perverts" who worked hand in glove with the idle rich, those lazy slackers—"big, fat, hog-jowled, weasel-eyed, pussy-lobsters." "Lord save us from off-handed, flabby cheeked, brittle boned, weak-kneed, thin-skinned, pliable, plastic, spineless, effeminate, ossified, three karat Christianity," Sunday thundered.[72]

One sermon, "The Fighting Saint," brought these themes together, as Sunday attacked both industrial capitalism and liberal Protestantism as enervating conspirators. "Men are feeding their muscle and bone and sinew into the commercial mill that grinds out the dividends . . . and the men who get the dividends sit by and watch it," he roared. The only solution was not the moral equivalent of war, but "moral warfare" itself. "Moral warfare makes a man hard. Superficial peace makes a man mushy," he argued. "The Prophets all carried the Big Stick." Don't tell me about the peaceful, gentle Jesus, Sunday admonished. "Jesus Christ could go like a six cylinder engine," he claimed. "I'd like to put my fist on the nose of the man who hasn't got grit enough to be a Christian."[73]

Here was a religion rippling with hard muscles, manly grit coupled with moral resolve, a faith that could move mountains. Like other masculinist efforts to counter feminization, Sunday's brawny theology did not extend to blacks or non-native-born Americans. "If they don't like it here, let 'em go back to the land where they were kennelled," he snarled.[74] And it was a potent mix: In a 1914 *American Magazine* poll of "the Greatest Men in the United States," Sunday tied for eighth place with Andrew Carnegie and Judge Ben Lindsey.[75]

Sunday was so successful that others quickly imitated his method. The Men and Religion Forward Movement of 1911–1912 was a church-based spinoff that sought to bring into Protestant denominations the virile ardor that Sunday inspired in his rural tent sermons and sought especially to bring men back into established churches. "The manly gospel of Christ should be presented to men by men," argued M&RF leader Henry Rood in "Men and Religion." Women "have had charge of the Church work long enough," agreed movement founder Fred Smith.[76] The movement "swept the country like a spiritual storm," according to one observer, increasing by up to 800 percent the number of men coming to church. The M&RF movement was most noted for organizing weeklong community-based revivals for young men and boys to help these revirilized Christians act ethically and manfully in their communities, "closing brothels, passing dance hall regulations, working for adequate garbage collection, or better housing regulations, or an open dialogue between business leaders and the city's unions."[77] For the men of the Men and Religion Forward Movement, manly religion implied strength and social concern.

TR, THE STRENUOUS LIFE, AND BULLY MANHOOD

The fin de siècle mission to thwart feminization and revirilize boyhood—and by extension, manhood—reached its symbolic apotheosis in Theodore Roosevelt. TR "epitomized manly zest for the new imperial nation in part because of his jaunty energy, but also because his image brought together both aspects of the new myth: the top rung of the ladder of social aspiration and the gladiatorial animal arena sensed at the bottom." America's self-proclaimed and self-constructed "real man," Roosevelt was, as he proclaimed, a completely Self-Made Man.[78]

Roosevelt's story of self-creation begins, as all such stories do, with his triumph over the body. He was, he recalled in his autobiography, "a sickly and delicate boy, [who] suffered much from asthma, and frequently had to be taken away on trips to find a place where I could breathe." On one of those trips, to Europe, he was seasick most of the time and rarely came on deck. Here was a "shy and timid boy, frail in body . . . thin, pale, asthmatic, outwardly the typical 'city feller,' " as the *Boy's Life of Theodore Roosevelt* put it. "Teedie," as his family affectionately called him, was a childhood wimp; his father constantly exhorted him to "make your body."[79]

Making his body was also a strategy for making his political image. Entering politics in the early 1880s, TR was called "Young Squirt" and "Jane Dandy" by the local press, and the *New York Star* threw in a little gay-baiting by calling him "our own Oscar Wilde." Roosevelt needed "to attain a state of manliness, and attempt to exorcise through exercise his effeminizing sickness, and at the same time . . .

attempt to masculinize and thereby strengthen his political position."[80] And where would a wimpy upper-class sissy go to make his body and thereby remake his political image?

Out west, of course. Roosevelt arrived in the Dakota territory in April 1885, determined to try his hand at ranching in the rapidly disappearing Old West. Like Owen Wister, Frederic Remington, and other eastern boys, Roosevelt had journeyed west to stake a claim on his manhood. On his arrival a reporter from the *Pittsburgh Dispatch* observed "a pale, slim young man with a thin piping voice and a general look of dyspepsia about him . . . boyish looking . . . with a slight lisp, short red moustache and eye glasses"—in short, the "typical New York dude." A local railroad man recalled "a slim, anemic-looking young fellow dressed in the exaggerated style which newcomers on the frontier affected, and which was considered indisputable evidence of the rank tenderfoot." Locals found him initially a laughingstock, calling him "Roosenfelder" and "Four Eyes" and "the Eastern punkin-lily." When he first mounted his horse, he tapped it and said meekly, "Hasten forward quickly there," which made local cowboys double over with laughter; the phrase soon became part of Badlands lore.[81]

But TR persevered and eventually triumphed over his effete dudeism, becoming the embodiment of "strength, self-reliance, determination," the three terms which defined his vision of manhood. He became a booster of the western cure, claiming that he owed "more than I could ever express to the west" because the frontier brings out manly virtues—mutuality, honor, self-respect—not the "emasculated milk-and-water moralities" of the eastern elite.[82] This personal credo for his self-making became the basis for a moral and political philosophy.

Using himself as the example, Roosevelt expressed fears that "overcivilization was sapping the strength of the civilized few, who therefore needed remedial training in barbarism, violence, and appropriation."[83] In two speeches, "The Strenuous Life" (1899) and "The Pioneer Spirit and American Problems" (1900), Roosevelt railed against "the cloistered life which saps the hardy virtues," the "flabbiness" and "slothful ease," and trumpeted the call for the "strenuous life." In G. Stanley Hall's terms, overcivilized adult men needed to recall more of their barbarous, prehistoric youthfulness. Roosevelt used his fears of feminization—of men with "small feet and receding chins"—to great political effect, equating individual manliness with national strength and international power:

> We cannot avoid the responsibilities that confront us in Hawaii, Cuba, Porto Rico, and the Philippines. All we can decide is whether we shall meet them in a way that will redound to the national credit, or whether we shall make of our dealings with these new problems a dark and shameful page in our history. . . . The timid man, the lazy man, the man who distrusts his country, the over-civilized man, who has lost the great fighting masterful virtues, the ignorant man, and the man of dull mind, whose soul is incapable of feeling the mighty lift that thrills "stern men with empires in their brains"—all these, of course, shrink from seeing the nation undertake its new duties; shrink from seeing us build a navy and an army adequate to our needs; shrink from seeing us do our share of the world's work, by bringing order out of chaos in the great, fair, tropic islands from which the valor of our soldiers and sailors has driven the Spanish flag. . . .
>
> I preach to you, then, my countrymen, that our country calls not for the life of ease, but for the life of strenuous endeavor. The twentieth century looms before us big with the fate of many nations. If we stand idly by, if we seek merely swollen, slothful ease and ignoble peace, if we shrink from the hard contests where men must win at hazard of their lives and at the risk of all they hold dear, then the bolder and stronger peoples will pass us by, and will win for themselves the domination of the world.[84]

Of course, not everyone was so taken with Roosevelt's strenuous manhood. Thorstein Veblen, John Dewey, and William James, for example, demurred from the national frenzy about bodybuilding and the sporting life that Roosevelt heralded. Dewey cringed at the "hunting psychosis" he saw, while Veblen saw sports as a case of "arrested spiritual development," and James cast Roosevelt's vision as adolescent ranting. In a letter to the *Boston Evening Transcript*, he wrote:

> Although in middle life, and in a situation of responsibility concrete enough, he is still mentally in the Sturm and Drang period of early ado-

lescence, [he] treats human affairs . . . from the sole point of the organic excitement and difficulty they may bring, gushes over war as the ideal condition of human society, for the manly strenuousness which it involves, and treats peace as a condition of blubberlike and swollen ignobility, fit only for huckstering weaklings, duelling in gray twilight and heedless of the higher life.[85]

A few singled out military heroics as a particularly disingenuous method for retrieving manhood. Joseph Dana Miller's "Militarism or Manhood?" (1900) posed the choice most starkly. To Miller, Teddy Roosevelt was a "splendid savage," whose "Rough Rider government is conspicuously lacking in those higher qualities which single out the man from among men." In fact, the battlefield was ill suited for demonstrations of manly valor:

> The anesthetics of battle smoke and battle music induce a sort of somnambulistic state in which prodigies of valor may be performed. . . . Most of the heroism exhibited on the battlefield is of the passive sort, disguised somewhat by the activity of maneuver, the noise of cannon, and the onslaught of cavalry. There is but a small individual initiative to the great fighting mass.

Instead of celebrating military manhood, Miller advocated a revision of the word *courage* to include being "true to conscience."[86]

Such throwbacks to barbarian forms of manhood were understood by some feminist women to bode ill for the advancement of equality. "I think a whole community of men in perfect physical condition would be very interesting, but extremely dangerous," wrote a woman in a letter to the editor of *Physical Culture* in 1901. And Charlotte Perkins Gilman worried, in her impassioned treatise *Women and Economics* (1899), about "the brutal ferocity of excessive male energy in the marketplace as in a battlefield" and the "destructive action of male energy in its blind competition," whether in sports, war, or business.[87] But few were persuaded by these critics, many of whom could be dismissed as whining women or their emasculated male sycophants.

The formation of the Rough Riders catapulted TR into the hallowed halls of American myth even during his lifetime. The symbolic capstone in TR's manly edifice, the Rough Riders consisted of twelve troops, all but one of which came from the western territories. This last, K troop, came from the East and was widely believed to be a collection of "swells" who had left their upper-class men's clubs, dress suits in their hands, to follow Roosevelt up San Juan Hill. And yet, though some may have worn "the broad brim hat and had the bronze cheek of the plains" while others "bore the unmistakable stamp of the student and club man," as one reporter wrote, all "mingled with easy good fellowship." The *Denver Post* reported (21 May 1898) in verse the western men's perspective:

> We was somewhat disappointed, I'll acknowledge, fur to see
> Such a husky lot o' fellers as the dandies proved to be,
> An' the free an' easy manner in their bearin' that they had
> Sort o' started the impression that they mightn't be so bad.
> There was absence of eye-glasses, an' of center parted hair,
> An' in social conversation they was expert on the swear,
> An' the way they hit the grub pile sort o' led us to reflect
> That our previous impressions mightn't prove so damn correct.

To which the *Chicago Tribune* (12 July 1898) responded two months later with the easterners' perspective:

> They scoffed when we lined up with Teddy,
> They said we were dudes and all that;
> They imagined that "Cholly" and "Fweddie"
> Would faint at the drop of a hat.
> But let them look there in the ditches,
> Blood-stained by the swells in the van,
> And know that a chap may have riches,
> And still be a man![88]

From TR's bully pulpit he promoted the strenuous life for individuals for their sake and as a grounding for the American Empire. He opposed policies as "half-and-half, boneless," and railed against opponents he called spineless sissies. Westward continental expansion had been "the central and all-important feature of our history," he wrote, and imperialist annexation completed the project. He promoted work as heroic, moralizing, and masculinizing and saw big capital and finance as emasculating effeminacy—he chastised the "moneyed and semi-cultivated classes" for "producing a flabby, timid type of character which eats away at the great fighting qualities of our race." He prescribed sports to develop a hardy masculinity—but only "the true sports for a manly race," like running, rowing, playing football and baseball, boxing and wrestling, shooting, riding, and mountain climbing. No president before or since has been a bigger promoter of exercise and sporting life, and no number of photos of Bill Clinton jogging, George Bush sailing or fishing, or (in another vein) Michael Dukakis driving a tank could make the point as emphatically as one photograph of TR in full hunting gear. In a 1900 essay, "The American Boy," TR echoed the same sentiments as Muscular Christians and bodybuilders:

> Forty or fifty years ago the writer on American morals was sure to deplore the effeminacy and luxury of young Americans who were born of rich parents. The boy who was well off then . . . lived too luxuriously, took to billiards as his chief innocent recreation, and felt shame in his inability to take part in rough pastimes and field sports. Nowadays, whatever other faults the son of rich parents may tend to develop, he is at least forced . . . to bear himself well in manly exercises and to develop his body—and therefore, to a certain extent, his character—in the rough sports which call for pluck, endurance, and physical address.[89]

Roosevelt celebrated the outdoors as an "arena for manly exertion," creating five national parks, sixteen national monuments, and fifty-one wildlife refuges in America's wilderness and organizing the Boone and Crockett Club to promote the strenuous life for young boys.[90] He sought personal refuge in the wilderness. As late as 1912, after the failure of the Bull Moose crusade, a fifty-three-year-old Roosevelt joined an expedition to probe the unknown regions of the Amazon. Encountering a river never before seen by a white man, Roosevelt was ecstatic—though the expedition cost the life of one of the explorers in an accident that nearly killed all of them. The river was named Rio Roosevelt by the Brazilian government. Asked why he risked his life for such a venture, he replied that he "had to go. It was my last chance to be a boy."[91]

TR consistently opposed coeducation and praised G. Stanley Hall's efforts to stem the tide of feminization. Although he supported woman suffrage "tepidly," he was more fervent in his support of women as mothers and furious at college-educated women who delayed childbearing or did not bear children at all. Accusing them of race suicide, TR suggested that women who did not bear at least four children be tried as traitors to America, much the same way as soldiers who refused to fight. A woman who "shirks her duty as wife and mother is . . . heartily to be condemned," he commented in an address to the Congress of Mothers in 1908. "We despise her as we despise and condemn the soldier who flinches in battle." Soldiers and mothers—this was the way TR saw the fulfillment of patriotic duty.[92]

As G. Stanley Hall had identified adolescence as a fragile stage requiring special attention to a rite of passage, so too did Roosevelt offer an adolescent nation the initiation rites to a new manhood. TR was the perfect embodiment of American-as-adolescent boy-man. His definition of manhood was reactive, defensive, an effort to repudiate a sickly childhood and his overdependence on his mother. To accomplish this end, Roosevelt engaged in a frenzied effort to appear a man in every possible guise; "changing frenetically from cowboy costume to safari suit to Rough Rider garb, Roosevelt shot more animals, rode more dusty trails, and risked his neck in combat" more than any American before John Wayne.[93] TR wore every conceivable hat—warrior, statesman, pioneer, cowboy, Rough Rider, president, father, historian, hunter, husband, naturalist, diplomat, and preacher—a well-rounded yet hardened manly presentation. For TR, manhood was a relentless test to be proved constantly and in every arena in which men find themselves. And it was enormously "attractive to men who feared their own impotence in an increasingly complex world."[94]

As for TR, so too for the typical American man, although on a far less grandiose scale. As turn-of-the-century American men had confronted social and economic limits to their ceaseless struggles to prove themselves, they had sought to preserve their workplaces as sites of self-making, shaped their bodies as disciplined instruments of their will to succeed, worked to rescue their sons from feminiza-

tion, created parallel institutions of nurture and solace for themselves, and occasionally escaped to a more pristine earlier world
where men were men and women virtually nonexistent. Yet all these
heroic efforts could not bring the relief that American men so desperately sought. As the nation faced a new century filled with new opportunities and new obstacles, the Self-Made Man would again
return to these themes, as well as invent some new ones.

Part Three

THE NEW MAN IN A NEW CENTURY, 1920–1950

CHAPTER 6

Muscles, Money, and the M–F Test

MEASURING MASCULINITY BETWEEN THE WARS

> Want to call it Men Without Women [because] in all of these
> [stories], almost, the softening feminine influence through
> training, discipline, death or other causes [is] absent.
> —Ernest Hemingway letter to Maxwell Perkins (1927)[1]

> Under ideal circumstances, the father should be an under-
> standing, tolerant but virile and decisive male. The mother
> should have the gentleness, patience, and passivity usually
> associated with womanhood. Any mixture, such as an
> effeminate father and an aggressive masculine mother is
> likely to be disconcerting to the child and accentuate
> homosexual tendencies.
> —Dr. George W. Henry (1937)[2]

In William Wellman's powerful film *Heroes for Sale* (1934), a World War I veteran returns home and tries to rebuild his life. Unable to find a job, he stoops to a terrible humiliation: He enters a pawnshop to hock his Congressional Medal of Honor. The pawnbroker is sympathetic but unwilling to offer any money. As the camera pulls away from their faces over the counter, we see that the entire display case is full of pawned medals. Heroism had lost its currency in the postwar world.

The end of the war was supposed to usher in a "return to normalcy," as President Warren G. Harding promised in 1920, a time not for "heroism but healing." And for American men, the postwar era was to be a period not of "agitation but adjustment." The turn-of-the-century crisis had been resolved—or at least temporarily muted. Wartime victories had allowed a generation of men to rescue a threatened sense of manhood, and the expanding peacetime economy augured well for economic success. In their work and in their families, middle-class men entered the decade optimistically convinced that they could be successful breadwinners.

But such reassurances soon gave way to a new restiveness. For one thing, as we've seen, military glory had proven elusive to the typical G.I. Joe, and cases of "paralysis, convulsions, paraplegias, tics and tremors of the battle-weary (and battle-shy) soldiers" flooded the psychiatric literature after the war.[3] For another thing, the workplace was anything but stable and reliable. The optimism ushered in by the Roaring Twenties was ushered out by the Great Depression and widespread unemployment in the 1930s. Never before had American men experienced such a massive and system-wide shock to their ability to prove manhood by providing for their families.

Even before the economic collapse of 1929, though, men's work was an increasingly unreliable proving ground, more the domain of the dull and the routine of George Babbitt than the arena of vaulting ambition and adventure of TR. Robert and Helen Lynd's masterful portrait of middle America, *Middletown* (1929), and its sequel, *Middletown in Transition* (1937), showed a people barely making do, clinging to traditional forms and unable to move beyond them, with high rates of unemployment, poverty, and divorce. Other social scientists saw a dramatic attenuation of social mobility during the decade and the rise of technicians and managers at the expense of ordinary workers.[4] Even the traditional image of the heroic toiler had become tainted by associations with bolshevism.

That's not to say that men weren't counseled to aim high. But frequently the targets were different. One sales manual urged readers to develop "the faculty of combativeness" by exercising each morning before going out to sell. "Combativeness functions through the shoulder and arm muscles as shown by the soldier, prize fighter, athlete, etc., and, well developed, it imparts a feeling of enthusiasm, physical vigor, and power of decision that no other faculty can give," wrote Clarence Darrow in a 1925 review of these manuals.[5] And rapid upward mobility brought no peace from anxiety; just different ones from lack of mobility. As Frederick Millard put it in his popular self-help book *What a Man Goes Through* (1925):

> Men are made nervous not so much, as a rule, by their business cares, as by various things they are doing that may become uncovered to a certain extent, or are liable to be uncovered at some particular time when they are just reaching a height where they want everything to run smoothly. It is when the express train is speeding along at the highest rate of speed that there is the most danger.[6]

Men certainly had it tough. One woman called for "a movement for the emancipation of men" in a letter to the editor of the *Nation*, while another writer asserted that "from a masculine standpoint life is not necessarily that unending round of Sunday dinners without dishwashing, that ever verdant series of love affairs without responsibility, that continuing vaudeville of adventure and daring which literary ladies imply it to be." There was, he concluded sadly, "no salvation in being born a man."[7]

Especially not once the Great Depression took hold. Wages plummeted and relief rolls swelled. The unemployment level rose from about 16 percent in 1930 to just under 25 percent barely three years later and remained almost as high for the rest of the decade.[8] With nearly one in four American men out of work, the workplace could no longer be considered a reliable arena for the demonstration and proof of one's manhood. And many men simply lost faith in a system that prevented them from proving their masculinity in the only ways they knew.

Even those men who still had jobs had a more difficult time proving their manhood in the 1930s. The competition was increasingly fierce, and the complexion of the American workforce seemed to many to grow increasingly dark. Racial exclusion and anti-immigrant nativism were again a recourse for some who searched for a foundation for secure manhood. Successive waves of immigrants were depicted as less mentally capable and less manly—either as feminized and effete or wildly savage hypermasculine beasts—and thus likely to dilute the stock of "pure" American blood. Henry Goddard's series of bogus mental tests, published in 1917, in which immigrants were given a battery of tests in English, led him to conclude that 79 percent of Italians, 80 percent of Hungarians, 83 percent of Jews, and 87 percent of Russians were "feeble minded." In 1923 Carl Bingham concluded definitively that there had been a "gradual deterioration in each class of immigrants" who had come to the United States in each succeeding five-year period since 1902. This deterioration was easily measured, he discerned, by the decreasing percentage of "nordic blood" in each group. (Bingham, incidentally, was no racist hack writer, nor did he toil at the margins of academic respectability. A psychology professor at Princeton, he was later secretary of the College Entrance Examination Board and the designer of the Scholastic Aptitude Test.)[9] Followers of Lathrop Stoddard, author of the bestseller *The Rising Tide of Color* (1920), envisioned a global struggle to the death between white and dark races.

Such themes echoed through the debates about the Immigration Act of 1924, which passed after bitter controversy and significantly reduced the number of immigrants allowed into the nation. Both the American Legion and the American Federation of Labor urged increasingly restrictive immigration policies, especially regarding Asians.[10] A particularly virulent campaign targeted Filipinos. Since the United States had acquired the Philippines during the Spanish-American War, Filipinos were classified as "American nationals" and therefore entitled to unrestricted immigration. And their number grew quickly, from only 406 Filipinos in the United States in 1910 to 5,603 in 1920 and 45,208 in 1930. Racist impulses were suffused with gender imagery, and this new immigrant group was tainted with the same gender slanders that earlier groups had been. "He is not our 'little brown brother,'" thundered the secretary of an agricultural association in California. "He is no brother at all! He is not our social equal." And as before, exclusion from brotherly equality rested on twin gender images; the Filipino was both too little and too much of a real man.

Racism and nativism bore the mark of gender, as if depicting "them" as less manly would make "us" feel more manly. So on the one hand, Filipinos were cast as effete and effeminate; small with delicate features, great dancers who possessed an obsessive concern with clothing and appearances. On the other hand, Filipinos were hypermasculine "jungle folk," "scarcely more than savages," with "primitive moral codes." Filipino sexuality was demonized. "The love making of the Filipino is primitive, even heathenish," and certainly "more elaborate," noted a deputy labor commissioner in 1930, while a businessman called them "hot little rabbits." In 1934 Congress passed the Tydings-McDuffie Act, giving the Philippines independence, in part so that Filipinos would no longer enjoy their status as American nationals, and thus their immigration could be restricted.[11]

Black men remained a most potent screen against which middle-class white men played out their masculinity. The widespread migration of blacks to northern cities (and within the South, from rural to urban areas) spurred recharged efforts to exclude blacks from public office and residential neighborhoods. Fewer than 10 percent of southern blacks lived in urban areas in 1890; by 1910 that percentage had more than doubled, reaching 25 percent in 1920 and 31.7 percent in 1930. A resurgent Ku Klux Klan flourished in the 1920s, especially in midwestern border states like Indiana. Lynchings and other forms of racist violence increased dramatically during the decade.

A special issue of The World Tomorrow in 1924 examined the re-emergence of the Klan with alarm. While one theologian criticized the Klan's "small boy buffoonery," anthropologist Alexander Goldenweiser's insightful cultural critique located the rise of the Klan in the "vacuity and dullness of our lives," the "insufferable boredom" that accompanied industrial society. The Klan, he argued, is "the back parlor of Main Street. It is the conventional, the mediocre, those whose outlook is narrow and whose imagination is deadened by routine, who seek stimulation in the activities of the secret brotherhood."[12]

Like the Klan, fraternal orders experienced a brief rise in popularity in the 1920s, but they also came in for increased criticism.

Though these roughly eight hundred secret societies met "a hunger which lies near the heart of gregarious mankind," as Devere Allen wrote, their rituals were obviously hokey:

> Once in so often you march around your lodgeroom in the wake of the Grand Exalter of the Holy Mackerel and absorb a certain luster from his glittering insignia. . . . You get the same thrill from the secret grip and password that you got from the gang which met after school in the Enchanted Haymow of the Sacred Neighborhood Barn.

and their politics were dangerous:

> Is it a healthy thing when so many Americans have to satisfy the normal craving for brotherhood by banding together on a basis which ineradicably mingles loyalty to one's own group with superiority and sometimes hostility to one's next door neighbor of another color, creed, or nationality?[13]

The Klan and other fraternal orders appropriated many of the iconographic images of Jesus first used by the Muscular Christians, declaring their campaign a "holy crusade" and depicting Jesus as "the unflinching, accomplishing, achieving Christ, because he was the purposeful, steadfast, determined Christ," as their national newspaper, *Searchlight*, put it in 1924.[14] But the Jesus who really caught the public's attention in the 1920s was a businessman. Bruce Barton's best-selling *The Man Nobody Knows* (1924) fused Muscular Christian images of Jesus with the persona of the modern corporate leader.

Typically, Jesus had been portrayed as "a frail man, under-muscled, with a soft face—a woman's face covered by a beard" and wearing a "benign but baffled look, as though the problems of living were so grievous that death would be a welcome release." Nonsense, railed Barton.

> A physical weakling! Where did they get that idea? Jesus pushed a plane and swung an adze; he was a successful carpenter. He slept outdoors and spent his days walking around his favorite lake. His muscles were so strong that when he drove the money changers out, nobody dared to oppose him!

With muscles "hard as iron" and nerves of steel, Jesus was extremely attractive to women and "the most popular dinner guest in Jerusalem." Most important, Jesus was the founder of a modern capitalist enterprise, harnessing his immense talents, organizational skills, and business acumen to create the first multinational corporation. "He picked up twelve men from the bottom ranks of business and forged them into an organization that conquered the world." Jesus, it turns out, was the epitome of the Self-Made Man, a successful entrepreneur who showed none of the anxieties and insecurities that so plagued his followers. He was the businessman's role model.[15]

At the same time that business was appropriating religious imagery, it also seized on the male-only retreats that had formerly been an escape from corporate culture. General Electric, for example, sponsored camps for lighting engineers and managers and brought in potential managerial recruits whose "behavior in sporting events, casual discussions, and the ceremonies of camp life gave officers of the company more insight into their strengths and weaknesses." Homosocial retreats had been harnessed to serve the corporation rather than provide solace away from corporate life or even, as in some earlier cases, serve as a form of resistance to corporate domination.[16]

These efforts to remasculinize the workplace through bonding and to exclude others from it echoed similar strategies in earlier decades, but they fell short of providing men with the security they seemed to promise. The chief problem seemed to be women, both at work and at home, as coworker, as mother, and as symbol. Everywhere men looked, there were women. Work itself was seen as increasingly feminized, with more women employed in increasingly feminine offices— hardly the world of real men at all. The enactment of woman suffrage in 1920 accelerated women's entry into the public sphere. By 1920 about one-half of all college students and one-third of all employed Americans were women.[17] The New Woman of the 1920s was that fast-talking, cigarette-smoking libertine known as the Flapper—an exciting and passionate sexual and gender nonconformist.

But many men did not find her especially enchanting. The public sphere has been "invaded" by the "gentler sex," warned Frederick Millard in *What a Man Goes Through*. "It may take a century or more for men to realize the situation and be sufficiently good sports to tolerate such changes," he conjectured, somewhat more presciently than he might have imagined. Architect Charles Loring recalled that the "offices of our grandfathers were without steel frames and files, without elevators and radiators, without telephones—and without skirts." One writer in *Fortune* magazine was disgusted with "this callipygian nation of silk knees, slender necks, narrow fingers, and ironic mouths which has established itself upon our boundaries," while another surveyed the modern office and found "an ocean of permanent waves." "Feminism really spells Masculinism," wrote Anthony Ludovici in 1927, since "exposure to the vicissitudes and asperities of the struggle for existence brings out the combative, predatory, and latent male side of female nature, and represses and impoverishes its dependent, peace loving and sequacious side."[18]

The acerbic journalist H. L. Mencken's *In Defense of Women* (1918) offhandedly praised women in the abstract while chastising feminists and suffragists as unhappy women incapable of getting a man to the matrimonial altar. Mencken portrayed American men as egoistic boobs—"complete masculinity and stupidity are often indistinguishable"—manipulated into marriage by conniving women. He saved his bitterest invective for men who supported feminism and would even stoop so low as to marry a woman's rights advocate.

> The iron-faced suffragist propagandist, if she gets a man at all, must get one wholly without sentimental experience. If he has any, her crude manoeuvers make him laugh and he is repelled by her lack of pulchritude and amiability. All such suffragists (save a few miraculous beauties) marry ninth-rate men when they marry at all. They have to put up with the sort of cast-offs who are almost ready to fall in love with lady physicists, embryologists, and embalmers.[19]

The acclaimed novelist Sherwood Anderson's astonishing little tract *Perhaps Women* (1931) echoes many of these same themes, but he drew a very different conclusion. Modern man is lost, Anderson wrote, "impotent" before the machine, which dominates industrial production. "The machines make me feel too small. They are too complex and beautiful for me. My manhood cannot stand up against them yet. They do things too well. They do too much." As a result,

Anderson wrote, in words reminiscent of Tocqueville a century earlier, man was a member of a lost sex with

> no definite connection with the things with which he is surrounded, no relations with the clothes he wears, the house he lives in. He lives in a house but he did not build it. He sits in a chair but he did not make it. He drives a car but he did not build it. He sleeps in a bed but he does not know where it came from.

But instead of urging women's exclusion, Anderson welcomed them, because he found "something still alive in the women that seems to be going dead in the men." Women, he believed, were "not enervated spiritually by the machines. They have not accepted the vicarious feelings of power, got from machines, as their own power." And so women, grounded still in the world of humanity, were men's only salvation.[20]

Few others agreed. For most men the Depression was emasculating both at work and at home. Unemployed men lost status with their wives and children and saw themselves as impotent patriarchs. And the consequences for men were significant. One New Jersey man spoke of his intense guilt as a father: "I haven't had a steady job in more than two years. Sometimes I feel like a murderer. What's wrong with me that I can't protect my children?"[21] And a young boy wrote to President and Mrs. Roosevelt about his father's plight. Concerned that his family would not get relief, the boy asked for help directly from the president. "My father, he staying home. All the time he's crying because he can't find work. I told him why are you crying daddy, and daddy said why shouldn't I cry when there is nothing in the house. I feel sorry for him. That night I couldn't sleep. The next morning I wrote this letter to you."[22]

Who was to blame? And what were men to do about it? The author Norman Cousins provided rather simpleminded answers. After noting that the unemployed ranks numbered about ten million, roughly the same number of women who were working, he suggested that we "[s]imply fire the women, who shouldn't be working anyway, and hire the men. Presto! No unemployment. No relief rolls. No Depression."[23] Other theories and solutions were not much more clear-

headed. One idea was to try and pin the blame on the wives for revic-
timizing their depressed nonbreadwinning husbands. As one psychiatrist explained it to journalist Studs Terkel, the men

> hung around street corners and in groups. They gave each other solace.
> They were loath to go home because they were indicted, as if it were
> their fault for being unemployed. A jobless man was a lazy good-for-
> nothing. The women punished the men . . . by withholding themselves
> sexually. By belittling and emasculating the men, undermining their pa-
> ternal authority, turning to the eldest son. These men suffered from de-
> pression. They felt despised, they were ashamed of themselves.[24]

Even if contemporary readers would not go as far as to blame the
women for reemasculating their husbands in some twisted incestuous plot, we cannot but feel compassion for men whose twin identities as worker and father/husband, a dual identity expressed in the
term "breadwinner," was suddenly eroded, seemingly beyond repair.

No wonder Dale Carnegie's *How to Win Friends and Influence People* (1936) was so instantly popular. Carnegie counseled readers away
from traditional measures of achievement like status, wealth, and
power—a wise move if one was going to be one of the era's few success stories. One's worth was not to be measured by standing out
from the crowd but rather by fitting in. Carnegie's self-help scheme
seemed to shift attention away from external trappings of success to
more internal forces, one's personality. But twentieth-century "personality" meant something very different from nineteenth-century
"character"—it meant a malleable instrument that could be applied
in social situations to elicit from others approval and advancement.
"You have a product and that product is yourself," Carnegie counseled his would-be salesmen readers. Men, Carnegie argued, could
shape their personalities to shape the forces around them and get
what they wanted.[25]

But the picture of men that emerges in the 1930s is far more
poignant than Carnegie's best-selling boosterism. In her pathbreak-
ing study *The Unemployed Man and his Family* (1940), the sociologist
Mirra Komorovsky provided a poignant description of the impact of
this dual erosion of the identities of father and worker. The unemployed man "suffers from deep humiliation" since he fails in his core

role as family provider. He appears bewildered, "as if the ground has gone out from under his feet."[26] Many of the men Komorovsky interviewed described the "humiliation within the family" as the "hardest part" of being unemployed. With their economic power eliminated, their status as head of the household is eroded and with it their sense of manhood. "When a man is at home all day he cannot possibly command as much respect as when he returns to the family for a few hours of concentrated conversation," noted one man, who felt himself to be a "fallen idol" without a job. "Before the Depression," says another, "I wore the pants in this family and rightly so. During the Depression I lost something. Maybe you call it self-respect, but in losing it I also lost the respect of my children, and I am afraid I am losing my wife."[27]

In the face of this humiliation, men turned increasingly to their sons. "The boy is building from infancy his conception of manhood, making little models in his thoughts of how he must behave to be a man," wrote one parental adviser, with words that must have reassured the unemployed fathers who were reading her words. "How false models in his thoughts must be when they are based on brief, superficial glimpses of his father."[28] By the 1930s three-fourths of American fathers said they regularly read magazine articles about child care, and nearly as many men as women were members of the PTA. "In the highest animal of all, man, we should expect to find the fullest development of a father's concern for his offspring," began one passage in a popular advice book from 1933. "A man would be lower than some beasts if he did not protect and aid his wife while she was bearing his child and if he did not do everything he could for it through all the years in which it needed his care."[29]

The workplace was too unreliable to enable men to prove their manhood; in fact, it eroded their authority at home. Many men returned to the home, as fathers and modest breadwinners (instead of as economic success stories), in the hope that by raising their sons to be successful men they could themselves achieve some masculine redemption. The popularization of psychology in the 1920s gave their efforts at domestic participation a real boost. Freudian ideas had made parental participation in child rearing a requirement of healthy gender development and appropriate sexual development. If a boy's behavior was feminine or a young girl's behavior was masculine, it was a sure sign that something had gone wrong in the child's psycho-sexual development, and it was feared that homosexuality might be the result. If women abandoned their traditional role as homemakers or if men abandoned their traditional role as breadwinners, it could easily send the wrong message to young children. Psychology thus weighed in with a new imperative in the re-separation of spheres, providing ammunition against women's efforts to enter the public sphere and ensuring, as Sinclair Lewis wrote in *Babbitt*, that "the realms of offices and of kitchens had no alliances."[30]

In the 1920s and 1930s many writers attempted to resolve parental anxieties by discouraging women from working outside the home and encouraging men to participate in domestic life. For exam-ple, some states passed laws that required that women teachers be fired when they married so they would be unable to attempt mother-hood and career. Popular magazines and advice manuals promoted both a "child care" movement and a "domestic science" movement meant to reassure women that motherhood and housework were deeply satisfying vocations whose importance could not be overesti-mated. Mother's Day, originally established to celebrate women's work *outside* the home (in civic projects such as public sanitation and as volunteers in hospitals during the Civil War), was transformed, via a mass-marketing campaign that delighted the nation's florists, into a celebration of traditional homemaking. Meanwhile, in 1924 the Na-tional Congress of Mothers' Clubs changed its name to the Parent-Teacher Association (PTA) in an effort to encourage fathers to join without fear of feminization.[31]

Some of the era's most popular psychological writers gave parents an increasing role to play in their children's development. J. B. Wat-son's enormously influential *Psychological Care of Infant and Child* (1928), a precursor to Dr. Benjamin Spock's post–World War II best-seller, implored parents to be actively involved with their children. "Children are made, not born," he wrote, but to Watson, the makers of children were women; one searches in vain through his work for specific references to fathers. "Parents" really meant "mothers," and the work's preoccupation was with the outcomes for the children, not for any intrinsic pleasures or important experience of the parents themselves. So while Watson promised mothers directly that they, too, could raise bankers, artists, merchants, if they set their minds to it, his interest was in the children's appropriate adjustment. And mothers must be especially attentive to the threat of overdoing maternal affection. In a chapter called "The Dangers of Too Much Mother Love," Watson cautioned readers against becoming the mother whose "heart is full of love which she must express in some way. She expresses it by showering love and kisses" upon her hapless children, threatening their independence and mental health, and transforming healthy little boys into whining, dependent mama's boys. "Mother love is a dangerous instrument," he declared. Mothers must guard against their own impulses in shaping the lives of their offspring, which could be accomplished by separating boys from girls and treating them differently. "Never hug [boys] and kiss them, never let them sit on your lap," Watson advised.[32]

Pushing women out did not assuage the pressure on young fathers: They were required, on the one hand, to be successful or at least competent and employed; on the other, to be active parents to their sons at home so that their sons would not remain overly attached to their mothers. Half a century before women claimed that they wanted to "have it all"—successful careers and warm, intimate family lives—men experienced having it all as an enormous headache.

Homosexuality hovered like a specter over anxious parents, who were convinced that effeminacy in young boys was a certain predictor of adult male homosexuality. About a third of Joseph Collins's *The Doctor Looks at Love and Life* (1926), one of the decade's best-selling advice books to parents, was devoted to male homosexuality. In general, he argued, the homosexual was effeminate and unmanly—a "man of broad hips and mincing gait, who vocalizes like a lady and articulates like a chatterbox, who likes to sew and knit, to ornament his clothing and decorate his face." Clement Wood's advice book *Manhood* (1924) tried to reassure anxious young men that homosexuality was a stage of development out of which they would soon, thankfully, pass. Wood maintained that a twelve-year-old boy's proclivities were 40 percent autosexual, 50 percent homosexual, and 10 percent heterosexual; by puberty the percentages shifted to 20, 30, and 50 percent, respectively.[33]

One popular song, "Masculine Women! Feminine Men!" (1926), ridiculed the entire reversal of sex roles to a catchy ragtime beat. While "Sister is busy learning to shave, / Brother just loves his permanent wave"; while "Auntie is smoking, rolling her own, / Uncle is always buying cologne"—no wonder the singer laments that "it's hard to tell 'em apart today." And the consequences are dangerous: "You go in to give your girl a kiss in the hall / But instead you find you're kissing her brother Paul."[34]

These anxieties about homosexuality and effeminacy quickly and decisively eroded the casual acceptance of the gay male subculture in major American cities. The late 1920s and 1930s witnessed a "pansy craze," as new fears of gay men were raised. Once, a gay man had been seen as "an effeminate fairy whom one might ridicule but had no reason to fear"; now, though, tabloid newspapers terrified and titillated their readers with stories of degenerate child molesters who committed acts of unspeakable depravity. Gender arrangements were now so fragile, it seems, that "even a glimpse of an alternative might endanger them." The closet was hastily built, and gay men immediately pushed into it.[35]

The inseparable pair of parental fears—feminized boys and homosexuality—led many educators and popular writers to counsel continued separation of boys and girls. The YMCA suggested in a 1926 project booklet that "former efforts in Boys' Work centered upon keeping boys busy at almost any activity in order to keep them away from evil associations and bad environments. What boys learned in these substituted activities was not a matter of great concern." Contact with girls could dilute boyhood purity, and idleness would breed evil thoughts and deeds. Strenuous exercise was thus even more vital to healthy boyhood; as William Allen White wrote in 1926:

> The boy of today, whose work is done by machinery, who lives in a house heated by oil, or gas, or who lives in an apartment where the janitor does the work, would grow flabby and weak if he had to depend upon the work that he could not do about the home. But he comes

home from the gymnasium and the ball field, renewed in body, and takes up his task of mastering the intricate problems of the radio and the motor-car, a young giant refreshed.[36]

Paternal involvement was seen as a central element in a healthy boy's development. The new fatherhood confirmed the new role of the psychologist as expert and the idea that the perilous project of shaping manhood began in the family, not in the workplace.

These new demands on parents were accompanied by increased marital tensions. In 1920 the nation recorded 7.7 divorces per one thousand marriages. Throughout the decade the number spiraled; between 1922 and 1926 there was one divorce for every seven marriages, and by 1927 there was one for every six—about sixteen times the rate for 1870.[37] One source of strain was men's efforts to juggle their roles as fathers and breadwinners, especially when many fathers weren't very good at child rearing and had been so poorly trained for it. Men were groomed for their work outside the home and had spent little time or energy developing the skills necessary for successful nurturing of children—patience, compassion, tenderness, attention to process.

Mocking fatherly incompetence became something of a boom industry in the popular press of the 1920s and 1930s, as in new comic strips like *Blondie* and plays like Clarence Day's *Life with Father* (1936). Dagwood Bumstead, Blondie's bumbling, incompetent, anti-hero husband, is the epitome of the breadwinner as boob:

> an untidy office worker who has to run every morning to catch the bus from his suburb; he is generally incompetent, inefficient, greedy (he is always sneaking into the kitchen to make the most incongruous sandwiches), sensuously lazy (outside the office and the kitchen he spends much of his time trying to take a nap on the sofa or laze in a hot bath), generally good tempered and easygoing but given to sudden and completely ineffective rages.

Dagwood isn't a *bad* man—he's "kind, dutiful, diligent, well meaning within his limits"—but he is a bad *man*, a model of the impotent patriarch, whose life would disintegrate without the quiet efficiency of his wife. He's so ineffectual that he doesn't even have the comic strip named after him![38] And Clarence Day, who said he saw more of his own father as an adult than as a child, portrayed Father as a blustering tyrant but one whose bark was decidedly worse than his bite.

If fatherhood was precarious, motherhood was out of the question. In one of their first films, *Their First Mistake* (directed by Hal Roach), Laurel and Hardy set up housekeeping together, and then decide to adopt a child without first consulting Ollie's wife. When she walks out, the two determine to raise the child alone. Before long, they are sleeping together, with the baby, in Hardy's marriage bed. In one scene Laurel sucks the bottle that Hardy holds. In another scene Hardy holds the bottle in his lap and strokes it so hard that the milk spurts out of it. Such hilariously homoerotic domesticity is soon shattered when the couple receive notice that Hardy's wife is suing for divorce and that Laurel is named as corespondent.[39]

These examples point to the difficulty men seemed to have grounding a sense of manly accomplishment in their performance as parents. The depression had forced many men to abandon their faith in the marketplace as certain to confirm their manhood. Masculinity had to be reconceived so that any man could achieve it and pass it on reliably to his sons. Here, again, psychology offered some solace. Masculinity could be redefined away from achievement in the public sphere and reconceived as the exterior manifestation of a certain inner sense of oneself. Masculinity could be observed in specific traits and attitudes, specific behaviors and perspectives. If men expressed these attitudes, traits, and behaviors, they could be certain that they were "real" men, regardless of their performance in the workplace. If a man failed to express these attitudes, traits, and behaviors, he was in danger of becoming a homosexual. A key psychological question for the 1930s, then, was whether homosexuality could be "cured" by a healthy dose of manhood.

Enter Lewis Terman, a Stanford psychologist best known as the creator of the Stanford-Binet intelligence test, the famous IQ test that measured supposedly innate intelligence. In a 1936 volume *Sex and Personality*, Terman and his associate Catherine Cox Miles reported on the development of an "M-F" scale that measured gendered behaviors, attitudes, and information by which parents could plot their child's "mental masculinity and femininity"—the successful acquisition of gender identity.[40] "If holding a job to support a family could no longer be counted on to define manhood," writes the contemporary psychologist Joseph Pleck, "a masculinity-femininity test could."[41] Terman and Miles were not the first behavioral scientists to attempt to measure masculinity and femininity and apply those measures to sexual orientation, but they were the most thorough. Their M-F scales included an inventory of 456 items and utilized state-of-the-art psychological personality tests—including Rorschach ink blots, projective tests that asked children to imagine themselves in various situations, and standard attitude and knowledge inventories—to position each test taker along a continuum from Masculinity at one pole to Femininity at the other.[42] An individual's answers to these tests, administered primarily to adolescents, both boys and girls, in junior high schools across the country, spelled success or failure in acquiring gender-appropriate identity. For those who failed, their gender-inappropriate personality could be seen as a kind of "early warning system" for future homosexuality. Parent-teacher conferences would be scheduled, and a variety of therapeutic interventions might be proposed, including, encouraging him to engage in more manly activities like sports and outdoor work, and prohibiting him from continuing what pleasure he might have taken from reading, painting, cooking, or listening to classical music.[43]

Never before had masculinity undergone such rigorous scrutiny and elaboration; never before had it seemed so urgent that it do so. Terman and Miles had recodified masculinity and femininity so that they could be measured and charted, thus encoding into science what had been historical and social arrangements. (I have included one of their sample tests, which was labeled the Attitude-Interest Analysis Test to disguise its purpose to test takers, as an appendix.) For example, some sentence completions made it clear that there were some things that men should—and should not—know:

1. Things cooked in grease are boiled (+), broiled (+), fried (-), roasted (+).

2. Most of our anthracite coal comes from: Alabama (-), Colorado (-), Ohio (-), Pennsylvania (+).

3. The "Rough Riders" were led by: Funston (-), Pershing (-), Roosevelt (+), Sheridan (-).
4. The proportion of the globe covered by water is about: 1/8 (-), 1/4 (-), 1/2 (-), 3/4 (+).

(To keep score in the way that Terman and Miles suggested, score a "+" for a masculine response and a "-" for a feminine one. I don't think they intended their own biases to be so transparent.)

A large set of items elaborated what men should and shouldn't feel; respondents were to quantify their emotional responses (a lot, some, a little, none) to explore the following emotions:

Anger: being called lazy, seeing boys make fun of old people, seeing someone cheat on an exam.
Fear: being lost, deep water, graveyards at night, Negroes.
Pity: a fly caught on sticky fly paper, a man who is cowardly and can't help it, a wounded deer.
Wickedness: boys teasing girls, indulging in 'petting,' not brushing your teeth, being a Bolshevik.[44]

The M-F test also included possible careers and their obvious sex typing, such as librarian, auto racer, forest ranger, florist, soldier, music teacher. There were also lists of character traits (loud voices, men with beards, tall women) that testees were asked to either like or dislike and a list of children's books (*Robinson Crusoe, Rebecca of Sunnybrook Farm, Little Women, Biography of a Grizzly*) that they either liked, disliked, or had not read. Another set of questions included a list of famous people one could either like or dislike (Bismarck, Florence Nightingale, Lenin, Jane Addams). Not having read a book or knowing about a famous person was seen as gender-conforming or nonconforming for both girls and boys. Other questions included what one might like to draw if one were an artist (ships or flowers); what one might like to write about if one were a newspaper reporter (accidents, theater); and where you might like to go if you had plenty of money (hunt lions in Africa or study social customs, learn about various religions or see how criminals are treated).

Finally, the test included some self-reporting about the respondent's own behaviors and attitudes. *Yes* or *no* items (here listed with the scoring of a *yes* answer) included:

Do you rather dislike to take your bath? (+)
Are you extremely careful about your manner of dress? (-)
Do people ever say you talk too much? (+)
Have you ever kept a diary? (-)

The M-F test was perhaps the single most widely used inventory to determine the successful acquisition of gender identity in history and was still being used in some school districts into the 1960s. The test also formed the basis for virtually all studies of gender-role acquisition ever since, including some of the most widely used psychological tests in our nation's history: the Strong Vocational Interest Blank (1943), the Guilford Temperament Survey (1936), and the Minnesota Multiphasic Personality Inventory (1972), still the most widely used complete personality inventory.[45]

Despite their comprehensiveness, Terman and Miles came up with results that were counterintuitive to the prevailing norms of the day. For example, they found that boys brought up "chiefly or only" by their mothers were somewhat more masculine than boys brought up by only their fathers or by both parents. It was equally true that girls raised "chiefly or only" by their fathers were slightly more feminine than those raised by only their mothers or by both parents. "So much for the necessity of a same-sex role model for learning cultural sex role norms!" writes one historian of psychology.[46]

Terman and Miles—and Terman's student, E. Lowell Kelly—also compared the scores of heterosexuals with those of "active" and "passive" homosexuals and found that male heterosexuals and active male homosexuals had very similar gender-role identities and that passive male homosexuals manifested a feminine gender-role identity. (The "normality" of the active homosexuals was theoretically finessed by the authors, whose theories required that all homosexuals be pathologized.) The authors argued that the etiology of homosexuality was always to be sought in the sinews of gender-role acquisition:

too demonstrative affection from an excessively emotional mother, especially in the case of a first, last, or only child; a father who is unsympathetic, autocratic, brutal, much away from the home, or deceased; treatment of the child as a girl, coupled with lack of encouragement or opportunity to associate with boys and to take part in the rougher masculine activities; overemphasis on neatness, niceness, and spirituality; lack of vigilance against the danger of seduction by older homosexual males.[47]

Here was one of the origins of the infamous "strong mother = gay son" theory, which held sway for many decades, well into the 1970s. Contemporaneous research by the psychiatrist George W. Henry came to similar conclusions, as have several significant subsequent studies.[48] Masculinity was now understood to be learned through the successful mastery of a variety of props. Freudian assumptions grounded the male sex role—a static, ahistorical container of attitudes, behaviors, and values that are appropriate to men and define masculine behavior.[49] A century after Henry Clay first declared us a nation of self-made men, American men were no closer to experiencing a secure, confident sense of themselves as men.

Of course, that didn't keep men from trying. And if acquiring all the traits and attitudes and behaviors that Terman and Miles had identified seemed too overwhelming, one could at least appear to have acquired them. As at the turn of the century, a masculine physique could signify success, physical strength could stand in for strength of character. Arms could make the man—or at any rate biceps and triceps could. At least that was true according to Charles Atlas, who stressed transformation of the body instead of the personality and taught successive generations of American men how to pump themselves up. Atlas provided an answer to the M-F test, a course of study the end of which was certain manliness.

Born in Italy in 1893, Angelo Siciliano came in 1910 to the United States, where he lived in a poor section of New York City with his mother. He was a scrawny young man, "a 97 pound runt . . . skinny, pale, nervous, and weak."[50] One summer day Angelo had the experience that changed his life: "One day I went to Coney Island and I had a very pretty girl with me. We were sitting in the sand. A big, husky, lifeguard . . . kicked sand in my face. *I couldn't do anything* and the girl felt funny. I told her that someday, if I met this guy, I would lick him." The girl quickly moved elsewhere on the beach, and Angelo, walking home, dejected, passed a large poster of the mythic Atlas lifting the weight of the world. He resolved at that moment to transform his body into one capable of heroic feats, and he adopted the name of his mythic hero.

After personally transforming himself into "the world's most perfectly developed man,"—the nation's "ranking collection of muscles," according to one reporter—the newly renamed Charles Atlas developed his technique of "dynamic tension," a muscle-making and -building technique designed to turn other "ninety-seven-pound weaklings" into real he-men.[51] His advertisements in boys' magazines and later in comic books asked, "Are You a Redblooded Man?" and "Do You Want to be a Tiger?" One text from his 1925 ads linked physical success to economic success. "It's the Tiger Men who grab everything they want these days. The new race of Tiger Men win the battles . . . in the mad, dizzy, jazzy marathon for personal success! They whiz by you in stunning limousines. They have fine homes and bulging bank accounts." Atlas built his first gymnasium in 1927, and during the Depression, business for this man-making machine was never better. By 1942 he was running the most successful mail-order business in the nation's history, and this "muscle maestro" boasted that he had added no less than six million pounds of solid rippling flesh to the American body.[52]

Atlas saw his mission as building "a perfect race, a country of perfect human masterpieces," a statement with dangerous overtones in 1942. Concerned with racial degeneration that derived from sedentary urban life, Atlas saw muscles and exercise as the route to national salvation. As one typical consumer of the Dynamic Tension system wrote: "Some time ago, I enrolled as one of your students. I was very skinny, with small bones. Enclosed you will find my picture taken after faithfully following your instructions. Today I feel that no man can rule or oppress me."[53]

This transformation of wimpy weaklings to "muscular mastodons" was soon echoed in one of the most famous fantasy heroes in history. In 1938 Clark Kent first magically transformed himself into the most courageous, heroic, manly man who had ever lived. Superman was so powerful that he wasn't really from this planet; his transformation was actually the Atlas program in reverse—a superhuman extraterrestrial who transforms himself into a wimpy bespectacled newspaper reporter in order to fit unnoticed into the emasculating metropolis. Yet as fantasy image, Superman gave a promise to every other obsequious American office worker: Behind those glasses and that mild-mannered demeanor beat the heart of the hero. As cartoonist Jules Feiffer writes, Clark Kent was

> Superman's opinion of the rest of us, a pointed caricature of what we were really like. Superman's fake identity was our real one . . . [if] the glasses and cheap suits, when removed, revealed all of us in our true identities [as supermen]—what a hell of an improved world it would have been![54]

Atlas's advertisements for his physical fitness regimen graced that first issue of *Superman* and virtually every issue since.

Superman and Clark Kent sanitized the gendered schizophrenia that had been the stuff of masculine fantasy for some time, making this version of Mr. Hyde every bit as respectable as Dr. Jekyll. And even more sexually chaste. As Clark constantly pursued Lois Lane, seeking the comforts of marital stability, Lois had eyes only for his more manly alter ego, who could not, and would never be, tied down into a life of domestic drudgery. What Clark craved, Superman avoided. Like Natty Bumppo and Huck Finn before him, Superman was also born to run—or rather, to fly.

Heroism was a masculine dream possible only in mythic fantasy or in daytime reverie. James Thurber's biting short story "The Secret Life of Walter Mitty," published in the *New Yorker* in 1939, opened a lens into the psyche of the henpecked husband as an emasculated daydreamer, whose wife has to remind him to wear his overshoes. In his fantasies, though, Mitty is so heroic that he even disdains a handkerchief as he stoically faces a firing squad.[55]

Another fantasy hero was the cynically crusty detective of novels and films. He first made his appearance in the late 1920s in the work of Dashiell Hammett and, in subsequent decades, in the stories by Raymond Chandler and Mickey Spillane. The detective thus joined Tarzan and myriad cowboy heroes as a vehicle for male escapist fantasy. Here, adventurous and cold men stalked the urban jungle, a world where women were either seductive vixens enticing men to their doom or angelic innocents needing their help (but never their marital commitment). The detective was the urban pioneer, making the world safe for women and children. He was, as Hammett wrote, a "little man going forward . . . through mud and blood and death and deceit—as callous and brutal as necessary."[56]

This new hard-boiled tough guy repackaged rugged artisanal manhood for modern urban audiences. Chandler's detective novels celebrated the autonomy of the private eye as Heroic Artisan; his essay "The Simple Art of Murder" provides a most eloquent description.

> Down these mean streets a man must go who is not himself mean, who is neither tarnished nor afraid. . . . He must be a complete man and a common man, yet an unusual man. He must be, to use a rather weathered phrase, a man of honor. He is neither a eunuch nor a satyr. I think he might seduce a duchess, and I am quite sure he would not spoil a virgin. If he is a man of honor in one thing, he's that in all things. He is a relatively poor man, or he would not be a detective at all. He is a common man or he could not go among common people. He has a sense of character or he would not know his job. He will take no man's money dishonestly, and no man's insolence without due and dispassionate revenge. He is a lonely man, and his pride is that you will treat him as a proud man or be very sorry you ever saw him.[57]

And Dashiell Hammett's private eye hero, Sam Spade, was more coldly cynical than his peers, a "defensive loner who is suspicious of all relationships, romantic and otherwise." Which made him all the more manly. "After the high minded detective heroes, their artistic leanings and their elaborate deductions," one ecstatic reviewer cooed when *The Maltese Falcon* was published in 1930, Sam Spade "is as startling as a real man in a shop window full of dummies. His actions and his language will shock old ladies."[58]

Less shocking, perhaps, were many of the era's most celebrated novels and films. But they were equally concerned with helping men cope with increased pressures, scale back their expectations, or at least provide momentary escape. There were rumblings of discontent among American men between the wars, and the fiction of the era expressed it eloquently. Some suggested that the traditional methods for self-making were unreliable in a modern world. For example, Ernest Hemingway's novels suggest the brittleness and vulnerability of male bonding, even as his impulse is to trust homosocial intimacy, especially when compared with relations with the opposite sex. Personally, Hemingway eschewed the upper-class gentility into which he had been born and embraced a rough-hewn artisanal manhood demonstrated and tested in the most highly ritualized ways—boxing matches, bullfighting, hunting, soldiering. His novels are also always about men's relationships with one another—fathers and sons, battle companions, friends on a fishing trip, fellow patients in a hospital, a couple of waiters preparing to close up shop, a bullfighter and his manager, a boy and a gangster. Only these "move him to simplicity and truth," writes Leslie Fiedler, although these men are almost always "maimed, unmanned, victimized." In a review of *In Our Time*, D. H. Lawrence said that Nick Adams, Hemingway's long-term protagonist, may have been "a type one meets in the more wild and woolly regions of the United States" but that he was only really "the remains of the lone trapper and cowboy."[59]

In *Men without Women* (1927), a short story collection, Hemingway's battle-scarred, weary warriors reveal a biting cynicism and emptiness at the core of modern American masculinity. In a hard-boiled, lean, and muscular prose Hemingway searches among the shards of European culture for a lost American manhood. The men are bullfighters, boxers, soldiers, hired gunmen, and the women are unwelcome—they're pregnant ("White Elephants"), prostitutes, deceivers, or fools. In one story, "Soldier's Home," Harold Krebs returns from the front only to feel suffocated in civilian life and tries to disengage from the world, to "live alone without consequences."

In *The Sun Also Rises* (1926), his first full-length novel, Jake Barnes and his comrades wander across the European continent searching for something to believe in. Like many of Hemingway's male characters, their scars leave them either incapable or uninterested in sexual passion with women, interested only in the most chaste bonds among men. Jake's shell-shocked impotence animates his rage at homosexuals and women and his sneering tone toward Lady Brett Ashley. "Somehow they [gay men] always made me angry," Jake says. "I know they are supposed to be amusing, and you should be tolerant, but I wanted to swing on one, any one, anything to shatter that supe-rior, simpering composure"—a composure that was at once, he thought, daintily ineffective and haughtily arrogant. But he reserves some of his bitterest invective for himself. "It is awfully easy to be hard-boiled about everything in the daytime," he admits, "but at night it is another thing."[60]

Other novelists turned their attention to characters who were cap-tives of their own illusions, captives of the American Dream and the vision of the Self-Made Man. Sinclair Lewis's character George Babbitt is a classic self-deceiver; this flabby, would-be-tough midwestern real-tor is constantly pumping himself up with phrases like "gotta hustle" and "real he-stuff." (He names his son Theodore Roosevelt Babbitt to ensure a hypermasculine lineage.) Babbitt's gushing about manhood, in a moment of "hysteric patriotism," at a realtors' convention reveals Lewis's critique of this small-town, small-minded masculine booster:

> The ideal of American manhood and culture isn't a lot of cranks sitting around chewing the rag about their Rights and their Wrongs, but a God-fearing, hustling, successful, two-fisted Regular guy, who belongs to some church with pep and piety to it, who belongs to the Boosters or the Rotarians or the Kiwanis, to the Elks or Moose or Red Men or Knights of Columbus or any one of a score of organizations of good, jolly, kidding, laughing, sweating, upstanding, lend-a-handing Royal Good Fellows, who plays hard and works hard, and whose answer to his critics is a square-toed boot that'll teach the grouches and smart alecks to respect the He-man and get out and root for Uncle Samuel, U.S.A.[61]

When Babbitt does rebel against this "duty of being manly," Lewis al-lows us to see through those illusions, thus giving to American litera-ture a synonym for disaffected suburban manhood.

Much of the era's fiction depicts men attempting to cope with forces that are far beyond their control. Jay Gatsby, in F. Scott Fitzger-ald's *The Great Gatsby*, was a Self-Made Man who rose "rapidly from poverty and obscurity to the highest pinnacles of wealth and power." Gatsby's fall is destined by his own illusions about self-making; he is ultimately "destroyed by an agency which he himself has brought into being."[62] Gatsby is, perhaps, the era's ultimate Self-Made Man, a

compassionate fraud, a hero whose tragic flaw is that he actually believes his own myth of self-creation as the way to realize the American Dream. Gatsby, as Nick puts it, "sprang from a Platonic
conception of himself"; shedding his former identity as Jay Gatz, he
"invented just the sort of Jay Gatsby that a seventeen-year-old boy
would be likely to invent, and to this conception he was faithful to
the end."

After his death, Gatsby's father, Mr. Gatz, shows Nick the young
Gatsby's copy of *Hopalong Cassidy*. Inside the back cover Jay had
neatly printed the word "Schedule," dated September 12, 1906. In
that brief passage, so reminiscent of Benjamin Franklin's prescriptions for self-making over a century earlier, Fitzgerald reveals the
tragedy of the myth of the Self-Made Man and also its allure:

Rise from bed . . . . 6.00 A.M.

Dumbbell exercise and wall scaling . . . . 6.15–6.30   "

Study electricity, etc. . . . . 7.15–8.15   "

Work . . . . 8.30–4.30 P.M.

Baseball and sports . . . . 4.30–5.00   "

Practice elocution, poise and how to attain it . . . . . . 5.00–6.00   "

Study needed inventions . . . . 7.00–9.00   "

GENERAL RESOLVES

No wasting time at Shafters or [a name, indecipherable]

No more smokeing or chewing

Bath every other day

Read one improving book or magazine per week

Save $5.00 [crossed out] $3.00 per week

Be better to parents

Here was a prescription for self-creation—perfecting body, mind, and
presentability. The realization of the Self-Made Man had become a set
of instructions for moral uplift.[63]

Gatsby's self-making took him from the humble Midwest to the
stately Long Island mansions of an aristocratic elite. By contrast,

John Steinbeck conferred a heroic dignity on the pained efforts of the working class to make themselves. No novelist captured the 1930s better than Steinbeck, whose powerful and poignant depictions of Americans' struggle to survive the depression found him a wide audience. Many of Steinbeck's novels center around men made marginal by economic hardship. "The roads became crowded with men *ravenous* for work, *murderous* for work," Steinbeck wrote in *The Grapes of Wrath* (1939). "What's it coming to?" asks Tom Joad. "Fella can't make a livin' no more. Folks can't make a livin' farmin'. I ask you what's it coming to?" And yet each offers temporary solace in human connections, so that the deep love between George and Lennie in *Of Mice and Men* (1937) or the resilience of the family bond, especially Ma Joad, in *The Grapes of Wrath*, offers the only hedge against the pain and isolation of economic marginality: "Guys like us got no fambly," says George to the simpleminded behemoth Lennie in the beginning of a story that is repeated throughout the novel. "They make a little stake and they blow it in. They ain't got nobody in the world that gives a hoot in hell about 'em—"

> "But not us," Lennie cried happily. "Tell about us now."
> George was quiet for a moment. "But not us," he said.
> "Because—"
> "Because I got you an'—"
> "An' I got you. We got each other, that's what, that gives a hoot in hell about us," Lennie cried in triumph.[64]

Such sentiments may seem "austerely mawkish" to contemporary readers, but Lennie's death is the highest expression of George's sacrifice and love.[65] Given how Steinbeck "traffics in the humble dreams of the lowliest workers in an age before social security and unemployment insurance," it is fitting that Aaron Copland was commissioned for the score of the 1939 film of the novel. In most of Steinbeck's novels, we also find a fanfare for the common man.[66]

A fanfare is also offered in the plays of Clifford Odets, who offered a sobering look at men's plight. In *Awake and Sing* (1935) and *Waiting for Lefty* (1935), Odets painted sympathetic portraits of men's search for their souls, for a reason to live, amidst the pain and humiliation of the economic crisis. Calling the American obsession with success a "peritonitis of the soul," Odets wrote against the myth of abundance and described instead the "unmanning fiscal panic" and the "demoralized resignation" that came with the fact of scarcity. In *Awake and Sing* the playwright creates a climate of humiliation and frustration that settles around the Berger household like "a thick fog," according to the theater critic John Lahr.[67] Each of the male characters tries to figure out ways to hedge against that creeping humiliation. Morty's success becomes a weapon to humiliate others, while Sam craves the invisibility of the shamed; stage directions describe Sam as "conditioned by the humiliation of not making his way alone."[68]

While Odets drew on the image of the Heroic Artisan as a model for the new proletarian man, other leftist polemicists used him as a weapon in cultural critique. Socialist critic Michael Gold, for example, called writers like Thornton Wilder a "typical American art pansy" who wrote "Chambermaid literature" with a "homosexual bouquet." "Send us a giant who can shame our writers back to their task of civilizing America," he wrote in *New Masses*. "Send a soldier who has studied history. Send a strong poet who loves the masses and their future. . . . Send an artist. Send a Bolshevik. Send a Man."[69] The Left, claimed these socialists, was more manly than the suburban middle class.

They seemed to get everything—artist, Bolshevik, and man—in the figure of Charles Chaplin, whose films captivated audiences in the 1930s just as his politics and romantic intrigues disillusioned many of them. Chaplin's films, especially *Modern Times* (1936), portray the assembly line as a site of humiliation and alienation, in which the worker is turned into a machine to serve omnivorous cannibalistic machines. Yet the individual working man is not the object of ridicule or even pity but rather, through humor, is rendered with both respect and pathos.

Chaplin was only one of a host of new American celebrities who emerged in the new film era of the 1920s and 1930s. Many early films promised fantasy escape from quotidian routine, and several also served as meditations on manhood. Cecil B. DeMille's *Male and Female* (1919), for example, was an adaptation of J. M. Barrie's play *The Admirable Crichton*.[70] In this film Crichton, a handsome, virtuous butler, possesses admirable manly qualities but is, by immutable circumstances of his birth, destined to serve his moral inferiors—rich courtiers who are languid and idle. The women's suitors are all portrayed as effete fops, while the liveries, butlers, and servants are given a kind of Lawrencian virility and rugged handsomeness. When the entire crew is stranded on a remote desert island, only Crichton is capable of teaching the others to survive, and he becomes the veritable "King of Babylon" as he carries Mary, the daughter of his master, onto the island, limp and lifeless. When the party is eventually rescued, it is not without some remorse and regret on Mary's part, now that she has experienced true virility. In the final scene Crichton serves Mary drinks on a tray. Order is restored, De Mille suggests, but at an enormous cost—the reemasculation of the Heroic Artisan.

Other films fueled fantasies of upward mobility in the midst of economic crisis. Busby Berkeley extravaganzas offered the glittering surfaces of being "in the money," while *It Happened One Night* (1934) and *Mr. Deeds Goes to Town* (1936) invited Americans on a breathless tour of the life of the newly wealthy elite. In the latter film Gary Cooper portrays a tuba-playing Clark Kent-type called Longfellow Deeds, who, by no virtue of his own, inherits millions and spends the largest part of the movie giving his money away, gaining his manhood as a paternalistic savior. Deeds thus reassured Americans that help was on the way, that upward mobility was just an inheritance away, and that the wealthy were really rather noble characters, capable of enormous generosity to those in need.

The enormously popular gangster movies presented the other side of the coin, a Depression-era countermyth of Self-Made masculinity. The gangster was depicted as a successful capitalist, a genuine Self-Made Man; the Mafia, we learned in these and later films calls its members "made men" when they've passed an initiation ritual test— a contract killing. But the gangster serves up the Self-Made Man in a negative cast. Only occasionally, as in *Angels with Dirty Faces* (1938), does the gangster become a positive role model, and then only when James Cagney feigns cowardice at his impending execution in order to dissuade a gang of young ruffians from following in his footsteps.

In 1939 American men got a choice of heroes in one of the most popular films of all time, *Gone With the Wind*—a choice that has persisted in Americans' minds, both male and female, for the ensuing decades. On the one hand, there was the chivalrous aesthete Ashley Wilkes, whose loyalty and dedication are both noble and effete, and on the other hand, there was Rhett Butler, a rogue and scoundrel, a man who thinks of no one but himself, a model of a Self-Made Man whose individualism prevents any connection with lofty noble contrivances such as country or honor. Guess whom Americans chose.

Gone with the Wind presented a crowning moment for both women and men. For women it was the fulfillment of the Victorian feminine fantasy—that a woman's love could transform an implacably self-centered scoundrel and turn him into a dutiful, though no-less, sexy husband. For men the contrast between Rhett and Ashley represented the fantasy triumph of the Self-Made Man as hero—competitive individualism and callous indifference both to other people and to political causes win out easily and are guaranteed to seduce even the most gorgeous and impetuous of women and transform them into loving and dutiful wives. Chivalry and the masculine devotion of the Genteel Patriarch were gone with the wind.

American men tried to come home, both literally and symbolically. And yet try as they might, they couldn't seem to ground their manhood on a firm footing. King Vidor's *The Crowd* (1928) offered a particularly poignant and bleak picture of the possibilities for this generation of Self-Made Men. The film's hero, Johnny Sims, is the "new man" for a new century. "There's a little man the world is going to hear from all right," his father exclaims when Johnny is born in 1900, at the dawning of the era. But Johnny does not do "something big" at all but rather takes a job as a faceless bureaucrat in a large insurance company, "a cog in an impersonal machine, undifferentiated from other men." He is part of the crowd.

Yet he longs for heroism, for success, to stand out from that crowd as a rugged individualist, a mythic American hero. He marries the lovely Mary, but even their romance cannot survive the absence of heroic opportunities for men. The couple lives in a shabby tenement, where daily annoyances slowly erode their love. When their youngest child dies in an automobile accident, Johnny falls apart and, bereft, quits his job. He ends up as a juggler, luring passersby into a local restaurant—a clown of a man who tries to hold many balls in the air at once. He is too cowardly to kill himself.

The film's final scene seems to offer Johnny a moment of surcease. As the camera pulls away from the close-up on his beaming face, though, we see a large audience at a theater, watching a show. Johnny is again, whether at work or at play, just another face in the crowd. Rarely has the cinema offered as bleak or as powerful an image of the dilemmas of twentieth-century American men.[71]

CHAPTER 7

"Temporary About Myself"

WHITE-COLLAR CONFORMISTS AND
SUBURBAN PLAYBOYS, 1945–1960

WILLY (longingly): Can't you stay a few days? You're just what
I need, Ben, because I—I have a fine position here,
but I—well, Dad left when I was such a baby and I never had
a chance to talk to him and I still feel—kind of temporary
about myself.
—Arthur Miller *Death of a Salesman* (1949)

"When it's all over . . . just think . . . being able to settle down
. . . and never be in doubt about anything." So said one aviator to his buddies in the 1944 film *Thirty Seconds over Tokyo*. And by
most calculations he should have been right. Employment had risen
dramatically during the war mobilization. Men had been able to
prove on the battlefield what they had found difficult to prove at the
workplace and in their homes—that they were dedicated providers
and protectors. Reports of battlefield heroism provided some sorely
needed manly templates. When the war took on the tone of a moral
crusade, saving the world from Nazi genocide and terror, the virtuous
tenor of military manhood was enhanced.

But war proved again to be only a temporary respite, and reentry

223

proved more difficult than many men had anticipated. The sanitized versions offered up by Hollywood movies little prepared their families for the lingering effects of the war.[1] Many films had muted both racial and ethnic tension and soldiers' longing for home and family by reconstituting the infantry squad as a kind of surrogate multicultural family, as men named Goldstein, O'Reilly, Vanelli, and Kowalski shared the same foxhole. But when men returned to their real families, life was not so simple.

One film that bucked the trend of postwar patriotic amnesia was William Wyler's *The Best Years of Our Lives* (1946). This poignant film chronicles the fitful reentry of three veterans: Al (Frederic March), a banker, who tries to reconcile his wartime experiences with his postwar life of relative ease and privilege; Fred (Dana Andrews), a glamorous flyer and war hero, who is haunted by nightmares and cannot find a decent job and whose hasty prewar marriage cannot survive the trials of separation and reentry; and Homer (Harold Russell), former star quarterback of his high school football team, who lost both his hands in the war and struggles to reveal his dependency to his steadfast fiancée. (One of the more innovative elements of the film was that Russell was actually a veteran who had lost both his hands, not an actor playing such a role.) Reentry was painful, and adjustments necessary. "Last year it was 'Kill Japs!' this year it's 'Make money!' " says Al on his first morning back from the war. But reintegration was possible, especially through the heroic compassion and generosity of the moral women who waited patiently and preserved the home front. Only through their support and understanding, it was suggested, was masculine recovery and repatriation possible for those returning vets.[2]

Advice columnists picked up these sentiments. Wives were urged to return to a docile domesticity to placate their wounded men. "He's head man again," reminded *House Beautiful*. "Your part in the remaking of this man is to fit his home to him, understanding why he wants it this way, forgetting your own preferences." If successful, *Good Housekeeping* predicted, their husbands should stop their "oppressive remembering" in about two to three weeks.[3] Sadly, such memories often lasted a very long time, and in some cases they never went away. War shock, difficulty reintegrating, unexplained lethargy, emotional mood swings, and nightmares were common.

After the war, psychiatrists probed past the military veneer to reveal a trembling terror underneath the soldier's bravado. Many soldiers in the Second World War, it turned out, could not fire their rifles and return enemy fire, and about 75 percent of all infantrymen rarely fired their weapons at all. A large number became incontinent in battle, and many men would "feign emotional disorder" in order to get out of the line of fire. The breakdown rate among the troops was higher than anyone predicted, as the "loss of personal freedom, sexual deprivation, physical misery, chronic exhaustion, and immersion in a chamber of horrors coalesced to produce strain beyond endurance."[4] In a startling volume of psychiatric reports on battle stress and emotional disorders published by the U.S. Army Medical Department in 1949, psychiatrists attempted to normalize men's battlefield anxieties. As one clinician put it, "in combat, most men have anxiety."[5] Indeed they did, but such claims set up the "Catch-22" that novelist Joseph Heller would later capture so brilliantly in his novel. Since stress and anxiety were normal, soldiers should not be excused from the front for displaying these symptoms but rather returned immediately. As one psychiatrist put it:

> The soldier is saying in effect that he feels he cannot subject himself further to this reaction. Management consists in pointing out to the soldier that these sensations represent a normal response to combat, not differing greatly from that experienced by men who have remained in the lines. The physiologic mechanisms may perhaps be explained in simple terms. Then the soldier must return to duty, either immediately, or after a few hours' rest at the aid station. Neither he nor the physician should expect that he will be relieved of the symptoms, since they are merely the normal autonomic response to fear in this soldier. It is as irrational to expect psycho-therapy to relieve or remove such symptoms as to expect it to prevent dampness and chilling during combat in inclement weather. The soldier must "learn to live with it."[6]

"Learning to live with it" became one of the dominant ways to maintain American manhood through the next decade.[7]

The difficulties in coping with the aftermath of the war were perhaps best expressed by the character Joseph Samuels, an insightful Jewish man, in Edward Dmytryk's film *Crossfire* (1947) just before he is murdered by Montgomery (Robert Ryan), a psychopathic anti-Semitic soldier. Describing postwar anomie, Samuels observes:

> I think maybe it's suddenly not having a lot of enemies to hate anymore. Maybe it's because for four years now we've been focusing our minds on . . . on one little peanut. [*Samuels holds up a peanut.*] The "win the war" peanut, that was all. Get it over, eat that peanut. [*Samuels eats peanut.*] All at once, no peanut. Now we start looking at each other again. We don't know what we're supposed to do. We don't know what's supposed to happen. We're too used to fightin'. But we don't know what to fight. You can feel the tension in the air. A whole lot of fight and hate that doesn't know where to go. A guy like you maybe starts hatin' himself. One of these days maybe we'll all learn to shift gears. Maybe we'll stop hatin' and start likin' things again.[8]

In this bleak film, however, most men are despondent and dissolute after the war, living in crowded hotel rooms, unable to return to their families or their previous lives. Only Mitchell (George Cooper), falsely accused of the murder, can go home again. "It'll be a bit rugged," says Robert Mitchum, as Mitchell is reunited with his wife, "but they'll be all right." All right, perhaps. But never the same.

One arena that provided the possibility of "likin' things again" was the family, and fatherhood loomed larger and larger as the war came to a close. It was often as fathers that men sought to anchor their identities as successes as men. First, the fathers who left their homes as soldiers were honored as heroes; those left behind found jobs in wartime production. Fathers were indispensable to the adequate development of their sons, to the provision for the family, and for the health of the nation. Fathers provided "masculine companionship and influence" to boys who "need a man who will take them to do 'men's things' in a 'man's way,'" as one columnist put it.[9] What's more, fathers need do nothing more than *be* fathers in order to serve this vital function. They didn't need to prove anything; they had already done so. Such ideas were particularly comforting to men who had come to manhood in the era of the Great Depression and the war because they faced a postwar world of limited opportunities and shrinking possibilities.

During the war the absence of so many fathers had been seen as a contributor to growing juvenile delinquency and other social problems. In 1943 the Memphis Tennessee Youth Service Council sponsored a drive to enlist men in the fight against delinquency. Several thousand men signed a promissory note pledging to spend a certain number of hours each week with their sons.[10] That same year congressional hearings over a proposed draft exemption for fathers centered around whether the manpower needs of the military could offset the need for social stability and fatherhood on the domestic front. The sponsor, Senator Burton Wheeler, and his supporters predicted dire consequences if the bill failed, including rising rates of juvenile delinquency and the "complete breaking down of the morale and the morals of the boys and girls" of the nation. To avoid this catastrophe, the social order required both a breadwinning father and a homemaking mother.

Opponents claimed that exemption would deplete the armed forces of necessary manpower and, they suggested, deprive these fathers of the opportunities to demonstrate their manhood. "There is, I know, a sufficient number of men in the father pool, who, if they were properly employed and were not working in department stores and other places, would be sufficient to fulfill the immediate manpower needs of the entire United States," argued Gen. Joseph McNarney against the amendment. However, he claimed, if fathers were exempted, that "particular class then is not required to furnish any effort for the successful completion of the war. If they see fit, they can still dress women's hair." Exemption from military service would emasculate fathers. The exemption amendment failed.[11]

In the increasingly suburban postwar world, fathers embodied masculinity—an idea confirmed by academic social science and psychology. "The process of transferring from the mother to the father is essential for emotional development, since the girl has to love and respect some man early in life if she is to grow up to marry one and the boy needs to have some male ideal if he is to wish to grow up to be a high type of man," wrote one social scientist.[12] Identification with father was central to the theories of Harvard sociologist Talcott Parsons, perhaps the most important social scientist of the postwar era, who attempted to develop a unified social science theory called structural functionalism. In a celebrated essay, "Certain Primary Sources and Patterns of Aggression in the Social Structure of the Western World" (1947), Parsons built on his earlier arguments for the emotional normality of the nuclear family, as father and mother embodied instrumental and expressive functions, both of which are necessary for social order and stability. Here, Parsons focused on the ways that the structure of the contemporary nuclear family produced specific problems, particularly the problem of adolescent male rebellion. The psychological requirement that the boy repudiate maternal nurture as the method of achieving healthy masculine identity means that his revolt against mother becomes a revolt against all he associates with femininity, including goodness. Becoming a "bad boy" becomes a positive goal, with important social consequences:

> Western men are peculiarly susceptible to the appeal of an adolescent type of assertively masculine behavior which may take various forms. They have in common a tendency to revolt against the routine aspects of the primarily institutionalized masculine role of sober responsibility, meticulous respect for the rights of others, and tender affection toward women. Assertion through physical prowess, with an endemic tendency toward violence and hence the military ideal, is inherent in the complex and the most dangerous potentiality.[13]

But the boy needs a father towards whom he can reorient his rebellion and grasp a positive identity. Father absence, caused by the occupational structure, makes this transition perilous; when the "boy does not have his father immediately available," he can develop a "large reservoir of repressed aggression," which can lead to a kind of "cult of 'compulsive masculinity.'" Parsons was loathe to locate masculine aggression in biological predisposition; he suggested that its cause was father absence and overdominant mothers.[14] Now strong mothers could be blamed for both gay sons and delinquent sons. Only by reestablishing the coherence of the traditional nuclear family could such problems be averted. These preoccupations became the standard fare of studies of delinquency in the 1950s, one of the growth areas of American social science.[15]

Pundits, too, went after mom—and with a vengeance. Philip Wylie's *Generation of Vipers* (1942) set the tone for a decade of mom-bashing and was followed in short order by David Levy's *Maternal Overprotection* (1943) and Edward Strecker's *Their Mothers' Sons* (1946).[16] Strecker, a consultant to the Surgeon General of the U.S. Army, attributed the unmanliness of those rejected by the military to their mothers' overprotectiveness.[17] Wylie, a disillusioned federal bureaucrat, went further, blaming mothers for virtually every characterological flaw among American men. Mom was a "destroying" angel, who rules her man by wiles and manipulation, and a cultural disease, "megaloid Momworship," ruled the land with narcissistic glee:

> Our land, subjectively mapped, would have more silver cords and apron strings crisscrossing it than railroads and telephone wires. Mom is everywhere and everything and damned near everybody, and from her depends all the rest of the U.S. Disguised as good old mom, dear old mom, sweet old mom, your loving mom, and so on, she is the bride at every funeral and the corpse at every wedding. Men live for her and die for her, dote upon her and whisper her name as they pass away, and I believe she has now achieved, in the hierarchy of miscellaneous articles, a spot next to the Bible and the Flag, being reckoned part of both in a way.[18]

Anthropologist Margaret Mead would have none of it. She painted a far less rosy portrait than Parsons did, given his expectation that a return to the nuclear family could ameliorate American men's restlessness. Nor did Mead buy Wylie's contention that the destruction of mother spelled the resurrection of manhood. In her brilliant dissection of the American character, *And Keep Your Powder Dry* (1942), a cultural critique that painted American masculinity as a retaliatory and vindictive hedge against fears and threatened humiliation, Mead worried about the consequences of continuing to pin gender identity on such outmoded ideals:

> Has the American scene shifted so that we still demand of every child a measure of success which is actually less and less possible for him to attain? . . . Have we made it a condition of success that a man should reach a position higher than his father's when such an achievement

(for the many) is dependent upon the existence of a frontier and an expanding economy?[19]

If American men were chronically restless and anxious, she argued, it was because of the contradictory cultural messages that form the backbone of male socialization.[20] "We teach them to be tough and to stand up for themselves, and, at the same time, teach them that aggression is wrong and should be suppressed, and, if possible repressed." As a result, American men are remarkable for a capacity to fight best only "when other people start pushing us around." Only in America do boys wear the proverbial chip on their shoulder, so that by waiting for someone to knock it off, he can "epitomize all the contradictory orders which have been given." Here is the typically American form of aggression—"aggressiveness which can never be shown except when the other fellow starts it; aggressiveness which is so unsure of itself that it has to be proved." Even our capacity for violence leaves us anxious and restless.[21]

Many of the chief sources of the decade's contradictory messages were cultural—from films to comic books. *Archie* comics, for example, begun in 1941, traded on masculine stereotypes in presenting Archie as the all-American high school kid. Archie plays off two negative archetypal poles familiar from previous decades of American history. Reggie Mantle and Dilton Doily, for example, represent two versions of the discredited Genteel Patriarch, imagined as either an unctuous upper-class fop (Reggie) or nerdy, egghead intellectual (Dilton). By contrast, the wiseguy and buffoon (Jughead) and the brawny, muscle-bound numskull (Moose), provide two examples of the discredited Heroic Artisan, depicted as wiseacre or Neanderthal. Archie steers down the middle of the road with just a hint of the impetuous smart aleck, the all-American guy who stands out by fitting in. And only he gets both Betty and Veronica (the blond, freshly scrubbed cheerleader and the somewhat darker, menacingly sexual brunette) to swoon over him. Archie is the Self-Made Man as Riverdale High School senior, even if he never manages to graduate.

The 1940s also resounded with voices of rage and pain, the voices of those groups of men who had historically been marginalized and emasculated by such self-made middle-class white men. The decade began with a violent scream from novelist Richard Wright, who, in *Native Son* (1940), and the more directly autobiographical *Black Boy* (1945), foretold a building black rage. As *Native Son* opens, Bigger Thomas's mother berates him for not being able to provide for a family: "We wouldn't have to live in this garbage dump if you had any manhood in you," she scolds. "You the most no-countenest man I ever seen in my life." Filled with shame, self-loathing, and rage, this encounter sets in motion the novel's violence and tragedy. When Bigger is finally captured—there have been eight thousand white men searching for him—the prosecutor calls for the death sentence as a reassertion of white manhood:

> the law is strong and gracious enough to allow all of us to sit here . . . and not tremble with fear at this very moment some half-human black ape may be climbing through the windows of our homes to rape, murder, and burn our daughters! . . . Every decent white man in America ought to swoon with joy for the opportunity to crush with his heel the woolly head of this black lizard.

When, at the novel's end, Bigger's mother visits him in prison and begs on her knees to Mrs. Dalton for Bigger's life, he is again "paralysed with shame" and feels "violated." In the coming decades black men turned that shame into anger and transformed white fears of black violence and sexuality into an attempt to reclaim their manhood. As Wright put it in his short story "The Man Who Was Almost a Man":

> The first movement he made the following morning was to reach under his pillow for the gun. In the gray light of dawn he held it loosely, feeling a sense of power. Could kill a man with a gun like this. Kill anybody, black or white. And if he were holding his gun, nobody could run over him; they would have to respect him.[22]

If rage was the new threat from the world of black men, anomie was its white counterpart. And anomie and masculinity were hard to reconcile. The cowboy or detective hero of the 1930s returned from the war with a darker, more sinister, and more sexual undertone in the film noir of the postwar era. Noir films utilized the conventions of true-crime and gangster dramas but offered virtually no avenues of masculine redemption. The heroes of noir films were grittier, tougher, colder, and far more cynical. Typically, the noir hero was a returning soldier who was alienated from the life he had left. "A guy like me after the war hates himself because he's scared to get going again," says the troubled veteran in *Crossfire* (1947). They were still less corruptible than the society they moved through but only because virtually everything in that world was already corrupt. Violence did not cathartically purge evil, nor did it even necessarily resolve the problems created by the plot. And forget about getting the girl and riding off into the sunset: The hero is nearly as likely to shoot her as marry her. Women are seductive temptresses—"alluring but ambitious *femmes fatales*"—who are as capable of the double cross and murder as men; not exactly the kind of equality that working women had in mind.[23]

Noir films had dark, viscous undercurrents of male sexual paranoia, of lugubrious forces out of control, of failure everywhere. Billy Wilder's films, especially *Double Indemnity* (1944) and *Sunset Boulevard* (1950), offer gloomy evocations of family disintegration, vacuous heroism, and the inability of the veteran to reintegrate into society. Raoul Walsh's *White Heat* (1949) suggests that the gangster can no longer pretend to be a heroic model of the Self-Made Man, a kind of alter ego to corporate conformists. *Dead Reckoning* (1947) suggests that the wartime leveling of class tension could not survive the peace. The bonds of friendship forged between two discharged paratroopers, Rip (Humphrey Bogart), a taxi driver, and Johnny (William Prince), a Yale-educated college professor, unravel as they travel together to receive medals for bravery in the war. The film turns into an anguished drama of the loss of those bonds in postwar America. Unstable and confused, and with the interjection of a woman, their abiding love forged in battle cannot survive.

Other works also took on the corrupting qualities of American society. Orson Welles's monumental film *Citizen Kane* (1940) provided a portrait of a man (loosely based on the life of newspaper magnate William Randolph Hearst) consumed by a cancerous greed and lust for power. Yet his downfall is caused, as was Jay Gatsby's, more by Kane's believing in the American Dream and in the American myth of self-made manhood than by his own moral failings. He believes his self-creation can transcend moral limits, turning him into an object of pity rather than veneration. What Kane (Welles) discovers is that even the creation of vast empires of wealth and power cannot compensate for the loss of childhood innocence and the intact, loving, nuclear family.

Perhaps the decade's most celebrated film star was Humphrey Bogart, a short, rather unattractive man who expressed the kind of reluctant heroism that both women and men found palpably masculine. As Clark Gable had done with Rhett Butler, Bogart often played a self-interested and selfish man who, during the course of the film, finds himself putting aside his self-centeredness and taking a moral and political stand for good. Bogart thus repudiates the Self-Made Man's dogged egoism; his characters become exemplary when they leave self-interest behind and act ethically. In this sense Bogart strikes a balance between self-made wealth and power and aristocratic virtue (without its class basis)—a tenuous balance that American men have found difficult to strike. In *Casablanca* (1942), for example, Bogart's character Rick retains his autonomy by not getting involved in other people's dramas, his detached demeanor mirroring American isolationism. In *To Have and Have Not* (1944), he plays a freewheeling adventurer who leases his boat out to tourists. Later, in *The African Queen* (1951), Bogart's Charlie Allnut doesn't particularly care about Germans and doesn't seem to know what the war is even about.

Yet in each film the transformative moment comes when he decides to act ethically: to facilitate the escape of a freedom fighter hunted by the Gestapo, or to blow up a German freighter, the *Louisa*. And in each case it is his love for a woman—Ingrid Bergman, Lauren Bacall, Katharine Hepburn—that provides the impetus for ethical manhood. None of these women sits atop a pedestal, passively adored; each is a leading actress, a powerful presence, and in Hepburn's case, his ally, accomplice, and mentor. Bogart's triumph is not through the conquest of these women—he doesn't even end up with two of them. Sacrifice of sexual desire, a most pivotal expression of self-interest, is necessary for the self-transcendence that is required of every real man as hero.[24]

Partnerships between women and men also were the axis around which the Spencer Tracy-Katharine Hepburn dramatic comedies revolved. Yet in most cases the tension between the couples was resolved by the woman's compromise and the reinscription of the nuclear family in which a wife subordinated her ambitions to her husband's. In *Woman of the Year* (1942), Hepburn's Tess Harding is a sort of superwoman—the efficient, smart, businesslike star reporter for a major New York City newspaper, whose feud with a crusty sports reporter, Tracy's Sam Craig, provides the comedic fuel for this renegotiation of the war between the sexes. Their marriage is the constant power struggle of the dual career couple, resolved in Hollywood fashion by Tess's capitulation and her return to Sam, recipe book in hand, ready to make domestic amends. She even takes his last name.

In *Adam's Rib* (1949) Tracy and Hepburn play married lawyers who find themselves arguing opposite sides of the same case. Hepburn wins in the courtroom by resorting to her "feminine wiles," but Tracy's revenge is exacted in their own relationship, as he bursts into tears as their relationship begins to unravel and she comforts him. To comfort the audience that Tracy wasn't *really* emasculating himself by crying, he later bursts into tears on cue to show Hepburn that men can be as manipulative as women, using feminine affect as well as women do to get their way. Thus can men outwoman women as an act of defiant manhood.

Arthur Miller's *Death of a Salesman* (1949) may be the most compelling portrait of the pathos of middle-class manhood and its consequences in literary history. Willy Loman, a tired, used-up salesman—a genuine "low-man"—is afraid to even take to the road. With his wife, Linda, he is alternately bullying and boastful, feeble and frightened. "I just couldn't make it, Linda," he tells her of his inability to get on the road as the play opens. "You know the trouble is, Linda, people don't seem to take to me," he confesses. When she reassures him, he says "I know it when I walk in. They seem to laugh at me." When she asks why, he says mournfully, "I'm not noticed."[25]

Willy's relationship to his absent brother Ben provides another axis around which the elegy for failed manhood is organized. Ben represents the road not taken for the Willy Lomans of the world, those stolid, middle-class American men, frightened into conformity and saddled with familial responsibilities. Ben went off for adventure, to be a hero on the frontier (Alaska). In Willy's soliloquies, rendered as conversations with Ben, Willy meditates on his own manhood and finds himself still feeling "temporary about myself." "Once in my life I would like to own something outright before its broken!" he exclaims. "I'm always in a race with the junkyard! I just finished paying for the car and it's on its last legs. The refrigerator consumes belts like a goddam maniac."[26]

Perhaps most tragic is the way in which Willy's failure becomes the mantle that he leaves to his sons, Biff and Happy. In their presence Willy sounds like a page out of Dale Carnegie boosterism. "It's not what you say it's how you say it—because personality always wins the day," he tells them. And so both of them avoid traditional expressions of manhood, alternately subscribing to Willy's idealized vision and hating him for their own failures. Biff rejects the life of the salesman as a "measly manner of existence," while confessing to his mother that he "just can't seem to take hold . . . of some kind of a life." Happy is equally restless and unhappy, seeking solace with women and believing himself better than anyone else. Happy's fantasy of upward mobility ends in isolation and recalls Tocqueville's statement in 1832 about American men building houses in which to pass their old age and then selling them before the roof is on:

> All I can do now is wait for the merchandise manager to die. And suppose I get to be the merchandise manager? He's a good friend of mine, and he just built a terrific estate on Long Island. And he lived there about two months and sold it, and now he's building another one. He can't enjoy it once it's finished. And I know that's just what I would do. I don't know what the hell I'm working for. Sometimes I sit in my apartment—all alone. And I think of the rent I'm paying. And it's crazy. But then, it's what I always wanted. My own apartment, a car, and plenty of women. And still, goddammit, I'm lonely.[27]

Biff's only response is an ineffectual invitation to go out west together. But even they know the frontier is closed.

It is Biff who in the end lashes out the hardest on Willy in what may be his only chance to break free of his father's illusions:

> Pop! I'm a dime a dozen and so are you! . . . I am not a leader of men, Willy, and neither are you. You were never anything but a hard-working drummer who landed in the ash can like all the rest of them!

And at Willy's funeral Biff's comment provides an epitaph for the new man of the postwar era. "He never knew who he was."[28]

Such a powerful indictment rolled across the lawns and rattled the windows of suburban housing developments for the entire decade of the 1950s. If the suburban breadwinner father didn't exactly know who he was, he could at least figure out who he wasn't. In the 1950s American men strained against two negative poles—the overconformist, a faceless, self-less nonentity, and the unpredictable, unreliable nonconformist. American middle-class men faced what I think of as the "Goldilocks dilemma," from that fairy-tale heroine's search for commodities (chairs, beds, porridge) that were not too something yet not too much the other side. Men had to achieve identities that weren't too conforming to the march of the empty gray flannel suits lest they lose their souls; but they couldn't be too nonconforming lest they leave family and workplace responsibilities behind in a frantic restless search for some elusive moment of ecstasy.

And they had to do it in surburban housing developments in which their homes were distinctive only in how uniform they were in design and decor. The suburbs had become a central fact of postwar America and the new arena for proving one's manhood. Over the first half of the century, suburban housing developments had gradually risen from a tiny slice of American dwelling to its majority form of housing. Thus, while men sought to define a normal masculinity, they situated themselves in a vast sprawl of "normalcy."

In our stereotypic image the 1950s was an era of quiet, order, and security. What we like to remember as a simple time, "happy days," was also an era of anxiety and fear, during which ideas of normality were enforced with a desperate passion. "The effort to reinforce traditional norms seemed almost frantic," writes the historian William Chafe.[29] The 1950s was a decade of containment.

No wonder Senator Joseph McCarthy so easily linked homosexuality and communism—both represented gender failure. McCarthy raged against both as "egg sucking phony liberals," effete eastern intellectuals, emasculated half men who, with their "pitiful squealing," had sold the country down the river and lost China and Eastern Europe through indecision and fear. "You can't hardly separate homosexuals from subversives," argued Senator Kenneth Wherry. "A man of low morality is a menace in the government, whatever he is, and they are all tied together." McCarthy's witch-hunt for "pinks, punks and perverts" uncovered a State Department that was "a veritable nest of Communists, fellow travelers, homosexuals, effete Ivy League intellectuals and traitors," according to one of the senator's aides.[30]

This link between intellectualism and effeminacy also contributed to the defeat of Adlai Stevenson in 1952 and 1956. Not only was Stevenson labeled "soft" on communism, but he was the classic "egghead." The candidate whom the *New York Daily News* called "Adelaide" used "tea cup words," which he "trilled" with his "fruity" voice, and was supported by "Harvard lace cuff liberals" and "lace panty diplomats." It's amazing that Stevenson—vilified as effeminate and weak, as was no other candidate since Martin Van Buren—got any support at all in his campaign against America's most recent warrior president.

The trappings of gender failure were all around us in the 1950s, and American men discovered what happened to men who failed, especially the sons of men who failed as breadwinners and fathers. They became homosexual, they became juvenile delinquents, they became Communists—soft, spineless dupes of a foreign power, who were incapable of standing up for themselves. Few experts really knew what a real man was; most were content to tell us what he was not. In part, as social scientists understood, the definition of masculinity had become so fuzzy because of the "conflicting nature of multiple role demands, lack of clear positive definitions . . . and the rigidity of role demands."[31] In J. D. Salinger's novel *The Catcher in the Rye* (1951), the decade's first antihero, Holden Caulfield, captured the increasing malaise of adolescent boys as they faced uncertain manhood. Confused about what it meant to be a man, about girls, about sex, Caulfield dreams a typically American male dream of escape:

> Finally, what I decided to do, I decided to go away. I decided I'd never go home again and I'd never go to another school again. I decided I'd . . . start hitchhiking my way out West. . . . [I]n a few days I'd be somewhere out West where it was very pretty and sunny and where nobody'd know me and I'd get a job. . . . I didn't care what

kind of job it was, though. Just so people didn't know me and I didn't know anybody.

Holden finds that those old masculine themes are more difficult these days. "You can never find a place that's nice and peaceful, because there isn't any. You may *think* there is, but once you get there, when you're not looking, somebody'll sneak up and write 'Fuck you' right under your nose."[32]

The adult man's version of Archie's pals proffered the corporate clone and the outlaw rebel to represent the two negative poles of American manhood against which men attempted to carve out meaningful lives. For Holden Caulfield, one was the terrifying future of most of his preppy classmates, the other the unrealizable goal of rebellion. These poles appeared in pop psychological advice books, academic social science, and virtually every cultural medium that men faced. How could men remain responsible breadwinners and not turn into docile drudges? How could men become active and devoted fathers—to make sure that their sons did not become sissies—and not turn into wimps themselves? How could men let their hearts run free with a wife and kids to support?

On these questions, both sides of the political spectrum seemed to converge. Several jeremiads argued that we were in danger of becoming—or that we had become—a nation of sheep. Ayn Rand's objectivist philosophy celebrated a cult of supreme egoism, as the only force capable of combatting the combination of big capital and the bureaucratic state that lulled the masses into a condition of soporific stupefaction. Real men, in her enormously popular books, like *Anthem* (1961), *Atlas Shrugged* (1957), and *The Fountainhead* (1943) (which were more thinly fictionalized political tracts than novels), battled heroically to live their own lives against the pressures of conformity. King Vidor's film of Rand's most famous work, *The Fountainhead* (1949), cast western- and war-movie hero Gary Cooper as the unrepentantly modernist architect Howard Roark, who struggles to realize his individual vision of form following function. Roark stands at the pinnacle of two triangulated relationships. The apparently central triangle involves Roark with his true love, Dominique Francon (Patricia Neal), and self-made newspaper magnate Gale Wynand

(Raymond Massey). Here, Wynand's waffling support reveals to both Roark and Dominique his ultimate failure as a man, and Roark eventually replaces Wynand as Dominique's husband, just as Wynand could not replace Roark as the object of her deepest love.

The purely homosocial triangle among Roark, Wynand, and the newspaper's pompous architectural critic, Ellsworth Tooey (Robert Douglas), reveals Rand's vision of manhood. Wynand, who escapes from Hell's Kitchen to become one of the wealthiest men in the city, is undone by the necessity of pandering to mass tastes and is ultimately ruined not by Roark but by Tooey, the effete intellectual. "You left to impractical intellectuals like me the whole field of ideas to corrupt as we please while you were making money," Tooey states in triumph. "You thought money was power. Is it, Mr. Wynand?" Here is the clash between the discredited Genteel Patriarch, now reduced to pretentious intellectual snobbery and clever manipulation, and Self-Made Masculinity, which has been so busy making money that it lost all semblance of heroic virtue.

Only Roark can rescue American society and, thus, American manhood as the resurgent Heroic Artisan, though in this right-wing incarnation he is an independent professional and decidedly non–working class. "Greatness comes from the independent work of independent minds," Roark claims in his defense, and it is his ideas which are his property. He rails against the "soulless collectivism" of mass society—whether capitalist or communist—which can only build "great big marble bromides" to the crassness of mass taste. (As if to make the contrast more potent, when Dominique first sees Roark he is a laborer in a granite quarry, holding erect a large drill in his sweaty, muscular forearms.) Only the professionalized artisan can stand against all the forces arrayed against him and redeem his manhood— and get the icily stunning woman to swoon with desire.

To critics on the left, the impersonal forces of mass society worked best for scions of big capital, who both manipulated potentially virtuous working people into blindly consuming things they neither needed nor wanted and kept middle-class men isolated and afraid. The psychologist Erich Fromm, for example, a wartime refugee from Germany's most celebrated intellectual hotbed, the Frankfurt School, criticized middle-class conformity in *Escape from Freedom* (1941) and

Man for Himself (1947). Fromm wrote of the "market orientation" of American men, through which the sense of self becomes anchored in activities and accomplishments and measuring up to social norms and standards. As a result, emphasis rests not on who the person is but on what the person has: It is what other people think of us that counts most. To Fromm, the contemporary alienated man was an individual who "has opinions and prejudices but no convictions, has likes and dislikes, but no will," and the new man was one who "escapes the burdens of freedom in group conformity."[33]

To other liberal critics the demands of corporate life had transformed potential marketplace men into frightened "little men," as the sociologist C. Wright Mills called them in *White Collar* (1953). Mills offered a relentless critique of this new middle-class manhood. In his view, the middle-class man was more pathetic than protean; he did "not threaten anyone" and did "not practice an independent way of life." He'd been "stood up by life,"

> living out in slow misery his yearning for the quick American climb. He is pushed by forces beyond his control, pulled into movements he does not understand; he gets into situations in which his is the most helpless position. The white collar man is the hero as victim, the small creature who is acted upon but who does not act, who works along unnoticed in somebody's office or store, never talking loud, never talking back, never taking a stand."[34]

Modern corporate capitalism had transformed a nation of small entrepreneurs—Self-Made Men—into a nation of hired employees. "Just as the working man no longer owns the machine but is controlled by it, so the middle class man no longer owns the enterprise but is controlled by it," Mills wrote. "The men are cogs in a business machinery that has routinized greed and made aggression an impersonal principle of organization."[35] Depersonalized cogs in the corporate machine also lost their sense of themselves as men. Their feelings were "deadened," and they felt "dwarfed and helpless," "worried and distrustful," "bored at work and restless at play," a "chorus, too afraid to grumble, too hysterical in their applause."[36]

Sociologist David Riesman's portrait of the social psychology of conformity, *The Lonely Crowd* (1950), revealed a diffuse anxiety among American men. The nineteenth-century American man was "inner-directed," animated by conviction and principle, Riesman argued; now, men had become "other-directed," concerned more with fitting in than standing out, "at home everywhere and nowhere." Modern man was animated by "anxiety rather than pride" and engaged in "veiled competition rather than openly rivalrous display."[37] Like Riesman, the historian Frank Tannenbaum argued in *A Philosophy of Labor* (1951) that the Industrial Revolution had "destroyed the solid moorings of an older way of life and cast the helpless workers adrift in a strange and difficult world."[38]

That world was made all the more strange by the changes in the workplace itself. Men faced more than emasculating demands and humiliating hierarchies; it was also getting quite crowded in there. Urban and suburban housewives alike ached to get back into the workplace from which they had been pushed after the war. Black men's anguished cry for full recognition of their manhood would not subside, as readers learned from Ralph Ellison's *The Invisible Man* (1952). And the winds of change began to erode the walls of white resistance in cases like *Brown v. Board of Education of Topeka* (1954), beginning, at least, the juridical integration of blacks into the American mainstream. And gay men were, it seemed, everywhere—in every florist shop or beauty salon and invading the suburban home to help wives decorate it.

Popular writers of all political stripes picked up these themes and translated them for mass-market readers. Vance Packard's books, such as *The Status Seekers* (1959) and *The Hidden Persuaders* (1957), frightened readers about the threats to their individualism from soft-voiced manipulators.[39] Business writer William H. Whyte's *The Organization Man* (1956) gave popular expression to these analyses, recognizing the irony of Dale Carnegie's method of winning friends and influencing people or Norman Vincent Peale's power of positive thinking.[40] Gone, Whyte argued, is the rugged individualist and in his place is a conception of "individualism *within* corporate life." Motivated more by a "passive ambition," urgently trying to belong, "obtrusive in no particular, excessive in no zeal," the future of these organization men is "a life in which they will all be moved hither and yon and subject to so many forces outside their control."[41]

Fiction writers, too, picked up the terrors of conformity. In Richard Matheson's *The Incredible Shrinking Man* (1953), an allegory of the disappearance of real manhood, it is financial failure that squeezes the hero, even before he gets hit with the chemicals that shrink him. The title of Sloan Wilson's novel *The Man in the Gray Flannel Suit* (1955) gave the era its most enduring rhetorical reference point, although the novel chronicles Tom and Betsy Rath's growing awareness that Self-Made Manhood is a trap, keeping men locked into soul-shattering routines of vicious competition and frenzied consumption.[42]

In a strange essay, "The White Negro" (1957), novelist Norman Mailer chafed at the fate of American men, who faced "a slow death by conformity with every creative and rebellious instinct stifled." In its stead Mailer offered a romanticized appropriation of the Negro as hipster-outsider—the delinquent, the hipster, the black man, the "male urban outlaw, living on the edge, searching out sex, using marijuana, appreciating jazz, finding momentary truth in the body":

> If the fate of twentieth century man is to live with death from adolescence to premature senescence, why then the only life-giving answer is to accept the terms of death, to live with death as immediate danger, to divorce oneself from society, to exist without roots, to set out on that uncharted journey into the rebellious imperatives of the self.[43]

Failure to undertake such a journey had significant political implications: These cookie-cutter men were raised for sameness, raised never to question authority, raised, some feared, to be unable to resist communism. Fears of brainwashing, especially after the Korean War, were also fears of loss of masculine control, of loss of will. That specter of hollow zombies incapable of individualistic resistance haunted America through the 1950s, as in *Invasion of the Body Snatchers* (1954), a transparent allegory of potential Communist takeover, and later *The Manchurian Candidate* (1962), in which the brainwashed emasculated soldiers take orders from a woman.[44]

On the other side of the tracks from respectable middle-class conformity lurked the dangerous men, the rebellious nonconformists, who threatened social stability, domestic harmony, and corporate responsibility. The decade's preoccupation with juvenile delinquency and the disheveled rebelliousness of the beatniks, or the new fears of effeminate homosexual men, provided several negative stereotypes against which American men played out their yearnings. In black leather on his motorcycle, the delinquent represented sexual and interpersonal power, control over himself and his environment. In a sense he was the era's Heroic Artisan, but this time cast entirely in negative terms. No wonder Beat poet Allen Ginsberg claimed that "the social organization most true to itself and to the artist is the boy gang"—here was the closest institution to the artisanal crafts shop of the eighteenth century, re-created with menacing, homoerotic overtones. The motorcycle gang of the 1950s was a descendant of the Arts and Crafts Movement's re-creation of the medieval guild—control over the machinery, individual autonomy, and mastery within a context of blood brotherhood. As Heroic Artisans themselves, the Beats had to create something, and what they created was the rhetoric of rebellion. They knew more what they were against—railing against the drone of self-made masculinity, the relentless pursuit of happiness through material possession—than what they were for. In his electrifying poem *Howl* (1956) Allen Ginsberg screamed at a Moloch "whose mind is pure machinery! Moloch whose blood is running money!"

Casting the nonconformist as negative role model, however tempting, also gave middle-class men a way to restore manhood, a manhood threatened by corporate and suburban sameness. As fathers they could prevent their sons from becoming delinquent, gay, Communist, or irresponsible beatniks.[45] Their return home was not the retreat of world-weary would-be warriors but a daring rescue mission, a campaign to save their sons.

That American boyhood was becoming a collection of sissies was "the overriding fear of every American parent," wrote anthropologist Geoffrey Gorer. "Are we staking our future on a crop of sissies?" asked a writer in *Better Homes and Gardens*. "You have a horror of seeing your son a pantywaist, but he won't get red blood and self-reliance if you leave the whole job of making a he-man of him to his mother."[46] Psychologists, child-development experts, sociologists, and educators all chimed in in a growing chorus of anxiety about the gender development of boys. Men had to be dedicated fathers to offset overdominant motherhood and to help their sons resist the temptations of gender nonconformity. On the other end of the feminized, potentially homosexual son lurked the other danger besetting American boyhood: the juvenile delinquent. Studies of delinquency were a growth industry in social science and psychology in the 1950s. Ironically, such seeming opposites as hypermasculine juvenile delinquency and hypomasculine homosexuality were traced to the same familial roots: the absent father and overdominant mother.

Talcott Parsons argued that the middle-class boy, dominated by his mother and with a weak identification with his father (whose absence made identification even more difficult), would be driven to prove himself by delinquent hell-raising. Parsons's student Albert Cohen's study *The Culture of the Gang* (1955) linked the sources of delinquency to the "masculine protest." Without adequate assurance that he is "indubitably, in his own eyes and those of the world around him," a man, the boy turns to dangerous methods of proof; "engaging in bad behavior acquires the function of denying his femininity and therefore asserting his masculinity."[47]

For working-class boys, Cohen claimed, the delinquent subculture provided not only grounds to demonstrate manly aggression but also an alternative work environment where men might experience success in deviant behavior and the chance to retaliate against those norms that they believed had emasculated them. Walter Miller's oft-cited study "Lower Class Culture as a Generating Milieu of Gang Delinquency" (1958) echoed this theme and tied it once again to smothering motherhood; the working-class boy's preoccupation with toughness was

> related to the fact that a significant proportion of lower class males are reared in a predominantly female household and lack a consistently present male figure with whom to identify and from whom to learn essential components of a "male" role. Since women serve as a primary object of identification during pre-adolescent years, the almost obsessive lower class concern with "masculinity" probably resembles a type of compulsive reaction-formation.[48]

The masculinity of working-class adolescents was thus, almost by definition, deviant; collectively, they were always in rebellion, not against a class, but against the "feminine principle" in society.[49]

In such studies hypermasculinity was a hedge, an effort to offset feelings of masculine inadequacy. If someone acted excessively masculine, these theories held, he must be the least secure in his manhood. Countless young boys must have heard the same message I did from my parents—that the local schoolyard bully was the boy who was "least secure," and therefore he had to keep "proving it" against boys who were smaller and weaker than he was. Thus did countless studies of hypermasculinity explain masculine excess as a compensation for insecure and anxious gender identity. In the celebrated studies that were collected in *The Authoritarian Personality* (1950), for example, psychologists at Berkeley and Yale determined that the personality complex of authoritarianism—which included racism, anti-Semitism, and general bigotry—was actually a form of "pseudo-masculinity," an effort to mask such gender insecurity. In the end, lead author Theodor Adorno wrote a year later, "the tough guys are the truly effeminate ones, who need the weaklings as their victims."[50]

It was not only for their sons, however, that men were advised to stay put in their suburban homes. Being a breadwinner and family provider remained the centerpiece of middle-class masculinity. It may have required subordinating one's heroic vision to a dull routine, but it was exactly that sort of compromise that separated the mice from the men. As it had earlier, academic social science added a scientific gloss to middle-class respectability and responsibility. "Virtually the only way to be a real man in our society is to have an adequate job and earn a living," wrote sociologist Talcott Parsons in 1959. "It is perhaps not too much to say that only in very exceptional cases can an adult man be genuinely self-respecting and enjoy a respected status in the eyes of others if he does not 'earn a living' in an approved occupational role." Real men were breadwinning men.[51]

They were family men, too, actively involved in the raising of their children. *Life* magazine declared 1954 the year of "the domestication of the American man," the climax of a decade of dedicated fatherhood and husbandry.[52] The 1950s elevated family life to a level of sacredness never before witnessed in our history. Family was ideology, as cultural historian Warren Susman observed. We watched "family-oriented TV" in the "family room," with "family size" packages of snacks; we traveled in "family cars" on "family vacations" and ate in "family restaurants."[53]

For men the celebration of the family was not supposed to be an emasculating retreat. "Being a father is not 'sissy' business," wrote a psychiatrist in *Parents* magazine in 1947. "It is an occupation," perhaps "the most important occupation in the world." When a man cooked, for example, in the family barbecue pit, he was achieving and expressing his masculinity. "When a barbecue goes into operation, it automatically becomes a masculine project," noted *Esquire* magazine's *Handbook for Hosts*. "After all, outdoor cooking is a man's job."[54]

Fathers of the new baby boom were told to get involved—but not *too* involved. "Of course I don't mean that the father has to give just as many bottles, or change just as many diapers as the mother," Dr. Benjamin Spock wrote in an early edition of his best-selling *Baby and Child Care*. "But it's fine for him to do these things occasionally. He might make the formula on Sunday." Social scientist Morris Zelditch agreed with this prescription for weekend nurturing, urging fathers to cross over only sparingly.

> Father helps mother with the dishes. He sets the table. He makes formula for the baby. Mother can supplement the income of the family by working outside. Nevertheless, the American male, by definition, *must* provide for his family. He is *responsible* for his support of his wife and children. His primary area of performance is the occupational role . . . and his *primary* function in the family is to supply an "income" to be the "breadwinner."

In fact, Zelditch concluded, there is "simply something wrong with the American adult male who doesn't have a 'job.'" The truly nurturing dad, emotionally expressive and available, Zelditch regarded as effeminate, with "too much fat on the inner side of his thigh."[55]

This conclusion presented an exceedingly thin line between feminization of the overdomesticated dad and the irresponsibility of the absentee father who was producing a generation of lost sons. One way to straddle that line was to pursue one of the myriad hobbies that suburban men were encouraged to develop. A hobby, like woodworking, or stamp and coin collecting, kept dad around the house, but not as a henpecked husband or domestic drudge—these were *his* hobbies after all. Some hobbies seemed designed simply to fill time and keep dad around, while others were trumpeted as lucrative side-lights to their breadwinner roles.[56] But virtually all were celebrated because they could bring dad and son together in a project that was theirs alone. The 1950s hobbies boom was thus more than a con-sumerist cornucopia designed to mindlessly fill leisure time. Hobbies could both salvage fathers and save sons.

Men needed help in fulfilling their domesticating mission. Much of the child-development literature aimed its advice specifically at fa-thers, many of whom were "not fully grown up and self-reliant them-selves" and therefore needed the help. *Parents* ran articles like "A Build-up for Dad," which began with basic Parenting 101 skills about how to interact with children and ran through attendance at PTA meetings, carpentry for tots, and sports. *Parents* also ran a column, ". . . Specially for Fathers," which gave monthly parenting tips. *Woman's Home Companion* reminded mothers that "fathers are par-ents too" and offered a pictorial collage of fathers in aprons feeding their children, helping them to make a boxcar, and teaching them about automobiles. Advertisements for a fourteen-volume *Childcraft* guide promised to inform anxious parents about everything they al-ways wanted to know about childhood but didn't know how to ask. Four volumes were specifically devoted to expert advice on "every phase of child development," including "what is normal and what is not," and tips on how to "direct your child's growth and character."[57]

One article in *American Home*, "Are You a Dud as a Dad?" sug-gested that fatherhood gave men the opportunity for achievement they might not receive in the workplace. "Here is one area of your life which doesn't depend on 'breaks' or ability, on education or money. A man can be a success as a father, a real 'dad,' if he cares enough to try." Fathers were counseled to share hobbies, laugh at their sons' jokes, and listen to their problems—"the kinds of things a fellow wants to talk over with a man."[58]

Television, the newly created carrier of entertainment for the whole family, rushed in quickly to give dad a boost. In shows such as *Ozzie and Harriet, Father Knows Best, Leave It to Beaver*, and *The Donna Reed Show*, fathers were seen as nurturing, caring, and devoted to their children.[59] They could always find the time to listen to their children's problems, to help with homework, or to ferry them around their suburban neighborhoods—partly because their jobs were so unimportant in the overall depiction of their lives. Who now remembers the occupations of Jim Anderson or Ward Cleaver?[60] Critic Mark Crispin Miller hints that this shift in emphasis away from the workplace and towards the family spelled the return of American man as the Heroic Artisan of the Home Front. "Since we almost never saw him working, we had no sense that there was any class above his own, and he had no competition in the class below him." Or as Ozzie Nelson put it, "by not designating the kind of work I did, people were able to identify with me more readily." An unemployed former bandleader, Nelson mostly sat around the house reading the newspaper and, in so doing, helped American men laugh at their retreat from heroic masculinity. Shows like *Bachelor Father* and *My Three Sons* centered around men raising children alone and proving to be adequate mothers and fathers rolled into one.[61]

By contrast, films and television shows about working-class men or childless men offered consolation to middle-class breadwinners and their sons. A few television shows cast the working-class family as a dysfunctional site of emasculated men or adult delinquents. If middle-class fathers were depicted as comfortably nondescript and devoted, working-class men were seen as both marital and workplace failures. Few working-class families on television seemed to have children. In *The Honeymooners*, for example, it was Ralph Cramden (Jackie Gleason), the crass blowhard, who played a male version of Lucy, while his wife, Alice (Audrey Meadows), played the female Ricky Ricardo; it was Ralph, after all, who was always coming up with harebrained schemes that left him humiliated and requiring rescue. In the childless working-class couple the man rants and raves, his emotions out of control, while his wife, cool and calm, rationally sets things right.

Without wives and children working-class men were transformed into wisecracking grown-up delinquents, like the well-named Sgt. Ernie Bilko (Phil Silvers) on *You'll Never Get Rich* (later *The Phil Silvers Show*). Bilko and his little platoon of thieves and con artists showed viewers that the army, once the site of heroic military manhood, was really a gigantic con game, staffed by inept bureaucrats and pursuing a Cold War that was nothing but a joke. Two decades before "the Fonz," Bilko was a middle-class delinquent with a heart of gold.

Most of the continuing cult audience seems to have misread the film version of Robert Linder's warning *Rebel Without a Cause* (1955) as a celebration of rebellion against dull conformity. To be sure, the movie turns on Jim's confrontation with his ineffectual father (played by James Dean and Jim Backus, respectively), who wears an apron in the scene as if to underscore his inability to relate to his desperately needy son. But it's also a celebration of the nuclear family—not the ones that the three teenage waifs were given by nature but rather the alternative family that they are able to create for themselves. Jim and Judy (Natalie Wood) find each other and together provide a home for Plato (Sal Mineo), whose wealthy parents are too preoccupied with their own lives to care at all about him. Plato's death enables Jim to hear his father's promise that he will "try to be as strong as you want me to be."

Not all working-class men were objects of middle-class ridicule, but they had to redeem themselves by subscribing to middle-class values. Retrieving one's manhood was not about the color of one's collar but about the values one held and the willingness to stand up for them. Take, for example, the characters played by Marlon Brando. More than any other actor of the era, Brando captured the repressed rage of the caged animal—recall his primal scream in *A Streetcar Named Desire* (1951), the adolescent alienation of the delinquent (*The Wild Ones* [1953]), and the brooding confusion of the stand-up working-class guy (*On the Waterfront* [1954]).[62]

Like Bogart's before him, Brando's characters follow a path of self-discovery that moves from dispassionate self-interest to ethical connection. In the beginning of *On the Waterfront*, which won the Academy Awards for Best Picture and Best Actor, Malloy is asked by the local priest where he stands, who he's with. "Me, I'm with me," Brando replies. He's a hero to the local neighborhood boys, but Brando himself is not taken in by his own hype. "I could have been a contender," the punch-drunk ex-fighter tells his brother Charley (Rod Steiger) in one of the film's most critical scenes. "I could have been somebody, instead of a bum, which is what I am."

From the ashes of his failed masculinity, Malloy finally acts ethically, manfully, confronting the corrupt union boss Johnny Friendly (Lee J. Cobb) and breaking the immoral code of masculine silence. And he takes the consequences—including the murder of his brother, the slaughter of his beloved pigeons, and one of the most savage beatings in film history—with a Christlike resignation. As Malloy rises from this terrible humiliation and walks fitfully towards the warehouse gates, he has reclaimed his manhood. He is no longer a bum. He can now go to work the waterfront, another working-class stiff remade as a working-class hero, confident that he is a real man.

For middle-class men, though, the work world offered none of those possibilities for manly redemption. It was as fathers, not as employees nor even as soldiers, that they experienced the autonomy and control that had once marked artisanal manhood. In one episode of *Leave It to Beaver* I especially remember as painfully familiar, Beaver and his class are asked by the teacher to describe what their fathers did during the war. Beaver, who considers his father "the neatest dad in the whole world," describes Ward as a veritable Audie Murphy, capturing dozens of enemy soldiers and dragging home enormous quantities of war booty. When challenged to back up his story, he breaks into his father's old footlocker only to discover a bunch of T squares and surveying instruments. Ward comforts Beaver, who is crushed by this obvious lack of heroism, by explaining that his role was important, too. "There were thousands of us in the service who weren't heroes. They put a man where they thought he could do the best job," he says. Thus, the past was symbolically and safely put away; so that, as the cultural critic Gerard Jones writes, "the day of the manly hero had yielded to the day of the builder, the planner, the quiet team player." And the dad.[63]

These periodic forays into masculine domesticity have returned men to home and family at various times in our history and in various guises—to provide adequate role models to potentially homosexual or delinquent sons or to remain a steadfast mate to wives and thus thwart those wives' ambitions, for example. Rarely, though, for the intrinsic pleasures of domestic life, which only the Genteel Patriarch probably enjoyed, and then only because his class position freed him from workplace obligations. Domestic retreat and caring fatherhood were little compensation for the restless anxiety that has continued to haunt American men; all that sober responsibility left a gaping void in the hearts of men, where once adventure, risk, and sexual passion had reigned. At least in their dreams.

By mid-century many of American men's traditional alternatives were gone. Of course, the frontier had all but disappeared. "No, no place to go," Carl says to Jody in John Steinbeck's story "The Red Pony" (1945). "Every place is taken. But that's not the worst—no, not the worst. Westering has died out of the people. Westering isn't a hunger any more. It's all done." Fraternal orders, once so popular, were now the objects of ridicule; men who joined, like Amos and Andy or Ralph Cramden and Ed Norton, were seen as working-class oafs seeking a night out with the guys and away from the little woman (who was probably bigger than he was).[64]

Of course, some of those methods retained some vitality.[65] Fitness guru Jack LaLanne recapitulated the American success story of re-creating the body as a way of reinventing the man. Like Charles Atlas a couple of decades earlier and Bernarr Macfadden at the turn of the century, LaLanne transformed his own "puny and embarrassing" physique into a physical marvel. As a youth LaLanne had been "a pathetic little world-hating, heart-aching boy" with an "ungovernable hunger for candy and soft drinks," who had grown thin, weak eyed, and weak spined. When his father died of a heart attack in his early forties—caused, LaLanne believed, by chronic "pooped-out-itis"— young Jack started exercising and eating wisely. From his humble origins as a calisthenics instructor in San Francisco in 1951, LaLanne became the star of the most widely viewed daytime television show on the air by 1960 and filled forty thousand orders a month for the Glamour Stretcher, his "whole gym on a rubber cord," offered to both bored housewives on perpetual diets and to men on the go who needed quick pick-me-ups.

LaLanne may have offered worldly ectomorphic salvation through an oversized rubber band, but many men wanted escape without any effort at all. So in the 1950s, as for over a century, it was to fantasy that middle-class men turned. So long as they remained reliable breadwinners and devoted dads, they could become wild and adventurous consumers, savoring real men's "true" adventures or grabbing fantasy thrills with traditional heroes like cowboys or with those delinquents with hearts of gold that Hollywood was fond of creating. It appeared that the more boring and dull the routine of men's work became, the more exciting and glamorous were their fantasies of escape.

None were more glamorous than those rhetorical returns to those thrilling days of yesteryear offered by the western. Over 10 percent of all fictional works published in the 1950s were westerns, and eight of the top ten television shows—a total of thirty prime-time television shows in all—were "horse operas."[66] Fifty-four western feature films were made in 1958 alone. Westerns provided the re-creation of the frontier, the "meeting point between civilization and savagery," where real men, men who were good with a horse and a gun, triumphed over unscrupulous bankers and other rogue versions of Self-Made Manhood. *The Lone Ranger* provided a new homosocial interracial couple in which the moral and innocent white Ranger, removed from society and left for dead, is then nursed back to health by the male mother and Native American spirit guide, Tonto. This deeply bonded couple, suspended in the liminal world between society and nature, allowed male viewers to experience an escape from the helplessness of childhood without having to succumb to adult responsibilities; the television show provided "a fantasy of the perpetuation of moral innocence and freedom from guilt into an adult world of power and aggression."[67]

Rodeos also experienced an unprecedented boom in popularity at the same time. Hailed as a "primitive, reckless and ruthless" sport that featured the "self-righteous virility" of its performers, the rodeo was part of a general cult of the cowboy. Families ran off to dude ranches to reestablish family togetherness through nature. Little boys thrilled to boy westerns like *Old Yeller* and television shows like *Lassie, My Friend Flicka*, and *Fury*—all love affairs between boys and their animals—while their fathers thrilled to grown-up shootouts and horseback chases.[68]

The cult of the cowboy's most celebrated hero, the man who best represented that "vanishing symbol of individualism in an age of togetherness and conformity," was an actor whose real name was Marion Michael Morrison.[69] But in this age of self-invention, Marion was urged by his agent and potential director to take a more manly name, preferably one composed of two first names, each with one syllable.

So Marion Michael Morrison became John Wayne, the only American who fought in every war in American history, a two-fisted loner who would not get tied down by domestic responsibility but always kept moving toward the edges of society, toward the frontier. For much of the 1950s and for all of the 1960s and even into the 1970s, Wayne topped popularity polls as the American man that other American men most admired. And in films like *Fort Apache* (1948), *Red River* (1948), and *Rio Grande* (1950), Wayne embodied a frontier masculinity as had no one else in this century since Theodore Roosevelt. He, too, spoke softly and carried a big stick, and he, too, lived the strenuous life—even if his cinematic sets were constructed so that he would appear too large for the tables and chairs at which he sat and even if he was filmed from a slight upwards angle to make him appear taller than his 6'4" frame! Describing his directorial debut in *The Alamo* (1960), which he also produced and in which he starred as Davy Crockett, Wayne saw his mission as "to remind people . . . that there were once men and women who had the guts to stand up for the things they believed." The way Wayne saw it, the Alamo was a metaphor for America: Mexicans against us; black and white, simple. "They tell me everything isn't black and white," complained Wayne. "Well, I say why the hell not?"[70]

One of Wayne's films, *The Man Who Shot Liberty Valance* (1962), provides a fitting coda for this era of mass conformity, men's retreat to the home as frightened fathers preventing the next generation's sexual deviance or adolescent rebellion, and men's escapist fantasies of rugged individualism, luxurious sensuality, and outdoorsy adventure. The film turns on a case of mistaken identity as Ransom Stoddard (James Stewart) is credited with killing Valance, even though it was really Tom Doniphon (John Wayne) who had done it. Rather than a climactic revelation and reversal of fortune, Doniphon lives out his life in obscurity, while Stoddard gets all kinds of glory and accolades, including Doniphon's girlfriend, as rewards for his putative heroism. Only Stoddard and his wife come to Doniphon's funeral. "The values remain," film critic Joan Mellon writes sadly, "but the men who profess them are no longer worthy."[71]

Perhaps even more central than the western, however, were the flights of sexual fantasy that captivated suburban men. The bevy of men's magazines that started up in the 1950s—such as *Male* (1950), *Real: The Exciting Magazine for Men* (1950), *Impact: Bold True Action for Men* (1957), and *True* (1956)—glorified the testing of manhood, whether it was in hand-to-hand jungle combat or against the primal forces of nature, but always with the sexual conquest of a large-breasted woman as a kind of masculine payoff. These hairy-chested outdoorsmen were real men, who took no guff from women. The magazine "stimulates his masculine ego at a time when man wants to fight back against women's efforts to usurp his traditional role as head of the family," crowed *True*'s editorial director.[72]

What was perhaps the decade's most significant cultural contribution to the stock of masculine escape hatches dispensed with the heroic warrior or grisly outdoorsman altogether. In the *Playboy* philosophy sexually alluring and available women were the reward for adventurous masculine consumerism, as they languidly draped themselves over the high-priced accoutrements of his bachelor pad. *Playboy* transformed the way men viewed women, separating them into distinct categories.[73] Wives were the enemy, mothers were abstractions to be venerated, and other women were soft playthings to be seduced. The playboy "loved women," but he "hated wives" as Barbara Ehrenreich put it.[74] Wives were "an idle class, a spending class, a candy-craving class," according to Philip Wylie; they turned healthy, sexy, fun-loving guys into domesticated Caspar Milquetoasts, "tweedy, corpulent, hornrimmed dollar chasers," who, as sex-starved wimps, give money, homes, clothing, and stability in return for . . . what? "It is her man who worries about where to acquire the money while she worries only about how to spend it, so he has the ulcers and she has the guts of a bear."[75]

First published in December 1953, *Playboy* instantly became "the Bible for the beleaguered male" and one of the most popular magazines in American history—an indication that it had struck a nerve with American men and, perhaps, an indication of men's yearning for something different from the hands they felt they had been dealt.[76] *Playboy*, Ehrenreich argues, attacked "the bondage of breadwinning," offering instead "a coherent program for the male rebellion: a critique of marriage, a strategy for liberation (reclaiming the indoors as a realm for masculine pleasure) and a utopian vision."[77] The playboy was all sexual prowess without responsibility, blemish-free sex fantasies with blemish-free nubile women. As the magazine's title intimated, American men experienced their manhood most profoundly when they were boys at play, not men at work.

Playboy offered men "a little diversion from the anxieties of the Atomic Age," as editor Hugh Hefner announced in the magazine's inaugural issue. But the elements of diversion were strikingly different from the usual masculine magazine fare. Other men's magazines may spend all their time "thrashing through thorny thickets or splashing about in fast flowing streams," Hefner wrote, but playboys "spend most of our time inside. We like our apartment. We enjoy mixing up cocktails and an *hors d'oeuvre* or two, putting a little mood music on the phonograph, and inviting in a female acquaintance for a quiet discussion on Picasso, Nietzsche, jazz, sex." The playboy was a domesticated bachelor, closer to the dandified Billy Dimple in *The Contrast* than either of the other male roles, a stereotypic ladies' man now offered up as a new model for manliness.[78]

It is therefore somewhat surprising that it was in the pages of *Playboy* that a mid-twentieth century debate about the feminization of American manhood was taking place. But it was a central tenet of the "Playboy philosophy" that women were not men's enemy; the magazine's editors and writers strove to carefully delineate the sources of masculine malaise, to celebrate some women even as it vilified wives and mothers. Philip Wylie, for example, announced the "womanization" of America in an article in 1958, followed four years later by a panel discussion on the topic.[79] Wylie cast a wide net in describing a "general male emasculation," carried out in large part by pushy protofeminists who sought "to invade everything masculine, emasculate it, cover it with dimity, occupy it forever—and police it." Bars now served "alcoholic substances with the hues and flavors of cake frosting" at "little Chinese tables you could tip over with a mere emphatic gesture." Through organized dances and Ladies Nights, women had even infiltrated men's clubs.[80]

Not only the public sphere but also the home had been completely feminized—"a boudoir-kitchen-nursery, dreamed up by women, for women, and as if males did not exist as males." In this colonization of domestic space, women had lots of help, first from male traitors, like interior decorators, who were of suspect sexuality, "usually males in form only—males emotionally so identified with the opposite sex they could rout reluctant husbands because their very travesty made men uncomfortable." And they'd also had help from husbands, who "defaulted" on their responsibilities and had turned into "flabby parodies of the physical male." Abandoning his role in imparting proper masculine socialization, his sons "grew up without paternal guidance and adult male companionship" and became "she-pawns" by age twelve.[81]

Masculine collaboration with these forces of cultural feminization was a dominant theme in other *Playboy* articles. In a later panel, artist Alexander King found the American man "no longer willing or ready to accept complete responsibility for the family as he did in my father's and grandfather's days," so that now he has "resigned his prerogatives, and by default, woman has taken over." Anthropologist Ashley Montagu, whose book *The Natural Superiority of Women* (1952) had ruffled more than a few feathers, also blamed men for women's noisome trouble in prescient language that equated racial and gender conflict in terms that would become familiar in coming decades. "The male is in the position to do what the whites could have done to make the so-called inferior races feel that they were as good as anyone else and no longer inferior. They didn't and will probably pay the penalty for it in the long run. And, similarly, males."[82]

Writer Norman Mailer stated the case most baldly. For Mailer, "masculinity is not something one is born with, but something one gains. And one gains it by winning small battles with honor. I'm saying that because there is very little honor left in American life, there is a certain built-in tendency to destroy masculinity in American men." This emasculation is not women's fault alone, Mailer argues. Sure, they've become "more selfish, more greedy, less romantic, less warm, more lusty, and also more filled with hate," but men have collaborated with them. And the consequences are catastrophic—far more homosexuality in 1962 than fifty years earlier, which he attributes to "a loss of faith in the country, faith in the meaning of one's work, faith in the notion of one's self as a man."[83]

One crucial difference between turn-of-the-century critiques of cultural feminization and those of the late 1950s, then, concerned the role of men. In the late nineteenth century men had resisted feminization, and when they could not, it was because the demands of the workplace prevented them from expressing their deep, now repressed, manhood. But the men of the 1950s seemed willing participants in their own emasculation, loving little lambs being led sheepishly to she-devil slaughter.[84]

Playboy's men were on a rescue mission. But amidst all the advertisements for high-end consumer products and the pinup photographs of lusciously large-breasted ladies, the magazine never offered a coherent political philosophy. On the one hand, work and family were the twin harnesses which constrained middle-class men from living out their playboy fantasies. *Playboy* encouraged men to search for a way to "break with the responsibilities of breadwinning, without, somehow, losing their manhood." For a while the male fled, as *Look* magazine had claimed in a 1958 feature series on the American male, "to the basement and busied himself sawing, painting, and sandpapering. But the women followed him, and today they are hammering right along with him. No place to hide there."[85] But on the other hand, below Wylie's clever conceits lay a lurking fear that overprotective mothers produced effeminate or delinquent sons. And underneath Mailer's masculine quest lay fears that men who abandoned meaningful work risked gender inversion. Men needed to rescue their sons and recommit themselves to their careers, that is, retrieve work and family as masculine preserves. Ultimately, it was fathers who might be able to resolve this tension. When men were bonding with their sons as dedicated fathers, they could legitimately claim homosocial freedom from their nagging wives. The stakes were high, the rewards potentially great.

As the 1950s drew to a close, American men still felt temporary about themselves, even more restless in the midst of even greater abundance than Tocqueville ever imagined. Responsible breadwinners and devoted fathers, they were still anxious about overconformity but unable and unwilling to break free of domestic responsibilities to become rebels on the run. Besides, they were *needed* at home to raise those sons to be real men. "I don't know what's the matter with us," says Betsy Rath to her husband, Tom, in Sloan Wilson's *The Man in the Gray Flannel Suit*. "Your job is plenty good enough. We've got three nice kids, and lots of people would be glad to have a house like this. We shouldn't be so *discontented* all the time."[86]

But discontented they were. Both husbands and wives yearned for something more, something neither could put a finger on exactly. Within a few years, though, Betty Friedan christened the discontent that women felt as the trap of "the feminine mystique" and began a movement that would bring to women the chance for a different life—fulfilling and equal. While the emerging feminist movement offered married suburban housewives hope for a life outside the domestic trap, their husbands also searched vainly for something, something they were unable to get from their work, from their relationships with their wives or their children, from their friends, and even, it turned out, from their fantasies. Men's efforts to hold fast to traditional manhood in the wake of the powerful currents of change in the 1960s and 1970s precipitated the contemporary masculine malaise.

Part Four

THE CONTEMPORARY
"CRISIS" OF MASCULINITY

The Masculine Mystique

How could we ever really know or love each other as long as
we kept playing those roles that kept us from knowing or
being ourselves? Weren't men as well as women still locked
in lonely isolation, alienation, no matter how many sexual
acrobatics they put their bodies through? Weren't men dying
too young, suppressing fears and tears and their own
tenderness? It seemed to me that men weren't really the
enemy—they were fellow victims, suffering from an outmoded
masculine mystique that made them feel unnecessarily
inadequate when there were no bears to kill.
—Betty Friedan *The Feminine Mystique* (1973)[1]

I n 1963 Betty Friedan's *The Feminine Mystique* resounded like a toc-
sin across the country, heralding the birth of a new wave of feminism. In June of that same year, Rev. Martin Luther King delivered
perhaps his most impassioned plea for racial equality, inviting his audience to dream with him of a time when the "grandsons of slaves
and the grandsons of slaveowners" would "sit down together at the
table of brotherhood."

There were even a few rumblings of discontent among men, rumblings which grew louder and more insistent as the decade progressed. The historian Arthur Schlesinger, Jr. noticed it in an article in
Esquire in November 1958:

What has happened to the American male? For a long time he seemed utterly confident in his manhood, sure of his masculine role in society, easy and definite in his sense of sexual identity. Today men are more and more conscious of maleness not as a fact but as a problem. The ways by which American men affirm their masculinity are uncertain and obscure. There are multiplying signs, indeed, that something has gone badly wrong with the American male's conception of himself.[2]

What had gone wrong? Actually very little was new, despite Schlesinger's anxious warning. Rather, the eminent historian had indulged in a bit of ahistorical nostalgia, as we often do during periods of uncertainty, suggesting that earlier times were happier, easier, and more stable times. As I've shown, this was a projection; those bygone days came weighted with their own gendered anxieties.

In the 1960s the "masculine mystique"—that impossible synthesis of sober responsible breadwinner, imperviously stoic master of his fate, and swashbuckling hero—was finally exposed as a fraud. The constant search for some masculine *terra firma* upon which to ground a stable identity had never provided firm footing for Self-Made Men; by the 1960s gradual erosion and uneasy footing had become a landslide. All the marginalized groups whose suppression had been thought to be necessary for men to build secure identities began to rebel. Friedan had finally named the "problem that has no name"—the confusion, self-blame, and anguish of women who had been told "to seek fulfillment as wives and mothers." For the second time in our history, women began to find their voices. At first, Friedan noticed, women spoke with "a tone of quiet desperation" about their problems, the same quiet desperation that Thoreau had observed among American men a century earlier. But soon that muted tone gave way to righteous indignation, as women were finally answering that old saw about what they wanted that Freud and countless other men had asked in bemused resignation. "I want something more than my husband and my children and my home" was the answer Friedan exclaimed we could no longer ignore.[3]

The civil rights movement challenged the exclusion of black people from full citizenship and, thus, the exclusion of black men from claiming their stake in American manhood. Gender images saturated militant black rhetoric, equating the demands for civil rights with a demand for full recognition of blacks as men. The gay liberation movement challenged the facile and false equation of homosexuality with failed gender identity, the popular misperception that gay men were not real men. And the counterculture, populated largely by the sons and daughters of the white middle class, challenged the illusions of suburban comfort and security. In a sense, the hippies represented another revolt of the sons against the fathers. In their long hair and flowing, feminine clothes, hippies rejected the corporate clone as a model for manhood. "Are You a Boy or Are You a Girl?" was the title of one popular song and the plaint of many a suburban parent.[4]

Even our earlier attempts to extend the frontier beyond national boundaries could no longer be relied upon. Despite JFK's inaugural promise of a New Frontier, the world was getting smaller, closing in on men seeking military heroism as a way to demonstrate manhood. By the middle of the decade, as we sank deeper and deeper in that morally indefensible political quagmire in Vietnam, many Americans came to realize that extending the frontier had consequences: The empire was striking back. And one of the most reliable refuges for beleaguered masculinity, the soldier/protector, fell into such disrepute as the news about Vietnam filtered home that even today Vietnam veterans are seen by some as having acted out an excessive and false hypermasculinity. Once a paragon of manly virtue, the soldier was now also coming to be perceived as a failed man.

The sustained, insisted demands for inclusion by those who have historically been marginalized did not begin in the 1960s, but it then became a permanent fixture in the national social and political agenda. And whether one welcomes them today to full economic, social, and political equality as the fulfillment of democracy's promise or dreads them with all the self-righteous indignation of the traditionally privileged, these groups are here to stay. They trumpet neither reveille for the Age of Aquarius nor taps for American culture, but they have irreversibly transformed the landscape on which American men have sought to test and prove their manhood.

Just as they had for over a century, many American men didn't take these new challenges particularly well, retreating to tired formulae of exclusion or escape. By the mid-1970s there were calls for "men's liberation" to free men from the restrictive roles to which they had been assigned. Men, it turned out, needed liberating, too. If middle-class white men couldn't beat 'em, perhaps they could join blacks, gays, and women in the ranks of the oppressed.

WORK

After all, the breadwinner role brought few of its anticipated rewards. By the 1960s American men felt increasingly alienated, stuck in a rut, unable to escape the dull monotony of a cookie-cutter corporate identity, a suit that was ready-made and waiting to be filled. These feelings resonated through all levels of American society, as successful businessmen, middle-class managers, and blue-collar workers all experienced alienation. The sociologist Robert Blauner's important study of factory workers, *Alienation and Freedom* (1964), identified several dimensions of alienation that were as pervasive for middle-class men as they were for blue-collar workers. Blauner argued that the experience of powerlessness (having no control over their actions on the job), meaninglessness (performing specialized tasks that they cannot relate to the whole), isolation (inability to identify with the firm or its goals), and self-estrangement (the lack of integration between their work and other aspects of life) led men to search for affirmation and identity outside the workplace, in the realm of consumption.[5]

It wasn't only industrial workers. A 1963 study of big business leaders asked:

> What is the point at which these men can stop, look back, and announce to themselves and their world that they have completed this long journey, that they will rest now? There does not seem to be such a point, for an essential part of the system is the need for the constant demonstration of one's adequacy, for reiterated proof of one's independence.[6]

And a Connecticut therapist described a middle-level manager at IBM:

> He's under constant fear and tension. He's constantly worried about whether he's going to get ahead or isn't he? He's not worried about

being dropped, but he's very worried about what people are thinking about him. He's been with IBM for something like eight years, and he hasn't moved ahead. He's putting the pressure on himself. It's him in relation to the society of IBM. He's afraid of taking the risk of getting a promotion, afraid he might not be able to handle the new responsibilities. He's also afraid of the competition. His idea is that if he fails, he'll look worse than if he didn't try at all. So he doesn't try. The failure becomes much more difficult for him to handle.

The pressure to be a successful breadwinner was a source of strain and conflict, not pride and motivation.[7]

In the 1960s the relentless striving and competition that had defined the Self-Made Man and the fears and anxieties that accompanied him were cast as the problem, not the cure. Self-making was now characterized as a disease, the type A personality—that impatient, driven, hostile, and competitive workplace successmonger, who, according to cardiologists, was far more prone to heart attacks and other stress-related diseases than his more calmly cooperative and accommodating type B brother. Immediately seized upon by psychologists and magazine writers, the type A man was, according to a *Business Week* article in 1964, "aggressive, hard-driving, vigorously competitive, continuously subject to deadline, and [subject to] an exaggerated sense of time urgency," while another observer saw his "restlessness, hyperalertness, explosiveness of speech, tenseness of facial musculature" as early warning signs of type A.[8] A 1974 study of one thousand seven hundred people over age eighty, including 129 people who were one hundred years old or older, found absolutely no "intense, driving, highly competitive business executive types in the whole bunch."[9] Literally sick at heart, Self-Made American men were driving themselves to early death.

Such relentless striving in the competitive crowd left men feeling isolated and alone. Loneliness, emptiness—these became the dominant terms in the era's cultural analyses of masculinity. The breadwinner role left men feeling like cogs in the corporate machine, and conspicuous consumption in sprawling suburban shopping malls were hardly a compensation. The pursuit of happiness promised by our Founding Fathers had become, as Philip Slater's compact indictment was titled, a "pursuit of loneliness"; our growing into manhood was, as Paul Goodman's equally insightful work had been titled a decade earlier, "growing up absurd"; and the culture of abundance was now what Christopher Lasch called a "culture of narcissism."

Each of these works brilliantly dissected the cultural malaise that lay at the heart of American self-making, the empty anxiety that sprang directly from the blind pursuit of a marketplace masculinity. The rugged individualism of the nineteenth century had been replaced by the shallow sociability of the modern American personality. Eagerly dependent upon the approval of others, the contemporary narcissist was not a gentle neo-hippy but a competitive, insecure manipulator. We could no longer have it both ways, Goodman had warned, maintaining "a conformist and ignoble system *and* . . . skillful and spirited men to man that system with."[10]

Only Charles Reich, in *The Greening of America* (1970), waxed optimistic in the face of these changes. To Reich, a Yale Law School professor, the cultural crisis was the dawning of a new age, in part exemplified by the hippies, and the new age signaled the birth of a new man. Reich's truncated history of America rested on the transitions in forms of consciousness. In Republican America (what Reich called Consciousness I) small businessmen and farmers, heirs to republicanism and frontier individualism, carved out the manhood of what I have called the Heroic Artisan, characterized by the Jeffersonian virtues of the yeoman and the autonomous shopkeeper. The turn of the century spelled the triumph of the organization man, the professional animated by hierarchy, marketplace rationality, and order (Consciousness II—roughly equivalent to what I have called Self-Made Masculinity.) But now (the late 1960s) Reich euphorically observed a new consciousness, Consciousness III, which replaced liberal marketplace individualism with a globally aware, environmentally sensitive, freely flowing androgynous cultural identity. Reich's breathless celebration of Consciousness III may have been premature, but his insight that hordes of American men were seeking to shed the burdens of preceding forms of consciousness suggested something significant in American culture.[11]

POLITICS

The emerging student movement also was uneasy about the possibilities for personal fulfillment promised by Self-Made Masculinity. The Port Huron Statement (1962), the founding document of the Students for a Democratic Society (SDS), is an anxious plea for a new definition of manhood. Contemporary society used men, treated them as "thing[s] to be manipulated . . . inherently incapable of directing [their] own affairs"; we had become docile and dependent. But the solution was not "egotistic individualism," which led only to "loneliness, estrangement, [and] isolation," but rather the exploration of our "unfulfilled capacities for reason, freedom and love" and our "unrealized potential for self-evaluation, self-direction, self-understanding, and creativity."[12]

For many young Americans, before personal fulfillment came a commitment to ending the war in Vietnam. The growing antiwar movement provided a new lens into the dynamics of American manhood in the 1960s and 1970s; the conflict between old and young, between hawks and doves, was also a test of wills, questions of loyalty became questions of standing up for what one believed. It was a central expression of the growing crisis of masculinity.[13]

The struggle between the Vietnam policymakers and the antiwar protestors held the gendered psyches of Washington policymakers up to a new lens. No longer did we lionize presidents and their cabinets as they stood fast against aggression, totalitarianism, and imperial expansion. Kennedy was, perhaps, the last president cast in that heroic mold, even though recent revisionist historians have significantly tarnished his image. Like both Roosevelts, Kennedy overcame the perceived burdens of his aristocratic family lineage and youthful infirmity or injury—a World War II hero on PT-109, Kennedy presented a youthful vigor, a hardy manhood that, despite his chronic back injury, made him as comfortable sailing or playing touch football with his family on the lawns of their Hyannisport home as he was leading the nation into the New Frontier. The shock wave that jolted the American psyche when Kennedy was assassinated in 1963 was, in part, that a man in the prime of his life, so vital and active, had been cut down by a sniper's bullet (or snipers' bullets). If Kennedy could be shot down, then the manhood he embodied was itself vulnerable.

The re-creation of the frontier loomed large in JFK's imagery. In his speech accepting the Democratic presidential nomination in 1960 in Los Angeles, Kennedy evoked the search for the frontier as the source of renewal and hope:

> I stand tonight facing west on what was once the last frontier. From the lands that stretch 3000 miles behind me, the pioneers of old gave up their safety, their comfort and sometimes their lives to build a new world here in the West. . . . [But] the problems are not all solved and the battles are not all won, and we stand today on the edge of a new frontier—the frontier of the 1960s, a frontier of unknown opportunities and paths, a frontier of unfulfilled hopes and threats.[14]

New frontier boundaries were drawn against communism and especially against the Russians—whether in the rice paddies of Vietnam, in building American bodies (through the President's Council on Physical Fitness), or in the space race. Exploring outer space offered the chance to win a war against the Russians without earthbound weapons and physical injury, and it also offered some new versions of American heroes. The astronaut was "the triumphant single-combat warrior," the "Cold Warrior of the Heavens," facing a challenge that was "ancient, primordial, irresistible," according to Tom Wolfe in his meditation on military masculinity couched as a portrait of aeronautical disillusionment, *The Right Stuff* (1979). Wolfe suggests that the astronauts, instead of being the triumphant reincarnation of the Heroic Artisan, were actually glamorized proletarians; each was little more than a passenger in his capsule—"a redundant component, a backup engineer, a boiler room attendant—in an automated system!"[15]

Kennedy's constant confrontations, both real and symbolic, with the Russians revealed a sense of manliness that was animated by a "keyed up, almost compulsive competitiveness," according to biographer Theodore Sorenson. Assembling around him the "best and the brightest," Kennedy saw many of his brief administration's tests as tests of manly resolve, from the Bay of Pigs crisis, to his own Vietnam policies, which began the rapid escalations of U.S. involvement. This foreign policy's aim, according to James McNaughton, assistant to Secretary of Defense Robert McNamara, was "70%—to avoid a humiliating U.S. defeat (to our reputation as guarantor) . . . 20%—to keep South Vietnam (and the adjacent territory) from Chinese hands . . . 10% to permit the people, of South Vietnam to enjoy a better, freer way of life."[16]

Kennedy managed to balance his compulsive competitiveness and aggression with a fresh-scrubbed handsome, energetic charisma—qualities that LBJ lacked in equal abundance. Johnson appears to have been so deeply insecure that his political rhetoric dripped with metaphors of aggressive masculinity; affairs of state seem to have been conducted as much with the genitals as with political genius. There was a lot at stake for LBJ, as David Halberstam noted in his monumental study, *The Best and the Brightest*:

> He has always been haunted by the idea that he would be judged as being insufficiently manly for the job, that he would lack courage at a crucial moment. More than a little insecure himself, he wanted very much to be seen as a man; it was a conscious thing. . . . [H]e wanted the respect of men who were tough, real men, and they would turn out to be hawks. He had unconsciously divided people around him between men and boys. Men were activists, doers, who conquered business empires, who acted instead of talked, who made it in the world of other men and had the respect of other men. Boys were the talkers and the writers and the intellectuals, who sat around thinking and criticizing and doubting instead of doing.[17]

Johnson's crisis of manliness contributed to, though of course it did not cause, the escalation of the war in Vietnam, his refusal to admit that the war was lost, or to see the error in the war in the first place. Bill Moyers, then President Johnson's press secretary, recalled that the president told him of his fear that if he withdrew from Vietnam, then McNamara and the other advisers would think him "less of a man" than Kennedy. When opposed by enemies real or imagined, Johnson questioned their manhood. "In decision making," Halberstam writes, "they proposed the manhood position, their opponents the softer, or sissy, positions." When informed that one member of his administration was becoming a dove on Vietnam, Johnson retorted, "Hell, he has to squat to piss." And as he celebrated the Christmas bombings of North Vietnam in 1966, Johnson declared proudly, "I didn't just screw Ho Chi Minh. I cut his pecker off." As Moyers noted, it was as if the war had become "a frontier test," with LBJ swearing, "by God I'm not going to let those puny brown people push me around."[18]

Nixon, too, was chronically afraid of appearing soft on communism—or on anything else. He was "afraid of being acted upon, of being inactive, of being soft, of being thought impotent, of being dependent on anyone else."[19] Nixon resolved to "overcome the weak-kneed, jelly backed attitude" of Congress and to press ahead with escalating the war in Vietnam, according to Barry Goldwater. When one Republican senator shifted his position on the war from hawk to dove, Vice President Agnew called him Christine Jorgensen, in reference to the most famous transsexual of the era. And in labeling anti-war protestors "effete intellectual snobs" and the press "nattering nabobs of negativism," speechwriter William Safire allowed Agnew to place into common currency the equation of manhood with support of the American war effort. Nixon's compulsive manhood formed an explosive amalgam with his political paranoia as he faced George McGovern, a soft-spoken ex-minister and college professor and the anti-war, Democratic presidential candidate in 1972. Nixon's desperate efforts to win, including the Watergate break-in and coverup, eventually brought him down and, with him, the nation's failed Vietnam policy.

In a sense, the Carter presidency was McGovern's vindication—here was another soft-spoken, deeply religious man, who made compassion and concern the apparent cornerstone principles of his domestic and foreign policy. But the "new man" represented by Carter proved to be a case of too much too soon for an American psyche still traumatized by defeat in Vietnam, the women's movement, and the relentless grind of urban problems. As the president in the resurgently masculinist 1980s, former actor Ronald Reagan would promise one last swing in the saddle for the western cowboy hero as president—and most Americans went happily along for the ride.

The erosion of confidence in a masculinity based on martial

virtues that attended our involvement in Vietnam was only part of the problem for American men in the 1960s and 1970s. Men were besieged at home; the social movements of those two decades—the women's movement, the civil rights movement, and the gay liberation movement—all offered scathing critiques of traditional masculinity and demanded inclusion and equality in the public arena. No longer could the marketplace and the political arena be the preserve of heterosexual white men. The very groups who had been so long excluded from American life were making their own claims for identity. And for manhood.

Black men, for example. James Baldwin's powerful essays and best-selling novels focused a tormented rage on white men's projections of their fears and longings on black men, a cultural psychosis that meant that the black man was "forced each day to snatch his manhood, his identity, out of the fire of human cruelty that rages to destroy it."[20]

As the civil rights movement of the mid-1960s enlarged to include movements for black power and black pride, so too did the rhetoric of gender. The Reverend Martin Luther King, Jr., asked America to live up to the promise of democracy by integrating and including black people into full humanity. In the 1968 sanitation workers' strike in Memphis, during which King was assassinated, workers carried signs that read, in bold block letters, "I *am* a man." Malcolm X developed a parallel political rhetoric that was equally gendered, as he spoke about reclaiming a manhood stolen from black men by white slavers and denied by two centuries of racist politics. "Malcolm was our manhood, our living black manhood!" exclaimed the actor and civil rights leader Ossie Davis, in the aftermath of Malcolm X's assassination. "This was his meaning to his people."

The Black Panther party, a militantly defiant organization, made black manhood a centerpiece of its appeal to young blacks. In the works of such Black Panther leaders as Huey Newton, Bobby Seale, and Eldridge Cleaver, there was a growing preoccupation with proving a manhood long suppressed and denied by racism. "We shall have our manhood. We shall have it or the earth will be leveled by our attempts to gain it," wrote Cleaver in *Soul on Ice* (1968), his incendiary manifesto of black liberation. The sight of hundreds of angry black men in military formations, carrying machine guns, preparing to fight for their rights, was a stirring sight to all who observed the Black Panthers—no doubt a terrifying sight to some but, also no doubt, an inspiring sight to many young black men facing the crippling realities of racism, unemployment, and inner city poverty.[21]

For some militants black pride meant pride in themselves as men, which led them to fuse their own homophobia with claims for manhood. "Most American white men are trained to be fags," with "weak and blank" faces with a "red flush" and "silk blue faggot eyes," asserted Amiri Baraka in his essay "american sexual reference: black male."[22] More than any of the others, Cleaver was preoccupied with black power as the vehicle to reclaim sexual potency. In an essay, "To All Black Women from All Black Men," Cleaver wrote about his struggle to "heal my castration"—the deep wound inflicted on black men through slavery and cultural dispossession. "Across the naked abyss of negated masculinity, of four hundred years minus my Balls . . . I feel a deep terrifying hurt, the pain of humiliation of a vanquished warrior . . . and a compelling challenge to redeem my conquered manhood." One of Cleaver's ideas of revolution was the rape of white women by black men, since such a violation was the ultimate violation of white male power. By raping "his" women, black men would be striking the ultimate blow against the white man. Such suggestions did not sit well with either his black sisters or with white women, who were themselves demanding that they cease to be the chattel of men.[23]

Women had a movement of their own for that purpose. Feminism posed perhaps the greatest challenge to a masculinity based on exclusion and affected men both personally and politically. For one thing, women had burst into public realms in sufficient numbers to really challenge the workplace, the classroom, and the political arena as homosocial preserves. For example, between 1968 and 1975 all but a small number of colleges and universities were opened to women— only a handful of college-educated American men currently under thirty-five has attended a single-sex institution of higher learning.[24] That's quite a change from the experiences of every other generation of men in U.S. history. Women were not only voting but voting for women candidates and supporting the ERA. In 1973 the Supreme

The Unmaking of the Self-Made Man: In the first decades of the twentieth century, former Heroic Artisans found themselves increasingly proletarianized, mere appendages to the machine. The world of work was increasingly competitive and crowded. *Top:* Charlie Chaplin as dispossessed worker in *Modern Times* (1936). *Bottom:* Police exam, New York City, 1931. (Photo courtesy of Bettman Archives)

Restoring Masculinity by Remaking the Body: Turn-of-the-century America went "sports crazy," as thousands of men sought to combat the enervating effects of their urban white-collar working lives with manly physiques, health regimens, and participation in sports. Muscular development revealed a Self-Made Man. The first professional bodybuilder, Eugen Sandow, used his sculpted body to become one of the world's most famous and wealthy men. Bernarr Macfadden promoted it all in his magazine *Physical Culture,* from muscle building, to clean living and healthy diet, to a "peniscope," a vacuum pump designed to enlarge the male organ. *Right:* Eugen Sandow. *Bottom:* Bernarr Macfadden. (Frontispiece from *The Virile Powers of Superb Manhood* by Bernarr Macfadden [New York: Physical Culture Publishing Company, 1900])

Manhood

How Strength and Vigor is Lost, and Manhood may be Restored by Self-Treatment

Wrecked

...BY...

Rev. W. J. HUNTER, Ph. D., D.D.   and   # Rescued

THIS is a most timely and important work, by one who has made a careful study of the subject, and brings to bear a thorough knowledge of general and sexual hygiene. For the want of the knowledge on sexual subjects this book contains many men are on a downward course, and by the use of it many could be saved from sexual weakness, restored to manly vigor and made capable of properly filling life's duties and become strong, manly men, instead of physical and social wrecks. We cannot better describe this work, which has received the highest praise from competent critics, than to publish the following from the

....TABLE OF CONTENTS....

CHAPTER I.—THE WRECK.

Primeval man—His dignity and purity—Some noble specimens of manhood still—Causes of the wreck—Ignorance of natural law—Poverty and lack of proper food—Stimulants and narcotics—Sexual perversions the crowning cause—Touches more than half the race—Puberty—When sexual passion abates in man—Rebukes to the clergy.

CHAPTER II.—AN ANCIENT WRECK.

Sensuality the sin of the ages—Proof that the flood was a direct punishment of sensuality—The Mosaic account critically examined—Testimony outside the Bible—Why Noah was spared—Perfect in his generations—Blameless in his sexual relations—The indecency of Ham—The old devil of sensuality—Circumcision; its meaning and its lessons—Sensuality the sin which caused the destruction of Sodom and the cities of the plain—Sensuality in the patriarchal age—The chastity of Joseph—A modern incident—Prostitution in the patriarchal age—The Mosaic economy—Sensuality the sin which destroyed the Cananites and surrounding nations —Sexual purity in the law of Moses.

CHAPTER III.—A MODERN WRECK.

The history of prostitution—The Christian era—The doctrine of chastity—The voice of the apostles and the life of the early Christians—No compromise with impurity—Modern civilization—Statistics of Prostitution—A startling testimony—The blood of the race poisoned by venereal diseases—Thirty thousand men daily infected in the United States—History of venereal diseases—A State document—National decay—Prevention better than cure—Licensed prostitution a failure—Roman laws for the regulation of prostitution —Facts and statistics of recent date—A threefold appeal.

CHAPTER IV.—A YOUTHFUL WRECK.

Masturbation—Puberty; its indications and sequence —Prevalence of the solitary vice—An ancient habit— Referred to in the law of Moses—Impossible to exaggerate its ruinous results—Testimony of medical experts and of educationalists—Duty of ministers—Duty of parents—Loss of semen is loss of blood—Results of its expenditure—Seminal emissions—Effects on the nervous system—Conservatism of nature—Where masturbation and marital excess do their most deadly work—A word to parents and boys—Quacks and charlatans—No medicine required to cure seminal emissions.

CHAPTER V.—A WRECK ESCAPED.

Continence of young men—Is continence possible?— Tremendous power of the sexual appetite—Created of God for the perpetuation of the race—Continence outside of wedlock is possible—None but impure men question this—Impure thoughts the chief cause of self-abuse and fornication—Testimony of Dr. Acton and his personal experience—How to live a continent life.

CHAPTER VI.—THE RESCUE BEGUN.

Does nature forgive?—Natural law is God's method of operation—Forgiveness in the moral realm a higher type than forgiveness in the natural realm— Nature repairs and restores when we cease to disregard her laws—Three letters to the author—Comments on the same—Difficult to convince the victim of seminal weakness that no medicine is needed—Cut loose from charlatans—Burn their pamphlets—High medical testimony that medicine is not required—Is marriage a cure?—The question answered—The habit abandoned—Helps and encouragements—A cure as certain as the rising of the sun—Old-time philosophy —An amulet—Perseverance and victory.

CHAPTER VII.—THE RESCUE CONTINUED.

Some earnest words—Imperative—Philosophy of the difference between nervous function and muscular power—Nervous sensation frequently evokes results in sensitiveness and debility—Strong drink—Tobacco and its effects on the nervous system—How to cure yourself of the tobacco habit without expense and without inconvenience—What to eat and drink—Employment— Exercise—Bathing—Sleep—Society.

CHAPTER VIII.—THE RESCUE COMPLETED.

The medical profession—If you must have medical advice, consult a resident physician—Beware of medical companies and sharks—They take your money and shorten your life—Additional testimony that medicine cannot cure seminal weakness—The parts affected—Their intimate relationship—The principal aggravating cause of seminal weakness—A flood of light on the subject—Special treatment without expense—An absolutely infallible remedy—A certain cure for piles, and relief for the suffering resulting from irritation of the bladder and enlargement of the prostate gland—It is your life—Worth a struggle—A man again.

This book is handsomely published in large clear type, bound in extra cloth, and wishing to co-operate with the author in his desire that all who need it might have it, it is sold at $1.00. Clergymen and teachers wanted to act as agents for this great work, for the bettering of man.

Manhood Wrecked and Rescued, sent postpaid, bound in cloth for	$1.00
With One Year's Subscription	1.25
With One Year's Subscription and Macfadden's Physical Training,	1.40

Physical Culture Pub. Co., TOWNSEND BLDG., 25th ST. AND BROADWAY, **New York City**

"Manhood Wrecked and Rescued" (Advertisement in *Physical Culture* v. 3, 1900)

Restoring Twentieth-Century Manhood: Depicting a rogue, conniver, and self-interested scoundrel, Rhett Butler revived Southern manhood, in contrast to Leslie Howard's aristocratic cavalier, who was now gone with the wind. In the 1950s, the self-made man returned as a bit of an aristocratic dandy in the image of the Playboy. With his smoking jacket, Danish modern furniture, and cigarette holder, the Playboy was neither a sexualized scamp nor working class hero, as the frontispiece illustration for the first issue of the magazine suggests. His idea was to invite a woman over to his well-appointed apartment for "a quiet discussion on Picasso, Nietzsche, jazz, and sex." *Top*: Studio still from *Gone With the Wind,* 1939. *Bottom*: Frontispiece, *Playboy,* December 1953; reprinted with permission of *Playboy* magazine.

Television Restores Domestic Patriarchy: As "family entertainment," watched in the "family room," early television shows reestablished the centrality of the father in the family, even as suburban men's working lives were increasingly distant from the home. That father was reinserted as the family's center of gravity held true whether they lived in a suburban development or in the jungle. *Top: Father Knows Best* replaces mom with dad. (Publicity photograph) *Bottom:* Tarzan and Jane recreate the nuclear family. (Publicity photograph)

Muscles Continue to Make the Man: Physical strength, once of significance in the real world, maintains profound symbolic importance in the making of Self-Made Men. Charles Atlas made a fortune promising to transform 97-pound weaklings into he-men, as have scores of his heirs to the muscle-building industry. At the Academy Awards presentation in 1992, Jack Palance showed that, despite his age, he was still man enough. *Right:* Charles Atlas advertisement. *Bottom:* Jack Palance does a set of one-armed pushups after his acceptance speech for Best Supporting Actor at the Academy Awards presentation, 1992. (Courtesy of Reuters/Bettman)

Expanding the Definition of Contemporary Manhood: The contemporary era has witnessed a constant challenge to a definition of masculinity based on exclusion of the "other"—women, gay men, black men, ethnic immigrants. And some men have challenged the behavioral restrictions that label men as "sissy." *Top:* Civil rights workers proclaim their manhood, Memphis, 29 March 1968. (Courtesy of UPI/Bettman Newsphotos). *Bottom:* Bruce Springsteen and Clarence Clemons, 1990. (Photo by Ebet Roberts; reprinted with permission)

The Continuing Masculine Allure of the Frontier: The demonstration of masculinity continues to have political currency, as candidates routinely are photographed in manly poses and costumes, and question their opponents' manhood. Patrick Buchanan donned a coonskin cap and bore a flintlock rifle as he grabbed for the mantle of Davy Crockett. *Top:* Pat Buchanan campaigns in Tennessee, March 1992. (Photo courtesy of Agence France-Presse). *Right:* Bill Clinton, near his childhood home, Hope, Arkansas. (Photo courtesy of Reuters/Bettman)

Court ruled in *Roe* v. *Wade* that women have the right to choose to terminate a pregnancy, thus allowing women to maintain control over their bodies—a right that men had been assuming for themselves since the Founding Fathers guaranteed men a sense of property in their own person.

Feminism also insisted that the women who were the victims of abusive masculinity—the battered wives, the abandoned families, the sexually abused young girls, the rape victims—be protected from men's violence and that the government institute policies to protect women from rape, sexual harassment, battery. At the same time as feminism demanded protection for victims, it also empowered women to claim autonomy in their personal lives, especially in inter-personal relationships with men. Women not only had the right to work but the right to sexual agency, a right to desire itself—perhaps, even, a right to orgasm. (The invention of the birth control pill pro-vided technical assistance to women and men who wanted to claim sexual pleasure independent of procreation.) Women had the right to choose the kinds of lives they wanted to lead. No longer to be con-signed to housework and child care, women could *choose* to be moth-ers, to have careers, to work around the home. As the Statement of Purpose of the National Organization for Women put it in 1966:

> We reject the current assumptions that a man must carry the sole bur-den of supporting himself, his wife, and family, and that a woman is au-tomatically entitled to lifelong support by a man upon her marriage, or that marriage, home, and family are primarily woman's world and re-sponsibility—hers to dominate—his to support.[25]

Of course, such sentiments had enormous implications for Ameri-can men, because feminism demanded that men change—that men cease abusing, raping, and battering women, that men begin to share in the daily chores around the household, and that they accept that women were working right alongside them. For many men, women's liberation meant increased anxiety, particularly sexual anxiety. After all, if women could now be more fully sexual, then men might fear sexual activity as a constant test, a "trial of manliness" that would find men perpetually wanting, according to British observer Myron Brenton in *The American Male* (1967). Women now had the right not only to respond sexually but also to initiate sexual activity; Brenton saw American men running away, in a somewhat spiteful escape, from women's sexual desires and right into impotence, decreased desire, homosexual encounters, affairs with other women, and visits to call girls.[26]

Animated by these fears, by the antipathy for women's entry into the public sphere, and by a growing resentment of any demands that they change, many men resisted women's efforts to either open up the public sphere or to transform the private sphere. Norman Mailer's *The Prisoner of Sex* (1971), itself a response to a feminist critique of his work, turned from a defensive plea to a meandering spiteful tirade, full of bathos and bombast. Confessing to exhaustion and confusion, Mailer moved back and forth, from calling his sexual instrument "the Avenger" to wincing at the "desperate bravado" that men exhibit in their "passion to be masculine."[27]

Academic works, like sociologist Steven Goldberg's *The Inevitability of Patriarchy* (1973), marshaled a limited and selective sample of anthropological and biological evidence to claim that women's liberation ran counter to the forces of nature and cultural stability, that male domination was encoded in the superior strength of the male. Male domination was universal, Goldberg claimed, and was therefore natural.[28] Conservative political theorist George Gilder also used a putative biological argument to support antifeminist claims in his books *Sexual Suicide* (1973) and *Naked Nomads* (1974). Men, Gilder argued, were biologically driven towards aggression, competition, and violence, naturally "disposed" to crime, drugs, and violence, and naturally "susceptible" to disease, and if women followed feminist ideals, they would abandon their traditional role as moralistic constraints on men's antisocial natures, and all hell would break loose. Since men were untamable, except in their traditionally responsible roles as father, husband, and breadwinner—he cites statistics that indicate that most violent crimes are committed by young men—then women's liberation would result in an anarchistic uprising among men, who would run rampant in an orgy of violence and aggression. And sex. Male sexuality is insistent and incessant; if not harnessed by women, there will be "aimless copulation," "slaked by masturbation and pornography" or uncontrolled promiscuous homosexuality.[29]

Gilder's solution was to reestablish the pedestal and replace women firmly on top of it. Women need to leave the public sphere and return to the home where they belong and where men desperately needed them to be. Feminists are their own worst enemies; "[a] society of wealthy and independent women will be a society of sexually and economically predatory males," he predicts. While his antifeminism is obvious, more subtle is the vehement rage at men. Gilder believes that masculinity is "at bottom empty, a limp nullity. While the female body is full of internal potentiality, the male is internally barren." Thus, men need women and society to help them define their place in the world because without women, men would be "destined to a Hobbesian life—solitary, poor, nasty, brutish and short."[30]

Popular magazines and books curried masculine resentment and resistance—not only in soft-core pornography, which boomed during the 1970s (*Playboy* and *Penthouse* became two of the five top-selling magazines in the country) but also in a host of new men's magazines promising deliverance from women. In a self-promotional advertisement a newly made-over *True* magazine recalled its earlier incarnation two decades before:

> one word describes the new TRUE magazine: MACHO. The honest-to-God American MAN deserves a magazine sans naked cuties, Dr. Spock philosophies, foppish, gutless "unisex" pap, and platform shoes. It's time for a refreshing change. . . . A hardy slice of adventure, challenge, action, competition, controversy. Including informative features that bring the American man and American values back from the shadows. Back from the sterile couches of pedantic psychiatrists. Back from behind the frivolous skirts of libbers.

The ad ended with as much a threat as a promise. "If you're a man, you'll like it."[31]

Gilder and other antifeminists prescribed traditional marriage and nuclear families, with one male breadwinner and one stay-at-home female homemaker, as the solution to the male malaise. Other cultural critics worried that such arrangements would again result in the feminization of American manhood. Echoing themes from the turn of the century, the sociologist Patricia Cayo Sexton observed a general "enervating trend" in American culture—a trend directly traceable to women's monopoly over child rearing and early education. In *The Feminized Male* (1969) Sexton argued that this "overexposure to feminine norms" at home and at school was turning American boys into a weak-willed bunch of sissies, "afflicted by excessive caution and a virtual incapacity to *do* anything in the real world."[32]

Sexton based her claims on her observations at several urban schools, where it seemed that the boys who were the most academically successful consistently scored the lowest on masculinity scales, especially the still-employed Terman and Miles M-F test. School "makes sissies out of many boys and feminizes many more by insisting that they act like girls" so that, in the end, "the more scholarly the men the lower their masculinity score tended to be."[33] Here again were all the fears of feminization from nearly a century earlier: that boys raised by women will be less manly than boys raised by men and that the configuration of the modern family turns boys into mushy little wimps.

Other writers followed suit. Hans Sebald's frantic and frightened tract *Momism: The Silent Disease of America* (1976) chronicled a generation of emotionally frustrated women whose career ambitions had been thwarted and who therefore sank despondently into professional motherhood, demanding of their children the career successes that they, the mothers, had never been able to achieve—and making "psychological wrecks" of their sons in the process. Echoing Philip Wylie's vituperative 1942 fusillade *Generation of Vipers*, Sebald exposed the "crippling peril" of Momism, the "hidden savagery" of "Mom's repressive transaction." His motto? "When Learning Masculinity, Don't Imitate the Teacher."[34]

Robert Ardrey, one of a host of popularizers of the new field of sociobiology, argued that the American mother is "the unhappiest female that the primate world has ever seen, and the most treasured objective in her heart of hearts is the psychological castration of husbands and sons."[35] A writer in *True* magazine called on his brethren to resist the civilizing pulls of feminization, which meant resisting the city as a source of domestication, hence enervation, since cities and their "suburban occlusions" are run by women and since "Gloria Whosits and whoever started the current thrombosis are city women."[36] Anthropologist Lionel Tiger was so concerned about gender blending that he advocated, in *Men in Groups* (1969), that urban planners place men's clubs in their plans for urban redevelopment to facilitate male bonding and provide men with a surcease from female invasion of the formerly homosocial workplace.[37]

In one of the decade's more humorous turns at cultural feminization and the relationship between gender identity and class, Tom Wolfe observed the ways in which the desire to appear masculine animated the activities of a bunch of preppy mama's boys. In the essay "Honks and Wonks" (1976) Wolfe drew a distinction between the street masculinity of the working class and that of preppy "honks" who "get hung up on the masculinity thing" because their manhood is always in question:

> It seems to me that when it comes to prep-school honks like Averell Harriman or Thomas Hoving—well, it doesn't matter how many worlds they have conquered or how old they are. As soon as they open their mouths, a bell goes off in the brains of most local-bred New York males: *sissy.* Here are a coupla kids who woulda got *mashed* in the street life.[38]

Preppies were feminized, Wolfe argues, by a class culture that shielded them from the harsher realities of masculine life. When they talked tough, they revealed their phony claims to masculine credentials.

Jewish men were also seen as feminized because they came from a religious culture that stressed morality and literacy; thus, they were seen as bookish and effete.[39] I recall, for example, marching in a protest demonstration against the war in Vietnam as an adolescent, when a heckler screamed at me to "go back to Russia, you Commie Jew faggot!" Though I was startled at the time by the venom of his accusations, stung by his rage, what is most significant to me now is the way that communism, Judaism, and homosexuality were so easily linked in his mind. All three, I came to understand, were not "real men."[40]

Jewish men inherited a legacy of gendered dismissal as gentle, intellectual, and moral. And generations of writers had moaned with pain at being left outside the hallowed gates of masculinity. The decade's most anguished cry came from Alex Portnoy, the angst-ridden antihero of Philip Roth's *Portnoy's Complaint* (1967), who screams to his psychiatrist, "Doctor, I can't stand anymore being frightened like this over nothing! Bless me with manhood! Make me brave! Make me strong! Make me *whole*!"[41] With the stereotypes of Jewish mothers as castrating and all-consuming, Jewish men were among the archetypal feminized men.[42]

Many Jews fought back, both rhetorically and politically. A generation of writers followed Norman Mailer into Jewish tough-guy poses. Some Jewish men began to articulate a vision of Jewish virility, a kind of "Muscular Judaism." In part, celebrating Zionist militarism in Israel was a vehicle by which American Jewry could come to terms with the Holocaust. If the Holocaust had feminized European Jewish men, who were castigated as incapable of protecting their families and were therefore led sheepishly to the slaughter, then supporting Israeli territorial expansion was a way to rescue one's manhood. And the discovery of Jewish resistance to Nazism gave Jewish men "Jewish Buffalo Bills" or "Jewish Tarzans," according to Arthur Koestler. Leon Uris's *Exodus* (1958) offered a new version of heroic Judaism. "We Jews are not what we have been portrayed to be," Uris told an interviewer immediately after the novel appeared. "In truth we have been fighters," as he wrote in a new preface to the paperback edition:

> [A]ll the cliché Jewish characters who have cluttered up our American fiction—the clever businessman, the brilliant doctor, the sneaky lawyer, the sulking artist—all the good folk who spend their chapters hating themselves, the world, and all their aunts and uncles . . . all those steeped in self-pity . . . all those golden riders of the psychoanalysis couch . . . all these have been left where they rightfully belong, on the cutting room floor.[43]

As I learned on that New York City street in 1965, the fears of feminization only partially cloaked a simmering homophobic fear, a fear that homosexuality was "spreading like a murky smog over the American scene," as Betty Friedan had put it in *The Feminine Mystique*. Hans Sebald claimed that the mother had "cast a spell" on young boys, "preventing them from developing normal heterosexual interest," so that the mother "bore the main responsibility" for sexual "deviance." Some parents worried that opening home economics courses to boys would "rob" boys of their masculinity and lead to "sexual deviance."[44]

Peter and Barbara Wyden's *Growing Up Straight: What Every Thoughtful Parent Should Know About Homosexuality* (1968) provided anxious parents with a set of early warning signs of homosexuality in their sons. "Pre-homosexual" boys were identified by their "unmasculine" behaviors, which were reinforced by overdominant mothers and absent fathers. For these vulnerable boys to become well-adjusted heterosexual men, fathers must become role models for their sons, and mothers must accept their husbands' place at the head of the family. Pre-homosexual boys grew up with inverted gender identities because they were taught the wrong things by parents who enacted reversals themselves. Only "sexually normal homes" could be certain to produce normal, heterosexual men.[45]

The gay liberation movement posited a strong riposte to the facile equation of homosexuality and masculine gender identity and made the counterclaim that gay men were as much "real" men as straight men.[46] Following the Stonewall riots of 1969, in which gay men fought back against a police raid on a Greenwich Village bar, and the subsequent birth of the Gay Liberation Movement, a new gay masculinity emerged in gay enclaves of America's major cities. In these "gay ghettos," the "clone," as he was called, dressed in hypermasculine garb (flannel shirts, blue jeans, leather) and had short hair (not at all androgynous) and a mustache; he was athletic, highly muscular. In short, the clone looked more like a "real man" than most straight men.[47]

And the clones—who constituted roughly one-third of all gay men living in the major urban enclaves of the 1970s—enacted a hypermasculine sexuality in steamy backrooms, bars, and bathhouses where sex was plentiful, anonymous, and very hot. No unnecessary foreplay, romance, or postcoital awkwardness. Sex without attachment. One might even say that, given the norms of masculinity (that men are always seeking sex, ready for sex, wanting sex), gay men were just about the only men in America who were getting as much sex as they wanted. And gay men were certainly making it plain that the traditional equation of gay man as failed man was no longer tenable. Gay liberation signaled that gay men, too, could stake their claim for manhood.[48]

Together feminism, black liberation, and gay liberation provided a frontal assault on the traditional way that men had defined their manhood—against an other who was excluded from full humanity by being excluded from those places where men were real men. It was as if the screen against which American men had for generations projected their manhood had suddenly grown dark, and men were left to sort out the meaning of masculinity all by themselves.

Enter "men's liberation," a curious mixture of a social movement and psychological self-help manual that emerged in the mid-1970s.[49] Media pundits often excoriated men's liberation as a bunch of middle-class white guys feeling left out of the fun of being oppressed and trying to jump on the liberation bandwagon. But men's liberation was more than merely a case of oppression envy. It's impulse, at least originally, came from the effort to take to heart the critiques of Self-Made Masculinity first voiced by the women's movement and later by the gay liberation movement. If men were supposed to be so powerful and oppressive, how come so many men were still living lives of quiet desperation—working in boring and unfulfilling jobs, trapped in unhappy marriages with little or no relationship with their children, with few, if any, close friends, isolated, lonely, and unaware of their feelings? "Male liberation calls for men to free themselves of the sex-role stereotypes that limit their ability to be human," announced Jack Sawyer in "On Male Liberation" (1970), a founding text of the new men's lib literature. Following his call, dozens of other works poured into the growing field, including Warren Farrell's *The Liberated Man* (1974), Marc Feigen Fasteau's *The Male Machine* (1975), Herb Goldberg's *The Hazards of Being Male* (1975) and *The New Male* (1979), Jack Nichols's *Men's Liberation* (1975), and two anthologies, Deborah David and Robert Brannon's *The Forty-Nine Percent Majority* (1976) and Joseph Pleck and Jack Sawyer's *Men and Masculinity* (1974).[50]

As women had sought liberation from restrictive stereotyped sex roles, so too did men begin to understand traditional masculinity as a burden, a form of oppression. "It's becoming clear to many of us that many of our most important inner needs cannot be met by acting in the ways we have been expected to act as men," noted the psychologist Pleck in an interview in 1973. The Berkeley Men's Center Manifesto counted the ways: "We no longer want to strain and compete to live up to an impossible oppressive masculine image—strong, silent, cool, handsome, unemotional, successful, master of women, leader of men, wealthy, brilliant, athletic, and 'heavy.'"[51]

At its core men's liberation provided a coherent critique of the Self-Made Man; in its eyes *he* was the failure. As a collection of dos and don'ts, the male sex role was a recipe for despair; given what it took to be a real man, few, if any, men could live up to the image, and hence all men would feel like failures as men. What's worse, the psychological costs of trying to live up to the image would lead men into lives of isolation and despair, of repressed emotion and deferred dreams. The blueprint for masculinity

> is a blueprint for self-destruction. . . . The masculine imperative, the pressure and compulsion to perform, to prove himself, to dominate, to live up to the "masculine ideal"—in short, to "be a man"—supersedes the instinct to survive. . . . Close examination of a man's behavior reveals a powerfully masochistic, self-hating, and often pathetically self-destructive style.

Our society is therefore full of "success-driven men at the end points of their success voyage, living in a nightmarish world of not knowing whom to trust, unable to find satisfaction in intimate contact, unaware of what they want and feel, and rigidly resistant to opening up in order to find out."[52]

Men's liberationists offered a systematic assault on what they called the male sex role, echoing many of the earlier critics of the workplace and family life that had attended the rise of Self-Made Manhood. For the first time in American history, outside of those small groups of Greenwich Village bohemians earlier in the century, men themselves were refusing to live up to the prescribed package of behaviors and traits that defined American manhood. They did not run off to the West, seeking to reclaim their manhood in the wilds of nature, nor did they escape into masculinist fantasies of adventure and heroic struggle. And they didn't seek to reclaim their manhood by the further exclusion of women, men of color, and gay men. (Some men's liberationists actually saw those movements as inspirational.) The very notion of Self-Made Masculinity was under siege—and from the very men who were supposed to live up to its ideals.

In the introduction to *The Forty-Nine Percent Majority*, the editors Deborah David and Robert Brannon brilliantly reduced the male sex role into four basic rules of manhood. The first and perhaps most important rule is "No Sissy Stuff": One can never do anything that even remotely hints of the feminine. The second rule, "Be a Big Wheel," indicates that masculinity is measured by power, wealth, success. The third rule reminds men to "Be a Sturdy Oak," since real men show no emotions, are emotionally reliable by being emotionally inexpressive. And finally, "Give 'em Hell" meant to exude an aura of manly daring and aggression. Always take risks, go for it. These four rules sum up the masculine predicament, and men "have been limited and diverted from whatever our real potential might have been by the prefabricated mold of the male sex role."[53]

How were men to free themselves from the prison of the male sex role? For one thing, men's liberationists wanted out of the corporate rat race, a "bland and boring" arena with little opportunity for self-expression or self-fulfillment. Being a big wheel was unsatisfying and deadening to real human experience. Work was "fraught with dehumanizing—i.e. unmanning—influences," wrote British critic Myron Brenton. As one thirty-six-year-old civil engineer told him, "I just don't get it. I've got everything. I really have. All the same, now and then, I get the feeling I'm in a prison or something. Happens when everything's on top of me, closing in, you know?" The rugged individualism of the Heroic Artisan was gone, as men sat "in lushly carpeted offices where the faint crackling of typewriters can barely be heard above Muzak," added Jack Nichols. As one corporate manager put it, "Every so often I feel like making it all disappear—start fresh. Hey, man, wouldn't you like to have been a pioneer?" one corporate manager confessed, while another added that he wanted to "chuck it all and take a raft down the Amazon!" In the absence of any sense of adventure, accomplishment, or fulfillment, men turn to accumulation of wealth. But as psychiatrist Robert Gould warned in a 1973 essay in *Ms.*, "Measuring Masculinity by the Size of a Paycheck," money was a "pretty insecure peg on which to hang a masculine image."[54]

Blue-collar workers suffered an even more dismally emasculating fate. One study found these men playing out "dramas of manliness in work settings" in everything they did—except their work. They wrote off white-collar workers as "desk jockeys" and "pencil pushers," who had sold out their manhood for the "dubious merits of a white shirt and a higher social status," while their reveling in off-color jokes, pornography, obscenities, and "adopting a stance of indifference as a form of self-protection" became demonstrations of working-class manliness. Men's liberationists rejected competition, aggression, and alienation and claimed that by changing men's roles, men's work would be an expression of their selves, not the repudiation of their humanity.[55]

At home, men's liberationists argued that men were equally disconnected and despairing. Being a sturdy oak meant denying or suppressing emotion and spontaneity. A "man isn't someone you'd want to have around in a crisis—like raising children or growing old together," wrote actor Alan Alda as he signed up for men's liberation. And male sexuality operated on the performance principle, not the pleasure principle; men turned sex into work, experiencing "performance anxiety" while they worked to "get the job done." Sex was a "dangerous encounter," the ultimate test of masculinity; our sex-role conditioning had destroyed "the potential for joyful, authentic, spontaneous, sexual responsiveness," according to Marc Feigen Fasteau. The male sex role reduces fatherhood to a "financial functionary" to children, forcing men to be not only absentee landlords in their homes but also absentee fathers with their children.[56]

If the traditional role models were unsatisfying, men needed to find new models for manhood. Theologians Thomas Hearn and Leonard Swidler returned to Jesus as masculine archetype but, this time, with exactly the opposite intentions of the Muscular Christians nearly a century earlier. To Swidler Jesus was a "feminist," while to Hearn he was a "sissy" who

> was given to feeling and expressing a wide range of the "tender" emotions; he wept without shame; he freely touched other men and even—I tremble to say it—kissed them. He was intuitive; he strongly sensed dependency on the human community as well as on the Father. He re-

sponded to beauty; he was touched with compassionate tenderness at the sight of suffering. He loved little children, and with kindred affection he regarded the birds of the air and the lilies of the field.[57]

Others proposed a desexualized androgyny by which women could get in touch with their "masculine sides" and men their "feminine sides" and thus both become whole people. A few suggested that gay men had already achieved such contact with their feminine sides, which explained what they took to be gay men's relative ease with intimacy, sensitivity, and emotion. Perhaps homosexual manhood could be a model for heterosexual men, who were, they suggested, still stifled by homophobic fears of expressing emotion or the need for physical contact with other men.

What virtually all men's liberationists promised was that by rejecting traditional masculinity, men would live longer, happier, and healthier lives, lives characterized by close and caring relationships with children, with women, and with other men.[58] Where they differed was over feminism. Some men's libbers, like Herb Goldberg, saw feminism as "unbalanced, unfair and psychologically invalid." Dismissing feminist leader Gloria Steinem, for example, Goldberg wrote that she concocted "a mixture of facts, half-truths, hyperbole, sweeping generalizations, and the fiery adjectives of an old-time preacher or charismatic crowd manipulator" in order to "castigate, in wholesale fashion, the *entire* male sex." Another feminist, he wrote, who "reacts with rage and fury at men for their alleged abuses" only "reveals her lack of perspective and empathy" for the ways in which—and this is a key insight for many men's libbers—"*men* have been trapped."[59]

Others saw feminism as providing half the answer: Just as women had to liberate themselves from their sex role, so too did men have to liberate themselves from their oppressive sex role. Warren Farrell, a self-proclaimed "liberated man" and convener of the National Organization for Women's Task Force on the Masculine Mystique, was masterful in providing role reversals that revealed to men what had been women's experience as sex objects. At the consciousness-raising groups he initiated, he organized male beauty contests to give men a sense of how traditional masculinity was experienced by those against whom it was deployed. Farrell believed that men could actually benefit from women's liberation; individually a man could be freed of the work pressure to be a woman's "security object" and thus be free to pursue his personal life with less stress and anxiety.[60]

But for some the personal was not merely psychological, and it did not involve the false equivalences between women's and men's experiences. The personal was political, and by confronting and challenging traditional masculinity, they believed they were simultaneously striking a blow for the liberation of women, black people, and gays and lesbians. Marc Feigen Fasteau believed that feminism implied both "women's and men's liberation," and Glenn Bucher's *Straight/White/Male* (1976) used gay liberation and black liberation as the starting points for a critique of traditional masculinity. According to Bucher and his colleagues, straight white men are dehumanized, but they are not oppressed; they are, rather, oppressors, and they must "restructure their identities and reroot themselves in a way of life that is not dependent upon the benefits of the status quo."[61]

Psychologist Joseph Pleck's work provided perhaps the most significant and sustained scholarly effort to expose the male sex role as a fraud. In his more polemical essays, "My Male Sex Role—and Ours" (1974) and "Men's Power with Women, Other Men, and Society" (1977), Pleck placed the psychological experience of men within a larger context of social and political oppression. In a style far more honestly self-revelatory than many of the other writers and with nary a hint of self-congratulation, Pleck argued that patriarchy has been a dual system of oppression, a system by which men have oppressed women and in which some men have oppressed other men, so that "to be a man with other men means to always fear being attacked, victimized, exploited, and in an ultimate sense, murdered by other men."[62]

Pleck's 1981 scholarly treatise *The Myth of Masculinity* provided the culmination of men's liberation theory as academic social psychology, challenging the basic explanation of gender development that academic psychology had been advancing since the mid-1930s. Rather than begin with the anxieties, stress, and pressures that men feel and from which therefore they need liberation, Pleck begins with a dissection of the male sex role itself. What he calls the Male Sex

Role Identity (MSRI) model is itself the problem; the MSRI model creates role demands that are so internally contradictory that no one could possibly live up to them. Trying to fulfill the role demands is the real source of stress in men's lives. For example, remaining cool under pressure on the one hand and giving 'em hell on the other hand pull men in opposing directions. Pleck argued that the MSRI was a testable hypothesis, not an established scientific fact; for that matter, he argued, the correlation between the prescribed behaviors and the feelings of secure manhood was actually very weak empirically. Even those men who conformed to the stereotypic definition didn't seem any more confident in themselves as real men. "How people continue to believe so fervently in values and norms according to which they can only be failures is an awe-inspiring phenomenon," he wrote.[63]

Instead of the MSRI, Pleck posited a model of Male Sex-Role Strain, which placed tension, contradiction, and anxiety squarely in the center of men's efforts to demonstrate manhood. Psychology was thus not going to be the liberator of men but was instead cast as the conduit for those very contradictory and confusing messages that kept us all in constant turmoil. It wasn't men as much as it was the prescription for masculinity that caused the crisis of masculinity and contributed to the oppression of women and minorities.[64]

Men's liberation drew some modest curiosity from cultural observers, some tentative and wary alliances with some feminist women, and a large amount of indifference from the majority of American men. But there were telling signs in popular culture that the times were changing. Traditional genres continued, but they were more popular when they offered twists on their own standard formulae. With hindsight we now see how these traditional genres were beginning to break down.

Take, for example, the grizzled tough-guy detective of classic film noir. *Marlowe* (1969), a resetting of Raymond Chandler's detective novel *The Little Sister* into hippie, drug-infested Los Angeles, uses the ironic sneer of James Garner to express the inability of the old genre to sustain men's hopes. Marlowe, a smoking, hard-drinking private detective, is enlisted to help a naive, innocent Kansas girl who is searching for her lost brother. During the course of the film, he suckers an Asian kung fu fighter (played by Bruce Lee), who had earlier trashed his office, into jumping to his death by calling him "just a little bit gay," thus simultaneously linking Asian immigrants and homosexuality and disposing of them both as threats to his manhood. Of course, it turns out that the naive little sister is also hopelessly corrupt, demonstrating once again that any faith in women—or even men's role as their protector—is faith misplaced and earnest effort manipulated.

The classic buddy film also tended to end in tragedy in the late 1960s and 1970s; what's more, the settings for these films became increasingly ironic in films like *Easy Rider* or *Midnight Cowboy*, both released in 1969. The male bonding celebrated in these films is a defensive reaction to traditional masculine failure; the men turn to each other because the world (and women) have failed them. In *Easy Rider* frontier escapism becomes a tamed delinquency, complete with an unsettling hallucinogenic drug experience; but the macho defiance is ultimately tragic, even as its misogynist core goes unchallenged. In *Midnight Cowboy* a de-eroticized homosexuality—an emotional, but not sexual connection—occurs in a highly ironic context: the failure of Joe Buck to establish himself as a stud. Instead, Joe finds love and success as a male mother, nursing the tubercular Ratso to his peaceful death.

Carnal Knowledge (1972) and *Deliverance* (1973) also recapitulated the buddy film, again with the bitter theme that masculine failure solidifies friendship. The bonding between Sandy (Art Garfunkel) and Jonathan (Jack Nicholson) is animated in "the mutuality of sharing and recounting sexual experiences," writes film critic Joan Mellers. In their characters the viewers got a sense of masculinity in transition. On the one hand, Sandy represents an effort, ultimately unsuccessful, to articulate a different, emotionally-based way of relating to women. By contrast, Nicholson's portrayal of Jonathan unflinchingly exposes the negative aspects of conventional success-oriented masculinity: He is unable to move beyond the "objectification-fixation-conquest" described by men's liberationists. This model proves so devastating that it becomes sexually deflating; Jonathan is impotent.[65]

Deliverance provided one of the era's signal films about both the dangers and redemptive possibilities of male bonding. Both novel and film begin as conventionally masculinist voyages of discovery

for Ed as he floats down the river with the darker, more earthily primal Lewis, his spirit guide in the masculine quest:

> Why on earth am I here? I thought. But then I turned back to the car to
> see what Lewis was doing, I caught a glimpse of myself in the rear win-
> dow. I was light green, a tall forest man, an explorer, guerilla, hunter. I
> liked the idea and the image, I must say. Even if this was just a game, a
> charade, I had let myself in for it, and I was here in the woods, where
> such people as I had got myself up were supposed to be. Something or
> other was being made good. I touched the knife hilt at my side, and re-
> membered that all men were once boys, and that boys are always look-
> ing for ways to become men. Some of the ways are easy too; all you
> have to do is be satisfied that it has happened.[66]

And the book underlines that such camaraderie is only possible outside any sexual relationship between men, that such a relationship
may undermine friendship. *Deliverance* simultaneously eroticizes and
glamorizes the friendship among the men while it de-eroticizes the
sexual scenes of homosexual rape. In a sense, the film graphically
provided one of the cinema's first clearly articulated feminist under-
standings that rape is a crime of power and violence and not a crime
of sexual desire—although the rape had to happen to a man for men
to understand this. What *Deliverance* expresses is a cautionary tale:
The male desire for escape from women is fraught with danger—danger from other men who are not so civilized that they can repress
their desires and from a nature whose wildness is actually a threat to
men's effort to prove themselves. In short, watch out, men: When
you escape from the civilizing constraints of women, you will rape
and murder each other.[67]

If men were made uneasy by these buddy films, though, and if the
rise of the gay liberation movement seemed to put all male friendships under a new homophobic scrutiny, then they could always take
refuge in the novels of Norman Mailer, who reassured his readers in
Why Are We in Vietnam? (1967) to:

> fear not, gentle auditor, they is men, real Texas men, they don't ding
> ding ring a ling on no queer street with each other, shit, no, they just
> talk to each other that way to express Texas tenderness than which

there is nothing more tender than a flattened pan-fried breaded paper-thin hard-ass Texas steak.[68]

When historian and playwright Martin Duberman, in his 1977 play *Visions of Kerouac*, dared to suggest any erotic possibilities in the male bonding between Dean Moriarty and Neil Cassady in Jack Kerouac's Beat novels, he was vilified by several critics as if he'd tainted one of the most redemptive, purest of masculine archetypes, buddy bonding on the road.

Three other films, all from 1971, offer eerily negative portraits of contemporary manhood. In *Straw Dogs* Dustin Hoffman plays an effete intellectual who with his wife rents a house in the English countryside. She holds him in contempt as unmanly. Later, she is raped by working-class thugs who doubt his ability to fight back. Yet when he finally does fight back, unaware of her rape, we know his manhood is not redeemed. In *Shaft*, a prototypical blaxploitation film of the era, Richard Roundtree plays a private detective—"a private dick that's a sex machine with all the chicks," as the theme song had it—who is always one step ahead of the rather nerdy white police officers on the case. Little wonder, in those sexually unrepressed 1970s, that black hypersexuality should have been so crassly depicted and equally dehumanized. And in *Play It Again Sam*, Woody Allen presents us with the first in a series of films about the revenge of the nerds, as yet another bespectacled wimp confesses that "most men are secretly tortured by not being Bogart." So Bogart returns as fantasy construction and imparts a series of lessons in manhood for Allen-as-nebbish-Everyman to follow. Men needed to reclaim their manhood; all they needed was the right role model.[69]

By the end of the 1970s, positive role models were increasingly hard to find. The end of the decade revealed the impotence of the stalwart friend in *The Deer Hunter* (1978); the saga of the Self-Made Man was retold as tragedy as in Geoffrey Wolff's *The Duke of Deception* (1979). Wolff's father was literally "the author of his own circumstances," able to "disassemble his history, begin at zero, and re-create himself"—but only because he completely fabricated his autobiography to suit his circumstances. The Self-Made Man turned out to be a con artist. Male bonding was equally bereft of meaning in Leonard Michaels's *The*

Men's Club (1978), in which a group of upper middle-class profession-als in Berkeley, California, imitate their wives' consciousness-raising group, only to find themselves more lost than before.[70]

On television the domestic patriarch of the 1950s and early 1960s had virtually disappeared, replaced by a working-class blowhard, Archie Bunker, or a bossy ignoramus, Mel, on *Alice*, behind whose back the waitresses rolled their eyes at his foolishness. On sitcoms like *Three's Company, Benson*, and *Night Court*, middle-class mas-culinity had become the butt of humor, not the object of veneration.

Star Trek revealed, perhaps more clearly, if unintentionally, than any other TV show, the growing crisis of masculinity. Here manhood was divided into two halves—the rational, abstract, and emotionally invul-nerable alien, embodied in Mr. Spock, and the aggressive, erotic, and intuitive traditional version of manhood, expressed by Captain Kirk. Here again was that most American of literary themes: cross-race (in this case cross-species) male bonding, although this time the white and nonwhite men were depicted as coequal. Neither was complete, and therefore neither could serve as a role model for the future. Full manhood could not even be reclaimed in space, the "final frontier."

One modestly hopeful sign was the emergence of a new vision of fatherhood, signaled, in part, by Dustin Hoffman's Academy Award–winning portrayal of Ted Kramer in *Kramer vs. Kramer* (1979). Masculine redemption for a failed marriage and a blind-alley career is found, as in the 1950s, in fatherhood, but this time with an ironic slap at feminism. We were invited to cheer when his ex-wife (Meryl Streep) finally decides to renounce her efforts to gain custody, since we have just witnessed the emergence of the sensitive new father from the chrysalis of an indifferent careerist. If put to the test, men turn out to actually be better "mothers" than women.

An old theme, perhaps, but it still didn't work. Masculinity could not be reclaimed in an arena so feminized. Nor could it be retrieved in outerspace aboard the *Enterprise*. The main theme of men's libera-tion—that changing men's *roles* would somehow magically transform the enormous economic and social structures that held those roles in place—revealed a theoretical naïveté that would easily sour into the whine of a new voice of victimhood. Men were still searching, but they still hadn't found what they were looking for.

CHAPTER 9

Wimps, Whiners, and Weekend Warriors

THE CONTEMPORARY CRISIS OF MASCULINITY
AND BEYOND

> The male of the past twenty years has become more
> thoughtful, more gentle. But by this process he has not
> become more free. He's a nice boy who pleases not only his
> mother but also the young woman he is living with.
> —Robert Bly *Iron John* (1990)

Ronald Reagan's presidency heralded "morning in America." Perhaps now American men would awaken to a new, recharged manhood for a new, ambitious, and aggressive era. We've often thought of the 1980s as a decade of the reassertion of pride, the retrieval of political and metaphoric potency for America and, hence, for the American man. In a replay of the frontier cowboy myth, America was once again sitting tall in the saddle, willing to take on all comers, asserting its dominance in world affairs. "Americans are now standing tall and firm," Reagan commented after the invasion of Grenada; columnists praised him for "stiffening our foreign policy"—as if this masculine country had been suffering from a nationwide bout with impotence. Symbolically, we even returned to Vietnam in our movies, answering John Rambo's plaintive question about his own return, "Do we get to win this time?" Wall Street was imagined as a Social Darwinist corporate jungle in which only the fittest could survive the frenzy of mergers and acquisitions.

But the manhood regained under Presidents Reagan and Bush was the compulsive masculinity of the schoolyard bully, defeating weaker foes such as Grenada and Panama, a defensive and restive manhood, of men who needed to demonstrate their masculinity at every opportunity. Men who feel powerful in their lives do not need to wear "power ties" or eat "power breakfasts" or "power lunches" as did yuppie arbitrageurs in the 1980s. Power is not something to be applied like a fashion accessory; it is both an inner confidence and security, as well as referring to a real hierarchical position. This kind of power American men still did not feel.

By some evidence American men were more confused in the 1980s than ever before. Who were their role models? John Wayne, who had dominated surveys of the American men that we most admired for over thirty years, was now absent from the list (and not merely because he had died). So were many politicians. Watergate and media revelations about other public figures so tarnished political life that our heroes would have to be drawn from elsewhere. Despite the writer Mark Gerzon's suggestion that in the 1980s we now could have *A Choice of Heroes* (1982), we had, in fact, a dearth of heroes.[1]

So instead, we sought out negative models to attack. The wimp, for example, emerged in the early 1980s. A virtual Great American Wimp Hunt repudiated the "new man" of the 1970s. Magazine articles and films had predicted that this new man—warm, sensitive, cuddly, and compassionate—would be the new hero of the 1980s. Betty Friedan, for one, was smitten; in a foreword to a new 1983 edition of *The Feminine Mystique*, she embraced Dustin Hoffman's *Tootsie* as the new man, whose experience masquerading as a woman "makes him a much better, stronger, more tender man." To Friedan this meant that America had "now clearly broken through and beyond the *masculine mystique* for man and woman to find such joyous adventure in being a woman." Not quite. As delightfully and playfully androgynous as they were, Hoffman's two new man films also had a darker side, implying that men could be not only better mothers than women (*Kramer vs. Kramer*) but also better *women* than women (*Tootsie*). The new man still emerged at the expense of women; he was not new enough for a truly egalitarian relationship with an equally strong woman.

But there he was anyway, the "sensitive New Age guy," poised as a masculine template for the decade, despite his receding hairline, flabby biceps, and enlarging waistline. In the film *Three Men and a Baby*, three swinging single men interrupt their routine sexual conquests to become surrogate "mothers" after a former lover drops off one's progeny—and they accomplish this feat without the slightest loss of a drop of androgen-laced manhood. In fact, they turn out to be even *more* attractive to women. Didn't Broadway Joe Namath model panty hose? And didn't Senator Paul Tsongas decide to resign from the Senate because, as he said, "[n]o man on his deathbed ever lamented that he spent too much time with his family"?[2]

Or what about John Lennon, ex-Beatle, pop superstar, Nixon "enemy." Lennon, who had earlier penned "Woman Is the Nigger of the World," one of the most feminist-inspired rock songs this side of Helen Reddy's "I Am Woman," opted out of pop superstardom to experience the simple joys of fatherhood and domestic bliss. "Isn't it time we destroyed the macho ethic?" he commented in an interview in 1980:

> Where has it gotten us all these thousands of years? Are we still going to have to be clubbing each other to death? Do I have to arm wrestle you to have a relationship with you as another male? Do I have to seduce her—just because she's a female? Can we not have a relationship on some other level?

Lennon concluded by confessing that he didn't "want to go through life pretending to be James Dean or Marlon Brando."[3]

But very few Americans bought the new man package. Alan Alda, Phil Donahue, Bob Newhart, and others could not fill the chasm left by cinematic machismo and political opportunism, despite the new man's vaunted decency, sensitivity, and liberal values.[4] Or, perhaps, because of them—as the new man was immediately on the defensive, afraid of being perceived as a sissy, a wimp. "Real men" hated wimps because they were so obeisant, as devoted as simpering puppies and just about as sexually compelling. The novelist George Stade, writing in the *New York Times Book Review* in 1984, bemoaned the current wimpiness of fictional male characters and lambasted novelists like Philip Roth, John Updike, and Leonard Michaels. "Their protagonists no longer venture forth; they retreat, admit defeat, take the heat, all with a sheepish grin," he brooded; they all have regressed "to the preadolescent condition of mama's boys, alternately bratty and eager to please." He yearned for a revival of manly literature, of sagas in which young boys sally forth to find and prove their manhood against the odds.[5]

Some women rejected the wimp as well. Wimps weren't interested in sharing power or equality, some women complained; they simply wanted to abdicate breadwinning responsibility. Equality, whether sexual or political, did not mean male passivity. A wimp lacks "a sense of purpose," including a sense of sexual purpose, one woman told an inquiring journalist. If a wimp were ever to sweep a woman off her feet, he'd probably help her up and make sure she was unhurt. "I appreciate a man wanting to please and all that," commented another woman, but wimps seemed to take it too far. "There's a lot of plaintive 'what do you like?' and 'what should I do?'" Far less common was a man with a "certain agenda," someone with "a sense of 'I like this and I know you're going to like it too.'" Some women openly regretted their demands that men become more emotionally expressive; it turned out they didn't like what the men wanted to express.[6]

Other women were a bit more sanguine. Film critic Janet Maslin, for example, found that the cinematic works of the wimp were "sweet"—a "celebration of the very sappiest good deeds and good intentions." In films such as 1988's Robert Redford's *Milagro Beanfield War*, Alan Alda's *A New Life*, and *Dominick and Eugene*, Maslin sensed something virtuous, even cinematically significant. Even in *A New Life*, Alda—"the pure embodiment of cloying, life-affirming hokum . . . the fullest flowering of wimp-mindedness"—had provided a film with "secret charms," which could provide pleasures even if one could barely admit to liking these films in mixed company.[7]

Some prominent men confessed their wimpiness—with a mea culpa of guilt-ridden angst that merely proved their critics' point. Television producer Mark Goodson confessed how his lifelong distaste for sports brought him humiliation and the terror of being found out that he was not a real man. Others were proud to be wimps. Novelist Paul Theroux called traditional manhood "pitiful, a little like having to wear an ill-fitting coat for one's entire life." The quest for manliness, he concluded, is "essentially right-wing, puritanical, cowardly, neurotic and fueled largely by a fear of women." Noel Perrin proclaimed himself an "androgynous man" and described his triumph over his dread of doing household repairs through using a manual called *Home Repairs Any Woman Can Do*. And the novelist Thomas Flanagan suggested that the "ways of the wimp" were the paths of integrity and virtue, not the marks of shame. After all, Flanagan argued, Hamlet is "literature's supreme example of the wimp"— he's "hesitant, indecisive, oppressed by an awareness of alternative possibilities . . . displays an unmanly love of language . . . [which is] sarcastic, sardonic, playful." And when Hamlet acted, he was decisive, littering Denmark with corpses, not least of them his own.[8]

But if all these men were wimps, who were the real men, the genuine articles? One index of the confusion engendered by this question was the popular reaction to a satiric little volume, *Real Men Don't Eat Quiche* (1982). Here, Bruce Feirstein jokingly enumerated the method in the madness of proving masculinity. All a man had to do in order to definitively demonstrate his masculinity was to follow the prescriptions of Flex Crush, a 225-pound truck driver, who, between hauling loads of nuclear waste, paused to define the meaning of manhood. And as Terman and Miles wrote in 1936, everything a man did, said, touched, ate, wore, thought, or felt played a role in the definition. It was a joke, but a joke that resonated. Here's a guy whose breakfast consists of "steak, prime rib, six eggs and a loaf of toast," wolfed down with side orders of flapjacks, a pound of bacon, and a pound of roofing nails, all the while "idly cleaning his 12-gauge shotgun." Feirstein mocks masculinity as much as he mocks quiche-eating wimps. The real man's revenge is as much a send-up of Rambo as it is of Donahue.[9]

The 1984 presidential election again brought the fear of the wimp into the center of the political arena.[10] Bumper stickers like "Mondale Eats Quiche" appeared on cars, and Republican Jeane Kirkpatrick accused the Democratic Party of being in the thrall of "San Francisco Democrats," a not-so-subtle reference to that city's substantial gay population. Although Mondale asked "where's the beef?" voters believed he didn't have the meaty temerity to take the helm. In the *New Republic* "TRB" summed up the Reagan presidency as a massive injection of anabolic steroids, making us "economically and militarily virile." Unfortunately, "steroids, like sedatives, have side-effects, and already our national testicles are starting to shrink."

Then–Vice President George Bush's comment after his 1984 televised debate with Democratic candidate Geraldine Ferraro that he "kicked a little ass last night" was more than a good ol' boy cliché; it revealed Bush's fear of being seen as a wimp, a fear that haunted him throughout his own campaign. If Reagan represented the triumph of the new-moneyed, gas-guzzling, right-wing cowboys, Bush offered a return to the "kinder and gentler" policies of traditionally aristocratic noblesse oblige. But the "manhood thing" kept getting in the way.

Americans have believed since Andrew Jackson's time that blue-blooded aristocrats—the Genteel Patriarchs—were indolent wimps, incapable of manly resolve. This notion, what the media dubbed "the wimp factor," plagued Bush's presidential ambitions. His state of residence was an ill-defined, ever-shifting combination of dowdy and aristocratic Kennebunkport, Maine, where well-bred Yalies like Bush had traditionally "summered," with brashly swaggering Texas— Houston, no less—home of the most venturesome of venture capitalists. He worked ceaselessly to offset upper-crust mannerisms, to stage photo opportunities to counter the public image that he was a "listless, indecisive man" who lacked "the drive to turn things around," as an editorial in the British *Economist* put it.[11] Turning a widely viewed television interview with newscaster Dan Rather into a rhetorical shoving match also seemed designed to bolster his manliness quotient. But asking for "just a splash" of coffee at a trucker's diner on a campaign swing proved equally emasculating.

Fortunately for him, he had some help in seizing the more-manly-than-thou mantle. Short, nerdy Democratic candidate Michael

Dukakis looked even more ridiculous riding around in a tank, complete with headgear, than Bush did in his hunting or fishing gear. One journalist found Dukakis's handshake "sort of wimpy," while another claimed that his predilection for dining at home with his family every evening while governor indicated that he was "Kitty whipped." Other pundits speculated about the candidates' food preferences—Bush's real-man pork rinds compared with Dukakis's fey fondness for coffee ice cream—and when Bush publicly banished broccoli from the White House menu, one got the feeling that Bush had to become the most powerful man in the world in order to get his way with a vegetable that, as a little boy, he had found yucky. Huck Finn triumphed over Aunt Sally after all.

Bush's years in office continued this preoccupation with demonstrating manhood. Immediately after his election journalists began to champion Bush as a "fighter, not a wimp"; "[t]he new George Bush looks rugged, even macho, standing chest deep in the Florida surf," noted *Newsweek*. "Something startling has happened to the man who was once marked as Ronald Reagan's lap dog. . . . George Bush walked into the polling booth as Clark Kent and emerged as the Beltway equivalent of Superman." Hyperbolic, yes—but also deliberate, calculated, and decisive. After the invasion of Panama, in which American forces deposed that nation's "strongman," Manuel Noriega, Bush celebrated that no one could call him "timid," that he was at last a "macho man." The press chimed in, hailing his "initiation rite," a demonstration of his "willingness to shed blood."[12]

The 1992 elections provided another dimension to Americans' fears of being seen as a wimp. That year, though, it was something about tasseled loafers, as H. Ross Perot prohibited his male assistants from wearing them and Bush accused Bill Clinton of being in the pockets of "that tassel-loafered lawyer crowd." The Bush campaign focused on Clinton's indecisiveness as indicating insufficient manhood. "Clinton reminds you of Woody Allen," commented Bush press secretary Torie Clarke, "sitting there giving you fourteen different explanations of why he did something and what caused him to do something and how that affects what he's doing today."

But the effort to outmuscle, outmacho one's opponent failed for one of the few times in American history. In 1992, the nation elected a man closer to the median age rather than someone old enough to be the national father, a candidate whose warm camaraderie with his contemporaneous running mate gave friendship a political valence, and a husband whose partnership-marriage with a career-oriented, savvy lawyer withstood publicly expressed difficulties, marital therapy, and antifeminist critics who had already castigated her as a ball-busting bitch. Bill and Hillary Rodham Clinton thus became the first two-career couple to ever occupy the White House; in Bill Clinton we seemed to have elected our first new man as president.

The honeymoon didn't last long. Pundits quickly heckled Bill as the henpecked husband hiding behind his connivingly careerist wife's business suit. Clinton's "character problem"—his indecisiveness, his apparent infidelities as a husband, and the venomous opposition his liberal "softness" evoked—has haunted him throughout his administration, and the erosion of support for his policies helped to make the current crop of right-wing Republican leaders appear leaner and meaner than ever.

These competing images indicate just how confused we've become as men. Magazine articles and self-help books vie for men's attention, prescribing a wide variety of antidotes for gender troubles. Many offer quick-fix solutions, continuing to bait us with the fear of the wimp, then sending us right back into the fray. Indiana University basketball coach Bobby Knight, for example, puts sanitary napkins in the lockers of his players to shame them as wusses and make them play more aggressively. (This is the same coach who, when asked by a television reporter how he handled stress, responded, "I think if rape is inevitable, relax and enjoy it.") Others seek to reclaim the proving ground from interlopers—like blacks, gays, and women. Many men seek to retrieve a lost manhood on a weekend retreat off in the woods where men beat drums and chant, initiate one another, and reclaim their "wild man" or "inner warrior." A few seek to overturn the traditional definitions of masculinity altogether, seeing in feminism or in gay liberation the possibilities of a new definition of manhood, a manhood based on compassion, trust, and nurturance.

If nothing else, though, the playing field has changed. The structural foundations of traditional manhood—economic independence, geographic mobility, domestic dominance—have all been eroding. The transformation of the workplace—the decline of the skilled worker, global corporate relocations, the malaise of the middle-class manager, the entry of women into the assembly line and the corporate office—have pressed men to confront their continued reliance on the marketplace as the way to demonstrate and prove their manhood. For some men the gender integration of the workplace may make success a hollow victory anyway. What's more, global economic trends augur poorly for younger men's ability to demonstrate manhood in traditional ways. Downward mobility is now more common than upward mobility for Americans in their twenties. Most Americans born in the suburbs in the 1950s and 1960s will never earn enough to afford to buy the houses they grew up in.[13] It now takes two incomes to provide the same standard of living that one income provided less than two generations ago. This generation may be the first in U.S. history that will leave its children poorer than itself. And despite the national exhilaration during the war in the Persian Gulf, the soldier now represents a somewhat tarnished image of manhood, not just because of Vietnam—since those veterans have been partially rehabilitated as pawns in other men's games, pawns whose survival indicates a kind of everyday heroism—but also because of the Tailhook incident and debates about gays in the military or about women entering all-male military colleges.

American men feel themselves beleaguered and besieged, working harder and harder for fewer and fewer personal and social rewards. Women have not only entered the workplace but demand entry into men's social clubs. There are even women Boy Scout troop leaders and scoutmasters. The criminalization of sexual harassment and date rape has left some men angry, and frightened of demonstrating manhood through sexual conquest. Many men say they experience a "fear of flirting," lest it be misunderstood and provide the possibility of allegations against them.[14] AIDS compounds the fears of disease with a demand for responsibility (i.e., wearing condoms). And men are tired. Epstein-Barr syndrome, the "Yuppie flu," is a mysterious enervating ailment that leaves its victims listless and tired—a 1990s version of neurasthenia.[15] What's a man to do?

SAVE THE MALES

If you ask a small but vocal group of men, we should return to the basics, revive the traditional version of Self-Made Manhood. The "old man," as opposed to the new man, is still around, not exactly enjoying a renaissance but far from slipping quietly into oblivion. The Reaganite retrieval of cowboy masculinity encouraged this crowd, even if the momentary reassertion of imperial dominance had more to do with the collapse of the opposing "evil empire" than it did with American virility and the feeding frenzy of corporate raiders, gobbling up smaller firms, produced a few extremely fat cats but failed to trickle down to the lower 95 percent of Americans.

These traditionalists—the "angry white males" of recent headlines—feel besieged by frenzied "feminazis" and a culture of entitlements, affirmative action, and special interests. They say they are sick and tired of being oppressed by women and dominated by impersonal bureaucracies—and they're not going to take it anymore! They experience feminism as an "emasculating force, for it exaggerates that familiar sense of unmanly guilt," and today's man is fed up with efforts to make him feel guilty. It's *men* who are the victims, they say. Politically, this resentment and anger has fueled a new gender gap, the preponderance of middle-class, middle-aged, straight white males who are listing constantly to the right. Raised to feel "entitled" themselves, they resent any entitlement program that gives anything to anyone else. "If I can't have what I'm entitled to," they seem to say, "then neither can you"—a new twist on the old exclusionary formula employed to retrieve a sense of manhood.[16] One writer fumed that he "will have none of the nonsense about oppressed and victimized women; no responsibility for the conditions of women, whatever that condition might be; none of the guilt or self-loathing that is traditionally used to keep men functioning in harness." And another writes that women "have always dominated me, directed me, intimidated me, loaded me with guilt, sometimes inspired me, oftentimes exploited or shamed me."[17]

In a flurry of reversals characteristic of this new "men's rights movement," these beleaguered men trot out a set of empirical inversions that make the rational mind reel. It's men, they tell us, who are the victims of sexual harassment by women, not the other way around. "The way young women dress in the spring constitutes a sexual assault upon every male within eyesight of them," writes William Muehl, a retired professor at the Yale Divinity School.[18] Men, they claim, are battered and abused by their wives far more frequently than the other way around; in fact, to hear them tell it, husband battery is one of the nation's most underreported crimes, and such men are in desperate need of shelters where they can feel safe from violent and abusive women. It's not that men abandon their families after divorce, the basic tenet of laws about child-support payments and alimony, but rather that vengeful wives and conniving lawyers have thwarted men's deep desires to maintain relationships with their children. Recent concern over sexual harassment and date rape have made men so vulnerable at home, in the workplace, and on the town that they don't know where to turn.[19]

Two groups of men lend their shrill voices to what the journalist Susan Faludi has called the backlash. On the one hand, besieged traditionalists prescribe a biologically or theologically based separation of spheres as the cure-all for men's malaise. If only women would get out of the public sphere and go back into the private sphere where they belong, these crusaders tell us, masculinity would be saved. Advocates of "men's rights," by contrast, use a somewhat different rhetoric, claiming that women have already achieved equality and that programs that favor women now serve to discriminate against men.

Many of these conservative traditionalist tracts echo the Social Darwinism of nineteenth-century antifeminists, as well as such 1970s conservatives as George Gilder. Journalist Nicholas Davidson's *The Failure of Feminism* (1987) claims that feminism attempted to reverse the law of nature, which is the law of male dominance. Sexually, for example, feminism demands the "impossible," such as "trying not to feel aggressiveness or dominance toward a woman when making love to her"—a statement with which the most radical feminist would probably agree. "It will be a sad day when men no longer see women as the objects of their lust," Davidson concludes mournfully.[20]

While Gilder and Davidson rely on Social Darwinism for their political conservatism, philosopher Michael Levin's *Feminism and Free-*

dom (1987) uses the rhetoric of radical libertarian individualism to argue that feminism is inimical to equality, in that it demands special protections and special privileges for women. "Although feminism speaks the language of liberation, self-fulfillment, options, and the removal of barriers, these phrases invariably mean their opposites and disguise an agenda at variance with the ideals of a free society" because "equality of outcome entails inequality of opportunity," he writes. But Levin, too, returns to the nuclear family as the foundation of the free society, since father absence is responsible for not only out-of-control masculinity but also feminism. "Nothing could have produced this degree of anger at men and hatred of self [i.e., feminism] but a childhood in which femaleness went unconfirmed by an ineffectual father, together perhaps with a dominant mother."[21]

Asa Baber, creator and writer of the "Men" column in *Playboy*, is probably the most widely read contemporary mouthpiece for the other version of male backlash, the "men's rights" movement. A column called "Men" in *Playboy*? you might ask. Isn't that just a little bit redundant? Not to Baber, who claims to speak for legions of men struggling against the rising red tide of "politically correct" feminism. "Men have now had 25 years of sexists calling us sexists," he writes about a feminism that is now "out of control" and which has become "an attack on masculinity itself." Baber celebrates manhood as if it's just come back into fashion. "It's fine to be male," he proclaims, "a glorious, sexual, humorous thing to be male."

Baber's book, *Naked at Gender Gap* (1992), a collection of his columns, rehearses the standard men's rights litany: Women should serve in the military to eliminate the sexism that forces only men to serve; men are the victims of discrimination in custody and divorce proceedings; men should have rights to determine whether or not a woman should have an abortion. Men have lost "power and control" while women reap all the benefits. They get out of military service— "there will never be equal rights for all in this country until that burden is shared by men and women"—and they also "perpetuate spousal violence almost as frequently as men."[22]

It's men, he whines, who are the real victims in America—victims of "antimale sexism," a veritable "sexual inquisition" making us "vulnerable in the extreme to false charges of sexual harassment." Feminists, he writes, have us "walking on eggshells." "All it takes to lynch a man these days is the accusation of rape."[23]

Baber is passionate about his rights as a father—from conception onwards. That fetus "is mine as much as yours," he encourages men to proclaim.[23] And after a divorce, Baber believes that men certainly should enjoy unimpeded visitation, equal custody, and the like—even if they were inactive as fathers *before* the divorce. Baber writes as if he had just discovered parental nurture, a controversial issue with a long history. Who, after all, has been asking—indeed begging, demanding, and cajoling—men to take a larger part in child care and housework all these decades?[24] Such inversions make the book a perfect illustration of men's rights rhetoric. Rather than express regret or take responsibility for the literal battery of women by men, Baber would rather complain about rhetorical "male bashing" by feminists when they verbally rail against men's violence.

Davidson, Levin, Gilder, and Baber provide a theoretical foundation for the men's rights backlash; Warren Farrell and Herb Goldberg make that theory into therapy. Once heralded as the most visible "liberated man" in the nation, Farrell seems to have completely abandoned his earlier support of feminism and now suggests that we "embrace traditional masculinity." To him, too, men are the oppressed sex. "Men are just as powerless as women in relationships," he asserts. In fact, it's men who are at a "psychological disadvantage" because they must initiate sexual contact, complains one of Farrell's followers. "I just want my fair share of the options." Farrell thus bridges the time warp between mid-seventies men's liberation rhetoric and the more vitriolic antifeminist men's rights cant.[25]

Farrell offers a list of the most important myths of manhood and proposes in their place a kind of Bill of Men's Rights.[26] Most central—men lack power. "Power is not earning money that someone else can spend and dying earlier so they can get the benefits." To Farrell, men are also: (1) not threatened by equality; (2) want love as much as women; (3) are as much the victims of discrimination as women; (4) are good fathers; (5) want equal rights to children; (6) do not earn a dollar for a woman's fifty-nine cents; (7) are battered as often as wives; and (8) are not in short supply.[27]

What's more, workplace discrimination against women is a femi-

nist falsehood. Take sexual harassment. "Consensual sex among employees," as he euphemistically calls it, is "courtship" when it works
and "harassment" when it doesn't. If there is a problem with em-
ployer-employee sex, it is because it "undermines the ability of the
employer to establish boundaries because the employer often feels
needy of the employee," he writes in a characteristic reversal. The notion of sexual harassment is discrimination against men, and Farrell
suggests that we need laws to protect men in the workplace.[28]

Farrell expands these dizzying counterfactuals to other arenas as
well. In academic settings, for example, sexual contact between professor and student may confer on the young woman "potential academic advantages over other students." And he likens workplace incest
to at home incest, which reverses family authority dynamics, since
"parental authority becomes undermined because the child senses it
has leverage over the parent." What a novel theory—incest affords
undue power to the young girl over her father's actions! And I suppose that he might find some statistics that reveal that 50 percent of
all participants in "family sex" report it to have been a positive experience.[29]

Rape, Farrell argues, is not, as feminists have argued, simply a
crime of violence. It's about sex. Younger, more attractive women are
8400 percent more likely to be raped than older women. The general
point that rape has a sexual component is, of course, not entirely
wrong despite the hyperbolic statistics. But to suggest that rape is a
crime of sexual frustration implies that if only women would put out
a little more often, rape rates would go down. And pornography is, to
Farrell, just another harmless way for men to cope with women's
miniskirt power, cleavage power, and flirtation power. Pornography
provides "access to a variety of attractive women without the fear of
rejection at a price we can afford." Women's "pornography," on the
other hand—books like *Smart Women, Foolish Choices* or *Women Who
Love Too Much*—is far more pernicious because it also objectifies the
opposite sex.[30]

Compared to the chameleon-like Farrell, men's liberationist Herb
Goldberg has been a model of consistency. Just as his 1970s books
sought to demolish the traditional definition of masculinity, so too
do his most recent works, such as *The New Male Female Relationship*

(1983), *The Inner Male* (1987), and *What Men Really Want* (1991). To Goldberg traditional masculinity remains a disease of disconnection, a "silent cancer"; men are "intimacy mechanics" who have all the right tools but are trying to fix a heartless, contentless machine. "Masculinity is an addiction," he says, echoing the latest trends in self-help.

Goldberg, however, blames women for these problems; he remains wedded to abdicating responsibility in the guise of equality and sharing. Since he claims that women support, encourage, and demand that men act this way, Goldberg gets to demolish traditional masculinity and blame women for its maintenance. "[M]ilitancy about women's rights is often a way of defensively avoiding recognition of one's own responsibility for helping to create the problem."[31]

The *real* victims in American society are men—so claim the political organizers who have built organizations around men's anxieties and anger at feminism, groups like the Coalition for Free Men, the National Congress for Men, Men's Rights, Inc. (MR, Inc.), and Men Achieving Liberation and Equality (MALE). These groups proclaim their commitment to equality and to ending sexism—which is why they are compelled to fight against feminism. For while feminism has actually given women *more* freedom than men enjoy, men are still responsible for initiating sexual relationships, for fighting in wars, and for paying alimony and child support. Feminism, they argue, is the most insidious and vexing form of sexism going. Feminist women are "would be castrators with a knee-jerk, obsessive aversion to anything male," writes Richard Doyle, an administrator of the Men's Rights Association, in his book *The Rape of the Male* (1986). Fred Hayward, the founder of MR, Inc., claims that men are the most common victims of violence, rape, abuse, and battery and that "women are *privileged* because they are more frequently *allowed* to raise children, while men are being *oppressed* by denial of access to children"—and it's women who control this situation. Another advises men who feel powerless in the face of divorce-court proceedings to "fight dirty and win" by exploiting their wives' vulnerabilities.[32]

Fathers' rights groups use a language of equality to take their revenge against women to court, to demand mandatory joint custody without demonstration of father's prior involvement. Jon Conine's *Fathers' Rights* (1989) provides handy advice to the father facing the loss of his children and displaces responsibility onto women and onto society as a whole. "Society cannot take away a father's rights to his children and expect him to cheerfully pay child support. Society cannot expect a father to make enough money to support two separate households. Society cannot afford to support mothers who choose not to work."[33] Fathers must have equal rights: the right to custody and the right to freedom from any burdensome alimony and child support. And men also need the right to choose—to choose whether a partner exercises her right to choose to terminate a pregnancy. Sidney Siller, divorce lawyer and *Penthouse* columnist, was so moved by feminist "inversions" that in 1983 he formed the National Organization for Men. NOM opposes affirmative action, forced collection of alimony and child support, and a single-sex military. "Men have been wimpified. They've been emasculated. We'd like to see them fight for their rights," says Siller.[34] Just not for their country—at least not alone.

Most advocates of men's and fathers' rights are disgruntled and divorced dads, who blame their wives and their wives' lawyers for their isolation and loneliness. Many now feel punished for their attempts to live up to a traditional definition of masculinity that was unrealizable from the start. Such a definition demanded that they renounce the pleasures of home—family, fatherhood, and friendships with women and with other men—to make an adequate living to support their families. They thought this behavior was a form of nurture, but now the bottom seems to have dropped out of their lives. Actually, men's participation with their children has steadily declined over time. Before World War I, men spent several hours a day with their children; they spent about two hours a day between the wars and about twenty *minutes* a day since World War II—roughly the inverse of their increasingly heated rhetoric about how much they want to be involved. Even if we can be sympathetic with their feelings of despair and gaping loneliness, knowing that it always attends the blind pursuit of the elusive ideals of Self-Made Masculinity, the men's rights analysis is so misguided, its inversions so transparent, its anger so displaced onto those who have traditionally been excluded, that it can hardly offer any man of reason a convincing picture of men's situation.[35]

But who needs accurate pictures with the Hollywood dream machine around? Though traditional masculinity's foundations and definition were eroding, that definition was still the stuff of fantasy; recent books and films have bolstered the masculine ego through fantasies of conquest and triumph against overwhelming odds. Though the western frontier was gone, it could be reconstituted on Wall Street. Capital, as one advertising jingle has it, "knows no boundaries." Popular biographies and autobiographies of Donald Trump and Lee Iacocca, movies like *Wall Street* and *Working Girl*, and novels like Tom Wolfe's *Bonfire of the Vanities* both celebrated and spoofed the primal glandular competition of male workplace rivalries. Donald Trump claimed that he had no interest in competing against women or weaker men; he saved all he had for competition with his peers. Manhood was still to be proved by a bulge—not the throbbing hypertrophied penis of pornographic fantasy but the bulging wallet.

Or bulging muscles. Hollywood currently regales American moviegoers with a parade of testosterone-infused superheroes like Steven Seagal, Sylvester Stallone, Jean-Claude Van Damme, Bruce Willis, and, of course, Arnold Schwarzenegger, who all seem to embody Stallone's admonition: "Screen characters seem more like young ladies than real men, and its time to reestablish the balance." In adventure stories like *Die Hard, Terminator, Rocky, Rambo*, and all their sequels and prequels, one lone real man is pitted against a horde of pretenders to the masculine crown—criminals, Vietnamese soldiers, unctuously well-dressed Eurotrash mobsters, cutthroat Japanese capitalists, and futuristic aliens; sometimes, it seems, all at once.[36]

The films of actor Michael Douglas suggest the pitfalls of these efforts to reinvigorate masculinity. Leaving aside his earlier buddy-film television persona on *The Streets of San Francisco*—the young, less streetwise, and more ethical cop, the sidekick to Karl Malden's hardened judiciousness—Douglas has emerged in the 1980s and 1990s as kind of politically incorrect polymath, "the poster boy for male fear of aggressive female sexuality."[37] In *Wall Street* he plays Gordon Gekko, an unscrupulous tycoon and financier whose cunning gamesmanship destroys other people's lives without remorse, only to be destroyed by his young protégé's late-developing scruples. In *The War Between the Roses*, Douglas reinvents his romantic team with Kathleen Turner but this time as a couple locked in a lethal pas de deux that gave new meaning to the phrase "till death do us part." The film's false equivalence between his demand that she give up her ambitions and devote herself to him and her demand that he take her a little more seriously works itself out with deadly consequences for both.

In a more recent spate of films—*Fatal Attraction* (1990), *Basic Instinct* (1991) *Falling Down* (1993), and *Disclosure* (1994)—Douglas gives masculine vengeance full force, usually against independent women invading the male turf. In *Fatal Attraction* the married-with-family Douglas's fling with a hot, single Glenn Close transforms her into a menacing she-devil who hounds him with demands for commitment while he tries to "ethically" extricate himself. She takes revenge on his family, even boiling the family bunny, only to end up murdered by Douglas's mousey wife—to the cheers of the audience. Single women are seductive, literally femmes fatale, likely to explode at the least opportunity.[38] In *Basic Instinct* Douglas again follows his lust into an encounter with a hot and potentially lethal single woman, while in *Disclosure* he is man enough to resist its consummation. Although his manhood is rescued in each case, it is only momentary. Women are never to be trusted—especially those who are single and sexually aware and active.[39]

In *Falling Down* Douglas offers an allegory of the besieged middle-class white male in today's society. Having bought into the American promise even after his layoff from the aerospace industry—his vanity license plate reads "D-Fens"—Douglas becomes progressively unhinged as the traditional props of white male privilege are shed. His efforts to reestablish himself lead to angry confrontations with virtually every group that has been historically excluded by Self-Made Masculinity—upwardly mobile, hardworking immigrants, young Latino men, a beautiful policewoman—all of whom he blames for his failures to cling to his tenuous grasp on economic security and mental stability. His death is the death of the dream of exclusion: Traditional masculinity cannot be resurrected, and even the old tried-and-true strategies of sexism, homophobia, and racism cannot keep the edifice from falling down.

ESCAPE ARTISTS

So where can men go to feel like men? This is one of the questions fueling the anger of the men's rights groups, who seek to prop up traditional definitions of masculinity in the ways that besieged men have always done: by clearing everyone else off the playing field. By reestablishing the early nineteenth-century separation of spheres between women and men and by excluding from full manhood the "other" men—men of color, gay men, non-native-born men—these men cling to the belief that a secure and confident gender identity is possible through the fulfillment of Self-Made Masculinity. This question is also the dominant theme for a new generation of masculinists, who see in contemporary arrangements a recipe for a new feminization of American culture parallel to the cultural feminization perceived at the turn of the last century.

At that time, masculinists argued that changes in the nature of work, the closing of the frontier, and changes in family relations had produced a cultural degeneracy—American men and boys were becoming feminized. Men searched for homosocial preserves where they could be real men with other men (fraternal lodges, Muscular Christian revival meetings) and sought vigorous ways to demonstrate their hardy manhood (wilderness retreats, dude ranches and rodeos, health and exercise crazes, evocations of martial glory), while they also sought ways to ensure that the next generation of young boys would not grow up to be an effete elite (Boy Scouts, single-sex classrooms, a fatherhood movement). Today, virtually every one of these strategies has been retrieved as a way to alleviate a growing sense of cultural malaise with American manhood. Contemporary masculinists believe that men are still wimps; they need to be rescued from the clutches of overprotective mothers, absent fathers, and an enervating workplace and need to rediscover themselves through a manly quest against a pitiless environment.

For some that environment is the contemporary workplace. As they sally forth into the urban jungle, today's middle-class men make themselves resemble their adventurous forbears through their fashionable clothes and masculinizing accessories. They wear Timberland shoes or cowboy boots, denim shirts, and aviator sunglasses; they drive Cherokees, Wranglers, Broncos, or Land Rovers; they splash on a little Aspen, Stetson, Chaps, or Safari cologne. As at the turn of the century, so too now—if manhood does not come from within, perhaps it can be worn. "When I dress in my suit each morning I feel like a knight going forth to battle and I love to fight hard and win in a hard bargaining session with a publisher," comments a literary agent.[40] But for most the workplace is no longer the literal testing ground. Tom Wolfe's satiric novel *The Bonfire of the Vanities* sounded a hilariously near-hysterical elegy for the yuppie 1980s, an era of bond traders, "head hunters," and arbitrageurs who were, for a time, the "masters of the universe."

If masculinity cannot be achieved at work, perhaps it can be achieved by working out. Men's bodies provide another masculine testing ground. Millions of American men participate in the current health and fitness craze—dieting, jogging and bicycling, exercising, consuming health foods and various bottled waters, and purchasing high-end fitness equipment. "Iron man" triathalons push men beyond normal physical limits to explore the boundaries of the body. Of course, this craze is not limited to men; women remain a steady market for fitness, health, and diet fads. Women have been steady consumers over the years in an effort to remain "feminine"—to shed unwanted pounds and turn back the hands of time. But men's interest in health and diet has matched women's only twice in our history—at the turn of the century and today—and men's sporadic interest in the body is prompted, I believe, by the collapse of the workplace as an area in which to test and prove masculinity. When our real work fails to confirm manhood, we "work out." Perhaps women's exclusion from the marketplace led them to turn first to the realm of consumption to achieve the perfect body, but today men are standing—or rather aerobicizing—right alongside of them. New magazines like *Men's Health* and countless muscle magazines celebrate the new male cult of the body.

A new subgenre of travel literature also re-creates the frontier and, with it, the western novel of the turn of the century and the popularity of the male-bonding war movie of the 1950s and 1960s. This strain of male travel writers ventures to difficult, inhospitable territories, exploring the boundaries of civilization, crossing the frontier into uncharted territory. Recent works such as Charles Nicholl's *Borderlines*, P. J. O'Rourke's *Holidays in Hell*, Tim Cahill's *A Wolverine Is Eating My Leg*, Nick Danziger's *Danziger's Travels: Beyond Forbidden Frontiers*, and Stuart Stevens's *Malaria Dreams* all find the journeyman/writer/hero hurtling through some jungle at the edge of civilization, testing manhood in a Land Rover. The global frontier remains open to middle-class white men who seek a confrontation with the "primitive" at the boundaries of civilization. It is also an escape from the feminizing city and an anxious quest to test one's manliness.[41]

Other fantasies reinvigorate military masculinity. Theologian Michael Pakaluk argues that young boys should play with toy guns because "Christian life essentially contains a warlike aspect, [and] the military virtues are essential to it"—although he does prescribe simple war toys to give the young boy ample room for imagination. Even without the theology, fantasy toys that drip with militarism have become the rage. Literary critic Susan Jeffords's fascinating studies of recent American war films and novels, *The Remasculinization of America* (1989) and *Hard Bodies* (1993), trace the cinematic and fictional efforts to return to the scene of defeat and retrieve lost manhood by rewinning lost wars.[42]

Some call for the literal remasculinization of America. For example, current debates over the entry of women and gays into the military are fueled by the presumed relationships between masculinity and military values. Brian Mitchell's *Weak Link: The Feminization of the American Military* (1989) claims that women's presence "inhibits male bonding, corrupts allegiance to the hierarchy, and diminishes the desire of men to compete for anything but the attentions of women." In his best-selling Vietnam memoir Philip Caputo suggests that male intimacy would be threatened by the integration of women:

The communion between men is as profound as any between lovers. Actually it is more so. It does not demand for its sustenance the reciprocity, the pledges of affection, the endless reassurances required by the love of men and women. It is, unlike marriage, a bond that cannot be broken by a word, by boredom, or divorce, or by anything other than death. Sometimes that is not strong enough.

Lest anyone confuse the imperatives of homosociality for homosexuality, Caputo conflates the debate about women in the military with the debate about gays in the military, noting that "the emotion of camaraderie is, of its nature, chaste. It may be more intense than what happens between male and female lovers, but it has to be nonsexual. It's not just women. Warriors can't be homosexual lovers either."[43]

Of course they can—and have.[44] Only a theory that casts male sexuality as a form of predatory domination, sexual attraction as lust for conquest, and emotional bonds as a form of property control could suggest that sexual bonds threaten emotional bonding among men. If sexual connection is about the possibility of deep emotional relationships, of love and commitment, then sexuality is no threat to military discipline—as long as everyone knows who everyone else is. Efforts to expel gays and lesbians from military service seem to be so easily paired with efforts to keep women from military equality because if women only were excluded, the homosocial military might be mistaken for a homosexual military.

Some contemporary masculinists echo the Muscular Christianity movement by recasting Jesus as a religious Rambo. The revival of evangelism, the journalist Carol Flake reports,

> brought with it a revival of muscular Christianity and a return to the social Darwinism of the athletic era. Jesus the teacher had become Christ the competitor. . . . From the pulpit, preachers prayed for winning seasons, sprinkling their sermons with so much athletic symbolism that they sometimes sounded like color commentators on TV sports broadcasts.[45]

One Jesuit priest claims that contemporary Christianity makes Jesus out to be a "bearded lady," while another calls him "Jesus, the Warm Fuzzy." "Christ wasn't effeminate," grumps televangelist Jerry Falwell. "The man who lived on this earth was a man with muscles. . . . Christ was a he-man!" Noting a "chronic absence" of men from church—only about one-third of American men attend church regularly, while nearly one-half of all American women do—one minister indicated that the long-term effects of cultural feminization of the church would be marginalization of the church, impoverishment of church life, and a coarsening of the tone of public society. What's a contemporary Muscular Christian to do?[46]

One minister suggested a program to bring men back to the church. This includes ministers adopting masculine styles themselves—giving firmer handshakes, learning about hunting and car repair—since "pastors often seem sissified." Develop programs for men, he counseled. "Provide a place where they can feel safe—a home turf—and you may be surprised how many will show up and open up." Another suggests portraying the Christian life as a manly life, a heroic quest for spiritual manhood. After all, religion is a man's vision, the church is a man's sacred space. And going forth to battle against evil, to bear witness and convert nonbelievers, to make the world whole—this is a man's job. "Jesus battles all forms of evil," writes one Jesuit priest, "but unlike other warriors his power does not kill." Other observers make no such distinction. "Sacred violence is the ultimate meaning of masculinity," writes one. The religious life is a heroic quest. The battle for men's souls is of cosmic importance; spirituality is "not equated with prissiness," and "Jesus, the Bible, and the house of God are not just for sissies and girls."[47] The enormous reponse to the Christian men's organization called the Promise Keepers is a testimonial to the sustained drawing power of a muscular Christian vision.

A recent book, *Jesus CEO*, repackages the corporate Jesus of Bruce Barton's 1924 work *The Man That Nobody Knows* into a contemporary Wall Street middle manager. Jesus, we are told, was in "constant contact with his boss," "demonstrated a sense of ownership of all things," "had a plan," was "willing to do an end run" to put it into effect. Jesus, it turns out, was a "turnaround specialist" who motivated his workers to become "a lean, mean marketing machine."[48]

Among the most visible campaigners for Muscular Christianity are Christian athletes. "You think because I've accepted Christ into my life, I'm passive," laughed baseball player Brett Butler. "I play hard. If Christ played this game, he'd slide right into the second baseman, and then he'd help him up. Christ was no wimp." A former teammate, pitcher Orel Hershiser, added that "[j]ust because I'm a Christian doesn't mean I'm a wimp." The Chicago Bears and New York

Giants held a joint prayer circle at midfield after they had spent sixty minutes bashing in each others' heads in their 1991 playoff game. Mark Eaton, the towering center for the Utah Jazz, thinks Jesus would have been a great basketball player. "He would have been one of the most tenacious guys out there. I think he'd really get in your face—nothing dirty, but he'd play to win." Another basketball player wants to prove that "Christians are not Casper Milquetoasts." Jocks for Jesus are visible in every sport, illustrating that the most manly of men can still experience salvation in religion and that the most religious of men need not appear unmanly.[49]

Some Christian athletes have made Muscular Christianity the basis for a second career. Bodybuilder John Jacobs, for example, founded "the Power Team," a group of massively muscular zealots who use a pumped-up theology as the basis for a kind of motivational preaching at revival-tent meetings around the country. "Jesus Christ was no skinny little man," Jacobs claims. "Jesus was a man's man." He and the other men's men perform circus feats of masculine strength, like breaking stacks of bricks or large blocks of ice with their bare hands. By equating masculinity with spiritual and physical power, Jacobs and his Power Team seek to retrieve a model of "an idealized Christian patriarchy."[50]

Some contemporary masculinists insist that the separation of the sexes is the only way to preserve what is different (and interesting) about either women or men. Writer Dotson Rader argued against co-education because young boys were biologically *inferior* to young girls in both fine motor skills and innate intelligence; thus, he argued, boys were at a *physical* disadvantage in the coed classroom.[51] Some collegiate fraternities resist coeducation, claiming the clubhouse preserves the best of manhood. In an "About Men" column in the *New York Times*, William F. Buckley fondly recalled his club years at Yale through the "dreams" of a younger member:

> Someday, damn it, we'll have a treehouse of our own. We'll build it out in the woods where Mother can't find us. And we'll eat when we want, what we want. We'll bring our friends. Have a secret club. And no girls.[52]

He must mean "gurls"—the boyhood misspelling that adorned many a cinematic boys' clubhouse, treehouse, or secret hideaway.

The search for the "fraternity house that wouldn't end" leads some grown-up men to promote the all-male club as a refuge. New Age masculinist writer Keith Thompson evokes turn-of-the-century fraternal orders when he claims that "a man needs a lodge"—a "retreat from concerns about money and work, family pressures, and . . . responsibility to roles." That's why men have fought so vigorously to protect single-sex men's clubs from integration, despite women's protests that these clubs reproduce men's power in society by providing informal arenas for networking and personal friendships to develop.[53]

But these homosocial preserves—single-sex colleges, fraternities, fraternal orders, men's clubs—are as much about the protection of men's privilege as they are arenas to facilitate closeness among men. At the Bohemian Grove, for example, America's elite men gather for a two-week bonding binge, an extended drunken fraternity stag party. But unlike the Masons, the Red Men, or Sigma Chi, this "overgrown boy-scout camp," this "college fraternity system transplanted from the campus to the redwoods," as one former employee put it, consists entirely of CEOs of *Fortune* 500 corporations, senators, congressmen, governors, and even presidents, vice presidents, and ex-presidents. Power brokers like George Shultz, Henry Kissinger, Ronald Reagan, and Richard Nixon mingle with corporate leaders like Thomas Watson and Lee Iacocca and celebrities like Walter Cronkite, all of whom have been regular clubbers. This "refuge for the weary heart," this "balm for breasts that have been bruised," according to members, invites America's upper-class white-male ruling class to experience the depths of their cohesive bonding through ritual contact with nature and one another. These clubs are "a means by which these values are transferred to the business environment"—that is, a mechanism of reproduction of class power. The obsessive exclusion of women and the only-recent grudging admission of a few black men (like Vernon Jordan) suggest that these retreats also serve a traditionalist agenda, regrounding masculinity on the exclusion of the various "others."[54]

The weekend retreat at Bohemian Grove begins as the men dance in a circle, throwing their worldly cares into the roaring bonfire that rises through the redwood trees into the night sky. (From that moment until the end of the encampment, they do not talk about business.) They retreat to lodges with names like Cave Man Camp—that's the one where Richard Nixon stayed. They don Native American war paint and masks, chanting and drumming, playing at rituals "full of schmaltz and nostalgia," as sociologist G. William Domhoff reports. And they bond, forging intimate, informal ties among the scions of business and government, cementing the allegiances of government and corporate power, and reassuring one another that they are all friends, all, really, on the same side.

Male bonding, Native American rituals, drumming, chanting, a virtual celebration of masculinity—sounds like the media descriptions of the new "men's movement," a motley collection of wounded men and their pop-psychological gurus, loosely led by poet and best-selling author Robert Bly. These men are conducting their own quest for their lost "deep" manhood in weekend retreats and workshops across the country.[55] By donning totemic animal symbols and reclaiming ancient myths of male bonding, these weekend warriors hope to tap into some primitive stream of essential masculinity, long buried by the feminizing worlds of work and home. This "mythopoetic" effort to retrieve deep manhood—the "inner warrior" or "wildman"—is by far the most interesting and seductive example of contemporary masculinism.

All across the country in the first few years of the 1990s, men have been in full-scale retreat, heading off to the woods to rediscover their wild, hairy, deep manhood. What are they retreating from? And what are they hoping to find? Perhaps the most celebrated purveyors of the search for the deep masculine are Robert Bly and Sam Keen, whose *Iron John* and *Fire in the Belly*, respectively, topped the best-seller lists for much of 1991. In *Iron John* Bly recounts a Grimm fairy tale as a timeless parable of male development. Here is a tale of separation from mother, frightening risk, a heroic quest, the scarring wound, and the recovery of manly virtue presented in a contemporary format to enable men to reclaim their "warrior" selves. And Keen provides a rough road map for a more individualistic psychospiritual quest for the grail of manhood. Contemporary mythopoetic masculinists speak eloquently to men's spiritual hunger, a deep longing for lives of meaning and resonance. Their weekend retreats allow men to break down the isolation and emotional repression that invariably attend efforts to demonstrate self-made manhood; here, they give voice, perhaps for the first time, to emotional needs for closeness and friendship with other men, to pain, confusion, and vulnerabilities that have long been suppressed in the confused efforts to prove the unprovable.

Like their turn-of-the-century forbears, contemporary masculinists, argue that men today are listless, lifeless, enervated, feminized. Psychologically, they claim that this is because men have not adequately separated from their mothers. The absence of the father at home and the disappearance of the apprenticeship system means that men have learned the meaning of manhood from women, especially from their mothers. Masculine authenticity was destroyed by the Industrial Revolution, Bly argues, because fathers abandoned their sons and went to work in factories. Mothers have also retained an incestuous dedication to their sons, excluding the father and keeping the boy dependent on her long after he needed to break away. Thus, "mythopoets" argue, the problem for men is incomplete separation, and so off they run to the woods, where they can escape the world of women—mothers, wives, and children—and workplace responsibility and drudgery. Here they can "bond" with each other, rediscover manly nurture, honor their ancestors as potential "mentors," and validate each other's, and hence their own, manhood.

Underneath all the trappings of mythopoetic manhood—the mythology, faux traditionalism, appropriated Native American and nonindustrial ritualism, bowdlerized Jungian archetypes, and evocations of non-Western initiation—lies a language that sounds more like the recovery movement than the strenuous life. Men, we hear, are also searching for their inner child, healing childhood wounds, and recognizing the addictive patterns characteristic of adult children. Men "suffer" in this society, argues Shepherd Bliss, partly because women maintain a monopoly on themes like oppression and powerlessness. "But women aren't victims," he insists. "We all know the power of women."[56]

The mythopoetic call of the wild runs into the same problems that faced turn-of-the-century masculinists. For one thing, they displace men's grown-up problems of economic contraction, political competition, social isolation, and interpersonal incompetence (the result of a definition of masculinity that is inseparably tied to performance in the marketplace, the bedroom, or the athletic field) onto overdominant motherhood and absent fatherhood. Our dilemmas have more to do with our adulthood than with a childhood struggle to wriggle free of clutching mothers or searching for absent fathers. As one critic argues:

> The massive contradiction between the public exhortation to aggressive individualism, and a social order in which most white-collar workers are embedded in massive organizations, is neatly resolved by transporting the scene of action into a mystic cult of masculinity. We can't all be Donald Trumps but, by God, we can be equally fierce in our hearts.[57]

As feminist psychoanalysts have argued, the problem with men isn't that they have not separated enough from mother, but that they have separated *too much*. The project of Self-Made Masculinity, of a manhood constantly tested and proved, becomes equated with a relentless effort to repudiate femininity, a frantic effort to dissociate from women. In daily life this translates to a devaluation of women, the psychological basis for sexism. Men had thus abandoned precisely those emotional skills that were most needed if women were to achieve equality: nurture, sensitivity, emotional responsiveness. But if mothers embody responsibility, care, and nurture, why would men's movement leaders counsel that we reject mother and run away, attempting to "heal the father wound"? Rather, we should heal the *mother* wound, close the gap between the mother who cared for us and the mother we've rejected. Reentering the domestic sphere through shared parenting, not flying in panic from it, would enable men to develop those emotional resources and allow their sons to experience nurturance and care as something that all adults do. Such reconnection is also about responsibility, at work and at home, such responsibilities as nurturance, compassion, and accountability—in short, responsibilities that have become equated with the conditions for emasculation, not demonstration of manhood. Frankly, I'd prefer more Ironing Johns and fewer Iron Johns.

And what are we to make of the search through mythic literature and non-Western cultures for the rituals that can usher in this new manhood? Mythopoetic weekend warriors evoke a misty preindustrial past through which to view our present dilemma. Keen, for example, believes that traditional life was harmonious and cooperative. Male and female, each in his or her sphere, living lives of meaning and coherence. Each gender is "half of a crippled whole." Men get the "feeling of power" and women get the "power of feeling"; men get the "privilege of public action" and women get the "privilege of private being." Keen quips as if these were equivalent.[58]

Other men's movement leaders utilize Jungian archetypes in their efforts to retrieve deep conscious manhood. Robert Moore and Douglas Gillette, in *King, Warrior, Magician, Lover* (1990) and the four-volume series that deals with each archetype separately, act as spirit guides to our archetypal reclamation. Their version of the king is no wimp but "aggressive, masculine, potent," "a warrior who enforces order within his kingdom and who may take military action to extend his kingdom."[59]

The search for the wild warrior within leads men's movement scions to wander through anthropological literature like postmodern tourists, as if the world's cultures were arrayed like so many ritual boutiques in a global shopping mall. Bly prefers nonindustrial primitivism, while Moore and Gillette search for the king in a breathless world historical tour, extracting images of kingship from ancient Egypt, seventh-century Tibet, the Aztecs, Incas, and Sumerians.[60] This is all slapped together in a ritual pastiche—part Asian, part African, part Native American. And all totally decontextualized. Rituals are deeply embedded in cultural life, and taking them out of that context is at least myopic, if not disingenuous.

Mythopoets celebrate cultures with elaborate rituals for men, all the while protesting that such rituals have nothing to do with women. Since the rituals exclude women, they must only be "about" men and manhood. But true traditional initiation ceremonies and sex-segregated mystical celebrations did not occur in a vacuum, and just as masculinist separation was not lost on feminists in the late nineteenth century, it is not lost on feminist women today. "The cry for revitalized initiation rites, for mentors, for sacred space, sounds ominously familiar—like a cry to reinforce the crumbling walls of those men's clubs whose primary interests were exclusion and self-perpetuation," writes the journalist Jill Baumgaertner.[61] In the real world women and men occupy the same cosmic planes—and they work desk to desk. Accessing an inner king that ignores or reduces woman's role—as wife, lover, friend, colleague, or mother—seems more like a celebration of the usurper or, at best, a benevolent despotism.

Which is how I understand all these middle-class white men beating drums, chanting Native American chants, and dancing to Native American dances. How, exactly, is this "spiritual colonialism," as one writer puts it, different from the Improved Order of the Red Men at the turn of the century, wearing war paint while whooping it up during fraternal initiation? Or for that matter, from the Tomahawk Chop? Perhaps the turn-of-the-century analogy is useful in another sense here. As I have argued earlier, in nineteenth-century minstrel shows white performers would don blackface in order to express racial anxieties as well as to gain access to emotions—longing for home and family (especially mother), urban loneliness from spatial displacement, confusions about modern life—that were denied expression by the rigidity of white manhood. Here were all these young Italian, Irish, and Jewish boys trying to make their way in a cold and unfriendly country, repressing their loneliness, and voicing a nearly "universal lamentation for homeland and birthplace." Blackface gave them access to those repressed emotions, as they sang of "mammy," the Swanee River, "de ol' folks at home"—in short, the simple joys of home and hearth. Of course, such behaviors would be seen as transparently racist today. But the mythopoets adopt what we might call "Redface"—the appropriation of putatively Native American rituals to allow privileged white men access to that set of emotions—community, spirituality, communion with nature—that they feel themselves to have lost and have therefore displaced onto Native American cultures.[62]

The search for the deep masculine is historically anachronistic, echoing late nineteenth-century masculinist complaints against the forces of feminization. But it is also developmentally atavistic, a search for lost boyhood, an effort to turn back the clock to the moment before work and family responsibilities yanked men away from their buddies. Wildman retreats are grown-up versions of the clubhouse with the sign saying No Gurls Allowed.[63] Sure, one must "wrestle with the wounds of childhood," but if one claims to be an "adult child," one uses the word "adult" only as an adjective—one remains the child. It is curious that these grown men, most of whom are between forty-five and sixty, identify more with the son in the Iron John fable. Identification with the son, the prince, reveals the traditional gender assumptions that lie at the heart of the masculinist project. The prince, after all, is the rightful heir to power; he will be the king. He is entitled to it, but he is not yet ready for it. So, too, manhood. Weekend warriors seem to believe themselves to be entitled to the power that is men's privilege. But they do not feel it yet. The mythopoetic retreats offer men a chance to reclaim their birthright, their right to power, and all the attendant privileges that derive from it. In that sense, it offers a subterranean, if inadvertent political program that reproduces and reinforces the existing power imbalances between women and men.

One thing, though, is clear: Bly, Keen, and the other leaders of the mythopoetic men's movement tap into a deep current of malaise among American men. The fears of feminization—that we have lost our ability to claim our manhood in a world without fathers, without frontiers, without manly creative work—have haunted men for a century. And nowhere have these fears been played out more fully for the past hundred years than in literature, film, and television. How else are we to understand the constant symbolic efforts to retrieve the lost father, to re-create the frontier testing ground, to experience romance and excitement in the workplace?

The deep bonds forged among soldiers have been celebrated in dozens of Vietnam films like *Platoon, Rambo, Full Metal Jacket*. Equally suggestive of the bonds forged in war are the films that evoke the life of the returning veteran. The warrior without a war is bereft, drowning in an anomic sea of meaningless routine. Films like *In Country* and *The Deer Hunter* provide the flip side to war movies, as men pick through the emotional rubble of a mundane postwar world in which deep meaning is no longer possible. Two films offer interesting contrasts. *Born on the Fourth of July* indicts not the mundane world for the collapse of meaning, but American foreign policy; Ron Kovic's heroic quest sets him against military masculinity, and he retrieves his manhood by becoming a tireless fighter against the very forms of manhood he had earlier proclaimed. And in *Casualties of War*, one young soldier challenges the bonding rituals of the others in his platoon, rituals that include the gang rape and murder of a young Vietnamese woman. Renouncing male bonding through violence and rape immediately brands him as less than a real man, his heterosexuality is questioned by the other soldiers, and later, his life is threatened, and he is nearly murdered by his brothers-in-arms. Male bonding, we are told, is certainly not a good thing for women—and it may not be a very good thing for men either, promoting excesses of violence and brutality, groupthink imperatives that obliterate individual responsibility, and an idealization of the warrior.

"Healing the father wound" as both the motivation for and the ultimate result of the masculine quest has been the theme of some of the most popular films of the past two decades. Take, for example, five of these decades' most popular films—a pair of alien movies, *E.T.: The Extra-Terrestrial* and *Close Encounters of the Third Kind*, offered by Steven Spielberg, and the *Star Wars* trilogy of George Lucas. In *Close Encounters* Richard Dreyfuss's character abandons his family and job to retrieve his childlike wonder in a call to a spiritual reawakening. In *E.T.* the void left by Elliot's father's abandonment of the family is filled by a cherubic alien whose power to heal families is motivated by the simple desire to go home. And in *Star Wars* Luke Skywalker undertakes the most mythopoetic journey of all, a spiritual quest in which the young Jedi Knight is initiated into warriorhood by male mentors Obi Wan Kenobi and Yoda; he is motivated as well by his sister Leia's love.[64] Skywalker defeats the evil emperor and redeems his archenemy, Darth Vader, who, it turns out, is Skywalker's long-lost father, transformed into a dark, menacing shadow warrior by addictions to power and wealth. The boy's quest literally heals the father wound and prepares him for adulthood as a heroic warrior.

In *Field of Dreams*, a search for boyhood innocence leads Kevin Costner's character to build a baseball field in his Iowa cornfield, an unconscious effort at reconciliation with the father who abandoned him long before. At the film's end the two are having a lazy catch on the mythic diamond. Baseball, that timeless masculine trope, has healed the father wound. In all these films the boy's quest to find himself, his inner child, also heals the father and provides the grounding for their reconciliation. Talk about family values![65]

Costner's epic *Dances with Wolves* reminds us that the western frontier is still the quintessential mythic site for demonstrating manhood. Like Owen Wister and every generation of American men since, we come to the western to experience the initiation into manhood and the mythopoetic quest reinscribed into buckskin and revolvers. The search for authentic experience, for deep meaning, has always led men back to the frontier, back to nature, even if it is inevitably the frontier of their imaginations. "I've always wanted to see the frontier," says Lieut. John Dunbar, "before it's gone."

Not only does Dunbar see the frontier, he is converted by it, like Roosevelt, Wister, and Remington before him. The slaughter of Pawnee attackers serves as Dunbar's ceremonial initiation. After the battle, where his introduction of high-level technology (repeating rifles) decimates the evil Indians, he writes in his journal that before that moment, he never really knew himself, but upon hearing his Sioux name, Dances with Wolves, "I knew for the first time who I really was." Unlike his real-life predecessors, Dunbar chooses not to return with his new vision to civilized life, here pictured as hopelessly venal and corrupt, but to go native, joining a tribe of Ogala Sioux on the trail of the vanishing buffalo and in full-scale retreat from the oncoming rush of white civilization. He finds his nonwhite spirit guides in Kicking Bird (Graham Greene), who brings him into the tribe, and Wind in His Hair (Rodney Grant), who finally accepts him and provides the coda of achieved equality for the film, shouting of their friendship. And of course, Dunbar gets the traditional reward for manhood regained: the beautiful woman, Stands with a Fist (Mary McDonnell), the white woman who had been raised by the Ogala (no miscegenation here!). Costner thus reinvents the heroic warrior as Rousseauian noble savage, inverts traditional cowboy and Indian mythologies (we cheer when the virtuous Indians kill the white soldiers), and retrieves lost manhood—a manhood that could never be achieved as long as our hero remains within the boundaries of eastern civilized life.

City Slickers transposes this mythic quest for manhood into the

1980s, as three yuppies—Mitch Robbins, Ed Furillo, and Phil Berquist, played, respectively, by Billy Crystal, Bruno Kirby, and Daniel Stern—resolve their midlife crises on a faux-western cattle drive that turns all too real as a test of manhood. Crystal's first foil is a seemingly ageless father figure/mentor (Jack Palance), who plays the genuine article, a real cowboy as ageless icon. His death releases Crystal and his friends to chase after the grail of manhood, which is pursued through the failure of several other characters. Crystal, Kirby, and Stern are successful in bringing in the herd of cattle; their initiatory moment is predicated on the failure of the others in their group—two rowdy ranch hands (traditional macho men), a father and son team of buppie dentists (black men), two effete and flabby Jewish ice-cream entrepreneurs (bespectacled Jewish wimps), and of course, a woman. The successful symbolic reclamation of manhood is possible for the white upper middle-class man only via the failure of the traditional "others," the exclusion of the other from that same mythic quest.

One ironic postscript illustrates the disjunction between the fantasy retrievals of lost manhood and its anxious and relentless real-life quest. As Jack Palance accepted the 1992 Academy Award for Best Supporting Actor for his performance in *City Slickers*, he noted that at seventy-seven years old, many movie producers had thought him washed up, too old to play these arduous roles. They're wrong, of course, he snarled, as he dropped to the floor of the stage to do a set of one-armed push-ups. Regaining his feet, he also boasted that he could "still get it up." In fantasy the quest to prove manhood ends at the Hollywood climax; in real life, it seems, it never does.

In *Unforgiven* Clint Eastwood, the embodiment of remorseless manhood, writes a countermyth, a story of manhood retrieved without redemption, without heroism. Eastwood plays William Munney, an aging widower, a failure as a father and domesticated farmer, who retrieves his manhood through cold, merciless, passionless murder. Like Crystal and his yuppie cronies, Eastwood reclaims his manhood via the failure of several others—English Bob (Richard Harris), a dandified British fop who stands in for the old aristocracy, revealed as just as brutal and vicious as the Self-Made Man (Bob made his living killing Chinese for the railroad); a cynical and sadistic sheriff, Little

Bill Daggett, (Gene Hackman), who reveals that the forces of law and order are as mercurial and lawless as those outside the law; Ned Logan (Morgan Freeman), a black comrade who has lost his ability to fight and whose death becomes the blood sacrifice Eastwood needs to complete his redemption; and the young Schofield Kid (Jaimz Woolvett), who wants to join the gang but who finds the reality of frontier virility so distasteful and horrifying that he returns home. When Eastwood reclaims his manhood, we realize that it is a manhood that no one in his right mind would want. The West is gone, we understand, and so too its supposed western heroes.[66]

But the masculinist descent to the primitive has resurfaced in another guise—the return of the monster as hypermasculine beast. How to explain films such as *Interview with the Vampire, Mary Shelley's Frankenstein, Bram Stoker's Dracula*, or *Wolf* except as contemporary versions of Tarzan or Buck? And like their predecessors, the descent to a primal, natural, animal-like masculinity can cut either way. In *Wolf* Jack Nicholson's transformation reconnects his character, a somewhat stuffily effete book editor, with a fierce, heroic, and sensual nature that civilized discourse had all but completely sapped. (Even his vision gets sharper.) But for James Spader, his rival, that same descent brings out a deeper cruelty, less concealed by social convention. Nicholson uses his descent to elevate his manhood, while Spader uses his as an invitation to unchecked depravity. Nicholson becomes a passionate lover, Spader a rapist.

Many of these themes resound in other cultural media. Popular music, for instance, for decades a form of masculine assertion—from teenage rebellion against work, family, and school to the wrenching passions of an awakening sexuality. A brief comparison between two of the most popular rock performers of the past decade can illustrate the different strategies and visions that men have embraced. Guns N' Roses insists angrily on exclusion, while Bruce Springsteen's career suggests a trajectory from rebellious rocker to responsible father.

Guns N' Roses has been among the nation's most successful hard rock bands; their *Use Your Illusion*, volumes 1 and 2 (Geffen Records), were the single fastest selling records in history. Record stores scheduled extra hours to handle the demand as fans lined up to buy the record as if they were buying concert tickets. Yet to hear them tell it, we should feel sorry for them. Like the advocates of men's rights, Guns N' Roses claims to be besieged on all fronts—as young working-class men by forces outside their control and as a rock band by demanding fans, tempting women, and rock critics who have held them accountable for the racial and sexual rage they have promoted. In one song, "One in a Million," lead singer Axl Rose sang about the newcomers to his neighborhood who were making life so difficult, who were potential harbingers of terrorism and disease:

> Immigrants and faggots
> They make no sense to me
> They come to our country
> And think they'll do as they please. . . .

At the end of the song, Rose warned both police and "niggers" to get out of his way.[67] On their most recent records it's no longer the invading hordes of immigrants, blacks, and gays streaming into white working-class neighborhoods. It's women, those seductive temptresses who really have all the power. "It's time for me to even the score," he screams in revenge in another song, echoing the men who would fight dirty and win.[68]

GN'R represent the worst tendencies of working- and middle-class white male politics, the politics of resentment and retaliation. Squeezed by a shrinking economy, ignored by politicians indifferent to their plight, they turn their rage on those just below them on the social ladder, those who are still hoping to land a piece of the American pie. Like David Duke's coded messages or Michael Douglas's *Falling Down*, GN'R tap into homophobia, racism, and sexism and make them the bases for their hard-edged rock. (In an increasingly segmented musical marketplace the excluded others have their say as well, in "women's" music, gay and lesbian cabaret acts, and in gangsta rap, in which misogyny and homophobia often serve as rhetorical counterpunches to racism. Predictably, it is only this last genre which has found a mass-market audience.)

What a contrast with Bruce Springsteen, named by *Rolling Stone* as the rock artist of the 1980s. The changes in Springsteen's style and substance reveal a surprisingly compelling vision of a direction for men in the 1990s. From his first rebellious record in the early 1970s and his breakthrough *Born to Run* (1975), Springsteen joined a venerable American cast of characters, latest in a line of "the last real man in America." And like Natty Bumppo, Huck Finn, or the Lone Ranger, he eluded domestic attachments while he set off in search of authenticity, freedom, and meaning—searching for manhood in an imagined America. "As a child, I felt the myth coming from everywhere, especially from television westerns with those big landscapes," he told one interviewer. "In rock music it was Chuck Berry, the cars, the guitars, the girls, the sense of endless highway and endless night and sexual power."[69]

And as it had done to every other "last real man," America let him down. Springsteen's lyrics painted a relentlessly bleak portrait of the downward spiral of the white working class. Rebuffed and rejected, he sought escape or solace in sex, cars, male camaraderie, adventure, and finally, in rock and roll itself. "Let's get out while we're still young," he sang on "Born to Run" (1975). But it all turned out to be illusory; there is no escape from the pain and dejection of life at the bottom. There was no relief from the working life, only darkness at the edge of town.

By contrast, his sound was energized, upbeat, anthemic. As if to underline the contradiction, Springsteen sang about the dead-end lives of workers, but his nickname was "The Boss." His hit song "Born in the U.S.A." embodied this contradiction. A desultory story of a returning Vietnam veteran, the song is also a jubilant celebration of hope in the American Dream—even as that hope is being dashed by unemployment and governmental bureaucratic indifference. The characters in his songs are classic American tragic figures, whose tragic flaw is that they believe in the Dream.

But Springsteen now seems to understand that the pain at the dead-end of dull routine in the factory life of his working-class father led him on his own quest for manhood, a quest that celebrated the traditional escape hatches for American men even as he saw their limits. The answers were to be found, not by fleeing the home, family, and domestic responsibility or through a mournful resignation to the traps of domesticated manhood, but by embracing them. On his recent records, *Human Touch* and *Lucky Town* (both 1992), and his newly penned "Blood Brothers" from his *Greatest Hits* album (1995), Bruce Springsteen has grown up. He makes his peace with the real world, seeing in his new experiences as husband and father the quotidian compromises that are the stuff of everyday heroism. And he's finally happy.[70]

EPILOGUE

TOWARD DEMOCRATIC MANHOOD

The old, recognized virtues have begun to lose their authority, they are no longer able to fulfill the religious, moral, intellectual and social demands of the contemporary soul. Man's soul seems to have grown bigger, it cannot fit any longer within the old molds. A pitiless civil war has broken out in the vitals of our age, has broken out, whether consciously or unconsciously in the vitals of every man abreast of his times—a civil war between the old, formerly omnipotent myth which has vented its strength, yet which fights desperately to regulate our lives awhile longer, and the new myth which is battling, still awkwardly and without organization to govern our souls.
—Nikos Kazantzakis (1971)[1]

There comes a moment when we stop creating ourselves.
—John Updike (1992)[2]

We, with love, shall force our brothers to see themselves as they are, to cease fleeing from reality and begin to change it.
—James Baldwin (1962)[3]

As we face a new century, American men remain bewildered by the sea changes in our culture, besieged by the forces of reform, and bereft by the emotional impoverishment of our lives. For straight white middle-class men a virtual siege mentality has set in. The frontier is gone and competition in the global marketplace is keener than ever. The current era, in which middle-class incomes seem to slip downward (in purchasing power) for the first time since World War II, makes pinning one's proof of manhood on the capacity to succeed as a breadwinner and provider increasingly perilous. The Self-Made Man, that model of manhood we have inherited as the only marker of our success as men, leads more than ever before to chronic anxiety and insecurity.

New issues have been raised by those groups formerly excluded from equality. Women demand both safety and choice—an end to date rape and sexual harassment and a secure right to choose how to respond to pregnancy. They want to enter the military, the fire department, and virtually every other male fraternity. Gay men and lesbians also want safety and choice—an end to discrimination and violence against them and the same right to enter the military, as well as increased research, funding, and compassion for people with AIDS. Black men demand structural solutions to the high levels of unemployment among young black men, levels which prevent an entire generation from achieving manhood in the usual way, as breadwinners, and they seek to develop separate schools for young black men to teach them less self-destructive means of coping with the persistence of racism. And new groups of immigrants continue to enter the American melting pot and refuse to melt, retaining cultural and ethnic differences as a hedge against assimilation, and becoming new targets for defensive rage.

As we have seen, men's responses to these new challenges have ranged from the angry resistance of men's rights groups to the defensive retreat to the cosmic archetypes of the mythopoets—exactly the responses of most American men to these challenges for the past 150 years. Bumper stickers advertise the driver's sexual prowess, informing us that divers "do it deeper," carpenters have "big tools," and rugby players have "leather balls." A legion of rock and rap singers boast of sexual prowess, about size, strength, and their ability to dominate and hurt women. The affluent still seek power, security, and strength in the names of their cars, clothes, and colognes. Many still equate a secure sense of themselves as men with the size of their bulges—from bulging wallets to bulging muscles to bulging crotches. And so every arena becomes a masculine testing ground: After a day's work we "work out," so that in the evening, with our wives or lovers, we can "get the job done" with our "tools" and thus calm our "performance anxiety."

And still it's not enough. On his deathbed Republican campaign strategist Lee Atwater recanted his dirty-tricks campaign style and repudiated the excesses of the Reagan-Bush era. "The 80s were about acquiring—acquiring wealth, power, prestige. I know. I acquired more wealth, power and prestige than most. But you can acquire all you want and still feel empty."[4] What we hear still is a shrill chorus of impotence, a frenzied assertion of power by those who do not feel powerful. And it is met by a cacophony of soothing therapeutic voices offering to heal the men who have been wounded in the struggle to prove themselves.

Even Flex Crush has returned to offer his opinions on the men of the 1990s. In *Real Men Don't Bond*, Bruce Feirstein presents a toned-down real man, now sporting a Gap T-shirt and eating fruit salad. He's even abandoned the nuclear waste business to drive a recycling truck. But he's still incendiary at men's continued confusion. "Jerks running around the forest, banging on drums, chanting to get in touch with their manhood. . . . Guys trying to find their masculinity at seminars." The problem today, though, "isn't wimps, or Phil Donahue, or even quiche," Crush informs us. "It's that we've become a nation of whiners." Everyone is so busy looking for their status as a victim that no one is taking responsibility for anything. Even Flex Crush is promoting responsible manhood![5]

But few men are calling into question the basis for all the resistance and retreat; few are examining the hinging of men's definitions of themselves as men with our position in a homosocial, competitive arena of the market. Current men's movements are often like psychological first aid, applying a salve to the wounds and then sending the men back out into the fray again. No wonder the men keep coming back—the cures aren't treating the root cause of the malady.

Efforts to ensure a feeling of masculinity by building the male body or controlling male appetites have made us powerful, muscular machines haunted by fears of our weakness.[6] From J. H. Kellogg's antimasturbatory frenzied fulminations to Teddy Roosevelt's bully manhood; from Bernarr Macfadden's physical culture to today's Iron Man triathlons, men have sought to prove their manhood by exercise, by acquiring the physical signs of strength, power, and domination. But there's always someone stronger, more physically fit, more powerful and dominating working out in the next gym. Working on the body becomes another example of proving manhood as a relentless test.

The strategies to preserve masculinity by exclusion have likewise failed. These efforts brought incredible power to men as a group, as opposed to women, and brought significant power to middle-class straight white men. But they have consistently left men without a feeling of empowerment. Men feel as beseiged today as ever. And the very men who are complaining loudest seem to be precisely those middle-class straight white men. From John Todd's admonitions against suffrage or women's education in the mid-nineteenth century to contemporary antifeminists and men's rights advocates; from Lathrop Stoddard's xenophobic racism at the turn of the century to David Duke today—propping up manhood by exclusion has never brought men the security and comfort of a stable gender identity.

We haven't found manhood by escaping either. From Rip Van Winkle to Robert Bly, men have sought the homosocial solace of the wilderness, the frontier, the West. Or the saloon, the fraternity, the clubhouse, the locker room. There they've healed their wounds by carving out a reprieve from the burdens of proof and reinvented themselves as warriors as a way to free themselves and rescue their sons from the feminizing clutches of women. But the respite has always been only temporary and must be constantly renewed, often in even more bizarre ritual appropriations, or else they may lapse into the same politics of resentment and exclusion. Men will be free, D. H. Lawrence wrote, "when they are in a living homeland, not when they are escaping to some wild west."[7]

No; these methods to restore or retrieve American manhood will fail as they have always failed throughout our history. Manhood cannot be regained by reasserting traditional privilege nor by retreats to these homosocial island hideaways. These efforts will fail because they ask the wrong questions, begin from the wrong premises. Self-control, exclusion, escape—these efforts fail because they still embrace the quest to prove masculinity in the first place and to do so in a public arena. They thus lead men on the historical and quixotic quest to demonstrate what can never be successfully, finally, demonstrated, to strive to achieve what can never be achieved. The trail blazed by the Self-Made Man is a spiral path leading only back to itself, to a relentless retesting of an unprovable ambition.

Self-Made Manhood is our legacy from nearly two centuries of American history; it feels as familiar as our skin. But it is not our nature; it has a history. It has changed from the embodiment of inner character and virtue to the muscle-building, wallet-bulging accoutrements of masculinity. And the meanings of manhood will continue to change. It is my hope that such changes not rehearse the failed strategies that have dogged our efforts to prove our manhood but that we accept the responsibility to consider other possibilities, other visions of manhood. The capacity to change, to grow, to learn from our past mistakes without centuries of evolutionary selection—this is also our legacy as human beings.

The American manhood of the future cannot be based on obsessive self-control, defensive exclusion, or frightened escape. We need a new definition of masculinity for a new century, a definition that is more about the character of men's hearts and souls than about the size of their biceps or their wallets. A definition that is capable of embracing differences among men and enabling other men to feel secure and confident rather than excluding them. A definition that centers around standing up for justice and equality instead of running away from commitment and engagement. We need a democratic manhood.

Democratic manhood means a gender politics of inclusion, of standing up against injustice based on difference. Some men have embraced feminism, gay liberation, and multiculturalism as a blueprint for the reconstruction of masculinity. Profeminist men believe, as Floyd Dell wrote at the turn of the century, that "feminism will make it possible for the first time for men to be free."[8] Profeminist men accept a wary alliance with those groups pressing for social change to embrace diversity and equality for women, people of color, and gay men and lesbians. Profeminist men believe that men's lives will only be healed when there is full equality for those people who have been traditionally excluded from their full humanity. The full, emotionally rich lives we have come to expect in modern times are possible only when all can taste the sweetness of freedom, and that is only possible if we change the meaning of manhood, wrest our identities away from the arena of competition, domination, and power, and reanchor them in the arena of accountability, responsibility, and hope.

This is not a call for androgyny, for a blurring of masculinity and femininity into a mélange of some vaguely defined "human" qualities. In difference, I believe, is heat, is passion—and I envision a masculinity and a femininity capable of heat as well as warmth. But I also question the facile equations—equality means sameness, difference means inequality—that frighten us away from attempting such a cultural redefinition. Our popular impressions of equality have always meant the obliteration of difference—in a word, sameness—and this has fueled the anxieties of American manhood for too long. We must begin to imagine a world of equality in which we also embrace and celebrate difference, a world in which our manhood is based more on our willingness to enlarge the arenas so that others may enter than our ability to shore up walls and fences to keep them out. It is a world in which successful achievement of identity is not reserved for those who happen to be of a specific gender, race, ethnicity, and sexual orientation but in which a secure and confident sense of oneself is part of the birthright of every American.

This will not be a noisy or violent revolutionary transformation but the result of countless quiet daily struggles by American men to free themselves from the burdens of proof. Democratic manhood requires both private and public commitments—changing ourselves, nurturing our relationships, cherishing our families, to be sure, but also reforming the public arena to enlarge the possibilities for other people to do the same. Along the way, we will find that much of what it has historically meant to be a man—strength, a sense of purpose, a commitment to act ethically, controlled aggressiveness, self-reliance, dependability—can be coupled with such newer masculine virtues as compassion, nurturing, and a fierce egalitarianism, which together may form a stronger and more resilient template for manhood in America.

We will have help on this road, often from the very people we have tried so desperately to keep out. Like feminist women, gay men and lesbians, and people of color. It has never failed to astonish me that so many people misinterpret the anger of feminist women, for example, as "male-bashing" or "man-hating." Feminist women, it seems to me, are quite justified in their anger at injustice and discrimination and their fears of violence and danger that together circumscribe their lives. But at its core feminism is, it seems to me, an optimistic worldview that sees men as capable of change and, with enough encouragement, even likely to change. The real "man-haters," it seems to me, are those right-wing zealots who believe that men cannot change their violent, abusive patterns and who argue that women must remain subordinate if only to keep men in line. Most feminists, by contrast, love men enough to believe in us.

The battle to prove manhood is a battle that can never be won. Only by renouncing the battle itself—not in resigned retreat but by joining the struggles of others for their rightful share of the sun— only then can we American men come home from our wars, heal our wounds, and breathe a collective sigh of relief.

APPENDIX

APPENDIX

ATTITUDE-INTEREST ANALYSIS TEST

READ THIS FIRST

You are asked to cooperate seriously and carefully in marking the items in this booklet. This is not an intelligence test. We want to find out something about the attitudes and interests of people in relation to their occupations, their home situations, and their hobbies. The items in this booklet have been selected by actual trial out of several thousand. More than 4,000 persons of different ages, occupations, and schooling have filled out test blanks like this one. We are trying to accumulate sufficient returns to discover what the actual standards of response are. Your answers are needed to help do this. Fill in all of the blanks on this page as indicated below. Please do not omit any of the items. All of the information is important. Do not look at the other pages of the booklet until you have finished filling in the blanks below.

Name.. Age........ Sex........ Race................

City .... State................

Underline one: Single,   Married,   Widowed,   Separated,   Divorced.

Amount of Schooling.

Mark highest point reached:

Yrs.	Grammar grades								High School				College				M.A.	Ph.D.
	1	2	3	4	5	6	7	8	1	2	3	4	1	2	3	4	5 6	7
																	M.A.	M.D.

Other schooling or courses................................

Profession or occupation................................

Previous professions or occupations if any:

(Married women list occupation before marriage)............

Specific hobbies or special interests such as playing baseball,   1. ....

choir singing, chess, collecting stamps, philanthropy.   2. ....

If ever married state for how many years: ....

If you have children state number of boys: .... girls: ....

How many brothers older than yourself reached 16 years of age? ....

How many brothers younger than yourself reached 16 years of age? ....

How many sisters older than yourself reached 16 years of age? ....

How many sisters younger than yourself reached 16 years of age? ....

Were both your parents responsible for your training up to the age of 16? ....

If not, please specify............

Underline the word that indicates your usual state of health: Robust, above-average, average, below-average, frail.

Mark a cross on each of the 12 lines below to indicate the amount of your interest in each subject or activity.

1. Travel	Much	Average	Slight or none
2. Out-door Sports	Much	Average	Slight or none
3. Religion	Much	Average	Slight or none
4. Mechanics	Much	Average	Slight or none
5. Social Life	Much	Average	Slight or none
6. Literature	Much	Average	Slight or none
7. Music	Much	Average	Slight or none
8. Art	Much	Average	Slight or none
9. Science	Much	Average	Slight or none
10. Politics	Much	Average	Slight or none
11. Domestic Arts	Much	Average	Slight or none
12. Pets	Much	Average	Slight or none

NOW READ THIS

Do not look at other parts of the booklet until you are ready to begin the test. When you are ready, turn at once to Exercise 1. Read the instructions carefully, marking the sample items as you come to them. Then go right on to the exercise itself. Work as rapidly as you can. As soon as you have finished Exercise 1 go right on to Exercise 2, then Exercise 3, and so on until you have finished the booklet. In each case read the directions with care, and work the exercise as rapidly as you can. It should take about 40 or 50 minutes to finish the booklet.

Time began test . . . .   Time finished test . . . .

Do not write in space below.

1	2	3	4	5	6	7
. . . .						
. . . .						

EXERCISE 1

DIRECTIONS: Look at the word in capital letters, then look at each of the four words which follow it.
For example:

   HORSE   cow   hay   race   swim

Draw a line under the word that seems to you to go best or most naturally with HORSE; that is, the word that HORSE tends most to make you think of.
Second example:

   AUTO   danger   gears   machine   ride

Draw a line under the word that seems to go best or most naturally with AUTO; the word that AUTO tends most to make you think of. Look at each of the words in the list below. In each case, draw a line under the word that goes best or most naturally with the one in capitals; the word it tends most to make you think of. Work rapidly; do not think long over any one.

EXERCISE 1.—Continued

1.[1] POLE   barber 0[2]   cat +   North −   telephone +
2. DATE   appointment −   dance +   fruit +   history +
3. BAR   drink +   prisoner −   sand +   stop −
4. SHARP   bright −   flat −   knife 0   pin +
5. TRUNK   baggage 0   elephant +   travel −   tree 0

6. ORDER   buy −   command +   neat −   quiet −
7. CASE   bottles +   container 0   doctor −   grammar −
8. POST   fence +   gate −   letter −   mail 0
9. TENDER   kind −   loving −   meat +   sore 0
10. JACK   cards −   money +   tool +   toy −

11. TRAIN   engine +   gown −   travel −   whistle −
12. DRAW   blood +   bridge +   pencil −   picture 0
13. BRACE   bit +   pair −   strap −   support −
14. FLY   airplane +   bird −   nasty 0   travel −
15. BOND   love +   paper −   security +   tie −

16. PASS   car 0   mountain +   over −   subject −
17. RAIN   clouds +   umbrella −   weather +   wet 0
18. BOOK   cover 0   paper +   print +   read −
19. PURE   good −   milk +   water −   white 0
20. MOON   light +   month 0   night −   round −

[1] The items in Exercises 1 and 2 were not numbered in the test blank, for fear of disturbing the associations. They are numbered here to facilitate reference to them.

[2] In this reproduction of the M-F test the response weights have been added. Responses followed by the sign "+" count one point toward masculinity, those followed by the sign "−" count one point toward femininity, those followed by "0" are neutral.

EXERCISE 1.—Continued

21. FLESH — blood – color – meat – soft –
22. DANGER — accident – caution + death – escape +
23. MODEST — bashful + good 0 nice 0 shy –
24. FRESH — cool – flirt 0 meat + stale +
25. COLOR — black + blind + blue – shade –

26. PICNIC — fun – hike 0 sandwich 0 Sunday +
27. WEDDING — bride – happiness – marriage + ring +
28. DUTY — God – honor 0 soldier + work –
29. GARDEN — flower – fruit + vegetable + weeds +
30. EMBRACE — arms – lover + mother 0 sin +

31. HOME — expenses – happiness – house + sleep +
32. BLUSH — red – rose – shame + smile +
33. BABY — cry + darling – infant – mother 0
34. FELLOW — boy – friend + good 0 pal 0
35. CHEAT — cards + clerk + crook 0 unfair –

36. ENJOY — food + happiness – jolly + laugh 0
37. DEVIL — dare 0 evil – hell + tempt –
38. JEALOUS — angry – green – lover + women +
39. DIMPLE — baby – cheek 0 hole 0 knee +
40. KNIGHT — armor + brave – Ivanhoe – man +

EXERCISE 1.—Concluded

41. LETTER	love +	news −	paper +	stamp 0
42. CELLAR	basement +	dark −	furnace 0	vegetables 0
43. TRUE	edge +	good −	soldiers +	story +
44. DESPISE	coward +	dirt −	dislike −	flirt 0
45. TWILIGHT	dark +	dusk −	morning 0	sunset +
46. FACE	enemy +	powder −	pretty +	wash 0
47. SPOON	fork +	pet +	silver −	soup +
48. CHEEK	blush +	girl +	nerve +	pink −
49. WORSHIP	church +	God −	hero 0	Sunday 0
50. LONGING	absence −	child +	home −	success 0
51. SACRIFICE	cards +	kill +	money 0	mother −
52. MARRIAGE	children −	divorce +	happy −	license 0
53. RULE	command −	footrule +	games +	obey −
54. BRAVE	fight +	honor −	protect +	soldier 0
55. FLOWER	fields 0	fragrant −	vase +	violet −
56. FAMILY	brother +	kind −	quarrel +	sister 0
57. SIXTEEN	age 0	foolish +	number −	years 0
58. ANGEL	death 0	Gabriel +	good −	heaven −
59. VAIN	peacock −	proud −	impossible +	useless +
60. MACHINE	engine −	Ford +	ride −	sew −

EXERCISE 2

Directions:—Here are some drawings, a little like ink blots. They are not pictures of anything in particular but might suggest almost anything to you, just as shapes in the clouds sometimes do. Beside each drawing four things are mentioned. Underline the one word that tells what the drawing makes you think of most.

Examples:—

baby
dog
man
squirrel

arm
flame
flower
tail

dog's head
glove
hand
horse's head

			Omission
1.*		jar 0 mail box − pipe + tombstone +	0
2.		ball bat − ham 0 pear + tadpole +	0
3.		candle 0 cup 0 hat + inkwell −	0
4		fish 0 mirror 0 snow shoe + spoon −	0

* See footnote 1 to Exercise 1.

EXERCISE 2.—Continued

5.

	Omission
brush	+
centipede	+
comb	−
teeth	−

Omission: 0

6.

ax	+
boat	+
chopper	−
moon	+

Omission: 0

7.

dish	−
ring	0
target	+
tire	0

Omission: 0

8.

bird house	0
flagpole	+
sword	−
torch	+

Omission: +

9.

fence	+
letter "E"	0
ship	0
tree	−

Omission: +

10.

babies	0
cloud	−
dancers	−
lovers	+

Omission: 0

11.

Indian	0
man hanged	+
scarecrow	−
tassel	−

Omission: 0

12.

chimney	−
coil	+
smoke	−
thread	−

Omission: 0

EXERCISE 2.—Concluded

13.

		Omission
bottle	0	0
cannon	+	
Indian club	—	
jug	—	

14.

		Omission
baby	+	0
bell	+	
idol	—	
incense	—	

15.

		Omission
fish	+	0
saxophone	+	
snake	0	
whip	0	

16.

		Omission
bat	+	0
flower	—	
goat	0	
star	—	

17.

		Omission
coal bucket	—	0
face	0	
kettle	+	
nose	+	

18.

		Omission
a man	0	0
bowl	—	
cup	—	
head	+	

EXERCISE 3

In each sentence draw a line under the word that makes the sentence true.

Example: America was discovered by BALBOA COLUMBUS DRAKE WASHINGTON

Work as rapidly as you can. Skip those you do not know.

		Omission
1.	Marigold is a kind of fabric + flower − grain − stone + ...	−
2.	Things cooked in grease are boiled + broiled + fried − roasted + ...	−
3.	The Yale is a kind of hammer 0 lock + screen 0 wrench 0	−
4.	We should drink tea from the cup − saucer + spoon + ...	0
5.	Pongee is a kind of cloth − drink 0 flower 0 game 0	+
6.	The most gold is produced in Alaska + New York 0 Tennessee − Texas −	−
7.	The earth moves around the sun in 7 days − 30 days 0 180 days − 365 days + ...	+
8.	A stately dance of colonial days was the minuet − polka + two-step 0 waltz + ...	+
9.	One must run fast in fruit basket − jackstones + tin-tin + wood-tag 0	+
10.	Beethoven is known as a composer − painter + poet + singer −	+
11.	Most of our anthracite coal comes from Alabama − Colorado − Ohio − Pennsylvania + ...	−
12.	The number of players on a baseball team is 7 − 9 + 11 − 13 0	0
13.	Eggs are best for us when deviled − fried + hard-boiled + soft-boiled −	0
14.	A loom is used for cooking + embroidering + sewing + weaving −	+
15.	Peat is used for fuel + pavement − plaster 0 road-making 0	−
16.	Marco Polo was a famous king 0 philosopher − traveler + warrior −	0
17.	Tokyo is a city of China − India − Japan + Russia 0	+
18.	The first American naval hero was Hull − John Paul Jones + Lawrence + Winslow −	−

EXERCISE 3—Continued

		Omission	
19. Daffodils are grown from bulbs — cuttings 0 seeds + shoots +	......	+	19
20. The baby found in the bulrushes was Jacob + Jesus + Moses — Paul +	......	0	20
21. The boomerang is an animal — plant 0 tool — weapon +	......	—	21
22. Minnehaha means falling leaves + laughing waters — running brooks + whispering pines 0	......	+	22
23. A correct expression is I have dove 0 I dived — He dove +	......	0	23
24. The "Rough Riders" were led by Funston — Pershing — Roosevelt + Sheridan —	......	—	24
25. The vessel which overcame the Merrimac was the Connecticut — Monitor + Old Ironsides —	......	—	25
26. About A.D. 1750 men's sleeves had bands + lace-ruffles — stiff cuffs + stripes +	......	+	26
27. A food with much the same food substance as rice is beans + peas + meat 0 potatoes —	......	+	27
28. A shilling is worth about 25 cts. + 50 cts. 0 $1.00 — $5.00 0	......	—	28
29. Punch and Judy are artists 0 dancers — musicians + puppets 0	......	—	29
30. "Speak for yourself" was said by Annabel Lee + Evangeline — Juliet + Priscilla —	......	0	30
31. The Erie Canal is in Canada — Ohio 0 New York + Pennsylvania 0	......	—	31
32. Red goes best with black — lavender + pink + purple +	......	+	32
33. Baby gets its first tooth at about 6 mos. — 12 mos. + 15 mos. + 18 mos. +	......	0	33
34. The mossy side of a tree is usually on the east — north + south 0 west 0	......	—	34
35. The state whose waters produce the most salmon is California 0 Maine — Massachusetts — Oregon +	......	0	35
36. Turpentine comes from coal + petroleum — trees + whales —	......	—	36
37. The number of persons on a jury in the U.S. is 8 0 12 + 16 — 18 0	......	—	37
38. The Madonna is a favorite subject for music + paintings — poetry 0 stories 0	......	+	38
39. The chief cause of the tides is the attraction of the moon + planets — sun 0 stars 0	......	—	39
40. The proportion of the globe covered by water is about $\frac{1}{8}$ — $\frac{1}{4}$ — $\frac{1}{2}$ — $\frac{3}{4}$ +	......	—	40
41. The turquoise is blue — red + white + yellow +	......	+	41
42. A plant "breathes" chiefly through its bark 0 leaves + roots — twigs 0	......	—	42

EXERCISE 3—Continued

		Omission	
43. Mica is an explosive 0 food + mineral + vegetable 0..........	—	43
44. Blue clashes worst with brown + gray + pink + purple —..........	0	44
45. A dinner hostess seats the guest of honor at her left 0 opposite + right —..........	0	45
46. A buffet is used for books 0 clothes + dishes — food —..........	+	46
47. Shinny is played with bats + clubs + nets — racquets —..........	—	47
48. When water freezes it contracts + expands — does neither —..........	—	48
49. The Roman numeral C equals 50 + 100 + 500 0 1000 —..........	—	49
50. Some think "moon over the right shoulder" means death 0 rain — sickness + wish fulfillment —..........	0	50
51. The amethyst is green + purple — white + yellow +..........	+	51
52. Ruth and Naomi are known for their devotion — hatred + pity 0 rivalry +..........	—	52
53. The length of a brick is 6 in. — 8 in. + 10 in. + 12 in.—..........	—	53
54. The number of Abou Ben Adhem's visions was 1 + 20 40 6 +..........	—	54
55. "Mennen's" is the name of cold cream + perfume + collar 0 talcum —..........	—	55
56. Barometers are used to measure air pressure + heat — humidity + rainfall —..........	—	56
57. Lobo was the name of a bear — crow + fox + wolf +..........	—	57
58. "Charades" is a running game 0 game of chance 0 guessing game — kissing game +..........	+	58
59. The number of ordinary steps in a mile is about 1,000 0 2,000 + 5,000 — 10,000 0..........	—	59
60. "Peter Pan" was written by Barrie — Kipling + Mark Twain + Stevenson +..........	—	60
61. Babies should be weaned at about 3 mos. + 6 mos. — 12 mos. — 2 yrs. +..........	0	61
62. The altitude record for airplanes is about 10,000 ft. — 20,000 ft. + 40,000 ft. + 60,000 ft. +..........	—	62
63. Limestone originated from granite — marble — sand 0 shells +..........	—	63
64. An animal that suckles its young is the alligator 0 shark — snake 0 whale +..........	—	64
65. A birthright was sold for a mess of pottage by Cain 0 Esau + Isaac — Judas 0..........	—	65

EXERCISE 3.—Concluded

	Omission
66. Beam scales illustrate the principle of buoyancy 0 elasticity 0 leverage + magnetism −	− 66
67. A character in "David Copperfield" is Betty + Uriah Heep − Sinbad + Oliver Twist + ...	− 67
68. A decisive Revolutionary battle was Gettysburg − New Orleans + Valley Forge − Yorktown + ...	− 68
69. "Nevermore" was spoken by a general + parrot 0 raven 0 woman −	− 69
70. A famous portrait painter was Rosa Bonheur 0 Mozart − Reynolds − Rubens + ...	+ 70

EXERCISE 4

Below is a list of things that sometimes cause anger. After each thing mentioned draw a circle around VM, M, L, or N to show how much it causes you.

VM means VERY MUCH; M means MUCH; L means A LITTLE; N means NONE.

1. Being blamed for something you have not done...... VM − M O L+ N O
2. Being called lazy...... VM − M O L O N +
3. Being called stupid...... VM − M O L+ N O
4. Being called a thief...... VM O M O L+ N −
5. Being deceived by a supposed friend...... VM − M O L O N O

6. Being disturbed when you want to work...... VM O M O L+ N −
7. Being snubbed by an inferior...... VM − M O L− N +
8. Being unexpectedly slapped on the back as a joke...... VM − M O L− N +
9. Hearing someone make fun of your clothes...... VM O M O L O N +
10. Hearing your political views ridiculed...... VM O M − L+ N +

11. Seeing boys make fun of old people...... VM − M + L+ N O
12. Seeing an honest official thrown out of office by politicians...... VM O M O L+ N −
13. Seeing a person laugh at a cripple...... VM − M + L O N +

EXERCISE 4—Continued

14. Seeing people disfigure library books................................. VM – M – L+ N+
15. Seeing someone cheat in an examination............................. VM – M 0 L+ N+
16. Seeing someone trying to discredit you with your employer...... VM + M 0 L+ N –
17. Seeing someone laugh when a blind man runs into an obstacle... VM – M+ L+ N+

Below is a list of things that often cause **fear**. After each thing mentioned draw a circle around VM, M, L, or N to indicate how much fear it causes **you**. Be honest and admit all the fears you have. Fears are not disgraceful.
VM means VERY MUCH; M means MUCH; L means A LITTLE; N means NONE.

1. Automobiles...........	VM 0	M –	L –	N+		11. Garter snakes...........	VM –	M –	L –	N+
2. Being lost...........	VM –	M –	L+	N+		12. Graveyards at night...........	VM –	M –	L 0	N+
3. Being in a closed room...........	VM –	M –	L 0	N+		13. Heart trouble...........	VM –	M+	L+	N+
4. Becoming deaf or blind...........	VM –	M+	L+	N –		14. Insects...........	VM 0	M 0	L 0	N 0
5. Bulls...........	VM –	M –	L+	N+		15. Lightning...........	VM –	M 0	L 0	N+
6. Burglars...........	VM –	M 0	L+	N+		16. Negroes...........	VM –	M –	L –	N+
7. Contagious diseases...........	VM 0	M+	L 0	N –		17. Pain...........	VM –	M 0	L –	N+
8. Deep water...........	VM –	M 0	L –	N+		18. Punishment in the next world..	VM 0	M 0	L –	N+
9. End of the world...........	VM –	M –	L –	N+		19. Thunder...........	VM –	M –	L –	N+
10. Floods...........	VM –	M –	L+	N+		20. Windstorms...........	VM –	M –	L –	N+

Below is a list of things that sometimes **cause disgust**. After each thing mentioned draw a circle around VM, M, L, or N to indicate how much disgust it causes **you**.
VM means VERY MUCH; M means MUCH; L means A LITTLE; N means NONE.

EXERCISE 4—Continued

	VM	M	L	N
1. An unshaven man	VM –	M –	L+	N+
2. A butcher shop	VM 0	M 0	L –	N+
3. A drunken man	VM –	M +	L+	N+
4. Crooked teeth	VM –	M –	L+	N 0
5. Food stains on clothing	VM –	M +	L+	N+
6. Foul language	VM –	M +	L+	N+
7. Gum chewing	VM –	M –	L+	N+
8. Mushy food in your mouth	VM –	M 0	L+	N+
9. Offensive breath	VM –	M +	L+	N+
10. Pimples	VM –	M 0	L+	N+
11. Sagging socks on a man	VM –	M –	L 0	N+
12. Seeing a woman smoking	VM –	M 0	L 0	N+
13. Sight of slimy water	VM –	M +	L 0	N+
14. Smell of decaying fish	VM –	M +	L+	N+
15. Soiled or ragged fingernails	VM –	M –	L+	N+
16. Spitting in public	VM –	M +	L+	N+
17. Untidy clothes	VM –	M +	L+	N+
18. Word "gent" used for gentle-man	VM –	M –	L+	N+

Below is a list of things that sometimes **arouse pity.** After each thing mentioned draw a circle around VM, M, L, or N to indicate how much pity it arouses in **you.**

VM means VERY MUCH; M means MUCH; L means A LITTLE; N means NONE.

	VM	M	L	N
1. A bee that is drowning	VM –	M 0	L 0	N+
2. A dog that must be killed for biting people	VM –	M 0	L+	N+
3. A man who is cowardly and can't help it	VM –	M +	L –	N+
4. An insane person	VM –	M +	L+	N+
5. An old person with a fatal disease	VM –	M +	L+	N+
6. An orphan girl	VM –	M +	L+	N 0
7. Overworked horses	VM –	M +	L+	N 0
8. Overworked children	VM –	M +	L+	N 0
9. A fly caught on sticky fly paper	VM 0	M –	L –	N+
10. An underfed child	VM –	M +	L+	N+

EXERCISE 4.—Continued

11. Very old people..........	VM −	M 0	L+	N+
12. A wounded deer..........	VM −	M+	L+	N+
13. A baby bird whose mother is dead...	VM −	M+	L+	N+
14. A wounded soldier who must beg for a living........	VM −	M+	L 0	N+
15. A young person totally paralyzed........	VM −	M+	L+	N 0

Below is a list of acts of various degrees of **wickedness or badness**. After each thing mentioned draw a circle around 3, 2, 1, or 0 to show how wicked or bad you think it is.

3 means "EXTREMELY WICKED"; 2 means "DECIDEDLY BAD"; 1 means "SOMEWHAT BAD"; 0 means "NOT REALLY BAD."

1. Picking flowers in a public park........	3 0	2 −	1+	0+
2. Stealing a ride on a truck........	3 −	2 −	1+	0+
3. Telling a lie to avoid punishment........	3 −	2+	1+	0+
4. Whispering in school........	3 +	2 0	1 −	0 0
5. Boys teasing girls........	3 −	2 −	1+	0+
6. Making fun of cripples........	3 −	2 +	1+	0 −
7. Using slang........	3 −	2 −	1+	0+
8. Breaking windows........	3 −	2+	1 0	0+
9. Boys smoking before they are 21........	3 −	2 −	1+	0+
10. Indulging in "petting"........	3 −	2 −	1+	0+
11. Moderate drinking........	3 −	2 0	1+	0+
12. Excessive drinking........	3 −	2+	1+	0 0
13. Putting pins on the teacher's chair........	3 −	2 −	1+	0+

EXERCISE 4.—Continued

	3	2	1	0
14. Swiping fruit out of orchards	−	0	+	+
15. Laziness	−	0	−	+
16. Going to bed without saying your prayers	−	−	+	+
17. Not brushing your teeth	−	0	+	+
18. Boys fighting	−	−	+	+
19. Being a slacker in time of war	0	0	+	0
20. Boy running away from home	0	−	0	+
21. Neglecting to study your lesson	0	−	0	0
22. Being a Bolshevik	+	−	0	0
23. Not standing up when the "Star Spangled Banner" is played	−	+	+	−
24. Drinking a great deal of coffee and tea	0	+	−	0
25. Being cross to your brother or sister	+	−	0	0
26. Shooting rabbits just for fun	−	0	+	+
27. Having fits of temper	0	−	+	+
28. Insulting the defenseless	−	+	+	0

In each comparison below draw a circle around 1 or 2 or S to show how well you like the things mentioned.
Around 1, if you like the FIRST thing better.
Around 2, if you like the SECOND thing better.
Around S, if you have the SAME LIKING for both.

1. (1) Make plans (2) Carry out plans.................... 1 + 2 − S 0
2. (1) Work involving many details (2) Work involving few details............. 1 + 2 − S 0
3. (1) Interesting work with small income (2) Uninteresting work with large income........ 1 − 2 + S +

EXERCISE 4—Concluded

4. (1) Give a report in writing   (2) Give a report verbally.............. 1 –   2 +   S +
5. (1) Work with men   (2) Work with women.............. 1 +   2 –   S –
6. (1) An auto with scruffy paint but excellent motor   (2) An auto with fresh paint but only fairly good motor.... 1 +   2 –   S –
7. (1) Live in the country   (2) Live in the city.............. 1 +   2 –   S +

EXERCISE 5

For each occupation below, ask yourself; would I like this work or not? If you would like it, draw a circle around L. If you would dislike it, draw a circle around D. If you would neither like nor dislike it, draw a circle around N. In deciding on your answer, think only of the kind of work. Don't consider the pay. Imagine that you have the ability to do the work, that you are the right age for it, and that it is equally open to men and women.

Don't stop to think long; answer fairly quickly.

	L	D	N
1. Architect	L +	D –	N –
2. Chef or cook	L –	D 0	N +
3. Auto racer	L +	D –	N +
4. Librarian	L –	D +	N +
5. Building contractor	L +	D –	N 0
6. Detective	L +	D –	N +
7. Nurse	L –	D +	N 0
8. Private secretary	L –	D +	N +
9. Journalist	L –	D +	N 0
10. Forest ranger	L +	D –	N 0
11. Dairyman	L +	D –	N +
12. Dressmaker	L –	D +	N +
13. Florist	L –	D +	N +
14. Stock breeder	L +	D –	N +
15. Optician	L –	D +	N –
16. Social worker	L –	D +	N 0
17. Music teacher	L –	D +	N –
18. Clerk in a store	L –	D +	N 0
19. Singer	L –	D +	N +
20. Preacher	L –	D +	N –
21. Novelist	L –	D +	N 0
22. Soldier	L +	D –	N 0
23. Draftsman	L +	D –	N –
24. Artist	L –	D +	N +
25. Bookkeeper	L –	D +	N +

EXERCISE 5—Continued

Do you like or dislike these people?

1. Men with beards	L +	D −	N +
2. Babies	L −	D +	N +
3. Infidels	L +	D +	N −
4. People with loud voices	L +	D −	N +
5. Argumentative people	L +	D −	N 0
6. Very forgiving people	L −	D +	N 0
7. Very quiet people	L +	D 0	N −
8. People who spend freely	L 0	D +	N −
9. People with gold teeth	L 0	D +	N −
10. Tall women	L −	D +	N +
11. Men who take the lead	L +	D 0	N −
12. Mannish women	L −	D +	N −

Do you like or dislike these?

1. Charlie Chaplin	L +	D −	N 0
2. Social problem movies	L −	D +	N +
3. Movie love scenes	L −	D +	N 0
4. Poetry	L −	D +	N +
5. Detective stories	L +	D −	N −
6. Stories of home life	L −	D +	N +
7. Adventure stories	L +	D −	N −
8. Comic supplements	L +	D −	N −
9. Radio magazines	L +	D −	N −
10. Chemistry	L +	D −	N −
11. Dramatics	L +	D +	N +
12. Ancient languages	L −	D +	N −
13. Civics	L +	D +	N +
14. Spelling	L −	D +	N +
1. Hunting	L +	D −	N +
2. Skating	L −	D +	N 0
3. Horseback riding	L −	D +	N +
4. Hopscotch	L −	D +	N +
5. Dare base	L −	D +	N 0
6. Drop the handkerchief	L +	D +	N 0
7. Chess	L +	D −	N 0
8. Charades	L −	D +	N +
9. Collecting flowers	L −	D +	N +
10. Cooking	L −	D +	N +
11. Studying lessons	L −	D +	N 0
12. Repairing a door latch	L +	D −	N 0
13. Parties and socials	L −	D +	N +
14. Being with one other	L +	D −	N 0
15. Strict Sunday laws	L +	D −	N −
16. Pet cats	L −	D +	N +
17. Near-beer	L +	D −	N 0
18. Coca cola	L +	D −	N 0
19. Cheese	L 0	D +	N −
20. Candies	L −	D +	N 0

EXERCISE 5—Continued

After each book you have read, put a circle around L, D, or N to show how well you like it. Skip those you have not read.

		Omission			
1.	Robinson Crusoe, by Daniel Defoe	−	L +	D −	N −
2.	Lorna Doone, by Richard D. Blackmore	+	L −	D +	N 0
3.	Through the Looking Glass, by Lewis Carroll	+	L −	D 0	N 0
4.	Westward Ho, by Charles Kingsley	−	L +	D +	N 0
5.	Daddy Long Legs, by Jean Webster	+	L −	D +	N +
6.	Peter Pan and Wendy, by J. M. Barrie	+	L −	D +	N +
7.	Huckleberry Finn, by Mark Twain	−	L +	D +	N −
8.	Rip Van Winkle, by Washington Irving	0	L −	D −	N 0
9.	The Wonder Book, by Nathaniel Hawthorne	0	L −	D +	N 0
10.	Bird's Christmas Carol, by Kate Douglas Wiggin	+	L −	D +	N +
11.	Rebecca of Sunnybrook Farm, by Kate Douglas Wiggin	+	L −	D +	N 0
12.	Christmas Carol, by Charles Dickens	+	L −	D +	N +
13.	The Man Without a Country, by Edward Everett Hale	0	L +	D −	N +
14.	Little Men, by Louisa Alcott	+	L +	D +	N +
15.	The Secret Garden, by Frances Hodgson Burnett	+	L −	D +	N +
16.	Captains Courageous, by Rudyard Kipling	−	L +	D −	N 0
17.	Little Lord Fauntleroy, by Frances Hodgson Burnett	+	L +	D +	N 0
18.	Boy's Life of Theodore Roosevelt, by Herman Hagedorn	−	L +	D 0	N 0
19.	Gulliver's Travels, by Jonathan Swift	−	L +	D −	N 0
20.	Biography of a Grizzly, by Ernest Seton-Thompson	−	L +	D 0	N 0

EXERCISE 5—Concluded

Omission
+ 0 —

21. Evangeline, by Henry W. Longfellow........ L— D+ N+
22. Tales from Shakespeare, by Charles Lamb.. L— D+ N+
23. Adventures of Sherlock Holmes, by Conan Doyle. L+ D— N—

Suppose you were an artist, what would you like to draw?
1. Fruits........ L— D+ N+
2. Children........ L— D+ N+
3. Horses........ L+ D— N0
4. Clouds........ L— D+ N+
5. Cats........ L— D+ N—

6. Flowers........ L— D+ N+
7. Tigers........ L+ D— N—
8. Ships........ L+ D— N—

Suppose you were a newspaper reporter, what would you like to write about, or report?
1. Accidents........ L+ D— N0
2. Sporting news........ L+ D— N—
3. Musical events........ L— D+ N+
4. Theatrical news........ L— D0 N+
5. News oddities........ L— D+ N0

6. Commercial news........ L+ D— N—

If you had two years to travel, with plenty of money, what would you like to see and do?
1. Visit Holland........ L— D+ N+
2. Hunt lions in Africa........ L+ D— N0
3. Spend a day in Westminster Abbey..... L— D+ N+
4. See London Bridge........ L— D+ N+
5. Visit many famous battlegrounds........ L+ D— N—

6. Visit many manufacturing plants........ L— D+ N+
7. See how people prepare their food........ L— D+ N+
8. Spend a year on a sailing boat........ L+ D0 N—
9. Study social customs........ L— D+ N+
10. See how criminals are treated........ L+ D— N—
11. Learn about various religions........ L— D+ N+

EXERCISE 6

Below is a list of famous characters. After each name draw a circle around L, D, or N to indicate whether you like that character. L means LIKE; D means DISLIKE; N means NEITHER LIKE NOR DISLIKE. Skip those you do not know anything about.

EXERCISE 6—Continued

	Omission	L	D	N
1. Jane Addams	0	L −	D +	N +
2. P. T. Barnum	−	L +	D +	N −
3. Bismarck	−	L +	D 0	N 0
4. Daniel Boone	−	L +	D −	N −
5. Aaron Burr	−	L 0	D +	N −
6. Kit Carson	−	L +	D −	N −
7. Cleopatra	−	L 0	D 0	N +
8. Christopher Columbus	−	L −	D +	N +
9. Oliver Cromwell	−	L +	D −	N +
10. Jefferson Davis	−	L +	D +	N 0
11. Jack Dempsey	+	L +	D −	N −
12. Lloyd George	−	L +	D +	N 0
13. Congressman Volstead	−	L +	D +	N 0
14. Booker T. Washington	−	L 0	D 0	N +
15. Ulysses S. Grant	−	L +	D −	N −

	Omission	L	D	N
16. Hearst, the publisher	−	L −	D +	N −
17. Herbert Hoover	0	L +	D −	N 0
18. Robert G. Ingersoll	−	L +	D −	N −
19. Thomas Jefferson	−	L 0	D +	N 0
20. Lenin	−	L +	D +	N +
21. Judge Ben Lindsay	−	L +	D +	N 0
22. Aimee McPherson	0	L 0	D +	N 0
23. Mussolini	−	L +	D 0	N −
24. Florence Nightingale	+	L −	D +	N +
25. Theodore Roosevelt	−	L 0	D −	N −
26. Billy Sunday	−	L +	D −	N +
27. Wellington	−	L +	D +	N 0
28. Woodrow Wilson	0	L −	D +	N +

Read each statement and consider whether it is **mostly true** or **mostly false.**
If it is mostly TRUE draw a circle around **T.**
If it is mostly FALSE draw a circle around **F.**
Work rapidly. Answer all.

	Omission	T	F
1. The face shows how intelligent a person is	0	T −	F +
2. The weak deserve more love than the strong	0	T +	F −

EXERCISE 6—Concluded

	Omission				
3. The world was created in six days of twenty-four hours each	—	T +	F 0		
4. One usually knows when stared at from behind	0	T —	F +		
5. Preachers have better characters than most persons	0	T +	F —		
6. Love "at first sight" is usually the truest love	0	T +	F —		
7. Girls are naturally more innocent than boys	0	T —	F 0		
8. Lincoln was greater than Washington	+	T 0	F 0		
9. Opportunity knocks but once for any man	—	T +	F 0		
10. The largest fortunes should be seized by the government and divided among the poor	—	T —	F +		
11. Children should be taught never to fight	0	T —	F +		
12. We should never give to beggars	0	T +	F —		
13. There should be perfect equality between men and women in all things	—	T —	F +		
14. Green-eyed people are not to be trusted	0	T +	F —		

EXERCISE 7

Answer each question as truthfully as you can by drawing a line under YES or NO.

1. Do you like most people you know?	YES +	NO 0
2. Did you ever have imaginary companions?	YES —	NO +
3. Do people often say you are too noisy?	YES —	NO +
4. Do you rather dislike to take your bath?	YES +	NO —
5. Have you been bossed too much for your own good?	YES +	NO —
6. Do you nearly always prefer for someone else to take the lead?	YES —	NO +
7. Do you feel yourself to be lacking in self-control?	YES +	NO —

EXERCISE 7—Continued

8. Are you extremely careful about your manner of dress?............................ YES – NO +
9. Do you work mostly by fits and starts?... YES 0 NO 0
10. Do you shrink from facing a crisis or difficulty?.................................... YES – NO +

11. Are you careful of your personal belongings?....................................... YES 0 NO 0
12. Do you worry much over possible misfortunes?..................................... YES – NO +
13. Are you much embarrassed when you make a grammatical mistake?............ YES – NO +
14. Are you worried when you have an unfinished job on your hands?.............. YES – NO +
15. Have you ever kept a diary?... YES – NO +

16. Do you like to go to parties, dances, or other social affairs?.................... YES – NO +
17. Do you ever feel that you are about to "go to pieces"?........................... YES – NO +
18. Are you often afraid of the dark?.. YES – NO +
19. Have you often fainted away?... YES + NO –
20. Can you usually sit still without fidgeting?.. YES – NO +

21. Do you usually enjoy your meals?.. YES – NO +
22. Have you the habit of biting your finger nails?..................................... YES – NO +
23. As a child were you extremely disobedient?... YES + NO –
24. Do you ever dream of robbers?... YES + NO –
25. Do people ever say that you talk too much?.. YES + NO –

26. Do you ever have the same dream over and over?................................ YES – NO +
27. Do people nearly always treat you right?.. YES – NO +
28. Were you ever expelled from school, or nearly expelled?........................ YES + NO –
29. Have you often been punished unjustly?... YES + NO –
30. Do you often get cross over little things?.. YES – NO +

EXERCISE 7—Concluded

31. Does it make you angry for people to hurry you? .... YES +   NO −
32. Can you stand as much pain as others can? .... YES +   NO −
33. Is it easy for you to get up as soon as you wake? .... YES +   NO −
34. Would you like to wear expensive clothes? .... YES −   NO +
35. Do you feel tired a good deal of the time? .... YES −   NO +

36. Do you ever walk in your sleep? .... YES −   NO +
37. Do you hear easily when spoken to? .... YES −   NO +
38. Are you often frightened in the middle of the night? .... YES −   NO +
39. Have you found school a hard place to get along in? .... YES +   NO −
40. Can you do good work while people are looking at you? .... YES +   NO −

41. Do you feel like jumping off when you are on a high place? .... YES −   NO +
42. Do you always remember to brush your teeth? .... YES −   NO +

Notes

INTRODUCTION: Toward a History of Manhood in America

1. Recently several works have appeared that have placed the gendered experiences of men at their center. The most significant of these new works in the social history of gender include Joe Dubbert, *A Man's Place: Masculinity in Transition* (Englewood Cliffs: Prentice-Hall, 1979); Peter Filene, *Him/Her/Self: Sex Roles in Modern America* (Baltimore: The Johns Hopkins University Press, 1986); E. Anthony Rotundo, *American Manhood: Transformations in Masculinity from the Revolution to the Modern Era* (New York: Basic Books, 1993); Peter Stearns, *Be a Man! Males in Modern Society* (New York: Holmes and Meier, 1979); Mark E. Kann, *On the Man Question: Gender and Civic Virtue in America* (Philadelphia: Temple University Press, 1991); G. J. Barker-Benfield, *The Horrors of the Half-Known Life: Male Attitudes Towards Women and Sexuality in Nineteenth-Century America* (New York: Harper and Row, 1976); David Pugh, *Sons of Liberty: The Masculine Mind in the Nineteenth Century* (Westport, Conn.: Greenwood Press, 1984).

   Some specific historical studies also place masculinity at the heart of their analysis, including Mark Carnes, *Secret Ritual and Manhood in Victorian America* (New Haven: Yale University Press, 1990); Mary Ann Clawson, *Constructing Brotherhood: Gender, Class and Fraternalism* (Princeton, N.J.: Princeton University Press, 1990); Michael Paul Rogin, *Fathers and Children: Andrew Jackson and the Subjugation of the American Indian* (New York: Vintage, 1975); Elliot Gorn, *The Manly Art: Bare-Knuckle Prize Fighting in America* (Urbana: University of Illinois Press, 1986); David Macleod, *Building Character in the American Boy: The Boy Scouts, YMCA and Their Forerunners* (Madison: University of Wisconsin Press, 1983);

Robert Griswold, *Fatherhood in America: A History* (New York: Basic Books, 1993).

Several anthologies also develop a more gendered notion of men's experiences, most notably Mark Carnes and Clyde Griffen, eds., *Meanings for Manhood: Constructions of Masculinity in Victorian America* (Chicago: University of Chicago Press, 1990); J. A. Mangan and James Walvin, eds., *Manliness and Morality: Middle-Class Masculinity in Britain and America, 1800–1940* (New York: St. Martin's Press, 1987); Elizabeth Pleck and Joseph Pleck, eds., *The American Man* (Englewood Cliffs: Prentice-Hall, 1980).

Works in literary criticism are also taking note of the applicability of a gender perspective to men's lives. See, for example, Leslie Fiedler, *Love and Death in the American Novel* (New York: Stein and Day, 1970); "The Male Novel," *Partisan Review* 37(1), 1970; and "Come Back to the Raft Ag'in Huck Honey!" in *Partisan Review*, June 1948; David Leverenz, *Manhood and the American Renaissance* (Ithaca, N.Y.: Cornell University Press, 1989); "The Last Real Man in America: From Natty Bumppo to Batman," *American Literary History* 3, 1991; and "Manhood, Humiliation and Public Life: Some Stories," *Southwest Review* 71, Fall 1986; Michael Paul Rogin, *Subversive Genealogy: The Politics and Art of Herman Melville* (New York: Knopf, 1983).

2. Thirty years ago social scientists would have only listed "class"; "race" was added about twenty-five years ago. Today "gender" has joined those two master statuses in an axiomatic trinity; when put together, they provide the most powerful analytic lens through which to view people's lives and the basis for most social scientific research.

3. Thomas Lacquer, *Making Sex: Body and Gender from the Greeks to Freud* (Cambridge: Harvard University Press, 1990), p. 22.

4. See Catharine Stimpson, *Where the Meanings Are: Feminism and Cultural Spaces* (New York: Methuen, 1988).

5. Natalie Davis, "Women's History in Transition: The European Case," *Feminist Studies* 3(3–4), 1976, p. 83.

6. Robert Bly, *Iron John* (Reading, Pa.: Addison-Wesley, 1990), p. 230.

7. Erving Goffman, *Stigma: Notes on the Management of Spoiled Identity* (Englewood Cliffs, N.J.: Prentice-Hall, 1963), p. 128.

8. The term "hegemonic masculinity" refers to that version that is used as a defining model of manhood is discussed in detail in R. W. Connell, *Gender and Power* (Stanford, Cal.: Stanford University Press, 1987), passim.

9. In its most basic formulation feminism offered women a symmetry between what one could observe in the social world and their individual experiences. At the social level, feminists argued, women were not "in

power." This was an empirical observation, easily apprehended by anyone who cared to look. Every board of trustees of every university, every board of directors of every law firm and corporation, every legislature at every level in every state in the country—all were illustrations that women, as a group, did not have power. Women were not *in power*, and individually, women did not *feel* powerful.

When this was applied to men's lives, however, something didn't compute. Certainly at the social level men *are* in power. But were you to complete that syllogism and present it to men—that their power means that individual men *feel* powerful—most men would look at you as if you were from another planet.

Some commentators have encouraged men to value individual experience over social analysis. Some proponents of "men's rights" claim that feminism's victory reversed old power dynamics; men, they argue, are now the victims of reverse discrimination. "You're right, you have no power," they said. "Women have the power now—in custody battles, in alimony, in the draft. Men are the real victims." And some of those who run weekend retreats designed to enable men to search for their deep, wild manhood also privilege those feelings. "You're right," they say. "You have no power. Let's go off to the woods and get some. Let's participate in the power ritual, drum the power drum, chant the power chant."

To a social scientist power is not a quality one can acquire by trooping off to mythic summer camp for a weekend with the boys. Power is an expression of the distribution of rewards and resources in a society; as such it is the property of groups, not individuals. That's not to say, of course, that certain individuals do not exercise power, nor does it require that we ignore the personal characteristics that some individuals possess that bring them significant power over others. At the individual level power is experienced as the ability to do the kinds of things in your life that you want to do. Men may feel powerless because they do not feel capable of making the choices they might like; but when you put all those "powerless" guys together, they turn into a very powerful group.

10. John Steinbeck, *Of Mice and Men* (New York: Scribners, 1937) p. 57. Note how Steinbeck uses the novel's only woman to offer these insights.

11. Cited in the *New York Times*, 3 January 1993. These ideas are not new but organize a significant amount of thinking about the construction of culture in general, as in Claude Lévi-Strauss and in feminist theory as well. As feminist theorist Luce Irigary writes:

The trade that organizes patriarchal societies takes place exclusively among men. Women, signs, goods, currency, all pass from one man to another or—so it is said—suffer the penalty of relapsing into the incestuous and exclusively endogamous ties that would paralyse all commerce. The work force, products, even those of mother-earth, would thus be the object of transaction among men only. This signifies that the *very possibility of the socio-cultural order would necessitate homosexuality*. Homosexuality is the law that regulates the socio-cultural order. Heterosexuality amounts to the assignment of roles in the economy; some are given the role of producing and exchanging subjects, while others are assigned the role of productive earth and goods. (See Luce Irigary, *New French Feminisms*, Elaine Marks and Isabelle de Courtivron, eds. [New York: Schocken, 1981], p. 107.)

Unlike Irigary, though, I argue that genital sexuality is not a requirement for homosociality as the foundation for masculinity; in fact, homophobia becomes a cultural requirement to separate the erotic charge that often accompanies homosocial interaction. I argue that historically masculinity is largely a homosocial enactment but that it is also an enactment among heterosexual men, and that homophobic fears of effeminacy ensure its heterosexuality. I develop these issues at greater length in "Masculinity as Homophobia: Fear, Shame, and Silence in the Construction of Gender Identity" in *Theorizing Masculinities*, Harry Brod and Michael Kaufman, eds. (Newbury Park, Calif.: Sage Publications, 1994), pp. 119–141.

12. Although my primary task is historical and sociological, there is also a psychological component to this process. In the classic Freudian model fear is the animating emotion that begins the process of change for the young boy. The fear of the father's power terrifies the boy to renounce his desire for his mother and identify with his father. This is the classic pattern to resolve the Oedipal crisis.

Such a story suggests several themes. First, it allows us to link gender identity with sexual orientation: The little boy's identification with father (becoming masculine) allows him to engage in sexual relations with women (he becomes heterosexual). This is the origin of how we can "read" one's sexual orientation through the successful performance of gender identity. Second, the fear that the little boy feels does not send him scurrying into the arms of his mother to protect him from his father. Rather, he believes he will overcome his fear by identifying with its source. In that sense, we become masculine by identifying with our oppressor.

There is a piece of the puzzle missing, a piece that Freud himself implied but did not follow up. If the pre-Oedipal boy identifies with mother, he *sees the world through mother's eyes*. Thus, when he confronts father during his great Oedipal crisis, he experiences a split vision: He sees his father as his mother sees his father, with a combination of awe, wonder, terror, *and desire*. And he simultaneously sees the father as he, the boy, would like to see him—as the object not of desire but of emulation. Repudiating mother and identifying with father only partially answers his dilemma. What is he to do with that homoerotic desire, the desire he felt because he saw father the way that his mother saw father? He must suppress it. Homoerotic desire is cast as feminine desire, desire for other men. Homophobia is the effort to suppress that desire, to purify all relationships with other men, with women, with children, of its taint and to ensure that no one could possibly ever mistake one for a homosexual. Homophobic flight from intimacy with other men is the repudiation of the homosexual within—never completely successful and hence constantly reenacted in every homosocial relationship. "The lives of most American men are bounded, and their interests daily curtailed by the constant necessity to prove to their fellows, and to themselves, that they are not sissies, not homosexuals," writes psychoanalytic historian Geoffrey Gorer. "Any interest or pursuit which is identified as a feminine interest or pursuit becomes deeply suspect for men."

13. Gen. S.L.A. Marshall, *Men Against Fire* (New York: Morrow, 1947); also cited in John Keegan, *The Face of Battle* (New York: Viking, 1976).

14. David Leverenz, "Manhood, Humiliation and Public Life: Some Stories," *Southwest Review* 71, Fall 1986, p. 451. Leverenz makes this haunting terror of emasculation the centerpiece in his brilliant analysis of the pantheon of mid-nineteenth-century American writers, *Manhood and the American Renaissance* (Ithaca, N.Y.: Cornell University Press, 1989).

15. David Leverenz, "Manhood, Humiliation and Public Life," p. 455.

16. My typology of masculine images does not conform to real individuals—there is no perfect Genteel Patriarch or Heroic Artisan or Marketplace Man. Each type represents what sociologist Max Weber called an "ideal type," a composite of traits that, in their pure form, constitute the ideal version of such a character. We will explore the contours of each type, and also describe the ways in which individual men have struggled to fit into the ill-fitting uniforms that each provides. Today, much of men's confusion stems, I believe, from the fact that we each contain elements of all three of these ideal types of manhood and that these parts often pull us in different directions. No one is fully able to live up to the demands of masculinity; we are all constantly struggling within and against these gender ideals. They are still with us, and they continue to animate the quest for manhood among American men.

17. Garry Wills, *Nixon Agonistes* (Boston: Houghton Mifflin, 1970), pp. 162–163.

CHAPTER 1: The Birth of the Self-Made Man

1. Royall Tyler, *The Contrast: A Comedy in Five Acts* (Boston: Houghton Mifflin, 1920). Some commentary on the play is offered in Ada Lou Carson

and Herbert L. Carson, *Royall Tyler* (Boston: Twayne Publications, 1979). See also Alexander Saxton, *The Rise and Fall of the White Republic: Class Politics and Mass Culture in Nineteenth-Century America* (New York: Verso, 1990), pp. 110–113.

2. Tyler, *The Contrast*, I, 1, p. 27.

3. Ibid., I, 2, p. 35.

4. Ibid., I, 2, pp. 32–33, pp. 38–39.

5. Manly's short soliloquy encapsulates what sociologist Max Weber would call, a century later, the Protestant Ethic. "We are both unhappy; but it is your duty to obey your parent—mine to obey my honour. Let us, therefore, both follow the path of rectitude; and of this we may be assured, that if we are not happy, we shall, at least deserve to be so" (IV, p. 99).

6. Tyler, *The Contrast*, III, 2, pp. 79, 82.

7. Ibid., V, pp. 112, 114–115.

8. My typology of masculine archetypes relies on several earlier efforts to map this terrain. See, e.g., Charles Rosenberg, "Sexuality, Class and Role in Nineteenth-Century America," *American Quarterly* 25, 1976; E. Anthony Rotundo, "Body and Soul: Changing Ideals of American Middle-Class Manhood," *Journal of Social History* 16, 1983, and "Learning About Manhood: Gender Ideals and the Middle-Class Family in Nineteenth-Century America," in *Manliness and Morality: Middle-Class Masculinity in Britain and America, 1800–1940*, J. A. Mangan and James Walvin, eds. (New York: St. Martin's Press, 1987); David Leverenz, *Manhood and the American Renaissance* (Ithaca, N.Y.: Cornell University Press, 1989). Rotundo's book *American Manhood: Transformations in Masculinity from the Revolution to the Present Era* (New York: Basic Books, 1993) appeared after this book was substantially completed; however, I have benefited greatly from the various articles which compose many of his chapters.

9. I use the term *artisan* here in a broader sense than just those men involved in urban craft production. What distinguishes the artisan, in my view, is his autonomy, his sense of integrity in manual labor, his calling. Thus, I also include the nation's independent farmers, the celebrated yeomen of Jeffersonian republicanism, who equally embraced the ideals of producerism.

10. Cited in Rotundo, "Learning About Manhood," p. 36.

11. Rotundo, "Body and Soul," p. 29

12. On this image, see, e.g., Jay Fliegelman, *Prodigals and Pilgrims: The American Revolution Against Patriarchal Authority, 1750–1800* (New York: Cambridge University Press, 1982), and David Pugh, *Sons of Liberty: The Masculine Mind in Nineteenth-Century America* (Westport, Conn.: Greenwood Press, 1983).

13. John Adams to Thomas Jefferson, 21 December 1819; in Cappon, ed.,

The Adams-Jefferson Letters, 1959; vol. 2, p. 549. John Hancock also warned against the dangers of luxury, writing: "Suffer not yourselves to be betrayed by the soft arts of luxury and effeminacy, into the pit digged for your destruction. Despise the glare of wealth. That people who pay greater respect to a wealthy villain, than to an honest upright man in poverty, almost deserve to be enslaved; they plainly shew that wealth, however it may be acquired, is in their esteem to be preferred to virtue." Cited in Philip Greven, *The Protestant Temperament: Patterns of Child-Rearing, Religious Experience, and the Self in Early America* (New York: Knopf, 1980), p. 351.

14. Charles Brockden Brown, *Edgar Huntley* [1799], 1928, p. xxiii; Washington Irving, *A Tour on the Prairies* [1835], John Francis McDermott, ed. (Norman: University of Oklahoma Press, 1956).

15. Fliegelman, *Prodigals and Pilgrims*, 1982, p. 224; see also Geoffrey Gorer, *The American People: A Study in National Character* (New York: Norton, 1964), and Winthrop Jordan, *White over Black* (Baltimore: Penguin, 1969), pp. 304–306.

16. Cited in Arthur M. Schlesinger, *Learning How to Behave: A Historical Study of American Etiquette Books* (New York: Macmillan, 1947), p. 12; letter 3. See also Charles M. Wiltse, *The New Nation, 1800–1845* (New York: Hill and Wang, 1961), p. 124.

17. Cited in Theodore P. Greene, *America's Heroes: The Changing Models of Success in American Magazines* (New York: Oxford University Press, 1970), p. 43.

18. Rev. Enos Hitchcock, *The Farmer's Friend* (Boston, 1793). Historian John Cawelti calls the work "the first Horatio Alger story in America," but I see Worthy's project less as upward mobility and more as self-improvement, so that he can play a larger role in the world and be more useful to others. In fact, as Cawelti notes, the work is best understood as "an attempt to persuade young men to eschew the promise of fame and fortune and to content themselves with the achievement of industry, self-discipline, and piety in the rank to which they were born." See John Cawelti, *Apostles of the Self-Made Man* (Chicago: University of Chicago Press, 1965), p. 32. On Franklin, see *The Autobiography of Benjamin Franklin* [1791] (New York: Doubleday, 1916), p. 129.

19. As political theorist Michael Rogin writes, "[p]atriarchy establishes a system of rules and restraints that preserve the self by denying gratification. It provides boundaried protection against the fears of merging and dissolution. The escape from patriarchy reawakens those fears." Michael Rogin, *Subversive Genealogy: The Politics and Art of Herman Melville* (New York: Knopf, 1983), p. 48.

20. Samuel Adams, *Writings*, vol. 4, pp. 236–238. David Pugh suggests a psy-

choanalytic tendency that continues to the present, as these restless sons "projected their anxieties onto the only parent left—the Mother—and displaced them by seeing in their enemies such female qualities as smothering maternalism and effeminate inaction that could only lead to the degeneration of democracy." Pugh, *Sons of Liberty*, p. xvii.

21. See Stephanie Coontz, *The Social Origins of Private Life* (New York: Verso, 1988), pp. 118, 168.

22. Nancy Cott, *The Bonds of Womanhood: Women's Sphere in New England, 1780–1835* (New Haven: Yale University Press, 1977), p. 3; Norman Ware, *The Industrial Worker, 1840–1860* (Boston: Houghton Mifflin, 1924), p. 37. On the emergence of the middle class, see Burton Bledstein, *The Culture of Professionalism: The Middle Class and the Development of Higher Education in America* (New York: Norton, 1976); Karen Halttunen, *Confidence Men and Painted Women: A Study of Middle-Class Culture in America, 1830–1870* (New Haven: Yale University Press, 1982); Mary Ryan, *Cradle of the Middle Class: The Family in Oneida County, New York, 1790–1865* (Cambridge: Cambridge University Press, 1981); Paul Johnson, *A Shopkeeper's Millennium: Society and Revivals in Rochester, New York, 1815–1837* (New York: Hill and Wang, 1978); Paul Boyer, *Urban Masses and Moral Order in America, 1820–1920* (Cambridge: Harvard University Press, 1978); David Brion Davis, *The Problem of Slavery in an Age of Revolution, 1770–1823* (Ithaca, N.Y.: Cornell University Press, 1975).

23. Hunt is cited in Arthur M. Schlesinger, Jr., *The Age of Jackson* (Boston: Little, Brown, 1953), p. 129. Thomas Low Nichols, *Forty Years of American Life* (New York, 1837), pp. 194–195. Cited in Nancy Cott, *The Bonds of Womanhood*, p. 60. Ralph Waldo Emerson, "Ode, Inscribed to W. H. Channing," in *The Poems and Translations of Ralph Waldo Emerson* (New York: Library of America, 1994), p. 119. Marketplace competition also received official sanction. In his advice book, *The Young Man's Friend* (1855), Rev. Daniel C. Eddy, the pastor of the Harvard Street Church in Boston, compared human life to a racecourse "in which a countless number of persons are contending for the prize." The prize was, of course, wealth, which was not only not a sin but a positive virtue. "There is nothing wrong in the accumulation of property; there is nothing wrong in a desire to have our needs approved by our fellowmen." Eddy's only caution was that we not become "inordinately attached" to wealth. It is "the *love* of money, and not money itself [that is the] root of all evil." Other books, like Charles Seymore's *Self-Made Men* (1859) and J. W. Kasey's *Young Man's Guide to Greatness* (1858), made similar arguments. See Rev. Daniel C. Eddy, *The Young Man's Friend* (Boston: Wentworth, Hewes, 1855), pp. 58, 129, 130.

24. Anonymous, *How to Behave* (New York, 1856), p. 124; cited in

Schlesinger, *Learning How to Behave*, p. 16. Webster is cited in Rotundo, "Body and Soul," p. 30. Francis Grund, *The Americans in their Moral, Social and Political Relations*, 2 vols. (London: Longman, Rees, 1837), vol. 1, p. 173. To be sure, it was only because women did not work that upward mobility provided a measure of manhood. The economic shift to the marketplace did not necessarily tie manhood to economic success, but the homosociality of the market, coupled with men's increasing insecurity about their manhood, made the market the ideal arena for demonstration and proof.

25. Cited in Michael Paul Rogin, *Fathers and Children: Andrew Jackson and the Subjugation of the American Indian* (New York: Vintage, 1975), p. 65. The American, Thomas Low Nichols, followed his return to the states from a European tour with the observation that

   There is no such thing in America as being contented with one's position. Everyone is tugging, scheming, to advance—to get ahead. . . . In Europe, the poor man, as a rule, knows that he must remain poor, and he submits to his lot, and tries to make the best of it. . . . Not so in America. Every little ragged boy dreams of being President or a John Jacob Astor. The dream may be a pleasant one while it lasts, but what of . . . the excited, restless, feverish life spent in the pursuit of phantoms? (Nichols, 1869, 1: 401–407)

26. Francis Grund, *The Americans in their Moral, Social and Political Relations*, 2 vols. (London: Longman, Rees, 1837), vol. 2, pp. 1–2, 5.

27. Charles Dickens, *American Notes for General Circulation* [1842] (New York: Penguin, 1972), pp. 141, 287, 285.

28. Ibid., pp. 289, 229. It should be noted that the two traits that seem most to have repulsed Dickens were slavery—"a most hideous blot and foul disgrace"—and American mens' habit of spitting all the time in public. Several times in his chronicle he pauses to rant against both.

29. Alexis de Tocqueville, *Democracy in America* [1840], George Lawrence, trans. (New York: Anchor, 1969) vol. 1, p. 314.

30. Ibid., vol. 2, p. 536.

31. Ibid., vol. 2, pp. 538, 627. He wrote further that

   He who has set his heart exclusively on the pursuit of worldly welfare is always in a hurry, for he has but a limited time at his disposal. . . . The recollection of the brevity of life is a constant spur to him. . . . This thought fills him with anxiety, fear and regret and keeps his mind in ceaseless trepidation which leads him to perpetually to change his plans and his abode. (2:162)

32. Cited in Irvin G. Wyllie, *The Self-Made Man in America* (New Brunswick, N.J.: Rutgers University Press, 1954), p. 10.

33. Calvin Colton, *Junius Tracts*, no. 7 (New York, 1844), p. 15. Also cited in Sellers, *The Market Revolution*, p. 238. Freeman Hunt's *Hunt's Merchant Magazine*, founded in 1839, also celebrated the cult of the Self-Made Man.

34. Kenneth Wayne, *Building the Young Man* (Chicago: A. C. McClurg, 1912), p. 18; Sam Osherson, *Wrestling with Love: How Men Struggle with Intimacy, with Women, Children, Parents, and Each Other* (New York: Fawcett, 1992), p. 291.

35. Kim Voss, *The Making of American Exceptionalism: The Knights of Labor and Class Formation in the Nineteenth Century* (Ithaca, N.Y.: Cornell University Press, 1993), p. 36. See also Sellers, *The Market Revolution*, pp. 152, 238; and David Leverenz, "The Last Real Man in America: From Natty Bumppo to Batman," in *American Literary History* 3, 1991, p. 757.

36. "It is not the wealthy that rule our legislative councils, in societies, in politics, in town meetings, and the everyday concerns of life; it is not the aristocratic part of our community that have sway over the rest; but it is the educated, the active, the intelligent" was the way one member of the Mechanics Institute put it in 1833. Cited in Sean Wilentz, *Chants Democratic: New York City and the Rise of the American Working Class, 1788–1850* (New York: Oxford University Press, 1984), p. 275.

37. Kathy Peiss, "Of Makeup and Men: The Gendering of Cosmetics," paper presented at a Conference on the Material Culture of Gender, Winterthur Museum, November 1989, p. 4.

38. John Adams, for example, wrote that monarchy would

    produce so much Taste and Politeness, so much Elegance in Dress, Furniture, Equipage, so much Musick and Dancing, so much Fencing and Skaiting, so much Cards and Backgammon; so much Horse Racing and Cockfighting, so many Balls and Assemblies, so many Plays and Concerts, that the very imagination of them makes me feel vain, light, frivolous. (cited in Philip Greven, *The Protestant Temperament*, p. 336)

    And Ralph Waldo Emerson warned that "[t]he world is full of fops who never did anything and who persuaded beauties and men of genius to wear their fop livery; and these will deliver the fop opinion, that it is not respectable to be seen earning a living; that it is much more respectable to spend without earning" (Ralph Waldo Emerson, *Works*, vol. 6, pp. 91–92).

39. See William R. Taylor, *Cavalier and Yankee: The Old South and the American National Character* (New York: George Braziller, 1961), p. 91; other quotes were cited in Bruce Curtis, "The Wimp Factor," in *American Heritage*, November 1989; and Mark Kann, *On the Man Question: Gender and Civic Virtue in America* (Philadelphia: Temple University Press, 1991), p. 246. France itself was increasingly cast as feminized.

40. T. Walter Herbert, *Dearest Beloveds: The Hawthornes and the Making of the Middle-Class Family* (Berkeley: University of California Press, 1993), p. 33.

41. Schlesinger, *The Age of Jackson*, pp. 23, 167; S. C. Allen is cited on p. 153.

42. The poem is in *Longfellow's Complete Poems* (Cambridge: Riverside Press, 1898).

43. Wilentz, *Chants Democratic*, p. 102; Allan Trachtenberg, *The Incorporation of American Culture: Culture and Society in the Gilded Age* (New York: Hill and Wang, 1982); Daniel Rodgers, *The Work Ethic in Industrial America, 1850–1920* (Chicago: University of Chicago Press, 1978), p. 19.

44. Walsh, cited in Lott, *Love and Theft*, p. 129; Mercein, cited in Howard Rock, *Artisans of the New Republic: The Tradesmen of New York City in the Age of Jefferson* (New York: New York University Press, 1984), p. 137; the poet is cited in Wilentz, *Chants Democratic*, p. 84. Tocqueville, *Democracy in America*, vol. 2, p. 48. Such statements indicate that later cultural critiques like David Riesman's *The Lonely Crowd* (New Haven: Yale University Press, 1950) might have overly romanticized the craftsmen of the early Republic in an effort to draw a contrast with contemporary society. The Heroic Artisan was often somewhat less than fully heroic. I am grateful to Bruce Nichols for pointing this out.

45. See Orestes Brownson, "The Laboring Classes," *Boston Quarterly*, July 1840, pp. 358–395.

46. Thompson writes that "[s]ocial intercourse and labour are intermingled; the working day lengthens or contracts according to the task—there is no great sense of conflict between labour and 'passing the time of day.'" Cited in Cott, *The Bonds of Womanhood*, p. 60.

47. Rock, *Artisans*, pp. 319, 129. I will return to this theme of American drinking habits in the next chapter.

48. See Wilentz, *Chants Democratic*, pp. 260–261.

49. Wilentz, *Chants Democratic*, p. 145; Paul Johnson, *A Shopkeeper's Millennium: Society and Revivals in Rochester, New York, 1815–1837* (New York: Hill and Wang, 1978), p. 6; Carroll Smith-Rosenberg, *Disorderly Conduct: Visions of Gender in Victorian America* (New York: Knopf, 1985), p. 83. See also Bruce Laurie, *Artisans into Workers: Labor in Nineteenth-Century America* (New York: Hill and Wang, 1989), esp. p. 38.

50. One English journalist in 1819, who remarked on men whose "only object is to accumulate in the aggregation of which, they are perfectly regardless of the wants of the Journeymen whom they employ"; cited in Wilentz, *Chants Democratic*, p. 167. See also Johnson, *Shopkeeper's Millennium*, pp. 57, 60, and Norman Ware, *The Industrial Worker, 1840–1860.* (Boston: Houghton Mifflin, 1924), p. xii.

51. "Is it the work of creation to be let out to hire?" asked Thomas Skidmore in *The Rights of Man to Property* in 1829, cited in Wilentz, *Chants Democratic*, p. 185. See also Charles Sellers, *The Market Revolution: Jacksonian America, 1815–1846* (New York: Oxford University Press, 1992); Thomas

Cochran and William Miller, *The Age of Enterprise* (New York: Harper and Row, 1961), esp. p. 26.

52. David Montgomery, *Citizen Worker: The Experience of Workers in the United States with Democracy and the Free Market During the Nineteenth Century* (New York: Cambridge University Press, 1994), p. 50. Of course, this is exactly what Marx meant when he wrote in *The Communist Manifesto* that capitalism destroyed all previous relationships among men and "left no other bond between man and man than narrow self-interest, than callous cash-payment." See Karl Marx and Frederich Engels, *The Communist Manifesto* (1848).

53. Cited in Laurie, *Artisans into Workers*, p. 64. See also Christopher Lasch, *The True and Only Heaven: Progress and Its Critics* (New York: Norton, 1991), esp. p. 203. In this sense, the working-class movement in America has never been, as Marx predicted, a revolutionary movement headed towards a new future; it was instead a defensive movement to protect the independence and workplace autonomy of the skilled craftsman and small shopkeeper from the indignities of proletarianization. It was a movement of retreat to the idealized past of the Heroic Artisan more than it was a progressive movement towards the proletarian socialist state.

54. The statistic and citation come from Alice Kessler-Harris, *Out to Work* (New York: Oxford University Press, 1982), pp. 47, 69. "From the perspective of skilled male workers, pressure to keep women out of certain jobs was the only way of saving their own," she writes. Labor historian Philip S. Foner notes that "[m]any skilled craftsmen saw the entrance of women into the job market as the major source of their problems." See *Women and the American Labor Movement* (New York: Free Press, 1982), pp. 13. "As they saw it, the more women workers hired, the more the wages of the skilled male workers would suffer"; *Foner*, p. 12. Women were also systematically excluded from the professions, especially law and medicine. See Kessler-Harris, p. 57 and passim. See also Susan Estabrook Kennedy, *If All We Did Was to Weep at Home: A History of White Working-Class Women in America* (Bloomington: Indiana University Press, 1979), and Barbara Mayer Wertheimer, *We Were There: The Story of Working Women in America* (New York: Pantheon, 1977).

55. Ware, *Industrial Worker*, p. 10. Foreign-born employers also were targets of nativist resentment; one early broadside tried to arouse the workers with an appeal to nativism and class-based solidarity:

Fellow Citizen—LET us support our independence! If we are Mechanics, Laborers, and Artizans—Why should we surrender our opinions, and our rights to the arbitrary mandate of a Tory Employer, and that employer, perhaps a foreign emissary! (cited in Rock, *Artisans*, p. 52).

56. See, e.g., Dale Knobel, *Paddy and the Republic: Ethnicity and Nationality in Antebellum America* (Middletown, Conn.: Wesleyan University Press, 1986).

57. David Roediger, *The Wages of Whiteness: Race and the Making of the American Working Class* (New York: Verso, 1991), p. 13. Contemporaries also saw the connection. "If this is not SLAVERY," as the *New York Evening Post* put it in June 1836, "we have forgotten its definition. Strike the right of associating for the sale of labor from the privileges of a freeman, and you may as well at once bind him to a master," cited in Schlesinger, *The Age of Jackson*, p. 196. Roediger argues that whites came to define blackness as all the things that they, the whites, didn't want to be, while at the same time, the things they secretly wanted, desired, and feared.

58. Eric Lott, *Love and Theft: Blackface Minstrelsy and the American Working Class* (New York: Oxford University Press, 1993), pp. 137, 53, et passim.

59. Frederick Jackson Turner, *The Frontier in American History* [1903] (New York: Holt, Rinehart and Winston, 1947), p. 253.

60. Bancroft, cited in Wilson Carey McWilliams, *The Idea of Fraternity in America* (Berkeley: University of California Press, 1973), p. 250; Tocqueville, *Democracy in America*, p. 278. See also Smith-Rosenberg, *Disorderly Conduct*, pp. 99, 101. As I recall, the bully must constantly be exhorted to pick on someone his own size, but he is also the one who's least secure about his masculinity and therefore has to prove it all the time—especially against those who are smaller and presumably weaker. That was, at least, the gender gospel according to my parents when advising that I not get drawn into fights with our local version.

61. Cited in Ron Takaki, *Strangers from a Different Shore: A History of Asian Americans* (New York: Viking, 1989), p. 94. Biography cited in Michael Paul Rogin, *Fathers and Children*, p. 141.

62. David Pugh, *Sons of Liberty*, p. 18. In his senate campaigns and later as president, he promoted "the world of independent producers, secure in their modest competence, proud in their natural dignity, confirmed in their yeoman character, responsible masters of their fate," as the genuine heroes of the American republic (Meyer, 1957, p. 32)

63. Gadsen and Jackson, both cited in Rogin, *Fathers and Children*, p. 199.

64. Jackson and Van Buren, cited in Rogin, *Fathers and Children*, pp. 287, 290–291. See also Marvin Meyers, *The Jacksonian Persuasion: Politics and Belief* (Stanford, Cal.: Stanford University Press, 1957), esp. p. 78.

65. Jackson, cited in Sellers, *The Market Revolution*, p. 308 (italics in original); cabinet as pimps cited in Pugh, *Sons of Liberty*, p. 28.

66. Schlesinger, *The Age of Jackson*, p. 291.

67. Cited in Robert Gray Gunderson, *The Log Cabin Campaign* (Lexington: University of Kentucky Press, 1957), pp. 102–105.

68. Crockett et al. cited in Gunderson, *The Log Cabin Campaign*, p. 114.
69. Cited in Pugh, *Sons of Liberty*, p. 28. One song, "Little Vanny," sung to the tune of "Rosin the Beau," captured the range of charges against Van Buren as a cowardly, effete dandy:

> You can't make a song to Van Buren
> Because his long name will not do;
> There's nothin' about him allurin'
> As there is about Tippecanoe!
>
> He never was seen in a battle,
> Where bullet and cannon shot flew
> His nerves would be shocked with the rattle
> Of a contest like Tippecanoe!
>
> While Harrison marched to the border,
> Sly Van stayed at home as you know,
> Afraid of the smell of gun-powder—
> Then hurrah for old Tippecanoe!
>
> Little Mat was too tender a dandy
> To shoulder a musket and go
> Where Harrison battled so handy
> As he did when at Tippecanoe!
>
> But snug in his pretty silk stockings,
> And dressed in his broadcloth all new,
> He roasted his shins in a parlor—
> Not fighting like Tippecanoe!
>
> And now with his gold spoons and dishes,
> He lives like a king with his crew;
> He'll feast on the loaves and the fishes
> Till we put in old Tippecanoe.

All songs are cited in Irwin Silber, *Songs America Voted By* (Harrisburg, Penn.: Stackpole Books, 1988), pp. 41, 36, 34, 35.

70. One of Taylor's campaign songs went:

> Oh Lewis Cass, he went to France
> King Phillippe showed him how to dance,
> He dressed him up in clothes so fine,
> Then let him come with him to dine.

71. Richard Slotkin, *The Fatal Environment: The Myth of the Frontier in the Age of Industrialization* (New York: Atheneum, 1985), p. 125.
72. Cited in John Updike, *Memories of the Ford Administration* (New York: Knopf, 1992), p. 229.

73. George G. Foster, *New York by Gas Light: With Here and There a Streak of Sunshine* (New York: Dewitt and Davenport, 1849), p. 101; see also Peter G. Buckley, "To the Opera House: Culture and Society in New York City, 1820–1860" Ph.D. diss., Department of History, SUNY at Stony Brook, 1984. On the link of artisanal republicanism and Anglophobic nativism, see Sean Wilentz, *Chants Democratic*, pp. 315–325.

74. Cited in *Account of the Terrific and Fatal Riot at the Astor Place Opera House* (New York: H. M. Ranney, 1849), p. 10. Other valuable sources on the Astor Place riots include Iver Bernstein, *The New York City Draft Riots* (New York: Oxford University Press, 1990), pp. 149–151; Harry Brinton Henderson III, "Young America and the Astor Place Riot," unpublished M.A. thesis, Columbia University, 1963.

75. *Account of the Terrific and Fatal Riot*, pp. 56–57.

76. "The Astor Place Riot," p. 227.

77. *Account of the Terrific and Fatal Riot*, p. 15.

78. On the B'hoys, see Peter Buckley, "To the Opera House," passim; George Foster, *New York by Gas Light*; and Sean Wilentz, *Chants Democratic*. Riots by young single men in New York were also directed towards upper-class brothels, combining "misogyny against sexually independent women" with class resentment that such women were financially out of the reach of the young men. See Timothy Gilfoyle, "Strumpets and Misogynists: Brothel 'Riots' and the Transformation of Prostitution in Antebellum New York City," *New York History*, January 1987, p. 61. See also Timothy Gilfoyle, *City of Eros: New York City, Prostitution and the Commercialization of Sex, 1790–1920* (New York: Norton, 1992), and Patricia Cline Cohen, "Unregulated Youth: Masculinity and Murder in the 1830s City," *Radical History Review* 52, Winter 1992, esp. p. 44.

79. For accounts of the events of the Astor Place riots, see Peter Buckley, "To the Opera House," passim; *Account of the Terrific and Fatal Riot at the Astor Place Opera House*, passim; Sean Wilentz, *Chants Democratic*; Harry Brinton Henderson III, "Young America and the Astor Place Riot"; and Iver Bernstein, *The New York City Draft Riots*.

80. *Account of the Terrific and Fatal Riot*, p. 19.

81. "The Astor Place Riot," p. 173; *Account of the Terrific and Fatal Riot*, pp. 24–28.

CHAPTER 2: Born to Run

1. Henry David Thoreau, *Walden* [1854] (New York: Signet, 1960), p. 10.

2. Charles Sellers, *The Market Revolution: Jacksonian America, 1815–1846* (New York: Oxford University Press, 1992), p. 246.

3. Such books were enormously popular. William Alcott's *The Young Man's Guide* (1833) ran through twenty-one editions by 1858. The first edition

of Daniel Eddy's *The Young Man's Friend* sold ten thousand copies. In 1857 Albert Barnes noted "the unusual number of books that are addressed particularly to young men" and the way in which "our public speakers everywhere advert to their character, temptations, dangers and prospects with deep solicitude"; cited in Joseph Kett, *Rites of Passage* (New York: Basic Books, 1977), p. 95.

4. *Onania* and Tissot's *A Treatise on the Diseases Produced by Onanism* are both reprinted in *The Secret Vice Exposed!* Carroll Smith-Rosenberg and Charles Rosenberg, eds. (New York: Arno, 1974).

5. "Men were preoccupied with the fear of a loss of sperm, connected as it was to the whole question of manhood and to a man's hopes for some kind of immortality. . . . Men believed their expenditure of sperm had to be governed according to an economic principle." G. J. Barker-Benfield, *The Horrors of the Half-Known Life: Male Attitudes Toward Women and Sexuality in Nineteenth-Century America* (New York: Harper and Row, 1976), pp. 180–181; see also esp. chaps. 15–16. Current research by James Martel examines the converging discourses about loss of fluids in the nineteenth century and the ways in which expenditure of sperm, water, and oil articulated with metaphoric constructions of gold mining in the American West.

6. Cited in G. J. Barker-Benfield, *The Horrors of the Half-Known Life*, p. 179.

7. Conformity to the spermatic economy indicated a form of conformity to the demands of marketplace masculinity. However, it also offered an undercurrent of resistance, "an alternative to the unchecked selfishness" of marketplace life, providing one arena in which the young man could experience successful marshaling of resources and a sense of moral discipline. See, e.g., E. Anthony Rotundo, *American Manhood*, p. 404. Quote about effeminated bodies is cited in T. Walter Herbert, *Dearest Beloveds: The Hawthornes and the Making of the Middle-Class Family* (Berkeley: University of California Press, 1993), p. 141.

8. He wrote that he had "seen some come to premature death, some in academic halls, some very quickly after leaving college and some having graduated with honors." John Todd, *The Student's Manual* (Boston: Lee and Shepherd, 1835), pp. 147–148. See also G. J. Barker-Benfield, "The Spermatic Economy," p. 173.

9. Sylvester Graham, *A Lecture to Young Men* (Providence: Weeden and Cory, 1834), pp. 25, 39, 73, 33–34, 58.

10. These included

Languor, lassitude, muscular relaxation, general debility and heaviness, depression of spirits, loss of appetite, indigestion, faintness and sinking at the pit of the stomach, increased susceptibilities of the skin and lungs to all the atmospheric changes, feebleness of circulation, chilliness, head-ache, melancholy, hypochondria, hysterics, feebleness of all the senses, impaired vision, loss of sight, weakness of the lungs, nervous cough, pulmonary consumption, disorders of the liver and kidneys, urinary difficulties, disorders of the genital organs, weakness of the brain, loss of memory, epilepsy, insanity, apoplexy—and extreme feebleness and early death of offspring. . . .

In part, the cautions against sexual expression were based on a volcanic theory of the orgasmic eruption. The nervous system, Graham warned, is almost unbearably fragile and is unable to bear "the convulsive paroxysms attending venereal indulgence":

The brain, stomach, heart, lungs, liver, skin—and the other organs—feel it sweeping over them, with the tremendous violence of a tornado. The powerfully excited and convulsed heart drives the blood, in fearful congestion, to the principal viscera—producing oppression, irritation, debility, rupture, inflammation, and sometimes disorganization;—and this violent paroxysm is generally succeeded by great exhaustion, relaxation, lassitude, and even prostration. (p. 20)

(Even in the early nineteenth century, it seems, men fell asleep after orgasm!)

11. Graham, *A Lecture*, p. 25. Graham feared that the daydreamer would succumb to "debility, effeminacy, disordered functions, and permanent disease, and even premature death, without the actual exercise of the genital organs!" In a primitive behaviorism, he suggested that seemingly harmless sexual fantasies would lead inevitably to desire and motivation, a blood-boiling lust, that must find an outlet, either with a woman or by oneself.

12. Gardner, cited in Barker-Benfield, *The Horrors*, pp. 272–273. See also John Haller and Robin Haller, *The Physician and Sexuality in Victorian America* (New York: Norton, 1977), p. 208. R. J. Culverwell, *Professional Records: The Institutes of Marriage, Its Intent, Obligations, and Physical and Constitutional Disqualifications* (New York, 1846), p. 75.

13. Other "remedies" are cited in Haller and Haller, *The Physician and Sexuality*, pp. 208–209.

14. Charles Dickens, *American Notes for General Circulation* [1842] (New York: Penguin, 1972), p. 292.

15. Cited in Sellers, *The Market Revolution*, p. 259.

16. Paul E. Johnson and Sean Wilentz, *The Kingdom of Matthias: A Story of Sex and Salvation in Nineteenth-Century America* (New York: Oxford University Press, 1994), p. 59; Sellers, *The Market Revolution*, p. 259.

17. James B. Finley, *Autobiography of Rev. James B. Finley; or, Pioneer Life in the*

West (Cincinnati: Methodist Book Concern, 1854), pp. 310–311. William Rorabaugh, *The Alcoholic Republic* (New York: Oxford University Press, 1979), pp. 14–15.

18. William Rorabaugh, *The Alcoholic Republic*, p. ix. Bourne is cited on p. 146. See also Donald Horton, "The Function of Alcohol in Primitive Societies," *Quarterly Journal of Studies on Alcohol* 4, 1943, pp. 199–320. Charles Sellers also writes that this binge was "fed primarily by the anxiety of self-making men." See Sellers, *The Market Revolution*, p. 260.

19. It is true that many of the leaders of this first temperance movement were male, mostly Protestant ministers—especially in contrast to the second temperance crusade, which was dominated almost entirely by women. But ministers occupied a kind of neutral zone between masculinity and femininity, as Ann Douglas and others have pointed out. As one man observed in 1830, clergymen were "a sort of people between men and women." Cited in Rorabaugh, *The Alcoholic Republic*, p. 220. See also Ann Douglas, *The Feminization of American Culture* (New York: Knopf, 1977).

20. Carroll Smith-Rosenberg and Charles Rosenberg, "The Female Animal," 1973, p. 353.

21. Tocqueville, *Democracy in America*, p. 240, 603.

22. Ibid., p. 587, 588.

23. Ibid., p. 601.

24. T. Walter Herbert, *Dearest Beloveds*, p. 187. See also John Mack Farragher, *Women and Men on the Overland Trail* (New Haven: Yale University Press, 1979), pp. 1–3.

25. Ruth Schwartz Cowan, *More Work for Mother: The Ironies of Household Technology from the Revolution to the Present* (New York: Basic Books, 1983), p. 64 See also Carroll Smith-Rosenberg, *Disorderly Conduct*, p. 85. John Gillis provided me with the information about child-rearing manuals.

26. See, e.g., David Rothman, *The Discovery of the Asylum: Social Order and Disorder in the New Republic* (Boston: Little, Brown, 1971).

27. John Demos, *A Little Commonwealth* (Boston: Little, Brown, 1970), pp. 177–178. See also Rogin, *Fathers and Children*, p. 63, and Cowan, *More Work for Mother*, pp. 66–67.

28. Cited in T. Walter Herbert, *Dearest Beloveds*, p. 14.

29. See Paul Johnson and Sean Wilentz, *The Kingdom of Matthias*, p. 106 and passim.

30. Buell, cited in Nancy Cott, *The Bonds of Womanhood*, p. 54. James Fenimore Cooper added, in *Notions of the Americas*: "Retired within the sacred precincts of her own abode, she is preserved from the destroying taint of excessive intercourse with the world. She makes no bargains beyond those which supply her own little personal wants, and her heart is not early corrupted by the baneful and unfeminine vice of selfishness. . . .

She must be sought in the haunts of her domestic privacy and not amid the wranglings, deceptions and heartburnings of keen and sordid traffic." (1836; 1:105)

31. See Cott, *The Bonds of Womanhood*, p. 63, Kessler-Harris, *Out to Work*, pp. 51, 71, and passim, and Kennedy, *If All We Did Was to Weep at Home*, p. 17. Social geographer Daphne Spain argues that the separation of spheres was one of the major historical building blocks of gender inequality, as women's second-class status "was reinforced by their segregation from men in the domestic sphere, in higher education, and in acceptable 'woman's occupations.'" Daphne Spain, *Gendered Spaces* (Chapel Hill: University of North Carolina Press, 1992) p. 197.

32. Meyers, *The Jacksonian Persuasion*, p. 52; Ward, 1962, p. 193. Ward argues that men paid a large price for this amoral public activity, becoming "an adjunct to the home"—a topic to which I will turn below.

33. Barbara Welter, "The Cult of True Womanhood," *American Quarterly*, Summer 1966, and Smith-Rosenberg, *Disorderly Conduct*, p. 13.

34. Cited in Sellers, *The Market Revolution*, pp. 242, 245. See also Barbara Welter, "The Cult of True Womanhood," esp. p. 152, and *passim*; Cott, *The Bonds of Womanhood*, p. 92.

35. Cited in Francesca Cancian, *Love in America: Gender and Self-Development* (New York: Cambridge University Press, 1987), pp. 21, 19.

36. Judd is cited in Ann Douglas, *The Feminization of American Culture* (New York: Knopf, 1977), p. 102. Eliza Farnham, *Woman and Her Era* (New York, 1864), p. 95. An article in *Godey's Magazine* in 1860 held that "the perfection of womanhood . . . is the wife and mother, the center of the family, the magnet that draws man to the domestic altar, that makes him a civilized being, a social Christian. The wife is truly the light of the home." Cited in Michael C. C. Adams, *The Great Adventure: Male Desire and the Coming of World War I* (Bloomington: Indiana University Press, 1990), p. 5.

37. E. Anthony Rotundo, *American Manhood*, chaps. 2–4.

38. Cited in T. Walter Herbert, *Dearest Beloveds*, p. 261.

39. Herbert, *Dearest Beloveds*, pp. 261, 262. Such an argument also suggests a historical origin to Robert Bly's evocations of mythic male bonding rituals that are said to retrieve some timeless, deep, essential masculine.

40. Eric Lott, *Love and Theft: Blackface Minstrelsy and the American Working Class* (New York: Oxford University Press, 1993), p. 196.

41. Committee on Female Labor and Commons, *Documentary History*, cited in Robert Max Jackson, untitled MS, chap. 4, pp. 5–8.

42. Cited in Christine Stansell, *City of Women* (New York: Knopf, 1986), p. 137. Committee on Female Labor and Commons, *Documentary History*, cited in Jackson, chap. 4, pp. 5–8.

43. Bram Dykstra, *Idols of Perversity: Fantasies of Women and Sexuality in Fin de Siècle America* (New York: Oxford University Press, 1986), p. 209. Todd, *Lectures to Children* (1834), sold over 200,000 copies, according to John Crandall, *Images and Ideals for Young Americans: A Study of American Juvenile Literature* (Ph.D. diss., University of Rochester, 1957), p. 70. See also John Todd, *Woman's Rights* (Boston: Lee and Shepard, 1867), p. 23.

44. Garfield, cited in Douglas, *The Feminization of American Culture*, p. 59; other citations in Michael S. Kimmel, "Men's Responses to Women's Educational Equality, 1848–the Present," in *Thought and Action* 8(2), 1993.

45. Todd, *Woman's Rights*, pp. 14, 26. Long cited in Susan B. Anthony, Elizabeth Cady Stanton, and Matilda Joslyn Gage, *History of Woman Suffrage* (New York: National Woman's Suffrage Association, 1887), vol. 1, pp. 853–854.

46. Historian Philip Greven observed three patterns of domestic patriarchy in eighteenth-century America, patterns which roughly parallel the three models of American manhood I have been developing. The *genteel* tradition placed the Genteel Patriarch in his role as father and revolved around an easygoing sensuousness and elegance. Fathers maintained an "inner security" free of the "burden of guilt and repression, or the tensions of anxiety." Their children thus "began their lives with a sense of self-worth, self-love, and self-confidence that set them apart from those reared in different ways," and were able to express both their "masculine" and their "feminine" impulses in the pursuit of sensuous and aesthetic pleasure and activity in public life of commerce, politics, and agriculture.

The *evangelical* father, following the Great Awakening, saw the child as inherently evil, passionate and uncontrolled; these "aggressively repressive" fathers, therefore, "insisted upon the decisive conquest of a child's will and the unconditional surrender of the child to the will of the parent." Authoritarian family government, with the father as absolute monarch, characterized the family systems of the lower-middling classes—the small shopkeepers, artisans, craftsmen—and many middle-class entrepreneurs; it stressed obedience, submission, and the denial of self, which was necessary to purge the child of his naturally aggressive masculine traits and instill in him the culturally induced "feminine" traits.

Finally, *moderate* fathers—urban entrepreneurs and merchants—were concerned less with breaking the wills of their children than with regulating and controlling them, shaping their characters. Moderate fathers saw childhood as a "process of growth and development" in which they, as parents, had a decisive early shaping influence but also a decreasing amount of influence. The moderate father promoted the greatest individual self-making in his son, thus allowing the widest latitude for individual

development and the greatest amount of moral responsibility for the outcome to be laid upon the children, not on the father. Sons of moderate fathers were the most plagued by the anxieties that attend the widest range
of individual choice. Thus had John Adams posed the question to himself: "Which, dear Youth, will you prefer? a Life of Effeminacy, Indolence
and Obscurity, or a Life of Industry, Temperance, and Honour?" And thus
did "virtue" advise him on which course to take:

> return to your Study, and bend your whole soul to the Institutes of the Law,
> and the Reports of Cases. . . . Let no trifling diversion or amuzement, or
> Company decoy you from your Books, i.e. let no Girl, no Gun, no Cards, no
> Flutes, no Violins, no Dress, no Tobacco, no Laziness, decoy you from your
> Books.

As a result of this self-administered individual child rearing, Adams
became "intensely ambitious" and yet also chronically "afraid of being
thought soft, indolent, passionate, and of being weak and subordinate,"
confessing once that "he could not look with complacency upon any man
who was in possession of more wealth, more honours, or more knowledge than himself."

Moderate fatherhood triumphed over both evangelical and genteel
fatherhood as the new demands of the industrializing American economy demanded more and more time, energy, and individual initiative
from men in the workplace. The workplace shifted from farm and household, through which fathers had passed several times daily, to the counting house, mill, factory, shop, and office, where work was defined by
wages and a clearly demarcated working day. See Philip Greven, *The
Protestant Temperament: Patterns of Child Rearing, Religious Experience
and the Self in Early America* (New York: Knopf, 1980); citations are on
pp. 274, 286, 309.

47. Pierce, cited in Cott, *The Bonds of Womanhood*, p. 120. E. Anthony Ro-
tundo, "American Fatherhood: A Historical Perspective," *American Behav-
ioral Scientist* 29(1), 1985, pp. 10, 13. Jay Fliegelman, *Prodigals and
Pilgrims*, p. 200. Adams cited in Dubbert, *A Man's Place: Masculinity in
Transition* (Engelwood Cliffs: Prentice-Hall, 1979), p. 23. Abbott, cited in
Mark Carnes, *Secret Ritual and Manhood in Victorian America* (New
Haven: Yale University Press, 1989), p. 111.

48. Carroll Smith-Rosenberg, *Disorderly Conduct*, p. 88.

49. David Leverenz, *Manhood and the American Renaissance* (Ithaca, N.Y.:
Cornell University Press, 1989), p. 165. Burroughs cited in Cott, *The
Bonds of Womanhood*, p. 64. Sellers argues that "[b]uffeted by the world's
fierce competition, they could brook no competition at home. A masculinity tested daily by competing makes required a domestic domain of

unquestioned mastery." See Sellers, *The Market Revolution*, p. 246. Mary Ryan argues that patriarchy's decline in the private sphere was accompanied by the rise of public patriarchy through the separation of spheres, which compensated men for their loss of domestic power. See Ryan, *Cradle of the Middle Class* (New York: Cambridge University Press, 1981), p. 102.

50. Henry David Thoreau, *Walden* [1854] (New York: New American Library, 1960).

51. Brownson converted to Catholicism because he felt it to be more manly and patriarchal. Brownson, cited in Barbara Welter, "The Feminization of American Religion, 1800–1860," in *Clio's Consciousness Raised*, Mary Hartman and Lois Banner, eds. (New York: Harper and Row, 1974), p. 139. See also Rotundo, "Learning About Manhood," p. 47.

52. This resistance to feminization, whether in the form of real women (mothers and wives) or against those cultural qualities of modern life that spell enervation and feminization (religion, education, workplace responsibilities, doing "brain work"), I call *masculinism*. Masculinism involves an effort to restore manly vigor and revirilize American men by promoting separate homosocial preserves where men can be men without female interference. Some masculinist efforts involve the symbolic appropriation of women's reproductive power, by developing distinctively masculine forms of ritual initiation and nurture—initiations that displaced maternal care with manly validation.

Masculinism is, at its center, resistance to femininity, to the forces that turn hard men into soft, enervated nerds; it is by escape from women and resistance to femininity that masculinists hope to retrieve their manhood. In their view, men had to wriggle free of these feminine, feminizing clutches—ironically the very clutches that male insecurity had created to free the workplace of female competition and to make the home into a man's castle. It was in the public sphere that men faced the greatest challenges to their manhood, where their sense of manhood was won or lost, and yet these anxieties were projected, instead, onto women as the bearers of enervating lassitude. Men were suddenly terrified of feminization in the very homes they had created, and now yearned to escape, or at least more clearly demarcate themselves, from women.

53. A similar process was evidenced in Britain, where the percentage of clean-shaven men pictured in the *Illustrated London News*, "the world's most venerable pictorial news magazine," dropped sharply from 1840, when about 40 percent were clean shaven, to a nadir of less than 10 percent clean shaven by 1885. See Dwight Robinson, "Fashions in Shaving and Trimming of the Beard: The Men of the *Illustrated London News*, 1842–1972," *American Journal of Sociology* 81(5), 1976, pp. 1134 (quote) and 1136 (for chart of percentages).

54. Whitman and *Harper's Monthly*, cited in William Leach, *True Love and Perfect Union: The Feminist Reform of Sex and Society* (New York: Basic Books, 1980), p. 217. On men and spectacles, see Paul E. Johnson and Sean Wilentz, *The Kingdom of Matthias* (New York: Oxford University Press, 1994), p. 94. Oliver Wendell Holmes, "The Autocrat at the Breakfast Table," in *Atlantic Monthly* 1, May 1858, p. 881. An 1851 issue of *Scientific American* celebrated the practicality of the American genius as against the ornateness and luxury of European inventions. See John Kasson, *Civilizing the Machine: Technology and Republican Values in America, 1776–1900* (New York: Grossman, 1976), p. 151. A wave of anti-European sentiment was fueled in part by masculine panic about feminization.

55. Although I will treat only the West in any detail here, there were other forms of masculinist resistance to cultural feminization. For example, much of the early nineteenth-century commune movement, from Fourierist phalanxes to Oneida, Brook Farm, and New Harmony, were efforts to restore manly dignity to men's work, to return men to the land, from which all integrity sprang. Idealizing the rapidly disappearing Heroic Artisan and yeoman farmer, these communes were, in this sense, reactionary and conservative efforts to retrieve and restore artisanal virtue as the artisan and yeoman were themselves being proletarianized. It is interesting that many of those efforts to restore the manly dignity of the Heroic Artisan did not do so at the expense of women, since many communal leaders actually supported women's equality. Masculinism could be a flight from a feminized *culture* and still promote women's equality. See Kimmel and Mosmiller, eds., *Against the Tide* (documents by John Humphrey Noyes, Robert Dale Owen, as well as Moses Harmon, Ezra Heywood, and other "sex radicals" in the latter half of the century).

56. Turner, *The Frontier in American History*, p. 92. (It is ironic that these same terms had been used almost two centuries earlier as a way to entice Englishmen to journey to the colonies.) See also Meyer, *The Jacksonian Persuasion*, p. 139. In 1836 a Massachusetts House committee saw the choice before young artisans and farmers as "the alternative of becoming essentially a manufacturing people, or of bidding adieu to their native hills . . . and following the rising glories of the west." Cited in Schlesinger, *The Age of Jackson*, p. 148. In the more recent work of literary critic David Leverenz, "to be aggressive, rebellious, enraged, uncivilized; this is what the frontier could do for the European clones on the East Coast, still in thrall to a foreign tyranny of manners." See Leverenz, "The Last Real Man in America," p. 763.

57. Flint, cited in Adams, *The Great Adventure*, p. 25; Timothy Dwight, *Travels in New England and New York*, 4 vols. (New Haven, 1821), vol. 2, p. 441; Crèvecoeur, cited in Roderick Nash, *Wilderness and the American Mind* (New Haven: Yale University Press, 1967), p. 30.

58. Francis Parkman, *The Oregon Trail: Sketches of Prairie and Rocky Mountain Life* [1849] (Boston: Little, Brown, 1892). Cited also in George M. Frederickson, *The Inner Civil War: Northern Intellectuals and the Crisis of the Union* [1965] (Champaign: University of Illinois Press, 1993), p. 34.

59. Webber wrote that "[t]he primitive virtues of a heroic manhood are all sufficient, and they care nothing for reverences, forms, duties, etc., as civilization has them, but respect each other's rights and recognize the awful presence of a benignant God in the still grandeur of mountain, forest, valley, plain, and river, through, among, and over which they pass." Such men, Webber wrote, "do not look back to society except with disgust." Charles Webber, *Old Hicks, the Guide; or, Adventures in the Comanche Country in Search of a Gold Mine*, 2 vols. (New York, 1855), vol. 1, p. 311.

60. Paula Mitchell Marks, *Precious Dust: The American Gold Rush Era, 1848–1900* (New York: William Morrow, 1994), p. 23.

61. Richard Stott, "The Geography of Gender in Nineteenth-Century America: Youth, Masculinity, and the California Gold Rush," paper presented at the 1991 Annual Meeting of the Organization of American Historians, esp. p. 6.; Rev. John Todd, 1871, pp. 44–45; C. W. Haskins, *The Argonauts of California* (New York, 1890), p. 73. Elisabeth Margo, *Taming the Forty-Niner* (New York, 1855), p. 8.

62. Stott, "The Geography of Gender," pp. 6, 8, 11; Marks, *Precious Dust*, p. 326. In such a world without women, men also retrieved the capacity for caring and nurture. "As a rule," observed one miner, "the men nursed their partners through these illnesses with as much tenderness as women." Cited in Marks, *Precious Gold*, p. 236.

63. Henry David Thoreau, *Walden*, pp. 10, 216, 66. Businessmen "come tamely home at night only from the next field or street, where their household echoes haunt, and their life pines because it breathes its own breath over again," he wrote, while workers "are so occupied with the factitious care and superfluously coarse labors of life that its finer fruits cannot be plucked by them." As a result, "[t]he laboring man has not the leisure for a true integrity day by day; he cannot afford to sustain the manliest relations to men; his labor would be depreciated in the market. He has no time to be anything but a machine"; pp. 142, 9.

64. Thoreau, *Walden*, pp. 142, 211.

65. That today thousands of men troop off to the woods to follow men's movement leader Robert Bly in a similarly stylized initiation process is, of course, part of the story I am telling. No wonder Bly calls Thoreau one of his heroes. In a recent poem Bly praises Thoreau for living so "extravagantly alone . . . keeping company with his handsome language." Robert Bly, "The Insatiable Soul," poetry reading at Scottish Rite Temple, San Francisco, 30 January 1993.

66. See Henry Nash Smith, *Virgin Land: The American West as Symbol and Myth* (Cambridge: Harvard University Press, 1950), p. 226; Turner, *The Frontier in American History*, John Mack Farragher, *Daniel Boone: The Life and Legend of an American Pioneer* (New York: Henry Holt, 1992), esp. pp. 6, 29, 66, 327–328. In that retreat was also rebellion; Boone sought to escape the fate of most men who become, as his biographer Gilbert Imlay put it, "mere machines of the state." All three men were, as Yale President Theodore Dwight wrote, "impatient of the restraints of law, religion, and morality"; the pioneer despises the "dull uniformity and monotony" of civilized life when "compared in his mind with the stirring scenes of wild western adventure," wrote David Coyner, in his fictionalized 1847 biography of Carson, *The Lost Trappers*, cited in Turner, *The Frontier in American History*, p. 251. All were fiercely anti-intellectual; Boone, for example, "rather eschewed books, parchment deeds, and clerky contrivances as forms of evil," as his biographer Timothy Flint put it, cited in Dubbert, *A Man's Place*, p. 35. And all were virtuous, embodying the hardiness and simplicity that characterized the Heroic Artisan, "drawing from association with uncultivated nature, not the rudeness and sensualism of the savage, but genuine simplicity and truthfulness of disposition, and generosity, bravery, single heartedness, to a degree rarely found in society," as one popular biographer portrayed Kit Carson in the *Rough and Ready Annual* of 1847, cited in Slotkin, *The Fatal Environment*, p. 204.

67. Slotkin, *The Fatal Environment*, p. 374.

68. The great Russian writer Maxim Gorky put it this way in his discussion of American literature: "As an explorer of the forests and prairies of the 'New World,' he blazes new trails in them for people who later condemn him as a criminal because he has infringed their mercenary and, to his sense of freedom, unintelligible laws. All his life he has unconsciously served the great cause of the geographical expansion of material culture in a country of uncivilized people and . . . found himself incapable of living in the conditions of this culture for which he has struck the first paths." Gorky is cited in Georg Lukacs, *The Historical Novel* (London: Merlin, 1962), p. 65.

69. Michael A. Lofaro, "Riprorious Shemales: Legendary Women in the Tall Tale World of the Davy Crockett Almanacs," in *Davy Crockett at Two Hundred*, Michael Lofaro and Joe Cummings, eds. (Knoxville: University of Tennessee Press, 1989), p. 26.

   As a suburban youngster in the late 1950s, I have the fondest memories of my own coonskin cap and the enormous role that Davy Crockett—or to be more accurate, Fess Parker—played in my life. Parker was, simply, the handsomest and ruggedest—in short, the manliest—man I had ever seen. A trip to the Alamo as an adult left me feeling saddened by

NOTES

the scale of the reality in comparison to the fantasy of heroic violent death.

Today the Alamo retains a special place in American spiritual iconography. The scene of a total massacre—one of the most lopsided losses in American military history, a loss at which everyone died—is recalled because it mobilized the nation to eventually expel the invading Mexicans. To visit the shrine today is to enter hallowed ground, a sacred space of sacrificial slaughter. Hushed tones only are appropriate. Silence—heroes died here. Remembering the Alamo is simultaneously a reverent recollection of racism (Mexicans as barbarian hordes) and military masculinity in the guise of deeply spiritual patriotism. It also serves as a monument to a retaliation far beyond the bounds of the initial offense, that distinctly American trait that Margaret Mead so eloquently unmasked in *And Keep Your Powder Dry*. The Alamo implies our victimization and thereby justifies our own slaughter of Mexicans since. I am grateful to Barbara Starr for her guidance both at the Alamo and in exploring my reactions to it.

70. This is, of course, not true of the novels by women, which were the best-selling works of fiction of the era.

71. To Leslie Fiedler, this marks the classical American novel as entirely different from the classical European novel, in which—as in, e.g., *Madame Bovary, Anna Karenina*, or *Jane Eyre*—the plot revolves around a heterosexual couple, struggling with issues of sexual fidelity, workplace responsibility, and family and domestic concerns; Leslie Fiedler, *Love and Death in the American Novel* (New York: Stein and Day, 1966), p. 181. That Fiedler's thesis has recently come under fire for its elitism and androcentrism should not blind us to the perceptiveness of his insights. See also David Leverenz, *Manhood in the American Renaissance* (Ithaca, N.Y.: Cornell University Press, 1989). Though both authors also discuss Herman Melville, I find neither as convincing as Michael Rogin, *Subversive Genealogy* (New York: Knopf, 1979).

72. Washington Irving, "Rip Van Winkle" [1820], in *Collected Stories of Washington Irving* (New York: Signet, 1963), pp. 43–57. Ever since Rip, writes Leslie Fiedler, "the typical male protagonist of our fiction has been a man on the run, harried into the forest or out to sea, down the river or into combat—anywhere to avoid 'civilization,' which is to say, the confrontation of a man and woman which leads to the fall to sex, marriage and responsibility"; Fiedler, *Love and Death*, p. 26.

Psychoanalyst Kenneth S. Lynn underscored the escapist theme in American literature in his disdainful essay "Adulthood in American Literature," in *Adulthood*, edited by E. Erikson (New York: Norton, 1978), pp. 237–247.

73. Fiedler, *Love and Death*, p. 214.

74. See Fiedler, *Love and Death*, p. 211 and passim.
75. Recent versions of this cross-race male bonding require the absence of any hint of sexual contact between the two men, and so one of them— usually the white man—is transformed into an overtly sexualized—and heterosexual—character. Thus do films like *Last of the Mohicans, Lethal Weapon*, and *Dances with Wolves* stress Natty's, Riggs's, and Lt. Dunbar's love interests. The man of color as native spirit guide remains relatively desexualized.
76. Danny Glover has consistently been cast in the role of the saner, soberer black man nurturing the white man, who totters on the brink of insanity. Not only in the *Lethal Weapon* series but also in *Grand Canyon*, where he rescues a white man (Kevin Kline) from a black gang and then helps him regain his sense of self and purpose, and in *The Saint of Fort Washington*, where he adopts a schizophrenic white homeless man (Matt Dillon) and claims him as his son. Only the *Nation*'s Stuart Klawans, one of America's most perceptive film critics, seems to have noticed this trend. "Come on down to the raft agin, Huck Honey!" he writes, cribbing Fiedler. See Stuart Klawans, "Short Takes," in the *Nation*, 13 December 1993, p. 744.
77. "The existence of overt homosexuality threatens to compromise an essential aspect of American sentimental life: the camaraderies of the locker room and ball park, the good fellowship of the poker game and fishing trip, a kind of passionless passion, at once gross and delicate, homoerotic in the boy's sense, possessing an innocence above suspicion." Fiedler, *Love and Death*, p. 143.
78. In his earlier novels Cooper groped for a way to develop his critique of the marketplace and his idealization of the natural man. In his 1821 novel *The Spy*, for example, his critique of one character, Harvey Birch, as a shrewd, acquisitive, Yankee peddler whose "love of money is a stronger passion than love of his kin" is less effective without another masculine archetype to play him off against. In 1823 he found that character in Natty Bumppo.
79. Christopher Lasch, *The True and Only Heaven* (New York: Norton, 1991), p. 94.
80. D. H. Lawrence, *Studies in Classic American Literature* (New York: Grove Press, 1967), p. 59. David Leverenz, "The Last Real Man in America," p. 754 and passim. See also Henry Nash Smith, *Wilderness*, p. 256; Cawelti, *Apostles of the Self-Made Man*, p. 78.
81. Cooper, *Last of the Mohicans*, p. 26. Bumppo returns to this theme of anti-intellectualism and the feminizing qualities of women throughout the novel:

"Book!" repeated Hawk-eye, with singular and ill-concealed disdain. "Do you take me for a whimpering boy at the apron string of one of your old gals; and this good rifle on my knee for the feather of a goose's wing, my ox's horn for a bottle of ink, and my leathern pouch for a cross-barred hand-kercher to carry my dinner? Book! What have such as I, who am a warrior of the wilderness, though a man without a cross, to do with books? I never read but in one, and the words that are written there are too simple and too plain to need much schooling; though I may boast that of forty long and hard-working years. (p. 132)

82. Cooper, *Last of the Mohicans*, p. 318. But Hawkeye's escape requires that he exchange clothes with David, the bespectacled bookworm with the golden song. "Are you much given to cowardice?" Hawkeye asks him. "My pursuits are peaceful, and my temper, I humbly trust, is greatly given to mercy and love," David responds, "a little nettled," Cooper tells us, "at so direct an attack on his manhood"; p. 323.

83. Cooper, *Last of the Mohicans*, p. 356.

84. Cooper, writes Marxist literary critic George Lukacs, "portrays the enormous historical tragedy of those early colonizers, who emigrated from England in order to preserve their freedom, but who themselves destroy this freedom by their own deeds in America." See Lukacs, *The Historical Novel*, pp. 64–65.

85. See Walt Whitman, *Leaves of Grass and Other Poems*. The phrase "athletic democracy" appears in "To Foreign Lands."

86. Cited in George Frederickson, *The Inner Civil War*, p. 30. Ralph Waldo Emerson argued in "Nature," that through contact with nature a man escapes "the sepulchers of the fathers" and "the keys of power are put into his hand." See Michael Rogin, *Subversive Genealogy*, p. 216. Like the others in the pantheon of the American renaissance—Thoreau, Whitman, Melville, Hawthorne—Emerson was "self-consciously deviant from the prevailing norms of manly behavior." On the one hand, he evidenced a "patrician disdain" for the young hustling men on the make. "Society is everywhere in conspiracy against the manhood of every one of its members," he wrote in 1841. But on the other hand, Emerson believed that manhood must be rescued from fading gentility. "Whoso would be a man must be a nonconformist," Emerson wrote epigrammatically. Leverenz, *Manhood and the American Renaissance*, pp. 159, 52, 107. Emerson's confusion, Leverenz suggests, stems from his early childhood humiliation by a severe and exacting father. To counter this fear of humiliation, Emerson employed "man-making words" in daily little pep talks with himself, employing a "willed optimism" to rouse himself from feelings of insecurity and inferiority (p. 7).

87. "The yeoman and the scholar—the yeoman and the man of the finest moral culture, though not the man of the sturdiest sense and integrity—

are two distinct individuals and can never be melted or welded into one substance," Hawthorne wrote (1954, p. 66). In his unfinished *Doctor Grimshawe's Secret*, Hawthorne contrasts American and English male cultures, exposing "the natural hatred of men—and the particular hatred of Americans—to an Aristocracy."

88. Leverenz, *Manhood and the American Renaissance*, pp. 279, 281. This is the same unconscious obsession, Leverenz argues, that fueled Melville's rage at the capitalist Leviathan that had consumed his own father, driven by marketplace failures to bankruptcy, insanity, and eventually suicide.

89. Like its female counterpart, this insanity is based, not on gender nonconformity, but on *over*conformity to impossible behavioral norms.

90. "The monsters of antebellum politics, like Jackson's Bank and Ahab's whale, were centers of hidden power, which explained the bourgeois's failure to master the world," writes Michael Rogin. "They have the power he wants, and the sensual materiality he experiences as resisting his will, and so he makes war against them." Rogin, *Subversive Genealogy*, p. 126.

91. Leverenz, *Manhood and the American Renaissance*, pp. 290, 294.

92. Even before the first Woman's Rights Convention was held in Seneca Falls in 1848, some American men supported women's equality—the right to vote, to enter the university, to work and receive equal wages, to own and control her own property after marriage. Thomas Paine had claimed, as early as 1776, that women had an "equal right to virtue." Charles Brockden Brown's first novel, *Alcuin* (1798), provided a sustained argument for women's rights in the form of a dialogue between a young man and an elderly woman, who instructs him about the position of women until he is forced to admit that his views of women were based on illogical prejudice and not reason. His later novels, especially *Edgar Huntly* and *Arthur Mervyn*, link this profeminist position to a critique of marketplace manhood. Mervyn's world is one of "failed fathers and ruined families," and Huntly is portrayed as a pathetic young man, so consumed with anxiety about his place in the competitive marketplace that he becomes, as Brown put it, "a formidable engine of destruction"—his gender insecurity cast as the signal cause of a propensity for violence. Brockden Brown is cited in Fritz Fleischmann, *A Right View of the Subject*, 1983, p. 137. For more about profeminist men before Seneca Falls, see my introduction to *Against the Tide: Pro-Feminist Men in the United States, 1776–1990*, Michael S. Kimmel and Thomas E. Mosmiller, eds. (Boston: Beacon Press, 1992), as well as sect. 1.

93. See, e.g., John Neal, "The Rights of Woman" (1843); Samuel May, "The Rights and Condition of Women" (1946); Theodore Weld, "Man's Disparagement of Woman in All Times and Climes" (1855)—all edited and reprinted in Kimmel and Mosmiller, eds., *Against the Tide*, pp. 82–93,

94–98, 297–299. See also William Thompson, *Appeal of One-Half of the Human Race* (New York, 1825), and *History of Woman Suffrage*, vol. 1.

94. Noyes linked slavery and women's sexual subordination explicitly in a short play, "Slavery and Marriage—A Dialog" [1850] (Woman's Rights Collection, Arthur and Elizabeth Schlesinger Library on The History of Women, Harvard University), and "Male Continence," reprinted in Kimmel and Mosmiller, eds., *Against the Tide*, pp. 338–341.

95. Owen argued that no man "ought even to desire that a woman should become the mother of his children, unless it was her express wish" and that a woman's "feelings, her interests, should be for him in this matter *an imperative law.*" Sexual desire, Nichols wrote, causes the brain to "glow with voluptuous ideas," so that men are "gallant, kind, attentive, and loving to women; ever seeking their favors; ever pressing their suit." Robert Dale Owen, *Moral Physiology* (New York: Wright and Owen, 1831).

Like Owen, Nichols was careful to insist on women's sexual rights and autonomy, that she alone should have the power to choose with whom and when to be sexual. "If a woman has any right in this world, it is the right to herself; and if there is anything in this world she has a right to decide, it is who shall be the father of her children. She has an equal right to decide whether she will have children, and to choose the time for having them." Nichols wrote in words that ring as powerfully today in light of recent attempts to erode women's rights to control their bodies. Thomas Gove Nichols, *Esoteric Anthropology* [1853] (New York: Arno, 1972), p. 100.

96. Walt Whitman, *Complete Poetry and Collected Prose*, Justin Kaplan, ed. (New York: Library of America, 1982), pp. 248, 1307; see also William Patrick Jeffs, " 'Man's Words' and Manly Comradeship: Language, Politics and Homosexuality in Walt Whitman's Works," *Journal of Homosexuality* 23(4), 1992.

The explicitly sexual component of these relationships has long been debated. On the one hand, some historians seem intent on desexualizing male comradeship; see, e.g., Donald Yacavone's "Abolitionists and the 'Language of Fraternal Love,' " in *Meanings for Manhood*. In his most recent novel John Updike declares categorically that "[t]hroughout most of history, men love one another, yes, but as spirits, not bodies; only our coarse materialist imaginations seek to deplatonize the masculine romances of the previous century." John Updike, *Memories of the Ford Administration* (New York: Knopf, 1992), p. 231.

I think Updike has it backward: It is only our contemporary discomfort with homoerotic relationships that lead us to *de*sexualize these relationships. Even if they were not genitally sexual and even if they did not culminate in orgasm, there can be little doubt that these relationships were deeply erotic and emotionally as well as sexually charged. The de-eroticization of these relationships impoverishes them, and us, considerably. See Martin Duberman, "Writhing Bedfellows," in *About Time* (New York: Dutton, 1991).

97. William Lloyd Garrison, "Intelligent Wickedness," reprinted in Kimmel and Mosmiller, eds., *Against the Tide*, pp. 212–214. Italics added.

98. In his speech as the cochair of the convention at Seneca Falls, Douglass claimed that women were

> justly entitled to all we claim for man. We go farther, and express our conviction that all political rights which it is expedient for man to exercise, it is equally so for woman. All that distinguishes man as an intelligent and accountable being, is equally true of woman, and if that government only is just which governs by the free consent of the governed, there can be no reason in the world for denying to woman the exercise of the elective franchise, or a hand in making and administering the laws of the land.

(reprinted in *History of Woman Suffrage*, vol. 1; also reprinted in Kimmel and Mosmiller, eds., *Against the Tide*, pp. 211–212). It is true that both Garrison and Douglass backed away from universal suffrage when faced with the "choice" between woman suffrage and black emancipation.

99. Cited in Arthur Schlesinger, "The Role of Women in American History," in *New Viewpoints in American History* (New York: Macmillan, 1922), p. 139.

100. Bennett is cited in Bertram Wyatt-Brown, "The Abolitionist Controversy: Men of Blood, Men of God," in *Men, Women and Issues in American History*, vol. 1, Howard Quint and Milton Cantor, eds. (Homewood, Ill.: Dorsey Press, 1975), p. 222. *New York Daily World*, 11 May 1866. *Baltimore Patriot* is cited in Nina Silber, *The Romance of Reunion: Northerners and the South, 1865–1900* (Chapel Hill: University of North Carolina Press, 1993), p. 22.

101. Phillips and Garrison are cited in Bertram Wyatt-Brown, "The Abolitionist Controversy," pp. 228, 233–234.

102. Whether the Civil War was a struggle between two competing visions of capitalism—one industrial, based on wage labor, and the other agrarian, based on slave labor—is the matter of significant debate. I tend to favor an interpretation that sees both as capitalist systems, each based on a different marketplace ideal of masculinity. See, e.g., Barrington Moore, *Social Origins of Democracy and Dictatorship: Lord and Peasant in the Making of the Modern World* (Boston: Beacon, 1966), and Immanuel Wallerstein, *The Modern World System*, vols. 1–3 (New York: Academic Press, 1974–1989).

103. All cited in David Shi, *The Simple Life* (New York: Oxford University Press, 1985), pp. 150, 151, 152.

104. Cited in Nina Silber, *The Romance of Reunion: Northerners and the South, 1865–1900* (Chapel Hill: University of North Carolina Press, 1993), p. 25.

105. H. Ford Douglass, cited in Richard Yarborough, "Race, Violence and Manhood: The Masculine Ideal in Frederick Douglass's 'The Heroic Slave,'" in *Frederick Douglass: New Literary and Historical Essays*, edited by Eric Sundquist (New York: Cambridge University Press, 1990), p. 169.

106. Frederick Douglass, *Narrative of the Life of Frederick Douglass, an American Slave* [1845] (New York: New American Library, 1968), p. 117.

107. Frederick Douglass, *My Bondage and My Freedom*, p. 247; *Narrative of the Life of Frederick Douglass*, p. 105. "Self-Made Men," in Frederick Douglass papers, Library of Congress, vol. 29, microform reel 18; cited also in Rafia Zafar, "Franklinian Douglass: The Afro-American as Representative Man," in *Frederick Douglass*, Eric Sundquist, ed., p. 113.

108. Thomas Wentworth Higginson wrote, in a volume of eulogies of Harvard's fallen sons, "there is no class of men in this republic from whom the response of patriotism comes more promptly and surely than from its most highly educated class." See George Frederickson, *The Inner Civil War*, pp. 156, 157.

109. Cited in Jon Cullen, "'I's a Man Now': Gender and African American Men," in Clinton and Silber, eds., *Divided Houses*, p. 85.

110. Douglass, cited in Lee Ann Whites, "The Civil War as a Crisis in Gender," in Clinton and Silber, eds., *Divided Houses*, p. 11. Two slaves are cited in Cullen, pp. 85, 91. Albery A. Whitman, *Not a Man, and Yet a Man* (Springfield, Ohio: Republic, 1877), p. 202.

111. Cited in Taylor, *Cavalier and Yankee*, p. 334. A century and a half before black supremacist professor Leonard Jeffries popularized these ideas, Yancey was suggesting that Southern *whites* represented the "sun people," while northern whites were the "ice people."

112. Memminger, cited in Eugene Genovese, *The World the Slaveowners Made* (New York: Vintage, 1969), p. 195. Huntley, cited in William R. Taylor, *Cavalier and Yankee: The Old South and the American National Character* (New York: George Braziller, 1961), p. 97. W. J. Cash, *The Mind of the South* (New York: Vintage, 1960), p. ix.

    Of course, such an idealized vision also had its contemporary detractors. Whitelaw Reid, a northern journalist who toured the South in 1865, found the Confederates less than adequate as soldiers, concerned primarily with social pretensions, "with feasting and dancing, and love making, with music improvised from the ball room," these ditzy socialites had "dashed into revolution as they would into a waltz"—impetuous, even feminine, in their overly emotional approach to war. Reid is cited in Nina Silber, "Intemperate Men, Spiteful Women, and Jefferson Davis" in Clinton and Silber, eds., *Divided Houses*, p. 286. Silber notes that dozens of songs, poems, cartoons, and newspaper accounts revealed Davis in women's clothes—a "feminized and feckless figure, who, in his ignoble flight, affirmed the southern system's violation of appropriate gender standards" (p. 284).

113. Genovese, *The World the Slaveholders Made*, p. 158. It was the market, not human nature, that created the Hobbesian war of each against all, Fitzhugh argued, for it "places all mankind in antagonistic positions and puts all society at war." George Fitzhugh, *Sociology for the South; or, The Failure of Free Society* (Richmond, 1854), p. 23. Even marriage had been corrupted, reduced to a "mere civil contract, entered into with no more thought, ceremony, or solemnity than the bargain for a horse." Ibid., pp. 194–195. The conservative Southern critique of the marketplace would resurface as part of the Populist platform half a decade later (see below, chapter 4).

114. William R. Taylor, *Cavalier and Yankee: The Old South and American National Character* (New York: George Braziller, 1961), pp. 48, 334.

115. Hale, cited in Taylor, *Cavalier and Yankee*, p. 133. Over half a century later, in her epic novel *Gone With the Wind*, Margaret Mitchell used this radical division between the competitive aggressive capitalist North and the lazy indolent Southern gentry to emasculate Ashley Wilkes, who, she wrote, came from "a line of men who used their leisure for thinking, not doing, for spinning brightly colored dreams that had in them no touch of reality."

116. "Jeff in Petticoats" is reprinted in Irwin Silber, ed., *Songs of the Civil War* (New York, 1960), p. 345. See Nina Silber, *The Romance of Reunion*, for a superb discussion of this event.

117. George Frederickson, *The Inner Civil War*, p. 183.

118. On the crisis see Peter Filene, *His/Her Self: Sex Roles in Victorian America* (Baltimore: The Johns Hopkins University Press, 1986), p. 78. See also John Higham, "The Reorientation of American Culture in the 1890s," in *The Origins of Modern Consciousness*, edited by John Weiss (Detroit: Wayne State University Press, 1965), for a classic historical statement of the problem and the variety of responses. Art historian David Lubin writes that "the emotional atrocities and guilts of war, the insecurity of the social Darwinist open market, and the ever-darkening cloud of feminism" all converged to create this crisis. David Lubin, *Acts of Portrayal* (New Haven: Yale University Press, 1985), p. 20.

119. Mark Twain, *The Adventures of Tom Sawyer*, p. 65.

CHAPTER 3: Men at Work

1. Madison C. Peters, *The Strenuous Career; or, Short Steps to Success* (Chicago: Laird and Lee, 1908), p. 22; Orison Swett Marden, *Power of Personality* [1899] (New York: Thomas Y. Crowell, 1906), p. 7.

2. C. Wright Mills, *White Collar* (New York: Oxford University Press, 1953), p. 63. Bruce Laurie, *Artisans into Workers*, p. 16.

3. Richard Edwards, *Contested Terrain: The Transformation of the Workplace in the Twentieth Century* (New York: Basic Books, 1979), pp. 23–28. Increasing rates of consolidation of ownership and the emergence of monopolies and trusts at the end of the century propelled these shifts in scale even further. Between 1898 and 1902 between one-fourth and one-third of all manufacturing capital stock of the nation underwent consolidation. See Edwards, p. 44.

4. Laurie, *Artisans into Workers*, p. 115. Rapid urbanization was also facilitated by the completion of the five transcontinental railroads, which linked eastern manufacturers with western markets.

5. Cited in Kett, *Rites of Passage*, p. 145.

6. H. L. Arnold and L. F. Faurote, *Ford Methods and the Ford Shops* (New York: Engineering Company Magazine, 1915), p. 328. Daniel Rodgers, *The Work Ethic in Industrial America, 1850–1920* (Chicago: University of Chicago Press, 1974), pp. 166–167.

7. Eliot, cited in Rodgers, *The Work Ethic*, p. 33; Greeley, cited in James F. Willard, *Union Colony at Greeley* (Denver: W. F. Robinson Printing Co., 1918), p. 1; Anthony Ludovici, "Women's Encroachment on Man's Domain," *Current History* 27, October 1927, pp. 21–22. The mechanic is cited in Kim Voss, *The Making of American Exceptionalism*, 1993, p. 82. Workers referred to these idealized early nineteenth-century Heroic Artisans as symbols by which to construct their resistance to proletarianization. And their efforts were partially successful, since Fordism and Taylorism were replaced by "human relations" management schemes in the 1930s.

8. Cited in William Leach, *Land of Desire: Merchants, Power and the Rise of a New American Culture* (New York: Pantheon, 1993), p. 161.

9. Henry Adams, *The Education of Henry Adams* (New York: Modern Library, 1931), pp. 247, 241. Being an investment is simultaneously about being "reduced" to a commodity and about being *valued* as such a commodity, so it carried a double valence for many observers.

10. James Platt, *Business* (New York. G. P. Putnam's Sons, 1889), p. vii. Rev. Russell Conwell, *Acres of Diamonds* (New York: Harper and Row, 1943), pp. 18, 21. Conwell was critical of inherited wealth; a rich father and mother often raise their son to be a "weak, little, lily-fingered sort of boy" (p. 32).

11. Melvin Adelman, *A Sporting Time: New York City and the Rise of Modern Athletics, 1820–1870* (Champaign: University of Illinois Press, 1986), p. 21; Thomas Cochran and William Miller, *The Age of Enterprise* (New York: Harper and Row, 1961), p. 230; George Frank Lydston, *Diseases of Society and Degeneracy (The Vice and Crime Problem)* (Philadelphia: Lippincott, 1904); Ronald Takaki, *Strangers from a Different Shore: A History of Asian Americans* (New York: Viking, 1989); Homer Lea, *The Valor of Ignorance* (New York: Harpers, 1909), p. 343.

12. James R. Grossman, *Land of Hope: Chicago, Black Southerners and the Great Migration* (Chicago: University of Chicago Press, 1989). See also Stanley Coben, *Rebellion Against Victorianism: The Impetus for Cultural Change in 1920s America* (New York: Oxford University Press, 1991), p. 72.

13. These laws segregated blacks in public spaces—buses, theaters, waiting rooms, schools, housing, hospitals, prisons, parks, amusements, toilets, restaurants, and drinking fountains. These laws were upheld by the Supreme Court in *Plessy* v. *Ferguson* in 1896, which declared constitutional facilities that were "separate but equal."

14. Cited in Grossman, *Land of Hope*, p. 167; cited in Laurie, *Artisans into Workers*, p. 158. Angela Davis argues that adding castration of black men for alleged sex crimes served to legitimate ideologically a largely economic process. White semiskilled workers feared the influx of low-paid black workers into the labor force and lynched them as a way of reducing the competition and terrorizing others into avoiding direct competition. But this led to sufficient public outcry against the practice. Alleging sex crimes, especially black men raping white women, legitimated the practice by playing on racialized fears of black male sexuality. The public outcries against lynching ceased. See Angela Davis, *Women, Race and Class* (New York: Random House, 1981).

15. See, among other sources, Cornelia Meigs, *What Makes a College? A History of Bryn Mawr* (New York: Macmillan, 1956), and Arthur Cole, *A Hundred Years of Mount Holyoke College: The Evolution of an Educational Ideal* (New Haven: Yale University Press, 1940). Holyoke was founded in 1837 as the Mount Holyoke Female Seminary and was changed into a full-fledged college by the 1880s.

16. Steven Seidman, *Romantic Longings: Love in America, 1830–1980*. (New York: Routledge, 1991), p. 68.

17. See Billington, 1967, p. 78; Daphne Spain, *Gendered Spaces* (Chapel Hill: University of North Carolina Press, 1992), p. 201. Some occupations were more amenable to gender transformation than others. For example, some occupations became feminized. In 1870 women composed 2 percent of all bookkeepers, cashiers, and accountants, 3 percent of office

clerks, 4 percent of all stenographers and typists, 20 percent of all librarians. Thirty years later women accounted for 29 percent of bookkeepers, 7 percent of office clerks, and 77 percent of stenographers and typists; by 1935 women composed 52 percent of bookkeepers, cashiers, and accountants, 35 percent of office clerks, over 90 percent of librarians, and fully 95 percent of stenographers and typists. See Barbara Reskin and Patricia Roos, *Job Queues, Gender Queues* (Philadelphia: Temple University Press, 1991), p. 11; and Stanley Coben, *Rebellion Against Victorianism*, p. 101. At the same time, the number of women in manufacturing fell significantly.

18. John Andrews and W.D.P. Bliss, *A History of Women in Trade Unions*, vol. 10 of *Report on Conditions of Woman and Child Earners in the United States*, S.Doc. 645, 61st Cong., 2nd sess. (Washington, D.C.: U.S. GPO, 1911), p. 48. See also Angel Kwolek-Folland, *Engendering Business: Men and Women in the Corporate Office, 1870–1930* (Baltimore: The Johns Hopkins University Press, 1994), pp. 4, 30.

19. Frederick Jackson Turner, *The Frontier in American History* [1893] (New York: Holt, Rinehart and Winston, 1947), p. 32. Turner often slept in a tent in his Cambridge backyard, explaining that he needed to get away from the city sometimes.

20. Here was a "democracy born of free land, strong in selfishness and individualism, intolerant of administrative experience and education, and pressing individual liberty beyond its proper bounds," Turner wrote. "The men of the 'Western World' turned their backs upon the Atlantic Ocean, and with a grim energy and self-reliance began to build up a society free from the dominance of ancient forms." Turner, *The Frontier*, pp. 32, 253; see also pp. 4, 23, 207. On Adams's germ theory, see also Daniel Patrick Moynihan, *Pandaemonium* (New York: Oxford University Press, 1993), p. 13.

21. Turner, *The Frontier*, p. 169; Horace Porter, "The Philosophy of Courage," *Century Illustrated Monthly Magazine* 36, May–October 1888, p. 253.

22. Hamlin Garland, *Jason Edwards, An Average Man* (Boston: Arena Publishing, 1892), p. v. In an 1896 speech Turner claimed:

> Americans had a safety valve for social danger, a bank account on which they might continually draw to meet losses. . . . No grave social problem could exist while the wilderness . . . opened wide its portals to all who were oppressed, to all who with strong arms and stout heart desired to hew out a home and a career for themselves. Here was an opportunity for social development continually to begin over again, wherever society gave signs of breaking into classes. Here was a magic fountain of youth in which America continually bathed and was rejuvenated. (Turner, cited in Smith, 1950, p. 297)

23. Cited in R. W. B. Lewis, *The American Adam* (Chicago: University of Chicago Press, 1957), p. 168.

24. Cited in Donald Worster, *Under Western Skies: Nature and History in the American West* (New York: Oxford University Press, 1992). Frank Norris lamented the disappearance of the frontier and its replacement with a consumer theme park in several novels as well as his essay, "The Frontier Gone at Last" (1902). Now, "only the imitation cowboys, the college bred fellows who 'go out on a ranch' carry the revolver or wear the concho. The frontier has become conscious of itself, acts the part of the Eastern visitor." To Norris this self-consciousness was a sign of "decadence" and "the passing of an epoch."

25. Cities had become the place to prove manhood. Albert Shaw observed that "New York now calls more strongly to the ambitious young men of the West and South than Chicago or the other Western centers call to the ambitious young men of the East. In short, the westward pioneering and developing trend of our American population is at an end." Albert Shaw, *The Outlook for the Average Man* (New York: Macmillan Company, 1907), p. 115.

26. Exclusion of nonwhites and women was linked to the resurrection of the Heroic Artisan as a white native-born man. "It is impossible to deal intelligently and thoroughly with the labor question without dealing with the immigration question," noted a spokesman for the American Iron and Steel Association in 1886. Cited in John Higham, *Strangers in the Land: Patterns of American Nativism, 1860–1925* (New York: Athenaeum, 1971), p. 51.

27. Cited in Richard Hofstadter, *Social Darwinism in America* (Boston: Beacon Press, 1955), p. 51. Social Darwinism "naturalized white male power by linking male dominance and white supremacy to human evolutionary development," as Gail Bederman argues. See Gail Bederman, "'Civilization,' The Decline of Middle-Class Manliness, and Ida B. Wells Antilynching Campaign (1892–4)," *Radical History Review* 52, Winter 1991. Most social Darwinists conveniently ignored the intent of Darwin's explication of the survival of the fittest—that he was explaining the survival of specific *species* that were able to adapt to changing conditions, not the survival of individual *members* of any particular species that adapted "better" than other members.

28. Charles Zueblin, *Democracy and the Overman* (New York: B. W. Huebsch, 1910). Zueblin warns that "[d]emocracy must accept the principle of the survival of the fittest, but see in the Anglo-Saxon and the Overman the worthy beneficiaries of opportunity. A superior race and civilization will follow the diffusion of opportunity, denied by its possessors to women and workmen, the children of the poor, the average citizen, and the people of color. The survival of the fittest may, by direction, become the survival of the best. Mastery by service is the salvation of men and of man" (pp. 60–61).

29. And he worried that they may not be up to the effort.

> In this ruthless struggle for existence carried on by human society, those who are weaker physically, intellectually, or morally must in the end yield to the stronger. . . . If, then, the black man cannot successfully compete with the white man, he is fated to be the victim of that natural selection which is constantly operating under our eyes in spite of everything, and he must eventually go under, in the more or less distant future.

Clemenceau is cited in George Frederickson, *The Inner Civil War: Northern Intellectuals and the Crisis of the Union* [1965] (Champaign: University of Illinois Press, 1993), pp. 192–193.

30. Eric Lott, *Love and Theft: Blackface Minstrelsy and the American Working Class* (New York: Oxford University Press, 1993), p. 122.

31. Lathrop Stoddard, *The Rising Tide of Color* (New York: Scribners, 1920), pp. 297–298. Madison Grant, *The Passing of the Great Race; or, the Racial Basis of European History* (New York: Scribners, 1916), pp. 68, 81; Homer Lea, *The Day of the Saxon* (New York: Harper Bros., 1912), pp. 234, 71; see also Homer Lea, *The Valor of Ignorance* (New York: Harper Bros., 1909).

32. St. Louis physician cited in John S. Haller, *Outcasts from Evolution: Scientific Attitudes of Racial Inferiority, 1859–1900* (Urbana: University of Illinois Press, 1971), p. 44; see also p. 117; anatomist cited in Stephen Jay Gould, *The Mismeasure of Man* (New York: Norton, 1981), p. 103. See also Nathaniel Shaler, "European Peasants as Immigrants," *Atlantic Monthly* 71, May 1893, who wrote that the "Negro has little or no more place in the body politic than he has in the social system." Other social scientists joined in, using their emerging field to give a scientific gloss on racialist doctrine. The white race, wrote anthropologist Josiah Nott in 1886, "is deteriorated by every drop of black blood infiltrated into it." (See "The Negro Race," *Anthropological Review* 4, July 1886, p. 111). And famed sociologist Edward Ross warned that the further influx of Asian immigrants would lead to the extinction of "true Americans." (He is cited in Stanley Coben, *Rebellion Against Victorianism*, p. 40).

33. Anatomist, cited in Stephen Jay Gould, *Mismeasure of Man*, p. 103.

34. Donnelly, cited in Ronald Takaki, *Strangers from a Different Shore*, p. 249. Gompers is cited in Alexander Saxton, *The Indispensable Enemy: Labor and the Anti-Chinese Movement in California* (Berkeley: University of California Press, 1971), p. 276; Agassiz, cited in Stephen Jay Gould, *The Mismeasure of Man*, p. 49; editor, cited in Richard Slotkin, *The Fatal Environment*, p. 185. William Bennett, editor of the *New York Herald*, further sexualized the experienced, suggesting that what began as rape might end up a happy marriage. "Like the Sabine virgins," he wrote, "she will soon learn to love her ravisher" (cited in Slotkin, p. 185).

Fears of diluting the purity of the white race with effeminate foreign blood permeated other social reform movements which did not have gender as their principle focus. For example, the eugenics movement fused racism, sexism, and scientific rationalization when they warned that the decreasing fertility rate among college-educated women and the increasing number of children born to immigrants was leading to "race suicide." Women were urged to leave the public sphere and return to the home to perform their patriotic duty and bear American children. From the 1870s through the 1920s, college-educated women were four times more likely to not marry and bear children than non-college-educated women—a statistic that fueled eugenicist notions that the "wrong" people were reproducing. Were these trends to continue, warned Harvard professor Edward Clarke in his influential *Sex in Education* (1873), "it requires no prophet to foretell that the wives who are to be mothers in our republic must be drawn from transatlantic homes." "The duty of maternity," statistician Frederick Hoffman wrote, "is one which no normally married woman can shirk" either physically or morally.

At the same time, eugenicists attempted to control the birthrate among non-native-born immigrant populations, demanding sterilization of those women who sought medical care or obstetric delivery of babies. Indiana enacted the first sterilization law in 1907; by 1915 twelve states had passed such measures. The National Conference on Race Betterment, which began in 1914, organized such proposals on a national scale. See Edward C. Clarke, *Sex in Education; or, A Fair Chance for the Girls* (Boston: James Osgood, 1873), p. 152. Frederick Hoffman, "The Decline of the Birth Rate," in *North American Review* 189, May 1909, p. 681. See also Richard Hofstadter, *Social Darwinism in America*, p. 162.

35. See Alexander Saxton, *The Indispensable Enemy*, pp. 272, 172. English, cited in John Haller, *Outcasts from Evolution*, p. 51; Californian John Miller believed dire consequences would result from intermarriage with Chinese immigrants. "Were the Chinese to amalgamate at all with our people, it would be the lowest, most vile and degraded of our race, and the result of the amalgamation would be a hybrid of the most despicable, a mongrel of the most detestable that has ever afflicted the earth"; cited in Ronald Takaki, *Strangers from a Different Shore*, p. 101.

36. Joseph Alfred Conwell, *Manhood's Morning; or, "Go It While You're Young": A Book for Young Men Between 14 and 28 Years of Age* (Vineland, N.J.: Hominus, 1896), p. 148. Such policies, advised Weir, fueled the growing labor movement's increasing militancy, as these "degenerate foreigners . . . are ready for any form of lawlessness and riot." James Weir, "The Methods of the Rioting Strikers as Evidence of Degeneration," in *Century* 48, October 1894, pp. 954, 953.

37. Cited in Alexander Saxton, *The Indispensable Enemy*, p. 59.
38. Editor cited in Richard Slotkin, *The Fatal Environment*, p. 469.
39. The document is printed in John C. Lester and David L. Wilson, *The Ku Klux Klan* [1884] (New York: Neale, 1905), p. 155.
40. *Prescript* is cited in John C. Lester and Daniel Wilson, *Ku Klux Klan* [1884] (New York: Neale Publishing, 1905), p. 155. The full prayer offered by the Klokard goes as follows:

> God give us Men! The invisible Empire demand strong
> Mind, great hearts, true faith and ready hands.
> Men who possess opinions and a will
> Men who have HONOR and men who will NOT Lie
> God give us men!
> Men who serve not for selfish bounty
> But real men, courageous, who flinch not at duty
> Men of dependable character; men of sterling worth;
> Then wrongs will be redressed, and right will rule the earth;
> God give us Men!

> The entire initiation ritual incorporates issues of nativism and manhood. When the "alien" approaches the Klavern for his "naturalization" (initiation), he is commanded by the Kladd to "Follow me and be a man." Cited in Joe Dubbert, *A Man's Place*, p. 68.

41. The APA and the ASRF both linked black emancipation to the International Jewish Conspiracy. Griffith depicted Reconstruction as "an orgy of looting and rape, loosed in a world of gallantry and grace by greedy invaders and bewildered ex-slaves: a saturnalia subdued only by the Christian Knights of the Klan, whose fiery crosses betoken the end of nightmare and the dawn of a new day." Leslie Fiedler, *What Was Literature: Class, Culture and Mass Society* (New York: Simon and Schuster, 1982), p. 193.
42. George Lydston, *Diseases of Society and Degeneracy*, p. 424. "Executed, they would be forgotten; unsexed and free, they would be a constant warning and ever-present admonition to others of their race," he wrote. South Carolina Senator Ben Tillman argued before Congress in 1907 that due process for black rapists circumvented men's manly feelings of revenge:

> [T]he white women of the South are in a state of siege. . . . Some lurking demon who has watched for the opportunity seizes her; she is choked or beaten into insensibility and ravished, her body prostituted, her purity destroyed, her chastity taken from her. . . . Shall men . . . demand for [the demon] the right to have a fair trial and be punished in the regular course of justice? So far as I am concerned he has put himself outside the pale of the

law, human and divine. . . . Civilization peels off us . . . and we revert to the . . . impulses . . . to kill! kill! kill!

An editorial in the *World* in December 1874, "A Southern Curse in a Northern Home," notes a rape of a white child by a black man as the consequences of "ghoul-like and emasculating influences" of philanthropic government, a turn-of-the-century precursor to George Bush's manipulation of Willie Horton's parole by Governor Dukakis in the 1988 presidential election. Salvation, the editorial continues, will come only when northern white men emulate their southern brethren and act on the intense longing for revenge "which every masculine man . . . must feel." Manhood can only be vindicated by a lynching—"one hour of Kansas with its hasty ropes"—and by this example, "the ruling race of Europe, of America, and of the world" will reassert itself over "all the ignorant and long brutalized races" around the world. Cited in Richard Slotkin, *The Fatal Environment*, p. 343.

43. California State Historical Library, San Francisco, MS. 2334.

44. Supporters of suffrage had claimed that women's natural virtue would purify the corrupt pit that politics had become, to which an editorial in the first issue (1890) of the journal of the Massachusetts Association Opposed to the Extension of Suffrage to Women gave this response:

> The belief that women will impart their tenderness and purity to politics is surely somewhat simple. They are tender and pure because their sphere has hitherto been the home, which is the abode of tenderness and purity. Thrown into the arena of political strife, the "angels," if experience may be trusted, instead of imparting an angelic character to the male combatants, would be in danger of losing it themselves. (Schlesinger Library, microfilm collection)

See also O. B. Frothingham, *Woman Suffrage: Unnatural and Inexpedient* (Boston, 1894), p. 5. For more about antifeminism as a strategy of redefining masculinity, see my "Men's Responses to Feminism at the Turn of the Century," in *Gender & Society* 1(3), 1987, and my introduction to *Against the Tide*.

45. Edward Clarke, *Sex in Education*, p. 128. Clarke's work was enormously influential, reprinted seventeen times between 1873 and 1886 alone, going through twenty-six editions by 1900, and also spurring several tracts and treatises in response; see David Tyack and Elisabeth Hansot, *Learning Together: A History of Coeducation in American Public Schools* (New Haven: Yale University Press, 1990), p. 151.

46. Zueblin, *Democracy and the Overman*, p. 96. Bok is cited in Vincent Vinikas, *Soft Soap, Hard Sell: American Hygiene in an Age of Advertisement* (Ames: Iowa State University Press, 1992), p. 52. Another editorialist wrote that

Women were not intended to work—not because work is ignoble, but because it is as disastrous to the beauty of a woman as is friction to the bloom and softness of a flower. She is to be kept from the workshop world, where innocence is snatched with rude hands, and softness is blistered into unsightliness. (cited in Daniel Rodgers, *The Work Ethic*, p. 208)

47. Cited in Richard Slotkin, *The Fatal Environment*, p. 237.
48. Angel Kwolek-Folland, *Engendering Business*, pp. 167, 168.
49. Harry Thurston Peck, "The Woman of To-Day and To-Morrow," in *Cosmopolitan* 27, June 1899, p. 154. Several did try—and eventually failed; e.g., *Blue Book* was launched in 1904 but was abandoned in the 1930s.
50. Frederick Douglass, introduction to *The Reason Why the Colored American Is Not in the World's Columbian Exposition*, Ida B. Wells, ed. (Chicago, 1892), p. 12. My account here draws from Gail Bed'erman's impressive essay, " 'Civilization. . . .'"
51. On 1850s gay male subculture, see Christine Stansell, *City of Women: Sex and Class in New York, 1789–1860* (New York: Knopf, 1986), pp. 90–92. George Lydston, *Diseases of Society*, p. 319; Jonathan Ned Katz, *Gay American History* (New York: Crowell, 1976) and *Gay/Lesbian Almanac* (New York: Harper and Row, 1983); George Chauncey, "Christian Brotherhood or Sexual Perversion? Homosexual Identities and the Construction of Sexual Boundaries in the World War I Era," *Journal of Social History* 19, 1985, p. 190. Gay capitals included New York, Boston, Washington, St. Louis, San Francisco, Milwaukee, New Orleans, and Philadelphia.
52. George Chauncey, *Gay New York: Gender, Urban Culture, and the Making of the Gay Male World, 1890–1940* (New York: Basic Books, 1994), pp. 133, 355.
53. *New York Medical Journal*, 1884, cited in Jonathan Ned Katz, *Gay/Lesbian Almanac*, p. 119; George Lydston, cited in Katz, p. 213; sailor cited in George Chauncey, "Christian Brotherhood . . . ," p. 192, and George Chauncey, *Gay New York*, p. 55. On psychiatric diagnosis see Elizabeth Lunbeck, *The Psychiatric Persuasion*, p. 237. See also M. W. Peck, "The Sex Life of College Men," *Journal of Nervous and Mental Disease* 62, 1925.
54. George Chauncey, *Gay New York*, p. 56.
55. Ibid., p. 57.
56. Ibid., p. 117. On the term "sissy" see Peter Stearns, *American Cool* (New York: New York University Press, 1994), p. 33.
57. Cited in George Chauncey, *Gay New York*, p. 179. This sentiment was echoed in the attacks on feminists as being lesbian. Dr. William Lee Howard wrote in 1900 that "the female possessed of masculine ideas of independence; the viragint who would sit in the public highways and lift up her pseudo-virile voice, proclaiming her sole right to decide questions

of war or religion, or the value of celibacy and the curse of women's impurity, and that disgusting anti-social being, the female sexual pervert, are simply different degrees of the same class—degenerates"; ibid., p. 122.

58. I don't intend to romanticize the life on the bum but merely suggest that outside the tightly drawn boundaries of marketplace masculinity, men have often found a surprising range of emotional resources they didn't know they had. See, e.g., Roger Bruns, *The Damndest Radical* (Urbana: University of Illinois Press, 1988), on Ben Reitman. For contemporary discussions see Timothy Nonn, "Tenderloin Men: Masculinities in an Urban Apocalypse" (unpublished paper, Graduate Theological Union, 1993); "Hitting Bottom: Homelessness, Poverty and Masculinity," in *Men's Lives*, M. Kimmel and M. Messner, eds. 3rd ed. (New York: Macmillan, 1994); and also Jeff McConnell, "Friendship Networks Among Homeless Men" (unpublished paper, Institute for Social Analysis, SUNY at Stony Brook).

59. Even before the nineteenth century, Charles Brockden Brown expressed uneasiness about the position of women and the relations between women and men. His first novel, *Alcuin* (1798), provided a sustained argument for women's rights in the form of a dialogue between a young man and an elderly woman, who instructs him about the position of women until he is forced to admit that his views of women were based on illogical prejudice and not reason. His later novels, especially *Edgar Huntly* and *Arthur Mervyn*, link this profeminist position to a critique of marketplace manhood. Mervyn's world is one of "failed fathers and ruined families," and Huntly is portrayed as a pathetic young man, so consumed with anxiety about his place in the competitive marketplace that he becomes, as Brown put it, "a formidable engine of destruction"—his gender insecurity cast as the signal cause of a propensity for violence. See also Fritz Fleischmann, *A Right View of the Subject: Feminism in the Works of Charles Brockden Brown and John Neal* (Erlangen: Palm and Enke, 1983); see also Michael S. Kimmel and Thomas E. Mosmiller, *Against the Tide: Pro-Feminist Men in the United States, 1776–1990, A Documentary History* (Boston: Beacon, 1992).

I would not go so far as to claim, in some grand linear causal way, that economic crises always produce crises of masculinity, but it does seem plausible that such economic shocks lead to a questioning of the values that underlie the system, which include but are not limited to constructions of masculinity.

60. Henry Ward Beecher, *Twelve Lectures to Young Men* (New York: Appleton, 1888), p. 8; Albert Shaw, *The Outlook for the Average Man* (New York: Macmillan, 1907), p. 26; Bouck White, *The Book of Daniel Drew* (New York: Doubleday, 1910), p. 144.

61. See Orison Swett Marden, *Pushing to the Front* (New York: Thomas Y. Crowell, 1894); *Success* (Boston: W. A. Wile, 1897), *The Secrets of Achievement* (New York: Thomas Y. Crowell, 1898), *Character, The Greatest Thing in the World* (New York: Thomas Y. Crowell, 1899), *The Power of Personality* [1899] (New York: Thomas Y. Crowell, 1906), *The Young Man Entering Business* (New York: Thomas Y. Crowell, 1903), *Optimistic Life* (New York: Thomas Y. Crowell, 1907), *He Who Can Thinks He Can* (New York: Thomas Y. Crowell, 1908), *The Crime of Silence* (New York: Physical Culture Publishing, 1915), *How to Get What You Want* (New York: Thomas Y. Crowell, 1917), *Prosperity* (New York: Success Magazine, 1922). H. L. Mencken, who despised Marden as a purveyor of homilies to the "booboisie," noted this success sarcastically, calling Marden "the most popular of American authors in Europe, and by immense odds" and estimated that twenty million copies of his books had been sold, including three million in twenty-five languages other than English. Mencken, cited in Gail Parker, *The Mind Cure in New England* (Hanover: University Press of New England, 1973), pp. 29–30.

62. Orison Swett Marden, *The Optimistic Life* (New York: Thomas Y. Crowell, 1907), p. 228. Marden, *Pushing to the Front* (New York: Thomas Y. Crowell, 1894), pp. 109, 105, 69.

63. Cited in Cindy Aron, *Ladies and Gentlemen of the Civil Service: Middle-Class Workers in Victorian America, 1840–1870* (New York: Oxford University Press, 1987), p. 188.

64. These paeans to salesmanship are culled from Angel Kwolek-Folland's fascinating study *Engendering Business*, pp. 87, 91, 173. The phrase "a nation of salesmen" is from Earl Shorris's book *A Nation of Salesmen* (New York: Norton, 1994). Of course, the last phrase about smiles and shines is from Arthur Miller's *Death of a Salesman*, to which I will turn in a later chapter.

65. Max Weber, *The Protestant Ethic and the Spirit of Capitalism* [1904] (New York: Scribners, 1970), pp. 41, 53.

66. Max Weber, *The Protestant Ethic*, pp. 181, 182.

67. Thorstein Veblen, *The Theory of the Leisure Class* [1899] (New York: New American Library, 1953). Veblen was also a fierce critic of gender relations. He argued that men saw women as mere adornments or, more accurately, as the beautiful mannequins whom they could adorn with useless and hence expensive baubles. Women were forced to dress, Veblen argued, as a way to "testify to the wearer's exemption from or incapacity for all vulgarly productive employment"—anything to show that "she does not occupy herself with anything that is gainful or is of substantial use." See also Thorstein Veblen, "The Barbarian Status of Woman," *American Journal of Sociology* 4, January 1899.

Other critics also scalded the upper class. Vernon Parrington described capitalist businessmen as a collection of predatory, unscrupulous creatures—those "primitive souls, ruthless, predatory, capable, single-minded men; rogues and rascals, . . . never hindered by petty scruples, never given to puling or whining—the raw material of a race of capitalist buccaneers"; cited in Lewis Coser, *Masters of Sociological Thought* (New York: Harcourt, Brace, 1967), p. 293.

68. Hitchcock, cited in Harvey Green, *Fit for America* (New York: Pantheon, 1986), p. 15; Homer Lea, *The Valor of Ignorance* (New York: Harper Bros., 1909), p. 58, 9.

69. Andrew Carnegie, cited in John Cawelti, *Apostles of the Self-Made Man* (Chicago: University of Chicago Press, 1965), p. 194.

70. James Weir, "The Methods of the Rioting Striker as Evidence of Degeneration," *Century* 48, October 1894, pp. 952–953.

71. James is cited in Richard Slotkin, *Gunfighter Nation: The Myth of the Frontier in Twentieth-Century America* (New York: Athenaeum, 1992), p. 153.

72. Letter to *Miner's Magazine* 6(74), 24 November 1904; letter to *Boston Labor Leader*, 19 February 1887; both cited in Andrew Neather, "'The Dignity and Grandeur of Perfect Manhood': American Workingmen's Gender and the Ideology of Organized Labor, 1885–1914," unpublished MS, Duke University, Department of History, 1992.

73. Cited in Christopher Lasch, *The True and Only Heaven*, p. 213. See also Larry Glickman, "A Living Wage: Political Economy, Gender and Consumerism in American Culture, 1880–1925" (Ph.D. diss., U. C. Berkeley, 1992), and James Davis, *The Iron Puddler: My Life in the Rolling Mills and What Came of It* (Indianapolis, 1922).

74. Cited in William Wyckoff, *The Workers* (New York: Scribners, 1899), pp. 111–112.

75. James Grossman, *Land of Hope*, p. 218; David Roediger, *The Wages of Whiteness: Race and the Making of the American Working Class* (New York: Verso, 1991); *Workingman's Advocate*, Chicago, January 1871, cited in Gerald Grob, *Workers and Utopia: A Study of Ideological Conflict in the American Labor Movement, 1865–1900* (Chicago: Quadrangle, 1969), p. 24.

76. Leon Fink, *Workingman's Democracy: The Knights of Labor and American Politics* (Urbana: University of Illinois Press, 1983), p. 23. See also Carroll Wright, "An Historical Sketch of the Knights of Labor," *Quarterly Journal of Economics* 1, 1887, pp. 137–168; Kim Voss, 1992; Bruce Laurie, *Artisans into Workers*, esp. chap. 4; Gerald Grob, *Workers and Utopia*; and Susan Levine, "Labor's True Woman: Domesticity and Equal Rights in the Knights of Labor," *Journal of American History* 70(2), 1983, pp. 330–331 and passim.

77. When confronted by a member who advocated excluding women from meetings, Powderly retorted, "I regret you entertain so poor an opinion of your wife, as to say of her that you would not allow her to mix among the lot of men who are sworn to defend her life, interest and reputation." What's more, Powderly answered, "She does not unsex herself by going where her father, brother, or lover goes in the evening. If the assembly is a bad place for a woman to go, it is a bad place for a man to go"; cited in Susan Levine, "Labor's True Woman," p. 331.

78. Steven Hahn, *The Roots of Southern Populism: Yeomen Farmers and the Transformation of the Georgia Upcountry, 1850–1890* (New York: Oxford University Press, 1983), p. 168. Corn prices, e.g., fell from 66¢ per bushel in 1866 to 31¢ in 1878 and by 1889 to as low as 10¢. Corn was often burned in place of higher-priced coal as fuel. As one farmer recalled:

> Many a time I have warmed myself by the kitchen stove in which ears were burning briskly, popping and crackling in the jolliest fashion. And if, as we sat around such a fire, watching the year's crop go up the chimney, the talk sometimes became bitter . . . who will wonder? (cited in Lawrence Goodwyn, *The Populist Moment*, New York: Oxford University Press, 1978, p. 195)

Cotton prices held firm at 11¢ per pound until 1890, when they dropped to 7.5¢ by 1892 and to less than 5¢ in 1898. Seven cents was considered the cost of production. Freight costs absorbed between one-third and one-half the price of corn, oats, and wheat. And a series of natural disasters—grasshoppers, wind, drought—exacerbated these social and economic problems. Throughout the South and Midwest, farmers were increasingly losing their farms and fields. In Kansas alone there were over eleven thousand farm foreclosures between 1889 and 1893. Aside from works by Hahn and Goodwyn, other significant works on populism include Donna Barnes, *Farmers in Rebellion: The Rise and Fall of the Southern Farmers Alliance and the People's Party in Texas* (Austin: University of Texas Press, 1984); Solon Buck, *The Agrarian Crusade: A Chronicle of the Farmer in Politics* (New Haven: Yale University Press, 1920); N. A. Dunning, *The Farmer's Alliance History and Agricultural Digest* (Washington: Alliance Publishing, 1891); John Hicks, *The Populist Revolt* (Minneapolis: University of Minnesota Press, 1931); Norman Pollack, *The Populist Response to Industrial America* (New York: Norton, 1966). Also see my " 'Disheveled Improvisation': Agrarian Resistance to Industrialization in the Late Nineteenth Century," in *Rethinking the Nineteenth Century: Contradictions and Movements*, Francisco Ramirez, ed. (Westport, Conn.: Greenwood Press, 1988).

79. *People's Party Paper*, cited in Hahn, *Roots of Southern Populism*, p. 282. See Bryan's "Speech Before the Democratic National Convention, Chicago,

1896," also known as the "Cross of Gold" speech, reprinted in *Life and Speeches of William J. Bryan*, edited by J. S. Ogilvie (New York: J. S. Ogilvie Publishing, 1896).

80. It is also evident in a less well-known work, *The Other Side* (1886), in which Martin Foran recounts the story of young Richard Arbyght (a homonym for the German word for "work"), a farm-bred boy who completes his apprenticeship as a cooper only to have the industry collapse before him. Tragedy strikes when his father is robbed and murdered by an urban rogue, who later becomes Richard's employer. In the end Richard recovers the stolen money, marries well, and supports his family by going into business for himself as a small capitalist, producing an unspecified "useful commodity."

81. "When Aunt Em came there to live she was a young, pretty wife. The sun and wind had changed her too. They had taken the sparkle from her eyes and left them a sober gray; they had taken the red from her cheek and lips, and they were gray also. She was thin and gaunt, and never smiled now. . . . Uncle Henry never laughed. He worked hard from morning till night and did not know what joy was. He was gray also, from his long beard to his rough boots, and he looked stern and solemn, and rarely spoke" (p. 2).

82. "How can I help being a humbug," the Wizard complains, "when all these people make me do things that everybody knows can't be done?" (p. 183).

83. I trust that my reading does not slight Dorothy, that protofeminist heroine whose sole desire is to return to Kansas, to her Aunt Em and Uncle Henry. Of course, Dorothy had the power to return the entire time, contained in her silver slippers, the new currency that Bryan claimed would help the farmers and workers retain their independence. I realize that there are feminist readings of *The Wizard of Oz* that stress the relationship between Dorothy and the various witches. Not only is Dorothy a feminist heroine, but the entire story has a feminist theme; it is, after all, her ambition and resolve that allows, enables, and encourages the men to undertake their quest in the first place. I trust that examining this redemptive quest for manhood by Dorothy's three friends can help to complete that picture.

84. On the Arts and Crafts Movement, see Eileen Boris, *Art and Labor: Ruskin, Morris and the Craftsman Ideal in America* (Philadelphia: Temple University Press, 1986); Althea Callen, *Women and the Arts and Crafts Movement* (New York: Pantheon, 1980); Alan Crawford, *C. R. Ashbee: Architect, Designer, and Romantic Socialist* (New Haven: Yale University Press, 1986); T. J. Jackson Lears, *No Place of Grace: Anti-modernism and the Transformation of American Culture* (New York: Pantheon, 1981); Gillian Naylor, *The Arts and Crafts Movement* (Cambridge: M.I.T. Press,

1971); Mary Ann Smith, *Gustav Stickley: The Craftsman* (Syracuse, N.Y.: Syracuse University Press, 1983); Peter Stansky, *Redesigning the World: William Morris, the 1880s, and the Arts and the Crafts* (Princeton, N.J.: Princeton University Press, 1985). See also my "Out of the Guilds and into the Streets: The Arts and Crafts Movement in England and the United States," in *Art, Ideology, and Politics*, J. Balfe and M. Wyszomirski, eds. (New York: Praeger, 1985), and "The Arts and Crafts Movement: Handmade Socialism or Elite Consumerism?" in *Contemporary Sociology* 16(3), 1987.

85. William Morris, *Selected Writings*, G.D.H. Cole, ed. (London: Nonesuch Press, 1948), p. 659. See also E. P. Thompson, *William Morris* (New York: Pantheon, 1977).

86. Eileen Boris, *Art and Labor: Ruskin, Morris and the Craftsman Ideal in America* (Philadelphia: Temple University Press, 1986), p. 165.

87. Cited in Alan Crawford, *C. R. Ashbee: Architect, Designer, and Romantic Socialist* (New Haven: Yale University Press, 1986), p. 37. For these reasons, though, Ashbee opposed women's entry into the guilds.

88. I take this phrase from the title of Ann Douglas's provocative and innovative study, *The Feminization of American Culture* (New York: Knopf, 1977).

89. Cited in Boris, *Art and Labor*, p. 76.

90. See, e.g., "Furniture for Men," *American Homes and Gardens* 1(4), October 1905.

91. "Will any one seriously contend that the North American continent should have been left forever in the hands of tribes whose sole use of their territory was to contravene the purposes of human life?" he asked; cited in Takaki, *Strangers from a Different Shore*, p. 269.

92. Lea, *The Valor of Ignorance*, p. 11.

93. Carl Schurz, "About War," in *Harper's Weekly* 42, 5 March 1898, p. 219.

94. William James, *The Varieties of the Religious Experience* (Boston, 1902). His later essay, "The Moral Equivalent of War," called for a national conscription of youth for an army to be enlisted against Nature to thereby restore youthful "manliness." Sarah Grand offered a similar critique of feminization but came to strikingly different conclusions. "Idleness and luxury are making men flabby," she wrote, so that men are beginning to "ask seriously if a great war might not help them pull themselves together." Her remedy was to make men work: "The best thing to cure men of their effeminacy would be to deprive them, all the idle and luxurious ones, of their incomes"; Sarah Grand, "The Man of the Moment," *North American Review* 158, May 1894, p. 626.

95. Interestingly, in the 1890s this militarist revival and imperial virility was accompanied by a cult of Napoleon. Three of the four best-selling magazines—*Century*, *McClure's*, and *Cosmopolitan*—ran serialized biographies

of Napoleon, who was venerated not for his tactical genius nor for his military heroism but for his "restless, gnawing hunger for undying renown"; not for his efforts to steer the course of the French Revolution and instill codified rational law into the formerly monarchical French legal system but because there was "something grand about his desire for fame." Napoleon's career had been turned into a turn-of-the-century version of *Lifestyles of the Rich and Famous*. See, e.g., William Sloane, "Life of Napoleon Bonaparte," *Century* 27, 1894; Ida Tarbell, "Napoleon Bonaparte," *McClure's* 3, 1894, and *All in the Day's Work: An Autobiography* (New York: Macmillan, 1939); and Viscount Wolsely, "The Young Napoleon," in *Cosmopolitan* 34, January 1903.

96. Cited in Peter Filene, *His/Her Self: Sex Roles in Victorian America* (Baltimore: The Johns Hopkins University Press, 1986), p. 324.

97. Lester Frank Ward, "Our Better Halves" *Forum* 6, November 1888. Charlotte Perkins Gilman called Ward "quite the greatest man I have ever known" and his essay "Our Better Halves" "the greatest single contribution to the world's thought since Evolution." Her life work was, in fact, to make his gynecocentric theory more readily accessible to all readers.

98. Lester Frank Ward, *Pure Sociology* (New York: Macmillan, 1903), p. 377; Lester Frank Ward, *Applied Sociology* (Boston: Ginn, 1906), p. 233.

99. On the rhetorics of support for feminism offered historically by profeminist men, see my introduction to *Against the Tide: Pro-Feminist Men in the United States, 1776–1990, A Documentary History*.

100. Max Eastman, *Enjoyment of Living* (New York: Harper, 1948), p. 310.

101. Floyd Dell, "Feminism for Men," *The Masses* 5(20), July 1917. The essay is reprinted in *Against the Tide*, pp. 361–364.

102. "What Do You Know About That!" *The Masses*, 1914, p. 7.

103. Dell, "Feminism for Men," in *Against the Tide*, p. 361.

104. The sexual and political contradictions of the Village bohemians has been explored by Ellen Kay Trimberger, "Feminism, Socialism and Modern Love: The Greenwich Village Radical," in *The Power of Desire*, edited by Ann Snitow, Christine Stansell, and Sharon Thompson (New York: Monthly Review Press, 1976), and Kevin White, *The First Sexual Revolution* (New York: New York University Press, 1993).

CHAPTER 4: Playing for Keeps

1. Henry James, *The Bostonians* [1885] (New York: Modern Library, 1984), p. 293.

2. This phrase comes most recently from Ann Douglas's *The Feminization of American Culture* (New York: Knopf, 1977).

3. Elliot J. Gorn, *The Manly Art: Bare-Knuckle Prize Fighting in America* (Ithaca, N.Y.: Cornell University Press, 1986), p. 192.

4. E. Anthony Rotundo, "Body and Soul: Changing Ideals of American Middle-Class Manhood, 1770–1920," *Journal of Social History* 16(4), 1983, p. 32.

5. David Riesman, *The Lonely Crowd* (New Haven: Yale University Press, 1950). On the transition from a "culture of production" to a "culture of consumption," see also Leo Lowenthal, "Twilight of the Mass Idols," in *Literature, Popular Culture and Society* (Palo Alto: Pacific Books, 1968).

6. Roberta J. Park, "Physiologists, Physicians, and Physical Education: Nineteenth-Century Biology and Exercise, Hygienic and Educative," in *Sport and Exercise Science*, J. W. Berryman and R. J. Park, eds. (Urbana: University of Illinois Press, 1992), p. 141.

7. Bernarr Macfadden, "An Open Letter to President Roosevelt," *Physical Culture*, vol. 18, 1907, p. 75. Frank Lloyd Wright, cited in Herbert Muschamp, *Man About Town: Frank Lloyd Wright in New York City* (Cambridge: M.I.T. Press, 1983), p. 13. Antiurbanism as a theme in the antimodernist critique of feminization is well discussed by T. J. Jackson Lears, *No Place of Grace: Anti-modernism and the Transformation of American Culture, 1880–1920* (New York: Pantheon, 1981).

8. Percentages of women teachers were even higher in major cities, such as New York (89%), Philadelphia (91.4%), Boston (89%), and Chicago (93.3%). See G. J. Barker-Benfield, *The Horrors of the Half-Known Life: Male Attitudes Towards Women and Sexuality in Nineteenth-Century America* (New York: Harper and Row, 1976), p. 21, and Earl Barnes, "The Feminizing of Culture," *Atlantic Monthly* 109, 1912, p. 772. Barnes writes that in half of U.S. cities in 1912, there were "virtually no men teaching."

9. The report did not specify the proper manner for having one's head punched. See Rabbi Solomon Schindler, "A Flaw in our Public School System," *Arena* 6, June 1892, p. 60; J. McKeen Cattell cited in William O'Neill, *Divorce in the Progressive Era* (New Haven: Yale University Press, 1967), p. 221. British report is mentioned in Luther Gulick, "The Alleged Feminization of Our American Boys," *American Physical Education Review* 10, September 1905, p. 214. Gulick himself played an important role in the efforts to counter this feminization as he rehabilitated and secularized the YMCA. I will discuss this further in the next chapter.

10. Alfred Cleveland, "The Predominance of Female Teachers," *Pedagogical Seminary* 12, September 1905, pp. 301, 303. A. Chadwick, "The Woman Peril," *Educational Review* 47, February 1914, pp. 115–116, 118.

11. See John Higham, *Strangers in the Land: Patterns of American Nativism, 1860–1925* (New York: Atheneum, 1970), pp. 78–79. Merwin, 1897, p. 838. O. S. Fowler, *Private Lectures on Perfect Men, Women and Children in*

Happy Families . . . (Sharon Station, N.Y.: privately printed by Mrs. O. S. Fowler, 1883), p. 5. William James argued that there is "no more contemptible type of human character than that of the nervous sentimentalist and dreamer, who spends his life in a weltering sea of sensibility and emotion, but who never does a concrete manly deed"; cited in Robert N. Bellah et al., *Habits of the Heart* (New York: Harper and Row, 1985), p. 120. See also Henry Childs Merwin, "On Being Civilized Too Much," *Atlantic Monthly* 79, June 1897.

12. Rafford Pyke, "What Men Like in Men," *Cosmopolitan* August 1902, pp. 405–406. Stillé, cited in Morris Fishbein, *A History of the American Medical Association* (Philadelphia: Saunders, 1947), pp. 82–83.

13. See George Chauncey, *Gay New York: Gender, Urban Culture and the Making of the Gay Male World, 1890–1940* (New York: Basic Books, 1994). I have discussed this in chapter 3.

14. See Kathy Peiss, "Of Makeup and Men: The Gendering of Cosmetics," paper presented at a Conference on Gender and the Material Culture, Winterthur Museum, 1989, p. 7; *Decorum* (New York, 1877), p. 320.

15. See William Leach, "Transformations in a Culture of Consumption: Women and Department Stores, 1890–1925," *Journal of American History* 71, September 1984; and also William Leach, *Land of Desire: Merchants, Power and the Rise of a New American Culture* (New York: Pantheon, 1993).

16. Orison Swett Marden, *Pushing to the Front*, p. 9; Kenneth Wayne, *Building the Young Man* (Chicago: A. C. McClurg, 1912), pp. 95–96, 167.

17. See George Chauncey, *Gay New York*, p. 80; see also Leonard Ellis, "Men Among Men: An Exploration of All Male Relationships in Victorian America," unpublished Ph.D. diss., Columbia University, 1982, passim.

18. Elizabeth Lunbeck, *The Psychiatric Persuasion: Knowledge, Gender and Power in Modern America* (Princeton, N.J.: Princeton University Press, 1994), p. 245; also p. 248. See also Ellis, "Men Among Men," pp. 127–128, and Richard Stivers, *A Hair of the Dog: Irish Drinking and American Stereotype* (University Park, Penna.: Pennsylvania State University Press, 1976).

19. Ted Ownby, *Subduing Satan: Religion, Recreation and Manhood in the Rural South, 1865–1920* (Chapel Hill: University of North Carolina Press, 1991). Such surcease could not and did not last long. Soon there would be other perceived enemies descending to the South, sent on a mission to incorporate the South into the American political economy or to reform racial segregation and achieve civil rights. But to southern men, they were coming to emasculate southern manhood, which in part explains the overtly sexualized images of civil rights workers and blacks, who would steal and defile southern womanhood. Emasculated men could not pro-

tect their womenfolk from these marauders; but a manhood animated by gendered race-rage could stop these forces in their tracks. From the Klan to George Wallace, Lester Maddox, and David Duke, demagogues have tapped white southern men's gendered rage at their emasculation by racial equality. See also Stuart A. Marks, *Southern Hunting in Black and White: Nature, History and Ritual in a Carolina Community* (Princeton, N.J.: Princeton University Press, 1991).

20. Cited in MacLean, 1994, p. 100. Cited in Barbara Franco, "The Ritualization of Male Friendship and Virtue: Nineteenth-Century Fraternal Organizations," paper presented at Winterthur Conference on The Gender of Material Culture, 9–11 November 1989, p. 8. See also Leonard Ellis, "Men Among Men," p. 168; and David Healy, *The Individual Delinquent: A Text-Book of Diagnosis and Prognosis for All Concerned in Understanding Offenders* (Boston, 1915).

21. L. Pierce Clarke, "A Psychological Study of Some Alcoholics," *Psychoanalytic Review* 6, 1919, pp. 270–271; Otto Juliusberger, "Psychology and Alcoholism," *Psychoanalytic Review* 1, 1913, p. 469; Karl Abraham, "The Psychological Relations Between Alcoholism and Sexuality," *International Journal of Psychoanalysis* 7, 1926, p. 4. See also Ellis, "Men Among Men," pp. 168–169.

22. See George Chauncey, *Gay New York*, p. 81.

23. George Ruskin Phoebus, "Civilization—Physical Culture," *Physical Culture* 3, 1900, pp. 21–22.

24. Hall, cited in Michael C. C. Adams, *The Great Adventure: Male Desire and the Coming of World War I* (Bloomington: Indiana University Press, 1990), p. 38.

25. Cited in James Whorton, "Eating to Win: Popular Concepts of Diet, Strength and Energy in the Early Twentieth Century," in *Fitness in American Culture*, Kathryn Grover, ed. (Amherst: University of Massachusetts Press, 1990), p. 111.

26. See, e.g., Harvey Green, *Fit for America: Health, Fitness, Sport and American Society* (New York: Pantheon, 1986). See also G. Carson, *Cornflake Crusade* (New York: Rinehart, 1957).

Cultural analysts have long understood that health reform was a simultaneous abandonment of hope for any larger-scale social and political transformation, as though changing the body could somehow compensate for failure to change the body social. One recent feminist historian writes that

the pursuit of personal fulfillment, well-being, and meaning through health may compensate for a belief that other, far larger aspects of one's life . . . are *not* controllable or ordered. Health and bodily perfectionism might be, in short, the ultimate metaphors for self-determination and choice amid cultural uncertainty and upheaval; they do indeed yield a self-directed, life-giving, empowering vision. (Susan Cayleff, *Wash and Be Healed: The Water-Cure Movement and Women's Health* [Philadelphia: Temple University Press, 1987], pp. 174–175)

See also Harvey Green, *Fit for America*, and Christopher Lasch, *The Culture of Narcissism* (New York: Norton, 1979).

27. Orison Swett Marden, *The Crime of Silence* (New York: Physical Culture Society, 1915), p. 48. On jealousy see Peter Stearns, *Jealousy: The Evolution of an Emotion in American History* (New York: New York University Press, 1989), esp. pp. 39–43, 154. One medical text in 1883 anthropomorphized and assigned political tendencies to male and female reproductive cells, claiming that "the male element is the originating factor, and the female the perpetuating factor; the ovum is conservative, the male cell, progressive"; William Keith Brooks, *The Law of Heredity* (Baltimore: J. Murphy, 1883) p. 94. See also Cynthia Eagle Russett, *Sexual Science: The Victorian Construction of Womanhood* (Cambridge: Harvard University Press, 1989), p. 94; and H. W. Foster, "Physical Education and Degeneracy," *The Independent* 52, 2 August 1900.

28. Joseph Alfred Conwell, *Manhood's Morning; or, "Go It While You're Young": A Book for Young Men Between 14 and 28 Years of Age* (Vineland, N.J.: Hominis, 1896), p. 197. O. S. Fowler, *Private Lectures on Perfect Men . . .* , p. 173; Bernarr Macfadden, *The Virile Powers of Superb Manhood: How Developed, How Lost, How Regained* (New York: Physical Culture Publishing, 1900), pp. 22, 29.

29. G. Douglas, "Social Purity," in *Official Report of the 12th International Christian Endeavor Convention* (New York, 1900), p. 254; Winfield Hall, *From Youth to Manhood* (New York: Association Press, 1900), p. 54. Hall was elaborate in his advice on the methods to avoid the evils of masturbation. He counseled boys and young men to sleep on hard beds, "throw your whole energy into your work," and perform a regimen of ritual ablution and purification: "Arise three quarters of an hour before breakfast every morning, take a cold sponge or shower bath; drink two glasses of cold water; dress and go out and walk around the block before breakfast" (p. 58). See also Martin Peck, "The Sex Life of College Men," *Journal of Nervous and Mental Disease* 62, 1925; and Albert Stearne, "Effects of Lascivious Conversations, Books and Companions in the Causation of Sexual Excess," *American Journal of Dermatology and Genito-Urinary Disease* 11, 1907.

30. See J. H. Kellogg, *Man the Masterpiece; or, Plain Truths Plainly Told About Boyhood, Youth and Manhood* (Burlington, Iowa: I. F. Segner, 1886), pp. 445–453; see also J. H. Kellogg, *Plain Facts for Old and Young, Embracing the Natural History and Hygiene of Organic Life* (Burlington, Iowa: I. F. Seg-

ner, 1888); Joseph Kett, *Rites of Passage* (New York: Basic Books, 1977), p. 165; John Money, *The Destroying Angel* (Buffalo: Prometheus Books, 1985); and T. J. Jackson Lears, *No Place of Grace*, p. 14.

31. Among the physical indicators Kellogg listed premature development, rounded shoulders, weak backs, stiffness in the joints, paralysis, awkward gait, lack of female breast development, paleness, acne, heart palpitation, epilepsy, and cold, clammy hands. Behaviors and attitudes that might be indicators included general debility, sudden change in disposition, lassitude, sleeplessness, mental lapses, fickleness, untrustworthiness, love of solitude, bashfulness, boldness, mock piety, confusion, nail-biting, capricious appetite, eating slate pencils, use of tobacco, hysteria, bed-wetting, unchastity of speech.

32. For girls Kellogg's remedies were equally gruesome. He claimed that he had found "the application of pure carbolic acid to the clitoris an excellent means of allaying the abnormal excitement, and preventing the recurrence of the practice in those whose willpower has become so weakened that the patient is unable to exercise entire self-control."

33. Henry Guernsey, M.D., *Plain Talks on Avoided Subjects* (Philadelphia, 1882). Cited in Haller and Haller, pp. 208–209.

34. Cited in Kevin Mumford, "Lost Manhood Found: Sexual Impotence and the Contradictions of Victorian Culture," unpublished MS, Stanford University, 1991, pp. 24–25.

35. I do not, of course, intend to argue that Freud is alone responsible for the deep cultural homophobia that continues to characterize American society. Rather, Freud was the first popular thinker to detach sexual orientation from biological or religious moorings and link it explicitly to gender identity. While his project was in part a reaction against Victorian prudery, it also seems to have sparked a widespread concern among anxious parents who wanted reassurance that their sons would turn out "all right."

    That homosexuals had recently begun to reveal their sexuality—especially in the celebrated trial of Oscar Wilde, followed avidly by Americans in the pages of the popular press and *Police Gazette*—added a graphic visual dimension to the terrors of emasculation by sexuality. The *Police Gazette* is especially revealing of masculine anxieties of the era. In addition to lurid tales of sexual depravity, the *Gazette* also featured advertisements for substances that promised to "cure sexual weakness, increase desire, and develop parts." See also Mumford, "Lost Manhood Found," p. 4.

36. I will return in the next chapter to this parental anxiety over child rearing and the ways in which pop psychology advised anxious parents to raise their sons to insure successful passage to heterosexuality and masculin-

ity. Here, however, I want to stress the way that the critique of cultural feminization articulated with the treatment of grown men's psyches. On this topic generally see Herman Adler, "Unemployment and Industry—a Study of Psychopathic Cases," *Mental Hygiene* 1, 1917.

37. Jarvis, cited in Barker-Benfield, *The Horrors of the Half-Known Life*, p. 29; Bryce, cited in John Starrett Hughes, "The Madness of Separate Spheres: Insanity and Masculinity in Victorian Alabama," in *Meanings for Manhood: Constructions of Masculinity in Victorian America*, M. Carnes and C. Griffen, eds. (Chicago: University of Chicago Press, 1991), p. 60; Philip Hamerton, *The Intellectual Life* (Boston: Roberts Bros., 1873), p. 5. See also Martin A. Berger, "Negotiating Victorian Manhood: Thomas Eakins and the Rowing Works," *masculinities* 2(4), 1994.

38. Cited in Spiller, 1990, p. 80. S. Weir Mitchell, *Gunshot Wounds and Other Injuries of Nerves*. On male hysteria and its link to military service, see Harold Evans, "Hysteria in the Male with Report of a Case," *Journal of the Association of Military Surgeons of the United States* 13, 1903; Richard Hutchings, "Hysteria As Manifested in the Military Service," *State Hospital Quarterly* 4, 1918–1919; Karl Menninger, "Hysteria in a Male as a Defense Reaction: A Case Report," *Boston Medical and Surgical Journal* 180, 1919; Aaron Rosanoff, "A Study of Hysteria, Based Mainly on Clinical Material Observed in the U.S. Army Hospital for War Neuroses at Plattsburgh Barracks, N.Y.," *Archives of Neurology and Psychiatry* 2, 1919; E. E. Southard, *Shell Shock and Other Neuropsychiatric Problems: Presented in Five Hundred and Eighty-Nine Case Histories from the War Literature, 1914–1918* [1919] (New York: Arno Press, 1973).

39. Elaine Showalter, *The Female Malady: Women, Madness, and English Culture, 1830–1980* (New York: Pantheon, 1985), pp. 175, 172, and 170–175 passim; see also Elaine Showalter, *Sexual Anarchy: Gender and Culture at the Fin de Siècle* (New York: Viking, 1990), and Spiller, 1990, p. 75.

40. George Beard, *American Nervousness*, 1881, p. 138; see also Tom Lutz, *American Nervousness, 1903: An Anecdotal History* (Ithaca, N.Y.: Cornell University Press, 1991); Edward Wakefield, "Nervousness: The National Disease of America," *McClure's* 2, February 1894; and Albert J. Underhill, "Sexual Neurasthenia in Men," *Journal of the American Medical Association* 60, 1913.

Mitchell agreed. In his best-selling *Wear and Tear: Hints for the Overworked* (1891), Mitchell observed:

the cruel competition for the dollar, the new and exacting habits of business, the racing speed which the telegraph and railway have introduced into commercial life, the new value which great fortunes have come to possess as means towards social advancement, and the overeducation and overstraining of our young people.

As a result of this "wear and tear," the "incessant cares of overwork, of business anxiety," Americans were suffering from "dyspepsia, consumption, and maladies of the heart"; S. Weir Mitchell, *Wear and Tear: Hints for the Overworked* (Philadelphia: Lippincott, 1891), pp. 28, 9, 67. Joseph Conwell also agreed; in *Manhood's Morning* he wrote that "[n]ervous prostration, nervous debility, neurasthenia, nervous dyspepsia, and other neurosis have become extremely prevalent, and seriously threaten the vigor and strength of our national physique." Conwell, *Manhood's Morning*, p. 206.

41. John Starrett Hughes, "The Madness of Separate Spheres," p. 57; see also John Haller and Robin Haller, *The Physician and Sexuality in Victorian America* (New York: Norton, 1977), esp. p. 217.

42. While most American experts diagnosed neurasthenia as a problem of the middle class, some Europeans added interesting twists on the problem. Richard von Krafft-Ebing, e.g., called neurasthenia the "American illness" and claimed that in Germany it was Jewish men who were the most susceptible to its debilities. The neurasthenic man is "an overachiever in the arena of commerce or politics" who "reads reports, business correspondence, stock market notations during meals, for whom 'time is money,'" Krafft-Ebing wrote. Jews "use too much of their brain in a restless striving for profit," which, he continued, "accounts for their higher percent mental and nervous ailments." See Sander Gilman, *Freud, Race and Gender* (Princeton, N.J.: Princeton University Press, 1993), p. 95.

43. See E. Anthony Rotundo, "Body and Soul," p. 28; Leon Fink, *Workingmen's Democracy: The Knights of Labor and American Politics* (Urbana: University of Illinois Press, 1983), p. 9; Delaware ad, cited in Kenneth Jackson, *Crabgrass Frontier* (New York: Oxford University Press, 1985), p. 138; John Muir, cited in David Shi, *The Simple Life: Plain Thinking and High Thinking in American Culture* (New York: Oxford University Press, 1985), p. 197; George Evans, "The Wilderness," *Overland Monthly* 43, January 1904, p. 33.

44. Roosevelt and Grinnell, 1893, pp. 14–15; Kent is cited in Roderick Nash, *Wilderness and the American Mind* (New Haven: Yale University Press, 1967), p. 153.

45. Woods Hutchinson, *Instinct and Health* (New York: Dodd and Mead, 1909). See also Martin Holbrook, *Eating for Strength; or, Food and Diet and their Relationship to Health and Work* (New York: Holbrook, 1888).

46. Although I will focus here on boxing and baseball, one could just as easily examine any number of sports. Take, e.g., bicycling. In 1894 a quarter of a million bicycles were sold in the United States, and the nation probably had over a million regular bike riders. In 1897 the League of Ameri-

can Wheelmen boasted 150,000 members. See A. H. Godfrey, "Cycling Clubs and the Spheres of Action," *Outing* 30, July 1897. Bicycling made men more moral, promoting "the clean, outdoor life, amid the tonic influences of fresh air, sunshine and the pleasant sights of nature, [and] remove[d] thousands of young men from the danger of debasing associations. Temperance is also promoted; no wheelman can safely use intoxicants for a cool, clear head and steady nerves are absolutely essential," wrote Sylvester Baxter, "Economic and Social Influences of the Bicycle," *the Arena* 6, October 1892, p. 583.

47. For some, sports were the moral equivalent of war for which William James yearned so eagerly. R. Heber Howe wrote that football, as well as service in the First World War, had "seen timid and retiring boys drive themselves through sheer character to become the most fearless and splendid examples of real manhood." R. Heber Howe, "Athletic Influence," in *The Education of the Modern Boy*, Alfred E. Stearns et al., eds. (Boston: Houghton Mifflin, 1928), p. 145.

48. Sargent, cited in Joe Dubbert, *A Man's Place: Masculinity in Transition* (Englewood Cliffs, N.J.: Prentice-Hall, 1979), p. 169. Fiske is cited in Donald Mrozek, *Sports and American Mentality* (Knoxville: University of Tennessee Press, 1983), p. 207. British paper, cited in Melvin Adelman, *A Sporting Time: New York City and the Rise of Modern Athletics, 1820–1870* (Champaign: University of Illinois Press, 1986), p. 284.

49. Walker and Wesleyan *Bulletin*, cited in Louise Knight, "The 'Quails': The History of Wesleyan University's First Period of Coeducation, 1872–1912," B.A. honors thesis, Wesleyan University, 1972. I am grateful to Ms. Knight for sharing her work with me. New York newspapers, cited in Melvin Adelman, *A Sporting Time*, p. 277. See also George Frank Lydston, *Diseases of Society and Degeneracy (The Vice and Crime Problem)* (Philadelphia: Lippincott, 1904), p. 582.

50. Frederic Paxson, "The Rise of Sport," *Mississippi Valley Historical Review* 4, September 1917, p. 146. See also Melvin Adelman, *A Sporting Time*, p. 83.

51. Cited in David Chapman, *Sandow the Magnificent: Eugen Sandow and the Beginnings of Bodybuilding* (Urbana: University of Illinois Press, 1994), p. 190.

52. Harvey Green, *Fit for America*, p. 215. On boxing, football, and baseball, see also Ellis, "Men Among Men," pp. 443–491, 491–542, 543–603, respectively. Boxing fan is cited in Michael C. C. Adams, *The Great Adventure*, p. 41. See, e.g., Duffield Osborn, "In Defense of Pugilism," *North American Review*, 1888.

53. Elliot Gorn, *The Manly Art: Bare-Knuckle Prize Fighting in America* (Ithaca, N.Y.: Cornell University Press, 1986), p. 138 and passim.

54. Ibid., p. 247.
55. Others included running, rowing, football, boxing, wrestling, shooting, riding, and mountain climbing.
56. Marshall, cited in Albert Spalding, *America's National Game* (New York: American Sports Publishing, 1911), p. 534. William McKeever, *Training the Boy* (New York: Macmillan, 1913), p. 91. Zane Grey, "Inside Baseball," *Baseball Magazine* 3(4), 1909. Much of the material in this section is condensed from my "Baseball and the Reconstitution of American Masculinity, 1880–1920," *Baseball History* 3, 1990.

    The historical literature on baseball and masculinity at the turn of the century is also discussed in several fascinating works, including Warren Goldstein, *Playing for Keeps: A History of Early Baseball* (Ithaca, N.Y.: Cornell University Press, 1989); Steven Reiss, *Touching Base: Professional Baseball and American Culture in the Progressive Era* (Westport, Conn.: Greenwood Press, 1980); and Steven Reiss, *City Games: The Evolution of American Urban Society and the Rise of Sports* (Champaign: University of Illinois Press, 1989).

57. Cited in Melvin Adelman, *A Sporting Time*, p. 173. Baseball was also heralded as promoting civic, as well as gendered, virtue. A. J. Spalding enumerated, alliteratively, in his *America's National Game* (1911):

    American Courage, Confidence, Combativeness; American Dash, Discipline, Determination; American Energy, Eagerness, Enthusiasm; American Pluck, Persistence, Performance; American Spirit, Sagacity, Success; American Vim, Vigor, Virility. (A. J. Spalding, *America's National Game*, p. 4)

    See also Peter Levine, *A. G. Spalding and the Rise of Baseball: The Promise of American Sport* (New York: Oxford University Press, 1985). Essayist Addington Bruce added:

    Physical fitness, courage, honesty, patience, the spirit of initiative combined with due respect for lawful authority, soundness and quickness of judgement, self-confidence, self-control, cheeriness, fair-mindedness, and appreciation of the importance of social solidarity, of "team play"—these are traits requisite as never before for success in the life of an individual and of a nation. (See H. Addington Bruce, "Baseball and the National Life," *Outlook* 104(13), May 1913, p. 105.)

58. As such, the masculinity reconstituted on the baseball field also facilitated a docility and obedience to authority that would serve the maintenance of the emerging industrial capitalist order. Thorstein Veblen argued that the sport "gives a product of exotic ferocity and cunning," a "rehabilitation of the early barbarian temperament," but its training regimen also "conduces to economic serviceability." Sports reproduced those character traits required by industrial capitalism, and participation by working-

class youths was hailed as a mechanism of insuring obedience to authority and acceptance of hierarchy (see Thorstein Veblen, *The Theory of the Leisure Class*, p. 204).

Veblen was one of many who were less than sanguine about sports' curative potential. His blistering critique of the nascent consumer culture suggests that organized sports are an illusory panacea. For the individual man, athletics are no sign of virtue, since "the temperament which inclines men to [sports] is essentially a boyish temperament. The addiction to sports therefore in a peculiar degree marks an arrested development of the man's moral nature." And culturally sports may be an evolutionary throwback, as they "afford an exercise for dexterity and for the emulative ferocity and astuteness characteristic of predatory life" (see *The Theory of the Leisure Class*, pp. 200, 203). And Boy Scout leader Ernest Thompson Seton thought that watching would lead to "spectatoritis" and turn manly men into "mollycoddles of the bleachers" (see Ernest Thompson Seton, "The Dangers of Athletic Training," *American Medicine* 13, 1907, p. 500).

59. Gunther Barth, *City People: The Rise of Modern City Culture in Nineteenth-Century America* (New York: Oxford University Press, 1980), pp. 190, 191. Of course, *real* parks were also a conscious attempt to bring nature to the city for its tonic renewal of masculine spirits, esp. in Frederick Law Olmsted's late nineteenth-century efforts, which utilized rougher, more natural forms instead of the manicured European garden. See Charles Beveridge, *The Papers of Frederick Law Olmsted* (Baltimore: The Johns Hopkins University Press, 1983).

60. Of significance here is that baseball spectatorship was also seen as muting or minimizing the pernicious effects of class struggle. Like the frontier, the baseball park was democratic:

> The spectator at a ball game is no longer a statesman, a lawyer, broker, doctor, merchant, or artisan, but just plain every-day man, with a heart full of fraternity and good will to all his fellow men—except perhaps the umpire. The oftener he sits in grand stand or "bleachers," the broader, kindlier, better man and citizen he must tend to become. (H. Addington Bruce, "Baseball and The National Life," p. 107)

"One thing in common absorbs us," wrote the Rev. Roland D. Sawyer in 1908, "we rub shoulders, high and low; we speak without waiting for an introduction; we forget everything clannish, all the petty conventionalities being laid aside." Novelist and former minor league ballplayer Zane Grey echoed these sentiments:

> Here is one place where caste is lost. Ragamuffins and velvet-breeched, white collared boys stand in that equality which augurs well for the future

of the stars and stripes. Dainty clothes are no bar to the game if their owner is not afraid to soil them.

Such celebrations of spectatorship also received the imprimatur of academic social science. "Persons of every economic, social, religious or intellectual class touch shoulders," wrote George Elliot Howard in the *American Journal of Sociology* in 1912. "They shout, thrill, and gesture in sympathy. They are just human beings, with the differentials of rank or vocation laid aside. They are 'deindividuated.' " See Rev. Roland Sawyer, "The Larger Side of Baseball," *Baseball Magazine* 1(6), 1908, pp. 31–32; Zane Grey "Inside Baseball," p. 12; George Elliot Howard, "Social Psychology of the Spectator," *American Journal of Sociology* 18, 1912, p. 44.

In this way, both as participant and spectator, baseball reconstituted a certain kind of masculinity—white and middle class. The baseball stands were as homosocial as any saloon but for some reason seemed less threatening, its male bonding more wholesome, its homosociality untainted by any sexualized social contact. Baseball was a popular amusement, controlled by the wealthy for the pleasure of the masses. In saloons, class resentment and rebellion had fermented alongside barley malt; hopes besides hops. Sons of Liberty knew John Barleycorn very well. Autonomous working-class homosociality threatened marketplace men in a way that spectatorship did not. Baseball perpetuated hierarchy even as it seemed to challenge it.

61. Taft here clearly refers to the solitary vice, as well as other feminizing indoor activities. Charles Murphy, "Taft, the Fan," *Baseball Magazine* 9(3), 1912, pp. 3–4.

62. Peter Filene, *Him/Her Self: Sex Roles in America* (Baltimore: The Johns Hopkins University Press, 1986), p. 139.

63. The mythical James and the real James were difficult to distinguish, in part because he fueled the myth himself. James embodied the republican virtue of the Heroic Artisan, promoting "the traditional world in which loyalty to family and friends took precedence over the greed and secularism the railroads had unleashed." Like Dick Turpin or Robin Hood (whose names he used when he signed letters, as if to claim a legacy with them), he "sought to reunite the community and reassert tradition by making the reluctant rich and powerful support the weak and defenseless." See David Thelen, *Paths of Resistance: Tradition and Dignity in Industrializing Missouri* (New York: Oxford University Press, 1986), pp. 74, 75. When the gang robbed a train in 1874, they examined the hands of all male passengers because they did not want to rob workingmen, but only the "plug hat gentlemen" whose hands were smooth and manicured.

64. Richard Slotkin, *The Fatal Environment*, p. 363.

65. James Robertson, "Horatio Alger, Andrew Carnegie . . . ," p. 251.

66. This repeats the pattern of women's novels from the first half of the century, where the heroines begin their quest for legitimacy as orphans or other kinds of outcasts.

67. On this see Marcus Klein, *Easterns, Westerns and Private Eyes: American Matters, 1870–1900* (Madison: University of Wisconsin Press, 1994), p. 13.

    Several British novels offer an interesting twist to this search for authentic grounding of masculine identity. While American heroes are searching for mentors in the absence of the father, British heroes or anti-heroes are literally creating themselves, whether by splitting or cloning ("Dr. Jekyll and Mr Hyde"), by transfusion (*Dracula*), by aesthetic duplication (*The Picture of Dorian Gray*), or by vivisection (*The Island of Dr. Moreau*). To be sure, English fiction offered many of the same escape hatches as American fiction, evoking the masculine quest (*She* or *The Man Who Would Be King*) and male bonding (*Heart of Darkness*). And of course, there's that elfin hero Peter Pan (1904), who pursues his fantasies of remaining a boy and not an adult by playing his identity off against Mr. Darling, the boring, mundane financier, whose public-sphere stature brings him no domestic patriarchal rewards (he is even jealous of the family dog), and against Captain Hook, the Englishman, free from the responsibilities of career and home that stunt the growth of the Darlings of the world. (Recall that Hook is a graduate of Eton and emphasizes playing by the rules and good form.) "No one is going to catch me, lady and make me a man," proclaims Peter. "I always want to be a little boy and have fun." No wonder. For more about these gendered fictional responses in Britain, see Elaine Showalter, *Sexual Anarchy*, 1990; Judith Walkowitz, "Jack the Ripper and the Myth of Male Violence," *Feminist Studies* 8, Fall 1982, and *City of Dreadful Delight: Narratives of Sexual Danger in Late-Victorian London* (Chicago: University of Chicago Press, 1992); and Michael C. C. Adams, *The Great Adventure*, 1990.

68. Alger subtitle is from *The Spider and the Fly* (1873); others from Marcus Klein, *Easterns, Westerns and Private Eyes*, p. 52.

69. Horatio Alger, *Luke Larkin's Luck*.

70. E.g., in *The Young Miner* it's a young Boston aristocrat, Lawrence Peabody, who serves as Tom's foil. Peabody is described as

    a young Boston clerk, who has spent several years behind a dry goods counter. He was soft and effeminate, with no talent for "roughing it" and wholly unfitted for the hard work which he had undertaken. He was deeply disappointed in his first work at gold hunting, having come out with the vague idea that he should pick up a big nugget within a short time that would make his fortune and enable him to go home a rich man. (p. 4)

    See also John Cawelti, *Apostles of the Self-Made Man* (Chicago: University of Chicago Press, 1965), p. 112.

71. Stephen Crane, *The Red Badge of Courage* [1895] (New York: Penguin, 1983). When more than one hundred historians, novelists, and journalists were asked by *American Heritage* magazine to name their favorite historical novel in U.S. history, *The Red Badge of Courage* was the most often mentioned—an amazing feat for a work of fiction in which virtually no women appear, the only exception being Henry Fleming's mother and she only in his memory. *Gone With the Wind, The Scarlet Letter*, and *War and Peace* were tied for second, another astonishing result, since those surveyed were specifically asked about *American* novels (*USA Today*, 30 September 1992).

72. In his famous short story "The Open Boat" (1896), Crane presents an allegory of baptism by fire, immersion, and regeneration; only after the ordeal of survival in a lifeboat can the men who did survive "then be interpreters" of life. Overcoming the first fear, the fear of death, the fear born of woman, is the masculine project, so that action can be motivated by the second—homosocial—fear. This process is Crane's version of the transition to adult manhood.

73. W. Churchill Williams, "Red Blood in Fiction," *The World's Work* 6(1), May 1903, p. 3694; Carman cited in T. J. Jackson Lears, *No Place of Grace*, p. 106. Leslie Fiedler claims that at the turn of the century, the male audience "reasserted itself." Leslie Fiedler, "The Male Novel," *Partisan Review* 37(1), 1970, p. 81.

74. Cited in Larzer Ziff, *The American 1890s: Life and Times of a Lost Generation* (New York: Viking, 1966), pp. 251, 252.

75. Frank Norris, *McTeague* [1899] (New York: New American Library, 1964); p. 7 and passim. See also Frank Norris, "The Frontier Gone at Last," *The World's Work* 3, February 1902.

76. Frank Norris, *Vandover and the Brute* (Garden City, N.Y.: Doubleday, 1914), p. 309. See also John Pettegrew, "The Return to Primal Man: The Psychology of Primitivism in Turn-of-the-Century Naturalist Fiction and College Football," *The Journal of Men's Studies* 2(1), 1993.

77. Frank Norris, *A Man's Woman*.

78. William Dean Howells, *The Rise of Silas Lapham* [1885] (New York: Harper and Row, 1958).

79. On Henry James see Alfred Habegger, *Gender, Fantasy, and Realism in American Literature* (New York: Columbia University Press, 1982), p. 255, and Kelly Cannon, *Henry James and Masculinity: The Man at the Margins* (New York: St. Martin's Press, 1994).

80. On Eakins see David Lubin, *Acts of Portrayal* (New Haven: Yale University Press, 1985), and Martin A. Berger, "Negotiating Victorian Manhood: Thomas Eakins and the Rowing Works," *masculinities* 2(4), 1994.

81. Ives, cited in Henry Cowell and Sidney Cowell, *Charles Ives and His Music*

(New York: Oxford University Press, 1955), p. 10. (It is unclear whether the spelling mistake in "feat" was an intentional double entendre or inadvertent.) See also David Noble, *The Progressive Mind, 1890–1917* (New York: Rand McNally, 1970), p. 131, and Rupert Wilkinson, *American Tough: The Tough-Guy Tradition and American Character* (New York: Harper and Row, 1986), p. 103. An article in the *New Republic* in 1915 also cited ragtime as distinctly American and the opposite of feminized European music. "No European music can or possibly could express this American personality." Hiram Moderwell, "Ragtime," *New Republic* 4, 16 October 1915, p. 286.

82. Vincent Scully, *Modern Architecture* (New York: George Braziller, 1974), p. 18; see also Robert Twombly, *Louis Sullivan: His Life and Work* (New York: Viking, 1986).

83. Johnson is cited in Henry Nash Smith, *The Virgin Land*, p. 122.

84. Wallace Stegner, cited in Ben Merchant Vorpahl, *My Dear Wister: The Frederic Remington–Owen Wister Letters* (Palo Alto: American West Publishing, 1972), p. ix. James Robertson, "Horatio Alger, Andrew Carnegie, Abraham Lincoln and the Cowboy," *Midwest Quarterly* 20, 1979, p. 253.

85. Frontier Days handbill and program, American Heritage Center, University of Wyoming Library, Laramie, W994-t-ch-fd, 1925. E. M. Bond, "The Cowmen's Carnival," *Sunset* 23(2), August 1909, p. 173. The Union Pacific Railroad was equally boosterish and with good reason—the railroad was an early sponsor of the rodeos and offered special package tours for easterners to Frontier Days:

> Here one may still see the real West of more than a quarter of a century ago—not a weak imitation after the manner of the tented Wild West Show known to the Easterner, but a realistic reproduction in which the actors play but once a year, and that for blood and the glory of a world's championship. It is no tamed Wild West Show under canvas, repeated day by day by tired performers. It is the "real thing," as the Cheyennes boastfully term it—and the increasing crowds from the East each year attest to its realism. It is the biggest show of its kind in all the world, and the only one in which the visitor may comfortably view the spectacular reproduction of the West as it was.

> Such authenticity included tableaux of Sioux warriors in full regalia during the intermissions between the events of the rodeo competition. Union Pacific program to 14th Annual Cheyenne Frontier Days, 1910, in American Heritage Center, University of Wyoming, Laramie, W994-t-ch-fd.

86. Bond, "the Cowmen's Carnival," p. 176; Jimmy Walker, "Rodeo Killers," *True West*, 1958; article in scrapbook at American Heritage Center, University of Wyoming, Laramie, Ro 614. See also *Saturday Evening Post*, 29 November 1919.

87. The cowboy is a man "in flight from his ancestors, from his immediate family, and from everything that tied him down and limited his freedom of movement," writes cultural critic Christopher Lasch, *The True and Only Heaven: Progress and its Critics* (New York: Norton, 1991), p. 39. To the cowboy, as Wallace Stegner puts it, civilization "meant responsibility, meant law, meant fences and homesteads, and water rights and fee-simple land ownership, meant women" (Stegner cited in Ben Merchant Vorpahl, *My Dear Wister*, p. ix). Robert Warshow put it most succinctly when he wrote that "the true enemy of the cowboy is the schoolmarm"; cited in Marcus Klein, *Easterns, Westerns, and Private Eyes*, p. 101.

88. Wright is cited in Mark Gerzon, *A Choice of Heroes* (Boston: Houghton Mifflin, 1983), p. 77.

89. The unattributed quotations above are all from Owen Wister's letters to his friend Frederic Remington and from an essay "The Evolution of the Cow Puncher" (1893), all in Ben Merchant Vorpahl, *My Dear Wister*, pp. xi, 81, 93, 94, and passim.

90. Owen Wister, *The Virginian* [1902] (New York: New American Library, 1979).

91. Cited in G. Edward White, *The Eastern Establishment and the Western Experience* (New Haven: Yale University Press, 1968), p. 124.

92. Jane Tompkins, *West of Everything: The Inner Life of Westerns* (New York: Oxford University Press, 1992), p. 136.

93. It was also an eroticized world, which has not escaped the notice of contemporary cultural critics. Robert K. Martin, for example, calls the western a "homoerotic cowboy romance" in which cowboys "gallop 'side by side' in furious flight from an increasingly feminine world in which they fear they will have no place; their search is ultimately for an imagined past before the civilizing entry of women." Robert K. Martin, "Knight Errant and Gothic Seducers: Representations of Male Friendship in Nineteenth-Century America," in *Hidden From History: Reclaiming the Gay and Lesbian Past*, M. B. Duberman, M. Vicinus, and G. Chauncey, eds. (New York: New American Library, 1989), p. 174. Of course, it was not only male camaraderie that was eroticized on the range; in the absence of women, several other props—like guns and horses—also carried that erotic charge.

94. "It is this note of manliness which is dominant through the writings of Mr. Wister," wrote Theodore Roosevelt in 1895:

> Beauty, refinement, grace, are excellent qualities in a man, as in a nation, but they come second . . . to the great virile virtues—the virtues of courage, energy, and daring: the virtues which beseem a masterful race—a race fit to fell the forests, to build roads, to found commonwealths, to conquer continents, to overthrow armed enemies. (Roosevelt, cited in G. Edward White, *The Eastern Establishment and the Western Experience*, p. 197)

On this point all reviewers agreed. William Dean Howells called it "a man's book throughout," and Morton Payne hailed it as "a man's book with not one touch of sickly sentiment." Frederic Taber Cooper notes it as a "thoroughly virile book." Morton Payne, review of *The Virginian* in *The Dial* 33, 1902, p. 242; Theodore Roosevelt, "A Teller of Tales of Strong Men" (a review of *Red Men and White* by Owen Wister), in *Harper's Weekly* 39, 1895, p. 1216; William Dean Howells, review of *Red Men and White* in *Harper's Weekly* 39, 1895, p. 2032; Frederic Taber Cooper, *Some American Story Tellers* [1911] (New York: Avon, 1968), p. 379. See also Sanford E. Marovitz, "Testament of a Patriot: *The Virginian*, the Tenderfoot, and Owen Wister," *Texas Studies in Literature and Language* 15, 1973, pp. 551–575. To contemporary feminist literary critic Madonne Miner, *The Virginian* is a "panegyric to American manhood" that ultimately fails—"a terrified, and decidedly unsuccessful, response to processes undermining traditional modes of manhood." Miner, "Manhood on the Make: Owen Wister's *Virginian*," *Men's Studies Review* 8(4), 1991, p. 15. See also her "Documenting the Demise of Manly Love: Owen Wister's *Virginian*," *Journal of Men's Studies* 1(1), 1992. I am grateful to Madonne Miner for her help in thinking through this section.

95. Donald Worster, *Under Western Skies: Nature and History in the American West* (New York: Oxford University Press, 1992), p. 80; Will J. Wright, *Six-Gun Society* (Berkeley: University of California Press, 1975), p. 152; Robert Murray Davis, *Playing Cowboys: Low Culture and High Art in the Western* (Norman: University of Oklahoma Press, 1992), p. 13. In Wister's fiction, as in many westerns, a tenderfoot narrator serves to bring the eastern reader into the western setting, and we see the West through his admiring and less-manly eyes.

96. The western hero is the living repudiation of the corporate clones of the eastern cities. Wister writes that the cowboy scorned the traveling salesman's "being too soon with everybody, the celluloid good fellowship that passes for ivory with nine in ten of the city crowd. But not so with the sons of the sage brush. They live nearer nature, and they know better." Wister, *The Virginian*, p. 16. Wister rededicated the novel in 1911 to Theodore Roosevelt.

Of course, the cowboy rides a horse, just as modern men's lives were increasingly dominated by steam- and gasoline-powered modes of transportation. The horse, literary critic Jane Tompkins aptly notes, represented "everything the bureaucratic, machine-run, rule-bound modern world would deprive them of—spontaneity, beauty, freedom from rules and routines, and the right to enjoy life"; Tompkins, *West of Everything*, 12, 102. By contrast, the automobile suppressed manhood, demanding a

sobriety and attention that precluded rambunctious animation. As Henry
Adams saw it in 1906:

> The typical American man had his hand on a lever and his eye on a curve in
> the road; his living depended on keeping up an average speed of forty miles
> an hour, tending always to become sixty, eighty or a hundred, and he could
> not admit emotions of anxieties or subconscious distractions, more than he
> could admit whiskey or drugs without breaking his neck. (Adams, cited in
> Diane Johnson, "Something for the Boys," *New York Review of Books* 16 Jan-
> uary 1992, p. 17)

97. Recalling Theodore Roosevelt, Wister recalled the days when "Ellis Island
    had not yet diluted Harvard." Interestingly, Wister's western egalitarian-
    ism halted before inequality based on race, gender, or even class. There
    are really two classes in America, he claimed, the "quality and the equal-
    ity." "It was through the Declaration of Independence that we Americans
    acknowledged the *eternal inequality* of man . . . [and] gave freedom to
    true aristocracy, saying 'Let the best man win, whoever he is.' . . . That is
    true democracy. And true democracy and true aristocracy are one and the
    same thing"; cited in Robert Murray Davis, *Playing Cowboys*, p. 14.
98. Louise Levathes, "Remington: The Man and the Myth," *National Geo-
    graphic*, August 1988, p. 226.
99. Remington, cited in Richard Slotkin, *The Fatal Environment*, p. 97; letter
    from Frederic Remington to Owen Wister, cited in Nixon O. Rush, *Fred-
    eric Remington and Owen Wister: The Story of a Friendship, 1893–1909*
    (Tallahassee: privately printed, 1961), p. 30; at University of California,
    Berkeley, Bancroft Library.
100. Louise Levathes, "Remington: The Man and the Myth," p. 226.
101. Jack London, *The Call of the Wild* [1903] (New York: Signet, 1975), p. 75.
102. In the last line of the book, Buck becomes both wolf and boy, so that now
    "he may be seen running at the head of the pack through the pale moon-
    light or glimmering borealis, leaping gigantic above his fellows, his great
    throat a-bellow, as he sings a song of the younger world, which is the
    song of the pack" (p. 102).

    I'm afraid I had precisely the opposite reaction to this book when I
    first read it at about age thirteen. I was heartbroken when Buck was dog-
    napped, and the only conclusion that would have pleased me, since I
    could only imagine this happening to my own little beagle puppy, was if
    Buck returned to his *real* family back in the garden in California, who
    were probably worried sick about him. Even in rereading the book, I was
    dismayed that once dognapped, we never again hear anything about the
    bereft family Buck leaves behind.
103. No wonder critics raved. "Such a primitive story, in the atmosphere of
    decadence and over-civilization which enveloped the turn-of-the-century

years, came to its readers as a bracing wind," writes one critic, while another thus assesses London's popularity:

the great elan and vigor that are properly associated with this country and its people emerge from his pages. Europe drained dry of such faculties, it is understandable that London's people, their concerns and their virtues, should have a nostalgic appeal that Europeans might even read of them as more credulous generations read of such heroic figures as Roland and Hector. (Harry Sylvester, *New York Times*, 19 August 1951)

Contemporary literary critic David Leverenz adds that "London unambivalently contrasts Buck's natural leadership with the degeneracy of [feminized] men. Nevertheless, ideal manliness thrives in Buck only because he becomes less and less human, more and more wild, while his admiring narrator—like Cooper—writes a 'wild' book about him for boy-men readers who feel trapped in the maturation and long for exotic virility." David Leverenz, "The Last Real Man in America: From Natty Bumppo to Batman," *American Literary History* 3, 1991, p. 761.

104. Jack London, *The Sea Wolf* [1904] (New York: Bantam, 1963), p. 13. Madonne Miner's suggestive essay, " 'It Will Be the (un)Making of You': Manhood Besieged in Jack London's *The Sea Wolf*," *Jack London Newsletter* 21, 1990, explores the homoerotic component to the struggle between Van Weyden and Larsen, illustrated in the palpably sensuous physicality of Van Weyden's description of his mentor.

105. Of course, for London, the stalwart socialist, there were also class themes present in his contrast between manly archetypes.

106. Edgar Rice Burroughs, *Tarzan of the Apes* [1912] (New York: Signet, 1966). When Jane first sees him, she is a captive of a great ape and Tarzan swings in on a vine to her rescue. Jane's "lithe young form flattened against the trunk of a great tree, her hands pressed against her rising and falling bosom, and her eyes wide with mingled horror, fascination, fear, and admiration—watched the primordial ape battle with the primeval man for possession of a woman—for her" (p. 155–156). When Tarzan has slain his foe, he grabs Jane's arm and she rebuffs him. "And then Tarzan of the Apes did just what his first ancestor would have done. He took his woman in his arms and carried her into the jungle" (p. 157).

107. Burroughs, *Tarzan*, p. 243. See also David Leverenz, "The Last Real Man in America," p. 759. In a sense, the male genre of adventure narrative has devolved into a romance novel; to civilize Tarzan, the novel becomes a sentimental "woman's" romance.

108. Cited in Jane Tompkins, *West of Everything*, p. 167, 33.

Toward the end of his life, Grey even attempted to graft George Washington into the frontier myth he had done so much to sustain. In a novel,

George Washington, Frontiersman, Washington begins an unbroken American tradition in which the West is the center from which American virtue springs. Washington is honest, self-made, and self-effacing. The novel leads up to the moment when Washington takes command of the armies of the Continental Congress. When he meets Daniel Boone, he exclaims admiringly: "Alone and self-sufficient in that wilderness!" See Zane Grey, *George Washington, Frontiersman*, edited with an introduction by Carlton Jackson (Lexington: University Press of Kentucky, 1994), esp. p. 137.

CHAPTER 5: A Room of His Own

1. "The father/husband was no longer the boss of the family enterprise but a breadwinner who carried the burden of supporting the entire family; his success or failure determined the family's economic well-being and its standing in the community. Moreover, a man's sense of himself as a man was tied up with his occupational success," writes Arlene Skolnick, *Embattled Paradise: The American Family in an Age of Uncertainty* (New York: Basic Books, 1991), p. 38. See also E. Anthony Rotundo, "Boy Culture: Middle-Class Boyhood in Nineteenth-Century America," in *Meanings for Manhood: Constructions of Masculinity in Victorian America*, M. Carnes and C. Griffen, eds. (Chicago: University of Chicago Press, 1991), p. 32; see also Susan Curtis, "The Son of Man and God the Father: The Social Gospel and Victorian Masculinity," in the same volume. Also see Steven Mintz and Susan Kellogg, *Domestic Revolutions: A Social History of the American Family* (New York: Free Press, 1988).

2. Cited in Dolores Hayden, *A Grand Domestic Revolution: A History of Feminist Design for American Homes, Neighborhoods, and Cities* (Cambridge: M.I.T. Press, 1981), p. 16; see also Susan Strasser, *Never Done: A Social History of Housework* (New York: Pantheon, 1982); Ruth Schwartz Cowan, *More Work for Mother: The Ironies of Household Technology from the Open Hearth to the Microwave* (New York: Basic Books, 1983); and Dolores Hayden, *Redesigning the American Dream: The Future of Housing, Work and Family Life* (New York: Norton, 1984).

3. Samuel Fraser, "What Are You Going to Do November Second?" addresses before the Livingston County Granges, Geneseo, New York, 1914 (Buffalo and Erie County Historical Society Library, Buffalo, New York), p. 2. Watson, is cited in Mintz and Kellogg, *Domestic Revolutions*, p. 108; see also Robert Griswold, "Divorce and the Legal Redefinition of Victorian Manhood," in *Meanings for Manhood*. Griswold also points out that the meaning of divorce differed. Men "took advantage of adultery, cruelty, or intemperance suits and secured a divorce, they ended their marital woes and enjoyed the freedom that was the birthright of their sex," while

women "secured immediate relief, but they also encountered a society that systematically denied them autonomy and independence." See p. 110.

Of course, such dire warnings were seriously misplaced, since fewer children, higher rates of divorce, and sexual behavior within marriage were all indicators of the increasing importance of the marital *relationship*—as opposed to family lineage—as the defining feature of domestic life.

4. A year later, in her novel *My Wife and I* (1870), Stowe stated the case like this: "We have heard much said of the importance of training women to be wives." Now it would be nice to have "something to be said on the importance of training men to be husbands." Cited in Margaret Marsh, "Suburban Men and Masculine Domesticity, 1870–1915," *American Quarterly* 40, June 1988, p. 174. See also Martha Bruere and Robert Bruere, *Increasing Home Efficiency* (New York: Macmillan, 1912). Other quotes cited in Marsh, p. 165. Some historians have cited Marsh's notion of Masculine Domesticity as a disconfirmation of my (and others') "crisis of masculinity" hypothesis, missing the way that fathers fused domestic nurture with retaliation against women's domestic power and men's resentment of women's role in their sons' emasculation. See, e.g., Clyde Griffen, "Reconstructing Masculinity from the Evangelical Revival to the Waning of Progressivism: A Speculative Synthesis," in Carnes and Griffen, eds. *Meanings for Manhood*, esp. pp. 183–184. The analogy with contemporary strands of the men's movement is striking. In the guise of encouraging active fatherhood, some contemporary advocates of masculine domesticity seek to wrest children away from mothers (esp. after divorce), while others seek to use fatherhood as a vehicle to encourage men to express deeply and distinctly masculine emotions.

5. One advice book counseled wives to "never allow the husband to be present" at childbirth. "If he is a man of sense and delicacy, he will not desire it, and if he is not, the more reason you should keep him out of your way." J. Jill Suitor found that husbands began attending the births of their children in the 1830s and continued until hospital births became common in the 1910s. J. Jill Suitor, "Husbands' Participation in Childbirth: A Nineteenth-Century Phenomenon," *Journal of Family History*, Fall 1981, p. 284 and passim.

6. Margaret Marsh, "Suburban Men and Masculine Domesticity," p. 166.

7. Margaret Marsh, "Suburban Men," pp. 176 and esp. 181. It is clear that masculine domesticity was actually a form of resistance, a reaction against women's putative control over domestic life.

8. This led to the conclusion of "blue for girls." See "Pink or Blue?" *Infants' Department*, June 1918; "What Color for Your Baby?" *Parents*, March

1939. The best contemporary historical account of children's clothing is in Jo Paoletti, "The Gendering of Infants' and Toddlers' Clothing in America," paper presented at the Conference on Gender and Material Culture, Winterthur Museum of American Culture, Wilmington, 1989. That toddlers of both genders are now dressed as little boys, i.e., in corduroy overalls, is part of the contemporary story.

9. E.g., Alfred Carleton Gilbert invented the Erector set, that conglomeration of girders and screws, because, as he put it, "I know what boys like"; cited in Paula Petrick, "The Self-Made Boy and the Scientific Capitalist: Gender and the Toy Industry, 1890–1920," paper presented at the Berkshire Conference on the History of Women, June 1990, p. 8.

10. J. Adams Puffer, *The Boy and His Gang* (Boston: Houghton Mifflin, 1912), p. 91.

11. Hall is cited in Peter Stearns, *American Cool* (New York: New York University Press, 1994), p. 31.

12. Albert Beveridge, *The Young Man and the World* (New York: Appleton, 1905). Dana cited in John Curtis Crandall, "Images and Ideals for Young Americans: A Study of American Juvenile Literature," 1825–1860, Ph.D. diss., University of Rochester, 1957, p. 92. Of course, both girls and boys might be feminized by reading novels, but such an outcome was a positive one for the girls.

13. Rev. William Forbush, *The Boy Problem: A Study in Social Pedagogy* (Boston: Pilgrim Press, 1901), p. 47. See also J. H. Tufts, "Feminization," *School Review* 17, January 1909. For a brilliant analysis of the fear of feminization and the opposition to coeducation in one school district, see Victoria Bissell Brown, "The Fear of Feminization: Los Angeles High Schools in the Progressive Era," *Feminist Studies* 16(3), 1990. Bissell Brown argues that the strategic solution to this problem was to undermine women and promote men—inviting more male teachers, canceling women's athletics, and creating more options for male high school students (like manual arts) and insisting on requirements for female students like domestic science courses.

14. G. Stanley Hall, *Adolescence: Its Psychology and Its Relations to Physiology, Anthropology, Sociology, Sex, Crime, Religion and Education*, 2 vols. (New York: Appleton, 1904). Hall's recapitulation theory earned him the title of "The Darwin of the mind." See also "How and When to Be Frank with Boys," *Ladies' Home Journal*, 1907; "The Awkward Age," *Appleton's Magazine*, August 1900, for more of Hall's thoughts on adolescence. See also his essays "Some Dangers in Our Educational System and How to Meet Them," *New England Magazine* 41, February 1907, and "Coeducation in the High School," *Addresses and Proceedings of the National Educational Association*, 1903, for his perspective on coeducation. Hall, of course, is

one of the nation's foremost popularizers of Freudian ideas; as president of Clark University, Hall invited Freud to lecture there on his only trip to the United States. See Dorothy Ross, *G. Stanley Hall: The Psychologist as Prophet* (Chicago: University of Chicago Press, 1972). See also Gail Bederman, Ph.D. diss., Brown University, 1992, and Lesley A. Diehl, "The Paradox of G. Stanley Hall: Foe of Coeducation and Educator of Women," in *American Psychologist* 41(8), August 1986. I am grateful to Gail Bederman and Lesley Diehl for sharing their work on G. Stanley Hall.

15. G. Stanley Hall, *Adolescence*, vol. 2, p. 562. Hall was not, obviously, enamored of the New Woman of the era, calling her "completely sterile" and the "apotheosis of selfishness":

> Despairing of herself as a woman, she asserts her lower rights in place of her one great right to be loved. . . . Failing to respect herself as a productive organism, she gives vent to personal ambitions; seeks independence; comes to know very plainly what she wants; perhaps becomes intellectually emancipated, and substitutes science for religion, or the doctor for the priest, with the all-sided impressionability characteristic of her sex which, when cultivated, is so like an awakened child. (2: 629)

> See also G. Stanley Hall, "Flapper American Novissima," *Atlantic Monthly* 129, June 1922. Hall actually believed that feminism was the fault of men, whose feminization was so complete that women had gotten sick of them:

> The more exhausted men become, whether by overwork, unnatural city life, alcohol, recrudescent polygamic inclinations, exclusive devotion to greed and pelf; whether they become weak, stopping, blear-eyed, bald headed, bow-legged, thin-shanked, or gross, coarse, barbaric, and bestial, the more they lose the power to lead woman or to arouse her nature, which is essentially passive. Thus her perversions are his fault. Indeed . . . it seems as if in human society, the processes of subordinating the male to the female . . . had already begun. If he is not worshipped as formerly, it is because he is less worshipful or more effeminate, less vigorous, and less able to excite and retain the great love of true, not to say great women. (2: 627–628)

16. Hall, *Adolescence*, vol. 2, p. 532; Hall, "How and When to Be Frank with Boys."
17. Hall, "The Awkward Age," p. 154. Even bullying other boys was understandable, Hall argued. "The boy's bullying is the soul-germ of the man's independence," he wrote, before citing approvingly one boy who was "over-bearing and cruel" to his sister, whom he had "perfectly terrorized," and another boy who forced his younger sister to kneel before him. Bullying helped boys develop manly independence, esp. if they bullied girls.

18. J. Adams Puffer, *The Boy and His Gang*, pp. 83, 142; Albert Beveridge, *The Young Man and the World*, p. 101.

19. Cited in Gail Bederman, Ph.D. diss., p. 30.

20. Although several colleges and universities were founded as coeducational, the great push for coeducation came in the decades after the Civil War, when the provisions of the Morrill Act prompted the founding of many of the nation's large state universities and also when other colleges and universities took up the question of women's admissions and educational and social segregation. See Rosalind Rosenberg, *Beyond Separate Spheres: Intellectual Roots of Modern Feminism* (New Haven: Yale University Press, 1982), and "The Limits of Access: The History of Coeducation in America," in *Women and Higher Education in American History*, J. Faragher and F. Howe, eds. (New York: Norton, 1988).

21. Wesleyan University Libraries, MS coll. 31, pp. 31–35. See also Louise Knight, " 'The Quails': The History of Wesleyan University's First Period of Coeducation, 1872–1912," B.A. honors thesis, Wesleyan University, 1972; Charles Emerick, "College Women and Race Suicide," *Political Science Quarterly* 24, June 1909. The material in this section is discussed further in my "Men's Responses to Women's Educational Equality, 1840–1990," *Thought and Action*, Spring 1993.

22. Wesleyan University *Argus* is cited in Knight, " 'The Quails'"; Hamilton is cited in Thomas Woody, *A History of Women's Education in the United States*, 2 vols. (New York: Science Press, 1929), vol. 1, p. 268.

    The debate about coeducation raged throughout the twentieth century, in part informed by fears of feminization of male students. See, e.g., Andrew Draper, "Coeducation in the United States," *Educational Review* 25, February 1903; Ely Van der Warker, "Is the Education of Women with Men a Failure?" *Harper's Weekly* 48, August 20, 1904; E. E. White, "Coeducation of the Sexes," *National Teacher* 2, 1872. For a general treatment of the debate, see Arnold Jack Keller, "An Historical Analysis of the Arguments for and Against Coeducational Schools in the United States," Ed.D. diss., Teachers College, Columbia University, 1971.

23. Wesleyan remained all-male until 1970. Both cited in Louise Knight, " 'The Quails,' " pp. 51, 50.

24. Cited in Thomas Woody, *A History of Women's Education*, vol. 2, p. 281. This policy was eventually abandoned by 1908 because it was so expensive and because students resisted it.

25. Eliot, letter to Lindley C. Kent, 30 March 1880; Schlesinger Library, A/K37 Lindley Kent. Eliot described himself as a "vocal foe of coeducation"; see Rosalind Rosenberg, *Beyond Separate Spheres*, p. 31. Uneasy about associating Harvard's name with women's education, Eliot informally invited selected members of Harvard's all-male faculty to tutor in the Society for the Collegiate Instruction of Women, colloquially known

as the Annex. Only after 1893, when the Annex was constituted as Radcliffe College, did women have a formal presence at Harvard. See Paul Buck, "Harvard Attitude Towards Radcliffe in the Early Years," *Massachusetts Historical Society* 74, May 1962; Marcia Graham Synott, *The Half-Opened Door: Discrimination and Admissions at Harvard, Yale and Princeton, 1900–1970*, Westport, Conn.: Greenwood Press, 1979.

26. University of California papers, cited in Lynn Gordon, *Gender and Higher Education in the Progressive Era* (New Haven: Yale University Press, 1990), p. 70. On Columbia see also Rosalind Rosenberg, *Beyond Separate Spheres*; Helen Lefkowitz Horowitz, *Alma Mater: Design and Experience in the Women's Colleges from their Nineteenth-Century Beginnings to the 1930s* (New York: Knopf, 1984), p. 134; Frederick Barnard, "Should American Colleges Be Open to Women As Well As to Men?" a paper presented to the twentieth Annual Convocation of the University of the State of New York at Albany, July 12, 1882; published by the Proceedings of the Convocation (Albany, 1882); Morgan Dix et al., "To the Trustees of Columbia College: A Report of the Select Committee on the Subject of Admission of Women to the College," 23 April 1884 (MS coll., Columbia University Library); Alice Duer Miller and Susan Myers, *Barnard College: The First Fifty Years* (New York: Columbia University Press, 1939).

Cornell, Michigan, and Wisconsin all accepted coeducation after vigorous debate. See James Angell, "Coeducation at Michigan University," *Pennsylvania School Journal* 29, 1881; Charlotte Conable, *Women at Cornell: The Myth of Equal Education* (Ithaca, N.Y.: Cornell University Press, 1977); Carl Becker, *Cornell University: Founders and Founding* (Ithaca, N.Y.: Cornell University Press, 1943); Wardon A. Curtis, "The Movement Against Coeducation at the University of Wisconsin," *Independent* 65, August 6, 1908; Patricia Foster Haines, "Women, Men and Coeducation: Historical Perspectives from Cornell University, 1868–1900," paper presented at the Berkshire Conference on the History of Women, 1976 (Schlesinger Library, Microfilm Collection, 244).

27. TR to GSH, 29 November 1899; Hall papers, Clark University, box 25, folder 18.

28. "The notion that our splendid women teachers are making mollycoddles of their boy students is utterly absurd. Why, women themselves are anything but mollycoddles in these days of basket-ball and athletic 'stunts' without number! They'd be the first to despise the 'feminine' boy—instead of petting him into being"; cited in Woody, *A History of Women's Education*, vol. 2, p. 514; See John Dewey, "Is Coeducation Injurious to Girls?" *Ladies' Home Journal* 28, 1911; "Education and the Health of Women," *Science* 6, 1885; and "Health and Sex in Higher Education," *Popular Science Monthly* 28, 1886.

29. On the coeducation debate see my *Against the Tide: Pro-Feminist Men in*

the United States, 1776–1990 (with Tom Mosmiller), part II. Dewey's comment about men who oppose coeducation is in a letter to President William Raney Harper of the University of Chicago, 25 July 1902 (University of Chicago Library, President's Papers, 1899–1925).

30. Joseph Kett, *Rites of Passage: Adolescence in America, 1790–the Present* (New York: Basic Books, 1977), p. 203; Gulick, cited in J. Adams Puffer, *The Boy and His Gang*, p. 127. Gulick went on to become the director of physical education for the New York City public schools in 1903 and was appointed to the first board of directors of the Boy Scouts of America in 1910. His wife founded the Camp Fire Girls. See also David Macleod, *Building Character in the American Boy: The Boy Scouts, YMCA and Their Forerunners, 1870–1920* (Madison: University of Wisconsin Press, 1983), and my review of Macleod, "It's a Boy's Life!" *Village Voice Literary Supplement*, April 1985.

31. George Bird Grinnell and Charles Sheldon, *Hunting and Conservation: The Book of the Boone and Crockett Club* (New Haven: Yale University Press, 1925), p. 534–535.

32. Rev. William Forbush, *The Boy Problem*, pp. 140, 98.

33. Baden-Powell, cited in Allen Warren, "Popular Manliness: Baden Powell, Scouting and the Development of Manly Character," in *Manliness and Morality: Middle-Class Masculinity in Britain and America, 1800–1940*, J.A. Mangan and J. Walvin, eds. (New York: St. Martin's Press, 1987), p. 203. Baden-Powell's successful repression of his own homosexual desires formed the basis of his idealization of the body and his repudiation of its activities. He was a virulent campaigner against masturbation, e.g., although he was fond of photograph collections of young naked men frolicking in the woods. And while he promoted what he called "the flannel shirt life," he also enjoyed cross-dressing and, as he called it, "skirt dancing." See also Michael Rosenthal, *The Character Factory: Baden-Powell and the Origins of the Boy Scout Movement* (New York: Pantheon, 1986), and Tim Jeal, *The Boy-Man: The Life of Lord Baden-Powell* (New York: William Morrow, 1990). Robert MacDonald's *Sons of the Empire: The Frontier and the Boy Scout Movement, 1890–1918* (Toronto: University of Toronto Press, 1993), extends the discussion of the Boy Scouts to Canada as well.

34. "My aim was to make a man," wrote Seton in *The History of the Boy Scouts*. "Baden-Powell's was to make a soldier"; cited in Betty Keller, *Blackwolf: The Life of Ernest Thompson Seton* (Vancouver: Douglas and McIntyre, 1984), p. 169. Not that Seton wasn't a devoted promoter of militarism, but he was less concerned with empire building than man making. He argued that a scout's duty was to bear arms for his country in time of need and that "there cannot be anything worse for this country than to have an organization of boys brought up to the mushy milk-and-water which is the stock in trade of the apostles of pacifism." Cited in

Keller, *Blackwolf*, p. 176. For general historical accounts of the Boy Scouts, see David Macleod, "Act Your Age: Boyhood, Adolescence, and the Rise of the Boy Scouts in America," *Journal of Social History* 16, 1982; David Macleod, *Building Character in the American Boy: The YMCA, the Boy Scouts and Their Forerunners* (Madison: University of Wisconsin Press, 1983); Jeffrey Hantover, "The Boys Scouts and the Validation of Masculinity," *Journal of Social Issues* 34, 1978.

35. In its first few years, the Boy Scouts of America promoted these two masculine templates in its iconic representation. Chief Scout Dan Beard had earlier promoted (for his Sons of Daniel Boone) a "buckskin man," the perfect vision of Anglo-Saxon manhood, a blond giant who stood six foot two in his moccasins. A rugged individualist, this virilized Yankee combined, Beard wrote, "the reckless, rollicking fun of Robin Hood with the rugged morals of Abe Lincoln." See Allan R. Whitmore, "Beard, Boys and Buckskins: Daniel Carter Beard and the Preservation of the American Pioneer Tradition," Ph.D. diss., Northwestern University, 1970, pp. 452–454; Ernest Thompson Seton, *Gospel of the Redman* (London: Psychic Press, 1937), p. 103. See also Robert MacDonald, *Sons of the Empire*, p. 33.

36. Frederick Jackson Turner, *The Frontier in American History* (New York: Holt, Rinehart and Winston, 1947), p. 358. Daniel Beard, *The Boy Scout Handbook* [1914] (Boy Scouts of America Publication, 1955), p. 12.

37. Cited in Robert MacDonald, *Sons of the Empire*, p. 142.

38. Seton cited in Keller, *Blackwolf*, p. 161. Here Thompson-Seton sounds remarkably like Professor Harold Hill in the Broadway musical *The Music Man*, that clever portrayal of the chronically restless, sexually irresponsible Self-Made Man, whose scam is to persuade midwestern municipalities of the need to organize a boys' band to counter feminization and urban decay.

The threat to manhood, Seton thought, was less individual women than consumer culture itself. In fact, Seton's wife, Grace, was one of Connecticut's most visible and active suffragists, undertaking extensive speaking tours to promote woman suffrage. Ernest was active in the state's Men's League for Woman Suffrage in their home state and spoke in an automobile campaign with his wife in 1912. In an article entitled "Woman Suffrage Is not Going to Break Up the Home," the *Bridgeport Herald* noted that both Setons "are full of enthusiasm for woman suffrage, and it is not astonishing to find whole squads of boy scouts ardent believers in Votes for Women" (15 September 1912). This suggests the difference between the masculinist critique of cultural feminization and the antifeminist efforts to push women out of the public sphere. See Grace Thompson Seton papers, Schlesinger Library.

39. Cited in Betty Keller, *Blackwolf*, p. 189.

40. In the first *Boy Scout Handbook*, Seton wrote:

> I yield to no one in enjoyment of the sight of those splendid specimens of our race, trained to perfection, and playing faultlessly; but my heart sickens at the reverse of the ideal—thousands of boys and young men, pale, narrow chested, hunched up, miserable specimens, smoking endless cigarettes, numbers of them betting, all of them learning to be hysterical as they groan or cheer in panic unison with their neighbors.

41. Seton, cited in Macleod, *Building Character*, p. 49; *Boy Scout Handbook*, p. 38.

42. Francis Shepardson, *The Beta Book: The Story and Manual of Beta Theta Pi* (published by Beta Theta Pi, 1927), p. 23. For more on the collegiate culture created by fraternities, see Helen Lefkowitz Horowitz, *Campus Life: Undergraduate Cultures from the End of the Eighteenth Century to the Present* (New York: Knopf, 1987). Here is the description of one late-nineteenth-century initiation ceremony at Yale: Each freshman is taken in hand by a particular sophomore, who at the appropriate moment guides him to a building "from which the sounds of pandemonium are issuing." Here's what happens next:

> A red devil in the passageway, assisted by a living skeleton redolent of phosphorous, quickly blindfolds him, and he is hurried upward. When he has reached an elevation apparently of several hundred feet, a new element in the continual din assure him that at last he is in the inquisitorial hall. But just as he begins to reply to the last nonsensical question put by an attendant fiend, some one jostles against him, and down, down, down he falls, until he strikes a blanket held in readiness for him. Then he flies up in the air again amid admiring shouts of "Go it, Freshie!" "Well done, Sub!" "Shake him up!" until a new candidate demands the attention of the tosses. Then he is officiously told to rest himself in a chair, the seat of which lets him down into a pail of water, though a large sponge probably saves him from actual wetting; his head and hands are thrust through a pillory, and he is reviled in that awkward position; he is rolled in an exaggerated squirrel wheel, a noose is thrown around his neck, and he is dragged beneath the guillotine, when the bandage is pulled from his eyes and the glare upon the glittering knife of block-tin which falls within a foot of his throat and cannot possibly go further. Being thus executed, he is thrust into a coffin, which is hammered upon with such energy that he is at length recalled to life, pulled out again, and made to wear his coat with the inside outward. This is a sign that the initiation is over. (Cited in Henry D. Sheldon, *Student Life and Customs* (New York: Appleton, 1901, pp. 172–173)

One wonders if the creators of this ritual knew about the various contemporaneous open-seated chairs designed to put a brake on adolescent sexual ardor and extinguish the impulse to masturbate that I mentioned in chapter 3.

43. Henry Sheldon, *Student Life and Customs*, p. 219. Fraternities also had their detractors, who saw their fraternal bonding as fraudulent and promoting exclusivity and rowdyism. One critic wrote that fraternities encouraged immorality and destroyed the relationship between parents and child. "They are a pretence, and thus at war with true candor and manliness," wrote Dr. Howard Crosby in 1869. "However harmless in their active operations or undertakings, however well composed in membership, the habit of secrecy is insidiously weakening to the foundations of frank truthfulness in the youthful mind. Sham is not only a mean thing, but it blocks the way to truth. . . . A lad who receives honour among his comrades because he wears a mystic skull and bones upon his breast will proportionately lose so much of his zeal for scholarship or all else that constitutes true worth."

One antifraternity pamphlet, *An Account of the Greek Letter Fraternities in the University of California* (Berkeley: "Occident" Publishing, 1883; Bancroft Library, University of California), called the fraternity system "the most serious evil that menaces the usefulness of the University" (p. 3). The anonymous author listed a train of abuses and problems stemming from the fraternity system, including demoralization because of unquestioned loyalty among brothers; continued reprimand and discipline of fraternity members; poor scholarship; cheating; publishing obscene literature; importing "several fast girls" from San Francisco to Berkeley for a party. Fraternities attracted men "of unquestioned morality and fair scholarship, and almost without exception . . . equally unquestioned mediocrity" (p. 39).

44. W. S. Harwood, "Secret Societies in America," *North American Review* 164, May 1897. In Missouri, e.g., Masons grew from fewer than 10,000 members in 1865 to more than 60,000 by 1914, while membership in the Odd Fellows increased from 4,000 to 93,000 in that same period. See David Thelen, *Paths of Resistance*, p. 157. See also Noel Gist, "Secret Societies: A Cultural Study of Fraternalism in the United States," *University of Missouri Studies* 15, October 1940.

My account of fraternal orders also draws on three contemporary studies. See Mark Carnes, *Secret Ritual and Manhood in Victorian America* (New Haven: Yale University Press, 1989); Mary Ann Clawson, *Constructing Brotherhood: Class, Gender and Fraternalism* (Princeton, N.J.: Princeton University Press, 1989); and two articles by Barbara Franco, "Fraternal Organizations and Industrial Society," paper presented at the Lowell Conference on Industrial History, 26–28 October 1989; and "The Ritualization of Male Friendship and Virtue in Nineteenth-Century

Fraternal Organizations," paper presented to Winterthur Conference on the Material Culture of Gender/The Gender of Material Culture, 9–11 November 1989. See my review of Clawson, "The Rites of Men," *Nation*, August 12, 1990.

45. James P. Carnahan, *Pythian Knighthood* (Cincinnati: Pettibone Manufacturing Co., 1909); also cited in Barbara Franco, "Fraternal Organizations and Industrial Society," p. 6.

46. Mary Ann Clawson, *Constructing Brotherhood*, p. 146. Nancy MacLean writes that "the values celebrated by fraternalists were those of early modern artisanal culture, in which male producer-proprietors prided themselves on their difference from and patriarchal domination over the women, youth, servants, and apprentices." See Nancy MacLean, *Behind the Mask of Chivalry: The Making of the Second Ku Klux Klan* (New York: Oxford University Press, 1994), p. 74.

47. "Fraternal members built temples from which women were excluded, devised myriad secrets and threatened members with fearful punishments if they should 'tell their wives the concerns of the order' and created rituals which reclaimed for themselves the religious authority that formerly reposed in the hands of Biblical prophets," writes Carnes, *Secret Ritual and Manhood*, p. 79.

48. Beharrell, cited in Carnes, *Secret Ritual and Manhood*, p. 84; A. B. Grosh, *The Odd Fellows Improved Manual* (Philadelphia, 1871). James Laird, of the Grand Lodge of Nebraska, endorsed a Masonic war against "destructive effeminacy" in 1876, arguing that "[w]hat Masons want, what the world wants, is not sympathy, not cooperation, not reform, not redemption, but strength" (cited in Carnes, *Secret Ritual*, p. 141).

Again, the parallels with the contemporary mythopoetic men's movement are striking. Today's masculinists also criticize American men for being too feminized—working tirelessly to please the women in their lives—and thus deadened inside. At the same time, their retreats offer men a safe place in which they can weep, express pain and longing, and begin to nurture and comfort one another through expressions of manly nurture. For me, fraternal orders and mythopoetic retreats raise the same question: Do men really need all this ritualistic hokum and bogus mysticism in order to be tender and caring with one another?

49. In fact, it was the most important thing that most of them did. Since many orders had upwards of fifty different ranks, at least one brother was moving up at virtually every meeting. One critic even charged that the order subverted friendship among the members, "since so much time was spent on initiation ceremonies that members never got a chance to know each other." In initiation we see most clearly the fusion of patriarchal theology and the masculine family. Cited in Carnes, *Secret Ritual and Manhood*, p. 1; Carnes offers vivid descriptions of these initiation rituals.

50. Unlike the love of mothers and wives, "[b]rothers love shall never cease," as the Red Men motto had it. Could one ask for a more graphic example of womb envy than initiation ritual—and this at the very moment that Freud was theorizing about how women grow up envying men! No wonder W. S. Harwood wrote in his 1897 essay that "there is a strange and powerful attraction for some men in the mysticism of the ritual. There is a peculiar fascination in the unreality of the initiation, an allurement about fine 'team' work, a charm of deep potency in the unrestricted, out-of-the-world atmosphere which surrounds the scenes where men are knit together by the closest ties [and] bound by the most solemn obligations to maintain secrecy"; W. S. Harwood, "Secret Societies in America," p. 622.

51. Mary Ann Clawson writes that "in constituting the lodge as a male-only preserve, fraternalism rejected the claims of domesticity and asserted the moral authority of masculine community." See Clawson, *Constructing Brotherhood*, p. 256; Gage is cited in Mark Carnes, *Secret Ritual*, p. 80.

52. On racial exclusion see Noel Gist, "Secret Societies," pp. 128–131; on the Klan in the 1910s and 1920s, see Kathleen Blee, *Women of the Klan: Racism and Gender in the 1920s* (Berkeley: University of California Press, 1991). "Since the Klan claimed to admit only men whose masculinity was unquestionable, the very act of joining the Klan conferred manhood," she writes (p. 43).

53. Jeffrey Charles, *Service Clubs in American Society: Rotary, Kiwanis, and Lions* (Champaign: University of Illinois Press, 1993), p. 7.

54. Club member, cited in G. Edward White, *The Eastern Establishment and the Western Experience* (New Haven: Yale University Press, 1968), p. 27. Another member wrote that each

> is as much at home as if he were in his own castle; the building . . . is kept with the same neatness and exactness, and [offers the same] comfort as a private dwelling. Every member is a master, without any of the cares or troubles of a master. He is always obeyed with alacrity. He can come when he pleases and stay away as long as he pleases. (Cited in Leonard Ellis, "Men Among Men: An Explanation of All-Male Relationships in Victorian America," Ph.D. diss., Columbia University, 1982)

> The YMCA also offered such domestic alternatives. The YMCA in Utica, New York, appealed for funds by pointing out that "[m]any a young man in this city . . . spends his days at work, perhaps in some mechanics shop, or mill, or in your stores, [and] when at night comes home has nowhere else to go, for at the best the little room he calls his own is no HOME to him"; cited in E. Anthony Rotundo, "Contending Passions," MS, chap. 6, p. 16.

55. The Bohemian Club still runs a weeklong drunken revel for America's

ruling elite at its Sonoma County retreat (although their homosocial intimacy was reportedly lubricated by the availability of prostitutes at local inns). See G. William Domhoff, *The Bohemian Grove and Other Ruling-Class Retreats* (New York: Harper and Row, 1974). Domhoff noted that at Bohemian Grove corporate CEOs and national and state legislators regressed in torpid imitation of a fraternity stag party laden with frontier, Native American mysticism; after ritual chants and bare-chested dancing around the central campfire, these scions of business symbolically threw away the cares of their corporate or political responsibilities.

56. On the decline of fraternalism, see Gist, "Secret Societies," esp. pp. 42–43; see also Carnes, *Secret Ritual*, and Clawson, *Constructing Brotherhood*. The quote about men being less anxious after World War I is from Mark Carnes, *Secret Ritual*, p. 153. While such a statement may be convenient to conclude a study of fraternal orders proper, it addresses neither the different institutional locations for those anxieties nor their persistence through the rest of the century. On the shift from fraternal lodge to corporate picnic, see David Nye, *Image Worlds: Corporate Identities at General Electric, 1890–1930* (Cambridge: M.I.T. Press, 1985).

57. Ann Douglas, *The Feminization of American Culture* (New York: Knopf, 1977), pp. 101, 113, 97, 17. Earl Barnes cited the sensational preaching and the emphasis on ritualism to explain women's dominance; see "The Feminizing of Culture," *Atlantic Monthly* 109, 1912, p. 776.

58. Cited in Douglas, *The Feminization of American Culture*, p. 91.

59. Cited in Ted Ownby, *Subduing Satan: Religion, Recreation and Manhood in the Rural South* (Chapel Hill: University of North Carolina Press, 1991), p. 14.

60. Norman Vance, *The Sinews of the Spirit: The Ideal of Christian Manliness in Victorian Literature and Religious Thought* (Cambridge: Cambridge University Press, 1985), p. 29.

61. Thomas Wentworth Higginson, "Saints and Their Bodies," *Atlantic Monthly* 1, 1858, pp. 587, 584. See also his "Barbarism and Civilization," *Atlantic Monthly* 7, 1861, pp. 51–61, and "Gymnastics" in *Atlantic Monthly* 7, 1861, pp. 283–302. See also "Muscular Christianity," *North Carolina Presbyterian*, 2 January 1867. On the British origins of Muscular Christianity, see George Worth, "Of Muscles and Manliness: Some Reflections on Thomas Hughes," in *Victorian Literature and Society: Essays Presented to Richard Altick*, J. R. Kincard and A. J. Kuhn, eds. (Columbus: Ohio State University Press, 1984).

62. Carl Case, *The Masculine in Religion* (New York, 1906); R. W. Conant, *The Manly Christ, a New View* (Chicago, 1904); Harry Emerson Fosdick, *The Manhood of the Master* (New York, 1911); Thomas Hughes, *The Manliness*

of Christ (Boston: Houghton Mifflin, 1880); Jason Noble Pierce, *The Masculine Power of Christ; or, Christ Measured as a Man* (Boston: Pilgrim Press, 1912); Kenneth Wayne, *Building the Young Man* (Chicago: A. C. McClurg, 1912); Bouck White, *The Call of the Carpenter* (New York: Doubleday, 1913).

Interestingly, just as American Protestants were creating Muscular Christianity, Viennese Jews were experimenting with Muscular Jewry. Max Nordau, the widely read literary critic and novelist, summoned Jewish men to the Bar Kokhba Gymnastic Clubs in 1903 in the name of "Muskeljudentum," or Muscular Jewry. See Paul Breines, *Tough Jews: Political Fantasies and the Moral Dilemma of American Jewry* (New York: Basic Books, 1990).

63. Kenneth Wayne, *Building the Young Man*, pp. 168, 169.
64. According to White, "an able-bodied person who is content to live upon [the backs of women and children] is deficient in manliness." White, *The Call of the Carpenter*, pp. 135–136.
65. "A free workingman compelled to compete with slave labor, he ate the bread of affliction and drank the cup of servitude. He was a day-laborer; he wore the mechanics dress; he belonged to what is now known as the tin-dinner-pail crowd." White, *The Call of the Carpenter*, p. 350. Other quotes from White, pp. 36, 38, 110, 171. White assures us that Jesus had a "splendid capacity for losing his temper" (p. 162).
66. White, *The Call of the Carpenter*, pp. 182, 333–334.
67. "The Master appeals to all that is strongest and most military in you," wrote Harry Emerson Fosdick in *Manhood of the Master*, p. 161. "A corrupt civilization becomes effeminate and is apt to go down before a simpler foe," wrote Alfred Mahan in *The Harvest Within*, p. 123. Citations from the Ku Klux Klan are from Nancy MacLean, *Behind the Mask of Chivalry*, p. 161.
68. Charles Sheldon's *In His Steps* sold about 23 million copies between its publication in 1896 and 1925, counseling the simple message to pattern our lives on the life of Jesus and always asking the simple question, "What would Jesus do?" Leaders of the Social Gospel movement linked social activism with Christian morality through their images of a manly savior. "If ever there was a manly man, it was Christ. He worked as a carpenter; he carried his manliness into his public ministry," wrote one social gospeler in 1912 in a typical liaison of public activism and Christian masculinity ("The Brotherhood Movement," 1912, p. 37). "The practical question for you is whether you are *man* enough to become a genuine Christian—man enough to give up the meanness of selfishness for the general good," wrote Josiah Strong in 1901. Walter Rauschenbusch, another leader, insisted that "there was nothing mushy, nothing sweetly

effeminate about Jesus"; rather, he was "a man's man," who "turned again and again on the snarling pack of His pious enemies and made them slink away." See Ronald Huff, "Social Christian Clergymen and Feminism During the Progressive Era," Ph.D. diss., Union Theological Seminary, 1974, and Susan Curtis, "The Son of Man and God the Father: The Social Gospel and Victorian Morality," in *Meanings for Manhood*, M. Carnes and C. Griffen eds. (Chicago: University of Chicago Press, 1991), esp. pp. 72–73.

Rauschenbusch explicitly challenged the pictorial images of Jesus in Protestant iconography. "[H]is attitude was not soft. He resisted. He fought. Even on the cross he fought. He never fought as hard as then. . . . Christian art has misrepresented him when it makes him suffer with head down. His head was up and he was in command of the situation." Walter Rauschenbusch, *Christianity and the Social Crisis* (New York: Macmillan, 1907), p. 263; see also Walter Rauschenbusch, *A Theology for the Social Gospel* (New York: Macmillan, 1918). Even earlier, in 1894, the "men's class" of New York City's Riverside Church was founded by Charles Evans Hughes and John D. Rockefeller to link robust Christianity and social service; noblesse oblige, as it were.

69. Gail Bederman, " 'The Women Have Had Charge of the Church Work Long Enough': The Men and Religion Forward Movement of 1911–1912 and the Masculinization of Middle-Class Protestantism," *American Quarterly* 41, 1989; *Delaware Republican*, 27 February 1915; cited in Paula Baker, *The Moral Frameworks of Public Life: Gender, Politics and the State in Rural New York, 1870–1930* (New York: Oxford University Press, 1991), p. 171; Alfred Stearns et al., *The Education of the Modern Boy* (Boston: Houghton Mifflin, 1928), p. 105; Roger A. Bruns, *Preacher: Billy Sunday and Big Time American Evangelism* (New York: Norton, 1992), p. 15.

70. William A. Sunday, "Why I Left Professional Baseball," *Young Men's Era* 19(30), 27 July 1893, p. 1. See also William T. Ellis, *Billy Sunday: The Man and His Message* (Philadelphia: Universal Book and Bible House, 1914) for long passages from Sunday's sermons. I am grateful to Tim Nonn for finding this volume for me. Quote from journalist is from Roger Bruns, *Preacher*, p. 137; see also p. 110. Other important secondary works on Billy Sunday include Lyle Dorsett, *Billy Sunday and the Redemption of Urban America* (Grand Rapids, Mich.: Eerdmans, 1991); William G. McLaughlin, *Billy Sunday Was His Real Name* (Chicago: University of Chicago Press, 1955).

71. Quotes from Sunday are cited in William McLaughlin, *Billy Sunday Was His Real Name*, pp. 141, 179; Bruns, *Preacher*, p. 15.

72. Cited in Bruns, *Preacher*, pp. 16, 121, 122, 284, 138. McLaughlin, *Billy Sunday Was His Real Name*, p. 175.

73. Cited in McLaughlin, *Billy Sunday Was His Real Name*, pp. 141, 177, 142.

74. Cited in Bruns, *Preacher*, p. 15.

75. Not everyone was enamored with Sunday, however. Emma Goldman denounced him as a "frothing, howling huckster," and Carl Sandburg denounced him in a poem, "To a Contemporary Bunkshooter" (1915), as a "bughouse peddlar of second-hand gospel . . . tearing your shirt . . . yelling about Jesus."

76. Henry Rood, "Men and Religion," *Independent* 71, 1911, p. 1364; Fred Smith, *A Man's Religion* (New York, 1913). See Gail Bederman, "'The Women Have Had Charge of the Church Work Long Enough,'" and Gary Scott Smith, "The Men and Religion Forward Movement of 1911–1912: New Perspectives on Evangelical Social Concern and the Relationship Between Christianity and Progressivism," *Westminster Theological Journal* 49(1), Spring 1987.

77. Quote from Gary Scott Smith, "The Men and Religion Forward Movement," p. 100; Gail Bederman, "'The Women Have Had Charge of Church Work Long Enough,'" p. 22.

78. David Leverenz, "The Last Real Man in America: From Natty Bumppo to Batman," *American Literary History* 3, 1991, p. 763. "Probably no finer illustration of American manhood has ever occupied the office of the presidency than Theodore Roosevelt" was how one contemporary observer put it. John Brisben Walker, "A Working Man in the Presidency," *Cosmopolitan* 32, 1901, p. 25. I have also relied on several contemporary accounts of Roosevelt, including Kathleen Dalton, "Theodore Roosevelt: Morality and Manliness in the Progressive Era," unpublished MS, 1979; "Why America Loved Teddy Roosevelt," in *Our Selves/Our Past: Psychological Approaches to American History*, Robert J. Brugger, ed. (Baltimore: Johns Hopkins University Press, 1981); William Davison Johnson, *TR: Champion of the Strenuous Life* (New York: Theodore Roosevelt Assoc., 1958); Bruce Miroff, *Icons of Democracy: American Leaders as Heroes, Aristocrats, Dissenters, and Democrats* (New York: Basic Books, 1993), pp. 158–199.

    Of course, TR himself was a frequent contributor to his own mythology. I have relied here on *Addresses and Papers of Theodore Roosevelt*, W. F. Johnson, ed. (New York: Unit Book Publishing, 1909); *The Works of Theodore Roosevelt*, 20 vols. (New York: Scribners, 1926), *Autobiography* [1913] (New York: Scribners, 1958); *The New Nationalism* (New York: Outlook, 1910); *The Letters of Theodore Roosevelt*, Elting Morrison, ed. (Cambridge: Harvard University Press, 1951).

79. Herman Hagedorn, *A Boy's Life of Theodore Roosevelt* (New York: Harper, 1918). One of the best-selling boys' books of all time, *A Boy's Life* made Roosevelt's journey a template for twentieth-century American men.

80. Tom Lutz, *American Nervousness* (1903), p. 79.
81. Roosevelt himself thought he looked smashing in his "sombrero, silk neckerchief, fringed buckskin shirt, sealskin chaparajos or riding trousers, and alligator hide boots" and with his "pearl-hilted revolver and beautifully finished Winchester rifle," he felt "able to face anything," as he wrote to his sister, cited in Donald Day, ed., *The Hunting and Exploring Adventures of Theodore Roosevelt* (New York: Dial, 1955), p. 47. See also G. Edward White, *The Eastern Establishment and the Western Experience*, p. 83, and John Eliot, "TR's Wilderness Legacy," *National Geographic*, September 1982, p. 344.
82. *Autobiography*, p. 76. The West, he wrote, "is no place for men who lack the ruder, coarser virtues and physical qualities, no matter how intellectual or how refined and delicate their sensibilities." *Ranch Life and the Hunting Trail* (1888), pp. 56, 10.
83. Tom Lutz, *American Nervousness* (1903), p. 28.
84. Theodore Roosevelt, *The Works of Theodore Roosevelt*, vol. 13, pp. 322–323, 331. With that speech Roosevelt catapulted to the head of a long list of American presidents, from Andrew Jackson to George Bush, who sought to prove their manhood through imperial aggression against smaller and weaker countries or cultures. From the Seminoles to the Philippines, from Panama (twice) to Grenada, the best strategy to promote war is to question the president's manhood.

    Of course, this concern was particularly salient at the turn of the century; as one California newspaper editorialized in the 1890s, "the ardor and strength of prime manhood is a much needed quality in American government, especially at this time, when all things political and all things social are in the transition stage"; cited in Bruce Curtis, "The Wimp Factor," *American Heritage*, November 1989, p. 44. Masculinist themes resounded across the political spectrum, as the campaign for James Garfield—"the workingman's best friend; ignoring fop and dandy"—or that between Benjamin Harrison, "the man who captured flags in battle's blazing track," and Grover Cleveland, "the cringing craven who would give them back," would attest (*Songbooks*, pp. 139, 140). Senator Roscoe Conkling continually characterized his opponents as "the man-milliners, the dilettanti and carpet knights of politics," whose stock-in-trade was "rancid, canting, self-righteousness" and who "forget that parties are not built up by deportment, or by ladies' magazines, or by gush." See Roscoe Conkling, *The Life and Letters of Roscoe Conkling*, Alfred Conkling, ed. (New York: Webster, 1889) pp. 540, 541. Even Woodrow Wilson eventually had to assert his manhood, since his early bookishness as president of Princeton did not outfit him for the manly heroism of the presidency of the nation. One article praised his transformation from the rarefied realm of Princeton, where he was "bulwarked by books," into a "boss wrecker of corrupt machine, and militant master of his party." See *Munsey's*, October 1911, p. 3.

85. Thorstein Veblen, *The Theory of the Leisure Class*, p. 168. Veblen delighted in castigating the "essential immaturity" of the sporting impulse. William James, "Governor Roosevelt's Oration," in *Works of William James: Essays, Comments and Reviews*, Frederick Burkhardt, ed. (Cambridge: Harvard University Press, 1987), pp. 162–164.

86. Joseph Dana Miller, "Militarism or Manhood?" *Arena* 24, October 1900, pp. 385, 386–388.

87. Amy Hardwicke, "A Woman's Idea of the Physical Culture Man," *Physical Culture* 4, 1901. Charlotte Perkins Gilman, *Women and Economics* [1899] (New York: Harper and Row, 1966), pp. 119, 126.

88. See "Muster Out Roll," reprinted in Roosevelt, *The Rough Riders*, pp. 238–269. *Santa Fe New Mexican*, 11 May 1898. These journalistic reports are cited in G. Edward White, *The Eastern Establishment*, p. 155.

89. Theodore Roosevelt, "The American Boy," 1900. Roosevelt's comment on continental expansion is from the foreword to the 1900 edition of *The Winning of the West*, vol. 1, pp. x–xi.

90. The quote is from George Frederickson, *The Inner Civil War: Northern Intellectuals and the Crisis of the Union* (Champaign: University of Illinois Press, 1993), p. 166. TR's boys' books, *The Wilderness Hunter* (1894), *American Big Game Hunting* (1894), and *Hunting in Many Lands* (1896), were written for the Boone and Crockett Club and became part of boy culture in the early twentieth century. As one of the founders of the American Museum of Natural History, Roosevelt linked Darwinian evolution, eugenics, and racism into a potent blend that the historian of science Donna Haraway ingeniously calls "Teddy Bear Patriarchy." See Donna Haraway, *Primate Visions: Gender, Race and Nature in the World of Modern Science* (New York: Routledge, 1989), chap. 3.

I admit to a very personal relationship to Teddy Bear Patriarchy. My great uncle, Morris Michtom, was one of those Americans who was completely mesmerized by this big-game hunting, rough and rowdy image of the president. An immigrant candy store owner and part-time tailor on the Lower East Side, Morris read about TR's hunting exploits and was particularly struck by a story of how TR refrained from killing a bear because he suddenly saw her small cub. Piecing together a little model of the bear cub from scraps of cloth, he sent it to TR in the White House, where the president was so pleased with his trophy that he displayed it in a magazine photograph. Within days Uncle Morris was deluged by Washington's political elite with requests for copies, and soon Morris had hired a collection of local neighborhood boys to manufacture these

"Teddy Bears." Morris Michtom founded the Ideal Toy Corporation the next year.

I also admit to having been completely taken in by TR's image in my youth. After devouring *A Boy's Life of Theodore Roosevelt*, I vividly recall a family outing to Sagamore Hill, TR's home and retreat in Oyster Bay, Long Island. His study was the manliest room I've ever encountered: animal rugs on the floor, deep rich leather chairs and book bindings, animal heads covering the dark brown wood paneling, and, most impressive to me, a chair made entirely from elephant tusks and covered with zebra skin. For years I kept a postcard of the room on the bulletin board at my desk and fantasized about the life that must have been lived in order to collect such trophies.

91. William Davison Johnson, *TR: Champion of the Strenuous Life*, pp. 138, 126–127.

92. If the "process of race decay continued in the United States and the British Empire, the future of the white race would rest in the hands of the German and the Slav," he wrote. Roosevelt, *Addresses and Papers*, p. 433; German and Slav quote cited in Richard Hofstadter, *Social Darwinism in American Thought* (Boston: Beacon Press, 1955), p. 189. Roosevelt also opposed women working, believing that it would work "change and disturbance" in American life, especially since it also produced the "decrease in marriage and especially in the birth rate." See *Addresses and Papers*, p. 275.

93. See Kathleen Dalton, "Theodore Roosevelt," p. 11. Dalton argues that even as he charged up San Juan Hill, TR "could not murder his invalid self" (p. 12).

94. Gail Parker, *Mind Cure in New England: From the Civil War to World War I* (Hanover, N.H.: University Press of New England, 1973), p. 34.

CHAPTER 6: Muscles, Money, and the M-F Test

1. Hemingway's letter is cited in Mark Spilka, *Hemingway's Quarrel with Androgyny* (Lincoln: University of Nebraska Press, 1990), p. 329.

2. George W. Henry, "Psychogenic Factors in Overt Homosexuality," *American Journal of Psychiatry* 93, p. 904.

3. See Elizabeth Lunbeck, *The Psychiatric Persuasion: Knowledge, Gender, and Power in Modern America* (Princeton, N.J.: Princeton University Press, 1994), p. 253; see also E. E. Southard, *Shell-Shock and Other Neuropsychiatric Problems: Presented in Five Hundred and Eighty-Nine Case Histories from the War Literature, 1914–1918* [1919] (New York: Arno, 1973); Harold Evans, "Hysteria in the Male with Report of a Case," *Journal of the Association of Military Surgeons of the United States* 13, 1903; Richard Hutchings, "Hysteria As Manifested in the Military Service," *State Hospital Quarterly* 4, 1918–1919; Aaron Rosanoff, "A Study of Hysteria, Based

Mainly on Clinical Material Observed in the U.S. Army Hospital for War Neuroses at Plattsburgh Barracks, N.Y.," *Archives in Neurology and Psychiatry* 2, 1919; Karl Menninger, "Hysteria in a Male as a Defense Reaction: A Case Report," *Boston Medical and Surgical Journal* 180, 1919.

4. Robert Lynd and Helen Lynd, *Middletown* [1929] (New York: Free Press, 1955); Robert Lynd and Helen Lynd, *Middletown in Transition* [1937] (New York: Free Press, 1966); see also Pitirim Sorokin, "American Millionaires and Multi-Millionaires," *Journal of Social Forces* 3, 1925, p. 636; and Thorstein Veblen, *Engineers and the Price System* (New York: Viking, 1921), and *The Technicians and Revolution* (New York: Viking, 1921).

5. Clarence Darrow, "Salesmanship," *American Mercury*, August 1925.

6. Frederick Payne Millard, *What a Man Goes Through* (Boston: Christopher Publishing House, 1925), p. 108.

7. Suzanne LaFollette quote and "These Modern Husbands," letter to the editor of the *Nation*, 12 January 1927, p. 39; both cited in Kevin White, *The First Sexual Revolution*, p. 178.

8. Labor Force Statistics, Series D 85-86: Unemployment, 1890–1970.

9. Henry H. Goddard, "Mental Tests and the Immigrant," *Journal of Delinquency* 2, 1917, p. 252; Carl C. Bingham, *A Study of American Intelligence* (Princeton, N.J.: Princeton University Press, 1923), pp. 111, 162; see also p. 180.

10. This wasn't new for organized labor, which had consistently followed a nativist line in their defense of the white Heroic Artisan. What was new was how easily this position fell into the American mainstream.

11. David Barrows, president of the University of California, testified before the U.S. Congress that the social problems of the Filipino were "almost entirely based upon sexual passion" because of his "lower nature." All cited in Ronald Takaki, *Strangers from a Different Shore: A History of Asian Americans* (New York: Viking, 1989), pp. 324–331.

12. Alexander Goldenweiser, "Prehistoric KKKs," *World Tomorrow* 7, March 1924, p. 81. See also F. Bohn, "Ku Klux Klan Interpreted," in *American Journal of Sociology* 30, 1925. For recent interpretive accounts, see Stanley Coben, *Rebellion Against Victorianism: The Impetus for Cultural Change in the 1920s* (New York: Oxford University Press, 1991), and Kathleen Blee, *Women of the Klan: Racism and Gender in the 1920s* (Berkeley: University of California Press, 1991).

13. Devere Allen, "Substitutes for Brotherhood," *World Tomorrow* 7, March 1924, pp. 74, 75. Charles Merz provided the estimate of 800 secret societies in "Halt! Who Comes There?" *New Republic* 35, 1923, and in "Sweet Land of Secrecy," *Harper's Magazine* 154, 1927. See also Nelson Crawford, "Nobility of the Campus," *American Mercury* 21, 1930, for a critical look at collegiate fraternities.

14. See Stanley Coben, *Rebellion Against Victorianism*, p. 138; see also Kathleen Blee, *Women of the Klan*.

15. Bruce Barton, *The Man Nobody Knows* (New York and Indianapolis: Bobbs-Merrill, 1924), pp. 43, 31, and passim. That this "self-made" man was, by doctrine, not in the least self-made did not seem to bother Barton and his followers. He remained an exemplar of manhood, even if now an Americanized man on the go.

16. David Nye, *Image Worlds: Corporate Identities at General Electric, 1890–1930* (Cambridge: M.I.T. Press, 1985), p. 96.

17. Newcomer, 1959, pp. 10–36.

18. Frederick Payne Millard, *What a Man Goes Through: Friendly Chats About the Battle of Life* (Boston: Christopher Publishing House, 1925), p. 66. Millard was also astute about the processes of social change, arguing that man would change "only when women force it upon him" (p. 68). A *Fortune* magazine writer is cited in Angel Kwolek-Folland, *Engendering Business: Men and Women in the Corporate Office, 1870–1930* (Baltimore: The Johns Hopkins University Press, 1994), p. 41; Charles Vanse, "How Well Do I Remember," *Equitable Spirit* 1(4), 1934 (also cited in Kwolek-Folland, p. 166); Anthony Ludovici, "Woman's Encroachment on Man's Domain," *Current History* 27, October 1927, p. 23.

19. H. L. Mencken, *In Defense of Women* (New York: P. Goodman Company, 1918), p. 135.

20. Sherwood Anderson, *Perhaps Women* (New York: Horace Liveright, 1931), pp. 42, 142.

21. Quoted in Steven Mintz and Susan Kellogg, *Domestic Revolutions: A Social History of American Family Life* (New York: Free Press, 1988), p. 138. See also R. S. Cavan, "Unemployment: Crisis of the Common Man," in *Marriage and Family Living* 21, 1959, which reviews studies of the Depression's impact on marital and family life.

22. Cited in Robert Griswold, "Fatherhood and World War II," paper presented to the Organization of American Historians annual meeting, April 1989, p. 2.

23. Cousins is cited in Alice Kessler-Harris, *Out to Work* (New York: Oxford University Press, 1982), p. 256.

24. Cited in Warren Sussman, *Culture as History: The Transformation of American Society in the Twentieth Century* (New York: Pantheon, 1984), p. 195.

25. But what Carnegie extolled as flexibility was criticized at the time as a doctrine of "the soft and . . . spineless citizens of a regimented state" instead of the "self-respecting and self-reliant men who made America," as Republican vice presidential candidate Frank Knox put it in 1936. Cited in Rupert Wilkinson, *The Pursuit of American Character* (New York: Harper and Row, 1988), p. 104. And Carnegie's mid-1930s flexible personality was reduced to impotent tears by Arthur Miller in 1949 and later soundly thrashed by the studies of bland conformity in the 1950s.

26. Mirra Komorovsky, *The Unemployed Man and His Family* (New York: Dryden Press, 1940), pp. 74–75. One is tempted to attribute the different tones in the two extracts—the psychiatrist's fixing blame on the castrating wife, and the sociologist's more structural explanation—on the different fields of inquiry and their analytic postures. One might, however, note that it is the *woman* researcher who exhibits far more compassion for all the members of the family than the male psychiatrist, who can only rescue the unemployed man by belittling his wife.

27. Komorovsky, *The Unemployed Man*, pp. 355, 357.

28. Lurine Pruette, *The Parent and the Happy Child* (New York: Henry Holt, 1932), p. 32. See also Robert Griswold, *Fatherhood: A Social History* (New York: Basic Books, 1993).

29. Roy Dickerson, *Growing into Manhood* (New York: Association Press, 1933), p. 21.

30. Sinclair Lewis, *Babbit* [1922] (New York: Signet, 1961), p. 97.

31. See Peter Filene, *Him/Her Self: Sex Roles in Modern America*, 2nd ed. (Baltimore: The Johns Hopkins University Press, 1986), p. 46, and Stephanie Coontz, *The Way We Never Were: American Families and the Nostalgia Trap* (New York: Basic Books, 1992).

32. John B. Watson, *Psychological Care of Infant and Child* (New York: Norton, 1928), pp. 5, 6, 12, 86, and esp. chap. 3; see also Warren I. Susman, *Culture as History: The Transformation of American Society in the Twentieth Century* (New York: Pantheon, 1984), p. 108, and Ben Harris, " 'Give Me a Dozen Healthy Infants': John B. Watson's Popular Advice on Child rearing, Women and the Family," in *In the Shadow of the Past: Psychology Portrays the Sexes*, Miriam Lewin, ed. (New York: Columbia University Press, 1984). I am grateful to Joseph Pleck for his comments on this point.

33. Joseph Collins, *The Doctor Looks at Love and Life* (New York: Doran, 1926), p. 73. Collins admitted that he had "known husky, articulate, self-opinionated, and even domineering" male homosexuals (p. 74). Clement Wood, *Manhood: The Facts of Life Presented to Man* (Kansas City: Haldeman-Julius, 1924). See also Kevin White, *The First Sexual Revolution: The Emergences of Male Heterosexuality in Modern America* (New York: New York University Press, 1992).

34. "Masculine Women! Feminine Men!" written by Monaco and Leslie, 1925; first recorded by Frank Harris in 1926 (Okeh Records, 40593). I am grateful to Jonathan Ned Katz for first bringing this song to my attention and for his delightful rendition of it for my class.

35. See George Chauncey, *Gay New York: Gender, Urban Culture and the Making of the Gay Male World, 1890–1940* (New York: Basic Books, 1994), pp. 354, 559–560. Gay men, Chauncey writes, were suddenly seen as "figures whose defiant perversity threatened to undermine the reproduction

of normative gender and sexual arrangements already threatened by the upheavals of the thirties" (p. 354).

36. Jodi Vandenberg-Daves, "Pursuing a Partnership Between the Sexes: The Debate over Programs for Women and Girls in the Young Men's Christian Association, 1914–1933," unpublished paper, University of Minnesota, 1991; William Allen White, *Boys—Then and Now* (New York: Macmillan, 1926), pp. 42–43.

37. See Thomas Woody, *A History of Women's Education in the United States* (New York: Science Press, 1929) vol. 2, p. 451; see also William O'Neill, *Divorce in the Progressive Era* (New Haven: Yale University Press, 1967).

38. Geoffrey Gorer, *The American People: A Study in National Character* (New York: Norton, 1964), pp. 48–49.

39. See the discussion of this film in George Chauncey, *Gay New York*, p. 325.

40. Lewis Terman and Catherine Cox Miles, *Sex and Personality* (New York: Russell and Russell, 1936), p. 3.

41. Joseph Pleck, *The Myth of Masculinity* (Cambridge: M.I.T. Press, 1981), p. 159, and passim. Pleck is the first psychologist to reexamine the M-F test and find it empirically untenable and internally contradictory.

42. That the inventory consisted of 456 items is a clear indication of the systematic quality—and the rather obsessive frenzy—of their efforts.

43. For more about Terman and the M-F test, see Henry L. Minton, "Femininity in Men and Masculinity in Women: American Psychiatry and Psychology Portray Homosexuality in the 1930s," *Journal of Homosexuality* 13(1), Fall 1986.

44. To score this section, give yourself a minus (-) for every answer in which you said that the thing caused "a lot" of the emotion—except for the answer "being a Bolshevik," which was obviously serious enough for even men to get very emotional about. On all the others, though, and through the entire test, high levels of emotion—regardless of the cause or the emotion—were scored as feminine.

45. The original sample upon which this MMPI was based, incidentally, was 54 male soldiers, 67 female airline employees, and 13 male homosexuals. See Joseph Pleck, *The Myth of Masculinity* (Cambridge: M.I.T. Press, 1981), p. 37. On the Strong Vocational Interest Blank, see Edward K. Strong, "Interests of Men and Women," *Journal of Social Psychology* 7, 1936, and Edward K. Strong, *Vocational Interests of Men and Women* (Stanford, Cal.: Stanford University Press, 1943). On the Guilfords' temperament survey, see J. P Guilford and Ruth P. Guilford, "Personality Factors S, E, and M and Their Measurement," *Journal of Psychology* 2, 1936. On all these tests, see James Harrison, "A Critical Evaluation of Research on Masculinity/Femininity and a Proposal for an Alternative Paradigm for Research on Psychological Differences and Similarities Between

the Sexes," unpublished Ph.D. diss., Union Theological Seminary, Columbia University, 1975; Joseph Pleck, "The Theory of Male Sex Role Identity: Its Rise and Fall, 1936 to the Present," in *In the Shadow of the Past: Psychology Portrays the Sexes*, Miriam Lewin, ed. (New York: Columbia University Press, 1984), pp. 205–225; and Pleck, *The Myth of Masculinity*, passim.

46. See Miriam Lewin, " 'Rather Worse Than Folly?' Psychology Measures Femininity and Masculinity, Part 1: From Terman and Miles to the Guilfords," in Miriam Lewin, ed., *In the Shadow of the Past: Psychology Portrays the Sexes*, p. 164.

47. Terman and Miles, *Sex and Personality*, p. 320. It might be noted that first, last, or only children probably composed over two-thirds of all children in the country.

48. See, e.g., George W. Henry, "Psychogenic Factors in Overt Homosexuality," *American Journal of Psychiatry* 93, 1937, and *Sex Variants: A Study of Homosexual Patterns*, vol. 1 (New York: Hoeber, 1941). For commentary see Henry L. Minton, "Femininity in Men and Masculinity in Women: American Psychiatry and Psychology Portray Homosexuality in the 1930s," *Journal of Homosexuality* 13(1), 1986. On subsequent measures see Lewin, " 'Rather Worse Than Folly?"

49. So significant is the development of the M-F test that Joseph Pleck places the emergence of the contemporary male sex-role paradigm in 1936. See Joseph Pleck, *The Myth of Masculinity*, and "The Rise and Fall of the Male Sex Role, 1936 to the Present," in *The Making of Masculinities*, Harry Brod, ed. (Boston: Unwin Hyman, 1987).

50. M. Zolotow, "You Too Can Be a New Man," *Saturday Evening Post* 214, 7 February 1942, p. 59. See also "Muscle Makers," *Time*, 22 February 1937.

51. Robert Lewis Taylor, "I Was Once a 97-Pound Weakling," *New Yorker*, 3 January 1942, p. 25.

52. Cited in Zolotow, "You Too Can Be a New Man," p. 60.

53. Ibid., p. 21.

54. Jules Feiffer, *Great Comic Book Heroes* (New York: Dial Press, 1965), p. 19. I am grateful to Susan Park for providing me a copy of her paper, "Lois Lane . . . Superwoman?" which helped clarify Superman's dual masculinity.

55. James Thurber, "The Secret Life of Walter Mitty," *New Yorker*, 18 March 1939.

56. I am grateful to George Robinson for this quote and for his enormous help in thinking through the genderedness of the era's films.

57. Raymond Chandler, *The Simple Art of Murder* (New York: Norton, 1968). See also Philip Durham, *Down These Mean Streets a Man Must Go: Ray-*

mond Chandler's Knight (Chapel Hill: University of North Carolina Press, 1963), and James Forman, *Softcover Manhood: The Rise of the Paperback and the Fear of Unmanliness, 1939–1959,* unpublished Ph.D. diss., University of Southern California, 1991.

58. Wexman, p. 27. Cited in Frank Krutnik, *In a Lonely Street: Film Noir, Genre, Masculinity* (New York: Routledge, 1991), pp. 42–43.

59. Leslie Fiedler, *Love and Death in the American Novel* (New York: Stein and Day, 1970), pp. 316–317. Sandra Gilbert and Susan Gubar, *No Man's Land: The Place of the Writer in the Twentieth Century,* vol. 1 (New Haven: Yale University Press, 1988), p. 36. D. H. Lawrence is cited in Mark Spilka, *Hemingway's Quarrel with Androgyny* (Lincoln: University of Nebraska Press, 1994), p. 179.

60. Quotes are from Ernest Hemingway, *The Sun Also Rises* (1927). Hemingway's power comes in part from his refusal of the possibility of relief from the torments of haunted manhood. When, in the book's final scene, Brett offers even modest comfort, Jake responds without illusion. " 'Oh, Jake,' Brett said, 'we could have had such a damned fine time together.' 'Yes,' I said. 'Isn't it pretty to think so?' "

61. Sinclair Lewis, *Babbit,* [1922] (New York: Signet, 1961), p. 155.

62. John Cawelti, *Apostles of the Self-Made Man* (Chicago: University of Chicago Press, 1965), p. 230.

63. F. Scott Fitzgerald, *The Great Gatsby* (New York: Scribners, 1925), pp. 99, 174.

64. John Steinbeck, *Of Mice and Men* [1937] (New York: Penguin, 1974), p. 104.

65. The phrase is Jim Hoberman's from his review of the film *Of Mice and Men* in the *Village Voice.*

66. In Steinbeck's later novel *The Winter of Our Discontent* (1961), we find the other side of the story. Ethan Allen Hawley is incapable of living up to his name, which evokes the rugged individualism of the Green Mountain Boys during the American Revolution. Well born, Hawley is an unsuccessful clerk in a grocery store, a patriarch without power or property. The efforts of this "gentle, moral good humored family man" to become a success transform him; he becomes ruthlessly cynical and "effectively alienate[s] himself from every important value he had always believed and or lived by. See Michael Messner, "The Fall of Patriarchy in *The Winter of Our Discontent,*" *masculinities* 2(3), 1994, p. 9.

But the successful Self-Made Man is isolated from others and incapable of friendship or connection. In the end all that seems to matter to Ethan is "[s]trength and success—they are above morality, above criticism. It seems, then, that it is not what you do, but how you do it and what you call it. Is there a check in men, deep in them, that stops or pun-

ishes? There doesn't seem to be. The only punishment is for failure."
John Steinbeck, *The Winter of Our Discontent*, p. 201.

67. John Lahr, "Waiting for Odets," *New Yorker*, 26 October 1992, p. 122. Like Odets, the Left continued to use the Heroic Artisan as a model for the New Socialist worker.

68. See Clifford Odets, *Waiting for Lefty*, in *Three Plays by Clifford Odets* (New York: Random House, 1935).

69. Gold is cited in David Savran, *Communists, Cowboys and Queers: The Politics of Masculinity in the Work of Arthur Miller and Tennessee Williams* (Minneapolis: University of Minnesota Press, 1992), p. 25.

70. Barrie, of course, was the British creator of Peter Pan, the boy who refused to grow up and assume manly responsibilities but rather wanted to always remain a boy and "have fun."

71. See Joan Mellon, *Big Bad Wolves: Masculinity in American Film* (New York: Pantheon, 1977), p. 29.

CHAPTER 7: "Temporary About Myself"

1. In reality, both the European and Pacific theaters yielded a collage of carnage and gore on a far greater scale than anything American soldiers had ever seen. Utah Beach on D-Day, e.g., was a "surreal hell" of landing craft picking their way through a sea of floating body parts, while all around there were "young men crying for their mothers, wetting and defecating themselves." Cited in Studs Terkel, *"The Good War": An Oral History of World War Two* (New York: Pantheon, 1985), p. 276.

2. See Sonya Michel, "Danger on the Home Front: Motherhood, Sexuality, and the Disabled Veterans in American Postwar Films," *Journal of the History of Sexuality* 3(1), 1992; and Kaja Silverman, "Historical Trauma and Male Subjectivity," in *Psychoanalysis and Cinema*, E. Ann Kaplan, ed. (New York: Routledge, 1990).

3. Cited in Michael C. C. Adams, *The Best War Ever: America and World War II* (Baltimore: The Johns Hopkins University Press, 1994), pp. 151, 150.

4. Adams, *The Best War Ever*, p. 112. This was made even more unsettling because the American military was far more selective than its European allies. Nearly one-third (32%) of all rejections from the military were for psychological reasons, and only the United States rejected men who might have *latent* homosexual tendencies, usually measured by a response that the opposite sex "frightened" the recruit or by his seeming discomfort when asked to strip naked during group physical examinations. See Allan Berube, *Coming Out Under Fire: The History of Gay Men and Lesbians in World War Two* (New York: Free Press, 1990), pp. 20–21.

5. Raymond Sobel, "The Battalion Surgeon as Psychiatrist," *Bulletin of the U.S. Army Medical Department*, suppl., November 1949, p. 38.

6. Stephen Ranson, "The Normal Battle Reaction: Its Relation to the Pathologic Battle Reaction," *Bulletin of the U.S. Army Medical Department*, suppl., November 1949, p. 6.

7. And living with it often meant suppression, both individually and culturally. John Huston's documentary about soldiers and shell shock, *Let There Be Light* (1948), was not shown until the 1980s because Army censors found the material about battlefield cowardice and trauma too threatening to anti-Communist morale building.

8. Cited in Frank Krutnik, *In a Lonely Street: Film Noir, Genre, Masculinity* (New York: Routledge, 1991), p. 210.

9. Cited in Griswold, "Fatherhood and World War II," p. 11.

10. See Daniel Boone, "No Substitute for Father," *Rotarian* 65, August 1944, and Robert Griswold, "Fatherhood and World War II," paper presented at the Organization of American Historians annual meeting, April 1989.

11. Cited in Griswold, "Fatherhood and World War II," pp. 5–6.

12. Ada Hart Arlitt, "How Separation Affects the Family," *Marriage and Family Living* 5, February 1943, p. 21.

13. Talcott Parsons, "Certain Primary Sources and Patterns of Aggression in the Social Structure of the Western World," in *Essays in Sociological Theory* (New York: Free Press, 1963), p. 309.

14. Later, he writes that boys

    refuse to have anything to do with girls. "Sissy" becomes the worst of all insults. They get interested in athletics and physical prowess, in the things in which men have the most primitive and obvious advantages over women. Furthermore, they become allergic to all expression of tender emotion; they must be "tough." This universal pattern bears all the earmarks of a "reaction-formation." It is so conspicuous, not because it is simply "masculine nature" but because it is a defense against a feminine identification. (Talcott Parsons, "Certain Patterns of Aggression," p. 171)

    In a later paper Parsons made it clear that full employment was a psychological necessity as well, since "virtually the only way to be a real man in our society is to have an adequate job and earn a living." Talcott Parsons, "The Social Structure of the Family," in *The Family: Its Function and Destiny*, Ruth Nanda Anshen, ed. (New York: Harper Bros., 1959), p. 271.

15. E.g., Arnold Green argued in 1946 that it was the sons of permissive and punishment-shunning mothers who turned out to have neurotic dispositions, not the sons of authoritarian and punitive parents. See Arnold Green, "The Middle-Class Male Child and Neurosis," *American Sociological Review* 11, 1946.

16. Philip Wylie, *A Generation of Vipers* (New York: Farrar and Rinehart,

1942); David Levy, *Maternal Overprotection* (New York: Columbia University Press, 1943); and Edward Strecker, *Their Mothers' Sons* (Philadelphia: Lippincott, 1946).

17. It should be noted, however, that Strecker used "mom" to describe all overprotective types, regardless of their gender, as well as institutions that coddled instead of confronted and challenged.

18. Philip Wylie, *A Generation of Vipers*, pp. 187–188. Readers of Wylie's book were invited to consider the following useful college courses: "How to Tell Your Mother from a Wolf," "Adventures in Mother's Four-Door Womb," and "Domestic Failures of Prominent American Women." In other aspects, Wylie's book is far more insightful: He indicts the educational system, mass media, and uncritical boosterism for lulling the American youth into mass passivity so that more pressing social problems are neither discussed nor addressed.

In Wylie's novel *The Disappearance* (New York: Holt, Rinehart and Winston, 1951) the world's men and women disappear from one another and inhabit separate worlds for four years, during which both sexes become aware of their mutual dependence. But the differences are revealing. In the absence of women, American and Russian political leaders unleash nuclear Armageddon, while in the absence of men, the women attend to the injured and attempt food rationing. Thus, Wylie argues, for all their individual rationality, men are collectively irrational without women around; by contrast, women, for all their supposed individual irrationality, are collectively far more rational than men. Taken together, then, Wylie's mom-bashing in *Generation of Vipers* and this novel suggest that it's a good thing when adult women act as moral constraints on adult men's excesses but a dreadfully feminizing thing when mothers act to constrain the excesses of their little boys.

19. Margaret Mead, *And Keep Your Powder Dry* (New York: Morrow, 1942), pp. 68–69.

20. And restless and anxious we are, Mead argued, "always moving on, always in his hopes, moving up, leaving behind him all that was his past," so that the typical American success story finds each man planning "to die in a position higher than the position in which he was born." However, this "carries with it an unfortunate need to deprecate the success of others at the same time that one maximates the success which one has attained oneself." Margaret Mead, *And Keep Your Powder Dry*, pp. 37, 65.

21. Ibid., pp. 142, 157, 151.

22. Richard Wright, *Native Son* (New York: Harper and Row, 1940), pp. 12, 273, 280. See also Richard Wright, *Black Boy* (New York: Harper and Row, 1945), and Richard Wright, "The Man Who Was Almost a Man," in *Eight Men* (Cleveland: World Publishing, 1961), p. 18.

23. Cited in James Greenberg, "In Film Noir, the Past Is Present and Perfect," *New York Times*, 6 February 1994, H9. On the genre see Krutnik, *In a Lonely Street*, and E. Ann Kaplan, ed. *Women in Film Noir* (London: BFI, 1978).

24. Something of the reverse occurs in *The Maltese Falcon* (1941), and then he rejects the woman because of his love for another man. I am grateful to Harry Brod and Jesse Berrett for pointing this out to me.

25. Arthur Miller, *Death of a Salesman* [1949] (New York: Penguin, 1986), p. 36.

26. Ibid., p. 73.

27. Ibid., p. 23; other citations from pp. 65, 22, 54.

28. Ibid., pp. 132, 138. Happy still can't let go and stubbornly insists that he's going to hang in there and show them that "a Loman" can and will be a winner.

29. Chafe is cited in Wini Breines, *Young, White and Miserable: Growing Up Female in the Fifties* (Boston: Beacon Press, 1992), p. 8.

30. Sen. Wherry is quoted in Max Lerner in the *New York Post*, 17 July 1950; both the Lerner article and McCarthy are cited in David Savran, *Cowboys, Communists and Queers: The Politics of Masculinity in the Work of Arthur Miller and Tennessee Williams* (Minneapolis: University of Minnesota Press, 1992), pp. 4–5. McCarthy's aide is cited in David Caute, *The Great Fear: The Anti-Communist Purge Under Truman and Eisenhower* (New York: Simon and Schuster, 1978).

31. Ruth Hartlet, "Sex Role Pressures and the Socialization of the Male Child," *Psychological Reports* 5, 1959, p. 468. Hartley's article and Helen Hacker's prescient "The New Burdens of Masculinity," *Marriage and Family Living* 3, 1957, indicated a growing understanding of the contradictory experiences of masculinity. Naturally, such an understanding was achieved first by female social scientists.

32. J. D. Salinger, *The Catcher in the Rye* (Boston: Little, Brown, 1951), pp. 198, 204. On Holden's confusion about girls and sex, see also pp. 63, 73.

33. Erich Fromm, *Escape from Freedom* (New York: Holt, Rinehart and Winston, 1941); Erich Fromm, *Man for Himself* (New York: Rinehart, 1947). See also Erich Fromm, *The Sane Society* (New York: Rinehart, 1955); Ronald J. Burke, "Managerial and Professional Men," *masculinities* 1(1–2), 1993.

34. C. Wright Mills, *White Collar* (New York: Oxford University Press, 1953), pp. ix, xii.

35. Ibid., pp. 108–109.

36. Ibid., pp. 110, 111, 353, xvii, 353. Mills argued that the discontinuity between new structures and institutions and our old ideals about artisanal integrity and entrepreneurial autonomy was deliberately manipu-

lated by those in power; i.e., that the anxieties and isolation of the middle-class white-collar man served the interests of what he would soon call "the power elite."

37. David Riesman, *The Lonely Crowd* (New Haven: Yale University Press, 1950), p. 47. Like Tocqueville before him, Riesman saw the pull towards conformity undermining individual autonomy and social freedom. See p. 307.

38. Frank Tannenbaum, *A Philosophy of Labor* (New York: Knopf, 1951); Tannenbaum is also cited in William H. Whyte, *The Organization Man* (New York: Anchor, 1956), p. 46.

39. Vance Packard, *The Status Seekers* (New York: McKay, 1959); Vance Packard, *The Hidden Persuaders* (New York: McKay, 1957).

40. Peale was influenced by Muscular Christianity and condemned "sissy religion" in his effort to reshape the American personality. See Carol V. R. George, *God's Salesman: Norman Vincent Peale and the Power of Positive Thinking* (New York: Oxford University Press, 1992).

41. William Whyte, *The Organization Man*, pp. 12, 147, 144.

42. Sloan Wilson, *The Man in the Gray Flannel Suit* (New York: Simon & Schuster, 1955).

43. Norman Mailer, "The White Negro" (San Francisco: City Lights Books, 1957), cited in Breines, *Young, White and Miserable*, p. 144.

44. In a sense, *The Manchurian Candidate* presents the most hysterical vision of Philip Wylie's "momism" ever recorded on film (including *Psycho*). Mother's love is so great for little Raymond that she breaks up his marriage, arranges to have him kidnapped, sets up an enormous Communist plot, then plans to double-cross her fellow saboteurs so that she and her son can rule the country! I should mention that Richard Condon, the author of the novel on which the film was based, was a superb parodist, so one's reading of both film and novel might also be taken as a parody of Wylie's and others' panic.

45. I recall my father, who costumed himself as a beatnik for Halloween in 1960; there in our comfortable suburban home, he wore a wig of long disheveled hair, large black-framed glasses, and a Greek fisherman's cap and smoked a pipe. What may have also been a flight of fantasy for him, it was also a setup of the Beats for ridicule, and my sister and I found his antics hilariously funny.

46. Cited in Elaine Tylor May, *Homeward Bound* (New York: Basic Books, 1988) p. 147.

47. Albert Cohen, *The Culture of the Gang* (New York: Free Press, 1955), pp. 163, 164. See also Joseph Pleck, *The Myth of Masculinity* (Cambridge: M.I.T. Press, 1981), pp. 96–106, which also suggests the empirical vacuity of such studies. My arguments here draw heavily on Pleck's discussion of the social scientific studies of delinquency.

48. Walter Miller, "Lower-Class Culture As a Generating Milieu of Gang Delinquency," *Journal of Social Issues* 14, 1958, p. 9.

49. See J. Rohrer and M. Edmonson, *The Eighth Generation* (New York: Harper, 1960), p. 163; cited in Pleck, *The Myth of Masculinity*, p. 97.

50. Theodor Adorno et al., *the Authoritarian Personality* (New York: Harper and Row, 1950), pp. 428, 405. Theodor Adorno, *Minima Moralia: Reflections from Damaged Life* [1955] (London: Verso, 1978).

51. Talcott Parsons, "The Social Structure of the Family," in *The Family: Its Functions and Destiny*, Ruth Nanda Ashen, ed. (New York: Harper Bros., 1959), p. 271. In perfect symmetry, the housewife, Parsons argued, was "the dominant mature feminine role." This was, of course, the "feminine mystique," and the rebellion against it prompted one of the century's most volatile and resilient social movements. Psychologist Bruno Bettelheim used the necessity of breadwinning to argue against men spending too much time in child care and housework. Although "the completion of womanhood is largely achieved through motherhood," he argued, "fulfillment of manhood is not achieved largely through fatherhood." Bruno Bettelheim, "Fathers Shouldn't Try to Be Mothers," *Parents'*, October 1956, p. 40.

52. Suburban fathers had to be careful, however, not to displace their wives, who had been counseled or coerced into returning to the home. This ideology was held firmly in place despite the statistical realities. In 1953 nearly one-third of all housewives were working outside the home (compared with less than one-fourth in 1941), and by 1957 32 percent of the labor force (22 million) were women, over half of whom were married. By 1960 there were twice as many working wives as there had been in 1950, and the number of working mothers had increased fourfold. See Harvey Levenstein, *Paradox of Plenty: A Social History of Eating in Modern America* (New York: Oxford University Press, 1993), p. 105.

53. Of course, as Susman points out, if we really felt so family oriented, we wouldn't have needed to label everything by it.

54. Psychiatrist is cited by Elaine Tylor May, *Homeward Bound: American Families in the Cold War Era* (New York: Basic, 1988), p. 143. *Esquire Handbook for Hosts* is cited in Levenstein, *Paradox of Plenty*, p. 132.

55. Spock is cited in Barbara Ehrenreich and Deirdre English, *For Her Own Good: 150 Years of Experts' Advice to Women* (New York: Anchor Books, 1975), p. 239. Morris Zelditch, "Role Differentiation in the Nuclear Family: A Comparative Study," in *Family, Socialization and Interaction Process*, Talcott Parsons and Robert F. Bales, eds. (New York: Free Press, 1955), p. 339. *Parents'* magazine offered articles like "Men Make Wonderful Mothers" to reassure men. See Peter Filene, *Him/Her/Self: Sex Roles in Modern America* (Baltimore: The Johns Hopkins University Press, 1986), pp. 172–173.

56. I vividly recall my father "justifying" his stamp collection in terms of its eventual value.

57. Elaine Tylor May, *Homeward Bound*, p. 148.

58. Cited in Elaine Tylor May, *Homeward Bound*, p. 149. Lots of frantic dads tried to squeeze in lots of buddy stuff with their sons on weekends, which were increasingly full of vehicles for male bonding as leisure activity.

59. See, e.g., Irwin Appelbaum, *The World According to Beaver* (New York: Bantam, 1984); Muriel Cantor, *Prime-Time Television: Content and Control* (Newbury Park, Calif.: Sage Publications, 1980); Muriel Cantor, "Prime Time Fathers: A Study in Continuity and Change," *Critical Studies in Mass Communication* 7(3), 1990; Clark Clifford, "Ranch House Suburbia: Ideals and Realities," in *Recasting America: Culture and Politics in the Age of the Cold War*, Larry May, ed. (Chicago: University of Chicago Press, 1989); Lisa Heilbronn, "Breadwinners and Loafers: Images of Masculinity in Fifties Situation Comedy," *masculinities* 2(3), 1993; Lynn Spigel, *Make Room for TV: Television and the Family Ideal in Postwar America* (Chicago: University of Chicago Press, 1992); Ella Taylor, *Prime-Time Families: Television Culture in Postwar America* (Berkeley: University of California Press, 1989).

60. Only when their wives sought to leave the homefront and enter the work world did men's occupations become important, as in *I Love Lucy*, where Lucy's scatterbrained plots to get out of the childless home set up each episode's reinscription of the traditional nuclear family.

61. Mark Crispin Miller, "Dads and Their Discontents," *Village Voice*, 25 November 1986, p. 45. See also Mark Crispin Miller, "Prime Time: Deride and Conquer," in *Watching Television*, Todd Gitlin, ed. (New York: Pantheon, 1986), p. 199. Ozzie Nelson is cited in Gerard Jones, *Honey I'm Home* (New York: St. Martin's Press, 1992), p. 92.

Miller argues that these 1950s sitcoms portrayed fathers so involved in family life and so uninterested in consumerism that advertisers grew anxious and corporate sponsors began demanding that fathers become better agents of consumption. By the 1960s fathers were again invisible, as on *Dennis the Menace* or *The Patty Duke Show*, or they relied on the magical powers of their wives, as in *I Dream of Jeannie* or *Bewitched*. The men in these shows were invariably underlings at work (ad agency execs always trying to please, NASA officers pushed around by higher-ranking officers, struggling television writers)—and the audience knew it.

62. Interestingly, Brando's first film, *The Men* (1950), finds him in a hospital ward filled with paraplegic World War II veterans.

63. Gerard Jones, *Honey I'm Home*, pp. 124–125. I was gratified that Jones also took this episode as emblematic of the show.

64. The hard-boiled private detective had also vanished. In *Kiss Me Deadly* (1954), e.g., Mike Hammer is a sweaty bum, who has no place in the

world of nuclear weaponry. Twenty years later, Elliot Gould transformed the P.I. into an ineffectual nebbish in Robert Altman's rendition of *The Long Goodbye* (1974). Only at the end of the film is he more than (less than?) completely passive.

65. Some middle-class men clung tenaciously to fantasies of self-invention. Two of the era's most honored social scientists, Robert King Merton (born Moskowitz) and Erik H. Erikson (born Erik Homburger), changed their names in an effort to reinvent themselves, the latter symbolically giving birth to himself and becoming his own son. (See, e.g., the obituary for Erikson in the *New York Times*, 13 May 1994, p. B9). Ironically, these were men who respectively celebrated the openness of American democracy as a meritocracy based on nothing but achievement and promoted the naturalness of accepting one's adult responsibilities as the pinnacle of self-fulfillment.

For black men such fantasies were also attractive. In Ralph Ellison's powerful novel *Invisible Man* (1952), the protagonist recalls his first exposure to the northern city:

My entire body started to itch, as though I had just been removed from a plaster cast and was unused to the freedom of movement. In the South, everyone knew you, but coming North was a jump into the unknown. How many days could you walk the streets of the big city without encountering anyone who knew you, and how many nights? You could actually make yourself anew.

66. Detective pulp novels continued, however, to be the most significant masculine fiction genre, probably doubling the number of westerns (Jesse Berrett, personal communication).

67. John Cawelti, *The Six-Gun Mystique* (Bowling Green, Ohio: Bowling Green University Popular Press, n.d.), pp. 2, 83.

68. See Jenni Calder, *There Must Be a Lone Ranger: The American West in Film and Reality* (New York: Tapplinger, 1974).

69. Martin Nussbaum, "Sociological Symbolism of the 'Adult Western,'" *Social Forces* 39, October 1960, p. 26.

70. On the Wayne iconography, see "John Wayne as the Last Hero," *Time*, 8 August 1969. There are also elements of autocritique of the very masculinity that Wayne projected. In *The Searchers* (1956) Wayne's excessive frontier masculinity prevents him from ever being reconciled to family life.

71. Joan Mellon, *Big Bad Wolves: Masculinity in American Film* (New York: Pantheon, 1977), p. 259.

72. Cited in Myron Brenton, *The American Male*, p. 30.

73. As they had in previous decades, some critics continued to blame women

for men's anxieties or unhappiness. Ferdinand Lundberg and Marynia Farnham's *Modern Woman: The Lost Sex*, e.g., took women to task for the renunciation of femininity in their masculinizing efforts to enter the workforce. Feminist aspirations produced "a deep illness," leading to unfulfilled husbands, confused children and chronically unfeminine unhappy wives. Ferdinand Lundberg (with Marynia Farnham), *Modern Woman: The Lost Sex* (New York: Harper Bros., 1947).

74. Barbara Ehrenreich, *The Hearts of Men: American Dreams and the Flight from Commitment* (New York: Anchor Books, 1983), p. 42.

75. Philip Wylie, *A Generation of Vipers*, pp. 48, 192, 207, 88. His solution to the dictatorship of wives was to "face the dynasty of the dames at once, deprive them of our pocketbooks when they waste the substance in them, and take back our dreams which, without the perfidious materialism of mom, were shaping up a new and braver world" (p. 205).

76. Myron Brenton, *The American Male* (London: George Allen and Unwin, 1967), p. 80.

77. Barbara Ehrenreich, *The Hearts of Men*, pp. 51, 50.

78. That Hefner thought women—unmarried and sexy, of course—were capable of a quiet discussion of modern art, continental philosophy, and avant-garde music, as well as a quiet discussion of sex, indicates that he actually saw them as *more* than the cuddly playthings of which he has constantly been accused. Coupled with the objectification of women for which *Playboy* has been vilified by both moralists and feminists, there was a sense that women were also competent participants in a highly refined and elegant art of seduction. With the mood music, mixed drinks (as opposed to straight shots of hard liquor), French language for the appetizers, and hints of European savoir faire, the playboy was anything but a "man's man." Hefner's critique of masculine boorishness bears more than a passing resemblance to the feminist critique that would emerge in the next decade. Men, Hefner counsels, should talk to their female acquaintances about art, philosophy, and music, as well as sex. (Were the word *sex* left off the list, such a mandate could be transported effortlessly to some early feminist arguments.) And to talk about sex? What "real man" did that? Wasn't that what women wanted men to do but what men were too uncomfortable to actually talk about? My argument here, of course, is not that *Playboy* articulated a protofeminist vision of a sensitive New Man, but that its mission presented a far more variegated set of meanings than is often thought. And some of those messages acted as counterweights to the objectification of the bare breast.

79. Philip Wylie, "The Womanization of America," *Playboy*, September 1958; *Playboy* panel, "The Womanization of America," *Playboy*, June 1962.

80. Wylie, "The Womanization of America," pp. 78, 77, 52.

81. Ibid., pp. 77, 79.

82. *Playboy* panel, "The Womanization of America," pp. 47, 134. Only one of the panelists, public relations director Edward Bernays, dissented. "I think that men, not as a conspiracy, but simply to maintain the old patterns, have created the illusion that women have many more equalities and rights than they actually have" (p. 46).

83. Ibid., p. 142. "There's been a change in the minds of most men about the function of marriage," Mailer continues, "which isn't necessarily that they're becoming weaker vis-à-vis their wives; it's that they've married women who will be less good for them in the home and more good for them in the world" (p. 44).

84. The first stirrings of the modern gay movement, with the founding of the Mattachine Society by Harry Hay in 1955 and the publication of the first homophile magazine *One* (1956), lent an even greater sense of cultural urgency to the sense of complicity by American men in their own emasculation.

85. Cited in Ehrenreich, *The Hearts of Men*, p. 51, 38.

86. Sloan Wilson, *The Man in the Gray Flannel Suit*.

CHAPTER 8: The Masculine Mystique

1. Betty Friedan, *The Feminine Mystique* [1963] (New York: Dell, 1983), p. 386. The citation is from the epilogue, published in 1973.

2. Arthur Schlesinger, Jr., "The Crisis of American Masculinity," *Esquire*, November 1958.

3. Friedan, *The Feminine Mystique*, pp. 15, 19, 32.

4. Leslie Fiedler argued in "The New Mutants" that the hippies wanted to become "not only more Black than White but more female than male." Cited in Mark Gerzon, *A Choice of Heroes: The Changing Faces of American Manhood* (Boston: Houghton Mifflin, 1982), p. 95.

5. Robert Blauner, *Alienation and Freedom* (Chicago: University of Chicago Press, 1964).

6. W. Lloyd Warner and James Abegglen, *Big Business Leaders in America* (New York: Atheneum, 1963), p. 83.

7. Cited in Myron Brenton, *The American Male* (London: George Allen and Unwin), p. 197.

8. Cited in Barbara Ehrenreich, *The Hearts of Men: American Dreams and the Flight from Commitment* (New York, Anchor, 1983), p. 83. Ehrenreich's description of cardiology's contribution to the revolt of men against their breadwinner role is both insightful and bitingly funny.

9. See Jack Nichols, *Men's Liberation* (New York: Penguin, 1975), p. 170.

10. Paul Goodman, *Growing Up Absurd* (New York: Vintage, 1960), p. 14. See also Philip Slater, *The Pursuit of Loneliness* (Boston: Beacon Press, 1970);

Christopher Lasch, *The Culture of Narcissism* (New York: Norton, 1979). Of course, what Slater, Goodman, and Lasch criticized, others made profitable in the growing market for self-help books, such as Robert Ringer's *Winning Through Intimidation* (1973) and Wayne Dyer's *Your Erroneous Zones* (1976), which counseled anxious readers to "go for it" regardless of the consequences.

11. Charles Reich, *The Greening of America* (New York: Simon and Schuster, 1970). On the other hand, I'm afraid, Professor Reich and I part ways on such sanguine projections. My analysis suggests that the crisis of Con II was resolved more by atavistic throwbacks to traditionalism and virile masculinist fantasies than by the emergence of a new consciousness. The 1960s did not usher in the Age of Aquarius but the Reagan Revolution of the 1980s—Rambo and Rocky, instead of the sensitive New Age guy.

12. Students for a Democratic Society, "The Port Huron Statement" (1962). It is reprinted in James Miller, *Democracy Is in the Streets* (New York: Simon and Schuster, 1988).

13. This is not to say that women were not involved in the antiwar movement nor in attempting to prop up the traditional gender complex. They were. But it is still true that much of the rhetoric revolved around questions of gender—from questions of sexuality and gender identity of the protestors to the accusations of hypermasculine frenzy against the perpetrators of My Lai. That the antiwar movement seemed to be so much a "men's movement" against the war made it increasingly clear to many women that the male-dominated Left was not going to address women's concerns, and indeed many male antiwar protestors agreed that women's place in the struggle against the war was "prone." Women's frustrations with the male-dominated Left was a significant spur to the development of an autonomous feminist movement in the early 1970s.

14. Quoted in the *New York Times*, 17 July 1960.

15. Tom Wolfe, *The Right Stuff* (New York: Farrar, Straus and Giroux, 1979), pp. 303, 367, 284. Here's how Wolfe describes the right stuff, the stuff that the astronauts believed they had and which they were prevented from expressing:

> a man should have the ability to go up in a hurling piece of machinery and put his hide on the line and then have the moxie, the reflexes, the experience, the coolness, to pull it back in the last yawning moment—and then to go up again *the next day* and the next day, and every next day, even if the series should prove infinite—and ultimately, in its best expression, do so in a cause that means something to thousands, to a people, to a nation, to humanity, to God. (p. 19)

For the most dire consequences of this mechanized bureaucratic masculinity in the space program, see Mark Maier's chillingly sober description of the *Challenger* disaster, "'Am I the Only One Who Wants to Launch?' Corporate Masculinity and the Space Shuttle *Challenger* Disaster," *masculinities* 1(1–2).

16. Cited in Marc Feigen Fasteau, *The Male Machine* (New York: McGraw-Hill, 1975), p. 162. David Halberstam writes that "[m]anhood was very much in the minds of the architects" of our Vietnam policy. "They wanted to show who had bigger balls." See Halberstam's *The Best and the Brightest* (New York: 1972).

17. Halberstam, *The Best and the Brightest*, p. 531.

18. Moyers is cited in Marc Feigen Fasteau, *The Male Machine*, pp. 172–173.

19. Bruce Mazlish, *In Search of Nixon* (New York: Basic Books, 1972), p. 116.

20. James Baldwin, *The Fire Next Time* (New York: Dell, 1962), p. 132. On racism as projection, see also p. 129.

21. Eldridge Cleaver, *Soul on Ice* (New York: Delta, 1968).

22. Baraka is quoted in bell hooks, *Black Looks* (Boston: South End Press, 1991), p. 98.

23. Eldridge Cleaver, *Soul on Ice*, pp. 188–189. It took nearly a decade for black women to publicly and visibly criticize Cleaver's misogyny, and when Michelle Wallace published her *Black Macho and the Myth of the Superwoman* (New York: Dial Press, 1979), she was vilified as a traitor to her race.

24. At this writing, the last two publicly funded all-male institutions—the Citadel and V.M.I., both military colleges—are attempting to fight off challenges to their policies of excluding women; only two or three private colleges remain all-male.

25. National Organization for Women, "Statement of Purpose," 1966.

26. Myron Brenton, *The American Male*, p. 165; see also p. 188.

27. Norman Mailer, "The Prisoner of Sex," first appeared in *Harper's* magazine in 1971 and later appeared as a book (see pp. 43, 45, 56 in the magazine version). Mailer emerges as far more of a traditionalist than earlier, even repudiating masturbation as a form of sexual pleasure because it "cripples people" and "turns them askew" and "steps up a bad and often enduring tension" (p. 84).

28. Steven Goldberg, *The Inevitability of Patriarchy* (New York: Morrow, 1973). See also Edward O. Wilson, *Sociobiology: The New Synthesis* (Cambridge: Harvard University Press, 1975), where evolutionary genetic selection sounds a lot like Social Darwinism. Sarah Blaffer Hrdy provides a blistering feminist critique of sociobiology in *The Woman That Never Evolved* (Cambridge: Harvard University Press, 1983).

29. George Gilder, *Sexual Suicide* (New York: Quadrangle, 1973), pp. 62, 11. See also George Gilder, *Naked Nomads* (New York: Times Books, 1974). In a review of a republication of *Sexual Suicide* (as *Men and Marriage*,

Gretna, La.: Pelican Publications, 1986), I argued that Gilder's "genius" is in linking together feminism, liberal intellectuals, and the welfare state as targets of right-wing resentment, thus providing a perfect platform for the Reagan Revolution. See *Society* 25(1), 1987, pp. 108–109. James Q. Wilson makes a similar argument to Gilder's in *The Moral Sense* (New York: Free Press, 1991).

30. Gilder, *Sexual Suicide*, p. 10. Barbara Ehrenreich argues that if a woman had written Gilder's books, she would have been vilified as a vicious manhater! See Barbara Ehrenreich, *The Hearts of Men*, p. 165.

31. Cited in David Pugh, *Sons of Liberty: The Masculine Mind in Nineteenth-Century America* (Westport, Conn.: Greenwood, 1984), p. 134.

32. Patricia Cayo Sexton, *The Feminized Male: Classrooms, White Collars and the Decline of Manliness* (New York: Random House, 1969), pp. 12, 4, 39. See also Patricia Cayo Sexton, "How the American Boy Is Feminized," *Psychology Today* 3(23), January 1970.

33. Sexton, *The Feminized Male*, pp. 55, 97. Sexton even explains the student radicalism on cultural feminization, the "college male's growing sense of having been duped and feminized by tasks assigned him in school" (p. 36). As a feminist, Sexton was cautious about blaming women themselves for the plight of their sons, suggesting that it was the traditional sexist division of labor that "consigns" women to the home and school and that also demands that fathers commute to work away from the home, "depriving" boys of adult male role models and leaving them to the "community of women" (p. 28). She goes so far as to demand the full-scale entry of women into the public sphere, so that more men will fill those places as child caregivers and elementary school teachers that women currently monopolize.

34. Hans Sebald, *Momism: The Silent Disease of America* (Chicago: Nelson-Hall, 1976), pp. 15, 65, 3, 86. Like Sexton (and most unlike Gilder), Sebald claimed that women's liberation might provide a hedge against momism. "What is badly needed, if we want to attain liberation from Mom, is breaking the sex line so that both men and women are free to choose occupations without being limited by traditional bias or senseless routine" (p. 275).

35. Ardrey is cited in Sebald, *Momism*, p. 169. See Robert Ardrey, *The Social Contract* (New York: Atheneum, 1970) and *The Territorial Imperative* (New York: Atheneum, 1966).

36. Ron Bishop, "The Big Squeal," *True*, January 1974, 28.

37. Lionel Tiger, *Men in Groups* (New York: Vintage, 1969), pp. 262–265.

38. Tom Wolfe, "Honks and Wonks," in *Mauve Gloves and Madmen, Clutter and Vine, and Other Stories, Sketches, and Essays* (New York: Farrar, Straus and Giroux, 1976), p. 222.

39. In his classic statement, *Anti-Semite and Jew* (1946), French philosopher Jean-Paul Sartre praised Jews as "the mildest of men . . . passionately hostile to violence"; cited in Paul Breines, *Tough Jews: Political Fantasies and the Moral Dilemma of American Jewry* (New York: Basic Books, 1990), p. 108. Breines's book is indispensable to understanding the rhetorical and real ways in which Jewish men fought back against such conceptions and the consequences for American Jewry of an Israeli government whose bellicose policies seem designed to reclaim manhood at the expense of others.

40. I have written about this event in discovering how my Judaism came to be part of my support of feminism in "Judaism, Feminism and Masculinity," in *A Mensch Among Men*, Harry Brod, ed. (Freedom, Cal.: Crossing Press, 1989). I am grateful to Harry Brod and Paul Kivel for helping me think through the relationship between Judaism and masculinity.

41. Philip Roth, *Portnoy's Complaint* (New York: Random House, 1967), p. 36.

42. Like countless other analysts, Roth blamed his lack of manhood on overdominant mothering. It was mothers who were "the outstanding producers and packagers of guilt in our time," mothers who created the grounds for homosocial competition and feelings of inadequacy. In one of the novel's more hilarious passages, Portnoy describes the process:

> *Pianist!* Oh, that's one of the words they just love, almost as much as *doctor*, Doctor. And *residency*. And best of all, *his own office. He opened his own office in Livingston*. "Do you remember Seymour Schmuck, Alex?" she asks me, or Aaron Putz, or Howard Schlong, or some yo-yo I am supposed to have known in grade school twenty-five years ago, and of whom I have no recollection whatsoever. "Well, I met his mother on the street today and she told me that Seymour is now the biggest brain surgeon in the entire Western Hemisphere. He owns six different split-level ranch houses all made of fieldstone in Livingston, and belongs to the boards of eleven synagogues, all brand new and designed by Marc Kugel, and last year with his wife and his two little daughters, who are so beautiful that they are already under contract to Metro, and so brilliant that they should be in college—he took them all to Europe for an eighty-million dollar tour of seven thousand countries, some of them you never even heard of, that they made just to honor Seymour, and on top of that, he's so important, Seymour, that in every single city that they visited he was asked by the mayor himself to stop and do an impossible operation on a brain in hospitals that they also built for him right on the spot, and—listen to this—where they pumped into the operating room during the operation the theme song from *Exodus* so everybody should know what religion he is—and that's how big your friend Seymour is today! *And how happy he makes his parents!* (pp. 98–99)

And like Eldridge Cleaver, Roth argues that one way for Jewish men to reclaim their manhood was by claiming the women of the oppressor. Sex with a non-Jewish woman was a symbolic occupation of the body of the real man's possession.

43. The two quotes from Arthur Koestler are from *Promise and Fulfillment: Palestine, 1917–1949* (New York: Macmillan, 1949), p. 67, and *Thieves in the Night* (New York: Berkley Books, 1960). Uris is cited in Paul Breines, *Tough Jews*, p. 54.

44. Friedan is cited in Steven Seidman, *Romantic Longings*, p. 137. See also Patricia Cayo Sexton, *The Feminized Male*, p. 200, and Hans Sebald, *Momism*, pp. 170, 140.

45. Peter Wyden and Barbara Wyden, *Growing Up Straight: What Every Thoughtful Parent Should Know About Homosexuality* (New York: Trident Press, 1968).

46. Of course, some gay lib theorists continued to argue for the sissy as an alternative role model for American manhood. See, e.g., Kenneth Pitchford, "The Effeminist Manifesto," and also Frank Rose, "Sissyhood Is Powerful," *Village Voice*, 15 November 1976.

47. For more on the birth of gay masculinity, see Seymour Kleinberg, "The New Masculinity of Gay Men," in *Alienated Affections* (New York: St. Martin's Press, 1980), and Martin P. Levine, "Gay Macho," Ph.D. diss. New York University, 1985. For further elaboration of Levine's argument, see his "The Life and Death of Gay Clones," in *Gay Culture in America: Essays from the Field*, Gilbert Herdt, ed. (Boston: Beacon Press, 1992). On Stonewall see esp. Martin Duberman, *Stonewall* (New York: Dutton, 1993).

48. On the proportion of gay men who were clones, see Alan Bell and Martin Weinberg, *Homosexualities: A Study of Diversity Among Men and Women* (New York: Simon and Schuster, 1978).

49. Several earlier works had set the stage for the emergence of men's liberation, including several works in academic social psychology on sex roles. Roger Brown, a social psychologist at Harvard, under whom Feigen Fasteau, Pleck, and Brannon had all studied, described the male sex role like this in his widely used textbook:

> In the United States, a *real* boy climbs trees, disdains girls, dirties his knees, plays with soldiers, and takes blue for his favorite color. When they go to school, real boys prefer manual training, gym, and arithmetic. In college, the boys smoke pipes, drink beer, and major in engineering or physics. The real boy matures into a "man's man," who plays poker, goes hunting, drinks brandy, and dies in the war. (Roger Brown, *Social Psychology* [Boston: Little, Brown, 1965], p. 161)

British journalist Myron Brenton found a deep yearning and malaise among American men in his book *The American Male* (1967), and he described how the patriarchal system, "with all its presumed advantages for men, has proved to be fairly costly to men" as well (p. 41). Journalist Robert Lipsyte, currently the conscience of sports journalism in his regular *New York Times* column, wrote a glib send-up of men's plight, *The Masculine Mystique*, in 1966, which posed a serious question: "Why have so many American men suffered so long in silence under so oppressive and restrictive a system, swallowing their true desires, often in fact, never knowing what their true desires are?" And even though Lipsyte keeps his tongue firmly in cheek, his anger at women surfaces as he describes the men's lot as the masculine mystique: "It is a man's inalienable responsibility to keep a woman warm with fur, full with food, large with child, and free from the demands of contributive endeavor." See Robert Lipsyte, *The Masculine Mystique* (New York: New American Library, 1966), pp. 17, 21.

50. See Jack Sawyer, "On Male Liberation," *Liberation* 15 (6–8), August–October 1970; Warren Farrell, *The Liberated Man* (New York: Random House, 1974); Marc Feigen Fasteau, *The Male Machine* (New York: Delta, 1975); Herb Goldberg, *The Hazards of Being Male* (New York: Nash, 1976) and *The New Male* (New York: New American Library, 1979); Jack Nichols, *Men's Liberation* (New York: Penguin, 1975); Deborah David and Robert Brannon, eds., *The Forty-Nine Percent Majority* (Reading, Mass.: Addison-Wesley, 1976); and Joseph Pleck and Jack Sawyer, eds., *Men and Masculinity* (Englewood Cliffs, N.J.: Prentice-Hall, 1974).

51. Pleck is cited in Barbara Katz, "Women's Lib Auxiliaries?" *National Observer*, 29 December 1973, p. 8; Berkeley Men's Center Manifesto (1973) is reprinted in Pleck and Sawyer, *Men and Masculinity*. Even conservatives got into the act, as right-wing fundamentalist Tim LaHaye put it:

> For the past thirty years, six foot four John Wayne has stalked through the American imagination as the embodiment of manhood. . . . He has left not only a trail of broken hearts and jaws everywhere, but millions of fractured male egos which could never quite measure up to the two-fisted ramrod-backed character who conquered the Old West. The truth of the matter is that no man could measure up to that myth in real life—not even John Wayne. (*Understanding the Male Temperament* [Charlotte, N.C.: Commission Press, 1977], p. 11)

52. Herb Goldberg, *The New Male*, pp. 17, 45.

53. Deborah S. David and Robert Brannon, eds., "The Male Sex Role—and What It's Done for Us Lately," in *The Forty-Nine Percent Majority*, p. 5 and passim.

54. Myron Brenton, *The American Male*, pp. 14, 15; Jack Nichols, *Men's Liberation*, p. 122; Robert Gould, "Measuring Masculinity by the Size of a Paycheck," *Ms.*, June 1973, p. 98.

55. Arthur Shostak, "Blue Collar Work," in *The Forty-Nine Percent Majority*, pp. 103, 101.

56. Alan Alda, "What Every Woman Should Know," *Ms.*, 1975; Feigen Fasteau, *The Male Machine*, p. 21; Herb Goldberg, *The Hazards of Being Male*, p. 118. Jack Nichols added that "[i]f men were communicating with children and were not remote from a child's scrutiny, each child might understand that masculinity does not mean being big, competitive, and domineering." Jack Nichols, *Men's Liberation*, p. 264.

57. Thomas Hearn, "Jesus Was a Sissy After All," *Christian Century* 87(40), October 1970, p. 1192; see also Leonard Swidler, "Jesus Was a Feminist," *Catholic World* January, 1971.

58. Here I differ with many of the critics of men's liberation, like Stephen Koch, who pierced the veneer of smug self-satisfaction and self-congratulatory style in many of the texts—he called Feigen Fasteau's *The Male Machine* "one of the most complacent, self-admiring, and snobbish books" he had ever read, a "nauseating display of almost mindless vanity"—and Barbara Ehrenreich, who cleverly critiqued men's liberation as an attempt to escape the burdens of responsibility that attended the breadwinner/provider role (see Stephen Koch, "The Guilty Sex," *Esquire*, July 1974, and Barbara Ehrenreich, *The Hearts of Men*). True enough: Many of these works *were* self-indulgent and smarmy, and several seemed to proffer men an escape from families and children and the transformation of the sober, responsible, marketplace man into a kind of New Age *Playboy* world, preoccupied with self-actualization at the expense of social change. But there was also something searching and sincere about several of these works, esp. those that struggled to embrace feminism as a way of challenging traditional manhood.

59. Herb Goldberg, *The Hazards of Being Male*, pp. 143, 104, 151. Goldberg led the antifeminist charge of men's liberation, focusing not on women's abdication of their traditional willingness to be the empathetic listeners but instead on the "sexist ways women behave toward men and the ways women reinforce male sexist behavior" (p. 251).

60. Warren Farrell, *The Liberated Man*, passim. Farrell and Goldberg were the chief targets of Barbara Ehrenreich's claim that men's liberation was really a New Age version of men's escape from breadwinner responsibility. Both tried to be decidedly apolitical. Farrell claimed the "need for liberation from the stereotypes," while Goldberg promised that these personal changes can be effected with great benefit to the man himself "*even if nobody else* changes"; personal liberation can "be worked at and reached without having to change the world in the process." Farrell, *The Liberated Man*, p. 4; Goldberg, *The Hazards of Being Male*, p. 256. Today Farrell spends much of his time arguing that men are the new victims of discrimination.

61. Marc Feigen Fasteau, *The Male Machine*, p. 60; Glenn Bucher, ed., *Straight/White/Male* (Philadelphia: Fortress Press, 1976), p. 111.

62. Joseph Pleck, "My Male Sex Role—and Ours," *WIN*, 11 April 1974; Joseph Pleck, "Men's Power with Women, Other Men, and Society: A Men's Movement Analysis," in *Women and Men: The Consequences of Power*, D. Hiller and R. Sheets, eds. (Cincinnati: Office of Women's Studies, University of Cincinnati, 1977).

63. Pleck, "My Male Sex Role," p. 15. This reliance on a static sex-role model of masculinity has come under significant criticism since the mid-1980s. Critics challenged the utility of a model that posits the early childhood sorting of biological males and females into these sex-role containers, which force both boys and girls to *adopt* attitudes and behaviors that are impossible and painful. Such models build in a false equivalence in the experiences of women and men, since the models themselves seem to suggest that boys are coerced into one role and girls coerced into another. (Some sex-role adherents tried to weasel out of that problem by suggesting that boys are forced into an "oppressor role," from which they would, of course, have to liberate themselves.) But the problem with sex-role theory was that it ignored or at least muted the significance of power in the construction of masculinity and femininity. Men have power over women, and some men exert power over other men (based on race, class, sexuality, ethnicity, etc.) The important task, then, was to theorize from this aggregate experience of men's power. See, e.g., R. W. Connell, *Gender and Power* (Stanford, Cal.: Stanford University Press, 1987); Michael S. Kimmel, "Towards Men's Studies," in *Changing Men: New Directions in Research on Men and Masculinity*, Michael S. Kimmel, ed. (Newbury Park, Cal.: Sage Publications, 1987); and T. R. Carrigan, R. W. Connell, and J. Lee, "Toward a New Sociology of Masculinity," *Theory and Society* 14(5), 1985.

   Many men's liberationists would be quick to point out that this aggregate power of men over women did not translate into men feeling powerful. In fact, although men are everywhere in power, most men do not feel powerful. But the collective power of men over women also established in men's minds their sense of entitlement to that share of power, the right to feel powerful. Men's feelings of powerlessness, then, were based on men's collective power and the individual experience of entitlement to that power. Such issues become very significant in current debates about "angry white males," who seem angry that their sense of entitlement is eroding.

64. In this way Pleck's work on men and masculinity prefigured Carol Gilligan's work about femininity—that psychology reproduced the problem instead of clarifying it. See, e.g., Carol Gilligan, *In a Different Voice* (Cambridge: Harvard University Press, 1982).

65. Joan Mellers, *Big Bad Wolves: Masculinity in American Film* (New York: Pantheon, 1977). I am grateful to Mike Messner for reminding me of the nascent feminist critique embedded in this film.

66. James Dickey, *Deliverance* (New York: Dell, 1970), p. 62.

67. See Carolyn Heilbrun, "The Masculine Wilderness of the American Novel," *Saturday Review*, 29 January 1972.

68. Norman Mailer, *Why Are We in Vietnam*? (New York: Putnam, 1967), p. 179. Mailer ironically opens the passage with a deliberate reference to the sentimental woman's novel of the nineteenth century, which frequently interrupted the narrative with an aside to the "gentle reader."

69. Even the most innocuously innocent escapism can be read as a meditation on Self-Made manhood. In one of Philip Slater's more biting works, *Earthwalk* (1975), he describes the best-selling *Jonathan Livingston Seagull* as an enchanting recapitulation of American men's worst qualities, a "puerile tale that glorifies overweening narcissism, compulsive striving, and schizoid alienation from the body." The story's hero, "a sort of avian Charles Atlas or self-made entrepreneur," has given his whole life over to his ambition of flying faster than any seagull has ever flown. A compulsive self-improver, Jonathan is the classic self-made bird; his "control needs are uncontrollable, and he is the helpless servant of his need for mastery." His relentless regimen of training finally pays off, and he sets a new speed record—214 miles per hour. "It was a breakthrough, the greatest single moment in the history of the Flock," chirps the author. But even that fails to satisfy Jonathan, and his further exploits guarantee him a literal immortality, not simply fame. "Even when he reaches a kind of heaven," Slater writes, "it turns out to be simply another gym, where the Superbirds spend 'hour after hour every day practicing flight, testing advanced aeronautics.' " See Philip Slater, *Earthwalk* (New York: McGraw-Hill, 1975), pp. 94–96.

70. Geoffrey Wolff, *The Duke of Deception* (New York: Avon, 1979), p. 7; Leonard Michaels, *The Men's Club* (New York: Farrar, Straus and Giroux, 1978).

CHAPTER 9: Wimps, Whiners, and Weekend Warriors

1. See Mark Gerzon, *A Choice of Heroes* (Boston: Houghton Mifflin, 1982). Gerzon makes the process seem entirely voluntary, as if individual men could come to the table of heroes and choose as one would choose dishes at a buffet.

2. Tsongas is cited in Sam Osherson, *Finding Our Fathers: How a Man's Life Is Shaped by His Relationship with His Father* (New York: Fawcett, 1987), p. 172.

3. The quote from John Lennon is from an interview in *Newsweek*, October 1978.

4. For an example, see Alan Alda's writing in support of feminism in *Ms.* magazine, especially his "Why Should Men Care?" and "What Women

Should Know About Men." The former essay is reprinted in Michael S. Kimmel and Thomas E. Mosmiller, eds. *Against the Tide: Pro-Feminist Men in the United States, 1776–1990* (Boston: Beacon Press, 1992).

5. George Stade in the *New York Times Book Review*, 1984.

6. Quotes are from Curt Suplee, "The Dawn of the Wimp," *Miami Herald*, 16 September 1984. Feminist writers, like Barbara Ehrenreich, were suspicious that the New Age "new man," the wimp, was really a capitalist's dream come true. In full-scale retreat from commitment, he also was preoccupied with consumption of high-end luxury goods. While she did not savor the wimpier virtues of open emotional expression, she also saw through the national wimp hunt as "the attempt to hector [men] back to paleolithic styles of masculinity" and "into line for the post-détente militarism of the 80s." Barbara Ehrenreich, "Hers," *New York Times*, 28 February 1985. See also Barbara Ehrenreich, "A Feminist's View of the New Man," *New York Times Magazine*, 1984.

7. Janet Maslin, "The New Man in Films," *New York Times*, 1988.

8. All these were in columns in the *New York Times Magazine*, which launched its "About Men" column in 1983. (The newspaper had had a weekly "Hers" column in the daily papers for about a decade by then.) These two currently alternate weeks in the magazine. These columns have been collected in *About Men: Reflections on the Male Experience*, Edward Klein and Don Erickson, eds. (New York: Poseidon, 1987).

9. Bruce Feirstein, *Real Men Don't Eat Quiche* (New York: Warner Books, 1982). Sure, it was a joke, and "everyone" got it. Except not everyone did. In an age of frantic efforts to shore up a besieged and confused manhood, Feirstein's best-seller was often given to young men with admonitions to follow its prescriptions. Several of my male students found it in their Christmas stocking in 1982, with cards similar to this one: "Here, you need this book. Dad." That *Real Men Don't Eat Quiche* was taken almost literally as a real-man's guide to the eighties indicated only how desperate American men were to prove their manhood and how pathetically silly they looked trying to do so.

10. Much of the material in this section on the 1984 and 1988 campaigns is drawn from Bruce Curtis's excellent essay, "The Wimp Factor," *American Heritage*, November 1989.

11. *Economist*, 30 May 1992, p. 32.

12. Barbara Ehrenreich, "The Warrior Culture," *Time*, 15 October 1990, p. 88.

13. See Katherine Newman, *Falling from Grace: The Experience of Downward Mobility in the American Middle Class* (New York: Free Press, 1988), and Barbara Ehrenreich, *Fear of Falling: The Inner Life of the Middle Class* (New York: Pantheon, 1989).

14. Lloyd Cohen, "Fear of Flirting," *New York Times*, 12 October 1991.

15. This is not to suggest that women are not equally susceptible to Epstein-Barr; in fact, women are more likely to be diagnosed with it. And women are and should be equally concerned about AIDS and other sexually transmitted diseases. But the interpretations of these diseases differ markedly by gender.

16. This trend was noted by countless observers during the 1994 political campaign. See, e.g., Susan Estrich, "The Last Victim," *New York Times Magazine*, 18 December 1994; Todd Gitlin, "Republicans Told White Guys: You *Can* Get It Up Again," *New York Observer*, 3 December 1994; and Rick Wartzman, "Clinton Is Still Struggling to Get Message Across to 'Angry White Males' Who Have Tuned Out," *Wall Street Journal*, 24 January 1995.

17. Ray Raphael, *The Men from the Boys* (Omaha: University of Nebraska Press, 1988), p. 167; Richard Haddad, "Feminism Has Little Relevance for Men," in *To Be a Man: In Search of the Deep Masculine*, Keith Thompson, ed. (Los Angeles: Jeremy Tarcher, 1991), p. 100; C. H. Freedman, *Manhood Redux* (Brooklyn: Samson Publications, 1985), p. 109.

18. "The Chaplain's Lament," letter to the editor of the *New York Times*, 12 June 1992.

19. These arguments are summarized conveniently in Warren Farrell, *The Myth of Male Power* (New York: Simon and Schuster, 1993).

20. Nicholas Davidson, *The Failure of Feminism* (Buffalo, N.Y.: Prometheus, 1987). Some radical feminists also think it is impossible for men to disentangle sexuality from violence and aggression, claiming that to men, sexuality *is* a form of violence and domination.

21. Michael Levin, *Feminism and Freedom* (New Brunswick, N.J.: Transaction, 1987), pp. 2, 3, 300. But see Susan Faludi, *Backlash: The Undeclared War Against American Women* (New York: Crown, 1991), for a portrait of Levin as sensitive father and supportive egalitarian husband even as he spews his antifeminist political rhetoric.

22. Asa Baber, *Naked at Gender Gap* (New York: Birch Lane Press, 1992), pp. 27, 50, 112.

23. Ibid., pp. 79, 92, 109, 138, 156, 169, 218.

24. And who, for that matter, has been preventing women from entering the military? Women have been struggling for that right—against men's resistance—for a long time.

25. Warren Farrell, "We Should Embrace Traditional Masculinity," in *To Be a Man: In Search of the Deep Masculine*, Keith Thompson, ed. (Los Angeles: Jeremy Tarcher, 1991); Farrell, interviewed in *Christian Science Monitor*, 29 February 1988, p. 24. Jerry Boggs, review of Davidson's *The Failure of Feminism, Transitions* 10(2), March/April 1990, pp. 10, 9.

26. These observations are based on my attendance at several of these workshops and lectures as well as on the promotional literature that he distributes.

27. Farrell's *The Myth of Male Power*. He explicitly disputes the statistic about wage disparities and reverses the idea that good men are hard to find, claiming that there are really many good men around, but they are ignored by women in the great American man shortage because they do not have the requisite class accoutrements.

28. Ibid., pp. 298, 293. Farrell's argument is echoed by Frederic Hayward, executive director of Men's Rights, Inc., in a letter to Ann Landers wherein he insists that men are harassed just as much as women in the workplace. See Ann Landers, "Men Harassed Just As Much As Women," *Marin Independent Journal*, 23 May 1992.

29. Farrell, *The Myth of Male Power*, pp. 301, 298.

30. Ibid., p. 310; Farrell at First International Men's Conference, Austin, Texas, October 1991.

31. See Herb Goldberg, *The New Male-Female Relationship* (New York: William Morrow, 1983), *The Inner Male* (New York: New American Library, 1987), and *What Men Really Want* (New York: Signet, 1991).

32. Richard Doyle, *The Rape of the Male* (St. Paul: Poor Richard's Press, 1986); Marcy Sheiner, "What Do Men Really Want . . . and Why Should We Care?" *East Bay Express*, 10 July 1992, p. 11. Of course, men are the most frequent victims of violent crimes of all kinds. What Hayward and his associates ignore is that men are both victimizer and victim, and that efforts to alleviate victimization require an analysis of the victimizers. I am always surprised, given men's rights advocates vaunted compassion for male victims of men's violence, that they would be so contemptuous of a social movement determined to end that very violence.

33. Jon Conine, *Fathers' Rights: The Sourcebook for Dealing with the Child Support System* (New York: Walker, 1989), p. 2.

34. Quoted in Daniel Gross, "The Gender Rap," *New Republic*, 16 April 1990, p. 13.

35. What we get instead from the men's rights advocates is "constant whining about how tough it is to be male, the relentless expressions of male anger and rage which seem rooted in paranoid delusions of institutionalized male victimization by women," according to one of the most trenchant critiques of the movement. See Mike Messner, review of *Men Freeing Men, Changing Men* 17, 1986, p. 32.

36. When these actors try to break free of the constraints of testosterone-infused fantasies, their audiences are rather merciless. Schwarzenegger's most recent films, *The Last Action Hero* and *Junior*, were decided flops in part because his traditional audience—young males—refused to see him

ironically satirize the genre or, worse, become pregnant and act "like a woman." See, e.g., Jeffrey Wells, "Ah-nuld's Baby Not As Big As Expected," *Newsday*, 8 December 1994, p. B9.

37. Terrence Rafferty, "Woman on Top," *New Yorker*, December 1994, p. 107.

38. It is interesting that in the film's original ending Close's character killed herself in mentally unstable despair, but focus groups demanded an ending more restorative of the family unit. The ending was rewritten and refilmed.

39. *Disclosure*, based on Michael Crichton's best-selling novel, is exemplary of men's rights reversals, suggesting that predatory, sexually aggressive, and unscrupulously ambitious women will prey upon men in the workplace to rise to power. Men's rights advocates want it both ways: men as victims of false accusations of sexual harassment and as victims of the harassment itself. See Caryn James, "Tales from the Corner Office," *New York Times*, 11 December 1994, p. B1.

40. Cited in Sam Keen, *Fire in the Belly: On Being a Man* (New York: Bantam, 1991), p. 66.

41. Charles Nicholl, *Borderlines* (New York: Viking, 1989); P. J. O'Rourke, *Holidays in Hell* (Boston: Atlantic Monthly Press, 1989); Tim Cahill, *A Wolverine Is Eating My Leg* (New York: Vintage, 1988); Nick Danziger, *Danziger's Travels: Beyond Forbidden Frontiers* (New York: Vintage, 1988); Stuart Stevens, *Malarian Dreams* (Boston: Atlantic Monthly Press, 1989). This retrieval of the tonic virtues of the wilderness is even appropriated by pricey health resorts and spas. Here's a pitch from one such resort, from a brochure sent to University of Arizona professors:

> Over 150 years ago, Henry David Thoreau realized that one's intellect is not completely developed until it is free to experience nature. To this end, Thoreau retreated to Walden Wood to "lose" himself and, in doing so, to discover himself.
>
> Here is your perfect excuse to discover yourself in the serene, natural beauty of Sedona's famous Oak Creek Canyon. The award-winning Los Abrigados Resort is pleased to offer this promotion to afford Arizona's university professor a unique opportunity to escape the harried world of classrooms and textbooks. After all, Thoreau would never have settled for a log cabin if 20 acres of Spanish-style architecture, an extensive health spa, pool and the world-class Canyon Rose Restaurant were available!

42. Michael Pakaluk, "War Games," *Crisis*, October 1991; Susan Jeffords, *The Remasculinization of America* (Bloomington: Indiana University Press, 1989) and *Hard Bodies: Hollywood Masculinity in the Reagan Era* (New Brunswick, N.J.: Rutgers University Press, 1993).

43. Brian Mitchell, *Weak Link: The Feminization of the American Military*

(Washington: Regnery Gateway, 1990); Philip Caputo, *A Rumor of War* (New York: Holt, Rinehart and Winston, 1977).

44. More than one observer has tried to remind these historically amnesiac critics of the sexual bonds forged among Greek troops or among Alexander the Great's celebrated armies. The current controversy about lifting the ban on gays in the military exposes male heterosexual panic that is as much about being the object of predatory male sexual lust as it is about male bonding. If heterosexual men will be seen by gay men in the way that they (heterosexual men) look at women, as the object of desire, it will be experienced as emasculating. Such a moment might offer the possibility for heterosexual men to achieve a new insight into women's experience and, perhaps, even to cease to treat women in the ways that they themselves do not want to be treated.

45. Carol Flake, *Redemptorama: Culture, Politics and the New Evangelism* (New York: Viking, 1984), p. 93.

46. Jerry Falwell is quoted in Frances Fitzgerald, *Cities on a Hill* (New York: Simon and Schuster, 1986), p. 166; Leon Podles, "Men Not Wanted," *Crisis*, November 1991. I am grateful to Tim Nonn for helping me think through this section.

47. William G. Thompson, "Men and the Gospels," *Catholic World*, May 1992, p. 105; Podles, "Men Not Wanted," p. 20; Tim Bayly, "Going for the Men," *Faith and Renewal*, July 1990.

48. Laurie Beth Jones, *Jesus CEO: Using Ancient Wisdom for Visionary Leadership* (New York: Hyperion, 1994). See also Jon Talton, "Author Describes Jesus As a Business Role Model," *St. Cloud Times*, 16 January 1995.

49. See *San Francisco Chronicle*, 15 August 1989; David Leon Moore, "Ballplayers Putting Faith in Christ," *USA Today*, 27 July 1991. Eaton is quoted in *Esquire*, January 1993, p. 67.

50. See Sharon Mazer, "The Power Team: Muscular Christianity and the Spectacle of Conversion," *Drama Review* 38(4), Winter 1994, pp. 162, 169. See also Meg Grant, "John Jacobs and His Team of Muscular Christians Give New Meaning to the Power of Faith," *People*, 8 February 1988.

51. Dotson Rader, "Against Coeducation," *Playboy*, January 1976.

52. William F. Buckley, "The Clubhouse," *About Men*, p. 256. Here's the next dream:

> I mean, it's a damn shame it's got to end. The fraternity and everything. Someday we should build us all a fraternity house that wouldn't end. And we could initiate our friends and go off and drink like freshmen and never graduate. Hell! Why build a fraternity house? Let's build a gigantic fraternity system! (p. 257)

53. Keith Thompson, "A Man Needs a Lodge," in *To Be a Man*, p. 254.

54. See G. William Domhoff, *The Bohemian Grove and Other Ruling Class Re-*

treats (New York: Harper and Row, 1974), p. 23 et al.; other quotes from Reed M. Powell, *Race, Religion and the Promotion of the American Executive* (Columbus: College of Administrative Science Monographs, no. AA-3, Ohio State University, 1969), p. 50.

55. Much of this section is drawn from "Reading Men: Men, Masculinity and Publishing," a review essay in *Contemporary Sociology*, April 1992, and from Michael Kimmel and Michael Kaufman, "Weekend Warriors: The New Men's Movement," in *Theorizing Masculinities*, Harry Brod and Michael Kaufman, eds. (Newbury Park, Cal.: Sage Publications, 1994). I have gathered some "profeminist" critiques of the mythopoetic men's movement and some responses by leaders of that movement in *The Politics of Manhood: Pro-Feminist Men Critique the Mythopoetic Men's Movement and Mythopoetic Leaders Respond* (Philadelphia: Temple University Press, 1995). I am grateful to Michael Kaufman for permission to draw from this material and for working these issues through in our seamless collaboration.

56. Quotes from Bliss are from Kenneth Guentert, "Returning to the Wound—an Interview with Shepherd Bliss," *Festivals* 7(1), February 1988, p. 7. Feminist women have been less than thrilled by the mythopoetic men's movement. See, e.g., the various essays in Kay Leigh Hagan, ed., *Women Respond to the Men's Movement* (San Francisco: HarperCollins, 1992); Jill Johnston, "Why Iron John Is No Gift to Women," *New York Times Book Review*, 23 February 1992; Diane Johnson, "Something for the Boys," *New York Review of Books*, 16 January 1992. In *Backlash*, Susan Faludi places Bly alongside Warren Farrell and Michael Levin as examples of the backlash.

57. R. W. Connell, "Drumming Up the Wrong Tree," *Tikkun* 7(1), 1991, p. 33.

58. Sam Keen, *Fire in the Belly*, pp. 208, 209. "The wounds that men endure, and the psychic scar tissue that results from living with the expectation of being a battlefield sacrifice is every bit as terrible as the suffering women bear from the fear and reality of rape," he adds, as another equivalent experience (p. 47). Keen's quips suggest, more than clever wordplay, a position that women's and men's experiences are separate but equal. I wonder if he'd want to change places with them.

59. Robert Moore and Douglas Gillette, *King, Warrior, Magician, Lover* (New York: HarperCollins, 1990). See also their *The King Within* (New York: William Morrow, 1992), *The Warrior Within* (New York: William Morrow, 1992), *The Magician Within* (New York: William Morrow, 1993), and *The Lover Within* (New York: William Morrow, 1994). I would have thought that after My Lai, Iraq, and Rodney King we'd want to tone down this fierce warrior for the new world order.

60. Their inner king comes complete with props and a soundtrack. A small

crystal pyramid is "a useful portable icon" and the music from *Spartacus* or *Ben Hur* is "particularly evocative of King energy." See Moore and Gillette, *The King Within*, pp. 215, 217.

61. Jill P. Baumgaertner, "The New Masculinity or the Old Mystification?" *Christian Century*, 29 May 1991, p. 596. In fact, there is some evidence that those cultures in which the men's rituals are most elaborately developed are those in which women's status is lowest. The best predictors of women's status, according to anthropologist Peggy Reeves Sanday, are women's postmarital property ownership and men's participation in child care. It turns out that ceremonial men's huts and elaborate initiation rituals are indicators of men's failure to participate in child care of young children; they fail in part because they are so busy with ceremonial and ritual life. Geographer Daphne Spain maps the spatial segregation of men's rituals and compares it with the spatial segregation of the Victorian American home. In each she finds that strict spatial segregation is invariably a contributor to women's lower status. See Peggy Reeves Sanday, *Fraternity Gang Rape* (New York: New York University Press, 1990); Daphne Spain, *Gendered Spaces* (Chapel Hill: University of North Carolina Press, 1992). For an explicit application of these ideas to the men's movement, see Daphne Spain, "The Spatial Foundations of Men's Friendships and Men's Power," in *Men's Friendships*, Peter M. Nardi, ed. (Newbury Park, Cal.: Sage Publications, 1992).

62. See Nina Silber, *The Romance of Reunion: Northerners and the South, 1865–1900* (Chapel Hill: University of North Carolina Press, 1993), p. 130.

63. Reading these celebrations of atavistic retreat, I am reminded of the first gang of boys I read about in my childhood. "We'll get the boys together and have the initiation tonight, maybe," says Tom Sawyer to his gang.

> "Have the which?"
> "Have the initiation."
> "What's that?"
> "It's to swear to stand by one another, and never tell the gang's secrets, even if you're chopped all to flinders, and kill anybody and all his family that hurts one of the gang."
> "That's gay—that's mighty gay, Tom, I tell you."
> (Mark Twain, *The Adventures of Tom Sawyer* (1876) [New York: Penguin, 1986], p. 245)

One must also be careful about the celebration of these male bonds. "Male bonding is not a vehicle for male-male emotional relationships, but rather a substitute for them," notes psychologist Joseph Pleck in *The Myth of Masculinity* (Cambridge: M.I.T. Press, 1981), p. 150.

64. The film also offers that traditional homosocial bond between the eager white man and his nonwhite (in this case, nonhuman primate) brother in the characters of Han Solo and Chewbacca. See Paul Hoch, *White Hero, Black Beast: Racism, Sexism and the Mask of Masculinity* (London: Pluto Press, 1979). I am grateful to Harry Brod for pointing this out to me.

65. Audience reaction to *Field of Dreams* was as gendered as for any "feminine" tearjerker or "masculine" western. When I saw the film, men in the audience found the last scene so touching and tender that one could hear sniffling and weeping from all corners of the theater. Their wives looked on perplexed. "They're having a catch," the men moaned with anguished feeling. "Yeah, so what," said their wives. "It's not like anything happened." In some other recent films sons teach their fathers how to be fathers.

66. Well, not quite. Journalists declared the summer of 1994 to be the summer of the return of the western: Costner returned as *Wyatt Earp*, and other westerns, like *Tombstone, Maverick* and *Have Gun Will Travel*, appeared. But this time around, the films failed to find much of an audience, and the reappearance of the western may be more a function of the absence of innovative vision in a Hollywood preoccupied with mining successful old television shows for new films.

    Ironically, perhaps, *Unforgiven* is the most profeminist film of the three discussed here. While Billy Crystal and his yuppie comrades retrieve their manhood to salvage their relationships with women and Kevin Costner's prize for his own initiation is the feistiest and most beautiful woman in the Ogala tribe, Eastwood attends to the needs and requests of strong and proud women (prostitutes, actually) but profits not at all from their plight. Eastwood has claimed in interviews that he has "always been extremely profeminist" and in recent films has developed strong women characters (one taught self-defense classes for women) to complement his own. (See Graham Fuller, "Liberal Harry," *Vogue*, December 1990, p. 126.) Eastwood has offered, rather than a celebration of traditional masculinity, a consistent and compelling critique of the cold-blooded manhood of the West, revealing it as empty and without mercy—in a word, unforgiven.

67. When asked to explain the song "Rolling Stone," Rose became defensive, as if the band meant no harm. "Nigger," he claimed, was "only a word to describe somebody that is basically a pain in your life"; he felt no need to apologize to gays. "I don't need them in my face, or, pardon the pun, up my ass about it."

68. And we rock critics—effete intellectual wimps—also come in for our share of abuse because we ask GN'R to be responsible about the possible influence of their venomous lyrics. In one song, the group calls out its critics by name and challenges them to a fistfight.

69. Springsteen is quoted in the *New York Times*, 9 August 1992. See also Barry Richards, "Bruce Springsteen and the Crisis of Masculinity," *Free Associations* 9, Fall 1987, and my reviews of various albums in *In These Times* and the *Guardian*.

70. For his most recent "Greatest Hits" record, Springsteen has reassembled his old band and recorded several new songs that underline his renunciation of the relentless quest. "Blood Brothers," in particular, looks back with deep fondness at what grown men have lost in giving up boyhood dreams, but without nostalgic longing—an especially difficult perspective to adopt.

Epilogue

1. Nikos Kazantzakis, *Report to Greco* (New York: Bantam, 1971).
2. John Updike, *Memories of the Ford Administration* (New York: Alfred Knopf, 1992), p. 362.
3. James Baldwin, *The Fire Next Time* (New York: Dell, 1962), p. 21.
4. Atwater is quoted in *The New Yorker*, 19 October 1992, p. 41.
5. Bruce Feirstein, *Real Men Don't Bond* (New York: Warner Books, 1992), pp. 7, 8.
6. For a graphic account of the fears of weakness among professional bodybuilders, see Allan Klein, *Little Big Man* (Albany: State University of New York Press, 1993); Sam Fussell, *Muscle: Confessions of an Unlikely Bodybuilder* (New York: Poseidon, 1991); Sam Fussell, "Bodybuilder Americanus," *The Male Body*, Laurence Goldstein, ed. (Ann Arbor: University of Michigan Press, 1994).
7. D. H. Lawrence, *Studies in Classic American Literature* (New York: Thomas Selzer, 1923), p. 9.
8. Floyd Dell, "Feminism for Men," *The Masses* 5(20), July 1917, p. 1.

BIBLIOGRAPHY

Abbott, Lyman. *Christianity and Social Problems*. Boston, 1896.

Abraham, Karl. "The Psychological Relations Between Alcoholism and Sexuality." *International Journal of Psychoanalysis* 7, 1926.

An Account of the Greek-Letter Fraternities in the University of California. Berkeley, Cal.: Occident Publication, 1883.

Account of the Terrific and Fatal Riot at the Astor Place Opera House. New York: H. M. Ranney, 1849.

Acton, William. *Functions and Disorders of the Reproductive System*. Philadelphia: Lindsay and Blakiston, 1875.

Adams, Brooks. *The Law of Civilization and Decay: An Essay on History*. New York: Macmillan, 1895.

Adams, Henry. *The Education of Henry Adams*. New York: Modern Library, 1931.

Adams, Michael C. C. *The Great Adventure: Male Desire and the Coming of World War I*. Bloomington: Indiana University Press, 1990.

——. *The Best War Ever: America and World War II*. Baltimore: The Johns Hopkins University Press, 1994.

Adams, Samuel. *The Writings of Samuel Adams*. Henry Alonzo Cushing, ed. 4 vols. New York: Putnam, 1908.

Adelman, Melvin L. *A Sporting Time: New York City and the Rise of Modern Athletics, 1820–1870*. Champaign: University of Illinois Press, 1986.

Adler, Alfred. *Cooperation Between the Sexes: Writings on Women, Love and Marriage, Sexuality and Its Disorders*. Edited and translated by Heinz Ansbacher and Rowena Ansbacher. New York: Jason Aronson, 1980.

Adler, Herman M. "Unemployment and Industry—a Study of Psychopathic Cases." *Mental Hygiene* 1, 1917.

Adorno, Theodor, et al. *The Authoritarian Personality*. New York: Harper and Row, 1950.

Agassiz, Louis. "The Diversity of Origin of the Human Race." *Christian Examiner* 49, 1850.

Alcott, William. *The Young Man's Guide*. Boston, 1833.

———. *The Boys Guide to Usefulness*. Boston: Waite, Peirce, 1845.

———. *The Young Man's Guide*. Boston: T. R. Marvin, 1846.

Alda, Alan. "What Every Woman Should Know." *Ms.*, 1975.

Allen, Devere. "Substitutes for Brotherhood." *World Tomorrow* 7, March 1924.

American Federationist XII, September 1905.

Anderson, Sherwood. *Perhaps Women*. New York: Horace Liveright, 1931.

Andrews, John, and W. D. P. Bliss. *A History of Women in Trade Unions*, vol. 10 of *Report on Conditions of Women and Child Earners in the United States*. Washington, D.C.: U.S. Government Printing Office, 1911.

Angell, James. "Coeducation at Michigan University." *Pennsylvania School Journal* 29, 1881.

Appelbaum, Irwin. *The World According to Beaver*. New York: Bantam, 1984.

Ardrey, Robert. *African Genesis*. New York: Atheneum, 1961.

———. *The Territorial Imperative*. New York: Atheneum, 1966.

———. *The Social Contract*. New York: Atheneum, 1970.

Arlitt, Ada Hart. "How Separation Affects the Family." *Marriage and Family Living* 5, February 1943.

Arnold, H. L., and L. F. Faurote. *Ford Methods and the Ford Shops*. New York: Engineering Company Magazine, 1915.

Aron, Cindy. *Ladies and Gentlemen of the Civil Service: Middle-Class Workers in Victorian America, 1840–1870*. New York: Oxford University Press, 1987.

Arthur, Timothy S. *Rising in the World*. New York, 1848.

———. *Advice to Young Men*. Boston: Phillips Sampson, 1855.

Ashworth, John. "The Jacksonian as Leveller." *Journal of American Studies* 14, 1980.

Astrachan, Anthony. *How Men Feel*. New York: Doubleday, 1986.

Baber, Asa. *Naked at Gender Gap*. New York: Birch Lane Press. 1992.

Bach, Richard. *Jonathan Livingston Seagull*. New York: Macmillan, 1970.

Baker, Paula. *The Moral Frameworks of Public Life: Gender, Politics and the State in Rural New York, 1870–1930*. New York: Oxford University Press, 1991.

Baker, Russell. "Gosh Ma! Nothing at All?" *New York Times*, 19 March 1991.

Baker-Fletcher, Garth. "Escape Artists." *Christianity and Crisis*, 13 January 1992.

Balch, William Ralston. *Garfield's Words: The Public and Private Writings*. Boston: Houghton Mifflin, 1881.

Baldwin, James. *The Fire Next Time*. New York: Dell, 1962.

Balswick, Jack O., and Charles W. Peer. "The Inexpressive Male: A Tragedy of American Society." In *The Forty-Nine Percent Majority*, David and R. Brannon, eds. Reading, Mass.: Addison-Wesley, 1976.

Banks, Russell. *Affliction*. New York: Harper and Row, 1989.

Banner, Lois. *Women in Modern America: A Brief History*. Harcourt Brace Jovanovich, 1984.

Barnard, Frederick A. "Should American Colleges Be Open to Women As Well As to Men?" Paper presented to the Twentieth Annual Convocation of the University of the State of New York at Albany, July 12, 1882; published in the Proceedings of the Convocation, Albany, 1882.

Barnes, Earl. "The Feminizing of Culture." *Atlantic Monthly* 109, 1912.

Barnum, Phineas T. *Art of Money Getting*. Philadelphia: International Publishing, n.d.

Barsness, John A. "Theodore Roosevelt as Cowboy: The Virginian as Jacksonian Man." *American Quarterly* 21 1969.

Barth, Gunther. *City People: The Rise of Modern City Culture in Nineteenth-Century America*. New York: Oxford University Press, 1980.

Barton, Bruce. *The Man Nobody Knows*. Indianapolis: Bobbs-Merrill, 1924.

Basch, Norma, *In the Eyes of the Law: Women, Marriage, and Property in Nineteenth-Century New York*. Ithaca, N.Y.: Cornell University Press, 1982.

Batten, Samuel Zares. "The Industrial Menace to the Home." Philadelphia: American Baptist Publication Society, 1914.

Baumgaertner, Jill P. "The New Masculinity or the Old Mystification?" *Christian Century*, 29 May 1991.

Baxter, Sylvester. "Economic and Social Influences of the Bicycle." *Arena* 6, October 1892.

Bayly, Tim. "Going for the Men." *Faith and Renewal*, July 1990.

Bean, Robert Bennett. "Some Racial Peculiarities of the Negro Brain." *American Journal of Anatomy* 5, 1906.

Becker, Carl. *Cornell University: Founders and Founding.* Ithaca, N.Y.: Cornell University Press, 1943.

Becker, Susan. *The Origins of the Equal Rights Amendment: American Feminism Between the Wars*. Westport, Conn.: Greenwood Press, 1981.

Bederman, Gail. " 'The Women Have Had Charge of The Church Work Long Enough': The Men and Religion Forward Movement of 1911–1912 and the Masculinization of Middle-Class Protestantism." *American Quarterly*, 1989.

———. " 'Civilization,' The Decline of Middle-Class Manliness, and Ida B. Wells Antilynching Campaign (1892–4)." *Radical History Review*, Winter 1992.

Beecher, Henry Ward. *Twelve Lectures to Young Men*. New York: Appleton, 1888.

Bell, Alan P., and Martin Weinberg. *Homosexualities: A Study of Diversity Among Men and Women*. New York: Simon and Schuster, 1978.

Beneke, Tim. "Pro-Feminist Man." *East Bay Express*, 27 March 1992.

Berg, Barbara. *The Remembered Gate: Origins of American Feminism; The Woman and The City*. New York: Oxford University Press, 1978.

Berger, Martin A. "Negotiating Victorian Manhood: Thomas Eakins and the Rowing Works." *masculinities* 2(4), 1994.

Bergler, Edmund. *The Revolt of the Middle-Aged Man*. New York: Grosset and Dunlap, 1954.

Berkeley Men's Center Manifesto. Berkeley, Cal.: privately printed, 1973.

Berman, David. "Male Support for Woman Suffrage: An Analysis of Voting Patterns in the Mountain West." *Social Science History*, 1987.

Bernard, Jesse. "The Good Provider Role: Its Rise and Fall." *American Psychologist*, 1981.

Bernstein, Iver. *The New York City Draft Riots*. New York: Oxford University Press, 1990.

Berryman, Jack W., and Roberta J. Pauk, ed. *Sport and Exercise Science: Essays in the History of Sports Medicine*. Urbana: University of Illinois Press, 1992.

Bertelson, David. *Snowflakes and Snowdrifts: Individualism and Sexuality in America*. Lanham, Md.: University Press of America, 1986.

Berube, Allan. *Coming Out Under Fire: The History of Gay Men and Lesbians in World War Two*. New York: Free Press, 1990.

Bettelheim, Bruno. "Fathers Shouldn't Try to Be Mothers." *Parents'*, October 1956.

Beveridge, Albert J. *The Young Man and The World*. New York: Appleton, 1905.

Beveridge, Charles E. *The Papers of Frederick Law Olmstead*. Baltimore: The Johns Hopkins University Press, 1983.

Bingham, John. "The Foot-Ball Questions." *DePauw Palladium*, 1897.

Bingham, Norman, ed. *The Book of Athletics and Out-of-Door Sports*. Boston: Lathrop, 1895.

Bishop, Ron. "The Big Squeal." *True*, January 1974.

Blackwell, Henry Browne. *Objections to Women Suffrage Answered*. Boston: Women's Journal pamphlet, 1896.

Blair, Karen G. *The Clubwoman as Feminist: True Womanhood Redefined, 1868–1914*. New York: Holmes and Meier, 1980.

Blauner, Robert. *Alienation and Freedom*. Chicago: University of Chicago Press, 1964.

Blee, Kathleen M. *Women of the Klan: Racism and Gender in the 1920s*. Berkeley: University of California Press, 1991.

Bledstein, Burton. *The Culture of Professionalism: The Middle Class and the Development of Higher Education in America*. New York: Norton, 1976.

Blumin, Stuart. *The Emergence of the Middle Class: Social Experience in the Industrializing City, 1760–1900*. Cambridge: Cambridge University Press, 1989.

Bly, Robert. *Iron John*. Reading, Mass.: Addison-Wesley, 1990.

Boggs, Jerry A. Review of Nicholas Davidson's *The Failure of Feminism*. *Transitions*, March/April 1990.

Bohn, F. "Ku Klux Klan Interpreted." *American Journal of Sociology*, 1925.

Bond, E. M. "The Cowmen's Carnival." *Sunset*, August 1909.

Boone, Daniel. "No Substitute for Father." *Rotarian*, August 1944.

Boone, Joseph A. "Male Independence and the American Quest Genre: Hidden Sexual Politics in the All-Male Worlds of Melville, Twain, and London." In *Gender Studies: New Directions in Feminist Criticism*, Judith Specter, ed. Bowling Green, Ohio: Bowling Green State University Popular Press, 1986.

Bordin, Ruth Birgitta Anderson. *Woman and Temperance: The Quest for Power and Liberty, 1873–1900* Philadelphia: Temple University Press, 1981.

Boris, Eileen. *Art and Labor: Ruskin, Morris and the Craftsman Ideal in America.* Philadelphia: Temple University Press, 1986.

Boydston, Jeanne. *Home and Work: Housework, Wages and the Ideology of Labor in the Early Republic.* New York: Oxford University Press, 1990.

Boyer, Paul. *Urban Masses and Moral Order in America, 1820–1920.* Cambridge: Harvard University Press, 1978.

Brashler, Bill. "The Man Behind 'Men.'" *Chicago Tribune Magazine*, 30 June 1991.

Braude, Ann. *Radical Spirits: Spiritualism and Women's Rights in Nineteenth-Century America.* Boston: Beacon, 1989.

Breines, Paul. *Tough Jews: Political Fantasies and the Moral Dilemma of American Jewry.* New York: Basic Books, 1990.

Breines, Wini. *Young, White and Miserable: Growing Up Female in the Fifties.* Boston: Beacon, 1992.

Brenton, Myron. *The American Male.* London: George Allen and Unwin, 1967.

Brigham, Carl C. *A Study of American Intelligence.* Princeton, N.J.: Princeton University Press, 1923.

Brisbane, Albert. *The Social Destiny of Man.* Philadelphia: C. F. Stockmeyer, 1840.

Brockden Brown, Charles. *Arthur Mervyn* [1793]. New York: Lovell, 1800.

———. *Edgar Huntly: or, Memoirs of a Sleep Walker* [1801]. New York: Macmillan, 1928.

———. *Alcuin* [1798]. New York: Grossman, 1971.

Brookhiser, Richard. "Deerslayer Helped Define Americans." *Time*, 9 November 1992.

Brooks, William Keith. *The Law of Heredity.* Baltimore: J. Murphy 1883.

"The Brotherhood Movement." In *The Gospel of the Kingdom*, March 1912.

Broun, Heywood. "The Happy Days of Baseball." *Brown's Nutmeg*, May 1939.

Brown, Victoria Bissell. "The Fear of Feminization: Los Angeles High Schools in the Progressive Era." *Feminist Studies*, Fall 1990.

Brown, William S. *The Capability of Women to Practice the Healing Act: A Lecture . . . Before the Ladies Medical Academy.* Boston: Ripley, 1859.

Brownson, Henry F., ed. *The Works of Orestes A. Brownson.* Detroit: Thorndike Nours, 1885.

Brownson, Orestes. "The Laboring Classes." *Boston Quarterly*, July 1840.

———. "Literature, Love, and Marriage." *Brownson Quarterly Review*, July 1864.

Bruce, H. Addington. "Baseball and the National Life." *Outlook* 104, 17 May 1913.

Bruere, Martha, and Robert Bruere. *Increasing Home Efficiency*. New York: Macmillan, 1912.

Bruns, Roger A. *Preacher: Billy Sunday and Big Time American Evangelism*. New York: Norton, 1992.

Bryan, William Jennings. "Speech Before the Democratic National Convention, Chicago, 1896." In *Life and Speeches of William J. Bryan*, J. S. Ogilvie, ed. New York: J. S. Ogilvie Publishing, 1896.

Bucher, Glenn R., ed. *Straight/ White/ Male*. Philadelphia: Fortress Press, 1976.

Buck, Paul. "Harvard Attitudes Toward Radcliffe in the Early Years." *Massachusetts Historical Society*, May 1962.

Buckley, J. M. *Oats or Wild Oats: Common Sense for Young Men*. New York: Harper, 1885.

———. *The Wrong and Peril of Woman Suffrage*. New York and Chicago: Revell, 1909.

Buckley, J. W. "The Education of Boys and Girls Together." *New York Teacher*, 1855.

Buckley, Peter G. "To the Opera House: Culture and Society in New York City, 1820–1860." Ph.D. diss., SUNY at Stony Brook, 1984.

Buckley, William F., Jr. "The Clubhouse." In *About Men*. New York: Simon and Schuster, 1987.

Burke, Ronald. "Managerial and Professional Men." *masculinities* 1(1–2), 1993.

Burnap, George W. *Lectures to Young Men*. Baltimore: John Murphy, 1848.

Burroughs, Edgar. *Tarzan of the Apes*. Chicago: McClurg, 1914.

Bushnell, Horace. *Woman Suffrage: The Reform Against Nature*. New York: Scribners, 1870.

Butterfield, Roger. *The American Past: A History of the United States . . . Engravings and Drawings*. New York: Simon and Schuster, 1947.

Byars, Ronald. "The Making of the Self-Made Man: The Development of Masculine Roles and Image in Antebellum America." Ph.D. diss., Michigan State University, 1979.

Bynum, Victoria. *Unruly Women: The Politics of Social and Sexual Control in the Old South*. Chapel Hill: University of North Carolina Press, 1992.

Cady, Edwin H. "The Strenuous Life as a Theme in American Cultural History." In *New Voices in American Studies*, Ray Browne, ed. West Lafayette, Ind.: Purdue University Studies, 1966.

Cahill, Tim. *A Wolverine Is Eating My Leg*. New York: Vintage, 1988.

Calder, Jenni. *There Must Be a Lone Ranger: The American West in Film and Reality*. New York: Tapplinger, 1974.

Callen, Anthea. *Women Artists of the Arts and Crafts Movement, 1870–1914.* New York: Pantheon, 1980.

Cantarow, Ellen. *Moving the Mountain: Women Working for Social Change.* Old Westbury, N.Y.: Feminist Press, 1980.

Cantor, Muriel. *Prime-Time Television: Content and Control.* Newbury Park, Cal.: Sage Publications, 1980.

———. "Prime-Time Fathers: A Study in Continuity and Change." *Critical Studies in Mass Communications* 7 (3), 1990.

Cappon, Lester Jene, ed. *The Adams-Jefferson Letters.* Chapel Hill: University of North Carolina Press, 1959.

Caputo, Philip. *A Rumor of War.* New York: Holt, Rinehart and Winston, 1927.

Cardin, Maren Lockwood. *The New Feminist Movement.* New York: Russell Sage Foundation, 1974.

Carnahan, James R. *Pythian Knighthood.* Cincinnati: Pettibone Manufacturing Co., 1909.

Carnes, Mark C. *Secret Ritual and Manhood in Victorian America.* New Haven: Yale University Press, 1989.

Carnes, Mark C., and Clyde Griffen, eds. *Meanings for Manhood: Constructions of Masculinity in Victorian America.* Chicago: University of Chicago Press, 1990.

Carrigan, T. R., R. W. Connell, and J. Lee. "Toward a New Theory of Masculinity." *Theory and Society* 15(4), 1985.

Carson, Ada Lou, and Herbert L. Carson. *Royall Tyler.* Boston: Twayne Publishing, 1979.

Carson, G. *Cornflake Crusade.* New York: Rinehart, 1957.

Case, Carl. *The Masculine in Religion.* New York: n.p., 1906.

Caute, David. *The Great Fear: The Anti-Communist Purge Under Truman and Eisenhower.* New York: Simon and Schuster, 1978.

Cavan, R. S. "Unemployment: Crisis of the Common Man." *Marriage and Family Living* 21, 1959.

Cawelti, John. *Apostles of the Self-Made Man.* Chicago: University of Chicago Press, 1965.

———. *The Six-Gun Mystique.* Bowling Green, Ohio: Bowling Green University Popular Press, n.d.

Cayleff, Susan E. *Wash and Be Healed: The Water Cure Movement and Women's Health.* Philadelphia: Temple University Press, 1987.

Chadwick, Adm. F. E. "The Woman Peril." *Educational Review* 47, February 1914.

Chafe, William H. *The American Woman.* New York: Oxford University Press, 1972.

———. *Women and Equality: Changing Patterns in American Culture.* New York: Oxford University Press, 1977.

————. *Paradox of Change: American Women in the Twentieth Century*. New York: Oxford University Press, 1991.

Chandler, Raymond. *The Simple Art of Murder*. New York: Norton, 1968.

————. *The Chandler Collection*. London: Pan Publications, 1983.

Chapman, David. *Sandow the Magnificent: Eugen Sandow and the Beginnings of Bodybuilding*. Urbana: University of Illinois Press, 1994.

Charles, Jeffrey. *Service Clubs in American Society: Rotary, Kiwanis and Lions*. Champaign: University of Illinois Press, 1993.

Chase, George C. *The Disruption of the Home*. Philadelphia: American Baptist Publication Society, 1912.

Chase, Thomas. *Liberal Education; Its Objects and Methods; an Address Delivered at the Opening of Bryn Mawr College, Pa.*

Chauncey, George, Jr. "Christian Brotherhood or Sexual Perversion? Homosexual Identities and the Construction of Sexual Boundaries in the World War I Era." *Journal of Social History* 19, 1985.

————. *Gay New York: Gender, Urban Culture and The Making of The Gay Male World, 1890–1940*. New York: Basic Books, 1994.

Chavasse, P. H. *Man's Strength and Woman's Beauty*. San Francisco: Jones Bros., 1880.

Christgau, Robert. "Are You Ready for Men's Liberation." *Ms.*, February 1974.

Clark, Kate Upson. *Bringing Up Boys: A Study*. New York, 1899.

Clark, Robert Judson, ed. *The Arts and Crafts Movement in America, 1876–1916*. Princeton, N.J.: Princeton University Press, 1972.

Clark, Rev. Rufus W. *Lectures on the Formation of Character, Temptations and Mission of Young Men*. Boston: John P. Jewett, 1853.

Clarke, L. Pierce. "A Psychological Study of Some Alcoholics." *Psychoanalytic Review* 6, 1919.

Clawson, Mary Ann. *Constructing Brotherhood: Class, Gender, and Fraternalism*. Princeton, N.J.: Princeton University Press, 1989.

Cleaver, Eldridge. *Soul on Ice*. New York: Dell, 1968.

Cleveland, Alfred A. "The Predominance of Female Teachers." *Pedagogical Seminary*, 12 Sept 1905.

Clifford, Clark E. "Ranch House Suburbia: Ideals and Realities." In *Recasting America: Culture and Politics in the Age of The Cold War*, Larry May, ed. Chicago: University of Chicago Press, 1989.

Clinton, Catherine. *The Plantation Mistress: Woman's World in the Old South*. Pantheon, 1982.

————. *The Other Civil War: American Women in the Nineteenth Century*. Hill and Wang, 1984.

Clinton, Catherine, and Nina Silber, eds. *Divided Houses: Gender and the Civil War*. New York: Oxford University Press, 1992.

Coben, Stanley. *Rebellion Against Victorianism: The Impetus for Cultural Change in 1920s America*. New York: Oxford University Press, 1991.

Cochran, Thomas, and William Miller. *The Age of Enterprise*. New York: Harper and Row, 1961.

Cohen, Albert. *Delinquent Boys: The Culture of the Gang*. New York: Free Press, 1955.

Cohen, Lloyd. "Fear of Flirting." *New York Times*, 12 October 1991.

Cohen, Patricia Cline. "Unregulated Youth: Masculinity and Murder in the 1830s City." *Radical History Review* 52, Winter 1992.

Cole, Arthur. *A Hundred Years of Mount Holyoke College: The Evolution of an Educational Ideal*. New Haven: Yale University Press, 1940.

Collins, Joseph. *The Doctor Looks at Love and Life*. New York: Doran, 1926.

Comfort, George F., and Ann Manning Comfort, M.D. *Woman's Education and Woman's Health*. Syracuse, N.Y.: Thomas Durston, 1874.

Comstock, Anthony. *Traps for the Young*. New York, 1883.

Conable, Charlotte W. *Women at Cornell: The Myth of Equal Education*. Ithaca, N.Y.: Cornell University Press, 1977.

Conant, Jennet. "The High Priced Call of the Wild." *Newsweek*, 1 February 1988.

Conant, R. W. *The Manly Christ, a New View*. Chicago: n.p., 1904.

Conine, Jon. *Father's Rights: The Sourcebook for Dealing with the Child Support System*. New York: Walker, 1989.

Conkling, Alfred R. *The Life and Letters of Roscoe Conkling*. New York: Webster, 1889.

Connell, R. W. *Gender and Power*. Stanford, Cal.: Stanford U. Press, 1987.

———. "Drumming Up the Wrong Tree." *Tikkun* 7(1), 1991.

Conway, Jill Ker. "Perspectives on the History of Women's Education in the United States." *History of Education Quarterly* 14(1), Spring 1974.

———. *The Female Experience in Eighteenth- and Nineteenth-Century America*. Pricenton, N.J.: Princeton University Press, 1985.

Conwell, Joseph Alfred. *Manhood's Morning; or, "Do It While You're Young." A Book for Young Men Between 14 and 28 Years of Age*. Vineland, N.J.: Hominis, 1896.

Conwell, Rev. Russell. *Acres of Diamonds*. New York: Harper and Row, 1943.

Coontz, Stephanie. *The Social Origins of Private Life*. New York: Verso, 1988.

———. *The Way We Never Were: American Families and the Nostalgia Trap*. New York: Basic Books, 1992.

Cooper, Courtney Ryley. "Ride 'Im Cowboy!" *Saturday Evening Post*, 29 Nov. 1919.

Cooper, Frederic Taber. *Some American Story Tellers*. New York: Avon, 1968.

Cooper, James Fenimore. *The Prairie*. New York: Holt, Rinehart, 1950.

———. *The Last of the Mohicans*. New York: Harper and Row, 1965.

Costello, John. *Virtue Under Fire: How World War II Changed Our Social and Sexual Attitudes*. Boston: Little, Brown, 1985.

Cott, Nancy F. *The Bonds of Womanhood: "Woman's Sphere"—New England, 1780–1835*. New Haven: Yale University Press, 1977.

———. *The Grounding of Modern Feminism*. New Haven: Yale U. Press, 1987.

Cowan, Ruth Schwartz. "Two Washes in the Morning and a Bridge Party at Night: The American Housewife Between the Wars." *Women's Studies* 3(2), 1976.

———. *More Work for Mother: The Ironies of Household Technology from the Open Hearth to the Microwave*. New York: Basic Books, 1983.

Cowell, Henry, and Sidney Cowell. *Charles Ives and His Music*. New York: Oxford University Press, 1955.

Crandall, John Curtis. "Images and Ideals for Young Americans: A Study of American Juveniles, 1825–1860." Ph.D. diss., University of Rochester, 1957.

Crane, Stephen. *Stories and Tales*. New York: Vintage 1959.

———. *The Red Badge of Courage*. New York: Penguin, 1983.

Crawford, Alan. *C. R. Ashbee: Architect, Designer and Romantic Socialist*. New Haven: Yale University Press, 1986.

Crawford, Nelson. "Nobility of the Campus." *American Mercury* 21, 1930.

Crèvecoeur, Hector St. John de. *Letters from an American Farmer* [1782]. New York: Fox, Duffield, 1904.

Crockett, David. *The Life of Martin Van Buren*. Philadelphia, 1895.

Cullen, Jim. "'I's a Man Now': Gender and African American Men." In *Divided Houses*, C. Clinton and N. Silber, eds. New York: Oxford University Press, 1992.

Culverwell, R. J. *Professional Records: The Institutes of Marriage; It's Intent, Obligations, and Physical and Constitutional Disqualifications*. New York, 1846.

Cunliffe, Marcus. *Soldiers and Civilians: The Martial Spirit in America, 1775–1865*. Boston: Little, Brown, 1968.

Curtis, Bruce. "The Wimp Factor." *American Heritage*, November 1989.

Curtis, George W. *An Address: A Vindication of the Right of Women to the Elective Franchise*. Speech delivered at the Women's Rights Convention, 15 May 1858. Women's Rights Collection, Schlesinger Library.

Curtis, Susan. "The Son of Man and God the Father: The Social Gospel and Victorian Morality." In *Meanings for Manhood*, M. Carnes and C. Griffen, eds. Chicago: University of Chicago Press, 1991.

Curtis, Wardon A. "The Movement Against Coeducation at the University of Wisconsin." *Independent* 65, 6 August 1908.

Czitrom, Daniel. "Bilko: A Sitcom for All Seasons." In *Popular Culture in America*, P. Buhle, ed. Minneapolis: University of Minnesota Press, 1989.

Dalton, Kathleen. "Theodore Roosevelt: Morality and Manliness in the Progressive Era." Unpublished MS, 1979.

———. "Why America Loved Teddy Roosevelt." In *Our Selves/Our Past: Psychological Approaches to American History*, R. J. Brugger, ed. Baltimore: The Johns Hopkins University Press, 1981.

Danziger, Nick. *Danziger's Travels: Beyond Forbidden Frontiers*. New York: Vintage, 1989.

Darrow, Clarence. "Salesmanship." *American Mercury*, August 1925.

David, Deborah S., and Brannon, Robert, eds. *The Forty-Nine Percent Majority: The Male Sex Role*. Reading, Mass.: Addison-Wesley, 1976.

Davidson, Nicholas. *The Failure of Feminism*. Buffalo, N.Y.: Prometheus, 1987.

Davies, Margery W. *Woman's Place Is at the Typewriter: Office Work and Office Workers, 1870–1930*. Philadelphia: Temple University Press, 1982.

Davin, Anna. "Imperialism and Motherhood." *History Workshop* 5, 1978.

Davis, Angela. *Women, Race and Class*. New York: Random House, 1981.

Davis, David Brion. "Ten Gallon Hero." In *The American Experience*, H. Cohen, ed. Boston: Houghton, Mifflin, 1968.

————. *The Problem of Slavery in an Age of Revolution, 1770–1823*. Ithaca, N.Y.: Cornell University Press, 1975.

Davis, Natalie. "Women's History in Transition: The European Case." *Feminist Studies* 3(3–4), 1976.

Davis, Robert Murray. *Playing Cowboys: Low Culture and High Art in the Western*. Norman: University of Oklahoma Press, 1992.

Day, Clarence. *Life with Father*. New York: Knopf, 1936.

Day, Donald, ed. *The Hunting and Exploring Adventures of Theodore Roosevelt*. New York: Dial, 1955.

Degler, Carl N. Introduction to *Women and Economics* by Charlotte Perkins Gilman. New York: Harper and Row, 1966.

————. *Is There a History of Women?* Oxford: Clarendon Press, 1975.

Demos, John. *A Little Commonwealth*. Boston: Little, Brown, 1970.

————. "The American Family in Past Time." *American Scholar* 43, Summer 1974.

————. "The Changing Faces of American Fatherhood: A New Exploration in Family History." In *Father and Child: Developmental and Clinical Perspectives*, S. Cath, A. Gurwitt, and J. Ross, eds. Boston: Little, Brown, 1982.

Deslandes, Leopold. *Manhood: The Causes of Its Premature Decline with Directions for Its Perfect Restoration, Addressed to Those Suffering from the Destructive Effects of Excessive Indulgence, Solitary Habits, etc.* Boston, 1843.

Dewey, John. "Education and the Health of Women." *Science* 6, 1885.

————. "Health and Sex in Higher Education." *Popular Science Monthly* 28, 1886.

————. "Is Coeducation Injurious to Girls?" *Ladies' Home Journal* 28, 1911.

————. "Letter to President William Raney Harper," 25 July 1902. University of Chicago Library, President's Papers, 1899–1925.

Dickens, Charles. *American Notes for General Circulation*. 1842. New York: Penguin, 1972.

Dickerson, Roy E. *Growing into Manhood*. New York: Association Press, 1933.

Dickey, James. *Deliverance*. New York: Dell, 1970.

Diehl, Lesley A. "The Paradox of G. Stanley Hall: Foe of Coeducation and Educator of Women." *American Psychologist* 41(8), August 1986.

Dix, Morgan, et al. "To the Trustees of Columbia College: A Report of the Selection Committee on the Subject of Admission of Women to the College," 23 April 1884.

Domhoff, G. William. *The Bohemian Grove and Other Ruling Class Retreats*. New York: Harper and Row, 1974.

Dorsett, Lyle. *Billy Sunday and the Redemption of Urban America*. Grand Rapids, Mich.: Eerdmann, 1991.

Doughty, Howard. *Francis Parkman*. New York: Macmillan, 1962.

Douglas, Ann. *The Feminization of American Culture*. New York: Knopf, 1977.

Douglas, G. "Social Purity." In *Official Report of the 12th International Christian Endeavor Convention*. New York, 1900.

Douglass, Frederick. Introduction to *The Reason Why the Colored American Is Not in the World's Columbian Exposition*. Ida B. Wells, ed. Chicago, 1892.

————. *Narrative of the Life of Frederick Douglass, An American Slave, Written by Himself*. B. Quarles, ed. 1845. Cambridge: Harvard University Press, 1960.

————. *My Bondage and My Freedom* (P. Foner, ed.). New York: Dover, 1969.

Doyle, Richard. *The Rape of the Male*. St. Paul: Poor Richard's Press, 1986.

Draper, Andrew. "Coeducation in the United States." *Educational Review* 25, February 1903.

Drimmon, Richard M. *Facing West: The Metaphysics of Indian-Hating and Empire Building*. Minneapolis: University of Minnesota Press, 1981.

Drummond, Henry. "Manliness in Boys—by a New Process." *McClure's* 2, December 1893.

Dubbert, Joe. *A Man's Place: Masculinity in Transition*. Englewood Cliffs, N.J.: Prentice-Hall, 1979.

Duberman, Martin. " 'Writhing Bedfellows' in Antebellum South Carolina: Historical Interpretation and the Politics of Evidence." *Journal of Homosexuality* 6(1/2), 1980–1981.

Duberman, Martin, Martha Vicinus, and George Chauncey, Jr., eds. *Hidden from History: Reclaiming the Gay and Lesbian Past*. New York: New American Library, 1989.

Dublin, Thomas. *Women at Work: The Transformation of Work and Community in Lowell, Massachusetts, 1826–1860*. New York: Columbia University Press, 1979.

Duffey, Elizabeth. *No Sex in Education; or, An Equal Chance for Both Girls and Boys*. Philadelphia: J. M. Stoddart, 1874.

Dunning, N. A. *The Farmer's Alliance History and Agricultural Digest*. Washington D.C.: Alliance Publishing, 1891.

Durham, Philip. *Down These Mean Streets a Man Must Go: Raymond Chandler's Knight*. Chapel Hill: University of North Carolina Press, 1963.

Dwight, Timothy. *Travels in New England and New York*. 4 vols. New Haven, 1821–1822.

————. *Advice to Young Men*. Boston: n.p., 1831.

————. *The Father's Book*. Springfield, Mass.: G. and C. Merriam, 1834.

Eddy, Rev. Daniel C. *The Young Man's Friend*. Boston: Wentworth, Hewer, 1859.

Edwards, Richard. *Contested Terrain: The Transformation of the Workplace in the Twentieth Century*. New York: Basic Books, 1979.

Eggleston, George Cary. *How to Make a Living (with Suggestions upon the Art of Making, Saving, and Using Money)*. New York: Putnam, 1875.

Ehrenreich, Barbara. *The Hearts of Men: American Dreams and the Flight from Commitment*. New York: Anchor, 1983.

————. "A Feminist's View of the New Man." *New York Times Magazine*, 1984.

————. *Fear of Falling: The Inner Life of the Middle Class*. New York: Pantheon, 1989.

————. "The Warrior Culture." *Time*, 15 October 1990.

Ehrenreich, Barbara, and Deirdre English. *For Her Own Good: 150 Years of Experts' Advice to Women*. New York: Anchor, 1979.

Eliot, Charles W. "The Higher Education of Woman." *Harper's Bazaar*, 1908.

Eliot, John. "T. R.'s Wilderness Legacy." *National Geographic*, September 1982.

Eliot, William. *Lectures to Young Men*. Boston: American Unitarian Association, 1882.

Ellis, Leonard Harry. "Men Among Men: An Exploration of All-Male Relationships in Victorian America." Ph.D. diss., Columbia University, 1982.

Ellis, William. *Billy Sunday: The Man and His Message*. Philadelphia: Universal Book and Bible House, 1914.

Ellison, Ralph. *Invisible Man*. New York: Random House, 1952.

Emerick, Charles Franklin. "College Women and Race Suicide." *Political Science Quarterly* 24, June 1909.

Erikson, Erik H. *Childhood and Society*. New York: Norton, 1963.

Ernst, Robert. *Weakness Is a Crime: The Life of Bernarr Macfadden*. Syracuse, N.Y.: Syracuse University Press, 1990.

Estrich, Susan. "The Last Victim." *New York Times Magazine*, 18 December 1994.

Evans, George S. "The Wilderness." *Overland Monthly* 43, January 1904.

Evans, Harold. "Hysteria in the Male with Report of a Case." *Journal of the Association of Military Surgeons of the United States* 13, 1903.

Fairchild, James Harris. *The Coeducation of the Sexes As Pursued at Oberlin College*. Hartford, 1868.

Faludi, Susan. *Backlash: The Undeclared War Against American Women*. New York: Crown, 1992.

Faragher, John Mack. *Women and Men on the Overland Trail*. New Haven: Yale University Press, 1979.

————. *Daniel Boone: The Life and Legend of an American Pioneer*. New York: Henry Holt, 1992.

Farnham, Eliza. *Woman and Her Era*. New York, 1864.

Farrell, Warren. *The Liberated Man*. New York: Random House, 1974.

————. *Why Men Are the Way They Are*. New York: McGraw-Hill, 1986.

————. "We Should Embrace Traditional Masculinity." In *To Be a Man: In Search of the Deep Masculine*, K. Thompson, ed. Los Angeles: Jeremy Tarcher, 1991.

————. *The Myth of Male Power*. New York: McGraw-Hill, 1993.

Faue, Elizabeth. *Community of Suffering and Struggle: Men, Women and the Labor Movement in Minneapolis, 1915–1945*. Chapel Hill: University of North Carolina Press, 1991.

Faulkner, William. *The Bear*. In *Three Famous Short Novels*. New York: Vintage, 1961.

Feiffer, Jules. *Great Comic Book Heroes*. New York: Dial Press, 1965.

Feigen-Fasteau, Marc. *The Male Machine*. New York: Delta, 1975.

Feirstein, Bruce. *Real Men Don't Eat Quiche*. New York: Warner, 1982.

————. *Real Men Don't Bond*. New York: Warner, 1992.

Ferguson, Frank. *The Young Man*. Boston, 1848.

Ferree, Myra Marx, and Beth Hess. *Controversy and Coalition: The New Feminist Movement*. Boston: Twayne Publishers, 1985.

Fiedler, Leslie. "Come Back to the Raft Ag'in, Huck Honey!" *Partisan Review*, June 1948.

————. *The Return of the Vanishing America*. New York: Stein and Day, 1969.

————. *Love and Death in the American Novel*. New York: Stein and Day, 1970.

————. "The Male Novel." *Partisan Review* 37(1), 1970.

————. *What Was Literature: Class, Culture, and Man Society*. New York: Simon and Schuster, 1982.

Filene, Peter G. *Him/Her/Self: Sex Roles in Modern America*. 2nd ed. Baltimore: The Johns Hopkins University Press, 1986.

Fink, Leon. *Workingmen's Democracy: The Knights of Labor and American Politics*. Urbana: University of Illinois Press, 1983.

Finley, James B. *Autobiography of Rev. James B. Finley; or, Pioneer Life in the West*. Cincinnati: Methodist Book Concern, 1854.

Fish, Carl Russell. *The Rise of the Common Man, 1830–1850*. New York: Macmillan, 1927.

Fishbein, Leslie. *Rebels in Bohemia: The Radicals of the Masses, 1911–1917*. Chapel Hill: University of North Carolina Press, 1982.

Fishbein, Morris. *A History of the American Medical Association*. Philadelphia: Saunders, 1947.

Fitzgerald, F. Scott. *The Great Gatsby*. New York: Scribners, 1925.

Fitzgerald, Frances. *Cities on a Hill*. New York: Simon and Schuster, 1986.

Fitzhugh, George. *Sociology for the South; or, The Failure of Free Society*. Richmond, 1854.

Flake, Carol. *Redemptorama: Culture, Politics and the New Evangelism*. New York: Viking, 1984.

Fliegelman, Jay. *Prodigals and Pilgrims: The American Revolution Against Patriarchal Authority, 1750–1800*. New York: Cambridge University Press, 1982.

Foner, Philip S. *Women and the American Labor Movement*. New York: Free Press, 1982.

Forbush, Rev. William. *The Boy Problem: A Study in Social Pedagogy*. Boston: Pilgrim Press, 1901.

Forman, James. "Softcover Manhood: The Rise of the Paperback and the Fear of Unmanliness, 1939 to 1959." Unpublished diss., University of Southern California, 1991.

Formani, Heather. *Men: The Darker Continent*. London: Mandarin, 1991.

Forster, Margaret. *Significant Sisters, The Grassroots of Active Feminism, 1839–1939*. New York: Knopf, 1985.

Fosdick, Harry Emerson. *The Manhood of the Master*. n.p., 1911.

Foster, George G. *New York by Gas Light: With Here and There a Streak of Sunshine*. New York: Dewitt and Davenport, 1849.

Foster, H. W. "Physical Education and Degeneracy." *Independent*, L11, 2 August 1900.

Fowler, Orson. *Perfect Men, Women and Children in Happy Families*. New York: Fowler and Wells, 1878.

———. *Private Lectures on Perfect Men, Women and Children in Happy Families*. . . . Sharon Station, N.Y.: privately printed by Mrs. O. S. Fowler, 1883.

Fox-Genovese, Elizabeth. "Androcrats Go Home!" *New York Times Book Review*, 4 October 1987.

Franco, Barbara. *Fraternally Yours: A Decade of Collecting*. Lexington, Mass.: Museum of Our National Heritage, 1986.

———. "Fraternal Organizations and Industrial Society." Paper presented at Lowell Conference on Industrial History, 26–28 October, 1989.

———. "The Ritualization of Male Friendship and Virtue: Nineteenth-Century Fraternal Organizations." Paper presented at Winterthur Conference on the Material Culture, 9–11 November 1989.

Frankfort, Roberta. *Collegiate Women: Domesticity and Career in Turn-of-the-Century America*. New York: New York University Press, 1977.

Franklin, Benjamin. *The Autobiography of Benjamin Franklin* [1791]. New York: Doubleday, 1916.

Fraser, Samuel. "What Are You Going to Do November Second?" Address before the Livingston County Grange, Geneseo, New York, 1914. Buffalo and Erie County Historical Society Library.

Frederickson, George. *The Inner Civil War: Northern Intellectuals and the Crisis of the Union*. New York: Harper and Row, 1965.

Freedman, C. H. *Manhood Redux*. Brooklyn: Samson, 1985.

Freeman, Jo. *The Politics of Women's Liberation*. New York: McKay, 1975.

Friedan, Betty. *It Changed My Life: Writings on the Women's Movement*. New York: Random House, 1976.

———. *The Feminine Mystique*. New York: Dell [1963], 1983.

Friedsan, H. J. "Bureaucrats as Heroes." *Social Forces* 32, 1954.

Fromm, Erich. *Escape from Freedom*. New York: Holt, Rinehart and Winston, 1941.

————. *Man for Himself*. New York: Rinehart, 1947.

————. *The Sane Society*. New York: Rinehart, 1955.

Fuller, Graham. "Liberal Harry." *Vogue*, December 1990.

Fussell, Edwin. "Valedictory Address to the Graduating Class of the Female Medical College of Pennsylvania, at the Tenth Annual Commencement, March 13 1861. . . ." Published by the class of 1861. Female Medical College of Pennsylvania Archives.

Fussell, Paul. *The Boy Scout Handbook and Other Observations*. New York: Oxford University Press, 1982.

Fussell, Sam. *Muscle: Confessions of an Unlikely Bodybuilder*. New York: Poseidon, 1991.

————. "Bodybuilder Americanus." In *The Male Body*, Laurence Goldstein, ed. Ann Arbor: University of Michigan Press, 1994.

Garfield, Arthur. *Campaign Song Book*. Washington, D.C., 1880.

Garland, Hamlin. *Jason Edwards, an Average Man*. Boston: Arena Publishing, 1892.

Gatlin, Rochelle. *American Women Since 1945*. Jackson: University Press of Mississippi, 1987.

Gaylin, Willard. *The Male Ego*. New York: Viking, 1992.

Genovese, Eugene D. *The World the Slaverholders Made: Two Essays in Interpretation*. New York: Vintage, 1971.

George, Carol V. R. *God's Salesman: Norman Vincent Peale and the Power of Positive Thinking*. New York: Oxford University Press, 1992.

Gerzon, Mark. *A Choice of Heroes: The Changing Faces of American Manhood*. Boston: Houghton Mifflin, 1982.

Gilbert, Sandra M., and Susan Gubar. *No Man's Land: The Place of the Writer in the Twentieth Century*. Vol. 1. New Haven: Yale University Press, 1988.

Gilder, George. *Sexual Suicide*. New York: Quadrangle, 1973.

————. "The Suicide of the Sexes." *Harper's*, July 1973.

————. *Naked Nomads*. New York: Times Books, 1974.

Gilfoyle, Timothy. "Strumpets and Misogynists: Brothel 'Riots' and the Transformation of Prostitution in Antebellum New York City" in *New York History*, January 1987.

————. *City of Eros: New York City, Prostitution and the Commericalization of Sex, 1790–1920*. New York: Norton, 1992.

Gillmore, Inez Haynes. *Angel Island*. New York: Plume, 1988.

Gilman, Sander. *Freud, Race and Gender*. Princeton, N.J.: Princeton University Press, 1993.

Gilmore, David. *Manhood in the Making: Cultural Concepts of Masculinity*. New Haven: Yale University Press, 1990.

Gist, Noel P. "Secret Societies: A Cultural Study of Fraternalism in the United States." *University of Missouri Studies* 15, October 1940.

Gitlin, Todd. *The Sixties*. New York: Times Books, 1988.

————. "Republicans Told White Guys: You *Can* Get It Up Again." *New York Observer*, 3 December 1994.

Gladden, Washington. *Tools and the Man*. New York: Houghton Mifflin, 1893.

Glickman, Lawrence. "A Living Wage: Political Economy, Gender and Consumerism in American Culture, 1880–1925." Ph. D. diss., University of California, Berkeley, 1992.

Goddard, Henry H. "Mental Tests and the Immigrant." *Journal of Delinquency* 2, 1917.

Godfrey, A. H. "Cycling Clubs Are Their Spheres of Action." *Outing* 30, July 1897.

Goffman, Erving. *Stigma*. Englewood Cliffs, N.J.: Prentice-Hall, 1963.

Goldberg, Herb. "Men's Lib." *Human Behavior*, April 1973.

————. *The Hazards of Being Male*. New York: Nash, 1976.

————. *The New Male*. New York: New American Library, 1979.

————. *The New Male-Female Relationship*. New York: William Morrow, 1983.

————. *The Inner Male*. New York: New American Library, 1987.

————. *What Men Really Want*. New York: Signet, 1991.

Goldberg, Steven. *The Inevitability of Patriarchy*. New York: William Morrow, 1973.

Goldenweiser, Alexander. "Prehistoric KKK's." *World Tomorrow* 7, March 1924.

Goldstein, Warren. *Playing for Keeps: A History of Early Baseball*. Ithaca, N.Y.: Cornell University Press, 1989.

Goldston, Robert. *The American Nightmare: Senator McCarthy and the Politics of Hate*. Indianapolis: Bobbs-Merrill, 1973.

Goodman, Paul. *Growing Up Absurd*. New York: Vintage, 1960.

Goodwyn, Lawrence. *The Populist Moment*. New York: Oxford University Press, 1978.

Gordon, Lynn. *Gender and Higher Education: The Progressive Era*. New Haven: Yale University Press, 1990.

Gorer, Geoffrey. *The American People: A Study in National Character*. New York: Norton, 1964.

Gorn, Elliot J. *The Manly Art: Bare-Knuckle Prize Fighting in America*. Ithaca, N.Y.: Cornell University Press, 1986.

Gould, Robert E. "Measuring Masculinity by the Size of a Paycheck." *Ms.*, June 1973.

Gould, Stephen Jay. *The Mismeasure of Man*. New York: Norton, 1981.

Graham, Patricia. "Expansion and Exclusion: A History of Women in American Higher Education." *Signs* 3, Summer 1978.

Graham, Sylvester. *A Lecture to Young Men*. Providence: Weeden and Cory, 1834.

Grand, Sarah. "The Man of the Moment." *North American Review*, May 1894.

Grant, H. Roger. *Self-Help in the 1890's Depression*. Ames: Iowa State University Press, 1983.

Grant, Madison. *The Passing of the Great Race; or, The Racial Basis of European History*. New York: Scribners, 1916.

Grant, Meg. "John Jacobs and His Team of Muscular Christians Give New Meaning to the Power of Faith." *People*, 8 February 1988.

Green, Arnold W. "The Middle-Class Male Child and Neurosis." *American Sociological Review* 11, 1946.

Green, Harvey. *Fit for America: Health, Fitness, Sport and American Society*. New York: Pantheon, 1986.

Greene, Theodore P. *America's Heroes: The Changing Models of Success in American Magazines*. New York: Oxford University Press, 1970.

Greiner, Donald J. *Women Enter the Wilderness: Male Bonding and The American Novel of the 1980s*. Columbia: University of South Carolina Press, 1991.

———. *Women Without Men: Female Bonding and the American Novel of the 1980s*. Columbia: University of South Carolina Press, 1992.

Greven, Philip. *The Protestant Temperament: Patterns of Child-Rearing, Religious Experience, and the Self in Early America*. New York: Knopf, 1980.

Grey, Zane. "Inside Baseball." *Baseball* 3(4), 1909.

———. *Riders of the Purple Sage*. New York: Harper and Brothers, 1912.

———. *George Washington, Frontiersman*. Edited with an introduction by Carlton Jackson. Lexington: University Press of Kentucky, 1994.

Grinnell, George Bird, and Charles Sheldon. *Hunting and Conservation: The Book of the Boone and Crockett Club*. New Haven: Yale University Press, 1925.

Griswold, Robert. *Family and Divorce in California, 1850–1890: Victorian Illusions and Everyday Realities*. Albany: SUNY Press, 1982.

———. "Fatherhood and World War II." Paper presented at the Organization of American Historians annual meeting, April 1989.

———. "Divorce and the Legal Redefinition of Victorian Manhood." In *Meanings for Manhood: Constructions of Masculinity in Victorian America*, M. Carnes and C. Griffen, eds. Chicago: University of Chicago Press, 1991.

———. "Ties That Bind and Bonds That Break: Children's Attitudes Towards Fathers, 1900–1930." In *Small Worlds: Children and Adolescents in America*, P. Petrick and E. West, eds. Lawrence: University Press of Kansas, 1992.

———. *Fatherhood in America: A History*. New York: Basic Books, 1993.

Grob, Gerald. *Workers and Utopia: A Study of Ideological Conflict in the American Labor Movement, 1865–1900*. Chicago: Quadrangle, 1969.

Grosh, A. B. *The Odd-Fellows Improved Manual*. Philadelphia, 1871.

Gross, Daniel. "The Gender Rap." *New Republic*, 16 April 1990.

Grossman, James. *Land of Hope in Chicago: Black Southerners and the Great Migration*. Chicago: University of Chicago Press, 1989.

Grozzman, Maximilian. "Femalization of Education." *Child-Study Monthly* 2, June 1896.

Grund, Francis. *The Americans in Their Moral, Social and Political Relations*. Boston, 1837.

Guentert, Kenneth. "Returning to the Wound—an Interview with Shepherd Bliss." *Festivals* 7(1), February 1988.

Guernsey, Henry. *Plain Talks on Avoided Subjects*. Philadelphia: 1882.

Guest, William. *The Young Man Setting Out in Life*. New York: American Tract Society, 1868.

Guilford, J. P., and Ruth P. Guilford. "Personality Factors S, E, and M and Their Measurement." *Journal of Psychology* 2, 1936.

Gulick, Luther H. "The Alleged Effeminization of Our American Boys." *American Physical Education Review* 10, September 1905.

———. "Does Your Work Drive You?" *The World's Work* 15(5), 1908.

———. *The Dynamics of Manhood*. New York: Association Press, 1918.

Gunderson, Robert Gray. *The Log Cabin Campaign*. Lexington: University of Kentucky Press, 1957.

Gusfield, Joseph R. "Status Conflicts and the Changing Ideologies of the American Temperance Movement." In *Society, Culture and Drinking Patterns*, F. Pittman and C. R. Snyder, eds. New York: Wiley, 1962.

———. *Symbolic Crusade: Status Politics and the American Temperance Movement*. Urbana: University of Illinois Press, 1963.

Hacker, Helen. "The New Burdens of Masculinity." *Marriage and Family Living* 3, 1957.

Hagan, Kay Leigh, ed. *Women Respond to the Men's Movement*. San Francisco: HarperCollins, 1992.

Hagedorn, Herman. *A Boy's Life of Theodore Roosevelt*. New York: Harper, 1918.

Hahn, Steven. *The Roots of Southern Populism: Yeoman Farmers and the Transformation of the Georgia Upcountry, 1850–1890*. New York: Oxford University Press, 1983.

Haines, Patricia Foster. "Women, Men and Coeducation: Historical Perspectives from Cornell University, 1868–1900." Paper presented at the Berkshire Conference on the History of Women, 1976.

Halberstam, David. *The Best and the Brightest*. New York: Random House, 1972.

Hale, Dennis. "Do Men Need Their Own Movement?" *Commonweal*, January 1974.

Haley, Bruce. *The Healthy Body and Victorian Culture*. Cambridge: Harvard University Press, 1978.

Hall, Donald. *Fathers Playing Catch with Sons*. San Francisco: North Point Press, 1985.

Hall, G. Stanley. "The Awkward Age." *Appleton's*, August 1900.

———. "Coeducation in the High School." In *Addresses and Proceedings of the National Educational Association*, 1903.

———. *Adolescence: Its Psychology and Its Relations to Physiology, Anthropology, Sociology, Sex, Crime, Religion and Education*. 2 vols. New York: Appleton, 1904.

———. "How and When to Be Frank with Boys." *Ladies' Home Journal*, 1907.

———. "Some Dangers in Our Educational System and How to Meet Them." *New England Magazine* 41, February 1907.

———. "Flapper American Novissima." *Atlantic Monthly* 129, June 1922.

Hall, Stuart. "The Toad in the Garden: Thatcherism Among the Theorists." In *Marxism and the Interpretation of Culture*, C. Nelson and L. Grossberg, eds. Urbana: University of Illinois Press, 1988.

Hall, Winfield. *From Youth to Manhood*. New York: Association Press, 1919.

Haller, John S. *Outcasts from Evolution: Scientific Attitudes of Racial Inferiority, 1859–1900*. Urbana: University of Illinois Press, 1971.

Haller, John, and Robin Haller. *The Physician and Sexuality in Victorian America*. New York: Norton, 1977.

Halttunen, Karen. *Confidence Men and Painted Women: A Study of Middle-Class Culture in America, 1830–1870*. New Haven: Yale University Press, 1982.

Hamerton, Philip Gilbert. *The Intellectual Life*. Boston: Roberts Brothers, 1873.

Haraway, Donna J. "The Biological Enterprise: Sex, Mind and Profit from Human Engineering to Sociobiology." *Radical History Review* 20, 1979.

Hardwicke, Amy. "A Woman's Idea of the Physical Culture Man." *Physical Culture* 4, 1901.

Hargreaves, John. *Sport, Power and Culture*. New York: St. Martin's Press, 1986.

Harrington, Henry. "Female Education." *Ladies' Companion* 9, 1838.

Harris, Ben. " 'Give Me a Dozen Healthy Infants': John B. Watson's Popular Advice on Childrearing, Women and the Family." In *In the Shadow of the Past: Psychology Portrays the Sexes*, Miriam Lewin, ed. New York: Columbia University Press, 1984.

Harrison, Brian. *Separate Spheres: The Opposition to Women's Suffrage in Britain*. New York: Holmes and Meier, 1978.

Harrison, James. "A Critical Evaluation of Research on Masculinity/Femininity and a Proposal for an Alternative Paradigm for Research on Psychological Differences and Similarities Between the Sexes." Unpublished Ph.D. diss., Union Theological Seminary, Columbia University, 1975.

Hartley, Ruth E. "Sex Role Pressures and the Socialization of the Male Child." *Psychological Reports* 5, 1959.

Hartmann, Susan M. *The Homefront and Beyond: American Women in the 1940s*. Boston: Twayne, 1982.

Harwood, W. S. "Secret Societies in America." *North American Review* 164, May 1897.

Haskins, C. W. *The Argonauts of California*. New York, 1890.

Hawthorne, Nathaniel. *Hawthorne's Doctor Grimshawe's Secret*. E. Davidson, ed. Cambridge: Harvard University Press, 1954.

Hayden, Dolores. *The Grand Domestic Revolution: A History of Feminist Design for American Homes, Neighborhoods, and Cities*. Cambridge: M.I.T. Press, 1981.

———. *Redesigning the American Dream: The Future of Housing, Work, and Family Life*. New York: Norton, 1984.

Healy, David. *The Individual Delinquent: A Text-Book of Diagnosis and Prognosis for All Concerned in Understanding Offenders*. Boston, 1915.

Hearn, Thomas K. "Jesus Was a Sissy After All." *Christian Century* 87(40), October 1970.

Heilbrun, Carolyn. "The Masculine Wilderness of the American Novel." *Saturday Review*, 29 January 1972.

Henderson, Harry Brinton, III. "Young America and the Astor Place Riot." Unpublished M.A. thesis, Columbia University, 1963.

Henry, Alice. *Women and the Labor Movement*. New York: Arno Press, 1971.

Henry, George W. "Psychogenic Factors in Overt Homosexuality." *American Journal of Psychiatry* 93, 1937.

———. *Sex Variants: A Study of Homosexual Patterns*. Vol. 1. New York: Hoeber, 1941.

Herbert, T. Walter. *Dearest Beloved: The Hawthornes and the Making of the Middle-Class Family*. Berkeley: University of California Press, 1993.

Hernton, Calvin. *The Sexual Mountain and Black Women Writers: Adventures in Sex, Literature and Real Life*. New York: Anchor, 1987.

Hersh, Blanche. *The Slavery of Sex: Feminist-Abolitionists in America*. Urbana: University of Illinois Press, 1978.

Hewitt, Nancy A. *Women's Activism and Social Change: Rochester, 1822–1872*. Ithaca, N.Y.: Cornell University Press, 1984.

Hewlett, Barry. *Intimate Fathers: The Nature and Context of Aka Pygmy Paternal Infant Care*. Ann Arbor: University of Michigan Press, 1991.

Hicks, John. *The Populist Revolt*. Minneapolis: University of Minnesota Press, 1931.

Higginson, Thomas Wentworth. "Saints and Their Bodies." *Atlantic Monthly* 1, 1858.

———. "Barbarism and Civilization." *Atlantic Monthly* 7, 1861.

———. "Gymnastics." *Atlantic Monthly* 7, 1861.

———. "The Higher Education of Woman." Paper read at the Social Science Convention, Boston, 14 May 1873. Women's Rights Collection, Schlesinger Library.

Higham, John. *Strangers in the Land: Patterns of American Nativism, 1860–1925*. New York: Atheneum, 1971.

Himmelstein, Jerome L. "The Social Basis of Antifeminism: Religious Networks and Culture." *Journal for the Scientific Study of Religion* 25(1), 1986.

Hirsch, Susan. *The Roots of the American Working Class*. Philadelphia: University of Pennsylvania Press, 1978.

Hirshey, Geri. "White Guys with Drums." *Gentleman's Quarterly*, December 1991.

Hitchcock, Rev. Enos. *The Farmer's Friend; or, The History of Mr. Charles Worthy, who, from being a poor orphan. . . .* Boston: I. Thomas and E. T. Andrews, 1793.

Hoberman, John. *Mortal Engines: The Science of Performance and the Dehumanization of Sport*. New York: Free Press, 1992.

Hoch, Paul. *White Hero, Black Beast: Racism, Sexism, and the Mask of Masculinity*. London: Pluto Press, 1979.

Hoffman, Frederick L. "The Decline of the Birth Rate." *North American Review* 189, May 1909.

Hofstadter, Richard. *The American Political Tradition and the Men Who Made It*. New York: Knopf, 1948.

———. *Social Darwinism in American Thought*. Boston: Beacon Press, 1955.

Holbrook, Martin. *Eating for Strength; or, Food and Diet in the Relation to Health and Work*. New York: Holbrook, 1888.

Holmes, Richard. *Acts of War: The Behavior of Men in Battle*. New York: Free Press, 1986.

hooks, bell. *Black Looks*. Boston: South End Press, 1991.

Hopkins, C. Howard. *History of the YMCA in North America*. New York: Association Press, 1951.

Horne, G. P. "Muscular Christianity." *Sandow's* 2, 1899.

Horowitz, Helen Lefkowitz. *Alma Mater: Design and Experience in the Women's Colleges from the Nineteenth-Century Beginnings to the 1930s*. New York: Knopf, 1984.

———. *Campus Life: Undergraduate Cultures from the End of the Eighteenth Century to the Present*. New York: Knopf, 1987.

Horowitz, Irving Louis. *C. Wright Mills: An American Utopian*. New York: Free Press, 1983.

Horton, Donald. "The Function of Alcohol in Primitive Societies." *Quarterly Journal of Studies on Alcohol* 4, 1943, 199–320.

"How It Feels to Be the Husband of a Suffragette." [no author listed, attributed to Frank McCullough]. New York, 1915. Women's Rights Collection, Schlesinger Library.

Howard, George Elliot. "Social Psychology of the Spectator." *American Journal of Sociology* 18, 1912.

Howard, William Lee. "Effeminate Men and Masculine Women." *New York Medical Journal*, 5 May 1900.

———. "Sexual Perversion in America." *American Journal of Dermatology and Genito-Urinary Diseases* 8(1), 1904.

————. *Confidential Chats with Boys*. New York: Edward J. Clode, 1911.

Howells, William Dean. Review of *Red Men and White* by Owen Wister. *Harper's Weekly* 39, 1895.

————. *The Rise of Silas Lapham*. New York: Harper and Row, 1958.

Hrdy, Sarah Blaffer. *The Woman That Never Evolved*. Cambridge: Harvard University Press, 1981.

Huff, Ronald P. "Social Christian Clergymen and Feminism During the Progressive Era, 1890–1920." Ph.D. diss., Union Theological Seminary, 1974.

Hughes, Thomas. *The Manliness of Christ*. Boston: Houghton Mifflin, 1880.

Humphrey, Herman. *Domestic Education*. Amherst, Mass.: Adams Publishing, 1840.

Hunter, William John. *Manhood Wrecked and Rescued: How Strength or Vigor Is Lost, and How It May Be Restored by Self-Treatment*. New York: Health Culture Co., 1900.

Hutchings, Richard H. "Hysteria As Manifested in the Military Service." *State Hospital Quarterly* 4, 1918–1919.

Hutchinson, Words. *Instinct and Health*. New York: Dodd and Mead, 1909.

Irigary, Luce. *New French Feminisms*. Elaine Marks and Isabelle de Courtivron, eds. New York: Schocken, 1981.

Irving, Washington. *A Tour on the Prairies* [1835]. Edited by John Francis McDermott. Norman: University of Oklahoma Press, 1956.

————. *The Legend of Sleepy Hollow, and Other Selections*. Edited by Austin McC. Fox. New York: Pocket Books, 1962.

Irwin, Inez Hayes. *The Story of the Woman's Party*. New York: Harcourt, Brace, 1921.

Jackson, James C. *The Sexual Organism and Its Healthful Management*. Boston: B. Leverett Emerson, 1861.

Jackson, Kenneth. *Crabgrass Frontier: The Suburbs in American History*. New York: Oxford University Press, 1985.

James, Caryn. "Tales from the Corner Office." *New York Times*, 11 December 1994.

James, Henry. *The Bostonians* [1885]. New York: Bantam, 1984.

James, William. "The Energies of Men" [1906]. In *Selected Papers on Philosophy*, edited by Ernest Rhys, ed. New York: 1927.

————. *Works of William James: Essays, Comments, and Reviews*. Frederick Burkhardt, ed. Cambridge: Harvard University Press, 1987.

Jeal, Tim. *The Boy Man: The Life of Lord Baden-Powell*. New York: William Morrow, 1990.

Jeffords, Susan. *The Remasculinization of America*. Bloomington: Indiana University Press, 1989.

Johnson, Diane. "Something for the Boys." *New York Review of Books*, 16 January 1992.

Johnson, Paul. *A Shopkeeper's Millennium: Society and Revivals in Rochester, New York, 1815–1837*. New York: Hill and Wang, 1978.

Johnson, William Davison. *TR: Champion of the Strenuous Life*. New York: Theodore Roosevelt Association, 1958.

Johnston, Jill. "Why Iron John Is No Gift to Women." *New York Times Book Review*, 23 February 1992.

Johnston, William. "An Address on Female Education." Delivered at Columbus, Ohio, 31 December 1844; Women's Rights Collection, Schlesinger Library.

Jones, Gerard. *Honey I'm Home*. New York: St. Martin's Press, 1992.

Jones, Laurie Beth. *Jesus CEO: Using Ancient Wisdom for Visionary Leadership*. New York: Hyperion, 1994.

Jordan, David Starr. *The Woman and the University*. San Francisco: Whitaker and Ray-Wiggin, 1910.

Jordan, Winthrop. *White over Black*. Baltimore: Penguin, 1969.

Jourard, Sidney. *The Transparent Self*. New York: Van Nostrand, 1971.

Juliusberger, Otto. "Psychology and Alcoholism." *Psychoanalytic Review* 1, 1913.

Julty, Sam. "A Case of Sexual Dysfunction." *Ms.*, November 1972.

Kaledin, Eugenia. *Mothers and More: American Women in the 1950s*. Boston: Twayne, 1984.

Kann, Mark E. *On the Man Question: Gender and Civic Virtue in America*. Philadelphia: Temple University Press, 1991.

Kaplan, E. Ann, ed. *Women in Film Noir*. London: British Film Institute, 1978.

Kasey, J. W. *Young Man's Guide to Greatness*. Published by the author, 1858.

Kasson, John F. *Civilizing the Machine: Technology and Republican Values in America, 1776–1900*. New York: Grossman, 1976.

Katz, Barbara. "Women's Lib Auxiliaries?" *National Observer*, 29 December 1973.

Kaufman, Michael. *Beyond Patriarchy: Essays by Men on Pleasure, Power and Change*. Toronto: Oxford University Press, 1987.

————, ed. *Cracking the Armour: Power, Pain and the Lives of Men*. Toronto: Viking, 1993.

Kazantzakis, Nikos. *Report to Greco*. New York: Bantam, 1971.

Keegan, John. *The Face of Battle*. New York: Viking, 1976.

Keen, Sam. *Fire in the Belly: On Being a Man*. New York: Bantam, 1991.

Keller, Arnold Jack. "An Historical Analysis of the Arguments for and Against Coeducational Schools in the United States." Ed.D. diss., Teachers College, Columbia University, 1971.

Keller, Betty. *Blackwolf: The Life of Ernest Thompson Seton*. Vancouver: Douglas and McIntyre, 1984.

Kellogg, J. H. *Plain Facts for Old and Young, Embracing the Natural History and Hygiene of Organic Life*. Burlington, Iowa: I. F. Segner, 1888.

————. *Man the Masterpiece; or, Plain Truths Plainly Told About Boyhood, Youth and Manhood*. Burlington, Iowa: I. F. Segner, 1906.

Kennedy, Susan Estabrook. *If All We Did Was to Weep at Home: A History of White Working-Class Women in America*. Bloomington: Indiana University Press, 1979.

Kerber, Linda. *Women of the Republic: Intellect and Ideology in Revolutionary America*. Chapel Hill: University of North Carolina Press, 1980.

————. " 'History Can Do It No Justice': Women and the Reinterpretation of the American Revolution." In *Women in the Age of the American Revolution*, R. Hoffman and P. Albert, eds. Charlottesville: University Press of Virginia, 1989.

Kerouac, Jack. *On the Road*. New York: Viking, 1955.

Kessler-Harris, Alice. *Out to Work*. New York: Oxford University Press, 1982.

Kett, Joseph F. *Rites of Passage*. New York: Basic Books, 1977.

Kimbrell, Andrew. "The Male Manifesto." *New York Times*, 4 June 1991.

Kimmel, Michael S. "Out of the Guilds and into the Streets: The Ideology and Organization of the Arts and Crafts Movement in England and the United States." In *Art, Ideology and Politics*, J. H. Balfe and M. J. Wyszomirski, eds. New York: Prager, 1985.

————. "Crackers and Flakes." *Nation*, 19 July 1986.

————. "The Cult of Masculinity: American Social Character and the Legacy of the Cowboy." In *Beyond Patriarchy: Essays by Men on Pleasure, Power and Change*, M. Kaufman, ed. Toronto: Oxford University Press, 1987.

————, ed. *Changing Men: New Directions in Research on Men and Masculinity*. Newbury Park, Calif.: Sage Publications, 1987.

————. "Men's Responses to Feminism at the Turn of the Century." *Gender & Society* 1(3), 1987.

————. "Judaism, Masculinity and Feminism." In *A Mensch Among Men: Explorations in Jewish Masculinity*, H. Brod. ed. Freedom, Cal.: Crossing Press, 1988.

————. "The Arts and Crafts Movement: Handmade Socialism or Elite Consumerism?" *Contemporary Sociology*, 1988.

————. " 'Disheveled Improvisation': Agrarian Resistance to Industrialization in the Late Nineteenth Century." In *Rethinking the Nineteenth Century: Contradictions and Movements*, F. O. Ramirez, ed. Westport, Conn.: Greenwood, 1988.

————. "Of Whales and Men." *Nation*, 10 July 1989.

————. "Sexual Devolution." *Nation*, 30 October 1989.

————. "Baseball and the Reconstitution of American Masculinity." *Baseball History* 3, 1990.

————. "The Music of the Spheres." *Nation*, 12 August 1991.

————. "The Invisibility of Masculinity in American Social Science." *Society*, September/October 1993.

————, ed. *The Politics of Manhood: Pro-Feminist Men Critique the Mythopoetic Men's Movement and Mythopoetic Leaders Respond*. Philadelphia: Temple University Press, 1995.

Kimmel, Michael S., and Michael Kaufman. "Weekend Warriors: The New Men's Movement." In *Theorizing Masculinities*, H. Brod and M. Kaufman, eds. Newbury Park, Calif.: Sage Publications, 1994.

Kimmel, Michael S., and Michael Messner, eds. *Men's Lives*. New York: Macmillan, 1989; 2nd ed., 1992; 3rd ed. Boston: Allyn and Bacon, 1995.

Kimmel, Michael S., and Thomas Mosmiller, eds. *Against the Tide: Pro-Feminist Men in the United States, 1776–1990: A Documentary History*. Boston: Beacon Press, 1992.

King, Florence. "The Niceness Factor: Good Guyism in America." *Harper's*, October, 1981.

Kinsey, Alfred C., Wardell Pomeroy, and Charles Martin. *Sexual Behavior in the Human Male*. Philadelphia: Saunders, 1948.

Kirk, William. "Shall We Have Sunday Baseball?" *Baseball* 1(3), 1908.

Kirtley, James S. *The Young Man and Himself*. Napierville, Ill.: Nichols, 1902.

Klein, Allan. *Little Big Man*. Albany: State University of New York Press, 1993.

Klein, Marcus. *Easterns, Westerns and Private Eyes: American Matters, 1870–1900*. Madison: University of Wisconsin Press, 1994.

Kleinberg, Seymour. *Alienated Affections*. New York: St. Martin's Press, 1980.

Knight, Louise. "The 'Quails': The History of Wesleyan University's First Period of Coeducation, 1872–1912." B.A. honors thesis, Wesleyan University, 1972.

Knobel, Dale. *Paddy and the Republic: Ethnicity and Nationality in Antebellum America*. Middletown, Conn.: Wesleyan University Press, 1986.

"Know Baseball, Know the American." *American* 76, September 1913.

Koch, Stephen. "The Guilty Sex." *Esquire*, July 1974.

Koestler, Arthur. *Promise and Fulfillment: Palestine, 1917–1949*. New York: Macmillan, 1949.

————. *Thieves in the Night*. New York: Berkley House, 1960.

Komisar, Lucy. "Violence and the Masculine Mystique." *Washington Monthly*, July 1970.

Komorovsky, Mirra. *The Unemployed Man and His Family: The Effect of Unemployment upon the Status of the Man in Fifty-Nine Families*. New York: Dryden, 1940.

Krutnik, Frank. *In a Lonely Street: Film Noir, Genre, Masculinity*. New York: Routledge, 1991.

Kupers, Terry. "Feminist Men." *Tikkun* 5(4), July 1990.

————. *Revisioning Men's Lives: Gender, Intimacy and Power*. New York: Guilford, 1993.

Kwolek-Folland, Angel. "Discoveries in the Meaning of Domesticity: Middle-Class Women and Cultural Change in the United States, 1870–1900." M.A. thesis, Kansas State University, 1982.

————. "The Gendered Environment of the Corporate Workplace, 1880–1930." Paper presented at a Conference on Gender and Material Culture, Winterthur Museum, 1989.

————. *Engendering Business: Men and Women in the Corporate Office, 1870–1930*. Baltimore: The Johns Hopkins University Press, 1994.

LaHaye, Tim. *Understanding the Male Temperament*. Charlotte, N.C.: Commission Press, 1977.

Lahr, John. "Waiting for Odets." *New Yorker*, 26 October 1992, pp. 119–122.

Lapham, Lewis. "La Difference." *New York Times*, 4 March 1983.

Laqueur, Thomas. *Making Sex: Body and Gender from the Greeks to Freud*. Cambridge: Harvard University Press, 1990.

Lasch, Christopher. *The Culture of Narcissism*. New York: Norton, 1979.

————. *The True and Only Heaven: Progress and its Critics*. New York: Norton, 1991.

Laurie, Bruce. *Artisans into Workers: Labor in Nineteenth-Century America*. New York: Hill and Wang, 1989.

Lawrence, D. H. *Studies in Classic American Literature*. New York: Thomas Seltzer, 1923.

Lea, Homer. *The Valor of Ignorance*. New York: Harper, 1909.

————. *The Day of Saxon*. New York: Harper Brothers, 1912.

Leach, William. *True Love and Perfect Union: The Feminist Reform of Sex and Society*. New York: Basic Books, 1980.

————. "Transformations in a Culture of Consumption: Women and Department Stores, 1890–1925." *Journal of American History* 71, September 1984.

————. *Land of Desire: Merchants, Power and the Rise of a New American Culture*. New York: Pantheon, 1993.

Lear, Martha Weinman. "The Second Feminist Wave." *New York Times Magazine*, 10 March 1968.

Lears, T. Jackson. *No Place of Grace: Antimodernism and the Transformation of American Culture, 1880–1920*. New York: Pantheon, 1981.

Leeman, Thomas. *Rites of Passage in a Student Culture*. New York: Teachers College Press, 1972.

Lemons, J. Stanley. *The Woman Citizen: Social Feminism in the 1920s*. Urbana: University of Illinois Press, 1975.

Lerner, Gerda. "The Lady and the Mill Girl: Changes in the Status of Women in the Age of Jackson." *American Studies Journal* 10 (1), 1969.

————. *The Grimke Sisters from South Carolina: Pioneers for Women's Rights and Abolition*. New York: Schocken Books, 1971.

————. *Black Women in White America: a Documentary History*. New York: Pantheon, 1972.

Lester, John C., and David L. Wilson. *Ku Klux Klan*. New York: Neale Publishing, 1905.

Levanthes, Louise. "Remington: The Man and the Myth." *National Geographic*, August 1988.

Levenstein, Harvey. *Paradox of Plenty: A Social History of Eating in Modern America*. New York: Oxford University Press, 1993.

Leverenz, David. "Manhood, Humiliation and Public Life: Some Stories." *Southwest Review* 71, Fall 1986.

————. *Manhood and the American Renaissance*. Ithaca, N.Y.: Cornell University Press, 1989.

————. "The Last Real Man in America: From Natty Bumppo to Batman." *American Literary History* 3, 1991.

Levin, Michael. *Feminism and Freedom*. New Brunswick, N.J.: Transaction Publishers, 1987.

Levine, Martin P. "Gay Macho: The Rise and Fall of the Homosexual Clone." Unpublished Ph.D. diss., New York University, 1985.

————. "The Life and Death of Gay Clones." In *Gay Culture in America: Essays from the Field*, Gilbert Herdt, ed. Boston: Beacon, 1992.

Levine, Peter. *A. G. Spalding and the Rise of Baseball: The Promise of American Sport*. New York: Oxford University Press, 1985.

Levine, Susan. "Labor's True Woman: Domesticity and Equal Rights in the Knights of Labor." *Journal of American History* 70 (2), 1983, 323–339.

————. *Labor's True Woman: Carpet Weavers, Industrialization and Labor Reform in the Gilded Age*. Philadelphia: Temple University Press, 1984.

Levy, David M. *Maternal Overprotection*. New York: Columbia University Press, 1943.

Levy, Emmanuel. *And the Winner Is . . . : The History and Politics of the Oscar Awards*. New York: Ungar, 1987.

Lewin, Miriam, ed. *In the Shadow of the Past: Psychology Portrays the Sexes*. New York: Columbia University Press, 1984.

Lewis, Alexander. *Manhood Making: Studies in the Elemental Principles of Success*. Boston: Pilgrim Press, 1902.

Lewis, R.W.B. *The American Adam: Innocence, Tragedy and Tradition in the Nineteenth Century*. Chicago: University of Chicago Press, 1957.

Lewis, Sinclair. *Babbitt* [1922]. New York: Signet, 1961.

Lichterman. Paul. "Making Sense of Masculinity." In *Comparative Social Research*, vol. 11. Westport, Conn.: JAI Press, 1989.

Lipsyte, Robert. *The Masculine Mystique*. New York: New American Library, 1966.

———. "Move Out of the Way: It's a Man's World." *New York Times* (wire service), 1991.

Lofaro, Michael A., ed. *Davy Crockett: The Man, the Legend, the Legacy. 1786–1986*. Knoxville: University of Tennessee Press, 1985.

Lofaro, Michael A., and Joe Cummings. *Crockett at Two Hundred*. Knoxville: University of Tennessee Press, 1989.

Longfellow, Henry Wadsworth. *Longfellow's Complete Poems*. Cambridge: Riverside Press, 1898.

Loring, Charles. "Office Buildings Now and Then." *Architectural Forum* 52, June 1930.

Lott, Eric. *Love and Theft: Blackface Minstrelsy and the American Working Class*. New York: Oxford University Press, 1993.

Ludovici, Anthony. "Woman's Encroachment on Man's Domain." *Current History* 27, October 1927.

Ludwig, Alfred. "Malingering in Combat Soldiers." *Bulletin of U.S. Army Medical Department* (Suppl.), November 1949.

Lukacs, Georg. *The Historical Novel*. London: Merlin, 1962.

Lunbeck, Elizabeth. *The Psychiatric Persuasion: Knowledge, Gender, and Power in Modern America*. Princeton, N.J.: Princeton University Press, 1994.

Lundberg, Ferdinand. *Modern Woman: The Lost Sex*. New York: Harper and Brothers, 1947.

Lutz, Alma. *Crusade for Freedom: Women of the Anti-Slavery Movement*. Boston: Beacon Press, 1968.

Lutz, Tom. *American Nervousness, 1903: An Anecdotal History*. Ithaca, N.Y.: Cornell University Press.

Lydston, George Frank. *Diseases of Society and Degeneracy: The Vice and Crime Problem*. Philadelphia: Lippincott, 1904.

Lydston, George Frank, and Hunter McGuire. *Sex Crimes Among the Negroes, Scientifically Considered*, 1893.

Lynd, Staughton. *Class Conflict, Slavery, and the United States Constitution*. Indianapolis: Bobbs-Merrill, 1967.

Lynn, Kenneth. "Adulthood in American Literature." In *Adulthood*, E. Erikson, ed. New York: Norton, 1976.

MacDonald, Robert H. *Sons of the Empire: The Frontier and the Boy Scout Movement, 1890–1918*. Toronto: University of Toronto Press, 1993.

Macfadden, Bernarr. *The Virile Powers of Superb Manhood. How Developed, How Lost: How Regained*. New York: Physical Culture, 1900.

———. "An Open Letter to President Roosevelt." *Physical Culture* 18, 1907.

MacIver, Robert M. *The Pursuit of Happiness*. New York: Simon and Schuster, 1955.

MacLean, Nancy. *Behind the Mask of Chivalry: The Making of the Second Ku Klux Klan*. New York: Oxford University Press, 1994.

Macleod, David, "Act Your Age: Boyhood, Adolescence, and the Rise of the Boy Scouts in America." *Journal of Social History* 16, Winter 1982.

———. *Building Character in the American Boy: The Boy Scouts, the YMCA and Their Forerunners*. Madison: University of Wisconsin Press, 1983.

Magill, Edward H. *An Address upon the Coeducation of the Sexes*. Philadelphia: Swarthmore College, 1873.

Mailer, Norman. *Why Are We in Vietnam?* New York: Putnam, 1967.

Male Teachers Association of New York City. "Are There Too Many Women Teachers?" *Educational Review* 28, 1904.

Mallan, John P. "Roosevelt, Brook Adams, and Lea: The Warrior Critique of the Business Civilization." *American Quarterly* 8, 1956, 216–230.

Mangan, J. A., and James Walvin. *Manliness and Morality: Middle-Class Masculinity in the Britain and America, 1800–1940*. New York: St. Martin's Press, 1987.

Mann, Horace. *A Few Thoughts for Young Men*. Boston: Lee and Shepherd, 1870.

Mansbridge, Jane J. *Why We Lost the ERA*. Chicago: University of Chicago Press, 1986.

Marden, Orison Swett. *Pushing to the Front*. New York: Thomas Y. Crowell, 1894.

———. *Success*. Boston: W. A. Wile, 1897.

———. *The Secrets of Achievement*. New York: Thomas Y. Crowell, 1898.

———. *Character, The Greatest Thing in the World*. New York: Thomas Y. Crowell, 1899.

———. *The Young Man Entering Business*. New York: Thomas Y. Crowell, 1903.

———. *The Power of Personality* [1899]. New York: Thomas Y. Crowell, 1906.

———. *Optimistic Life*. New York: Thomas Y. Crowell, 1907.

———. *He Who Can Thinks He Can*. New York: Thomas Y. Crowell, 1908.

———. *The Crime of Silence*. New York: Physical Culture Publishing, 1915.

———. *How to Get What You Want*. New York: Thomas Y. Crowell, 1917.

———. *Prosperity*. New York: Success Magazine, 1922.

Margo, Elisabeth. *Taming the Forty-Niner*. New York, 1855.

Marks, Stuart A. *Southern Hunting in Black and White: Nature, History and Ritual in a Carolina Community*. Princeton, N.J.: Princeton University Press, 1991.

Marovitz, Sanford E. "Testament of a Patriot: *The Virginian*, the Tenderfoot, and Owen Wister." *Texas Studies in Literature and Language* 115, 1973.

Marshall, Samuel Lyman Atwood. *Men Against Fire: The Problem of Battle Common in Future War*. New York: William Morrow, 1947.

Martin, Robert K. "Knights-Errant and the Gothic Seducers: The Representation of Male Friendships in Mid-Nineteenth Century America." In *Hidden from History: Reclaiming the Gay and Lesbian Past*, Martin Duberman, Martha Vicinus, and George Chauncey, Jr., eds. New York: New American Library, 1989.

Martin, Waldo. *The Mind of Frederick Douglass*. Chapel Hill: University of North Carolina Press, 1984.

Mathews, William. *Getting On in the World; or, Hints on Success in Life*. Chicago: Griggs, 1873.

May, Elaine Tylor. *Homeward Bound: American Families in the Cold War Era*. New York: Basic Books, 1988.

Mazer, Sharon. "The Power Team: Muscular Christianity and the Spectacle of Conversion." *Drama Review* 38(4), Winter 1994.

Meigs, Cornelia. *What Makes a College: A History of Bryn Mawr*. New York: Macmillan, 1956.

Mencken, H. L. *In Defense of Women*. New York: P. Goodman Company, 1918.

Menninger, Karl A. "Hysteria in a Male as a Defense Reaction: A Case Report." *Boston Medical and Surgical Journal* 180, 1919.

Michel, Sonya. "Danger on the Home Front: Motherhood, Sexuality and Disabled Veterans in American Postwar Films." *Journal of the History of Sexuality* 3(1), 1992.

Millard, Frederick Payne. *What a Man Goes Through: Friendly Chats About the Battle of Life*. Boston: Christopher Publishing House, 1925.

Minton, Henry L. "Femininity in Men and Masculinity in Women: American Psychiatry and Psychology Portray Homosexuality in the 1930s." *Journal of Homosexuality* 13(1), 1986.

Miroff, Bruce. *Icons of Democracy: American Leaders as Heroes, Aristocrats, Dissenters, and Democrats*. New York: Basic Books, 1993.

Montgomery, David. *Citizen Worker: The Experience of Workers in the United States with Democracy and the Free Market During the Nineteenth Century*. New York: Cambridge University Press, 1994.

Moody, Richard. *The Astor Place Riot*. Bloomington: Indiana University Press, 1958.

Moore, Barrington. *The Social Origins of Dictatorship and Democracy*. Boston: Beacon, 1966.

Moore, David Leon. "Ballplayers Putting Faith in Christ." *USA Today*, 27 July 1991.

Moore, Robert, and Douglas Gillette. *King, Warrior, Magician, Lover*. New York: HarperCollins, 1991.

———. *The King Within*. New York: William Morrow, 1992.

———. *The Warrior Within*. New York: William Morrow, 1992.

———. *The Magician Within*. New York: William Morrow, 1993.

———. *The Lover Within*. New York: William Morrow, 1994.

Morain, Thomas. "The Emergence of the Women's Movement, 1960–1970." Ph.D. diss., University of Iowa, 1974.

Morgan, David H. J. *Discovering Men*. New York: Routledge, 1992.

Mott, James, and Lucretia Mott. *Life and Letters*. A. D. Hallowell, ed. Boston: Houghton Mifflin, 1884.

Mrozek, Donald J. *Sport and American Mentality*. Knoxville: University of Tennessee Press, 1983.

―――. "The Habit of Victory: The American Military and the Cult of Manliness." In *Manliness and Morality: Middle-Class Masculinity in Britain and America, 1800–1940*, J. A. Mangan and J. Walvin, eds. New York: St. Martin's Press, 1987.

Muehl, William. "The Chaplain's Lament." Letter to the editor of the *New York Times*, 12 June 1992.

Mumford, Kevin. "Lost Manhood Found: Sexual Impotence and the Contradictions of Victorian Culture." *Journal of the History of Sexuality*, 1992.

Mumford, Lewis. *The Brown Decades: A Study of the Arts in America, 1865–1895*. New York: Dover, 1931.

Murphy, Charles. "Taft, the Fan." *Baseball* 9(3), 1912.

Muschamp, Herbert. *Man About Town: Frank Lloyd Wright in New York City*. Cambridge: M.I.T. Press, 1983.

"Muscle Business." *Fortune*, 17 January 1938.

"Muscle Makers." *Time*, 22 February 1937.

"Muscular Christianity." *North Carolina Presbyterian*, 2 January 1867.

Nash, Roderick. "The American Cult of the Primitive." *American Quarterly* 18, 1966, 517–537.

―――. *Wilderness and the American Mind*. New Haven: Yale University Press, 1967.

Naylor, Gillian. *The Arts and Crafts Movement*. Cambridge: M.I.T. Press, 1971.

Nelson, Claudia. *Boys Will Be Boys: The Feminine Ethic and British Children's Fiction, 1857–1917*. New Brunswick, N.J.: Rutgers University Press, 1991.

Newman, Katherine. *Falling from Grace: The Experience of Downward Mobility in the American Middle Class*. New York: Free Press, 1988.

Newton, Huey P. *Revolutionary Suicide*. New York: Harcourt, 1973.

Nicholl, Charles. *Borderlines*. New York: Viking, 1989.

Nichols, Jack. *Men's Liberation*. New York: Penguin, 1975.

Nichols, Thomas Low. *Forty Years of American Life*. London: Longmans, Green, 1874.

Nissenbaum, Stephen. *Sex, Diet and Debility in Jacksonian America*. Westport, Conn.: Greenwood, 1980.

Noble, David. *The Progressive Mind, 1890–1917*. Chicago: Rand McNally, 1970.

Nordau, Max. *Degeneration*. New York: H. Fertig, 1968.

Norris, Frank. *A Man's Woman*. New York: Doubleday, 1900.

―――. "The Frontier Gone at Last." *The World's Work* 3, February 1902.

―――. *Vandover and the Brute*. Garden City: Doubleday, 1914.

―――. *McTeague*. New York: New American Library, 1964.

Nott, Jonah. "The Negro Race." *Anthropological Review* 14, July 1886.

Nussbaum, Martin. "Sociological Symbolism of the 'Adult Western.'" *Social Forces* 39, October 1960.

Nye, David E. *Image Worlds: Corporate Identities at General Electric, 1890–1930*. Cambridge: M.I.T. Press, 1985.

Oakley, Ann. *Women's Work: The Housewife, Past and Present*. New York: Vintage, 1974.

Odets, Clifford. *Waiting for Lefty*. In *Three Plays by Clifford Odets*. New York: Random House, 1935.

O'Donnell, Edward. "Women as Bread Winners—the Error of the Age." *American Federationist*, October 1897.

O'Malley, William J. "The Grail Quest: Male Spirituality." *America*, 9 May 1992.

O'Neill, William. *Divorce in the Progressive Era*. New Haven: Yale University Press, 1967.

————. *Everyone Was Brave: The Rise and Fall of Feminism in America*. Chicago: Quadrangle Books, 1969.

————. *American High: The Years of Confidence, 1945–1960*. New York: Free Press, 1986.

Ong, Walter J. *Fighting for Life: Contest, Sexuality and Consciousness*. Ithaca, N.Y.: Cornell University Press, 1981.

Oppenheimer, Valerie Kincade. *The Female Labor Force in the United States: Demographic and Economic Factors Governing Its Growth and Changing Composition*. Westport, Conn.: Greenwood, 1976.

O'Rourke, P. J. *Holidays in Hell*. Boston: Atlantic Monthly Press, 1989.

Osborn, Duffield. "Defense of Pugilism." *North American Review*, 1888.

Osherson, Samuel. *Finding Our Fathers: How a Man's Life Is Shaped by His Relationship with His Father*. New York: Fawcett, 1989.

————. *Wrestling with Love: How Men Struggle with Intimacy, with Women, Children, Parents, and Each Other*. New York: Fawcett, 1992.

Ownby, Ted. *Subduing Satan: Religion, Recreation and Manhood in the Rural South*. Chapel Hill: University of North Carolina Press, 1991.

Packard, Vance. *The Hidden Persuaders*. New York: D. McKay, 1957.

————. *The Status Seekers*. New York: D. McKay, 1959.

Pakaluk, Michael. "War Games." *Crisis*, October 1991.

Palmer, Bruce. *"Man over Money": The Southern Populist Critique of American Capitalism*. Chapel Hill: University of North Carolina Press, 1980.

Paoletti, Jo B. "The Gendering of Infants' and Toddlers' Clothing in America." Paper presented at Conference on Gender and the Material Culture, Winterthur Museum, 1989.

Park, Roberta J. "Physiologists, Physicians and Physical Educators: Nineteenth-Century Biology and Exercise, *Hygienic* and *Educative*." In *Sport and Exercise Science*, J. W. Berryman and R. J. Park, eds. Urbana: University of Illinois Press, 1992.

Park, Susan. "Lois Lane . . . Superwoman? The Impact of World War II on Gender Relationships." Unpublished paper, University of California at Berkeley, Department of History, 1992.

Parke, Ross. *Fathers*. Cambridge: Harvard University Press, 1981.

Parker, Gail Thain. *Mind Cure in New England: From the Civil War to World War I*. Hanover, N.H.: University Press of New England, 1973.

Parker, Theodore. *"A Sermon on the Public Function of Women."* 27 March 1853. Schlesinger Library, microfilm collection.

Parkman, Francis. *The Oregon Trail: Sketches of Prairie and Rocky Mountain Life* [1849]. Boston: Little, Brown, 1892.

Parsons, Talcott. "The Social Structure of the Family." In *The Family: Its Function and Destiny*, Ruth Nanda Anshen, ed. New York: Harper and Brothers, 1959.

Paxson, Frederic, "The Rise of Sport." *Mississippi Valley Historical Review* 4, September 1917.

Payne, Darwin. *Owen Wister: Chronicler of the West*. Dallas: Southern Methodist University Press, 1985.

Payne, Morton. Review of *The Virginian* by Owen Wister. *Dial* 33, 1902.

Peck, Harry Thurston. "The Woman of To-Day and of To-Morrow." *Cosmopolitan* 27, June, 1899.

———. "What a Father Can Do for His Son." *Cosmopolitan* 33, October, 1902.

Peck, Martin W. "The Sex Life of College Men." *Journal of Nervous and Mental Disease* 62, 1925.

Peiss, Kathy. "Of Makeup and Men: The Gendering of Cosmetics." Paper presented at Conference on Gender and Material Culture, Winterthur Museum, November 1989.

Peters, Madison C. *The Strenuous Career; or, Short Steps to Success*. Chicago: Laird and Lee, 1908.

Patrick, Paula. "The Self-Made Boy and the Scientific Capitalist: Gender and the Toy Industry, 1890–1920." Paper presented at the Berkshire Conference on the History of Women, June 1990.

Pettegrew, John. "The Return to Primal Man: The Psychology of Primitivism in Turn-of-the-Century Naturalist Fiction and College Football." *Journal of Men's Studies* 2(1), 1993.

Phillip, Robert. *The Young Man's Closet Library*. New York: n.p., 1857.

Phillips, David Graham. "Restless Husbands." *Cosmopolitan* 51, August 1911.

Phoebus, George Ruskin. "Civilization—Physical Culture." *Physical Culture* 3, 1900.

Pierce, Jason Noble. *The Masculine Power of Christ; or, Christ Measured as a Man*. Boston: Pilgrim Press, 1912.

Pillsbury, Parker. "The Morality of Nations." Address delivered before the American Equal Rights Association, 1867. Schlesinger Library, microfilm collection.

"Pink or Blue." *Infants' Department*, June 1918.

Pivar, David. *Purity Crusade: Sexual Morality and Social Control, 1868–1900*. Westport, Conn.: Greenwood, 1973.

Platt, James. *Business*. New York: G. P. Putnam's Sons, 1889.

Playboy Panel. "The Womanization of America." *Playboy*, June 1962.

Pleck, Joseph. "My Male Sex Role—and Ours." WIN, 11 April 1974.

————. "Men's Power with Women, Other Men and Society: A Men's Movement Analysis" in *Women and Men: The Consequences of Power* (D. Hiller and R. Sheets, eds.) Cincinnati: Office of Women's Studies, University of Cincinnati, 1977.

————. *The Myth of Masculinity*. Cambridge: The M.I.T. Press, 1981.

————. "The Theory of Male Sex Role Identity: Its Rise and Fall, 1936 to the Present." In *In the Shadow of the Past: Psychology Views the Sexes*, M. Lewin, ed. New York: Columbia University Press, 1984.

Pleck, Joseph, and Elizabeth Pleck, eds. *The American Man*. Englewood Cliffs, N.J.: Prentice-Hall, 1980.

Pleck, Joseph, and Jack Sawyer, eds. *Men and Masculinity*. Englewood Cliffs, N.J.: Prentice-Hall, 1974.

Podles, Leon. "Men Not Wanted." *Crisis*, November 1991.

Pollack, Norman. *The Populist Response to Industrial America*. New York: Norton, 1966.

————. *The Humane Economy: Populism, Capitalism and Democracy*. New Brunswick, N.J.: Rutgers University Press, 1990.

Porter, Horace. "The Philosophy of Courage." *Century Illustrated Monthly* 36, May–October 1888.

Potter, David, M. *People of Plenty: Economic Abundance and the American Character*. Chicago: University of Chicago Press, 1954.

Powell, Reed M. *Race, Religion and the Promotion of the American Executive*. College of Administrative Science Monograph no. AA-3. Columbus: Ohio State University, 1969.

Puffer, J. Adams. *The Boy and His Gang*. Boston: Houghton Mifflin, 1912.

Pugh, David. *Sons of Liberty: The Masculine Mind in Nineteenth-Century America*. Westport, Conn.: Greenwood, 1984.

Pyke, Rafford. "What Men Like in Men." *Cosmopolitan*, August 1902.

Rader, Dotson. "Against Coeducation." *Playboy*, January 1976.

Rafferty, Terrence. "Woman on Top." *New Yorker*, December 1994.

Ranson, Stephen W. "The Normal Battle Reaction: Its Relation to the Pathologic Battle Reaction." *Bulletin of United States Army Medical Department* (suppl.), November 1949.

Raphael, Ray. *The Men from the Boys: Rites of Passage in Male America*. Omaha: University of Nebraska Press, 1988.

Rauschenbusch, Walter. *Christianity and the Social Crisis*. New York: Macmillan, 1907.

————. *A Theology for the Social Gospel*. New York: Macmillan, 1918.

Ray, Jefferson Davis. *Meant for Men*. Nashville: Broadman Press, 1939.

Reed, James. *From Private Vice to Public Virtue: The Birth Control Movement and American Society Since 1830*. New York: Basic Books, 1978.

Reich, Charles. *The Greening of America*. New York: Simon & Schuster, 1970.

Reiss, Steven. *Touching Base: Professional Baseball and American Culture in the Progressive Era*. Westport, Conn.: Greenwood, 1980.

————. *City Games: The Evolution of American Urban Society and the Rise of Sports*. Champaign: University of Illinois Press, 1989.

Remington, Frederic. "Cracker Cowboys of Florida." In *Frederic Remington: Selected Writings*, Peggy and Harold Samuels and Frank Oppel, eds. Secaucus, N.J.: Castle, 1981.

"Report of the Male Teachers Association of New York City." *Educational Review* 23, 1902.

Reskin, Barbara, and Patricia Roos. *Job Queues, Gender Queues*. Philadelphia: Temple University Press, 1991.

Richards, Barry. "Bruce Springsteen and the Crisis of Masculinity." *Free Associations* 9, 1987.

Riesman, David. *The Lonely Crowd*. New Haven: Yale University Press, 1950.

Roberts, Gerald F. "The Strenuous Life: The Cult of Manliness in the Era of Theodore Roosevelt." Ph.D. diss., Michigan State University, 1970.

Robertson, James. "Horatio Alger, Andrew Carnegie, Abraham Lincoln and the Cowboy." *Midwest Quarterly* 20, 1979.

Robinson, Dwight E. "Fashions in Shaving and Trimming of the Beard: The Men of the *Illustrated London News*, 1842–1972." *American Journal of Sociology* 81(5), 1976.

Robinson, Forrest G. "The Roosevelt-Wister Connection: Some Notes on the West and the Uses of History." *Western American Literature*, Summer 1979.

Rock, Howard. *Artisans of the New Republic: The Tradesmen of New York City in the Age of Jefferson*. New York: New York University Press, 1984.

Rodgers, Daniel T. *The Work Ethic in Industrial America, 1850–1920*. Chicago: University of Chicago Press, 1974.

Rogin, Michael Paul. *Fathers and Children: Andrew Jackson and the Subjugation of the American Indian*. New York: Vintage, 1975.

————. *Subversive Genealogy: The Politics and Art of Herman Melville*. New York: Knopf, 1983.

Rood, Henry. "Men and Religion." *Independent* 71, 1911.

Roosevelt, Theodore. "The Manly Virtues and Practical Politics." *Forum* 17, July 1894.

————. "A Teller of Tales of Strong Men." Review of *Red Men and White* by Owen Wister. *Harper's Weekly* 39, 1895.

————. "The Essence of Heroism." *Youth's Companion* 75, 18 April 1901.

————. *Addresses and Papers of Theodore Roosevelt*. W. F. Johnson, ed. New York: Unit Book Publishing, 1909.

————. *The New Nationalism*. New York: Outlook, 1910.

————. *Autobiography*. New York: Scribners, 1913.

————. *The Works of Theodore Roosevelt*. 20 vol. New York: Scribners, 1926.

————. *The Letters of Theodore Roosevelt*. E. Morrison, ed. Cambridge: Harvard University Press, 1951.

Rorabaugh, William J. *The Alcoholic Republic: An American Tradition*. New York: Oxford University Press, 1979.

Rosanoff, Aaron J. "A Study of Hysteria, Based Mainly on Clinical Material Observed in the U.S. Army Hospital for War Neuroses at Plattsburgh Barracks, N.Y." *Archives of Neurology and Psychiatry* 2, 1919.

Rose, Frank. "Sissyhood Is Powerful." *Village Voice*, 15 November 1976.

Rosen, Ruth. *The Lost Sisterhood: Prostitution in America, 1900–1918*. Baltimore: The Johns Hopkins University Press, 1982.

Rosenberg, Charles. "Sexuality, Class and Role in Nineteenth-Century America." *American Quarterly* 25, 1973.

Rosenberg, Rosalind. *Beyond Separate Spheres: Intellectual Roots of Modern Feminism*. New Haven: Yale University Press, 1982.

————. "The Limits of Access: The History of Coeducation in America." In *Women and Higher Education in American History*, J. Faragher and F. Howe, eds. New York: Norton, 1988.

Rosenthal, Michael. *The Character Factory: Baden-Powell and the Origins of the Boy Scout Movement*. New York: Pantheon, 1986.

Ross, Dorothy. *G. Stanley Hall: The Psychologist as Prophet*. Chicago: University of Chicago Press, 1972.

Roth, Philip. *Portnoy's Complaint*. New York: Random House, 1969.

Rothman, David. *The Discovery of the Asylum: Social Order and Disorder in the New Republic*. Boston: Little, Brown, 1971.

Rothman, Sheila. *Woman's Proper Place: A History of Changing Ideals and Practices, 1870 to the Present*. New York: Basic Books, 1978.

Rotundo, E. Anthony. "Body and Soul: Changing Ideals of American Middle-Class Manhood, 1770–1920." *Journal of Social History* 16(4), 1983.

————. "American Fatherhood: A Historical Perspective." *American Behavioral Scientist* 29(1), 1985.

————. "Learning About Manhood: Gender Ideals and the Middle Class Family in Nineteenth-Century America." In *Manliness and Morality: Middle-Class Masculinity in Britain and America, 1800–1940*, J. A. Mangan and J. Walvin, eds. New York: St. Martin's Press, 1987.

————. "Romantic Friendship: Male Intimacy and Middle-Class Youth in the Northern United States, 1800–1900." *Journal of Social History* 23(1), 1989.

————. "Boy Culture: Middle-Class Boyhood in Nineteenth-Century America." In *Meanings for Manhood: Constructions of Masculinity in Victorian America*, M. Carnes and C. Griffen, eds. Chicago: University of Chicago Press, 1990.

————. *American Manhood: Transformations in Masculinity from the Revolution to the Present Era*. New York: Basic Books, 1993.

Rudy, Arthur, and Robert Peller. "Men's Liberation." *Medical Aspects of Human Sexuality* 6(9), 1972.

Rush, Nixon O. *Frederic Remington and Owen Wister: The Story of a Friendship, 1893–1909*. Tallahassee: privately printed, 1961.

Russ, William Ward. "Our Boys." *Outlook* 54, 1896.

Russett, Cynthia Eagle. *Sexual Science: The Victorian Construction of Womanhood*. Cambridge: Harvard University Press, 1989.

Ryan, Mary P. *Cradle of the Middle Class: The Family in Oneida County, New York, 1790–1865*. New York: Cambridge University Press, 1981.

————. *Womanhood in America: From Colonial Times to the Present*. New York: Franklin Watts, 1983.

Sabo, Donald F., and Ross Runfola, eds. *Jock: Sports and Male Identity*. Englewood Cliffs, N.J.: Prentice-Hall, 1980.

Salinger, J. D. *The Catcher in the Rye*. Boston: Little, Brown, 1951.

Samons, Jeff. *Beyond the Ring: The Role of Boxing in American Society*. Urbana: University of Illinois Press, 1988.

Sanday, Peggy Reeves. *Fraternity Gang Rape*. New York: New York University Press, 1989.

Sandburg, Carl. "To a Contemporary Bunkshooter" [1915]. In *Complete Poems*. New York: Harcourt, Brace, 1950.

Sanford, R. Nevitt. *Self and Society*. New York: Atherton, 1966.

Savran, David. *Communists, Cowboys and Queers: The Politics of Masculinity in the Work of Arthur Miller and Tennessee Williams*. Minneapolis: University of Minnesota Press, 1992.

Sawyer, Jack. "On Male Liberation." *Liberation* 15(6–8), August–October, 1970.

Sawyer, Rev. Roland D. "The Larger Side of Baseball." *Baseball* 1(6), 1908.

Saxton, Alexander. *The Indispensible Enemy: Labor and the Anti-Chinese Movement in California*. Berkeley: University of California Press, 1971.

————. *The Rise and Fall of the White Republic: Class Politics and Mass Culture in Nineteenth-Century America*. New York: Verso, 1990.

Scharf, Lois. *To Work and to Wed: Female Employment, Feminism and the Great Depression*. Westport, Conn.: Greenwood, 1980.

————. and Joan M. Jensen, eds. *Decades of Discontent: The Women's Movement, 1920–1940*. Westport, Conn.: Greenwood, 1983.

Schindler, Rabbi Solomon. "A Flaw in our Public School System." *Arena* 6, June 1892.

Schlesinger, Arthur M. *Learning How to Behave: A Historical Study of American Etiquette Books*. New York: Macmillan, 1947.

Schlesinger, Arthur M., Jr. *The Age of Jackson*. Boston: Little, Brown, 1953.

————. "The Crisis of American Masculinity." *Esquire*, November 1958.

————. *The Disuniting of America*. Knoxville: Whittle Direct Books, 1991.

Schurman, Paul. "Male Liberation." *Pastoral Psychology* 35(3), 1987.

Schurz, Carl. "About War." *Harper's Weekly* 42, 5 March 1898.

Schwab, Charles M. *Succeeding with What You Have*. New York: Century, 1917.

Schwartz, Milt. Interview with Shepherd Bliss. *Sober Times*, September 1991.

Scully, Vincent. *Modern Architecture*. New York: George Braziller, 1974.

Seale, Bobby. *Seize the Time*. New York: Random House, 1970.

Sebald, Hans. *Momism: The Silent Disease of America*. Chicago: Nelson-Hall, 1976.

Seidler, Victor J. *Re-creating Sexual Politics: Men, Feminism and Politics*. London: Routledge, 1991.

———. *Unreasonable Men: Masculinity and Social Theory*. London: Routledge, 1993.

———, ed. *The Achilles' Heel Reader: Men, Sexual Politics and Socialism*. London: Routledge, 1991.

Seidman, Steven. *Romantic Longings: Love in America, 1830–1980*. New York: Routledge, 1991.

Sellers, Charles. *The Market Revolution: Jacksonian America, 1815–1846*. New York: Oxford University Press, 1992.

Seton, Ernest Thompson. "The Dangers of Athletic Training." *American Medicine* 13, 1907.

———. *Gospel of the Redman*. London: Psychic Press, 1937.

Sexton, Patricia Cayo. *The Feminized Male: Classrooms, White Collars and the Decline of Manliness*. New York: Vintage, 1969.

———. "How the American Boy Is Feminized." *Psychology Today* 3(23), January 1970.

Seymore, Charles. *Self-Made Men*. New York: Harper and Brothers, 1857.

Shackford, James Atkins. *David Crockett: The Man and the Legend*. Chapel Hill: University of North Carolina Press, 1956.

Shaler, Nathanial. "European Peasants as Immigrants." *Atlantic Monthly* 71, May 1893.

Shaw, Albert. *The Outlook for the Average Man*. New York: Macmillan, 1907.

Sheiner, Marcy. "What Do Men Really Want . . . and Why Should We Care?" *East Bay Express*, 10 July 1992.

Sheldon, Henry D. *Student Life and Customs*. New York: D. Appleton, 1901.

Shepardson, Francis. *The Beta Book: The Story and Manual of Beta Theta Pi*. Beta Theta Pi, 1927.

Shepherd, E. R. *True Manhood: A Manual for Young Men: A Guide to Physical Strength, Moral Excellence, Force of Character, and Manly Purity*. Chicago: Sanitary Publishing, 1888.

Shepherd, E. S. "Contribution to the Study of Indeterminacy." *American Journal of Urology and Sexology* 14(6), 1918.

Shi, David. *The Simple Life: Plain Living and High Thinking in American Culture*. New York: Oxford University Press, 1985.

Shostak, Arthur. *Blue Collar Life*. New York: Random House, 1969.

Showalter, Elaine. *The Female Malady: Women, Madness, and English Culture, 1830–1980*. New York: Pantheon, 1985.

———. *Sexual Anarchy: Gender and Culture at the Fin-de-Siècle*. New York: Viking, 1990.

Shyrock, R. H. "Sylvester Graham and the Popular Health Movement, 1830–1870." *Mississippi Valley Historical Review* 18, 1931.

Silber, Irwin. *Songs America Voted By*. Harrisburg: Stackpole Books, 1988.

Silber, Nina. "Intemperate Men, Spiteful Women and Jefferson Davis." in *Divided Houses*, C. Clinton and N. Silber, eds. New York: Oxford University Press, 1992.

———. *The Romance of Reunion: Northerners and the South, 1865–1900*. Chapel Hill: University of North Carolina Press, 1993.

Silverman, Kaja. "Historical Trauma and Male Subjectivity." In *Psychoanalysis and Cinema*, E. Ann Kaplan, ed. New York: Routledge, 1990.

Simmel, Georg. "The Sociology of Secret Societies." A. Small, trans. *American Journal of Sociology* 11, 1906.

———. "The Alpine Journey" [1897]. *Theory, Culture and Society* 8, 1991.

Sinclair, Upton. *The Jungle*. New York: Doubleday, 1906.

Sklar, Kathryn Kish. *Catherine Beecher: A Study in American Domesticity*. New Haven: Yale University Press, 1973.

Skolnick, Arlene. *Embattled Paradise: The American Family in an Age of Uncertainty*. New York: Basic Books, 1992.

Slater, Philip. *The Pursuit of Loneliness*. Boston: Beacon Press, 1970.

———. *Earthwalk*. Garden City, N.Y.: Anchor, 1974.

———. *Footholds*. New York: Dutton, 1977.

Sloane, William. "The Life of Napoleon Bonaparte." *Century* 27, 1894.

Slotkin, Richard. *Regeneration Through Violence: The Mythology of the American Frontier, 1600–1860*. New York: Atheneum, 1973.

———. *The Fatal Environment: The Myth of the Frontier in the Age of Industrialization*. New York: Atheneum, 1985.

———. *Gunfighter Nation: The Myth of the Frontier in Twentieth-Century America*. New York: Atheneum, 1992.

Smith, Gary Scott. "The Men and Religion Forward Movement of 1911–1912: New Perspectives on Evangelical Social Concern and the Relationship Between Christianity and Progressivism." *Westminster Theological Journal* 49(1), Spring 1987.

Smith, Henry Nash. *Virgin Land: The American West as Symbol and Myth*. Cambridge: Harvard University Press, 1950.

Smith, Mary Ann. *Gustav Stickley: The Craftsman*. Syracuse, N.Y.: Syracuse University Press, 1983.

Smith, Matthew Hale. *Successful Folks: How They Win*. Hartford: American Publishing, 1878.

Smith, Orren E. *Manhood: A Study of Male Vitality*. Indianapolis: Sentinel Printing, 1910.

Smith-Rosenberg, Carroll. *Disorderly Conduct: Visions of Gender in Victorian America*. New York: Knopf, 1985.

Smith-Rosenberg, Carroll, and Charles Rosenberg. "The Female Animal: Medical and Biological Views of Woman and Her Role in Nineteenth-Century America." *Journal of American History* 2, 1973.

———, eds. *The Secret Vice Exposed! Some Arguments Against Masturbation*. New York: Arno Press, 1974.

Sobel, Raymond. "The Battalion Surgeon as Psychiatrist." *Bulletin of the U.S. Army Medical Department* (suppl.), November 1949.

Sochen, June. *The New Woman: Feminism in Greenwich Village, 1910–1920*. New York: Quadrangle Books, 1972.

———. *Herstory: A Record of the American Woman's Past*. New York: Knopf, 1974.

———, ed. *The New Feminism in Twentieth-Century America*. Lexington, Mass.: D. C. Heath, 1971.

Sokolow, James, *Eros and Modernization: Sylvester Graham, Health Reform, and the Origins of Victorian Sexuality in America*. Rutherford, N.J.: Fairleigh Dickinson University Press, 1983.

Solomon, Robert. *The Bully Culture: Enlightenment, Romanticism and the Transcendental Pretense, 1750–1890*. Totowa, N.J.: Rowman and Littlefield, 1992.

Sorokin, Pitirim. "American Millionaires and Multi-Millionaires." *Journal of Social Forces* 3, 1925.

Southard, E. E. *Shell Shock and Other Neuropsychiatric Problems: Presented in Five Hundred and Eighty-Nine Case Histories from the War Literature, 1914–1918* [1919]. New York: Arno Press, 1973.

Spain, Daphne. *Gendered Spaces*. Chapel Hill: University of North Carolina Press, 1992.

———. "The Spatial Foundations of Men's Friendships and Men's Power." In *Men's Friendships*, P. Nardi, ed. Newbury Park, Calif.: Sage Publications, 1992.

Spalding, Albert. *America's National Game*. New York: American Sports Publishing, 1911.

Spigel, Lynn. *Make Room for TV: Television and the Family Ideal in Postwar America*. Chicago: University of Chicago Press, 1992.

Spilka, Mark. *Hemingway's Quarrel with Androgyny*. Lincoln, Neb., University of Nebraska Press, 1994.

Spillman, W. J. "The Country Boy." *Science* 30, 1909.

Stall, Sylvanus. *What a Young Man Ought to Know*. Philadelphia: n.p., 1897.

Standing Bear (Chief). "What the Indian Means to America." In *The American Frontier*, C. M. Babcock, ed. New York: Holt, 1965.

Stansell, Christine. *City of Women: Sex and Class in New York, 1789–1860*. New York: Knopf, 1982.

Stansky, Peter. *Redesigning the World: William Morris, the 1880s and the Arts and Crafts*. Princeton, N.J.: Princeton University Press, 1985.

Stearne, Albert. "Effects of Lascivious Conversations, Books, and Companions in the Causation of Sexual Excess." *American Journal of Dermatology and Genito-Urinary Disease* 11, 1907.

Stearns, Alfred E., et al. *The Education of the Modern Boy*. Boston: Houghton Mifflin, 1928.

Stearns, Peter. *Be a Man! Males in Modern Society*. New York: Holmes and Meier, 1979.

———. "Men, Boys and Anger in American Society, 1860–1940." In *Manliness and Morality: Middle-Class Masculinity in Britain and America, 1800–1940*, J. A. Mangan and J. Walvin, eds. New York: St. Martin's Press, 1987.

———. *Jealousy: The Evolution of an Emotion in American History*. New York: New York University Press, 1989.

———. *American Cool*. New York: New York University Press, 1994.

Steinbeck, John. *The Grapes of Wrath*. New York: Viking, 1939.

———. *The Winter of Our Discontent*. New York: Viking, 1961.

———. *Of Mice and Men* [1937]. New York: Penguin, 1974.

Stevens, Stuart. *Malaria Dreams*. Boston: Atlantic Monthly Press, 1989.

Stevens, Walter Le Conte. "The Admission of Women to Universities." New York: S. W. Green, 1883.

Stimpson, Catharine. *Where the Meanings Are: Feminism and Cultural Spaces*. New York: Methuen, 1988.

Stivers, Richard. *A Hair of the Dog: Irish Drinking and American Stereotypes*. University Park, Pa.: Pennsylvania State University Press, 1976.

Stoddard, Lathrop. *The Rising Tide of Color*. New York: Scribners, 1920.

Stone, I. F. "Machismo in Washington." *New York Review of Books*, 18 May 1972.

Storrs, Richard Salter. *Manliness in the Scholar*. New York. A.D.F. Randolph, 1883.

Stott, Richard. "The Geography of Gender in Nineteenth-Century America: Youth, Masculinity and the California Gold Rush." Paper presented at the 1991 annual meeting of the Organization of American Historians.

Stouffer, Samuel, et al. *The American Soldier*. 2 vols. Princeton, N.J.: Princeton University Press, 1949.

Strasser, Susan. *Never Done: A History of American Housework*. New York: Pantheon, 1982.

Strecker, Edward. *Their Mothers' Sons: The Psychiatrist Examines an American Problem*. Philadelphia: Lippincott, 1946.

Stricker, Frank A. "Socialism, Feminism and the New Morality: The Separate

Freedoms of Max Eastman, William English Walling and Floyd Dell, 1910–1930." Ph.D. diss., Princeton University, 1974.

Strong, Edward K. "Interests of Men and Women." *Journal of Social Psychology* 7, 1936.

———. *Vocational Interests of Men and Women*. Stanford, Cal.: Stanford University Press, 1943.

Suitor, J. Jill. "Husbands' Participation in Childbirth: A Nineteenth-Century Phenomenon." *Journal of Family History*, Fall 1981.

Summerbell, Martyn. *Manhood in Its American Type*. Boston: Richard C. Bidger, 1916.

Sunday. William A. "Why I Left Professional Baseball." *Young Men's Era* 19(30), 27 July 1893.

Suplee, Curt. "The Dawn of the Wimp." *Miami Herald*, 16 September 1984.

Susman, Warren I. *Culture as History: The Transformation of American Society in the Twentieth Century*. New York: Pantheon, 1984.

Swidler, Leonard. "Jesus Was a Feminist." *Catholic World*, January 1971.

Symes, Lillian. "The New Masculinism." *Harper's Monthly* 161, January 1930.

Synott, Marcia Graham. *The Half-Opened Door: Discrimination and Admission at Harvard, Yale, and Princeton, 1900–1970*. Westport, Conn.: Greenwood, 1979.

Takaki, Ronald. *Iron Cages: Race and Culture in Nineteenth-Century America*. New York: Knopf, 1979.

———. *Strangers from a Different Shore: A History of Asian Americans*. New York: Viking, 1989.

———. *A Different Mirror: A History of Multicultural America*. Boston: Little, Brown, 1993.

Talton, Jon. "Author Describes Jesus as a Business Role Model." *St. Cloud Times*, 16 January 1995.

Tannenbaum, Frank. *A Philosophy of Labor*. New York: Knopf, 1951.

Tarbell, Ida. "Napoleon Bonaparte." *McClure's* 3, 1894.

———. *All in a Day's Work: An Autobiography*. New York: Macmillan, 1939.

Tavris, Carol. *The Mismeasure of Woman*. New York: Simon and Schuster, 1992.

Taylor, Ella. *Prime-Time Families: Television Culture in Postwar America*. Berkeley: University of California Press, 1989.

Taylor, Karen. "Patriarchy and Male Oppression: Suffering the Responsibilities of Manhood." In *Transcending Boundaries*, P. Free and J. Coggleshall, eds. New York: Bergin and Garvey, 1991.

Taylor, Robert Lewis. "I Was Once a 97-Pound Weakling." *New Yorker*, 3 January 1942.

Taylor, William R. *Cavalier and Yankee: The Old South and American National Character*. New York: George Braziller, 1961.

Terkel, Studs. *"The Good War": An Oral History of World War Two*. New York: Pantheon, 1985.

Terman, Lewis, and Catherine Cox Miles. *Sex and Personality*. New York and London: McGraw-Hill, 1936.

Thelen, David. *Paths of Resistance: Tradition and Dignity in Industrializing Missouri*. New York: Oxford University Press, 1986.

Thomas, Mary Martha. *The New Woman of Alabama: Social Reform and Suffrage, 1890–1920*. Tuscaloosa: University of Alabama Press, 1992.

Thomas, Thaddeus P. "Why Equal Suffrage Has Been a Success." Harrisburg: Pennsylvania Woman Suffrage Association. Schlesinger Library, microfilm collection.

Thomas, William I. *Sex and Society*. Chicago: University of Chicago Press, 1907.

Thompson, Keith, ed. *To Be a Man: In Search of the Deep Masculine*. Los Angeles: Jeremy Tarcher, 1991.

Thompson, William G. "Men and the Gospels." *Catholic World*, May 1992.

Thoreau, Henry David. *Walden* [1854]. New York: New American Library, 1960.

Thurber, James. *Thurber Country: A Collection of Pieces about Males and Females, Mainly of Our Own Species*. New York: Simon and Schuster, 1953.

Thurber, James, and Elliot Nugent. *The Male Animal* [a play]. New York: Samuel French, 1941.

Tiger, Lionel. *Men in Groups*. New York: Random House, 1969.

Tilton, Theodore. "The Rights of Woman: A Letter to Horace Greeley." New York, 1871. Schlesinger Library, microfilm collection.

Toby, Jackson. "Violence and the Masculine Mystique: Some Qualitative Data." *Annals of the American Academy of Political and Social Science* 36(4), 1966.

Tocqueville, Alexis de. *Democracy in America* [1832]. New York: Anchor, 1969.

Tompkins, Jane. *West of Everything: The Inner Life of Westerns*. New York: Oxford University Press, 1992.

Trall, Russell T. *Sexual Physiology: A Scientific and Popular Exposition of the Fundamental Problems of Sociology*. New York: Miller and Wood, 1867.

Traubel, Horace, "The Soul of the Workman and His Work." *Artsman* 3, July 1906.

Tufts, J. H. "Feminization." *School Review* 17, January 1909.

Turner, Frederick Jackson. "Contributions of the West to American Democracy." *Atlantic Monthly* 91, 1903.

———. "The Significance of the Frontier in American History." In *The Early Writings of Frederick Jackson Turner*, F. Mood, ed. Madison: University of Wisconsin Press, 1938.

———. *The Frontier in American History*. New York: Holt, Rinehart and Winston, 1947.

Tuttle, William M., Jr. *"Daddy's Gone to War": The Second World War in the Lives of America's Children*. New York: Oxford University Press, 1993.

Twain, Mark. *The Adventures of Huckleberry Finn* [1884]. New York: Bantam, 1981.

———. *The Adventures of Tom Sawyer* [1876]. New York: Penguin, 1986.

Twombley, Robert. *Louis Sullivan: His Life and Work*. New York: Viking, 1986.

Tyack, David, and Elisabeth Hansot. *Learning Together: A History of Coeducation in American Public Schools*. New Haven: Yale University Press, 1990.

Tyler, Robert L. "My Woman Problem, and Ours." *American Man*, Spring 1984.

Tyler, Royall. *The Contrast: A Comedy in Five Acts* [1787]. Boston: Houghton Mifflin, 1920.

Tyrrell, Ian R. *Sobering Up: From Temperence to Prohibition in Antebellum America*. Westport, Conn.: Greenwood, 1979.

Underhill, Albert J. "Sexual Neurasthenia in Men." *Journal of the American Medical Association* 60, 1913.

Updike, John. *Memories of the Ford Administration*. New York: Knopf, 1992.

Valverde, Mariana. " 'When the Mother of the Race is Free': Race, Reproduction, and Sexuality in First Wave Feminism." In *Gender Conflicts: New Essays in Women's History*, F. Iacovetta and M. Valverde, eds. Toronto: University of Toronto Press, 1992.

Vance, Norman. *The Sinews of the Spirit: The Ideal of Christian Manliness in Victorian Literature and Religious Thought*. Cambridge: Cambridge University Press, 1985.

Vandenberg-Daves, Jodi. "Pursuing a Partnership Between the Sexes: The Debate over Programs for Women and Girls in the Young Men's Christian Association, 1914–1933." Unpublished paper, Department of History, University of Minnesota, 1991.

Vander Warker, Ely. "Is the Education of Women with Men a Failure?" *Harper's Weekly* 48, 20 August 1904.

Vanse, Charles. "How Well Do I Remember." *Equitable Spirit* 1(4), 1934.

Veblen, Thorstein. *The Theory of the Leisure Class* [1899]. New York: New American Library, 1953.

Vinikas, Vincent. *Soft Soap, Hard Sell: American Hygiene in an Age of Advertisement*. Ames: Iowa State University Press, 1992.

Vorphal, Ben Merchant. *My Dear Wister: The Frederic Remington-Owen Wister Letters*. Palo Alto: American West Publishing, 1972.

Voss, Kim. *The Making of American Exceptionalism: The Knights of Labor and Class Formation in the Nineteenth Century*. Ithaca, N.Y.: Cornell University Press, 1993.

Wakefield, Edward. "Nervousness: The National Disease of America." *McClure's* 2, February 1894.

Walker, Don. D. "Wister, Roosevelt and James: A Note on the Western." *American Quarterly* 12, 1960.

Walker, Francis. "College Athletics." *Harvard Graduates* 2, 1893.

Walker, John Brisben. "A Working Man in the Presidency." *Cosmopolitan* 32, November 1901.

Walker, Jimmy. "Rodeo Killers." *True West*, 1958.

Walkowitz, Judith R. "Jack the Ripper and the Myth of Male Violence." *Feminist Studies* 8, Fall 1982.

———. *City of Dreadful Delight: Narratives of Sexual Danger in Late-Victorian London*. Chicago: University of Chicago Press, 1992.

Wallace, Michelle. *Black Macho and the Myth of the Superwoman*. New York: Dial Press, 1979.

Walsh, William S. "The Conceited Sex." *North American Review* 159, 1894.

Walters, Marianne. "The Co-Dependent Cinderella Who Loves Too Much Meets Iron John." Lecture at the 15th Annual Family Therapy Network Symposium, Washington, D.C., March 1992.

Walters, Ronald. "The Erotic South: Civilization and Sexuality in American Abolitionism." *American Quarterly* 25, May 1973.

———, ed. *Primers for Prudery: Sexual Advice to Victorian America*. Englewood Cliffs, N.J.: Prentice-Hall, 1973.

Wandersee, Winifred D. *On the Move: American Women in the 1970s*. Boston: Twayne, 1988.

Ward, Lester. "Broadening the Way to Success." *Forum* 2, 1886.

———. "Our Better Halves." *Forum* 6, 1888.

———. *Pure Sociology*. New York: Macmillan, 1903.

———. *Applied Sociology*. Boston: Ginn, 1906.

———. *Dynamic Sociology; or, Applied Social Science*. 2 vols. New York: D. Appleton, 1926.

Ware, Norman. *The Industrial Worker, 1840–1860*. Boston: Houghton Mifflin, 1924.

Ware, Susan. *Beyond Suffrage: Women in the New Deal*. Cambridge: Harvard University Press, 1981.

———. *Holding Their Own: American Women in the 1930s*. Boston: Twayne, 1982.

Warner, Charles Dudley. "The Subjection of Man." *Harper's New Monthly* 80, May 1890.

Warner, W. Lloyd, and James Abegglen. *Big Business Leaders in America*. New York: Atheneum, 1963.

Warren, Allen. "Popular Manliness, Baden-Powell, Scouting and the Development of Manly Character." In *Manliness and Morality: Middle-Class Masculinity in Britain and America, 1800–1940*, J.A. Mangan and J. Walvin, eds. New York: St. Martin's Press, 1987.

Wartzman, Rick. "Clinton Is Still Struggling to Get Message Across to 'Angry White Males' Who Have Tuned Out." *Wall Street Journal*, 24 January 1995.

Watson, John B. *Psychological Care of Infant and Child*. New York: Norton, 1928.

Wayne, Kenneth H. *Building the Young Man*. Chicago: A. C. McClurg, 1912.

Webber, Charles. *Old Hicks, the Guide; or, Adventures in the Comanche Country in Search of a Gold Mine*. 2 vols. New York: Harper and Brothers, 1848.

Weir, James. "The Methods of the Rioting Striker as Evidence of Degeneration." *Century* 48, October 1894.

Weiss, Richard. *The American Myth of Success: From Horatio Alger to Norman Vincent Peale*. New York: Basic Books, 1969.

Wells, Jeffrey. "Ah-nuld's Baby Not As Big As Expected." *Newsday*, 8 December 1994

Welter, Barbara. "The Cult of True Womanhood." *American Quarterly*, Summer 1966.

———. "The Feminization of American Religion, 1800–1860." In *Clio's Consciousness Raised*, M. Hartmann and L. Banner, eds. New York: Harper and Row, 1974.

Wertheimer, Barbara. *We Were There: The Story of Working Women in America*. New York: Pantheon, 1977.

"What Color for Your Baby?" *Parents'*, March 1939.

Wheeler, John. *Touched with Fire: The Future of the Vietnam Generation*. New York: Avon, 1984.

Whipple, Edwin P. *Success and Its Conditions*. Boston: James R. Osgood, 1871.

White, Bouck. *The Book of Daniel Drew*. New York: Doubleday, 1910.

———. *The Call of the Carpenter*. New York: Doubleday and Page, 1913.

White, E. E. "Separate Education of Boys and Girls." *Common School Journal* 13, 1851.

———. "Coeducation of the Sexes." *National Teacher* 2, 1872.

White, G. Edward. *The Eastern Establishment and the Western Experience*. New Haven: Yale University Press, 1968.

White, Kevin. *The First Sexual Revolution: The Emergence of Male Heterosexuality in Modern America*. New York: New York University Press, 1992.

White, William Allen. *Boys—Then and Now*. New York: Macmillan, 1926.

Whites, LeeAnn. "The Civil War as a Crisis in Gender." In *Divided Houses*, C. Clinton and N. Silber, eds. New York: Oxford University Press, 1992.

Whitman, Albery A. *Not a Man, and Yet a Man*. Springfield, Ohio: Republic Printing, 1877.

Whitman, Walt. *Complete Poetry and Collected Prose*. J. Kaplan, ed. New York: Library of America, 1982.

Whitmore, Allan R. "Beard, Boys and Buckskins: Daniel Carter Beard and the Preservation of the American Pioneer Tradition." Ph.D. diss., Northwestern University, 1970.

Whorton, James. "Physiologic Optimism: Horace Fletcher and Hygienic Ideology in Progressive America." *Bulletin of the History of Medicine* 55, 1981.

———. *Crusaders for Fitness: The History of American Health Reformers*. Princeton, N.J.: Princeton University Press, 1982.

Wiegman, Robyn. "Negotiating the Masculine: Configurations of Race and Gender in American Culture." Ph.D. diss., Department of English, University of Washington, 1988.

———. "Feminism, the *Boyz*, and Other Matters Regarding the Male." In *Screening the Male: Exploring Masculinity in Hollywood Cinema*, S. Cohan and I. Hark, eds. New York: Routledge, 1992.

———. "Fiedler and Sons." Unpublished MS, Indiana University, 1992.

———. "The Anatomy of Lynching." *Journal of the History of Sexuality* 4(1), January 1993.

Wilder, Burt Green. *What Young People Should Know*. n.p., 1875.

Wilentz, Sean. *Chants Democratic: New York City and the Rise of the American Working Class, 1788–1850*. New York: Oxford University Press, 1984.

Wilkinson, Rupert. *American Tough: The Tough-Guy Tradition and American Character*. New York: Harper and Row, 1986.

———. *The Pursuit of American Character*. New York: Harper and Row, 1988.

Willard, James F. *Union Colony at Greeley*. Denver: W. F. Robinson Printing, 1918.

Williams, W. Churchill. "Red Blood in Fiction." *World's Work* 6(1), May 1903.

Wills, Garry. *Nixon Agonistes*. Boston: Houghton Mifflin, 1970.

———. "Goodbye to Boxing." *New York Review of Books* 35(2), 18 February 1988.

Wilson, Edward. *Sociobiology: The New Synthesis*. Cambridge: Harvard University Press, 1975.

Wilson, Sloan. *The Man in the Gray Flannel Suit*. New York: Simon and Schuster, 1955.

Wilson, Woodrow. *The New Freedom*. New York: Doubleday, 1913.

Wiltse, Charles M. *The New Nation, 1800–1845*. New York: Hill and Wang, 1961.

Winn, Will H. "The Negro: His Relation to Southern Industry." *American Federationist* 4, February 1896.

Wister, Owen. *Red Men and White*. New York: Harper and Brothers, 1896.

———. *The Virginian* [1902]. New York: New American Library, 1979.

Wittgenstein, Ludwig. *Culture and Value*. Chicago: University of Chicago Press, 1980.

Wohl, R. Richard. "The 'Country Boy' Myth and Its Place in American Urban Culture: The Nineteenth-Century Contribution." In *Perspectives in American History*. New York: Cambridge University Press, 1969.

Woldenberg, Susan. "Modern Man Is Revolting!" *Los Angeles Reader* 9(8), 5 December 1986.

Wolfe, Tom. *Mauve Gloves and Madmen, Clutter and Vine, and Other Stories, Sketches, and Essays*. New York: Farrar, Straus and Giroux, 1976.

————. *The Right Stuff.* New York: Farrar, Straus and Giroux, 1979.

Woloch, Nancy. *Women and the American Experience.* New York: Knopf, 1984.

Wolsey, Viscount. "The Young Napoleon." *Cosmopolitan* 34, January 1903.

"Women in Business 2." *Fortune* 12, August 1935.

Wood, Clement. *Manhood: The Facts of Life Presented to Men.* Girard, Kans.: Haldeman-Julien, 1924.

Woods, Frederick A. "City Boys Versus Country Boys." *Science* 29, 1909.

Woody, Thomas. *A History of Women's Education in the United States.* 2 vols. New York: Science Press, 1929.

Woolfolk, Robert, and Frank Richardson. *Sanity, Stress and Survival.* New York: Signet, 1978.

Worster, Donald. *Under Western Skies: Nature and History in the American West.* New York: Oxford University Press, 1992.

Worth, George J. "Of Muscles and Manliness: Some Reflections on Thomas Hughes." In *Victorian Literature and Society: Essays Presented to Richard Altick*, J. R. Kincard and A. J. Kuhn, eds. Columbus: Ohio State University Press, 1984.

Wouk, Herman. *The Caine Mutiny.* Garden City: Doubleday, 1951.

Wright, Carroll. "An Historical Sketch of the Knights of Labor." *Quarterly Journal of Economics* 1, 1887.

Wright, Gwendolyn. *Moralism and the Model Home: Domestic Architecture and Cultural Conflict in Chicago, 1873–1913.* Chicago: University of Chicago Press, 1985.

Wright, Harold Bell. *When a Man's a Man.* Chicago: Book Supply, 1916.

Wright, Richard. *Native Son.* New York: Harper and Row, 1940.

————. *Black Boy.* New York: Harper and Row, 1945.

————. "The Man Who Was Almost a Man." In *Eight Men.* Cleveland: World Publishing, 1961.

Wyatt-Brown, Bertram. "The Abolitionist Controversy: Men of Blood, Men of God." In *Men, Women and Issues in American History*, vol. 1, H. Quint and M. Cantor, eds. Homewood, Ill.: Dorsey Press, 1975.

Wyckoff, William. *The Workers: An Experiment in Reality.* 2 vols. New York: Scribners, 1899.

Wyden, Peter, and Barbara Wyden. *Growing Up Straight: What Every Thoughtful Parent Should Know About Homosexuality.* New York: Trident Press, 1968.

Wylie, Philip. *Generation of Vipers.* New York: Rinehart, 1942.

————. *The Disappearance.* New York: Holt, Rinehart and Winston, 1951.

————. "The Womanization of America." *Playboy*, September 1958.

Wyllie, Irvin G. *The Self-Made Man in America.* New Brunswick, N.J.: Rutgers University Press, 1954.

Yagoda, Ben. "The True Story of Bernarr Macfadden." *American Heritage* 33(1), December 1981.

Yarborough, Richard. "Race, Violence, and Manhood: The Masculine Ideal in Frederick Douglass's 'The Heroic Slave.'" In *Frederick Douglass: New Literary and Historical Essays*, E. Sundquist, ed. New York: Cambridge University Press, 1990.

Young, James Harvey. *The Medical Messiahs: A Social History of Health Quackery in Twentieth-Century America*. Princeton, N.J.: Princeton University Press, 1967.

Zafar, Rafia. "Franklinian Douglass: The Afro-American as Representative Man." In *Frederick Douglass: New Literary and Historical Essays*, E. Sundquist, ed. New York: Cambridge University Press, 1990.

Zelditch, Morris. "Role Differentiation in the Nuclear Family: A Comparative Study." In *Family, Socialization and Interaction Process*, T. Parsons and R. F. Bales, eds. New York: Free Press, 1955.

Ziff, Larzer. *The American 1890s: Life and Times of a Lost Generation*. New York: Viking, 1966.

Zolotow, M. "You Too Can Be a New Man." *Saturday Evening Post* 214, 7 February 1942.

Zueblin, Charles. *Democracy and the Overman*. New York: B. W. Huebsch, 1910.

Zunz, Olivier. *Making America Corporate, 1870–1920*. Chicago: University of Chicago Press, 1992.

Index

Abbott, John S. C., 58
Abolitionism, 70–73
Abortion, 114, 273
Acres of Diamonds (Conwell), 85
Acton, William, 54
Adams, Charles Francis, 58
Adams, Henry, 84
Adams, Henry Baxter, 87
Adams, John, 16, 19
Adams, John Quincy, 34
Adams, Samuel, 21
Adam's Rib (film), 234
Admirable Crichton, The (Barrie), 218
Adolescence, 162-164, 166, 187
Adolescence (Hall), 161, 162
Adorno, Theodor, 245
Adventures of Tom Sawyer, The (Twain),78
Advice books and manuals, 45-48, 49, 53,54,
    57, 102, 128, 140, 202, 203
Advice to Young Men (Arthur), 46
African Queen, The (film), 233
Agassiz, Louis, 92
Agnew, Spiro, 270
Alamo, The (film), 253
Alcohol, 48–51, 101, 124–126
Alcott, William, 46
Alda, Alan, 283, 293, 294
Alger, Horatio, 142, 143
Alienation and Freedom (Blauner), 264
Allen, C. S., 28
Allen, Devere, 196
"American Boy, The" (Roosevelt), 186
American Male, The (Brenton), 273
American Nervousness (Beard), 134

American Notes for General Circulation
    (Dickens), 24
American Revolution, 18–19, 21, 72–73
Americans, The (Grund), 23–24
"American Scholar, The" (Emerson), 28
American Woman's Home, The (Beecher and-
    Stowe), 159
Anderson, Sherwood, 198–199
And Keep Your Powder Dry (Mead), 229–230
Andrews, E. A., 57
Angels with Dirty Faces (film), 219
Anthem (Rand), 238
Antifeminism, 90, 96–97, 274–275
Anti–Semitism, 91–92
Antiwar movement, 267
Appearance, 28, 60, 120, 123–124,
    126–127, 183, 210–212, 310, 314,
    332
Applied Sociology (Ward), 113
Apprenticeship, 30, 32, 83
Archie comics, 230
Architecture, 147–148
Ardrey, Robert, 276
Aristocracy, 19, 21, 25, 28
Arthur, Timothy, 46
Arts and Crafts Movement, 110–111
Ashbee, C. R., 110
Ashcan School, 147
Astor Place riot, 41–42
Atlas, Charles, 210–212, 251
Atlas Shrugged (Rand), 238
Atwater, Lee, 331
Authoritarian Personality, The, 245
Awake and Sing (Odets), 217, 218

Babbitt (Lewis), 202, 215
Baber, Asa, 302–303
Baby and Child Care (Spock), 246
Backwoodsmen, 63–64
Baden–Powell, R. S. S., 157, 168
Baldwin, James, 271, 329
Bancroft, George, 34
Bank of the United States, 34, 35–36
Baraka, Amiri, 272
Barrie, J. M., 218
Barton, Bruce, 33, 196
Baseball, 137, 139–141
Baseball Players Practicing (Eakins), 147
Basic Instinct (film), 308
Basketball, 137, 138
Baum, L. Frank, 108–110
Baumgaertner, Jill, 320
Beard, Daniel, 169
Beard, George, 98, 134–135, 137
Beatniks, 243
Bederman, Gail, 178
Beecher, Catherine, 159
Beecher, Henry Ward, 50, 102
Bellows, George, 147
Bennett, James Gordon, 72
Benton, Thomas Hart, 147
Berkeley, Busby, 219
Best and the Brightest, The (Halberstam), 269
Best Years of Our Lives (film), 224
Beveridge, Albert J., 157, 164
Bingham, Carl, 194
Birth control, 114, 273
Birth of a Nation (film), 95
Black Boy (Wright), 231
Black men, 33, 73–75, 85–86, 91, 92, 95–96,
        107, 139, 195, 231, 241, 271, 330
Black Panther party, 271–272
Blauner, Robert, 264
Bliss, Shepherd, 317
Blithedale Romance (Hawthorne), 69
Blix (Norris), 145
Blondie, 205–206
Bly, Robert, 5, 291, 316, 317, 332
Bogart, Humphrey, 232, 233, 289
Bohemian Grove, 315–316
Bok, Edward, 97
Bonfire of the Vanities (Wolfe), 307, 310
Book of Wealth, The (Hunt), 23
Boone, Daniel, 63–64
Boone and Crockett Club, 168, 186
Boosterism, 200, 235
Born on the Fourth of July (film), 321–322
Bostonians, The (James), 117–118, 146
Bourne, Edward, 49
Bourne, Randolph, 114

Boxing, 137, 138–139, 164
Boy and His Gang, The (Puffer), 163–164
Boy Scouts of America, 168–170
Bram Stoker's Dracula (film), 325
Brando, Marlon, 249
Brannon, Robert, 282
Breadwinner role, 20, 200, 245, 246, 264,
        265
Brenton, Myron, 273, 282
Bridgeman, Howard Alan, 176
Brown, Antoinette, 57
Brown, Charles Brockden, 19
Brown, John, 72
Brownson, Orestes, 29–30, 60, 117
Brown v. Board of Education of Topeka (1954),
        241
Brueres, Martha, 159
Brueres, Robert, 159
Bryan, William Jennings, 108, 110
Bryce, Peter, 133
Buchanan, James, 39
Buchanan, Pat, 64
Bucher, Glenn, 285
Buckley, William F., 314
Buddy films, 287–288
Buell, Rebeccah Root, 54
Building the Young Man (Wayne), 27
Buntline, Ned, 41
Burnap, George, 46
Burroughs, Charles, 59
Burroughs, Edgar Rice, 152, 154
Bush, George, 186, 292, 296–297
Butler, Brett, 313

Caesar's Column (Donnelly), 92
Calhoun, John C., 76
Calhoun, T. J., 133
California Gold Rush, 61–62
Call of the Carpenter, The (White), 177–178
Call of the Wild (London), 152–153
Capitalism, 21, 22, 36, 84
Caputo, Philip, 311–312
Carman, Bliss, 144
Carnal Knowledge (film), 287
Carnegie, Andrew, 105, 180
Carnegie, Dale, 200, 235, 241
Carnes, Mark, 173
Carpenter, Edward, 110
Carson, Kit, 63
Carter, Jimmy, 270
Casablanca (film), 233
Cass, Lewis, 39
Casualties of War (film), 322
Catcher in the Rye, The (Salinger), 237–238
Catch-22 (Heller), 225

Cattell, J. McKeen, 121
Cereals, 127–129
Chafe, William, 236
Chandler, Raymond, 212, 213, 286
Chaplin, Charles, 218
Chauncey, George, 98–100, 126
Chevalier, Michel, 24
Cheyenne's Frontier Days, 148, 149
Chicago Black Sox scandal, 139, 141
Child development, 201–205, 243, 247
Childhood development, 158, 160
Chinese Exclusion Act (1882), 85, 108
Choice of Heroes, A (Gerzon), 292
Citizen Kane (film), 232–233
City Slickers (film), 323–324
City Wilderness, The (Wood), 120
Civil rights movement, 78, 261, 262–263,
    271
Civil War, 72–78, 94, 151
Clansman, The (Dixon), 95
Clarke, Edward, 96
Clay, Henry, 26, 210
Cleaver, Eldridge, 271, 272
Clemenceau, Georges, 91
Clinton, Bill, 186, 297–298
Clinton, Hillary Rodham, 298
Close Encounters of the Third Kind (film), 322
Clothing, children's, 160–161
Coalition for Free Men, 305
Cody, Buffalo Bill, 148
Coeducation debate, 162–167, 187, 315
Cohen, Albert, 244
Collins, Joseph, 203
Colonial America, 18
Colton, Calvin, 26
Columbian Exposition (1893), 98
Communism, 236, 237, 277
Communist Manifesto, The (Marx and Engels),
    42
Companionate marriage, 158–159
Conine, Jon, 306
Conspicuous consumption, 104
Contrast, The (Tyler), 13–17, 25, 27, 39, 255
Conwell, Joseph, 129
Conwell, Russell, 85
Cooper, Gary, 219, 238
Cooper, James Fenimore, 66–68
Copland, Aaron, 217
Cott, Nancy, 22, 54
Counterculture, 263
Cousins, Norman, 199
Cowan, Ruth Schwartz, 53
Cowboys, 148–150, 300
Cox, Samuel Sullivan, 90–91
Craft guilds, 32

Crane, Stephen, 142, 144
Creek War of 1813/14, 34
Crèvecoeur, Hector St. John, 20, 61
Crime of Silence, The (Marden), 128
Crockett, Davy, 37–38, 63, 64
Crossfire (film), 226, 232
Cross–race male bonding, 65–66
Crowd, The (film), 220–221
Cult of True Womanhood, 54
Cultural feminization, 118–124, 132, 146,
    150, 256–257, 309, 313
Culture of the Gang, The (Cohen), 244
Culverwell, R. J., 48
Custer, George Armstrong, 142

Dana, Mrs. S. B., 161–162
Dana, Richard Henry, 61
Dances with Wolves (film), 323
Darrow, Clarence, 193
Date rape, 299, 301, 330
Davidson, Nicholas, 301, 303
Davis, Jefferson, 77
Davis, Natalie Zemon, 3
Davis, Ossie, 271
Day, Clarence, 205, 206
Day of the Saxon, The (Lea), 91, 111–112
Dead Reckoning (film), 232
Death of a Salesman (Miller), 223, 234–236
De Beauvoir, Simone, 1
Declaration of Independence, 18–19
Deer Hunter, The (film), 289, 321
Deerslayer, The (Cooper), 67
Delany, Martin, 71
Deliverance (film), 287–288
Dell, Floyd, 114–116, 333
DeMille, Cecil B., 218, 219
Democracy and the Overman (Zueblin), 91
Democracy in America (Tocqueville), 13
Democratic manhood, 333–335
Democratic Vistas (Whitman), 105
Dens, 111, 158
Department stores, 123
Detective novels, 212–213, 286
Dewey, John, 115, 166–167, 183
Dickens, Charles, 24–26, 48
Disclosure (film), 308
Discovery of the Great West (Parkman), 61
Divorce, 159, 205, 303, 305
Dixon, Thomas, 95
Dmytryk, Edward, 226
Docine, G. W., 48
Dr. Jekyll and Mr. Hyde (Stevenson), 145
Doctor Looks at Love and Life, The (Collins),
    203
Domhoff, G. William, 316

Dominick and Eugene (film), 294
Donahue, Phil, 293
Donnelly, Ignatius, 92
Double Indemnity (film), 232
Douglas, Ann, 176
Douglas, G., 129
Douglas, Michael, 307–308, 326
Douglas, Robert, 239
Douglass, Frederick, 71, 73–74, 98
Douglass, H. Ford, 73
Doyle, Richard, 305
Drew, Thomas, 53
Duberman, Martin, 289
Dude ranches, 135, 136, 252, 309
Dueling, 95, 124
Dukakis, Michael, 186, 296–297
Duke, David, 326, 332
Duke of Deception, The (Wolff), 289
Dwight, Theodore, 58
Dwight, Timothy, 61

Eakins, Thomas, 135, 147
Eastman, Max, 114–116
Easy Rider (film), 287
Eaton, Mark, 314
Edgar Huntley (Brown), 19
Edis, Robert, 127
Education, 57, 86, 96, 162–167, 187
Effeminacy, 8, 19, 21, 92, 93, 99, 100, 105,
    106, 125, 186, 203, 204, 237
Ego, 131–132
Ehrenreich, Barbara, 254
Eliot, Charles, 166
Eliot, Samuel, 84
Ellison, Ralph, 241
Emancipation Proclamation, 90
Emerson, Ralph Waldo, 23, 28, 73, 87
Engels, Friedrich, 42
English, William, 93
Enjoyment of Living (Eastman), 114
Epstein–Barr syndrome, 299
Escape, 9, 44, 59–70, 87–89, 155, 251–257,
    263, 309–325, 332–333
Escape from Freedom (Fromm), 239
Esoteric Anthropology (Nichols), 70
E.T.: The Extra–Terrestrial (film), 322
Evans, George, 88, 136
Evans, Hiram Wesley, 178
"Evolution of the Cowpuncher" (Wister), 152
Exclusion, 9, 44, 89–100, 107, 116, 263,
    332, 333
Exodus (Uris), 278

Facial hair, 123
Factory system, 30, 31, 53

Failure of Feminism, The (Davidson), 301
Fairchild, James, 167
Falling Down (film), 308, 326
Faludi, Susan, 301
Falwell, Jerry, 312
Family size, 158–159
Farmers, 82, 84, 108
Farmer's Friend, The (Hitchcock), 20
Farnham, Eliza, 55
Farrar, Eliza W. R., 48
Farrell, Warren, 284–285, 303–304
Fasteau, Marc Feigen, 283, 285
Fatal Attraction (film), 308
Fatherhood, 52, 58, 158–160, 201–203,
    205–206, 226–228, 243, 245–250,
    283, 290
Father's Book, The (Dwight), 58
Fathers' Rights (Conine), 306
Fathers' rights groups, 305–306
Feiffer, Jules, 212
Feirstein, Bruce, 295, 331
Female labor, 56–57, 87, 197–198, 241
Feminine Mystique, The (Friedan), 261, 278,
    292
Feminism and Freedom (Levin), 301–302
"Feminism for Men" (Dell), 115
Feminism (*see* Women's movement)
Feminized Male, The (Sexton), 276
Ferraro, Geraldine, 296
Fiedler, Leslie, 66, 214
Field of Dreams (film), 322
54th Massachusetts regiment, 74
"Fighting Saint, The" (Sunday), 180
Filipinos, 194–195
Finley, James, 48
Finney, Charles, 22
Fire in the Belly (Keen), 316
Fiske, G. Walter, 137
Fitzgerald, F. Scott, 215–216
Fitzhugh, George, 76
Flake, Carol, 312
Flanagan, Thomas, 295
Flappers, 197
Fletcher, Horace, 127
Flint, Timothy, 61
Formation of a Manly Character, The (Peck), 46
Forrest, Edwin, 40–41
Fort Apache (film), 253
Fountainhead, The (Rand), 238–239
Fowler, O. S., 122, 129
Frankfurt School, 239
Franklin, Benjamin, 20–21, 104, 216
Fraternal organizations, 171–175, 195–196,
    309, 315, 320
Fraternities, 170–171, 314, 315

Frederick, Christine, 158
Frederickson, George, 74, 77
Freed blacks, 78, 85, 86
Freud, Sigmund, 131–133, 174, 262
Friedan, Betty, 26, 258, 261, 278, 292
Fromm, Erich, 239–240
Frontier (see West)
Frost, John, 26

Gage, Matilda Joslyn, 174
Gangs, 163–164, 243
Gangster movies, 219
Gardner, Augustus Kingsley, 47
Garfield, James, 57
Garland, Hamlin, 88
Garrison, William Lloyd, 50, 71, 72
Gay liberation movement, 263, 271,
    279–280, 288, 330
Generation of Vipers (Wylie), 229, 276
Genovese, Eugene, 76
Genteel Patriarch, 9, 16–20, 27–28, 39, 76,
    77, 154, 220, 230, 239, 250, 296
Gerzon, Mark, 292
Ghost Dance, 94
Gilder, George, 274–275, 301, 303
Gillette, Douglas, 316
Gilman, Charlotte Perkins, 135, 184
Ginsberg, Allen, 243
Goddard, Henry, 194
Goffman, Erving, 5
Gold, Michael, 218
Goldberg, Herb, 284, 303, 304–305
Goldberg, Steven, 274
Goldenweiser, Alexander, 195
Gold rush, 61–62
Goldwater, Barry, 270
Gompers, Samuel, 92
Gone With the Wind (film), 219–220
Goodman, Paul, 266
Goodson, Mark, 295
Gorer, Geoffrey, 243
Gorn, Elliot, 118, 139
Gould, Robert, 282
Graham, Sylvester, 46–47, 50, 69, 127, 129,
    136
Grant, Madison, 91
Grapes of Wrath, The (Steinbeck), 217
Great Depression, 192–194, 199–201, 206
Great Gatsby, The (Fitzgerald), 215–216
Great Migration, 85
Greeley, Horace, 60, 84
Greening of America, The (Reich), 266
Greenwich Village bohemians, 113–116, 281
Grey, Zane, 140, 155
Griffith, D. W., 95

Grinnell, George Bird, 136
Growing Up Straight: What Every Thoughtful
    Parent Should Know About Homosexu-
    ality (Wyden and Wyden), 279
Grund, Francis, 23–24, 28
Guernsey, Henry, 131
Guilford Temperament Survey, 209
Gulick, Luther, 167, 177
Guns N' Roses, 325–326
Gyms, 126–127

Haikie, William, 128
Halberstam, David, 269
Hale, Sarah, 76
Hall, G. Stanley, 127, 161–164, 166, 167,
    171, 182, 187
Hall, Winfield, 129
Hamerton, Philip, 133
Hamilton, F. W., 165
Hammett, Dashiell, 212, 213
Hapgood, Hutchins, 114
Hard Bodies (Jefford), 311
Harding, Warren G., 192
Harper, William, 165–166
Harrington, Henry, 54
Harrison, William Henry, 36–38
Harwood, W. S., 171
Haskins, C. W., 62
Hawes, Joel, 176
Hawthorne, Nathaniel, 28, 56, 69
Hawthorne, Sophia, 46, 56
Hayward, Fred, 305
Hazing, 163, 164
Health crazes, 46–48, 120, 126–130, 309,
    310
Hearn, Thomas, 283
Hefner, Hugh, 255
Heller, Joseph, 225
Hemingway, Ernest, 191, 214–215
Henri, Robert, 147
Henry, George W., 191, 210
Hepburn, Katharine, 233–234
Herbert, T. Walter, 28, 56
Heroes for Sale (film), 191
Heroic Artisan, 9, 16–18, 20, 27–35, 37, 39,
    64, 68, 84, 101, 105, 106, 108, 116,
    138–139, 142, 177, 213, 218, 230,
    239, 243, 266, 268
Hershiser, Orel, 313
Hidden Persuaders, The (Packard), 241
Higginson, Thomas Wentworth, 71, 177
Hippies, 263, 266
Hitchcock, Edward, 105
Hitchcock, Enos, 20
Hobbies, 246–247

Hobos, 101
Holmes, Oliver Wendell, 60
Homestead Act (1862), 93
Homosexuality, 98–100, 110, 122, 125, 126,
        132, 202–204, 206, 207, 209–210,
        214–215, 236, 237, 241, 243, 244,
        256, 263, 272, 277–280, 284, 312,
        326
Homosociality, 7–8, 26, 61–62, 110, 125,
        197, 312, 332
Honeymooners, The (television show), 248
"Honks and Wonks" (Wolfe), 277
Household Engineering (Frederick), 158
Howells, William Dean, 146
Howl (Ginsberg), 243
How to Get Strong and How to Stay So
        (Haikie), 128
How to Win Friends and Influence People
        (Carnegie), 200
Huckleberry Finn (Twain), 59
Hughes, Thomas, 177
Hunt, Freeman, 26
Hunt, Thomas, 23
Hunting, 125, 136
Huntley, David, 75
Hutchins, Robert Maynard, 167
Hutchinson, Woods, 137
Huxley, Aldous, 1
Hysteria, 133, 134

Iacocca, Lee, 307
Immigrants, 32, 83, 85, 90, 93, 108, 194, 330
Immigration Act (1924), 194
Imperialism, 111, 185
Incest, 304
In Country (film), 321
Incredible Shrinking Man, The (Matheson),
        242
In Defense of Women (Mencken), 198
Industrialization, 78, 81–83
Industrial Revolution, 9, 241, 317
Inevitability of Patriarchy, The (Goldberg), 274
Influence of Sea Power upon History, The
        (Mahan), 111
Ingraham, Prentiss, 148
Intellectualism, 237
Intellectual Life, The (Hamerton), 133
Intermarriage, 91
Interview with the Vampire (film), 325
Invasion of the Body Snatchers (film), 242
Invisible Man, The (Ellison), 241
Iron John (Bly), 291, 316
Irving, Washington, 19, 41, 65
It Happened One Night (film), 219
Ives, Charles, 147

Jackson, Andrew, 33–36, 50, 69
Jacobs, John, 314
James, Frank, 105–106
James, Henry, 118, 146
James, Henry, Sr., 176
James, Jesse, 141–142
James, William, 112, 183–184
Jarvis, Edward, 132–133
Jefferson, Thomas, 16, 19, 27, 33
Jefford, Susan, 311
Jesus, 177–180, 196–197, 283–284,
        312–314
Jews, 91–92, 171, 277–278
Jim Crow laws, 86
Johnson, Jack, 139
Johnson, Laura Winthrop, 148
Johnson, Lyndon B., 269–270
Johnson, Paul, 48
Jones, Gerard, 250
Jordan, Vernon, 315
Judd, Sylvester, 54
Jungle, The (Sinclair), 120
Juvenile delinquency, 227, 228, 242–244

Kazantzakis, Nikos, 329
Keen, Sam, 316, 319
Kellogg, J. H., 127, 129–130, 332
Kelly, E. Lowell, 209
Kennedy, John F., 267–269
Kent, William, 136
Kerouac, Jack, 289
Kilmer, Joyce, 112
King, Alexander, 256
King, Martin Luther, Jr., 261, 271
King, Warrior, Magician, Lover (Moore and
        Gillette), 319
Kingsley, Charles, 177
Kirkpatrick, Jeane, 296
Knight, Bobby, 298
Knights of King Arthur, 168
Knights of Labor, 30, 107–108
Knights of St. Crispin, 106
Koestler, Arthur, 278
Komorovsky, Mirra, 200–201
Kramer v. Kramer (film), 290, 293
Ku Klux Klan, 95, 174, 178, 195

"Laboring Classes, The" (Brownson), 29–30
Labor movement, development of, 106–107
Lacquer, Thomas, 3
Lahr, John, 218
LaLanne, Jack, 251
Lasch, Christopher, 266
Last of the Mohicans, The (Cooper), 66
Laurel and Hardy, 206

Lawrence, D. H., 67, 214, 332
Lazarus, Emma, 85
Lea, Homer, 91, 105, 111–112
Leatherstocking Tales (Cooper), 66–68
Leave It to Beaver (television show), 250
Lectures on Science and Human Life (Graham), 46
Lectures to Young Men (Burnap), 46
Lecture to Young Men, A (Graham), 46
Lennon, John, 293
Lethal Weapon series, 66
Letters from an American Farmer (Crèvecoeur), 20
Leverenz, David, 8
Levin, Michael, 301–303
Levy, David, 229
Lewis, Sinclair, 202, 215
Life with Father (Day), 205, 206
Lincoln, Abraham, 39
Lindsey, Ben, 180
Lives of American Merchants (Hunt), 26
London, Jack, 152–154
Lonely Crowd, The (Riesman), 119, 240–241
Lone Ranger, The (television show), 252
Long, James, 58
Longfellow, Henry Wadsworth, 28
Loring, Charles, 198
Lott, Eric, 32, 33
Lowell, Charles Russell, 68–69
Lucas, George, 322
Ludovici, Anthony, 84, 198
Lydston, George, 95
Lynching, 86, 96, 195
Lynd, Helen, 192
Lynd, Robert, 192

Macfadden, Bernarr, 100, 121, 127–129, 251, 332
Macready, William, 39–41
Madison, James, 16
Mahan, Alfred Thayer, 111
Mailer, Norman, 242, 256, 257, 274, 278, 288–289
Malcolm X, 271
Male and Female (film), 218–219
Male bonding, 65–66, 69–70, 170, 173, 197, 287–290, 316, 322
Maltese Falcon, The (Hammett), 213
Mamet, David, 7
Manchurian Candidate, The (film), 242
Man for Himself (Fromm), 240
Manhood (Wood), 203
Man in the Gray Flannel Suit, The (Wilson), 242, 257–258
Manly Art, The (Gorn), 139

Manners Maketh Man (Docine), 48
Man Nobody Knows, The (Barton), 196, 313
Man's Woman, A (Norris), 145–146
Man the Masterpiece (Kellogg), 129
Man Who Shot Liberty Valance, The (film), 253
"Man Who Was Almost a Man, The" (Wright), 231
Marble Faun, The (Hawthorne), 55
Marden, Orison Swett, 81, 102–103, 128
Marlowe (film), 286–287
Marshall, Edward, 140
Marx, Karl, 42
Mary Shelley's Frankenstein (film), 325
Masculine domesticity, 159–160
Maslin, Janet, 294
Massey, Raymond, 239
Masturbation, 45–48, 128–131, 134
Maternal Overprotection (Levy), 229
Matheson, Richard, 242
Matthias, Prophet, 53
McCarthy, Joseph, 236–237
McGovern, George, 270
McKeever, William, 140
McNamara, Robert, 269
McNarney, Joseph, 227
McNaughton, James, 269
McTeague (Norris), 145
Mead, Margaret, 229–230
Meat eating, 136–137
Meigs, Charles, 54
Mellers, Joan, 287
Mellon, Joan, 253
Melville, Herman, 41, 43, 69–70
Memminger, M., 75
Men Achieving Liberation and Equality (MALE), 305
Men and Religion Forward Movement, 180–181
Mencken, H. L., 198
Men in Groups (Tiger), 277
Men of Tomorrow, 168
Men's Club, The (Michaels), 289–290
Men's clubs, 315, 319
Men's League for Woman Suffrage, 114, 115
Men's liberation, 280–290
Men's magazines, 254–257, 275
Men's Rights, Inc., 305
Men's rights movement, 300–306, 309, 330
Mental illness, 133
Men without Women (Hemingway), 214
Mercein, Thomas, 29
M–F scale, 206–210, 276
Michaels, Leonard, 289–290, 294
Middletown in Transition (Lynd and Lynd), 192

Middletown (Lynd and Lynd), 192
Midnight Cowboy (film), 287
Milagro Beanfield War (film), 294
Miles, Catherine Cox, 206–210, 276, 295
Militarism, 95, 112, 299, 302, 311
"Militarism or Manhood?" (Miller), 184
Millard, Frederick, 193, 197–198
Miller, Arthur, 223, 234–236
Miller, Joseph Dana, 184
Miller, Mark Crispin, 248
Miller, Walter, 244
Mills, C. Wright, 240
Minnesota Multiphasic Personality Inventory, 209
Minstrel shows, 32–33, 320
Mr. Deeds Goes to Town (film), 219
Mitchell, Brian, 311
Mitchell, S. Weir, 133–135, 150
Moby Dick (Melville), 43, 69–70
Modern Times (film), 218
Momism: The Silent Disease of America (Sebald), 276
Mondale, Walter, 296
Monogamy, 113, 114
Montagu, Ashley, 256
Montgomery, David, 31
Moore, Robert, 319
Moral Physiology (Owen), 70
Moran (Norris), 145
Morrill Act (1862), 86
Morris, William, 110
Mount Holyoke College, 57, 86
Moyers, Bill, 269, 270
Muehl, William, 301
Muir, John, 136
Muscular Christianity, 177–181, 196, 283, 309, 312–313
Music, 147, 325–328
My Bondage and My Freedom (Douglass), 74
Myth of Masculinity, The (Pleck), 285

Naked at Gender Gap (Baber), 302–303
Naked Nomads (Gilder), 274
Namath, Joe, 293
National Congress for Men, 305
National Geographic, 120
National Organization for Men (NOM), 306
National Trade Union, 56–57
Native Americans, 34–35, 90, 93–94, 169, 316, 317, 320
Native Son (Wright), 231
Nativism, 90, 107, 194, 195
Natural Superiority of Women, The (Montagu), 256
Nature (Emerson), 87

Neurasthenia, 134–135, 150, 299
Newhart, Bob, 293
New Life, A (film), 294
Newton, Huey, 271
Nichols, Jack, 282
Nichols, Thomas Gove, 23, 70
Nixon, Richard M., 270
Noir films, 231–232
Norris, Frank, 144–146
Not a Man, and Yet a Man (A. Whitman), 74
Noyes, John Humphrey, 70
Nuclear family, 228, 249, 302

Odets, Clifford, 217–218
Of Mice and Men (Steinbeck), 7, 217
Ogle, Charles, 37
Oneida commune, 70
"On Male Liberation" (Sawyer), 280
On the Waterfront (film), 249–250
Optimistic Life, The (Marden), 102
Oregon Trail, The: Sketches of Prairie and Rocky Mountain Life (Parkman), 61
Organization Man, The (Whyte), 241
Origin of the Species (Darwin), 90
Osherson, Sam, 27
Owen, Robert Dale, 70
Ownby, Ted, 124

Packard, Vance, 241
Painting, 147
Pakaluk, Michael, 311
Palance, Jack, 324
Parent–Teacher Association (PTA), 202
Parkman, Francis, 61, 88–89, 91
Parsons, Talcott, 227–229, 244, 245
Passing of the Great Race, The (Grant), 91
Pathfinder, The (Cooper), 67
Patten, Gilbert (Burt Standish), 142
Paxson, Frederic, 138
Peale, Norman Vincent, 241
Peck, George, 46
Peck, Harry Thurston, 97
Perhaps Women (Anderson), 198–199
Perkins, Maxwell, 191
Perot, H. Ross, 297
Perrin, Noel, 295
Persian Gulf war, 299
Peters, Madison, 81
Peyote cult, 94
Philippines, 194, 195
Phillips, Wendell, 71, 72
Philosophy of Labor, A (Tannenbaum), 241
Pierce, Sarah, 58
Pillsbury, Parker, 71
Pioneers, The (Cooper), 66

"Pioneers! O Pioneers!" (Whitman), 60
"Pioneer Spirit and American Problems, The"
    (Roosevelt), 182
Plain Facts for Young and Old (Kellogg), 129,
    130
Plain Talks on Avoided Subjects (Guernsey),
    131
Platt, James, 85
Play, 167–171
Playboy, 254–257
Play It Again Sam (film), 289
Pleck, Joseph, 207, 281, 285–286
Populists, 30, 108–110
Pornography, 304
Porter, Horace, 88
Port Huron Statement (1962), 267
Portnoy's Complaint (Roth), 278
Post, C. W., 127
Powderly, Terrence, 107–108
Power of Personality (Marden), 81
Prairie, The (Cooper), 67
Prescript of the Order of the Ku Klux Klan, 95
Presidential manhood, 38–39, 267–270,
    296–298
Prince, William, 232
Princess Casamassima, The (James), 146
Prisoner of Sex, The (Mailer), 274
Producerism, 29–30, 34, 105
Promise Keepers (Christian men's organiza-
    tion), 313
Prostitution, 106
Protestant Ethic and the Spirit of Capitalism,
    The (Weber), 104
Psychological Care of Infant and Child (Wat-
    son), 202
Puffer, J. Adams, 163–164
Punishment, 163
Pure Sociology (Ward), 113
Pushing to the Front (Marden), 102
Pyke, Rafford, 122

Racism, 33, 90, 91, 92, 95–96, 107, 194,
    195, 326
Rader, Dotson, 314
Ragged Dick (Alger), 143
Railroads, 82, 93
Rand, Ayn, 238
Randolph, Sir William, 18
Rape, 95–96, 273, 304
Rape of the Male, The (Doyle), 305
Rauh, Ida, 114
Reagan, Ronald, 270, 291–292, 296
Real Men Don't Bond (Feirstein), 331
Real Men Don't Eat Quiche (Feirstein), 295
Rebel Without a Cause (film), 249

Recapitulation, theory of, 162
Red Badge of Courage, The (Crane), 142, 144
Redford, Robert, 294
"Red Pony, The" (Steinbeck), 251
Red River (film), 253
Reich, Charles, 266
Religion, 50, 53–54, 60, 175–181, 196–197,
    283–284, 312–314
Remasculinization of America, The (Jefford),
    311
Remington, Frederic, 135, 136, 147,
    151–152, 155, 182, 323
Restlessness, 24–25
Retreats, 197, 298, 309, 315–321, 332–333
Revere, Paul, 16
Rice, William North, 167
Riders of the Purple Sage (Grey), 155
Riesman, David, 119, 240–241
Right Stuff, The (Wolfe), 268
Rio Grande (film), 253
"Rip Van Winkle" (Irving), 65
Rising Tide of Color (Stoddard), 91, 194
Robinson, William, 131
Rodeos, 148–149, 252, 309
Roediger, David, 32
Roe v. Wade (1973), 273
Rogin, Michael, 34
Rood, Henry, 180
Roosevelt, Franklin D., 267
Roosevelt, Theodore, 110, 135, 136, 140,
    166, 168, 181–187, 253, 267, 323,
    332
Rorabaugh, William, 49, 51
Rose, Axl, 326
Roth, Philip, 278, 294
Rotundo, E. Anthony, 55
Rough Riders, 184–185
Rush, Benjamin, 21
Ruskin, John, 110

Safire, William, 270
"Saints and Their Bodies" (Higginson), 177
Salesmen, 103, 193
Salinger, J. D., 237–238
Saloons, 124, 125
Sandow, Eugen, 138
Sanger, William, 114
Sargent, D. A., 137
Sawyer, John, 280
Schaffer, Peter, 143
Schindler, Solomon, 121
Schlesinger, Arthur M., Jr., 261–262
Scientific management, 83
Scott, Winfield, 39
Seale, Bobby, 271

Sea Wolf, The (London), 153–154
Sebald, Hans, 276, 278–279
Second Great Awakening, 50, 54, 60
Second Sex, The (De Beauvoir), 1
"Secret Life of Walter Mitty, The" (Thurber),
　212
Self–control, 9, 44–50, 333
Self Made Men in America (Frost), 26
Self–Made Men (Seymore), 26
Sellers, Charles, 49
Seminole Indians, 35
Seneca Falls Convention, 57, 71
Sex and Personality (Terman and Miles), 206
Sex in Education (Clarke), 96
Sexism, 33, 107, 113, 326
Sexton, Patricia Cayo, 275–276
Sexual behavior, 45–48, 50, 51, 128–132,
　273–274
Sexual harassment, 273, 299, 301, 302, 304,
　330
Sexual Impotence (Robinson), 131
"Sexual Morality and Modern Nervousness"
　(Freud), 131
Sexual Neurasthenia (Beard), 134
Sexual Suicide (Gilder), 274
Seymore, Charles, 26
Shaft (film), 289
Shaving, 123
Shaw, Robert Gould, 74
Shell shock, 133–134
Shepardson, Francis, 171
Showalter, Elaine, 134
Siller, Sidney, 306
"Simple Art of Murder, The" (Chandler),
　213
Sinclair, Upton, 120
Sissies, 8, 100, 122, 147, 185, 243, 276
Slater, Philip, 265–266
Slavery, 32, 50, 71–74
Sloan, John, 147
Slotkin, Richard, 64
Smith, Fred, 180
Social Darwinism, 90–93, 96, 101, 301
Socialism, 106, 116
Social Purity Movement, 125
Sorenson, Theodore, 268
Soul on Ice (Cleaver), 271
Southern manhood, 28, 75–78, 124–125
Space program, 268
Spanish–American war, 152, 194
Spencer, Herbert, 90
Spheres, separation of, 50–59, 70, 157–158
Spielberg, Steven, 322
Spillane, Mickey, 212
Spock, Benjamin, 202, 246

Sports, 9, 118, 126, 135, 137–142, 170, 183,
　186, 313–314
Springsteen, Bruce, 325–328
Stade, George, 294
Star Trek (television show), 290
Star Wars trilogy, 322
Status Seekers, The (Packard), 241
Steinbeck, John, 7, 217, 251
Steinem, Gloria, 284
Stevenson, Adlai, 237
Stevenson, Robert Louis, 145
Stickley, Gustav, 110, 111
Stillé, Alfred, 122
Stimpson, Catharine, 3
Stoddard, Lathrop, 91, 194, 332
Stowe, Harriet Beecher, 159
Straight/White/Male (Bucher), 285
Straw Dogs (film), 289
Strecker, Edward, 229
Streetcar Named Desire, A (film), 249
Strenuous Career, The (Peters), 81
"Strenuous Life, The" (Roosevelt), 182
Strikes, 31, 87
Strong Vocational Interest Blank, 209
Student movement, 267
Students for a Democratic Society (SDS), 267
Student's Manual, The (Todd), 46
Suburbs, 236
Success magazine, 102, 105
Suffrage, 57, 70, 96, 114, 115, 197
Sullivan, John L., 139
Sullivan, Louis, 147–148
Sumner, William Graham, 90
Sun Also Rises, The (Hemingway), 214–215
Sun Dance religion, 94
Sunday, Billy, 177, 179–180
Sunset Boulevard (film), 232
Superb Manhood (Macfadden), 128
Superman, 211–212
Survival of the fittest, 90, 91
Susman, Warren, 245
Swidler, Leonard, 283
Swimming Hole, The (Eakins), 147

Taft, William Howard, 141
Tannenbaum, Frank, 241
Tarzan of the Apes (Burroughs), 154
Taylor, Buck, 148
Taylor, Frederick Winslow, 83
Taylor, Zachary, 39
Teachers, 121, 162, 167, 202
Technological change, 83, 158
Temperance movement, 49–50, 125
Tennis, 137, 138
Terkel, Studs, 200

Terman, Lewis, 206–210, 276, 295
Textile industry, 82
Texts and Pretexts (Huxley), 1
Their First Mistake (film), 206
Their Mothers' Sons (Strecker), 229
Theory of the Leisure Class, The (Veblen), 104
Theroux, Paul, 295
Thomas, M. Carey, 166
Thompson, E. P., 30
Thompson, Keith, 315
Thompson Seton, Ernest, 169–170
Thoreau, Henry David, 43, 44, 60, 62–63, 262
Three Men and a Baby (film), 293
Thurber, James, 212
Tiger, Lionel, 277
Tilton, Theodore, 71
Tissot, S. A., 45
Tocqueville, Alexis de, 9, 13, 25–26, 29, 34, 50, 55, 104, 199, 235, 257
Todd, John, 46, 57, 62, 332
To Have and Have Not (film), 233
Tompkins, Jane, 150
Tootsie (film), 292, 293
Toys, 161
Trachtenberg, Alan, 82
Tracy, Spencer, 233–234
Training the Boy (McKeever), 140
Trall, Russell, 127
Traubel, Horace, 110
Travels in New England and New York (Dwight), 61
Treatise on the Diseases Produced by Onanism, A (Tissot), 45
Trollope, Frances, 176
Trump, Donald, 307
Truth, Sojourner, 97–98
Tsongas, Paul, 293
Turner, Frederick Jackson, 33, 60–61, 87, 169
Twain, Mark, 59, 78
Twelve Lectures to Young Men (Beecher), 102
Two Years Before the Mast (Dana), 61
Tydings–McDuffie Act (1934), 195
Tyler, John, 31
Tyler, Royall, 13–17, 21, 27, 39
Type A personality, 265

Unemployed Man and his Family, The (Komorovsky), 200–201
Unemployment, 106, 192, 193, 199–201
Unforgiven (film), 324–325
Unions, 31, 56, 106–107
Updike, John, 294, 329
Urbanization, 82, 83, 85–86
Uris, Leon, 278

Valor of Ignorance, The (Lea), 111
Van Buren, Martin, 35–38, 237
Vandover and the Brute (Norris), 145
Van Vleck, John, 167
Varieties of Religious Experience, The (James), 112
Veblen, Thorstein, 103, 104–105, 183
Vegetarianism, 137
Vidor, King, 220, 238
Vietnam war, 263, 267–271, 299, 321–322
"Village Blacksmith, The" (Longfellow), 28
Villard, Oswald Garrison, 115
Virginian, The (Wister), 150–152
Visions of Kerouac (Duberman), 289
"Voluntaries" (Emerson), 73

Waiting for Lefty (Odets), 217
Walden (Thoreau), 43
Walker, Frances, 137
Wall Street (film), 307–308
Walsh, Mike, 29
Walsh, Raoul, 232
War, 34, 72–78, 94, 133–134, 151, 152, 184, 194, 223–226, 263, 267–271, 291, 292, 299, 321–322
War Between the Roses, The (film), 308
Ward, Lester, 113
War of 1812, 34
Washington, George, 14, 19
Watergate, 270, 292
Watson, John B., 159, 202–203
Wayne, John, 252–253, 292
Wayne, Kenneth, 27, 123–124
Weak Link: The Feminization of the American Military (Mitchell), 311
Webber, Charles, 61
Weber, Max, 103–104
Webster, Daniel, 23
Weir, James, 105
Weld, Theodore, 50
Welles, Orson, 232–233
Wellman, William, 191
Wells, Ida, 98
West, 44, 60–64, 68, 78, 87–89, 135, 136, 148–150, 182
Westerns (novels, films , television shows), 150–152, 154–155, 252, 253
What a Man Goes Through (Millard), 193, 197–198
Wheeler, Burton, 227
When a Man's a Man (Wright), 149–150
Wherry, Kenneth, 236
Whigs, 36, 37
White, Andrew D., 167
White, Bouck, 177–178

White, William Allen, 204–205
White Collar (Mills), 240
White Heat (film), 232
"White Negro, The" (Mailer), 242
Whitman, Albery A., 74–75
Whitman, Walt, 60, 68, 70–71, 105, 110
Why Are We in Vietnam? (Mailer), 288–289
Whyte, William H., 241
Wilder, Billy, 232
Wilder, Thornton, 218
Wild Ones, The (film), 249
Wild West Show, 148
Wilentz, Sean, 48
Willard, Emma, 57
Williams, W. Churchill, 144
Wills, Garry, 9
Wilson, Sloan, 242, 257–258
Wimps, 292–298, 309
Wise, Stephen, 115
Wister, Owen, 135, 136, 150–152, 155, 182, 323
Wizard of Oz, The (Baum), 108–110
Wolfe, Tom, 268, 277, 307, 310
Wolf (film), 325
Wolff, Geoffrey, 289
Woman of the Year (film), 234
Woman suffrage, 57, 70, 96, 114, 115, 197
Women and Economics (Gilman), 184
Women's movement, 3, 10, 70–72, 86, 112–116, 271, 272–274, 276, 280, 284, 300–305, 333–335

Women's Studies, 3
Wood, Clement, 203
Wood, Robert, 120
Work ethic, 104
Working Girl (film), 307
Workplace, 2, 26, 29–31, 82–84, 103, 193, 264–266
Worth and Wealth (Hunt), 26
Wright, Frank Lloyd, 121, 148
Wright, Harold, 149–150
Wright, Richard, 231
Wyden, Barbara, 279
Wyden, Peter, 279
Wyler, William, 224
Wylie, Philip, 229, 254, 255, 257, 276

Xenophobia, 33

Yancey, William Lowndes, 75
Yeats, William Butler, 7
"Yellow Wallpaper, The" (Gilman), 135
You'll Never Get Rich (television show), 248–249
Young Man and the World, The (Beveridge), 157
Young Man's Guide, The (Alcott), 46
Young Man's Own Book, The (Farrar), 48
Young Men's Christian Association (YMCA), 167, 204

Zelditch, Morris, 246
Zueblin, Charles, 91